FAR-FLUNG AND FOOTLOOSE

Books by E. J. Kahn, Jr.

FAR-FLUNG AND FOOTLOOSE

Pieces from *The New Yorker*
1937–1978

by E. J. Kahn, Jr.

Preface by William Knapp

THE PUTNAM PUBLISHING GROUP
New York

Copyright © 1979 by E. J. Kahn, Jr.

All rights reserved. This book, or parts thereof,
must not be reproduced in any form without permission.
Published simultaneously in Canada by Academic Press Canada
Limited, Toronto

Library of Congress Cataloging in Publication Data

Kahn, Ely Jacques, date.
  Far-flung and footloose.

  I. Title.
AC8.K27 1979   081   79-15636
ISBN 0-399-12428-4

PRINTED IN THE UNITED STATES OF AMERICA

This book is affectionately and gratefully dedicated to all the people at The New Yorker, *past and present, who devote their skills to making writers look better than they probably are.*

Contents

10

Foreword

How Easy Is Easy to Edit?

by William Knapp

Ely Jacques Kahn, Jr., known around *The New Yorker* as Jack, has told me that the launching of his career at the magazine, some forty-two years ago, was almost entirely a matter of serendipity. By way of explaining that "forty-two years," which gives pause when one looks at Jack and decides that he still resembles a reasonably youthful leprechaun, it should be said that he was all of twenty years old at the time. The story of his hiring begins with the fact that, in the course of a comfortable childhood, he made some trips to Europe, and, in the course of one of these, he met an African chieftain who was travelling in the British Isles. Recalling the meeting much later, as a senior at Harvard, he wrote a graceful little piece about it. (My hasty classifications for writing are "graceful," "disgraceful," and "all other.") Although he claims that at this time he harbored no burning literary ambitions, someone had, in fact, by then performed the useful service of introducing him to a literary agent—who had already sold a piece of his to a national magazine. (Aside from a brief stint on something, by that time already defunct, called the *Harvard Journal*, the indigenous publications did not particularly engage his attention; he had, as I was to do several years later, tried out for the college newspaper, *The Crimson*, but, like me, was impelled to abandon the effort through lack of encouragement.) Anyway, he minded his studies and his own other business, and was somewhat skeptical when the agent suggested submitting his piece, entitled "My African Potentate," to *The New Yorker*. Thus he was mildly surprised to learn that there had been a letter from Wolcott Gibbs to the agent accepting the piece.

Subsequently, Kahn received a summons to the *New Yorker* office, where, during his Easter vacation, he had a moderately nervous interview with St. Clair McKelway, another brilliant writer, who then was in the midst of a relatively brief tenure as Harold Ross's Managing Editor (an edgy sort of relationship that James Thurber dealt with in "Ross and The New Yorker").

After a few weeks of suspenseful silence, Kahn received a call from McKelway, who informed him that, if the idea suited him, after graduation he could come down to 25 West 43rd Street and start work as a Talk of the Town reporter at twenty-five dollars a week.

The idea did appeal to Kahn, and the consequences fill the better part of five large looseleaf volumes in what *The New Yorker* calls its library and many other publications would call the morgue. Kahn's collected works, as it happens, now outnumber those of any other *New Yorker* writer. I estimate the total, very roughly, at well over two hundred by-lined factual articles, several score fiction pieces and poems, and about three hundred Notes and Comment and Talk of the Town pieces. (I feel obliged to explain, for the sake of all those who have filled pauses at parties by asking me, "Who writes the Talk of the Town now?" that there are two separate and distinct categories; what we call "Comment" covers the usually untitled opinion pieces that lead off the main editorial section of the magazine; what we call "Talk" makes up the balance of that section; the latter pieces are usually more or less factual and bear very brief, unrevealing titles. Both sorts of pieces are written, at this point, by a variety of people, including Kahn.)

I asked Jack whether, at the outset of his career, he had envisioned the building of any such huge literary or journalistic monument. Absolutely not, he said, thus joining the long list of brilliant creators I have known who neither invite nor anatomize their muse, but simply get on with it, with a minimum of fuss and chatter. In fact, my general formula is: The more brilliant a person is in his or her field, the less vocal self-advertisement he or she indulges in. I have carefully had to insert the word "vocal" here, because Jack has recently unburdened himself of a book entitled "About *The New Yorker* and Me." In this, he mentions that I have edited a good deal of his work, and, at one point, he quotes me as telling a colleague that he (Kahn) was "easy to edit." Writerlike, he begins, in the book, to brood about this. ("Is that good or bad?") My first reaction is that, against the background of the number of pieces I have just enumerated, which contain something like two and a half million words, it is far too late for Kahn to decide that he is going to be a prima donna. What I meant when I made the remark to my colleague, Derek Morgan, was that Kahn had always accepted the maddening complexity of *The New Yorker* editing process philosophically and graciously, which is more, I'm afraid, than I can say for a few of his colleagues, to whom the process seems to come as more or less a total surprise each time it takes place.

I once attempted to describe the process in question to a writer for *The New York Times*, and, among other things, I told him that each sentence in a *New Yorker* fact piece (or long nonfiction piece, to give it a more exact designation) is read an estimated fifteen times. This does not mean by fifteen different people, but at least seven are usually involved. The sequence begins when the writer hands his manuscript to William Shawn, our editor, with whom he has presumably discussed the project in some detail at its inception. The odds are approximately nine-to-one that the man who has done the writing is among our approximately fifty staff writers, a group for whom submitting ideas and obtaining reactions to them is relatively easy. In earlier times, there was much more tendency to assign stories from voluminous "idea books," but Shawn seems to believe, logically, that a writer will do a better job on a subject he has come up with himself.

The author's next problem is an agonizing, but usually short-lived, one. Will the piece be accepted? First of all, Shawn was a legendary speedreader before most of us knew there was such a thing. Second, he is aware of the author's agony, as he is aware of most agonies around the office. Customarily, he will swiftly terminate this one with a call to the author, if he can find him. I have received one such call on a Saturday afternoon, at home in Connecticut, and can testify to its restorative powers. If one could be tipped off that a call was imminent, he should be prepared to record it, for use as a morale builder in some future black moment, saving it like very good whisky or some other prime anodyne.

I have no idea whether Kahn attempts to hasten this part of the process, but I can testify that he is not among the writers who then start worrying about which editor on the staff is going to handle their piece, and if so, how soon. Because of his many obvious preoccupations, Bill Shawn may take a little while to pass the piece along to one of the non-fiction editors, and, during the interval, writers—I exclude Kahn—begin to fear all sorts of dire eventualities: Shawn may change his mind; some editor who they think has treated them badly in the past will get the piece; it may be given to someone who has just been hired from *Hustler* and has no notion of *New Yorker* editing. Then the writer may hear, over the bush telegraph or perhaps by directly asking Shawn, which editor is likely to be assigned. He may even hear it from the editor himself. Ordinarily, the editor is put under surveillance. Does he really have the piece? Is he really working on it? When will it be in galley?

In a delightful reminder-list titled "Theory and Practice of Editing *New Yorker* Articles," Gibbs wrote, "Preserve the author's style if he is an author and has a style." I try to follow this rule—an easy one in the case of Kahn—a man not given to hiding essential facts, like Easter eggs, in obscure corners, or to the creation of impenetrable grammatical thickets. If Jack has a weakness, it is for an occasional unworkable pun or irresistible—to him— piece of humor, from which the editor must gently dissuade him. Jack's manner, in these cases, is one of mild regret ("Oh gee, I *liked* that") but after throwing himself on the mercy of the court, he is usually prepared to accept its judgment. At this stage, anyway, when the editor is doing what he considers the essential preliminary editing—including the insertion of foolish queries and the substitution of his own clichés and prejudices for the author's—the author may reveal either a mounting apprehension or a realization of roughly what the editor is trying to accomplish and why. Kahn is in the latter category. He appears to believe that the editor is doing his job because he derives satisfaction from it, rather than as an effort to work out his aggressions and his frustrations over not being a writer himself. Furthermore, Jack does not *hover*, as some writers may do over an editor, rather like a police helicopter. Some may curl their necks like flamingoes over the editor's desk in an effort to see just what the editor is up to, while at least one I have known, otherwise a good friend, has unlimbered and lit up numberless small odious cigars over my desk, apparently in the hope that incipient nausea will cause me to push his copy aside unmarked. Unless he has been unable to resist an unusual number of not-quite-workable jokes, Kahn's copy usually needs to be only very lightly marked—the primary basis for my calling him "easy to edit."

Before long, the piece will come through in galley, and the writer's next anxiety begins to take over: When will it appear in the magazine, if ever? I believe Jack is one of the writers who, over years of experience, has grasped the idea that the magazine's editor, like a farmer planting his fields or a museum director planning an exhibit, must, for each issue, balance all of the material at hand in terms of space, basic nature, and general harmony. So schedules come and go, and writers and editors fret. The only certain signs that publication is imminent—and veterans like Kahn wait for them as patiently as possible—are the arrival on the editor's desk of, first, what is known as a "Gould Proof" and next of a proof from *The New Yorker's* Checking Department.

Eleanor Gould Packard is our wizard of usage—our resident composite of H.W. Fowler and Sir Ernest Govers. For some thirty years she has patiently trudged through each article, pencil and eraser poised, calling attention to grammatical gaffes, factual booby traps, clichés, non-sequiturs, and other horrors from which *The New Yorker* is supposed to be—and in considerable part thanks to her is—free. She makes her observations on galley proofs to which, as you might imagine, writers exhibit a broad spectrum of reactions—ranging from almost complete disbelief that they could ever be accused of so many transgressions against the language they love, to a feeling that the whole thing is a plot in which their style is being savaged, to a feeling that an honest and remarkable professional is at work and their piece will, by and large, be the better for it.

Much the same goes for reactions to *The New Yorker's* unique Checking Department, in which eight dedicated and well-educated people, male and female, attempt to verify every factual statement that an author has made in a piece. (The difference between their job and that of *Time* researchers, for instance, is that the latter have, in many cases, helped to dig up the facts in a piece, and therefore develop a vested interest in those same facts: "This *must* be right; I put it here.") In setting up the Checking Department, years ago, Harold Ross obviously hoped to encourage the sort of dispassionate skepticism that typifies the best sort of journalism. A *New Yorker* checker will go a long way, often telephonically, to prove an author wrong—without malice, of course—and an author will do well, at the outset, to give the checkers as much source material, preferably printed, as he can. Recently a checker was heard on the trans-Atlantic phone ascertaining from an English informant that a principal road out of London was, in fact, known as the M-1 Motorway. Ultimately, and sometimes after considerable in-house litigation, the writer and the editor realize that they ignore the checkers' findings at their peril. A recent flap over where a noted restaurant got its fish brought this home to all concerned.

I am reminded of some lines of Chesterton's:

> You cannot hope to bribe or twist
> By God, the British journalist.
> Nor, seeing what the chap will do
> Unbribed, is there any reason to.

My variant is:

> You cannot hope to scare or fool,
> By God, the New Yorker checking pool,
> And if you hold some nugget back
> A libel lawyer will be on your track.

A veteran of the Checking Department, now retired, has told me that years ago E. J. Kahn had a reputation for being somewhat coy with his research material. But he has long since, I gather, outgrown this habit. And he has learned to remain calm through the elaborate series of subsequent events: reading page proofs; receiving queries on same from Mr. Shawn and from a whole new team made up of a page editor and a proofreader; dealing with more queries from the checker. But I had better stop praising Kahn's *panache:* He will decide to become more difficult, and my boss will decide that my job is easier than it is.

These pieces will give you an idea of Jack Kahn's ingenuity, curiosity, grace, humor, and his endless capacity for discovery and elucidation. Gibbs and McKelway were on the right track.

(William Knapp is a senior editor of The New Yorker.)

Author's Note

The words contained hereinafter (a word I've been waiting forty-two years to use) represent something less than ten percent of those I've had printed in *The New Yorker*. About ten percent of the contents of this book, to pursue this tithing for a moment, has appeared in earlier books of mine; but inasmuch as most of these are now out of print, and as this fraction consists of pieces I've particularly liked for one reason or another—one reason being that readers have let me know that *they* particularly liked them—I am wedging them once again between hard covers.

This collection is being presented chronologically, in part because I couldn't think of any better arrangement. It reflects fairly accurately, I guess, my interests over the years. Nearly every reportorial subject I have tackled for *The New Yorker* has been one of my own choice. Some of the people I've done Profiles on that are hereinetc. excerpted (the magazine is commendably gracious about the amount of space it allows writers, and there isn't room enough to run them *in toto*), I would probably not elect to write about today; but at the time I pestered them they appealed strongly to me and would also appeal, I naturally hoped, to others.

It will become apparent to anyone leafing through the pages that follow that, unlike many contributors to *The New Yorker*, I have never had any single compelling area of interest, or expertise. In an era of increasing specialization, I have always been—conceivably for lack of any alternative—a generalist. I am restless. I get bored if I dwell too long in any field of inquiry. I like to travel, and to describe what I see and hear and feel. That is not unusual, but I am lucky enough to be able to earn a living by, if not my wits, my senses. Specialist though I may not be, my answer to the oft-asked question "Whom do you *New Yorker* people think you're writing for, anyway?" can be and is anything but general: I write for one person—the editor-in-chief of that magazine. Since its inception in 1925, there have been but two such individuals—Harold Ross and William Shawn. They have been the constituency whose approving vote I have sought. That so much of the eyes-only copy I have submitted for their perusal has received their imprimatur has been my continuing good fortune.

—E. J. K.

New York, New York

1 June 1979

My African Potentate

ACCRA, Gold Coast Colony.—Sir Ofori Atta, the blue-black ruler of one of Britain's African Gold Coast states, put justice above fatherly affection today and jailed two of his sons for stealing one of his golden crowns.— *Associated Press dispatch.*

I know Sir Ofori Atta. Of all my acquaintances, I can truthfully say that he is the only African potentate—at least the only African potentate who rules 250,000 people in the state of Akim Abuakwa. I have known him for many years, but up to the moment have never been able to convince anyone of it. People just won't believe there is such a place as Akim Abuakwa.

Sir Ofori and I met nine years ago, when I was eleven. I was travelling in Europe with my sister, aged thirteen, and my grandparents. Our journey had taken us to Edinburgh, where it left my sister and me perched on a balcony of the massive North British Hotel, looking out over the broad course of Princes Street. Had we read the newspapers, we should have known that the long procession of cars that crawled up the concourse contained royalty. We should have known that the blanketed figures who stepped out of the first few cars of the cavalcade were members of the retinue of the short, stout man in the purple robe who ducked his head to keep his golden crown from hitting the roof of the car—Sir Ofori Atta.

But we didn't know. Being Americans, we guessed that it was part of a circus, or an initiation. Being children, we guessed that it was some personage from an imaginary world. Being curious, we went down to the lobby to investigate.

The hotel was in a flurry of excitement. Assistant managers in morning coats raced up and down the corridors, bowing and scraping and occasionally glancing apprehensively at their distinguished guest and his entourage.

Uncomfortably dressed civic officials proudly cleared a way for their swarthy prize. The only person who didn't seem to care about the whole procedure was Sir Ofori. We decided then and there that we liked him.

My sister and I were not without experience in associating with the great. We cared not at all for the prestige that royalty bestows upon its acquaintances, and we had a healthy spirit of adventure that scoffed at social convention. Several weeks before, we had met Prince Henry of the House of Hohenzollern, a tired old man who talked of ships. Then we had spent a few hours with Gustav Stresemann—not royalty, but at that time a powerful figure in Europe. So, with typical American confidence, we decided to arrange a meeting with His Majesty.

Minor difficulties didn't faze us. We had no idea what language Sir Ofori spoke; we were limited to English and a smattering of French and German. We were not even sure where the Gold Coast was. But fortunately my sister had some reputation as an artist. She was always being commissioned to draw birthday posters and illustrate place cards; our house is filled with ungainly "Welcome Home" signs with which she has at some time or other greeted a homecoming aunt or uncle. So we got some paper and a bottle of India ink, and in no time we had produced a letter decorated with a wreath of marginal embellishments, most of them pictures of a boy and girl gazing wide-eyed at a huge man with a crown on his head, holding a spear in one hand as he sat on the back of a pygmy tiger. It was a pretty fine letter.

The next problem was that of transmission. We had no faith in the hotel employees, who would obviously be unsympathetic to our cause. We received no assistance from our grandparents. Grandfather, slumped in a chair, grumbled "What?," then "Who?," and then "Atta who?" After a while he got up and muttered "Attaboy!" and wandered chuckling into the other room. Grandfather, we decided, was not an adventurer at heart.

A call to the desk gave us His Majesty's room number. Stepping out of the elevator hesitantly, we walked down the hall toward his suite, losing confidence at every step. As we neared his door, from adjoining rooms appeared the largest Negroes we had ever seen. We were pretty small then, and everyone seemed unnecessarily big, but these men, clothed from head to foot in nothing but blankets, as far as we could see, were certainly larger than any normal six-foot American. They stared at us silently, without expression, and drew their doors shut. We stood in front of Sir Ofori's door for a moment, stooped and slipped the note underneath, and then ran down the corridor as fast as we could. We were appalled at our temerity.

A few minutes later there was a knock at our door and an assistant manager entered, informing us that His Majesty would be glad to give us an audience in half an hour. My grandmother, who had heard somewhere that cannibalism was not wholly extinct, was alarmed. Grandfather told her not to worry; he said that King George didn't go around knighting people who planned to eat American children in hotel rooms.

When we knocked on His Majesty's door, a voice said, "Come in." That was an encouraging note of civilization.

It is difficult to make a royal chamber out of a hotel room, but Sir Ofori's men had done their best. He was seated in the centre of the room, on a raised chair. His crown rested on a cushion nearby. His purple robe, girt at the waist by a sash, flowed to his feet, which were encased in golden sandals. Around him stood more of the blanketed figures, towering over him. In a corner of the room, dressed in a navy-blue suit, stood a little Negro boy. A couple of newspaper reporters were looking out of a window.

"How do you do?" said a cultured English voice. The voice was His Majesty's. We didn't know whether to kneel or to bow, so we walked up and shook hands.

Conversation was easy. Born in Africa, Sir Ofori had been sent to Oxford as part of his preparation for the post he was destined to inherit. He spoke English and German fluently, and told us of his plans to include both these languages in the curricula of his native schools. He was very much interested in our schooling; asked us what courses we took and how our schools were run, and told us that he had two sons of his own back home, whom he would like us to meet. We never suspected that they were plotting the whole while to steal his crown. Our manner of speech amused him. Our American slang was a distinct contrast to the courtly conversation of Buckingham Palace.

In its dispatch about the crown, the Associated Press also tells how the King, when he visited England, brought with him a deputy drinker, to help him out when there was too much drinking for even a King to cope with. He didn't tell us about that, figuring, perhaps, that we were too young to understand, but he did tell us about a much more interesting member of his troupe: the little boy in the corner.

Akim Abuakwa is probably a lot more civilized than the average African state, but many native traditions are still treated with the utmost respect. And one of these was responsible for the boy. He had no official title, but the natives looked upon him as the King's spirit. As soon as Sir Ofori ascended the throne, the boy was delegated to spend the rest of his life in the King's company. Should anything happen to the boy, the natives believed that the same fate would overtake their ruler, and consequently the boy's life was almost as precious to them as that of their sovereign. It was not an intolerable life for the boy; except for Sir Ofori, he was probably treated with more care and respect than any of his fellow-countrymen. We wanted to speak to him, but unfortunately Sir Ofori was the only member of his party who could speak English. During our visit with the King, the boy was up against one of the most difficult situations he had ever had to cope with.

As a matter of fact, he was scared speechless, not of us, but of a danger he had never even dreamed of: a victrola. In some mysterious manner, music was being transmitted to him. He searched in vain for instruments, and was eventually reduced to glaring suspiciously at the box from which the sounds issued. The King knew what a victrola was, but his servants did not. They huddled around the boy, protecting him from any evil spirit the box might engender.

After a while Sir Ofori summoned Grandfather, whom he wanted to meet. Grandfather came down grudgingly, took one look at the big black men who were standing around the room, and decided it was no fit place for us. He was somewhat placated by Sir Ofori's cultured speech, but was still uneasy. So we prepared to depart.

Sir Ofori had mentioned casually that his state contained a lot of diamonds for which he could find no use. We thought he wouldn't mind if we asked for one, and so we did. He was very nice about it; said we should write him when we got home, and he would send us one right away.

When we got to New York, we did write him, thanking him in advance for the diamond. But we never got an answer. We have always suspected that the Post Office threw the letter away, along with all the notes that our less fortunate contemporaries were sending to Santa Claus.

April 3, 1937

This was the first piece I had in *The New Yorker*, written while I was a senior at Harvard. Wolcott Gibbs was the editor who handled it. I got to the Gold Coast myself—by then it was Ghana—in 1970, but never did make it to Akim Abuakwa.

Paddles and Cards

The Hi-Li is probably the biggest thing to hit New York since the yo-yo, some ten years ago. You may not recognize the name, but you have certainly seen hundreds of Hi-Lis in action; they're those paddles with rubber balls attached by elastics with which office boys and urchins in general while away the time these days. Hi-Lis come in two models, the standard and the de luxe, which retail, respectively, for a dime and a quarter. What you do with a Hi-Li is to hit the ball with the paddle, trying to get it to bounce back so you can hit it again. This sounds easy, but it isn't. The pamphlet given purchasers of Hi-Lis gravely says, "The child (or adult—for that matter) who will stick with a Hi-Li with determination until they master it shows real character"—an admirable sentiment, even if the prose style would horrify O. O. McIntyre. Difficult as the manipulation of a

Hi-Li is, it's on record that a six-year-old child in Cincinnati kept it up for four hours once, stopping only because he had a dinner engagement.

Hi-Lis are manufactured by something named the K & E Enterprises. For the past five years K & E have been putting on intensive sales campaigns in cities all over the country. Last year, in Chicago, two million Hi-Lis were sold, in the course of a six weeks' drive. The New York territory was saved for the last because the promoters were frankly terrified of its possibilities. In the second week of their campaign, when we checked up on the local sales, a million and a half had already been sold. There are a hundred trained demonstrators working in stores, and two hundred and sixteen movie theatres are showing a special slow-motion sound picture which demonstrates the fine points of Hi-Li. There is also a Mr. Bill Chappell making personal appearances on stages here and there. Mr. Chappell possesses the rather oppressive accomplishment of being able to manipulate five Hi-Lis at once: two in each hand and one in his teeth. The New York *American* and the aforementioned two hundred and sixteen movie theatres are sponsoring a Hi-Li contest, in which the first prize is a bicycle. There are also a hundred and twenty-five lesser prizes, and every contestant is, willy-nilly, presented with a Baby Ruth candy bar, said to be rich in dextrose.

The late John D. Rockefeller's favorite card game, it may be worthy of note at this time, was a Parker Brothers number called Numerica. News of Mr. Rockefeller's death brought about a mild revival of interest in Numerica, about fifteen people calling up Parker Brothers to ask where they could purchase it. Numerica was copyrighted in 1894, and has never sold very well, Parker Brothers told us. Their best customer for the game was Mr. Rockefeller himself, who used to buy a dozen decks at a time, to give to his friends. Parker Brothers advertised Numerica for a while as "Mr. Rockefeller's game," but this didn't do much good, so they gave it up. The game seems to appeal principally to mild people who would like to play rummy or old maid, but son't like to have a deck of real cards about the house. Instead of suits, a Numerica deck has four different colors, and the cards are severely numbered from one to thirteen, instead of having symbols and faces. Patient people could play stud poker with a Numerica deck by remembering, for example, that a ten, eleven, twelve, thirteen, and one, all in green, constitute a royal spade flush, but it hardly seems worth the trouble.

June 19, 1937

My debut in the Talk of the Town.

No Hits, No Runs

If you follow baseball you know all about how history was made in Brooklyn last week; how, in the first big-league night baseball game in these parts, Johnny Vander Meer of the Cincinnati Reds pitched his second straight no-hit, no-run game, to the utter astonishment of 40,000 Brooklyn residents who'd have given you a million to one that it couldn't be done—and who probably will give you a thousand to one now that it won't be done again. Well, we were there that memorable night, observing the ceremonies in the company of a fellow named Eddie, who introduced himself as soon as we'd taken our seat by turning and saying, "Cheez, whadda mob! Ain't never been nuttin like it in Brooklyn." It was a mob so big, in fact, that the Fire Department ordered the gates closed more than half an hour before the game began. We will report at once that night baseball is entirely successful and express the opinion that it ought to be adopted all over the East. The one drawback we could see is that, with daylight-saving time, the game has to wait an uncomfortably long time for darkness.

The Brooklyn crowd was partially lulled through the twilight by Jesse Owens, who wore an Olympic track suit and essayed, among other things, to race 120 yards over ten hurdles against a Brooklyn outfielder just plain running. Jesse lost by eight yards, and you probably could have got two million to one against Vander Meer then. "The hell with this track meet!" yelled Eddie. "Play ball!" Through it all a band played doggedly from a point behind home plate and an American Legion drum corps paraded in centrefield. The lights went on at 8:37 to a practically unanimous "Oh," and the players took on an unreal air, as if they were running around in Technicolor. Babe Ruth walked across the field (loud cheers), a man in a white coat offered autographed bats (small size a quarter, large size fifty cents), and a plane flew over advertising the show at Radio City Music Hall. It seemed pretty much like an everyday ball game at that point except for the seven huge light towers and a sign on top of the scoreboard: "YOUR HOUSEHOLD ELECTRIC BILL IS WORTH MONEY." This may have been addressed to the Dodgers themselves, whose lighting bill for the evening, we were later advised, was equal to that of 1,500 householders. Six hundred and fifty floodlights are used to illuminate the field, producing a total of 1,200,000 candlepower, enough, the Dodgers announced irrelevantly, to light 447 miles of highway. The Dodgers' management is convinced that if you read a newspaper at second base you'd have ten times as much light as in your own home. Of course, if a ballplayer tried to do this, Eddie would make a terrible fuss, and probably he'd be traded. All told, the installation cost $100,000. One Dodger official is reputed to have remarked, "We could get it back easy if we had a ball club."

At the start of the game all the Brooklyn rooters were notably blood-thirsty, sparing neither players nor umpires the sting of their scorn. Eddie, for instance, instead of calling the Dodgers by their proper names, such as Kiki, Buddy, Blimp, and Cookie, addressed them all merely as "Dopey"—all but Manager Burleigh Grimes, whom no true Brooklynite calls anything but Boily. When a Brooklyn pitcher was hit by a batted ball and carried off on a stretcher, Eddie yelled cheerfully, "Dopey broke his leg. They'll have to shoot him now." As the game progressed and the crowd began to root for Vander Meer, Eddie lapsed into silence; at the end, when the pitcher had finally done the impossible, he whispered to us, "It could only happen in Brooklyn," and rushed off to join the crowd milling around the Cincinnati dugout. The outcome of the game and the subsequent delirious excitement were probably a disappointment only to a party of ten men representing a current movie. They stood stolidly, elbow to elbow, each with a letter on his largely unnoticed back, spelling out "Y-E-L-L-O-W J-A-C-K."

June 25, 1938

Real Sheik

The arrival in these parts of His Excellency Sheik Hafiz Wahba, Envoy Extraordinary and Minister Plenipotentiary of His Majesty King Ibn Saud of Saudi Arabia, during the revival of "The Sheik," starring Rudolph Valentino, and "The Son of the Sheik," starring Rudolph Valentino, was naturally open to suspicion as a Hollywood publicity stunt, but we were definitely assured that it wasn't and thereupon went to interview the Sheik at the Waldorf-Astoria. In the bedroom we found a non-Arabian, red-faced man, dressed simply in a pair of shorts, who sat gazing thoughtfully at a couple of whisky bottles; and another American, in a brown suit, who was arguing over the telephone about steamship reservations. We readily gathered that the Sheik had been assigned a small inside cabin and that this was unthinkable for the head of a tribe, which is what his title signifies. This distressing state of affairs was finally settled with the aid of the Texas Oil Company, apparently as a sort of courtesy to the two men, who are with the Standard Oil Company of California and had travelled across the country with the Sheik. Lots of oil in Arabia, you know.

While we waited to see the Sheik, the two men offered determinedly to tell us something about his life. "He has a genial and pleasant personality," the first one announced as he was getting into his shirt. "And a keen sense of humor," added his colleague. "How old is he?" we asked. "Forty-six," said one man. "We-ell," said the other, "better just put him in his forties." We put him there, and learned further that this was his first trip to America, though he's been all over Europe and Asia, mostly by airplane. The reason he came here was that he was delegated to represent Saudi Arabia at the opening of a mosque in Tokyo; being relatively so near the United States, the Sheik decided to stop off here on his way back. He travelled without a retinue, at least until Standard Oil got hold of him, and wore ordinary Western clothes except when paying a formal call on the President and having his picture taken. On such occasions he donned the accepted garb of a Sheik: embroidered headcloth (*kaffiyah)*, decorated with two bands of gold and leather (*agal)* at the crown, and two white robes—a *zubool* underneath and an *aba* over that. While on the Coast, we were told, he met Myrna Loy, Clark Gable, and Fanny Brice, and also visited a broadcasting studio. "Better mention the Huntington Library and the Planetarium, too," the red-faced man added. "Put a little culture in the damned thing." He thereupon pulled on his pants.

Evading a bearded man who turned up and wanted to tell us about the number of Arabs in Detroit, we went into another room and found the Sheik himself, a small man with a black mustache and beard and dark-rimmed glasses, who spoke English haltingly. "I am very happy for this visit to America," he said right off. He told us that ordinarily he divides his time between London and Saudi Arabia, which has a population of five million and includes the holy cities of Medina and Mecca. The Sheik was governor of Mecca fifteen years ago and has a home there, as well as a palace in Riyadh, the capital of the country. "Big palace?" we asked. "Oh no," he said. "I'm a small Sheik." While he was in New York, he wanted to see the Valentino pictures, but was too busy attending dinners and luncheons and greeting fellow-Arabs, of whom there are fifty thousand here. "I like to see what ideas they have about a Sheik," he said, "but anyhow it's not my son. It's another Sheik's son." This drew loud laughter from the red-faced man, who had got dressed and joined us, and now escorted us to the door. "No cracks about his harem now, pal," he said. "What harem?" we asked. "No cracks, pal," he said. "O.K., pal," we said, and bowed our way out.

July 16, 1938

Our Pushing Correspondents
A Goat Among Sheep

NEWPORT, R. I., AUG. 17

In the minds of many newspaper readers, the début of Miss Lesley Hyde Ripley at Newport will probably go down in history as the society brawl of the year. Actually it was a quiet, uneventful affair, little different from any other dance, if a bit more exclusive. Wine, women, and song were available in suitable quantities. The wine was good, the song was good (the best tune being "The Flat Foot Floogee with the Floy Floy"), and the women for the most part were just about what you'd find at any Eastern college dance. Naturally, the Newport glamour girls, glorified in picture and print, were there, and so were the débutantes, glamour girls of tomorrow. An unusually large number of glamour girls and débutantes had long, straight, blond hair that fell to their shoulders. This made them look pretty much alike from the back. As a matter of fact, they looked pretty much alike from the front, too. They danced with apparently unlimited energy and fixed, determined smiles. While they were dancing—at least while they were dancing with me—they said practically nothing but "Uh?" (with a rising inflection) or occasionally "Uh-huh" (with a certain finality). In general, the young ladies wore flowers and the elderly ones, who sat grimly at ringside tables, wore jewels. There were quite a few of these elderly ladies, ladies with snow-white hair and rather heroically cheerful faces. There didn't seem to be so many old gentlemen about. The few I saw wore tail coats and looked like British colonels. Most of the young men wore dinner jackets, white or black, and looked pretty much the same, front and back and from the side. Although I overheard one stag say, "These are the most fantastic-looking people I've ever seen," they didn't seem fantastic to me.

The day after the party the society columnists, who had already given Miss Ripley a buildup worthy of any movie star, really let go with both barrels. As far as I am concerned, the shells were blanks. In the *Daily News*, Nancy Randolph bubbled, "And you should have seen the ones that couldn't get in, lacking the necessary engraved invitations, passports, or letters from their Senators. The entire Newport police force was commandeered to surround the Ripley residence and separate the invited sheep from the gate-crashing goats." Miss Randolph set the cost of the party at $75,000. Barclay Beekman of the *Mirror* declared feverishly that Lesley had "skyrocketed to fame as the top débutante of the United States." He set the cost of this ascent at $10,000. Up in Boston, the *Post* front-paged a story telling how the Ripleys had flung a police guard around their estate to forestall any kidnapping attempts. "Each unknown person was questioned and barred, a procedure never before employed at coming-out parties," New Englanders learned. The *Post* set the cost at $8,500. I had the feeling, after reading all the papers, that I had just been mooning the night before and had missed a great deal. That may be. I'm not, I must confess, what the newspapers call a trained observer.

I hadn't intended to go to the party and the Ripleys had not intended me to come. I happened to be in Newport, which has always seemed an unlikely place to be except maybe during Tennis Week, and on my way home from dinner with some friends, who had talked a good deal about the publicity the Ripley party was getting, I decided to go by and look at the crowds that would be looking at the Ripleys' residence. I took a taxi and told the driver to stop somewhere near the house. This, we soon found, could not be done. The taxi might as well have tried to park in the Holland Tunnel on a Friday afternoon in midsummer. There were plenty of police around, all right, but they were simply directing traffic, and when they spotted me sitting in a taxicab in a white dinner jacket they very efficiently saw to it that I was not delayed. Inexorably they urged the taxicab on until it drew up at the house. The only thing for me to do seemed to be to get out. Here at the door more policemen were busily engaged in trying to move everyone into the house as fast as possible, acting with the firmness of subway guards. They were being assisted by a gray-haired man with a mustache, who I later found out was Mr. Ripley. I had a glimpse of the driveway, trimmed with yellow lights, and the trees beyond, hung with blue and orange lights, giving a quaint World's Fair effect, and then I was inside, in a baronial hallway, with a distinguished-looking butler inclining his head toward me and obviously expecting me to tell him my name. I told him as nice-sounding a one as I could think of in all that confusion and he murmured an approximation of it to a rather square lady in a red-and-white dress who was standing at my left. Next to her was a wholesome-looking sunburned girl in green, with some white orchids on her shoulder. These two were Mrs. Ripley and her daughter Lesley. Mrs. Ripley smiled halfheartedly and pressed my hand; Lesley didn't smile at all—just looked at me dully and held out her hand. I said, "How do you do?" and they said, at almost the same time, "So glad you . . . " and their voices trailed off. With Mr. Ripley busy outside the door, Mrs. Ripley and her daughter constituted the entire receiving line. I had counted on something bigger, but I decided to stay anyway, and went on in, an innocent goat, to join the sheep.

There were no cards of admission, not even a list of invited guests at the entrance, such as is usually found at débutante parties. I learned later that the Ripleys had dispensed with a check list on the evidently sound theory that most of the goats would be scared off by the rumors of the elaborate precautions taken to keep them from crashing the party. A few were denied admittance in the course of the evening, but these, I was told, had made the mistake of sidling up to the front door in a shifty manner, with silly grins on their faces. Three others had been thrown out because they had had the bad judgment to say that they were Beverley Bogert, who happens to be Mrs. Ripley's brother-in-law and nephew.

What aroused public interest in the Ripley début more than anything else was the large, rectangular ballroom that had been built specially for the occasion and was to be torn down the day after the party. Estimates of its cost varied from $2,000 to $25,000; the correct figure was probably around $15,000. An architect I spoke to said he wouldn't try to duplicate it for less, and a guest at the dance, a house-wrecker by trade, said it looked very substantial to him. "I could pull it down in a day, though," he said, tapping the wall professionally. As to the total cost of the dance, one guess seemed to be as good as another. A presumably reliable source, a cousin of the Ripleys, told me casually at the bar that the evening represented an expenditure of at least $30,000, which sounded reasonable enough. The dance pavilion itself was thoroughly described in the newspapers, and everyone who reads the society pages knows that the ceiling was of latticework, into which had been entwined a great deal of smilax and several dozen blue and white bulbs; that the five window openings on the harbor side were equipped with window seats and silver-and-pink awnings; and that the interior walls were covered with plaster to give a stucco effect. The pavilion was about a hundred feet long and twenty-five wide. Opposite the window openings were five arched passages leading to the porch of the house proper, where tables had been placed for supper and breakfast. Additional tables were at the south end of the pavilion. At the north end the orchestra sat in an alcove on a series of platforms, with Meyer Davis in front, framed in a leafy archway. He stayed there from eleven o'clock until seven the next morning, and I never saw him sit down once. "Maybe some people think it is good publicity," Mr. Davis was quoted as saying in one of the papers the next day, "but for me, if the public really believes that the music cost any such nonsensical price as ten thousand dollars, I'll never be engaged again." A couple of days before this, Mr. Davis had been interviewed on the same subject by the New York *Post*. "I'm getting ten thousand dollars flat," he had said, adding that it wouldn't be the first time, either. I think he earned whatever it was he got.

Lesley Ripley does not qualify as a glamour girl despite her enviable quota of newspaper linage, not to speak of her lineage. Her social career is officially just beginning, and glamour girls are supposed to be established heartbreakers, capable of handling college boys, bankers, and princes with equal nonchalance. If her altogether admirable attitude toward her own party is any indication of her outlook on social life in general, I do not think she will ever become a glamour girl, and I think that will be fine. When I danced with her, which was of course the correct thing to do, she remarked that she had no idea who a lot of her guests were, and she didn't seem to care much, either. A reciprocal feeling was shown by some of the male guests, who asked me, well along in the morning, when they thought it was time they did their duty, to point her out to them. I directed their attention to a girl wearing white organza, with gardenias in her hair, who looked good-natured. Since the avowed function of a débutante party is to introduce the débutante to potential husbands, and since the Ripleys were paying out roughly thirty dollars a head (a butler stationed at the front door with a counting device told me there were exactly 980 guests), this lack of coöperation seemed a pity, and yet praiseworthy at the same time. Lesley was very popular, of course, and she danced doggedly throughout the night with a brave if slightly muscular smile. Between four-twenty and four-thirty she was stuck with John Jacob Astor III.

During most of the evening only a small percentage of the guests were on the dance floor at any one time. They wandered into the bar, only a short walk from the pavilion, or sat outside on marble benches and wicker chairs, looking at the harbor. The Ripleys' yacht, Elfreda, was anchored a few hundred yards offshore under a gay rigging of yellow lights. Spotlights were focussed on the trees around the house and electric lights shone in the bushes. All these improvements on nature, while they formed a pleasant setting, served also to attract hordes of mosquitoes, which buzzed about merrily and attacked people. Once, while I was slapping one on my neck, I saw a Swope brush one off his forehead—a rather high forehead, incidentally.

Conversation at the dance centred chiefly around the decorations, the expense, the approach of Tennis Week, and a few coming marriages. There was some excitement over the fact that John Jacob Astor III had just spoken to Eileen Gillespie for the first time since they broke their engagement all over the newspapers.

During the five hours I was there, between one and six, the proceedings were not varied by even so much as a supper intermission. The buffet tables, at the south end of the pavilion, were kept stocked with food all night, and the guests wandered over to eat creamed chicken or cold meats or lobster or salmon or sandwiches whenever they felt like it. Early in the morning there was a general switch to scrambled eggs, sausages, and milk. The system made it easy on everybody except Meyer Davis and his men. When I left, at six o'clock, I hadn't seen a single person who was obnoxiously or even amusingly drunk. The only one who was close to it was an amiable fellow who came up to me and said, "Want to earn my gratitude?" I said "Certainly," whereupon he said, "Just cut in on the girl with the blue dress." "Which girl in which blue dress?" I asked. "Oh," he said unhappily, "I hadn't thought about that," and wandered away.

If dignity was the keynote of the party, as I think it probably was, Mr. Davis and his men seemed determined to do their part. They played a relatively large number of waltzes and decorous fox trots, with a few rumbas thrown in to keep the crowd on its toes. Every now and then they'd burst into something hot, but they played with restraint, and with solemn faces. Nobody did the Big Apple, and only a few daring couples indulged in the shag, notably one tireless middle-aged lady with red hair who shagged no matter what the music was or what her partner was doing. It was interesting, and possibly significant, that the song most frequently played was "I Married an Angel," and that not once during their eight-hour stand did the orchestra break into that other current favorite, "Oh Mama," the

29

lyrics of which include the blunt phrase "Please get that man for me."

The sky began to lighten at five o'clock, and by five-thirty it was practically daylight. A few of the dancers deserted the floor to go outside and look at the harbor, strolling along green-painted strips of carpet that had been laid out on the lawns. I strolled outside myself. The grass was littered with cigarette butts, bits of fruit from Old-Fashioned glasses, and a few wilted corsages. In the morning light the dance pavilion looked curiously out of place, like a merry-go-round in a churchyard. The lights on the yacht were out, and behind it, a quarter of a mile or so away, was a cruiser, perhaps stationed there to foil any kidnap plots from overseas. I walked around the grounds and looked at the gardens, but at six o'clock, I decided I had had enough and left. My feet hurt, and besides it suddenly seemed silly for me to be standing there watching a lot of people in evening clothes who were dancing in broad daylight to the strains of "Flat Foot Floogee." Believe it or not.

August 27, 1938

I might have inadvertently, and disastrously, used the name "Beverley Bogert" myself, had I not known one of the gentlemen who rightly bore it—a classmate of mine at college. The *nom de bal* I chose was "Sanderson Weekes," an amalgam of the two most elegant names on *The New Yorker's* editorial roster—Sanderson Vanderbilt and Hobart G. Weekes. The magazine's editors must have had qualms about my duplicity, for they did not append my own name to this piece—merely my initials.

Hearstlings

Probably the best opportunity the public has of seeing the *Journal & American* homing pigeons in action is during the local games of the World Series, when they circle about the field to get their bearings for the dash to the roof of the Journal & American Building at 220 South Street. Their flight to the office lasts about nine minutes and they make it possible for the *Journal* to print Joe DiMaggio's smiling face thirty-eight minutes after he crosses home plate, which leaves ample time to put the paper on sale by the end of the game. This is how it works: As a photographer snaps the picture, a colleague in the press box writes the caption on onion paper. He then takes the photographer's camera and, after putting it in a black bag which has openings for his hands, removes the film, rolls it up with the paper, and inserts both into a small metal capsule. This he fastens with adhesive tape to the leg of one of a dozen pigeons which have been brought to the Stadium in a canvas-covered crate. The bird is tossed into the air and, after two circles around the park, makes for home.

The *Journal's* pigeons, now 170 in number, began operating three and a half years ago. Mostly they covered the arrival of ships. Lately they have taken on all sorts of assignments: horse races, football games, and calamities. During the 1936 flood, when mechanical means of communication failed, they brought pictures from Hartford, more than a hundred miles away, in a little over two hours. Their longest flight was 161 miles, from the Queen Mary steaming westward on her maiden voyage. The first *Journal* pigeon got home three hours after being released, making the trip almost twice as fast as the Queen Mary, and the others came in a few moments later. The pigeons had been sent to England to sail back on the liner. The *Journal* birds are cared for by a staff of five men. Only half a dozen pigeons go out on small stories, but when Corrigan arrived fifty of them covered the event, some from an airplane which took air views. After the pictures had been snapped, the plane flew low over the Journal Building so that all the birds had to do was dive down to their cote. They made it in eight to eleven seconds. All the pigeons can fly a mile a minute. The unofficial record belongs to a bird which made it from a Philadelphia football game at 73.8 miles an hour, aided by a strong tail wind. Each one goes on an average of three assignments a week and not one has ever failed to come home.

The *Journal* is the only local paper using pigeons, but the Acme picture service has some. During the recent hurricane a considerably ruffled Acme bird landed on the *Journal* roof, along with some *Journal* pigeons, with a full load of film. The *Journal* men attribute this unusual happening to the fact that the bird wore a heavy harness and had been flying against the wind, and they also suspect that he hadn't been well trained. After they had fed and watered the pigeon, they threw him back into the air, without his pictures. These were delivered later by a slow messenger. In the early days of pigeon reporting, the *Journal* birds wore harnesses on their backs, and one bird, released at Hawthorne, N. Y., got his wing caught in his harness and had to land. He was picked up in the Bronx walking south in a straight line. The pads of his feet were worn through. The man who found him called the *Journal* and was told to send him home in a taxi, with the windows closed, which he did. The *Journal* is fond of its pigeons, and they are loyal to their keepers, who call them the "cooing Hearstlings." The men are especially proud of one scoop the birds scored. When Jimmy Walker returned from Europe a couple of years ago, pictures were flown from the boat together with an autographed story by the ex-Mayor, and by the time Jimmy landed, a photographer was waiting at the pier to take a picture of him buying a paper with his picture and story in it. Whereupon *that* picture was rushed by pigeon for the next edition, which presumably reached Walker at the door of his hotel.

October 8, 1938

I used to spy on Jimmy Walker when he had weekend trysts with Betty Compton at a house next door to my parents' summer place in Westchester County, but so far as I know no lurking photographer ever caught me in the act, or him.

Exiles in Princeton

With both Thomas Mann and Einstein settled in Princeton, that community could easily advertise itself as a centre of German intellectualism. Dr. Mann has rented a large red-brick house at 65 Stockton Street, a short distance from the campus, and lives there with Mrs. Mann and whichever of his six children are at home. Ever since he left Germany, the author told us in his library the other afternoon, he has wanted to live in a university town. Princeton opened the way by appointing him Lecturer in the Humanities. He is giving six lectures, four in English to the public and two in German to advanced students, on four subjects: Goethe, Wagner, Freud, and his own book, "The Magic Mountain." He writes his lectures in German and his wife translates them into English. He will continue to write in German no matter what Hitler does. His only composition in English to date, aside from a few letters, has been his speech at a pro-Czechoslovakian meeting in Madison Square Garden a couple of months ago. At the moment he is at work on a novel based on the life of Goethe. Dr. Mann says this will be a "tragi-comic little thing." He writes about three hours every morning, starting directly after breakfast. His afternoons are devoted to reading and answering correspondence. His wife serves as his secretary.

The Manns took out their first citizenship papers last May, about the time the author was completing a lecture tour. On this trip so many people wanted to hear him that frequently the police had to be called out. In Cleveland the excitement was so great that Dr. Mann thought the cops were present to shield him from enemies. He had scarcely regained his calm when two days later, in Toronto, he and Mrs. Mann awoke to find a note under their door reading, "We've got you now," or words to that effect. The Manns ran next door to the room of their lecture agent. It was ultimately revealed that the note had been left for the agent by some ribald friends of his who had made a mistake in doors. We found Dr. Mann troubled not only about the Nazis but about a Christmas tree, which he didn't realize could be purchased in Princeton. The library is his favorite room. He writes there at a large desk which he sneaked away from Hitler by a ruse, sending it to a friend in France, near the border. On the desk are the bronze head of a Siamese warrior, a wooden figure of a servant taken from an Egyptian tomb, and half a dozen medals, one of which was presented to him by President Hindenburg in the old days for his services to German culture. He took another from a case and handed it to us with the remark that it was heavy—"and solid gold, too." We admired the sculptured figures on one side and the bas-relief of a head on the other, and the inscription, "Nobel."

Before he moved to Princeton, Dr. Mann had frequently visited Einstein there. The two men were friends in Germany. Now they meet for lunch or dinner at each other's homes or at the home of Dr. Mann's other translator, Mrs. Lowe-Porter. Einstein is no longer regarded as a campus novelty in Princeton. There is a story to the effect that one time none of his neighbors' radios would work and a repairman who was called attributed this to the presence of a certain type of electric heating pad in the vicinity. They eliminated every house but Einstein's, and then sent a timid delegation there. Einstein readily admitted he had such a device but insisted on illustrating, by a bewildering series of mathematical calculations, that his heater couldn't possibly cause trouble. The neighbors nodded politely but, nudged by the repairman, asked if he would mind if they bought him a different kind of heater. Einstein agreed, and after they got him a new pad all the radios worked.

December 10, 1938

Distant Music

Our favorite spectacular fact about "The American Way," starring Fredric March (in person), is that the music which accompanies it doesn't come from an orchestra pit and isn't recorded, either. It originates in a studio above the Center Theatre proper, is picked up by two microphones, and piped to a pair of loudspeakers in the auditorium. That's the Rockefeller Way. The reason for this is that the Kaufman and Hart opus requires a forestage, which could only be built over the orchestra pit. We looked into the situation one night last week and found ourself, after some involved travelling around the theatre building, outside a door on the seventh floor which bore a sign saying, "IMPERATIVE—DO NOT KNOCK AT THIS DOOR WHILE MUSIC IS PLAYING." Not hearing any music, we knocked and were let in by Oscar Levant, who composed much of the music for the show, arranged all of it, and conducts the orchestra. There were sixteen musicians with him, some in their shirtsleeves, one needing a shave, and all sitting on gilded chairs that the Rockefellers acquired for "The Great Waltz." The walls were hung with cloth and the floor was heavily carpeted, to absorb echoes, Mr. Levant explained. He sat us on a gilt chair next to a mike and warned us not to sneeze.

To keep Mr. Levant in touch with the action onstage six stories below, there are three signal lights: a blue one, a white one, and a red one. Blue means "Get ready," white means "Go," and red means "Stop." In case these should fail, there is a supplementary mike, from which a tinny voice says "Go ahead," or whatever is necessary, when the white light flashes on. The lights, and voice, are operated by Jack Kennedy, one of the show's seven stage managers, who stands in the wings and instructs not only the orchestra but also a man named Spong in the first mezzanine. Mr. Spong turns the loudspeakers on and off and a mistake on his part would be serious. When they're not playing, the musicians, who have already exhausted the stories of their lives, tell each other jokes that a mixed audience might find upsetting.

The orchestra's longest stretch of continuous playing is six minutes, during the intermission. The musicians' intermissions during the play vary in length from one minute to eighteen. At our visit the men smoked and played cards during these and we chatted with Mr. Levant, who has never seen "The American Way" and probably never will unless he loses his job. He told us that the sign outside the door of his room—which used to be a dressing room for extras—was absolutely essential. One night a flutist fainted and a nurse who was sent up to attend him banged on the door so insistently that Mr. Kaufman, who was in the audience below, asked Levant later why the hell he had suddenly added a bass drum to the orchestra. None of the actors ever talks to the isolated musicians except Eve Abbott, a warmhearted bit player who rides up on the elevator during one of her long waits and visits them.

Besides his own compositions, Mr. Levant plays parts of Victor Herbert's "American Fantasy," MacDowell's "In Autumn," and, of course, "The Star-Spangled Banner." For the funeral scene, he rescored a Bach prelude from "The Well-Tempered Clavichord." "That music transcends the ordinary funeral march," he told us defensively. He's perhaps best known as the composer of such popular tunes as "Lady, Play Your Mandolin," "Lovable and Sweet," and "If You Want the Rainbow"—either as that or as the musical-question answerer on the radio hour Information Please—but his real interest is in writing serious music. He has composed a piano sonatina, a piano concerto, and a suite for orchestra which includes a dirge for his friend George Gershwin. Of late he's been frequently commended for his wittiness, and we asked for a few quotable examples. "Well," he said, "once when I was going to play a piece by Brahms on the air, they asked me if I'd mind cutting it. I said I wouldn't but they might hear from Brahms in the morning. And another time I was in bed telephoning somebody late at night and I said, 'I'll have to hang up now or

I'll be too sleepy to take my sleeping pill.'" He also gave us an example of Gershwin's wit. He and Gershwin were travelling on a train together once and sharing a drawing room. Gershwin went to bed in the lower berth and Levant in the upper. After they'd got settled, Gershwin observed, "The difference between a minor and a major talent."

April 1, 1939

Just A Débutante

A few days after Christmas a committee including Elsa Maxwell and the Grand Duchess Marie selected the eleven most glamourous people of 1938. A few observers might have questioned the attribution of glamour to Orson Welles, the Duke of Windsor, Neville Chamberlain, Anthony Eden, Vera Zorina, the angelic ballet dancer; Alice Marble, the singing tennis player; Countess Barbara Hutton Mdivani Haugwitz-Reventlow, or the movie stars Danielle Darrieux, Hedy Lamarr, and Bette Davis, but no one could have expressed surprise at the eleventh name on the list: Brenda Diana Duff Frazier, who, the committee announced, had "made the American débutante the most attractive young woman alive."

The citation was unnecessary and in a sense untrue. If Brenda has made the American débutante anything, she has made her unhappy. She may even have delivered an involuntary *coup de grâce* to the antiquated coming-out system, which today is less of a concern to the débutantes themselves than to a few high-priced social secretaries and some mothers whose daughters are not, to use a word, photogenic. She has, with a very few exceptions, driven the other New York débutantes right into the undesired privacy of their homes by taking considerably more than her share of the public notices. There were about four hundred débutantes in New York City this past season, and Brenda's newspaper linage probably outnumbered all theirs put together. On occasion, when some of them were sitting in a night club with Brenda and a couple of boys, a picture would be taken, but before being printed would be trimmed to include only Brenda and one of the escorts, not necessarily her own. She has, or should have, discouraged all the press agents in the world by realizing, in a short and giddy year, their wildest dreams, without paying for the help of any of them. She needs a press agent about as much as she needs a nickel for a cup of coffee. Like her fellow-debs, she felt elated, when their season started, at the prospect of some flattering publicity, and last November she commissioned the Burrelles Press Clipping Bureau to keep track of her journalistic life. That turned out badly for everyone but the clipping bureau. During the next six months, Brenda received some five thousand different items (at the not inconsiderable rate of five cents apiece) and abandoned whatever sentimental notions she had fostered of pasting up a scrapbook for her old age.

Much of the news about Brenda which is served to her public is garnished with inaccuracy, a typical item being that she was running around with a jai-alai player when, as a matter of fact, she had never even seen the game played. Brenda makes no attempt to curb the imaginative press. Only once has she complained against its unflagging concern over her emotions. That was one evening when she was in bed with a cold and read in an early edition of the *Daily News* that she had been seen with somebody in the Stork Club the same night. She telephoned the society department the next morning to express polite displeasure. On the whole, Brenda's relations with the press have been cordial if not intimate. She has a high opinion of Maury Paul, with whom she coöperated to publicize the cleansing charms of Woodbury's soap by accompanying his testimonial with her picture in an advertising campaign. She feels well disposed toward Walter Winchell, who, though he had been writing familiarly about her for months, never met her formally until early in April of this year. Winchell was so impressed then that he promptly coined a new word for her, "celebutante," and offered her a ride in his car, which is equipped with special police-radio receiving apparatus and a siren. She hadn't gone, at last reports.

Miss Frazier was seventeen at the time of her début and is just celebrating her eighteenth birthday this week. Outside of the fact that she is a year younger than most of her fellow-débutantes, there is nothing terribly unusual about her. She is neither the richest, the most pedigreed, nor the most beautiful of the winter's debs. She is a nice combination of the three, however, and possesses in addition certain characteristics seemingly demanded of a top-ranking glamour girl: dark hair cut to shoulder length, a dead-white complexion, and a positive reaction to a camera. These gifts of nature had belonged to Eleanor ("Cookie") Young, who took over Newport, and Gloria ("Mimi") Baker, who took over Bob Topping, but Brenda's appearance wasn't studied. As a matter of fact, she never met Miss Young, the founder of glamour, until they were introduced at a night club early this May. "I've heard a lot about you," said Brenda cordially, as the flash bulbs popped to record this historic occasion. "I've heard a lot about you, too," said Cookie graciously.

The properties of glamour are not in themselves very impressive. In Brenda's case they are a small, thin mouth; wavy blue-black hair, which she is incessantly combing; deep-set, staring eyes; and round, full cheeks, over which she sometimes pulls a few stray locks of hair while having her picture taken or portrait painted. Consistently late hours have given her face a brittle, doll-like look, much as if her features had been painted on. Some of them, of course, have. She uses a deep-red lipstick, to match her long fingernails, which she manicures herself. She lengthens her short eyebrows by pencilling them down in a curve around the corners of her eyes. She doesn't have to bleach her face; her complexion has always been pale. It is one of the banes of her relatively baneless existence, in fact, that no matter how many applications of oil or hours of exposure she submits to, she is unable to get any more suntanned in two months at Nassau than the average shopgirl can on a summer afternoon at Coney Island. If Brenda looks pretty much the same in all her pictures, which are usually somewhat flattering, it is probably because she has the habit of raising her eyebrows, which makes her seem continually amazed. She talks in a high, shrill voice. Among her own set, which, for the most part, deals conversationally in social trivialities, she is regarded as an intellectual leader. "She talks about life and things," they say.

The theoretical climax of any débutante's season is her own coming-out party. Brenda happened to have a cold at the time, and the tabloids reported this with all the gravity that might attend the last earthly hours of a dying king or queen. Brenda's ball at the Ritz, despite her indisposition, was a gala affair, disturbed only by uninvited cameramen. Her mother, Mrs. Watriss, who had decided that on this one night at least Brenda should remain pictorially unchronicled, barred all photographers but Jay Te Winburn, who was commissioned to record the occasion for Brenda's future entertainment. This was an admirable idea, but Mrs. Watriss underestimated the resourcefulness of the *Daily News*, which dressed half a dozen of its most attractive young men in tailcoats and supplied them with a room in the Ritz. From there they drifted casually into the ballroom, armed with concealed candid cameras. One, who decided that the chances of taking his own shots without being observed would be slim, sneaked up behind Mr. Winburn and, every time that fast-working gentleman laid down an exposed plate to pick up a fresh one, slipped it under his coat. After a spell he strolled out and sent his collection to the *News*. Another stationed himself on the bandstand, disguised as a musician. While waiting for an opportunity to begin shooting, however, he was recognized by another jealous photographer, a Russian free-lancer, who had managed to get in, but without his camera. The Russian reported the presence of the *News* man to Brenda, who had him thrown out and then had the Russian thrown out too. She just stared blankly at one *News* man who was perched in a box overlooking the dance floor, making faces at her to hold her attention. She took him for one of the thousand guests, many of whom she had never seen before. By the time the last edition of the *News* went to press, the whole story was ready in pictures: Brenda greeting Mrs. Cornelius Vanderbilt and Elsa Maxwell; Brenda chatting with a host of young men; Brenda being, so the caption read, kissed by an anonymous admirer. The society reporters grew

37

hysterical over the guests, the food, the music, and the cost (which was reported to have been as high as $60,000), and Elsa Maxwell complained subsequently that she hadn't been able to get a chicken sandwich. The only missing detail was: Who had kissed Brenda? The *News* didn't know, and neither did a society press agent whom the paper called in early in the morning to identify the cast of characters. Brenda refused to say who he was and maintained that he had only been whispering, anyhow. That remark got no more attention than Mrs. Watriss's anguished statement, printed in subsequent editions, that the party had actually cost just under $16,000— which, as deb parties have gone, is neither little nor much.

As the season rolled merrily along, Brenda became a convenient peg on which to hang everything from doubtful humor to obscenity. She had become a national institution, like the doughnut. As a matter of fact, she and the doughnut coöperated once, to the considerable benefit of the doughnut if not to her. In order to help a photographer get an unusual picture, which was fast becoming a difficult feat, she obligingly dunked a doughnut. The picture appeared in two national magazines and was incorporated into the institutional advertising not only of the doughnut industry but of the Shell Union Oil Corporation, which used it, apparently, on the farfetched ground that to be a successful dunker you had better dunk doughnuts made in machines lubricated with Shell. An orchid was named after her, and lots of girls who shouldn't began wearing strapless evening gowns.

Brenda was at first amused by this notoriety. She became less amused on discovering that her autograph was apparently so valuable a commodity that people would use physical pressure to get it—sometimes twenty or thirty people at once. The family's social secretary found herself suddenly cast in the rôle of diplomatic agent between Brenda and people with ideas for something called Brenda Linen, interviewers from the high-school press, and college boys telephoning from Wyoming. Then there was the problem of fan mail, which came in at the rate of ten letters a day. There were billets-doux in Italian, French, and German, and others from Australia, New Zealand, and the Orient. A thirteen-year-old boy asked for a hundred dollars with which to buy a car, a girl in the West for a set of Louis XVI bedroom furniture, a struggling musician for a grand piano. Almost every letter requested financial help, and in certain seemingly worthy cases, like that of a woman whose small son had never seen the circus, Mrs. Watriss fulfilled the demands. College boys all over the country invited Brenda to their proms and offered to pay Mrs. Watriss's expenses as chaperone if necessary. A mother sent Mrs. Watriss a picture of her son, suggesting pleasantly that it would be nice if the kids could get together. A group at Cornell offered Brenda her choice of any escort there, provided she brought a strapless evening gown to one of their dances. All such invitations were refused. Brenda has, in fact, never been to a college prom.

During the deb season, Brenda has actually spent less time in New York than most of her contemporaries. On three occasions, once for two months, she has gone to visit her grandparents in Nassau, a resort she likes almost as much as it likes her. Her approach on one journey was heralded by a prose poem in the editorial columns of the Nassau *Daily Tribune*, which referred to her as a "delicate little creature of God's own personal creation" and ended tremulously by predicting that "Brenda Frazier is no flower of this season alone but . . . will continue perennially green—a thing of beauty, and a joy forever." Her departure from New York on this particular trip was hysterically recorded by the press, which omitted no details, not even that she had utterly amazed the other passengers on the medium-priced Munargo by doing a lovely Conga on deck. In Nassau, as in New York, photographers tagged along after her, and distance could not prevent her local fans from glimpsing her leading an orchestra, sunning herself on the beach, and winning a competition known as the hurdle dance—a kind of inverted high jump in which the bar is lowered progressively to within a few inches of the floor while the contestants squirm underneath it.

Nassau was also the scene of her first dickerings with the motion-picture industry. One company offered her fifty thousand dollars to make a single picture, and another a five-year contract at a hundred thousand a year, but Mrs. Watriss put her foot down and Brenda refused to accept either offer. If Brenda had had her own way, she might have gone to Hollywood, because it would have made possible the achievement of one of her two ambitions; to build herself a lodge on a lake shore in the Adirondacks. (The other ambition, somewhat easier if less exciting to realize, is to continue her study of languages.) While toying with the idea of the movies, Brenda was lectured at some length by one of her escorts about the soulless atmosphere of Hollywood. Later, when he discovered that a rival had been given a screen test because of his friendship with Brenda, the first fellow tried to have one made, too, just to be prepared in case she changed her mind. She probably won't. If she signed a movie contract, it would be too easy for her critics to point to her astonishing quota of publicity as a premeditated plot, and she would stop being the most unproductive public figure of the era, next to Charlie McCarthy, and become just an ordinary celebrity, a word she dislikes having applied to herself. "I'm not a celebrity," she says. "I don't deserve all this. I haven't done anything spectacular. I haven't done anything at all. I'm just a débutante."

June 10, 1939

Excerpts from a Profile.

Tables For Two
Getting Away from It All

There are moments in the life of the most tractable escort when he gets tired of looking for that remote country nook, and gets equally tired of ashes flying into his drink, tablecloths flapping around his knees, and views of the city at dusk. He even gets tired of stars. Looking for a nice, smoke-filled retreat to take a girl to last week, this fugitive roof gardener wandered first into Mother Kelly's new Miami Room, at 130 East Fifty-eighth Street, and found himself practically out of doors again. There are stars on the ceiling and the room is filled with remembrances of nature—photomurals of a Florida beach, paintings of race horses, and imitation palm trees, transplanted, I suppose, from whatever warehouse bears the same relationship to night clubs that Cain's had to the theatre. The place is air-cooled and seems very spacious, perhaps because it has a relatively large dance floor. I imagine that Mother Kelly, who is, as you're probably tired of hearing, a man, would be only too glad to cover part of it with extra tables if the necessity arose. You'll find plenty of room, though, to do the World's Fair Hop and whatnot to music supplied by Jerry Livingston's band, one of those outfits featuring three violins and a lot of gourd-shaking.

Dozens of familiar places have yielded neither to the weather nor the Fair as yet, although there's a tendency at this time of year for night-club proprietors to close up shop suddenly and retire to the mountains, or the beach, or another night club. The Famous Door, at 66 West Fifty-second Street, is not only open but generally filled to its elastic brim now that Count Basie is back with a band as good, and as loud, as it ever was. Don't go there if you have a quiet, restful evening in mind. Basie, who belongs to the fight-fire-with-fire school, overcomes the heat outside by the simple method of manufacturing more of his own within. If you're not prepared to be half blown out of the place by the brass section, drop the whole idea. Or go down the street to the Hickory House, at 144 West, where you can hang onto the circular bar while the band plays inside it—a setting I have found difficult to explain to Fair visitors. The magnet that draws me to the Hickory is not the trick bar but Hazel Scott, a curly-haired girl who is somewhat of an institution there. Miss Scott, who acts like an almost grown-up pickaninny, probably because she is one, just sits at the piano, singing or playing or laughing at the customers, and everybody, including herself, has a wonderful time. The band right now is Wingy Mannone's.

Rumors are floating around that the present tenants of Fifty-second Street are going to be trampled someday in the onward march of Rockefeller Center, but there are no indications yet of an exodus. New places, shiny and confident, continue to open, and close, with celerity. One of the latest (to open, and, I trust, not to close) is the Troc, at 53 West. It has a band headed by Bobby Hackett, whose trumpet-playing you've probably heard somebody compare to Bix Beiderbecke's. I'm not going to get into that argument, but I do think it's a pity Hackett had to get himself involved with a full-sized fourteen-piece band. That's a larger number than he used to have in the Village, and I'm not sure that the extra men have helped him any.

At Nick's, 170 West Tenth Street, Bud Freeman, the saxophonist, has herded together some of his cronies, including Pee Wee Russell and Eddie Condon, and they're producing as solid swing as you could ask for at any time. In addition, there's Zutty Singleton, the marvellous drummer who plays with a piano-and-clarinet accompaniment. Occasionally this threesome is augmented by Nick himself at another piano, sizzling like one of his steaks.

If you want to make a clean break with the great outdoors, try the Village Vanguard, at 178 Seventh Avenue South (11th), which was mentioned briefly in this column several months ago. If the Vanguard were to put in air-conditioning, even, it would probably scare away a lot of its regular patrons, an informal group who are as likely as not to be in play suits or shirtsleeves. Don't let this scare you away, though. What makes the place worth visiting is its entertainment, as clever a revue as any in town, written, directed, and acted by five engaging young people whose professional experience could be inscribed on the head of a swizzle stick. Their material is the type of stuff you've seen in "Pins and Needles," but the accent is nonpolitical, though decidedly satirical. Currently, they're putting on a forty-five-minute show based roughly on the subject of magazines, and, like any revue, it has its high spots. You'll be sorry when you leave that there isn't any published sheet music for "Young Man with a Kazoo" or "Picketing the Fair," so you could learn the words yourself.

The Vanguard kids, who call themselves the Revuers, go on twice a night—at 10:15 and 12:15, approximately—every day but Sunday and Monday. If you know about the place but haven't been there in a month or so, you'll be glad to hear that it has finally obtained a liquor licence and that you won't have to bring your own supplies any more and feel as if you were doing something slightly illegal. In the postwar days, the Vanguard was the hangout of indigent poets who read their latest epics aloud and subsisted on the coins thrown to them by other patrons. Nobody throws anything any more, and if there are poets around, they're no more active than poets in any other cellar. None of the Revuers, incidentally, is over twenty-three. They write a new show whenever they feel like it and also construct their own scenery (a decorated wooden screen), which costs them about two dollars a production. If you go on Wednesday, which is variety night, you'll see a potpourri of their best numbers.

August 5, 1939

For nearly two years, I covered night clubs for *The New Yorker*. I signed my "Tables for Two" departments "Check"—this in recognition of the magazine's unflinching and admirable policy that its operatives, known or anonymous, refrain whenever humanly possible from accepting free drinks or other favors. The above was my first offering, and in it I paid deserved tribute to the then uncelebrated Revuers, though I foolishly omitted to mention any of their names, among these the later celebrated Judy Holliday, Betty Comden, and Adolph Green.

Mabel's Tony

We dropped in on Mabel Dodge Luhan, who, as you've undoubtedly heard, is back in town reviving her salons of yesteryear, largely to ask her about her celebrated, and fourth, husband, Tony, a Pueblo Indian who is due to come to New York from their home in Taos, New Mexico, sometime in February. Mrs. Luhan, a lady whose low black bangs are now slightly tinged with gray, told us that Tony, who, like herself, is over sixty, will probably not have too good a time here; he visited the city before and, as a confirmed outdoors man, objects to having everything go on under roofs. He likes hockey matches at the Garden and wrestling, however, and the singing in musical shows. He dislikes oysters, and Mrs. Luhan doubts that he'll react much more favorably toward her salons, if he attends any. "He would probably get little pleasure out of such topics as civil liberties and 'Finnegans Wake' and psychiatry," she said, referring to recent discussions *chez* Luhan. Tony has never read any of his wife's four volumes of "Intimate Memories," in which he is a featured character. He has never read anything in English, in fact, and can speak it only haltingly, even after seventeen years of married life with Mabel. He prefers Spanish, in which she is far from fluent, but they get along fine anyhow. When they're apart he sends letters to her in English, which he dictates to a New Mexican friend. Mabel's letters to Tony are read to him. She has never attempted to learn his Indian dialect and it's probably just as well; a philologist went to Taos several years ago, intending to compile a native grammar, and left after three months, completely discouraged by the acquisition of fifty-eight personal pronouns.

Tony's full name is Antonio Lujan; almost all the Pueblo children are baptized at an early age by Spanish priests, and are accordingly given

42

Spanish names. The discrepancy in spelling between his surname and his wife's is attributable to her resentment of her Eastern friends' mispronunciation of Lujan, which is pronounced "Luhan." Tony has an Indian name, too, but has never told his wife what it is, being reserved about Indian affairs practically to the point of complete silence. "In the beginning I used to ask him about things like that," Mrs. Luhan told us, "but he never answered." She doesn't mind this a bit; Tony lives his life, she lives hers (and writes about it), and everything is amicable. She has never been inducted into his tribe and maintains that such honorary gestures have no significance among Indians—only among newsreel editors and Republican Presidents. She does have an Indian name, though, which Tony gave her long ago: White Hawk. She once named a horse after Tony.

In New York, Mr. Lujan will wear regular city clothes; in Taos he wears a blanket and devotes himself to the tribe's affairs and to farming. "He is always in a field," Mrs. Luhan said. He also hunts, bagging such local game as deer, quail, duck, elk, and antelope, most of which the household eats along with chickens, turkeys, apples, plums, pears, and numerous green vegetables that it raises. Tony gets on reasonably well, his wife said, with her artistic and literary friends, but if he is bored with any of them, "he just fades away." His chief purpose in coming East is to see the Commissioner of Indian Affairs in Washington, John Collier, who is an old friend of the Luhans, or Lujans. Mr. Collier got his job in 1933, partly because Tony went to Washington and convinced both President Roosevelt and Secretary Ickes that Collier was the Indians' friend. Tony will stop off in Washington on this trip to discuss Indian business with Collier and Ickes; Mrs. Luhan thinks he is probably going to ask them to give his tribe a flour mill.

February 3, 1940

No Ice, Please

It may not matter to the sportswriters or anyone else, but I am going to hang up my skates. The popularity of figure-skating has made it impossible for me to continue a career which I began twenty-odd years ago, when I was not yet three. I made this astonishingly early start partly because there was a convertible tennis-courts-to-rink place right down the street from my house, and partly because an elderly aunt of mine, not quite clear about my age, sent me a pair of double-runners for Christmas, when a picture book made of indestructible cloth and colored with digestible vegetable dye would have been more appropriate. I soon became the best double-runner man, weight for age, in the block. Later, when I had achieved single-runner status, the one Christmas present I could always accurately foretell was a season ticket to the rink. I cite these facts to prove that I was a conscientious skater. I was also a pretty good one, in my line, and at the age of twelve managed, with the help of a generous handicap, to finish third in an informal Saturday-morning speed-skating race at Iceland.

For years I held stubbornly to the theory that figure-skating was a pastime suitable for delicate ladies and a few spry old gentlemen, and that the truly sensible way for a man to act on ice was to tie himself into a pair of long racing blades and skate as fast as possible in a wide, masculine circle. That may not have been the universal point of view, but it was mine and I cherished it until the spread of the Sonja Henie influence made it untenable. Girls, delicate or not, now take to the ice and try to emulate Miss Henie even if they haven't nice legs, and boys brush up on their figure eights so they can waltz with the girls or get a job in Hollywood. During the height of my skating career, more than ten years ago, there were no skating movies, and if you happened to get entangled with a girl at the rink, you simply pulled her around it three or four times, following the circular, counter-clockwise movements of the pack.

This counter-clockwise business is important, because to my mind it constitutes the major difference between what might be called the Henie school of thought and my own. Miss Henie and I must have started skating about the same time, if under different conditions. She had unlimited ice in Norway and could skate in any old direction without running into anyone. I couldn't. Aside from rare occasions when the rink wasn't crowded, I had to skate round and round, counter-clockwise. If I tried for one moment to break away from the moving circle, an attendant would dash over and thrust me back in or make me sit down.

Despite this restriction, I enjoyed skating and was proud of my skill. My family was rather proud of my skill, too, and for one birthday presented me with a pair of custom-built, Blue Streak, sixteen-inch tubular racers, which were almost as long as I was and considerably more dangerous. I loved them. I drew pictures of them in all my textbooks and, in order to give them the proper care, invested my savings in a sharpening stone and a set of vises. I spent hours tenderly grinding the edges of the blades and shining them with a special chamois cloth. I rented a locker at the rink so that I wouldn't have to put on my skates while sitting on the warped wooden benches occupied by boys who had only fourteen- or fifteen-inch blades. This turned out to be an uplifting move, because the next locker belonged to an ex-member of an Olympic skating team whom I was eventually permitted to address by his first name. On Saturdays and Sundays, when the rink was so well patronized that ordinary speed-skating was out of the question, he used to clear a small space in the middle of the ice and tear around in a tight, swift circle, with other racers hot in pursuit. I would hurl myself boldly into this curious procession and hang on as long as I could, nearly grazing the ice with my left arm and often alarming my mother, who would peer in occasionally and see me flying by, inches ahead of an Olympic skater who, for all she (or I) knew, was just about to trample me in his mad dash to nowhere.

I more or less abandoned skating when I went to college, and didn't take it up again until one afternoon a few weeks ago, when a girl invited me to join her at a skating club to which she belonged. I dug up my old sixteen-inchers out of a closet, discovered I could still get into them, and, feeling pleasantly excited, walked over to the rink. When I got there I found it exclusively occupied by lady figure-skaters, who stared at my long blades as if they thought they had been borrowed from the New-York Historical Society. The girls were all wearing abbreviated skirts and whirling and pirouetting like something out of Darryl F. Zanuck. The ice itself seemed much glassier than the ice of my memories.

I began to skate around cautiously in my old-fashioned way, but the other skaters didn't coöperate. Each of them had staked out her own little claim and was practicing complicated figures there, which made it difficult for me to proceed in any comfortable, circular fashion. Finally the girl who had invited me suggested that we try to skate around together a couple of times. Halfway through the first lap we were confronted by the awful spectacle of a young lady bearing down on us backward, one leg in the air high over her head, à la Henie. I tried to do the only thing possible under the circumstances. I attempted a sharp right-hand turn. This unfamiliar maneuver sent me into a tail spin, and I crashed to the ice. Naturally, since I was holding onto my partner, she went down too. After regaining her feet and brushing the particles of snow off her velvet skirt, she looked at me pityingly and said maybe we ought to stop and have a bite to eat.

We stopped, and I don't think I'll ever start again. As long as Sonja reigns, there is no point to my going on. I can only skate counter-clockwise.

February 24, 1940

Oh No, Bonnie, Oh No!

No matter how hard I try to keep away from them, I always seem to be wandering head on into publicity stunts. I think it's high time this stopped, and I feel especially strongly about it because of what happened last Thursday night, or rather Friday morning. I had been to a party and, at about three o'clock, stopped in at the Stork Club for a nightcap. At a table near the bar I saw a press agent who works for the Columbia Broadcasting System, and with whom on a couple of previous occasions I had had pleasant nightcaps. He asked me to join him, and introduced me to a few other men at the table. We chatted for about an hour. Then I suggested to the press agent that he come out and have some breakfast with me, but he urged me to go along with his group to a rather special breakfast party he was involved in. My resistance was low, and I went along.

Two hours later I was riding over Governors Island in a United Airlines plane (NC16072), eating scrambled eggs and sausages with Bonnie Baker, a pretty young lady who has gained much fame and prosperity recently from having sung the words "Oh" and "Johnny" more times than I would even like to think about, much less hear. If on paper this seems a sudden transition, I can only plead that it was a sudden transition when it happened, too. Maybe I ought to go back a little.

We left the Stork Club and stood on the street for a couple of minutes. Our group at that time included the press agent, an advertising man from Lord & Thomas, a reporter from the *World-Telegram* and one from the United Press, an executive from the Columbia Broadcasting System, and a short, dark man whose precise status in the gathering I was never able to figure out at all, not even when, later on, he leaped to his feet in the plane and shouted, "I'm Lindbergh!" Well, anyway, we were standing outside the Stork Club, at four-fifteen in the morning, waiting, I was told, for the *Times*. The *Times* turned up sleepily a moment later, having been routed from his bed, and we rode off wildly toward Flushing, some of us in a cab, others in a private car. I think I was in the car, but I am not sure of anything now. We were about halfway across the upper level of the Queensboro Bridge before I learned that our destination was LaGuardia Airport, that there we were to meet a plane which had left Chicago carrying Miss Baker, Orrin Tucker and his band, and a few odd people named Oh Johnny, and that we were supposed to climb into the plane seats vacated by all the musicians except Miss Baker and Mr. Tucker, and to accompany that couple on an early-morning flight. The trip had been thought up, as nearly as I could make out, by Lucky Strike cigarettes, on whose Hit Parade program Tucker's band is now playing; by Lord & Thomas, representing Lucky Strike; by C.B.S., over whose network the Hit Parade is broadcast; by the Columbia Record Corporation, which makes records of "Oh Johnny, Oh Johnny, Oh!"; by Columbia Artists, Inc., which feels coöperatively inclined toward any project conceived by its fellow-Columbians; by United Airlines, which owned the plane; and by the New Yorker Hotel, which, for some obscure promotional reason, was providing the breakfast. I don't want anyone ever to tell me again that big businesses can't get together.

At the airport we were joined by a dozen or so others, including three photographers, a couple of subsidiary press agents, another reporter, three song-pluggers, and a Columbia Record man carrying a portable phonograph and copies of every record made by Mr. Tucker and Miss Baker. "They're our million-dollar babies," he said fondly, referring, I gathered from subsequent remarks of his, both to the records and to their creators. After we had stood around for a while watching the sky get lighter, one of the song-pluggers cried wildly and pointed up at an inbound plane. My press-agent friend said dreamily, "Just as we got to the Stork they were leaving Chicago, and I've never even been in Chicago." I was beginning to wish he had been in Chicago instead of at the Stork.

Miss Baker and Mr. Tucker descended from the plane, or tried to, amid a great flashing of bulbs and plugging of songs, both of which they withstood gracefully. Bonnie was wearing a fur coat and a black hat with a long red feather. Orrin was wearing gray spats. Bonnie yelled "Hello," with the accent, of course, on the "o." Then innumerable pictures were taken of her—standing with Tucker, standing with the whole band, signing her autograph, kneeling beside the phonograph with her mouth open to singing width, leaning against a truckload of suitcases and instrument cases, and in many other poses.

After standing around in the cold doing nothing for a while, we boarded the plane. When I had finished strapping myself into my seat, I looked up and noticed that on the door leading to the pilots' compartment were three name plates, evidently prepared by someone typographically unfamiliar with Miss Baker's favorite diminutive. The plates said:

Captain	Oh Johnnie Pincomb
1st Officer	Oh Johnnie Martin
Stewardess	Oh Johnnie Johnson

We took off at 5:45, to the quavery strains of "Oh Johnny, Oh Johnny, Oh!"—courtesy of the portable phonograph. Miss Baker didn't seem displeased when the phonograph ran down with a whine and stopped. Miss Johnson began passing around breakfasts of sliced oranges, cereal, eggs and sausages, toast, and coffee, and the photographers, in search of new angles on Miss Baker's eating habits, crawled about furiously, taking at least one picture to her every bite. I managed to slip into the seat next to her and she told me that the band had finished a vaudeville stand in Chicago just before embarking, that no one had slept on the way East, and that during the remainder of the day they were to attend a publicity luncheon, rehearse for the Hit Parade, and then play all night for dancing at the Waldorf-Astoria. My expressions of sympathy were cut short by a photographer who leaned across me and asked her, "Are you single?" Miss Baker said yes. "Well, can we line up a romantic angle anywhere?" he asked. "Not with the boys in the band," Bonnie said firmly. "Maybe with one of the pilots, though." The photographer asked, "Which Johnny do you want?," and Miss Baker answered sensibly, "The one that isn't driving." The photographer wandered off and came back with a uniformed young man who said, in answer to one of the reporters' questions, "I'm Oh Johnny Pincomb. My middle name is Billy." "Well, here we go again," said Miss Baker to Oh Johnny Billy Pincomb as the flash bulbs went off. "Yes, Ma'am," he said.

I remember vaguely flying above Manhattan, Brooklyn, Queens, and unidentifiable parts of New Jersey and Staten Island. We were in the air for over an hour and by the time we got down, shortly before seven, I was not sorry to leave even Miss Baker. She didn't seem sorry to leave any of us, either, and I didn't blame her. After a few dozen more pictures of her were taken, just to finish things off consistently, we started back for New York in an airline bus. On the way the *Times* man began unconsciously to hum "Oh Johnny," then stopped with a conscious shudder. The press agent who had got me into it all said ecstatically, "This is an opium-smoker's dream, this story." But I knew it had been no dream, this story; no dream was ever made on stuff as tough as this.

April 13, 1940

Over the years, I have used a number of signatures in *The New Yorker* other than my own. This piece was attributed, inescapably, to "Oh J. Kahn, Jr."

Why I Don't Believe In Superman

When I read a while ago that a Nazi newspaper had protested against the activities of Superman, holding them to be offensively pacifistic, I decided to get acquainted with the fellow. After all, it isn't every comic-strip character who is singled out for such personal attention. Little Orphan Annie was once attacked by the *Daily Worker*, but that isn't very eventful and she had been around for years anyhow. Superman, on the other hand, is a comparative newcomer—just a year and a half old. In that short time he has been furiously active and, I found by collecting some old newspapers recently and leafing through them, undeniably pacifistic, though not in the ordinary, do-nothing sense of the word. If Superman disapproves of a war, he simply stops it. When, for example, Blitzen and Rutland went to war in his strip, he grabbed up Dictator Amork of Blitzen and General Gotha of Rutland. Tucking one under each arm, he flew to the trenches and there instructed them to fight it out on a man-to-man basis in full view of their assembled and hitherto embattled forces. You know what happened; they began to pull one another's hair, the softies, and the soldiers threw down their arms in disgust, thus ending the war instantly for lack of participants.

Superman can take wars in his stride, or flight, because he is impervious to attack. Bullets spin off his superskin like raindrops off a windshield, and once, when a rascal attempted to whack him over the head with a heavy club, the weapon bounced back so fast off Superman's superskull that it knocked his assailant cold.

At the start of Superman's career it was hinted that he could leap an eighth of a mile, hurdle a twenty-story building, and outrun an express train. It has since developed that he can also outrun a bullet, swim an ocean without puffing, demolish an airliner by meeting it head on in mid-air, and change the course of a forest fire by breathing heavily on it. He can knock out eleven burly pugilists in exactly one second, divert a flood by barehandedly digging a pit a mile long in a few minutes, and win a rather one-sided combat with a battleship by pushing it close to shore and then walking out of the water holding the ship up over his head. "Nothing less than a bursting shell could penetrate his skin," his authors once crowed, and they have lived up to their words. Bayonets, when thrust at him, crumple into so much scrap steel, and the Princess Tania, one of several young ladies who have crossed his impressive path, ruined a perfectly good dagger by trying to drive it into his hide. Superman was momentarily dazed after a collision with a loaded torpedo, but when in form he can project himself right through the side of a ship, and destructive implements are generally his dish. Not long ago somebody fired a cannon at him from a distance of a few yards. He caught the cannon ball in one hand, remarking, "Nice curve on that ball! Wanta play catch, eh?," and threw the ball back at the cannon, shattering it to bits.

Superman has had three identities. Originally he was Kal-l, the infant son of Jor-l and Lora, a nice young couple living on the planet of Krypton. Kal-l arrived on earth by means of a rocket ship into which his parents had thoughtfully inserted him just before Krypton burst into fragments and disappeared. Kal-l matured into Superman, and abandoned his given name forever, in one frame of a single comic strip. He decided almost immediately to become a newspaper reporter and, in his own words, to dedicate himself "to helping the oppressed, and seeing that truth and right triumph." As a reporter, he is called Clark Kent, and his disguise consists of a business suit and a pair of spectacles. Nobody has yet exposed Kent as Superman, though Princess Tania once gave him a nasty turn by remarking that he reminded her somehow of Superman, who had once rescued her and her father, King Boru of Rangoria, from the most awful predicaments.

As Kent, Superman pretends to be a miserable coward, and therefore, before doing anything superhuman, he has to get rid of his reportorial garb. He does this so swiftly that Ed Wynn's most notable change of costume seems by comparison like the performance of a reluctant turtle. Superman's basic outfit is a Buck Rogersish affair with a cape flowing behind it and a high-school football emblem on its chest. He always wears this under his Kent outfit, an arrangement which may be unsanitary but is efficient. When about to go off on a spectacular errand, he dumps his Kent clothes in any old corner, returning to them as unerringly as a homing pigeon. Sometimes he gets them back on without seeming to have returned to them at all. For instance, he swims an ocean as Superman, having left his sack suit in an alley, and comes back by transport plane, wearing the identical suit. This sartorial implausibility has taken away just about all the admiration I ever had for him.

Now, here is a typical Superman episode. It lasted for thirteen days (thirteen newspaper days, that is, not including Sundays, when Superman, in color, is engaged in entirely different and conflicting activities). Superman starts off by depositing his reporter's clothes in an ashcan next to the building occupied by the *Morning Star*, his paper. Then he picks up a low character named the Weasel and flies around for a spell with the Weasel under his arm. After five submachine guns have been emptied into his chest (not even a powder burn to show for it), he wraps the machine guns around the necks of the gunmen; stops a speeding car by grabbing its bumper; lifts up the car and shakes out two men and a girl; rescues the girl, who happens to be Lois Lane, a reporter he is unsuccessfully trying to date up as Kent (though she, the unintuitive dope, loves Superman); demolishes the car and leaps into the air to catch Lois, who by this time has been whisked into a plane and has fallen out at an altitude of several thousand feet; deposits her on the ground; flies up again and rips a wing off the plane that dropped her; and gets back to earth just in time to retrieve Lois from some quicksand into which she has clumsily stumbled. A moment later he's back in his office, with his tie knotted neatly, as Clark Kent. Economic conditions being what they are, I maintain that while all this was going on somebody would surely have poked into that ashcan, found Kent's suit, and perhaps exposed Superman before he could get around to Barney's and pick up a substitute.

Superman's best performance, to my mind, was given the night Lois broke down and asked him, as Kent, up to her apartment for a real home-cooked dinner. While she was in the kitchen stirring up something, he slipped out a window, doffed his suit, swam through a sea, destroyed a submarine that was attacking King Boru's yacht, got slapped by Princess Tania, and returned to the apartment, fully dressed, before the dinner had cooled. Lois, however, had noticed his brief absence and become embittered. She dropped a few dishes and threw him out hungry. Oh, I forgot. In between he also telephoned a story to his paper.

It's barely possible, of course, that Kent's clothes might have lain untouched where he dropped them during both these expeditions, but here are a couple of other cases, and what are you going to do about *them?* Superman, dressed as Kent, is tossed out of a boat by some gangsters. He swims along under water for a few miles wearing all of his Kent clothes but his suit coat, which he has clearly shed somewhere in the water. He gets to a dock and there removes the rest of his Kent disguise. Having won a brief race with a bullet, overcome the gangsters, and gone off carrying their boat with him, he turns up at the office again dressed as Kent and with *even his coat on*, neatly pressed and not in the least damp. And how about the time he takes off his suit in mid-air while clinging to the outside of an airplane in which, as Kent, he had been riding? His pants, you'd think, would drift off into space, but a few strips later he is back in the plane, dressed respectably as Kent, adjusting his safety belt.

I am willing to believe that Superman can fly, that his skin is impregnable, that he could beat up Paul Bunyan with both hands tied to his feet, and that he will never get to first base with Lois, who is a rather ill-tempered girl and probably not worthy of his super-attentions anyhow. I am not willing to believe, however, that he can handle human problems like dressing with such inexplicable ease. Tying a shoelace is tying a shoelace, after all, and super-strength will only break the lace. Until something is done to clear up this slight matter of logic, I am going to agree with the Germans that he is a subversive influence. If he reads this and gets sore, though, I hope he takes care of Goebbels first.

June 29, 1940

Dummy, Dummy!
Who's Dummy?

With the exception of my grandfather, all of the bridge players I know often glance at the summaries of bridge hands carried in the newspapers. My grandfather does not care to have his simple, rugged game altered by the gratuitous advice of experts, but other bridge-fanciers take occasional delight in having unfolded for them the mysteries of the Vienna coup or the triple squeeze. A few weeks ago, while reading the *Sun*, I noticed a report on the progress of the Masters' Individual Bridge Championship, an annual affair as important to bridge fans as the individual shoot at Sea Island, Georgia, is to skeet-shooters. "The final round," said the *Sun*, "produced a few spectacular results, one of the most outstanding being a hand on which most North and South players reached a small slam and made an extra trick." The *Sun* forthwith printed a box score of the hand and the accompanying bidding, as follows:

South, dealer. Neither side vulnerable.

S—A K Q J
H—K 4 3
D—A Q 9
C—Q 4 2

S—10 3 2
H—9 8 6 5
D—K 8 7
C—8 6 5

S—8 7 6 4
H—J 10
D—6 4 3 2
C—10 7 3

S—9 5
H—A Q 7 2
D—J to 5
C—A K J 9

The bidding:

Lebhar South	Glick North	Fry Jr. Jacoby	Fry North
I C	I S	South	Pass
I N T	6 N T	I C	Hymes
7 N T	Gerst	Double	East
Fuchs	East	Ap-pleyard	2 S
		West	
West	Pass	I S	
Pass	Pass	All Pass	
Pass			
All Pass			

Any bridge player, even my grandfather, would admit that the results indicated by this chart are spectacular. At first glance, they are also somewhat puzzling. I carried the item around with me for a while, studying it at odd moments, and I finally decided that I could understand it and moreover reconstruct from it the scene at that bridge table. It wasn't an easy job; none of the participants in the game was credited by the *Sun* with saying more than a word or two at a time, and I had to figure out the intervening thoughts and reactions solely from my meagre knowledge of the temperament of bridge players. My reconstruction begins just after the cards were dealt. At that point, I figure, the reporter assigned to the tournament, a young man with little or no sense of direction, asked the four men at the table to tell him exactly where they were sitting, to ensure the accuracy of his account. This is what they said, and why the said it:

LEBHAR: South. (*Lebhar is a sound, sensible fellow. He is sitting South and would naturally say so.*)

GLICK: North. (*He doesn't hear the "Sun's" question, as he is telling a kibitzer named Fuchs the title of a play he has recently seen. Actually, Glick is sitting West.*)

FRY, JR.: Jacoby. (*This answer is just silly. It will become clear, as we go on, that Fry, Jr., is a spirited but alarmingly absent-minded fellow. He's sitting North.*)

FRY: North. (*Playing against his son in major competition always makes him nervous. He knows he's sitting East but decides that the other players are having fun with the "Sun" reporter and that he'll string along; he doesn't want to seem old-fashioned.*)

After these geographical preliminaries, the men hitch up their chairs and get down to the serious business of bidding:

LEBHAR: One club. *(With three and a half quick tricks, he'd be a fool not to say it.)*

GLICK: One spade. *(He figures that if he tosses in a psychic bid, he might confuse his opponents.)*

FRY, JR.: South. *(Obviously, he's badly rattled.)*

FRY: Pass. *(He can't decide exactly what is going on, so he'll bide his time.)*

LEBHAR: One no trump. *(Although the bidding appears to be screwy, he hopes things will get straightened out. He holds a powerful hand and wants to play it.)*

GLICK: Six no trump. *(Having bluffed originally, he might as well go the whole hog, he thinks. This is the final round of the tournament and the other players are getting on his nerves; he'd like to get the hell out of the joint and into a Turkish bath.)*

FRY, JR.: One club. *(Hopelessly muddled by now, he remembers dimly that Lebhar said "One club" a while back. Fry, Jr., is peculiarly fascinated by everything Lebhar says and often repeats his partner's words, just because he likes the way they sound.)*

FRY: Hymes! *(An ejaculation. Any father might say it under the circumstances.)*

LEBHAR: Seven no trump. *(He's furious.)*

GLICK: Gerst. *(He is evidently asking Gerst, an elderly retainer at the bridge club, to come over and empty an ashtray into which Lebhar has been angrily depositing the shredded remnants of a scoring pad.)*

FRY, JR.: Double. *(Aside from the fact that he is doubling his own partner's bid, this is a perfectly proper remark.)*

FRY: East. *(He has suddenly remembered what he should have said way back at the beginning and is trying to straighten himself out.)*

LEBHAR: Fuchs. *(Mr. Fuchs, the kibitzer, has remained commendably quiet so far. Now Lebhar is requesting him to pay exceptionally careful attention. Most people, when playing a seven-no-trump contract, doubled, insist on having an outside witness looking on, so that if they are successful they will have impartial corroboration for the story they plan to tell their wives.)*

GLICK: East. *(This is an aside, addressed to Fry. Glick is simply acknowledging Fry's last word and is saying, in effect, "Oh—East. You mean you should have said that before.")*

FRY, JR.: Appleyard. *(The word "East" started him off on a train of thought, too. Its destination happens to be an appleyard he was fond of as a boy. As he says this, he looks in a happy, reminiscent way at his father.)*

FRY: Two spades. *(There is no rational explanation for this; perhaps it's a typographical error.)*

LEBHAR: West. *(Close, but not an exact transcription. What Lebhar is actually saying is "Gerst." The ashtrays need emptying again. Besides, Lebhar wants a drink, quick.)*

GLICK: Pass. *(He feels that the sooner this is over, the better.)*

FRY, JR.: West. *(A statement undoubtedly based on Lebhar's "Gerst," which Fry, Jr., misunderstood. Since he has been parroting Lebhar all along, it is illogical to expect him to stop now. If he had heard Lebhar say "Gerst," he would have said "Gerst," too.)*

FRY: *(He is speechless by now, and no wonder.)*

LEBHAR: Pass. *(He would be happy if they cut out the kidding and laid down some cards.)*

GLICK: Pass. *(If only the rest of the boys would follow his example!)*

FRY, JR.: One spade. *(He thinks he is imitating Lebhar again, but is so confused, what with his father glaring at him and the rest of the boys drumming angrily on the table, that by mistake he imitates Glick instead.)*

FRY: *(Still speechless.)*

LEBHAR: Pass. *(He's grimly determined to keep a grip on himself, no matter what.)*

GLICK: *(He has passed twice already, so this time he just nods.)*

FRY, JR.: All pass! *(Being absent-minded, he has failed to notice that the other players have done little but pass for some time. Fry, Jr., probably thinks he is doing them a favor by issuing this sweeping order to stop the bidding. They'd have stopped by themselves long ago if it hadn't been for him.)*

FRY: *(He doesn't say anything; isn't even thinking of bridge.)*

LEBHAR: All pass! *(It took quite a while, but he has finally collapsed under the strain and has begun to imitate Junior. It is a tribute to Lebhar's durability that he held out as long as he did.)*

The *Sun's* comment on this extraordinary episode was a masterpiece of subtle criticism. "Score for Fuchs and Gerst on this hand," it said, "was minus 1,520." I do not blame the *Sun* for losing patience with the contestants and attributing the whole mess to a couple of fellows who we know were merely dumping ashes and leaning on shoulders. Perhaps the only man who really relished this singular incident was my grandfather. I showed him the story and his eyes lit up. "Those so-called experts play like a lot of damn fools," he said. "I could have bid the hand better myself."

May 31, 1941

Curve Balls

After reading those letters about curve pitching in baseball which have been appearing in the rearward pages of this magazine, we concluded that the best thing to do was consult some contemporary ballplayers and get their best, and possibly final, word on the subject. Accordingly we headed for the Yankee Stadium, and made it, by a slightly curved route, about two hours before game time. Gaining entrance to the field via the Yankee dugout, we found Paul Schreiber, the Yanks' batting-practice pitcher, who throws somewhat more baseballs during the course of a season than his more celebrated colleagues. We had counted on this in the first place, for we had met Schreiber, having done a little story on him a couple of years ago. Our instinct was to get onto a friendly personal basis with the Yanks. Mr. Schreiber, not to keep you in suspense, believes implicitly in the existence of the curve ball. He snorted with indignation and tobacco juice at the theory that curves are an optical illusion. "If balls don't curve, they do some mighty funny things," he said. He added that he doubted if anybody could throw a straight ball. "Even a plain fast ball has a little hop on it—an inch or two," he said. "When a pitcher throws a curve, it looks, from his point of view, as if it breaks a foot and a half. Why, I've thrown drop curves that headed for the letters on a batter's shirt and were caught by the catcher level with his belt."

Schreiber led us out to home plate, where Joe Gordon, the Yankee second baseman, was standing in a batting cage, engaged in hitting practice. Frank Crosetti, another infielder, was pitching to him. "Man here wants to see a curve ball, Joe," said Schreiber. "Throw a curve ball, Frank," said Gordon. We got behind the cage and stood directly in front of the pitch, which was a wide-breaking curve, unless, of course, it was an optical illusion. Gordon hit it on the nose and said, "See that ball curve? Throw another, Frank." Crosetti threw another, which Gordon missed. "Curved too much," he said, with a kind of tolerant leer.

We went back to the dugout with Schreiber and met Charlie Stanceau, another pitcher; Frenchy Bordagaray, an outfielder; and Tim Sullivan, a bat boy. Unanimously, they looked at us peculiarly and agreed that pitched balls curve. Stanceau, in what was a burst of eloquence for a ballplayer, said, "It curves. It must do something. It goes around there. It *moves*. We always figured it was caused by wind resistance against the seams." "It's the way you snap your fingers," said Schreiber, which was the most scientific explanation we got from the Yanks. "It must curve," blurted Stanceau. "Why, I could throw a ball sidearm and make it break forty feet." "Not forty feet, you couldn't," said Schreiber. "Don't give me that." Schreiber then said we'd better get out of the dugout, as the boss might show up and bawl everybody out. In general, we had a very definite feeling that the ballplayers regarded us as so stupid there wasn't much use talking to us.

July 19, 1941

By the time this Talk of the Town piece appeared, I had been drafted into the army.

Nothing Up His Sleeve

Joseph Dunninger maintains that every human being is telepathic to some degree and that he himself just happens to have been endowed with unusual mental equipment for transmitting and receiving thoughts. He began to take serious notice of these gifts when he was in his teens. He developed the novel habit of casually informing his parents, after hearing a telephone or doorbell ring, of the identity of the caller. "Naturally, they were amazed and dumfounded," he says. Dunninger still occasionally dumfounds an acquaintance who has telephoned him by triumphantly announcing the caller's name before any words have been exchanged. He also has a highly developed knack of remembering telephone voices and once told a comparative stranger who had called up, "I can hear a voice on the telephone and remember it for thirty years. Call me back thirty years from now."

Dunninger has been putting on demonstrations of telepathy at parties as well as on stages almost since he became aware of his abilities in that line. As a professional mind-reader, he has naturally often been accused of having accomplices, and, as Dunninger, he naturally stands ready to present $10,000 to anybody who can prove such a dastardly accusation. Since 1928, he has appeared, without accomplices, at dozens of dinner parties attended by fashionable minds and at larger functions of organizations like the International Association of Milk Dealers, the National Hardwood Lumber Association, and the National Freight Traffic Golf Association. Many of these affairs are for men only, and his business manager, a performers' agent named Frances Rockefeller King, is proud of her ability to book him for them. "People come in and ask me for a girl show," she says, "and I give them Dunninger." Miss King is perhaps his greatest fan. "You ought to see him quiet a lady drunk by threatening to read her mind," she says admiringly. Dunninger has received as much as $1,500 for a single evening of mind-reading. Like all magicians and mentalists, he is reluctant to disclose any of his methods. He has about sixty or seventy engagements a year, and at most of them he warms up with a few card tricks and then passes around slips of paper, requesting his audience to put down dates, addresses, telephone numbers, or questions like "What was my mother's maiden name?" Dunninger instructs the crowd to concentrate hard on their questions, and then, without bothering to collect the slips, begins calling out answers. He is astonishingly accurate. He has by such procedure read the mind and so won the respect of every President from Theodore Roosevelt on, of Pope Pius XII (when he was Cardinal Pacelli), of the Duke of Windsor (when he was the Prince of Wales), and of the Countess Haugwitz-Reventlow (when she was Barbara Hutton). The Cardinal momentarily confused him by thinking in Latin; Dunninger says he could visualize the words clearly enough, but they just didn't seem to make sense. The others, however, thought in English and were easy. "The Prince concentrated the word 'Johnny,' all too simple a name," says Dunninger, reminiscing in a strange, transitive way. "When I got it, the Prince said, 'I'd love to have the folks see this.' The King and Queen! Rather a unique comment, wasn't it? Barbara Hutton concentrated a nice thought: 'If you have two loaves of bread, sell one and buy a lily.' You can grasp the significance, naturally."

Dunninger rarely indulges in extracurricular mind-reading, although he is fond of doing magic on the side and sometimes astonishes companions by causing lighted cigarettes to vanish or pencils to emerge from the air. People who have seen him in action tell him now and then that he ought to be the world's greatest stud-poker player, but he modestly disagrees. "I cannot look a man in the eye and read his thoughts," he says. When acquaintances look him in the eye and ask him just to read a few of their more obvious thoughts, he is apt to look back at them severely and say, "Would you ask a doctor who removed appendixes to prove his ability by removing one for you? Mine is hard work, requiring great concentration. I lose from two and a half to three pounds a performance." Dunninger, a fastidious man, hastens to explain that his lost weight has nothing to do with perspiration. "Energy," he says mysteriously. Occasionally he sacrifices a little energy when it seems likely that the newspapers will mention the effort. When his car was stolen a few years ago he thought hard and told the police where to look for it, enabling them to find it almost instantly, wrapped around an "L" pillar. Another time, when he was suing a janitor for $50,000 as a result of a fall that injured his arm and compelled him to abandon mind-reading for a few months, he concentrated a prediction that the jury would award him $2,750, which it did. Both these incidents were considerably reported by the press, with which Dunninger has frequent and amiable relations. He keeps a huge collection of scrapbooks but rarely bothers to look at any of them except the one he calls his first-page book, a volume reserved for items about himself which made the front page.

Dunninger dislikes being thought of as a crusader, but for the last sixteen years, as chairman of a loosely organized scientific body called the Universal Council for Psychic Research, he has been tilting away at mediums in a crusading manner. He began to devote himself to the cause in June, 1923, a banner year in which he also sufficiently hypnotized a man by radio to enable some friends to stick pins into the fellow without making him jump. That year, too, a magazine called *Science & Invention* offered a prize of $10,000 for spiritistic phenomena of a physical nature which Dunninger, one of the magazine's editors, could not reproduce or explain. A few months later an additional award of $1,000 was offered by Joseph F. Rinn, a psychic investigator who had helped to expose such distinguished mediums as

Eusapia Palladino of Italy and Margery of Boston and who had debated publicly with Sir Arthur Conan Doyle and Sir Oliver Lodge, both of whom believed it was possible to communicate with the spirit world. In 1925 Dunninger, in the name of the Universal Council, added an offer of $10,000 to the fund, and in 1926 Mrs. Harry Houdini, widow of the magician, did likewise. The sum of $31,000 was available for a short time only; Mrs. Houdini and Rinn withdrew their offers after a while. At present the sum to be won is $15,000—Dunninger's original $10,000 and $5,000 put up by the *Scientific American*, whose editors have recently organized a Committee for the Investigation of Psychic Phenomena, of which Dunninger, naturally, is chairman.

Since Dunninger became interested in spirits, some two hundred thousand letters have been sent to him or the groups of which he is chairman by people who claim to be in almost daily touch with one ghost or another. Currently, this mail is filtered by the staff of the *Scientific American*, which brings the least illegible and least illiterate parts of it to his attention. Whenever a man claims he can levitate a chair without employing mechanical devices, Dunninger gets in touch with him. "After the second or third letter I often have the complete answer," Dunninger says. "I inquire into the *modus operandi*. Then, when he says that in order to levitate the chair he burns incense, keeps a full glass of water at the foot of his bed, and sleeps on his left ear, I know he's cracked." When Dunninger has reason to believe that a correspondent is sincere, or at least uncracked, he attempts to make it possible for the person to demonstrate his talents in the presence of the psychic-phenomena committee. Recently, Dunninger tried unsuccessfully to arrange séances for a couple of mediums who employ *modi operandi* of a rather striking nature. One of them promised that if he were seated in the electric chair at Sing Sing, he would produce the spirit of Ruth Snyder, with whom he was eager to converse. The other, with an equally nice flair for morbidity, guaranteed that if he were brought together with an obliging corpse, he would persuade it to talk to him.

Dunninger has supervised some two hundred and fifty test séances, most of which have produced little in the way of tangible spiritistic phenomena. The mediums who have appeared before him have generally explained that they failed to do better because no self-respecting spirit would be seen dead in a room with Dunninger. With Dunninger looking on intently and sometimes clutching their arms and legs, countless mediums have gone into trances, hundreds of tables have wobbled in darkened rooms, and thousands of words have been chalked up on slates. Often such seeming improbabilities occur after the mediums have been bound with ropes. Exhibitions of that sort do not faze Dunninger, who is adept at getting out of ropes himself and used to make a practice of escaping from a safe when he was in vaudeville, until one evening he was accidentally locked in without a screwdriver and had to be dragged out, breathing heavily. At test séances he frequently has himself trussed up inside a cabinet and then proceeds to duplicate the mediums' performances or go them one better, activating three floating trumpets for every two conjured up by a medium.

Like most séances, Dunninger's test ones are held in almost total darkness, but mediums have the privilege of instructing a photographer to take a flashbulb picture whenever they feel sure that some spiritistic presence is in the room. One medium, who was thought to be securely roped and had made a piece of white paper flutter in front of the cabinet in which he was locked, called loudly for a picture of this astonishing event, but called a little too soon; when the negative was developed one could see not only the paper but, holding it, the medium's hand, which he had intended to withdraw just as the camera shutter clicked. To date, Dunninger's tests have failed to reveal any photographic evidence of spirits. He does not often have to wait for the development of photographs to confute a medium. One singularly gifted lady medium, who insisted on holding her séance near the top of the Empire State Building because of the spot's relative closeness to the spirit world, puzzled him briefly with a series of seemingly inexplicable raps. He soon figured out that she was equipped with an unusual set of toes, which she could cause to snap loudly inside her shoes. "I cannot duplicate that effect," he apologized later. "I am not a toe-snapper." The lady, while flattered, wouldn't admit that his theory was correct. Dunninger's most persistent adversary was Nino Pecoraro, a frail Italian medium skilled at extricating himself when tied up in ropes and getting back into them after creating a lively clatter which he unassumingly credited to spirits. In the nineteen-twenties, Dunninger matched his prowess with Pecoraro's twenty times, in a series of séances, both of them squirming in and out of ropes on monotonously even terms. In 1931, to Dunninger's immense satisfaction, Pecoraro confessed in a newspaper interview that he had no mediumistic powers and was an outright fake.

Dunninger frequently exposes mediums who have not applied for a hearing and would be just as happy if they had never met him at all. When a Hindu arrived in this country six years ago with the reputation of being able to walk without discomfort on white-hot coals and with the evident intention of putting on a few profitable demonstrations of this art, he was greeted with a statement by Dunninger in which the magician offered not only to duplicate the visitor's footwork but also to pick some white-hot coals up in his hands, to dip his hands into gasoline and set fire to them, and to engage in other pyrotechnical diversions. "I am Public Enemy Number One for phony fakirs," Dunninger announced at the time, no doubt thoroughly disillusioning the Hindu about American hospitality. In that capacity, Dunninger has distressed many mediums by invading their headquarters and subjecting them to his scrutiny. A few years ago, in an investigating mood, he called unexpectedly upon a lady medium in Harlem who weighed close to three hundred pounds. "When I got to her place," he says, "she peered out and said, 'You look like Dunninger, the world's greatest hater of mediums. No, you're better-looking. You can't be him. Come in.'" Dunninger, not offended, went in, and when the lady asked if he wanted to communicate with any particular spirit, he capriciously put in a bid for a mythical horse named Edna. He was presently kicked painfully in the shins, presumably by Edna, who, the medium said, was that glad to see him. Dunninger, who would never kick a horse, or a medium, himself, decided that the lady had changed her mind and had identified him as the world's greatest hater of mediums. Before limping out to the comparative safety of the street, however, he stayed around to watch the lady produce some ectoplasm from her mouth. While she lay trancelike on a couch, he stepped up boldly and examined the ectoplasm. "I leaned over and poked it delicately," he reported later. "I peeled off a little bit and examined it. Madame had introduced a marshmallow."

November 29, 1941

From a Profile

The Army Life
The Natives

One of the permanent effects of this war, no matter what happens at the peace tables, will be a decline in movies with South Sea Island settings. American soldiers who have returned from the Southwest Pacific will be unable to refrain from laughing out loud at the alluring women and romantic scenery exposed to their knowing, skeptical gaze, and Hollywood will have to change its line. If Dorothy Lamour and her luscious colleagues want to get out before it's too late, I'd suggest that they toss aside their wraparounds and dress themselves in Central European finery. This would assure them of a chance, for a while at least, to impersonate, imaginatively, seductively, and no doubt profitably, the belles of one of the few areas American soldiers have not yet thoroughly explored. Nobody in the movies or anywhere else is going to get very far trying to convince Americans who have been in New Guinea, for instance, that it is a garden spot or that its ladies are lovely, passionate flowers. I have seen a lot of them and have seen a lot of American soldiers near them, but I have not seen any soldier so much as hold hands with one of them. Some of us, admittedly, have stared with interest at their eccentric shapes, but it has always been in a purely academic way. For the men of Papua, the women there may have a certain charm, but to us transients they are an unseemly bunch. I'm sure that they would say, and have said, the same of us.

Leaving the gross subject of sex aside, I'd say that the better we American soldiers have come to know the permanent residents of this island, the more we've appreciated them. At times they have been our sole supply lines, as valuable as a railroad and somewhat surer. A railroad can always be blown up. When Japanese planes come toward a procession of native carriers, however, they merely dive into the jungle. Sometimes, to be sure, they remain there for two or three days, but almost invariably they come out again. Each group of natives working for us has a military organization of its own. The ranking member is a native police boy, often proudly wearing corporal's stripes, who carries an old-fashioned rifle. I have never seen a police boy fire his weapon and have no idea whether or not it is loaded, but it commands vast respect among his mates, who are unarmed and carry only a rolled-up fibre sleeping mat, a handful of tough vines, a long pole, and forty pounds of Allied impedimenta. Each group is also supervised by an Australian belonging to an organization called Angau—Australian New Guinea Administrative Union, I think the letters stand for—who tries to soothe his men when the Zeros approach, accompanies them up and down the difficult trails, and makes sure that none of them is carrying more or less than his allotted load of forty pounds.

Before beginning a jungle march, we dump into a pile the extra equipment we can't carry ourselves, and the natives gather around it like children examining gifts, while the Angau man, without the aid of scales, judiciously lifts each object and estimates its weight. Most of the natives, after receiving their assignments, work in pairs, toting eighty pounds between them. They tie their load to a pole with their vines, put the pole on their shoulders, and then stride swiftly down the trail. They are incredibly fast. One day, when my company had to move thirteen miles, the natives started off just as we did. We were still about four miles from our destination, panting unashamedly, when we met the natives strolling back with their poles and rolled-up vines, heading for home as if they didn't have a care in the world. Covering twenty-five miles a day for ten days in a row apparently doesn't strike them as anything noteworthy, but, in view of the fact that their wives act as porters when their own families move, I imagine they don't find the work agreeable.

The majority of the natives we have encountered are friendly and loyal to the Allied cause. By their standards of physical beauty we are certainly no more handsome than the Japs, but they are on our side. For one thing, they are well paid, and for another, they have sensibly concluded, even without benefit of military commentators, that the white star of the Americans is the advisable one to get hitched to. Furthermore, they just don't like the Japanese. When bringing one of our wounded back from the front lines, four of them will carry the litter gently and a fifth will walk alongside, holding a palm leaf over the injured man's face. They take no special pains when given the task of hauling back an enemy casualty. Some natives have been employed by the Japs, who, at the time of their initial landing at Buna last summer, coerced one whole local tribe into coöperating with them and in addition imported native carriers from New Britain. We captured half a dozen of these natives one afternoon, and when they were brought to our headquarters a couple of hours later, the natives who were there took delight in spitting on them.

The captive natives looked wilder than our own. They were liberally streaked with white paint, appeared cannibalistic, and would have fitted in perfectly with any casting director's preconceived notions of medicine men. Our carriers go in less heavily than they do for bodily adornment. Some of our men, though, are tattooed here and there, many of them wear flowers in their bushy hair (the women, however, do not), most of them dye their teeth a sickly reddish brown with betel-nut juice, and a few, evidently dudes, treat their hair with this same clinging substance, causing it to turn an astounding reddish-orange color.

We scarcely consider the natives curiosities, probably because they are no odder than anything else in the vicinity. They are, besides, a comparatively subdued group, never pounding tom-toms, indulging in orgies, or dancing until all hours. Every now and then, to be sure, we hear shrill, frightening cries and assume that one of them is beating his wife, but the practice doesn't appear to be any more prevalent here than back home and is apparently condoned by the victims. Both men and women are notably modest. Although they wear practically no clothes, they nevertheless, for example, bathe as demurely as our dowagers. I have never seen a native older than eight or nine, in or out of the water, completely naked.

Comparatively few of the natives understand English, but it doesn't much matter, since we rarely have an occasion to engage them in prolonged conversation. The Angau men are well versed in their gruff dialect and serve as interpreters whenever we have any important messages to convey. Several of the police boys, moreover, are slightly better acquainted than their compatriots with our language and can usually pass the good word along. In emergencies, or quandaries, we can always fall back on sign language. I have rarely heard anyone here talking to anyone else in pidgin English. There are a handful of natives who can even manage our irregular verbs, which they have learned to do from missionaries, but they are otherwise thoroughly un-Anglicized, or un-Americanized. For instance, they never use mosquito nettings, without which we wouldn't dream of going anywhere unless we absolutely had to. The natives just let the mosquitoes bite them, and accordingly most of them have malaria from time to time. Many of them are sprinkled with sores which have a tendency not to heal and which turn into itching, festering, tropical ulcers. Some of the natives, too, are afflicted with a strange skin disease that covers their bodies with grayish scales. We sedulously avoid those so decorated. The natives, by the way, don't believe that by constant exposure to malarial mosquitoes they will acquire immunity; they just don't care. This attitude was shared by one Australian I know who has lived in New Guinea for twenty years as the overseer of a rubber plantation. He once told me that he never bothered with a netting and never took quinine as a preventive against malaria. I asked him if he didn't get sick. "Certainly," he said. "How often?" I asked. "Oh, every three weeks or so," he replied.

That the natives and the Americans basically have little in common is perhaps best proved by the fact that the former regard bully beef as a treat and gobble up the stuff as eagerly as we would go for breast of guinea hen. However, they seem less concerned than one might expect with white man's magic, showing practically no interest in our radios and cameras. Unlike all natives of fiction, they are neither excited nor terrified when someone attempts to snap their picture. They just take photography for granted. Also, instead of standing around gaping when we turn on the radio, they listen contemptuously a moment or two and then walk away. The natives are no fools.

April 10, 1943

There were thirty-nine of these pieces altogether. This was No. XXIX.

Notes and Comment

A soldier friend of ours, here on leave, chanced to notice, some hours after a night on the town, that a little sticker had been pasted on the sweatband of his hat, advertising the Stork Club. He had spent a few hours there, and he concluded that the job had been done by a hatcheck girl, presumably under orders. He dropped the matter (and the sticker) there, but we are not prepared to dismiss it so lightly. We have long admired the skillful and relentless way in which the Stork Club has burrowed its way into the public consciousness, but this is going too far. Furthermore, Mr. Billingsley's evident assumption that the inside of a man's hat constitutes an effective billboard seems to us unwarranted; a man rarely looks at the inside of a hat unless he thinks he has picked up somebody else's by mistake. We regard the move as a serious violation of man's privacy, a furtive intrusion into a niche where man's own initials have long stood in unmolested dignity. If a man wants to put additional data inside his hat, it should be his secret and personal business. Perhaps the Stork Club pastes its stickers on the outside of civilian hats, and the other method applies only to military men, on the theory that the War Department might object to any outward tampering with the uniform. If that is so, we trust that the Army will not take it lying down.

March 4, 1944

Notes and Comment

This is a footnote for anyone who may be compiling a treatise on juvenile delinquency and would like to use it. Between our home and the nearest subway station lies a drab and dingy section where the streets are almost always full of children who, for want of a grassy arena, must make them serve as a playground. On our way to and from the office, we have often thought that the neighborhood children, in this age of reputed adolescent lawlessness, are in many respects the most scrupulous observers of rules we know of. Watching their games, most of which involve bouncing an old ball off the sides of buildings and pedestrians, we have noted that every infraction of the local ground rules is promptly followed by a heated huddle, in which the offender is called before, and bows to, the neighborhood bar of justice. This recognition of established order, this willingness to abide, if sometimes with the forearm twisted upward behind the back by representatives of communal authority, this realization that a man, no matter what his size or strength, may not bounce the ball above a certain level of the wall at the expense of his fellowmen, seem to us much more pronounced in these children than in many of their elders or their elders' governments.

The other evening we came upon a youthful crowd solemnly gathered around a modest bonfire. The central figure was a grimy boy of about fourteen, a notoriously dangerous age, who was holding a piece of cloth in his hands. A soldier and his girl joined the circle, and the lad asked, eagerly, "This is right, isn't it?" The soldier nodded. "Dame wanted to get rid of it and threw it out the window," the boy said indignantly. "Like an ordinary piece of garbage. See," he said to the other youths, "I told you it had to be done like this." We peered over a couple of shoulders to find out what was going on and saw the boy carefully fold the last unconsumed piece of an American flag and lay it gently on the fire.

December 15, 1945

Notes and Comment

In our own part of the world, the anxieties of the honorable gentlemen of Congress still center on the past. Last week they picked and pecked away at the eminent specialist whose diagnosis of an ailing China was eagerly awaited by a world by no means immune to infection. General Marshall's voice, we read, was a little weaker on his sixth day of testifying about Pearl Harbor, but his inquisitors, working in relays, had lost none of the relish with which they were poking into the clouds of the past, trying desperately to find some individual, dead or alive, on whom they could pin the responsibility for the day of infamy. We did some poking ourself, into that strange body of folksy literature that comprises our legislative records, and refreshed our memories of the ancient times of 1940 and 1941, when a good deal of congressional energy was devoted to questioning General Marshall, who had made suspicious proposals that Congress do something about strengthening the nation's means of defense.

Did General Marshall, we wondered, recall, as he testified this time, the day in August, 1940, when he had to plead for funds before a Senate subcommittee? Did he recall how Senator Nye had said, "Of course, General, we can entertain a hope that developments abroad in the next few months will be such that we can abandon a considerable part of this program, can we not?" and how he had replied, "Senator, I am sorry that I cannot entertain any such hope at present. My fear is not that I am recommending too much but rather that I may find at some time in the future that I recommended too little"?

Did Marshall reflect on the day in April, 1941, when he told a Senate committee how Congress had trimmed an Army request for funds to garrison Alaska—a not inconceivable point of attack—from twelve million dollars to nothing, and how an appropriation for domestic military maneuvers had been drastically cut? That resulted in the following dialogue:

SENATOR BREWSTER: When you speak of that cut, by whom was that cut?
GENERAL MARSHALL: By the Congress.
SENATOR BREWSTER: Not by the Budget?
GENERAL MARSHALL: No, sir.
SENATOR BREWSTER: The Budget recommended the larger sum?
GENERAL MARSHALL: Yes, sir.

Did General Marshall remember how, over and over again, he had had to explain the same things to different groups of congressmen, because you could hardly expect one legislator to read what had been said to another legislator? Did he recall the lengthy dialogues with Senator Reynolds of North Carolina, the endless exchanges with Senator Wheeler of Montana? Did he remember how, in July of 1941, he begged Congress to make a decision—any decision, but a decision—on a bill extending the term of service of young men already in the Army, and how, finally, a few weeks later, the House passed the bill by one vote? We shall probably never know what he thought, but pending his return from what we hope will be a fruitful mission, we are filing our data in the bulging files of our Wind on Capitol Hill Department.

December 22, 1945

Hats On

Our buoyant Mr. Stanley is safely back from the wars, and when he reported for work last week, we immediately sent him on an expedition to Danbury for an investigation of men's hatlessness, a condition about which we had been wondering. Stanley left the office hatless and returned wearing a new, fur-felt snap-brim. They wouldn't let him leave Danbury without a hat. He has turned in the following memorandum:

"Danbury is *the* hat town. It's so hat-conscious that one hotel has a Mad Hatter Tap Room & Grill, and a dine-and-dance joint is called the Hat Box. Danbury terribly disappointed in New York, because New York most hatless city in country. Some manufacturers attribute this to the present trend toward informality in masculine dress, but one guy (*fifty* hats in *his* wardrobe) thinks the trouble may be intellectuals are inclined not to wear hats and New York is full of intellectuals. Fellow who advanced this theory said I was foolish to go without a hat. He said, 'The first time your mother ever took you out, she covered your head with a baby carriage. If your skull were as thick as an African savage's, you might not need a hat, but you got to protect your head, spine, eyes, and the back of your neck.' Danbury itself not hundred-per-cent hatted. Many hat factories used to have a rule no employees could come to work without a hat, but no more. Sign at the entrance to one factory office: 'Notice to Salesmen. Our buyers have been instructed not to give interviews to hatless salesmen. It is to your interest to wear a hat when calling at this office.' Asked one fellow about the notion that hats cause baldness, and he damn near exploded. 'We made a survey and found that people who wear hats have fewer harmful bacteria on their heads than people who don't,' he said. 'We made another survey and found that only seven per cent of adult Americans believe that old wives' tale about baldness anyhow. That's as low a percentage as you can hope for, because a survey in 1943 showed that six per cent of the people didn't know who the President was.'

"Hatlessness not so rampant as it seems. Only twelve per cent of all men *never* wear hats. Thirty-two per cent always wear hats. Hat men are chiefly concerned with the other fifty-six per cent, influenced by season, weather, time of day, occasion, so on. Hatters think in terms more of hat owners than of hat wearers. Ninety-eight per cent all men over forty-five own at least one hat. Percentage in younger age groups progressively smaller. College students worst. Only seventy per cent of college men own hat. When hat people asked college men if they considered hats important to personal appearance, sixty-two per cent said no. Sixty-eight per cent of World War II vets said yes. Hat manufacturers encouraged by this. Discouraged, however, by other statistics: early this century, U.S. had 25,000,000 males old enough for hats, and annual production of fur-felt hats was 36,000,000; just before war, 50,000,000 hat-males, but production of felts only 22,000,000. (Post-war production nowhere near saturation point.) Some hat manufacturers blame themselves for hatlessness; say they haven't made hats comfortable enough. Others blame retail salesmen. One fellow said to me, 'A salesman tells a customer, "Here's a lovely hat. It'll go with anything." Hell, he shouldn't say that. He should sell different hats to go with different ensembles.' Frank Lee, of Lee Hats, who sponsors Drew Pearson, said one trouble is that hat men have been concentrating on round-oval heads for years and have ignored long-oval men. Now they're making long-oval hats for long-oval heads. I'm a round-oval. Drew Pearson long-oval, always wears hat.

"Hatters began a big advertising drive last winter to encourage hat wearing. They'd tried that sort of thing before. Years ago, Lee ran ads like one showing girl saying into phone, 'Yes, if you'll wear a hat this time.' Now industry running ads like 'Wear a hat. It gives you that look of importance!' and 'Wear the right hat with the right outfit.' They're working on men through women, too. Put ads in women's magazines to plug men's hats. But women themselves going hatless these days and this feared bad effect on men. Industry out to convince women that men can't be properly courteous without hats. Made a survey about *that*, too. Fifty-nine per cent women dislike seeing men hatless. Hat men also trying to get women to tell men that their hats, if any, look old. This angle the result still another survey. Industry asked retail salesmen why men buy hats. Forty per cent of replies said mostly bad condition old hats, forty-eight per cent said mostly some dame."

Welcome home, Stanley.

September 28, 1946

The genesis of this Talk piece was characteristic of its era: Harold Ross had the impression that men weren't wearing hats as much as had been their wont, and he wanted to look into that.

Notes and Comment

The generals and admirals of five nations who comprise the Military Staff Committee of the United Nations, and who have been working on a martial approach to peace, are flying to North Dakota next week to hunt pheasants in the valley of the Mouse River, at the invitation of the Junior Association of Commerce of Minot, North Dakota. We read about this just after we had read an advertisement in this very magazine showing an alert young fellow crouching by a limbless tree, a gun on its way to his shoulder, his gaze fixed intently on some distant target. "Happy man!" said the accompanying text, in contrast to the captions that until lately accompanied illustrations of men in this stance. "Out where he loves to be! Waiting to test his eye and aim . . . and equipped for the fullest enjoyment of his favorite sport!" His sport, of course, was hunting. Perhaps there is a good deal to be said for such efforts of commerce to persuade trained marksmen to busy themselves with shots not fired in anger. Good luck to the happy men of the Military Staff Committee, out where they love to be, in the valley of the Mouse. May their eyes be clear, their aim true, their weapons accurate, and the pheasants plentiful. And then, having had their fill of the whining bullet and the itching trigger finger, may they return refreshed and determined to the shores of the lake called Success.

October 12, 1946

Phenomenon

Because it was in 1943 that Frank Sinatra caught on, his popularity has often been called a by-product of the war, the theory being that young women turned to him as compensation for the absence of their young men. Some of his ill-wishers have even blamed him for the wartime increase in juvenile delinquency. A great many psychologists, psychiatrists, psychopathologists, and other experts on the psyche have tried to define the relationship between Sinatra and young womanhood. "A simple and familiar combination of escapism and substitution, to be expected in times of high emotional stress," said one. "Mass frustrated love, without direction," declared another. "Mass hysteria," said a third; "mass hypnotism," said a fourth; "increased emotional sensitivity due to mammary hyperesthesia," said a ninety-seventh. One of the editors of the *New Republic*, a journal of opinion, went on a safari to the Paramount while Sinatra was in season there and reported that in his opinion many members of the audience had seemed to find in the man on the stage a "father image," and added, "Perhaps Frankie is more important as a symbol than most of us are aware." A romantic psychologist attributed Sinatra's eminence to "a sort of melodic strip tease in which he lays bare his soul. His voice," he continued "haunts me because it is so reminiscent of the sound of the loon I hear in the summer at a New Hampshire lake, a loon who lost his mate several years ago and still is calling hopefully for her return." Sinatra's appeal to his fans, whether they think of him as a father, a hypnotist, or a widowed loon, can probably be ascribed simply to the desperate chemistry of adolescence. Some of his more rabid admirers have conceded guiltily that they may cast off a tiny bit of the love they bear for him when they get married, and it is perhaps significant that when the president of a Sinatra fan club in New Zealand became engaged, she resigned her office, and that when she broke her engagement, she applied for reinstatement. In Detroit, early this summer, a radio station conducted a "Why I Like Frank Sinatra" contest. Among the fifteen hundred essays submitted was one that read, "I think he is one of the greatest things that ever happened to Teen Age America. We were the kids that never got much attention, but he's made us feel like we're something. He has given us understanding. Something we need. Most adults think we don't need any consideration. We're really human and Frank realizes that. He gives us sincerity in return for our faithfulness."

Sinatra has male fans, too, including twenty members of the crew of a Navy vessel, who, just before their departure for the atom-bomb tests at Bikini, asked him for a photograph to pin up on a bulkhead. For a while, there was a Sinatra fan club whose membership requirements were nearly as exacting as the Union League's; you not only had to be a male and to admire Sinatra, but you also had to be named Frank yourself. His fans are, however, overwhelmingly young women. Their versions of the effect he has on them are, on the whole, more daintily phrased than the callous judgments of the psychologists. "I shiver all the way up and down my spine when you sing," a girl wrote Sinatra, "just like I did when I had scarlet fever." "After the fourth time I fell out of a chair and bumped my head," said another, "I decided to sit on the floor in the beginning when I listen to you." And when a local radio station held an essay contest to find out "Why I Swoon at Sinatra," the prize-winning answer, which could readily serve as the basis of a song lyric, was "If lonesome, he reminds you of the guy away from your arms. If waiting for a dream prince, his thrilling voice sings for you alone."

Sinatra is skilled at giving each of his listeners the impression that she is the particular inspiration of, and target for, the sentiments he is proclaiming. While singing to an audience, he rarely gazes abstractedly into space. Instead, he stares with shattering intensity into the eyes of one trembling disciple after another. Though his fans usually greet his appearance with loud acclaim, occasionally they are as hushed as if they were in church, and in some fan-club publications all pronouns of which he is the antecedent are reverently capitalized. Sinatra handles his kids, as he calls them, with artful skill. "I never saw anything like the way he milks 'em and kicks 'em around," one Broadway theatrical agent said as he emerged, in a daze, from a Sinatra show at the Paramount. Experienced comedians appearing as guests on Sinatra's weekly radio program have been so perplexed by the antics of his studio audiences that they have lost all sense of timing and gone up in their lines. Sinatra, on the other hand, is unperturbed when his chaotic fans are screaming, shivering, and falling off chairs. Never was a man more attuned to the discord of his accompaniment. His fans seemingly will do almost anything he tells them to, and it is fortunate for the rest of the population that he does not have a hankering for, say, arson. Their obedience falters only when he asks them to keep quiet, as he usually does just before a broadcast. "It's like trying to tell the tide not to come in," the producer of his program has said. Sinatra fans have a party line, like Communists. Lately they have been preaching self-control. It was once policy to make as much noise as possible, but the older hands among them now profess to disapprove of squealing unless Frankie does something so wonderful that you can't help yourself. They are reduced to helplessness by, for one thing, Sinatra's celebrated use of glissando; whenever he slides gently from one note to another, their admiration is exceedingly open-mouthed. They insist that they do not really scream but merely murmur "Ooh" or "Aah," but to the unaccustomed ear the bleat of many lambs can sound as harsh as a lion's roar. The girls are currently puzzled by a throbbing dilemma. They fear that if they don't continue to react boisterously to their idol, other citizens, by now conditioned to hearing him only over the strident obbligato of their affection, will conclude, an intolerable idea, that he is losing his grip. "What can a poor fan do?" one of them asked recently.

Sinatra fans express their devotion to him in odd ways. They sign letters "Frankly yours" or "Sinatrally yours," and they begin postscripts not with "P.S." but with "F.S." They try, as nearly as is feasible for young women, to dress as he does. Once, after he had absentmindedly appeared in public with the sleeves of his suit coat rolled up, thousands of other coat sleeves were tortured out of shape. The fans pin club buttons not only over their hearts but also on their socks, and they inscribe his name on sweaters and coats. One of them painstakingly inked the titles of two hundred Sinatra songs on the back of a beer jacket. Another braided her hair and tied up one braid with a ribbon labelled "Frankie" and the other with one labelled "Sinatra." A girl whose arm he had accidentally brushed while trying to escape from a pack of fans wore a bandage over the spot for two weeks, to prevent anybody else from brushing it. Another became the envy of her gang when, after Sinatra had checked out of a hotel room, she got into it before the maids did and escaped with a cigarette butt and a half-used packet of matches, both of which she assumed he had touched. After he had left a restaurant, an equally lucky girl got to his table ahead of the bus boy and managed to polish off a bowl of cornflakes he had unquestionably touched. Girls have plucked hairs from his head and, at somewhat less trouble to him, have collected clippings of his hair from the floors of barbershops. One Sinatra fan carries around in a locket what she insists is a Sinatra hangnail. Souvenir-hunting young ladies broke into his Hasbrouck Heights, New Jersey, house after he had moved out of it in 1944 and incestuously made off with a discarded bundle of old fan mail, some of which they had doubtless written themselves. So that some girls could get his autograph, others have momentarily immobilized him by throwing themselves sacrificially beneath the wheels of his car.

No entertainer's audience is more resolute than Sinatra's. Five New York girls borrowed their parents' savings of two thousand dollars and went to Montreal to hear him sing at a theatre there. The expedition was a failure. For one thing, he had left Montreal two weeks before, and for another, they had to flee from a rooming house so precipitately, to escape some police who were tracking them down, that they abandoned forty precious photographs of Sinatra they had brought along as luggage. One stay-at-home fan has listed in a notebook every song he has sung over the air in the past three years, and another takes down his broadcasts in shorthand and transcribes them, so that she will have something to read at night. Among his other fans are a girl who saw one of his movies so often that she memorized the dialogue, which she then wrote out and mailed to Sinatra; a girl who made a hundred and twenty-one pilgrimages to a movie in which he appeared only in one brief scene; and a girl who announced, after her fifty-ninth viewing of another Sinatra movie, that he spoke fourteen hundred and seventy-six words in it, not counting the lyrics of songs.

Sinatra's evolution, in the past two years, into a crusader for civil liberties and a political orator has delighted his fans. They are impressed by the knowledge that they are pledged to an entertainer of such versatility, and they look down upon the more limited idols of other fans. "Van Johnson," one Sinatra fan said in disparagement of an actor who has quite a few fans of his own, "hasn't done a darn thing for anybody except sit around and look cute." While Sinatra was stumping for Roosevelt in 1944, his fans dutifully put on buttons saying, "Frankie's for F.D.R. and so are we," and took to nagging at their parents to vote a straight Sinatra ticket. The Sinatra-fan-club papers run editorials condemning intolerance and urging their readers to cut down on ice-cream sodas so that they can contribute—in Sinatra's name, of course—to humanitarian causes. Last winter, the National Foundation for Infantile Paralysis collected money for its March of Dimes by conducting a popularity contest at a stand in Times Square. Passersby were invited to drop change into any one of forty-eight bottles, each labelled with the name of an entertainer. As soon as the local Sinatra clubs heard of the competition, they mobilized for action, and when the coins were finally counted, it was discovered that Sinatra's bottle contained nearly twice as much money as that of the runner-up, Bing Crosby.

Sinatra has undoubtedly made his fans tolerance-conscious and persuaded them to champion the rights of minority groups, but on the whole they have not learned to be tolerant of critics of Sinatra. When Ben Gross, the radio editor of the *Daily News*, remarked that he did not consider Sinatra the greatest singer in the world, one Sinatra fan wrote him that she "would love to take you to Africa, tie you to the ground, pour honey on you, and let the ants come and bite you to pieces," and another that "you should burn in oil, pegs should be driven into your body, and you should be hung by your thumbs." For unwavering loyalty to the man of their choice and antipathy for his detractors, Sinatra fans have no peers. He likes the color blue; so do they. He likes chocolate and pistachio ice cream; so do they. It was once reported that he had switched from purple to brown fountain-pen ink; many of them changed theirs, too, and one girl, who had just bought a large supply of purple and couldn't afford not to use it up, decided to write letters three times as long to expedite the exhaustion of her supply. Before the Joe Louis-Billy Conn fight this summer, Sinatra's New York fans learned that Sinatra's pal Toots Shor was rooting for Conn. The fans, assuming that no true friend of the singer would differ with him on an important matter and that therefore Sinatra must be for Conn, too, began rooting for the challenger. Just before the fight, Sinatra came to New York, and the fans learned that he not only was favoring Louis but had bet fairly heavily on him. Impassively switching their party line, the fans were solidly behind the champion from there on in.

Sinatra's fans can be demure enough young ladies when they are by themselves, and even en masse they are not always disorderly, but they have nevertheless compiled an impressive record of shenanigans from coast to coast. In 1943, when Sinatra was on his way to Hollywood, to fulfill a movie contract with Radio-Keith-Orpheum, the studio anticipated, and may just possibly have inspired, trouble at the railway station when it requested an escort of twenty-five policemen to protect Sinatra on his arrival. R.K.O. then decided to have him disembark secretly at Pasadena instead of publicly at Los Angeles. This secret was whispered over the radio. R.K.O. sent a collection of bit players to Pasadena to welcome Sinatra, in case his fans had missed hearing the whisper. They hadn't. Five thousand of them met the train, and in the ensuing turmoil at least one girl bit at least one reporter in the arm. In Boston, Sinatra was once welcomed at a station by three thousand young women. One of them, clutching wildly at him, missed and gashed a detective with her fingernails, and another, perhaps enraged by a local newspaper's report that the singer was contributing all his fan mail to a wastepaper drive, made a flying tackle at him from a divan in a hotel lobby. She missed, too. Some months later, when Sinatra was to appear in a Boston armory, the management had the seats bolted to the floor. In Chicago, Sinatra fans broke a few windows of a train on which he had just arrived, and another time there an enthusiastic young miss, trying to hand him a bouquet of flowers, knocked down a bishop who happened to be in her way. In San Francisco, fifty-six girls lined up at four in the morning outside a theatre in which he was singing, to wait for the box office to open, and were arrested for violating a local wartime curfew. Sinatra protested to the police, in their defense, that they had not stayed up late but had merely arisen early. A plane in which he was travelling landed at the Detroit airport just before the arrival of a car bearing Secretary of War Patterson, for whom a police escort had been provided. The Secretary took a quick look at the crowd closing in on Sinatra and told the escort to take care of him instead. In Pittsburgh, a candy store next to a theatre into which Sinatra had been booked prudently boarded up its windows ahead of time, and the schools prepared for his arrival by decreeing expulsion as the penalty for inexplicable absenteeism. As a rule, any public appearance by Sinatra is a guarantee of at least a modest riot, and some of his old, experienced friends are no longer willing to accompany him to a rendezvous with his impulsive public. "You can enjoy that sort of thing for five minutes," one of them remarked, "but six minutes is too goddam much."

Nowhere are Sinatra's fans more exuberant than in New York, and nowhere in New York is their exuberance more spirited than at the Paramount, where in the past four years the singer has made four appearances, covering eighteen weeks in all. The Paramount is the shrine of their disorder. "No holds are barred there," a Sinatra fan said cheerfully a few weeks ago. "That's the home of swoon." Sinatra has broken the house records almost everywhere he has appeared, but not at the Paramount, for when he is there many of his fans literally consider the theatre their home and spend the day in it, occupying a seat through half a dozen shows for the price of one ticket. A girl who sat through fifty-five stage and screen shows in the three weeks of Sinatra's last tour of duty at the Paramount quivers with remorse when she recalls that during his first engagement there she left after one performance. She points out that she was only twelve then, but she says, "I die every time I think of it." The management of the theatre, trying desperately to increase the turnover, has resorted to various devices in an attempt to clear the house. It has, for instance, required young patrons who bring box lunches to check them in the lobby. This rule is difficult to enforce. Many fans hide sandwiches, candy bars, and other emergency refreshment in their purses and under their clothes. Furthermore, those who comply with the rule paralyze the operation of the cloakroom by milling around it when they finally depart and complaining bitterly that they deposited a peanut butter on white instead of the pressed ham on rye the attendant is trying to palm off on them. The theatre tries to book as inferior a movie as possible to complement Sinatra, hoping that recurrent flashes of mediocrity on the screen will discourage fans from waiting around for the next stage show, but the fans either take naps or turn their backs to the screen and chat with one another during the picture.

Before Sinatra opens at the Paramount, the management summons its ushers to a lecture on a special kind of tolerance and warns its staff to watch out for patrons' attempts to reach the performer's dressing room by sneaking underneath the stage. Sinatra's recent appearances there have been big parties in which the audience has participated almost as fully as the paid hands. At the final performance of an engagement in the fall of 1945, Sinatra and the spectators joined in singing "Auld Lang Syne." A year before, while Sinatra was on the Paramount stage, an eighteen-year-old boy sitting in the orchestra threw three eggs at him. One hit its mark. The orchestra swung into "The Star-Spangled Banner," but a lively fracas developed anyway. In the course of it, the assistant manager of the theatre suffered a sprained finger while helping to save the assailant from being mauled to death. A fifteen-year-old young lady who had been sitting next to the egg thrower said afterward, "I grabbed him right after the third egg. I got in a couple with my handbag. My friend hit him with her binoculars." (Sinatra fans, even when seated in the second or third row, often use binoculars.) Sinatra, unwounded, forgave his foe, and the audience took up a collection and later interrupted the show again to present the singer with four large bouquets of flowers. Even during shows not featured by assault, the fans usually present him with at least one large bouquet. At the Paramount, he has received innumerable other gifts, including a loving cup, a heart-shaped arrangement of carnations, a golden key (the card explained that he already possessed the hearts it would unlock), two Teddy bears, and a portable bar.

Ever since the Sinatra tide began to swell, it has been alleged that his popularity, though perhaps not altogether undeserved, is not altogether uninspired, either. Some people have even come right out and blamed the whole business on press-agentry. George Evans, who has been Sinatra's press man for nearly four years, was once quoted by a newspaper reporter as having said that he had urged girls to moan and suffer unaccountable dizzy spells at the Paramount. He has frequently offered to donate a thousand dollars to the favorite charity of anyone who could prove that "a kid was given a ticket, a pass, a gift, or a gratuity of any kind in any shape or manner at all to go in and screech." Recently, perhaps because of the inflationary nature of the times, Evans has raised the stakes to five thousand. He does not maintain, though, that Sinatra's acclaim has always been entirely spontaneous. "Certain things were done," he says mysteriously. "It would be as wrong for me to divulge them as it would be for a doctor to discuss his work."

The word "swoon," now inseparably attached to Sinatra, was firmly tied to him in an imaginative item that two press agents for the Riobamba, a New York night club in which he toiled in the spring of 1943, persuaded a gossip columnist to publish. Its import was that women were swooning and otherwise acting up all over the joint. One of the few actual cases of coma induced by Sinatra's singing turned out to be simply the result of malnutrition; a young lady had been waiting in line outside a theatre nearly all night and then had sat through seven shows without nourishment. Many other girls, however, have obligingly lost consciousness for a moment to accommodate photographers.

To many unenlightened visitors to Evans' office, at 1775 Broadway, the place looks pretty much like any other press agent's headquarters, but to Sinatra fans it is mecca. Though Sinatra is scarcely ever there, it is the nerve center for the vast activities of his fans, whom Evans undeniably eggs on. "It's almost like a public service," he explains in extenuation. "If the kids weren't doing this, they'd be doing something less elevating." He maintains liaison with most of the Sinatra fans through a middle-aged widow named Marjorie Diven, who sits in a cluttered cubicle stacked to the ceiling with scrapbooks, photographs, card files, and unanswered fan mail. Many Sinatra fans would consider it a treat to be permitted to help Mrs. Diven paste up clippings and slit envelopes, but ordinarily only fan club presidents enjoy the privilege. This system serves the double purpose of giving club members aspiring to office an extra incentive and of providing Evans with a certain amount of superior unpaid clerical assistance. Sinatra's fans have huge respect for Mrs. Diven, and she has been elected to honorary membership in hundreds of their clubs. "Marj is just about the busiest person I have ever seen," one of the girls has said. Sinatra fans hardly ever use last names. "Calling Frank Mr. would be as silly as calling my mother Mrs.," said one recently. They call Evans, who has a married son, George. They are, though, rather afraid of him and try hard not to annoy him, for fear of getting in bad with Frank.

Marj has been handling Frank's fans for George since the spring of 1944. Hers is so much a labor of love that she keeps at it nights and weekends. "People think it's strange that I take this business so seriously," she says, "but I've seen many things it does that go beyond the eye. There was a sixteen-year-old girl in Alsace-Lorraine who, maybe because of some war experience, was suspicious of all men but Frank. Why, she wouldn't even trade stamps. After she wrote in, I got in touch with a forty-five-year-old male fan in Iceland—the serious, responsible type—and had him write her a couple of letters. Five months later, she wrote Frank and asked if it would be all right if she wrote back to the man in Iceland, and I said yes. Now she's happy; she sleeps with his letters under her pillow. We in New York cured that girl in Alsace-Lorraine with the help of a man in Iceland."

Mrs. Diven has organized Sinatra cells in many foreign places, including Ceylon, Nigeria, and the Isles of Wight and of Man. His fans in Argentina, she says, are the most excitable and those in England the most reserved. "Turkey is becoming very Sinatra-conscious," she announced matter-of-factly one day. She tries to get domestic fans to correspond with ones abroad, and has organized the Adopt a Foreign Fan Association. "I wrote for your picture three months ago and haven't got it yet," a fan reported to Sinatra, "but I got a wonderful friend in Canada." Mrs. Diven, who is without doubt the world's greatest expert on the Sinatra fan, has a clear image of what she thinks is the typical one. "She's a fourteen-year-old girl living in a small town," she says. "She never gets to see anybody except her family, who haven't much money, and her schoolmates. She's lonely. On the way home from school, she stops at a drugstore for an ice-cream soda and picks up a movie magazine. She reads about Frank's life and it sounds wonderful: a pretty wife, two children—a boy and a girl—plenty of money, a home in Hollywood near the other movie stars. She writes him a letter. She imagines he gets about six or seven letters a day, and she visualizes him at his breakfast table, with her letter propped against the toaster. She calculates how long it will take for his answer to her to come back. When the time arrives and she hears the postman coming, she runs down the lane to her mailbox, one of those wobbly rural boxes. She keeps this up for three weeks, while her family makes fun of her. It's the thought of that fourteen-year-old girl running down that lane to that wobbly mailbox that makes me sympathetic to the fans."

Of the five thousand fan letters Sinatra receives a week, few ever feel the comforting warmth of his toaster. Nearly all, no matter how they are addressed, eventually end up in Evans' office. New York fans who have visited the place and made this discovery are sometimes disillusioned. "Why the devil do I write him every Wednesday night?" cried one girl, up to the top of her bobby sox in other fans' mail. Most of the letters are either requests for photographs, renditions of certain songs, or buttons off his suits, or else are run-of-the-mill expressions of admiration. (There are also many postcards, which Mrs. Diven simply puts aside until her office gets unbearably cramped. Then she throws them out, as many as fifty thousand at a time.) There are, in addition, a few crackpot notes and a quantity of appeals for information, advice, or comfort. A surprisingly large number of young people think Sinatra is omniscient and thus qualified to answer such questions as "What does a girl do whose world seems to have come to an end?" or, as a fourteen-year-old boy put his problem, "Do you think you should talk to your best girl about sex?" Some of the most ticklish queries are tackled by Evans himself, perhaps the only press agent on Broadway who spends an hour or so a day telling young women how to get over being wallflowers at dances. "Not every girl can be popular," he writes, and suggests that they take up the piano. Mrs. Diven, a prodigious correspondent, answers all other letters that seem to require a reply, signing herself as Sinatra's secretary. "I wonder what he *really* thinks about the kids," she once remarked, when no kids were present. On the whole, Sinatra thinks well of them, since they have helped to make him what he is. He is usually patient with them, but now and then he admits that their aggressiveness exasperates him, and an article, entitled "If My Daughter Were Seventeen," that appeared a while ago under his signature in *Photoplay*, contained the statement "Personally, I've always admired girls who have a certain amount of reserve."

November 2, 1946

From Part II of a three-part Profile.

Happy

On the coldest morning of last week's cold snap, we resolutely dispatched our man Stanley to the Central Park Zoo, to see how the polar bears were making out. He returned in a couple of hours, rubbing himself with snow, and reported that they were doing considerably better than he was. There are two polar-bear enclosures in Central Park, Stanley found, each occupied by a male and a female—Jimmy and June on the left as you face the bear cages, and a rather commercially named couple, Soc and Cony, on the right. On mild days, five black bears in neighboring cages keep them company, but the blacks do not enjoy low temperatures and in cold weather spend most of their time under cover, though not in a state of complete hibernation. During Stanley's visit, they stayed holed up—sensibly, he thought—in two of the small interior lairs beneath the rocks on which the bears like to pace. All four polar bears, however, were outside, Soc and Cony playfully wrestling, Jimmy and June sitting on their haunches, scratching themselves and sniffing the bracing wind that cut through the Park. All the bears, Stanley noted, exhaled a frosty breath. At the time of his inspection, only two other visitors were present, a mother and her young daughter, and the mother was clearly anxious to move on. "Don't you think we've had enough, dear?" she said earnestly. Her daughter ignored this direct question and stared at Soc as he plunged into a pool of running water and splashed about.

Stanley looked up Mr. Al Sirignano, the bears' keeper, and, standing before the cages as they stamped their feet and blew on their hands, they discussed the incredible climatic preferences of polar bears. "They *love* this weather," said Mr. Sirignano. "It's *never* too cold for them. I don't think they ever feel the cold at all. What they like most of all is a blizzard. Next to that, they like to stay on the highest rock, because up there the wind hits them the hardest." Mr. Sirignano said "Excuse me" and paused to take a sheet of Kleenex out of his pocket and blow his nose. "They never go inside at all, except in the summer," he resumed. "Notice where Jimmy's lying now, right on the ice. If there isn't any ice, they make their own. They jump into their pools, and climb out and shake themselves hard, and that way they get ice. The other day, I was standing near Soc when he took a swim. He splashed water all over my arm, and in a moment I had ice on my sleeve."

Mr. Sirignano told Stanley that each pair of polar bears eats a bucket of horse meat and fish (butterfish or mackerel) daily, as well as enough bread to make eighteen household-size loaves. The males outeat their mates by a considerable margin, but then they outweigh them, too—six hundred pounds to four hundred and fifty. Mr. Sirignano doesn't enter their cages unless all the inmates are at the other end. He is convinced that the bears recognize him because he feeds them, and he is just as convinced that they do not like him, or any other human being, for that matter.

"All they got to do is give you a shove and you're a goner," he said. Stanley asked him if the polar bears seem contented, what with being cooped up all the time and the scarcity, from their standpoint, of cold weather. "If they weren't happy, they wouldn't eat," Mr. Sirignano told him. "And they'd mope. Do they look to you like they're moping?" Stanley agreed that they did not. Cony was rubbing her back dreamily against an ice-coated rock and Soc was licking her ear. Stanley asked his guide if many visitors came to see the polar bears on extremely cold days. "You know how it is," said Mr. Sirignano. "People come and people go, like dribs and drabs. Always they're asking me if the polar bears catch cold, but they don't—not that I ever heard of." He stopped and blew his nose again. "We get our feet a little wet," he continued, "and we've got a cold. These bears go swimming on a day like this and stay in the water for five, ten, maybe fifteen minutes, and just keep splashing away. It seems funny when you stop and think about it."

February 15, 1947

Notes and Comment

Louis B. Mayer told the House Committee he wouldn't know a Communist if he saw one. Later he testified that three writers in his employ had been mentioned to him as Communists, and he named them. The newspaper accounts added that among the movies written by one of them, Lester Cole, was "The Romance of Rosy Ridge," and when we learned that this picture was currently playing at Loew's Forty-second Street, we sent our man Stanley over to see it, with instructions to watch especially for subversive propaganda and to report back. Lest we inadvertently distort the sense of Stanley's notes in attempting to rephrase them, here they are, just as he turned them in:

"Wish I knew shorthand. This a post-Civil War costume-&-dialect picture, & what with everybody in cast mumbling & me taking notes in dark, can't guarantee accuracy my version dialogue. Anyhow, picture begins with M-G-M lion & 'Ars gratia artis.' Un-American phrase? Lester Cole did screen play all right—said so on screen. Most pictures have either Guy Kibbee or Thomas Mitchell, & this one has both. Van Johnson is star. How much more American can you get? Plot involves Confederate-minded family with old man (Mitchell) unwilling forgive & forget. Van Johnson is Union vet. Wanders along playing mouth organ, moves in with family, falls in love with daughter (Janet Leigh—cute). Masked night riders burning barns, stirring up trouble between Union & Confederate sympathizers in Missouri. Nobody dares help neighbors harvest crops, because have to protect own barns. Van finally breaks down ill will. Also shoots four men & horse with five bullets; beats up fifth guy barehanded, thus disposing of barn-burners; gets girl; rides off toward horizon with her at end, like close of FitzPatrick Traveltalk. Elapsed time: 1 hr., 45 min. This not entire story, but hard to keep awake. At least I absorbed more of movie than fellow next to me, who fell asleep moment Van started in on that mouth organ.

"As to possible propaganda lines, near start of picture somebody says, 'Peace is achieved by the good will of people & not by flourishing strokes of a pen.' Might be Senator Taft line. There's little boy (guess you couldn't make picture like this without little boy), who says he always carries a fishing rod with him, in case he happens to run across any fish. Would say too frivolous & opportunistic an attitude toward life's grim realities to be politically harmful. Guy Kibbee flatly disapproves of barn-burning, believes in property rights. Somebody asks Van explain difference between right & wrong. He says, 'To me, right is lots o' things, like plantin' your fields an' havin' rain fall on 'em, like havin' songs to sing when your heart is right.' He said more along that line, but I got lost. Also said, 'Rain water tastes better'n sassprilla.' Statement allowed to go unanswered. Point debatable, I should say. Twice during picture, Kibbee, trying to get arguments settled, urges everyone present to be democratic & to take a vote. This accepted American way for resolving squabbles? Possible un-American note when two women are discussing what to wear to party & one says, 'Shucks, Maw, dressin' purty ain't everythin'.' Possible current allusion when Van says, 'The war's over, but some people, 'stead o' lookin' for friends, are lookin' for trouble.'

Crack at somebody here? Twice during picture, Van, barefooted & carrying shoes over shoulder, explains that they're good-wearing shoes, and so he wants to preserve them. Honest toil, neighborly love, thrift stressed throughout. Van says of dead soldier buddy & himself, 'We both wanted to make this country a free country, for folks—all folks—to live in.' Pinko sentiment, maybe? Noticed one thing. Communists supposed to be exploiting plight of Negroes in South nowadays. Well, this about Civil War issues & not a single Negro in it, not even one in background strummin' on ol' banjo. I'd give it clean bill of health but wouldn't want anyone to think I recommend seeing it."

November 1, 1947

Notes and Comment

Walter Winchell, who has commendably been responsible for the collection of a great deal of money to be used in the fight against cancer, is currently offering a ten-thousand-dollar mink coat to that citizen who, along with a one-dollar contribution to the fund, provides him with the best answer, in twenty words or less, to the question "What is a Communist?" The first answer that comes to our mind is "A Communist is what a certain columnist would probably call anybody who dared venture the opinion that Mr. Winchell's injection of this problem into a worthy, non-political, philanthropic cause is an example of the kind of tasteless foolishness that supplies the U.S.S.R. with arguments, whether sound or unsound, against some of the aspects of contemporary American life." Our answer is thirty-seven words over the maximum, but we doubt that we'd have won the prize anyhow.

November 22, 1947

Ooff!! (Sob!) Eep!! (Gulp!) Zowie!!!

Al Capp is perhaps without an equal among contemporary fairy-tale composers in his ability to proceed with engaging plausibility from a ludicrous premise to a preposterous conclusion. "My readers have a hard time," he said a while ago. "They have to learn to accept the incredible as the normal run of things." His readers can be divided into three categories, corresponding to the three levels upon which "Li'l Abner" is constructed. The base level is in the Bam!!!-and-Zowie!!!! tradition, a broad, slapstick foundation of frenzied adventure, such as hair-raising chases, violent fights, and people hanging by their fingertips from the edges of precipitous cliffs. Readers of all ages who like to browse on this level are apt to be quite concerned about the outcome of Capp's elaborate and giddy plots, and those who get a chance always ask him whether Li'l Abner is ever going to marry the heroine of the strip, a handsome but vacuous young lady named Daisy Mae Scragg, whose love for Abner is equalled only by his distaste for her entire sex. Capp is sometimes tolerant of, but always bored with, people who make this inquiry about this foolish young couple, and he refers to them brusquely as "Abner fans." Readers who indicate to him that they are especially pleased with the middle, or socially significant, level of his work, and who ask him when he is going to take another poke at radio commercials or the United States Senate, are, he thinks, much more estimable citizens, and he calls them, approvingly, "disgusting Abner fans." The third level, sometimes of microscopic dimensions, consists of bits of Rabelaisian humor, often so adroitly covered up that, like rare archeological treasures, they are less likely to be spotted by children at play than by people who set out looking for them. These mischievous escapades in print amuse Capp more than anything else about his work, and the thought that few of his readers share this enjoyment with him depress him. If, however, he were to make these touches more obvious, it is possible that his strip might be banned not only in Boston but in Springfield, Charlotte, and San Antonio as well.

When Capp encounters a reader who enjoys not only the two lower levels but the nuances on Level Three, he confers on the fellow the highest possible token of his esteem, the designation of "slobbering Abner fan." People who have thus been honored realize that the title is a compliment, since "slob" is one of Capp's favorite nouns. "To me, the word 'slob' has a great deal of force and humor," he has said. "It's one of those really choice and charming words." It is not regarded with the same fervor by the United Feature Syndicate, whose editors feel obliged to tone down Capp's material when they detect something that particularly worries them. (A United Feature man was once described by a sympathetic friend as a "quivering Abner fan," and a piece of promotional literature that the syndicate issued a couple of years ago said, with perhaps unconscious wistfulness, "You never know what's coming next when it comes off the pen of the creator of 'Li'l Abner.'") One of Capp's favorite characters is a Dogpatch girl called Moonbeam McSwine, whose name indicates her paradoxical nature, since although she is uncommonly good-looking, she detests bathing and prefers the company of hogs to that of men. Six years ago, Capp had her say, "Ah is a lazy good-fo'-nothin' slob!" Somebody in the United Feature offices gave this confessional a scrubbing on its way to the public, and when it finally appeared in print it read, "Ah is a lazy good-fo'-nothin'!" Capp was distressed by the disappearance of what to him had been the only really charming word in the sentence, but he cheered up a few years later when he succeeded in having Daisy Mae, a girl of profound delicacy, call Moonbeam McSwine a slob.

Capp is not a self-effacing man, but he has stubbornly resisted the temptation to consider himself, as many of his fellow-citizens do, the world's greatest contemporary comic-strip artist. He feel that he is merely one of the two greatest, the other being Milton Caniff, the gifted inventor of "Terry and the Pirates" (now being done by another man) and at present the shepherd of "Steve Canyon." Capp's estimate seems to be shared by the School of Education of New York University, which, when it revealed, not long ago, that it planned to conduct a study of "the cartoon narrative as a medium of communication," said that Caniff and Capp were the only two cartoon narrators who were slated to take part in the inquiry. Caniff does not share Capp's shy reluctance to put one man at the top of the list; Caniff puts Capp there. "Al's the best of us all," he said recently. "To me, he is the only really funny man in the funnies business." Capp's professional honors are numerous. For one thing, he was the first comic-strip creator (a noun used in the business to describe anyone who both writes and draws a strip) to introduce parodies of other comic strips into his own. For another, he was the first comic-strip man to effect a profitable tieup, in his strip, with commercial broadcasting. Last year, he collaborated on a song about Li'l Abner and, after persuading several important radio vocalists to plug it, worked them into the plot of his strip. Then, on whatever day they were scheduled to sing the number, caricatures of them appeared in "Li'l Abner" and mentioned their broadcasts. Considering that comic strips have to be put together several weeks before publication and that radio programs are often torn apart at the last minute, the fact that Capp managed to synchronize events in the two media was impressive.

Capp has done a great many things other comic-strip artists might well be afraid to attempt. "The funnies have always avoided the enormous comic gold mine of sex," he once said. He was not referring to his own strip. When a song entitled "Six Lessons from Madame La Zonga," which he did not help compose, was at its height, Capp introduced into "Li'l Abner" an engaging and romantic character named Adam Lazonga. "He was a perilous experiment," Capp wrote to a friend, "because he was the master of how to woo, Dogpatch style—a kinda wooing the details of which were never very clear to the reader or to me, but which was superior to all other styles—and because he had won loving cups in exhibitions of Dogpatch-style wooing the world over. It was a nervous moment when I let him loose in the nation's family newspapers. Readers were shocked as it dawned on them what he was famous for doing, but delighted by his courtly and genteel way of doing it, and his dignified attitude toward his work."

It is generally believed that Capp created Li'l Abner in his own image. Cartoonists' characters frequently take after their masters, and there is no doubt that Yokum bears a superficial resemblance to Capp; both are big, black-haired, broad-shouldered men, and both are constantly getting into scrapes. People who have studied Yokum and Capp, however, sometimes think that Li'l Abner does not resemble Capp nearly as much as Capp resembles him. Abner and his fellow-Dogpatchers are noticeably fond of the words "gulp" and "sob." So is Capp. He regularly uses both these words in conversation nowadays, but he did not do so until after his hillbillies had started doing it. The characters in "Li'l Abner" are partial to such adjectives as "horrible," "repulsive," "miserable," "loathsome," and "revolting." So is Capp. When he was a young art student, he did not markedly employ vigorous modifiers of this sort, but today, at thirty-eight, he uses them a good deal. He calls his favorite readers "slobbering Abner fans" and he calls himself, when he is feeling particularly self-indulgent, "a monster." A philologist who recently happened to spend a quiet, sociable evening going around town with him and who made a note, just for the hell of it, every time Capp uttered certain picturesque words, reckoned the next morning that his companion had emitted eighteen "revoltings," twenty-two "loathsomes," an even thirty "miserables," forty-three "horribles," seven "gulps," three "sobs," and, as he spotted various professed admirers of his art, seventeen "slobberings."

When Capp is invited to a party, he is apt to reply, just as if he lived in Dogpatch, "How do we dress—informal or shoes?" He is by no means, however, an exact personification of his hero. Yokum is always indifferent, and sometimes even rude, to attractive young women. When Capp is at, say, the Copacabana and a showgirl bobbing by his table winks at him, he always politely winks back. Li'l Abner has been shown to be fond of mayonnaise, which he eats in sandwiches also containing a side of bacon, a loin of pork, a sausage or two, a few sliced bananas, butter, and ketchup. Capp has a delicate stomach, and while he often vexes it with highly spiced foods and then tries to appease it with huge draughts of bicarbonate of soda, he does not like mayonnaise. Once he horrified a mid-morning lady radio commentator, on whose program he was appearing as a guest and whose sponsors included a mayonnaise company, by ad-libbing a sharp indictment of the stuff, concluding with a recommendation that all the mayonnaise in the world be dumped into an immense vat and that all the people in the world who like mayonnaise jump into it.

Capp does not consider the similarities between Yokum and himself, such as they are, of any account. "There is no more logical basis for saying that I resemble Abner," he is reputed to have declared, "than for saying that Albert Payson Terhune resembled a collie." Temperamentally, nevertheless, Capp is an excellent example of a man's nature imitating his art. Like Li'l Abner, he is impulsive, optimistic, reckless, energetic, seemingly childlike but far shrewder than most of the people he associates with, and unshakably confident about his ability. Capp has been described by a former business associate as "a fierce ego in action, coupled with astounding ingenuity." Many of Capp's friends believe that the exceptional liveliness of his imagination is a result of his having lost his left leg at the age of nine in a street accident. He gets around nimbly these days on a wooden prosthesis, but he has always hankered to be more powerful physically than his disability has permitted him to become. In his teens, he used to raise a piano stool above his head over and over again to develop his muscles; lately he has been taking exercises at a gymnasium. He has a great compassion for people who are handicapped in any way, physically, economically, or socially—an attitude undoubtedly inspired, at least in part, by his own handicap. During the war, Capp wrote and illustrated an autobiographical comic book entitled "'Al Capp,' by Li'l Abner," a hundred thousand copies of which were distributed by the Red Cross to disabled service men. In it, Capp's father says, speaking of his son's intense concentration on art after his accident, "It's nature's law of compensation. The loss of some of his physical activity has resulted in increasing his mental activity!! It never fails!!"

Some of Capp's boyhood friends point out, as proof of the working of this law, that while his head appeared to be of routine proportions when he was a lad, his hat size is now seven and seven-eighths. Capp is inclined to make light of this formidable measurement, but he is nonetheless rather proud of his head, and he hardly ever conceals it under a hat. He has a glossy, abundant crop of hair and usually lets it grow quite long. He frets incessantly about it, and for twenty years he has been belaboring his scalp with vibrators, ointments, tonics, hot and cold towels, and eerie rays. He does not conceal his worries about his hair, and often tells dinner companions about a chronic waking nightmare from which he professes to suffer. "Every now and then," he says, "I get up positive that by evening I'll be totally bald. I go into a panic. I stagger to my drawing board and draw pictures of myself with all my hair on. Then I erase all the hair. Then I draw on a toupee and try to make it look real, but it never does. It's the most hideous, harrowing horror anyone could go through." Five years ago, according to Capp, he retired early one morning determined to arise bright and early that noon and spend six hours doing six comic-strip advertisements for Cream of Wheat, for which he was being paid two thousand dollars an ad. "I woke up knowing that a foul disease would eat up my hair during the day," he says. "I made an emergency appointment for two in the afternoon with the best dermatologist in town. I got to his office on the dot, but he was having a leisurely lunch and arrived forty-five minutes late. I was furious. When he finally showed up, he glanced at my head, gave me a prescription for some loathsome unguent, and dismissed me. The whole examination took three minutes. Then he sent me a bill for twenty dollars. He'd wasted forty-five minutes' worth of my Cream of Wheat time that day, so I sent him a bill for fifteen hundred dollars and told him he could deduct his twenty before paying it. 'I'm sorry you made no use of my time,' I said in an accompanying note, 'because it's costing you so much.' He stopped sending me bills after a while, but I kept billing him on the first of every month for two years. It was an incident typical of my refusal to pay bills and of my lovable bad temper."

It is also an incident typical of the terrible conflict that is constantly going on between Capp's memory and his imagination. His imagination, being much the stronger, usually wins. What probably happened in this case was that a practical joker told him that his hair seemed to be thinning, that he went to see a hair specialist a few days later, that he was told his hair was not thinning, that he was sent a bill for ten dollars, and that he paid it. Capp regards himself as a storyteller, not a mere cartoonist, and he is unable to tell any story, including that of his life, without embellishing his remarks with harmless and diverting fictions. "I have it on the very best information," a close friend of his said recently, "that Al was born in three different places." Capp was born, as even he will admit when pressed, in New Haven, on September 28, 1909. His name was, and still is, Alfred Gerald Caplin, but he unofficially abbreviated it in 1934, when he began writing and drawing "Li'l Abner." His father—an industrial-oil salesman—and mother, both natives of Latvia, came to this country when they were children, and were brought up in New England. Alfred is the oldest of four children. His two brothers, Jerome and Elliott, and his sister, Madeline, are all involved, one way or another, with comic strips. Jerome is Alfred's right-hand man, as general manager of Capp Enterprises, Inc., of which Alfred is president and Elliott vice-president. The corporation, in which Alfred is a majority stockholder, was set up a year ago with the ultimate objective of handling the rights on such "Li'l Abner" byproducts as comic books, toys, costume jewelry, and ladies' blouses. Madeline is a press agent; one of her principal accounts is her brother Al. Elliott is an official of the Parents' Institute, which publishes, in addition to *Parents' Magazine*, seven high-toned monthly comic books directed by Elliott, including *True Comics*, which consists of illustrated presentations of historical events. He is also a comic-strip author himself; he writes the continuity for a syndicated strip called "Dr. Bobbs." It is his opinion that his brother has no rival in the business. "Oh, the things Al can do!" Elliott once said. "You know, I honestly believe he uses the word 'merely' better than anyone else in the world."

According to "'Al Capp,' by Li'l Abner," its subject was interested, when he was a boy, in sports, girls, and hitchhiking, and had a lush head of hair. "At the age of 3, Li'l Mistah Capp had growed up to be a fine yung joovy-nile de-linkwunt," the biography says. "Now that he is growed up he clames to of bin a champeen kid athleet. The brootal facks is, he warn't no better'n the averidge. . . . He had a li'l talent fo' drawrin' but no more'n the averidge as any fool kin planely see." Actually, Capp had considerable talent, possibly inherited from his father, who was an accomplished, though amateur, cartoonist and who amused his children by drawing comic strips for them. Al began turning them out himself when he was eleven. As soon as he had finished a sequence, which took him about a week, his brothers and sister would sell copies to other children in the neighborhood for two or three cents. The Caplins moved from New Haven to Brooklyn for a year, and there, in somewhat peculiar circumstances, Al became conscious of the greater commercial potentialities of pictorial art, which now brings him, before taxes, nearly a quarter of a million dollars a year. "I was thrown into a big public school," Capp says, "just when its principal had agreed to turn over fifty students—twenty-five brilliant children and twenty-five degenerates—to a man who was conducting an educational experiment. I think I was supposed to be one of the smart kids and that the morons were supposed to benefit by association with us, but it worked the other way around. The experiment went on for a couple of months, and it made thieves and monsters and perverts out of us nice kids. It was horrible, like a leper colony. The boy directly in back of me spent all day drooling over French postcards; the one in front of me kept picking his neighbor's pocket. We never got any textbooks or anything, and to pass the time away I used to draw a lot. Well, one day a twelve-year-old boy—a rapist, I think—sidled up to me and said, 'Jeez, you're a good drawrer.' He offered me a quarter for an indelicate portrait of the teacher, and when I had no idea what he was talking about, he described in detail what he wanted. I was just a kid from the country, but soon I became an expert in pornography. My price was a quarter a drawing, and with twenty-five steady customers, I was doing fine until I got so many commissions that I started taking extra work home and my father found out about it." The fables narrated by the classic storytellers of history generally have finished on a tidy moral note, and Capp's story ends, appropriately, with the man in charge of the experiment being committed, soon after its conclusion, to an insane asylum.

November 29 and December 6, 1947

From a two-part Profile.

Our Snowbound Correspondents
Gilroy Was Here

SCARBOROUGH-ON-HUDSON

My grandfather, who is now going on eighty-nine, was just about my present age in 1888, so I was eager to get together with him after the recent meteorological to-do to match my experiences in the storm against his recollections of his earlier experiences. It wasn't until a week after the start of the New Year that I had a chance to drop in on Grandpa at his Manhattan apartment. He said right off the bat that he hadn't paid too much attention to the great snow of '47, having spent December 26th and 27th happily and comfortably absorbed in his fourteenth reading of "Nicholas Nickleby," but—and here he seemed to be following the line that most old-timers, according to the newspapers, hastily adopted when they woke up on the 27th—it was altogether meaningless and misleading to make comparisons in terms of official estimates of totals of snow-inches, and we youngsters couldn't possibly begin to imagine the cutting wind and the biting cold of '88, not to mention the drifts. Ah, those drifts! Why, he said, half closing his eyes, he could remember a ten-foot mountain at the corner of Broad and Beaver—or was it Maiden Lane?—that was so formidable that when a man with a pair of brewery horses tried to . . .

I brashly started to relate my own adventures in Westchester County, where my wife and I and our infant son have been living in a two-story cottage since July, but Grandpa quickly interrupted me. "How come you didn't spend the night of the twenty-sixth on one of those stalled commuters' trains, as everybody else in Westchester did?" he asked sternly. I replied that I hadn't gone to my New York office the day after Christmas, having made plans to do some skiing with my wife. "Didn't go to work!" said Grandpa triumphantly. "When I was your age, I worked twelve hours a day six days a week, and a man who didn't even *try* to get to his office during the Blizzard wouldn't have dared admit it to a stranger, much less to a member of his own family." To change the subject, I asked Grandpa to tell me what he considered the biggest difference—aside, of course, from wind velocity and temperature—between the two storms. "Machines," he said firmly. "In my day, we didn't have Sno-Gos or any mechanical plows, and we didn't have subways, or trucks, or automobiles. You should have seen those brewery horses at Broad and Beaver. The driver was a big, beefy chap in a fur hat that covered his whole face except for his eyes, and there were icicles hanging from his eyebrows that must have reached nearly to his nose, and those horses were snorting like dragons when they breathed, and while I was standing there, next to that twelve-foot drift, the fellow with the icicles down to his chin and I suddenly heard this faint little baby cry come from somewhere, and . . . "

Grandpa was certainly right about the machines. But for the gasoline engine, my experiences in the great snow of 1947 would have been so embarrassingly trivial that I could hardly have counted on them to lure my own grandchildren to my knee and hold them there, wide-eyed, while, between chuckles, I reminisce. As it is, because of machines, I have some hope of being able to keep the little beggars' mouths agape. December 26th began quietly enough in Scarborough. When my alarm clock went off at eight-thirty and I reluctantly got up (my grandfather has never stayed abed later than seven-fifteen in his life, he often tells me), it was snowing hard, and there were three or four inches of the stuff on the ground, according to an unofficial estimate I made from the bathroom window. I was so little impressed, however, that when I drove to the railroad station at nine to pick up the morning papers, I didn't even stop at the local gas station to have my chains put on. Traffic was flowing smoothly on the old Albany Post Road, which is only twenty feet from our house, and, besides, I had always figured I could put the chains on myself if I needed them, a theory that had never, incidentally, been confirmed. We really do live only twenty feet from the Post Road. A spry crow would hardly have to take to wing to leap from our bedroom, upstairs, to the Post Road. On many nights in the past, in fair weather, when the upstate trucks came thundering down the road on their way to New York, our beds had actually quivered.

Anyway, as the snow piled up that White Friday, we dropped the notion of going skiing, and I kept myself occupied by shovelling a footpath from our front door to our garage, a hundred feet away. Every couple of hours, I went outside and worked on my path, and as the walls of snow flanking it increased in height, I became aware of the seriousness of the situation. On one of my trips to the garage, I tried to put my chains on. No luck. By then, it didn't matter much, because our driveway was already impassable, but I wanted to keep a path clear from the house to the garage; living in a motorized age, I had, I suppose, a blind faith in my machine, and even if the machine couldn't perform its customary services for me, I was determined not to be out of touch with it. So I shovelled diligently through the afternoon and early evening.

My wife fed the baby and put him to bed, and then she cooked dinner. The groceries we had ordered over the telephone that morning hadn't been delivered, but we had enough canned food, we figured, to last us for three or four days. We finished dinner at about nine o'clock, and my wife said she thought she'd wash her hair, and went upstairs. A few minutes later, she called to me to come up, and when I did, she pointed out the bathroom window to the Post Road, where, through the still-falling snow, we could dimly make out a half-dozen motionless vehicles. "Some people are walking around out there," she said, "and it seems to me that I haven't felt any traffic moving for quite a while. Maybe the road's blocked." We put on ski boots and tramped out to the highway. Traffic had stopped, all right, some of it in the middle of the road; trucks and cars were stalled all over the place. As we approached one giant truck-trailer with "Ruppert's Beer" prominently inscribed on it, a fellow got out of the truck cab and shuffled toward us, blowing on his hands. We asked him what was up. Well, he said, he'd been stuck there for a couple of hours. Some other drivers and passengers had taken refuge in a nearby church, he told us, but he had decided to wait around, in the hope that a snowplow would come along and open up the road. While we were talking to him, four other men climbed out of three other trucks, stalled not far away, and walked over. We invited them all in to have a cup of coffee, assuring them that if a plow came by, they'd be able to hear it from our house. They waded back home with us. There were, in addition to the Ruppert man, a man driving a moving van to its base in New Jersey and his helper, a boy of around eighteen; the driver of a tobacconist's truck heading south from Peekskill; and an old man. During the night, which the inadequacies of the machine age were to permit us to spend together, the old man never said anything, so I have no idea who he was or where he was going; all I know about him is that he was, when my wife and I first saw him, entirely blue. He was wearing dark-blue clothes, he had a heavy beard of dark blue, and the unshaven portion of his face was light blue.

When the five men got inside our house, we noticed that the Ruppert man was shivering and that his clothes were wet. He had been fussing with his chains, he said. My wife told him to go up and take a shower and, while his pants were drying, to put on some gray flannel slacks of mine. He didn't want to at first, but she was insistent. I took him upstairs, gave him the pants, and remarked that I'd been having some trouble with my chains, too. Meanwhile, downstairs in the kitchen, my wife had started making coffee and sandwiches. By the time they were ready, the Ruppert man had bathed, changed, and joined the rest of us. After a while, the tobacco man reported that from the bathroom window he'd seen somebody else walking on the Post Road. I went out to investigate and ran into another beer driver—a Schaefer man. I told him he might as well come in and get warm. He seemed reluctant, but when I said that we already had a Ruppert man in the house, he brightened and said that in that case he'd be glad to. Then we saw, staggering toward us through the snow, a woman, two little boys, and a man carrying something wrapped in a blanket—a baby boy, it turned out. The father was a used-car dealer from Schenectady. They didn't have to be urged to join us. As I was leading this squad past our garage, I saw a flickering light inside it. I went in. The moving-van driver was holding a flashlight, and the Ruppert man, back in his own pants and down on his knees, was putting my chains on my car.

Back in the house, my wife, who had seen us coming, was heating a big caldron of soup. Assorted soup, I guess you could call it, since the ingredients consisted of all the cans we had on hand—one cream-of-asparagus, two split-pea, a vegetable-with-beef, a black-bean, two pepper-pot, and a consommé. When I told her we had another beer-truck man, she reflected for a moment and then insisted that he go upstairs, take a shower, and put on my gray flannel pants. He didn't particularly want to take a shower, and his pants were reasonably dry, but he didn't argue.

The tobacco man soon went to sleep on a living-room sofa, with his hat on. The rest of the group began feeding the three little boys. I went outside to see how everything was going in the garage and, having got that far, decided to make one more survey of the highway. I came back with an Army officer from Virginia, his wife, and their daughter, aged five. By the time we got inside the house, my wife had inserted all the leaves in our dining-room table, put chairs around it, lighted some candles, and turned on the lights on our Christmas tree, and was presiding over a lively supper party, the menu of which included the assorted soup, canned compote of fruit, and some mince pie left over from Christmas. Since there were truck drivers present, the meal began, of course, as well as ended, with coffee.

It was midnight when our group finished drying the dishes. The radio had been announcing repeatedly that driving conditions were terrible, but we all still felt that the road was bound to be opened up soon. A couple of the truck drivers telephoned their dispatchers and said they expected to be rolling again shortly. The Ruppert man put the dishes away. The Schaefer man and the mother of the three boys got into an earnest chat about progressive education. The Army officer revealed that he was in the Signal Corps, and I suggested that he might be able to do something about a defective string of lights on our Christmas tree. He replied, apologetically, that he was cryptographer. The wife of the Schenectady man told us that her name was Gloria, that her husband's name was George, and that their sons also had six-letter names beginning with "G"—Gerald, Gordon, and Gilroy. My wife seized an opening to tell about how the speeding trucks on the Post Road made our beds rattle at night. The drivers listened thoughtfully, and the moving-van man said, "You know, once a cop stopped one of our boys and dragged him off his seat and into a house along a dip on the Post Road, a house even closer to the highway than yours. The cop didn't say anything to the driver, just shoved him inside the front door, and the driver looked around, and it was awful what he saw—cracked mirrors, and broken cups and plates, and goodness knows what all else—and he thought to himself, 'My God, this might be *my* home,' and he got back on his seat and drove away, and pretty soon the word got around, and not any of us have gone by that house ever since at more than twenty miles per hour."

At twelve-thirty, I called the police and told the sergeant on duty that if he wanted to move any of the nearby vehicles abandoned on the Post Road and couldn't find the drivers, our house would be a likely place to make inquiry. I asked the sergeant when he thought traffic would get going. "Not before morning," he said. I asked him what I should advise the drivers to do. "Tell 'em to stay put," he said. We didn't have quite enough beds, couches, and cots in the house, so three men had to sleep on the floor. My wife got everybody billeted, and at one-thirty she and I decided to go to bed ourselves. Fifteen minutes later, we heard the roar of a motor outside and rushed to a window. A snowplow was lumbering south on the Post Road, weaving in and out among the stalled vehicles. It got abreast of our house, stopped, turned around, and headed back north. I went downstairs, with the idea of reporting that the road was now partly open in one direction. Everybody was asleep except the Ruppert man, who was fixing the lights on our Christmas tree. I didn't disturb anyone.

My wife and I were awakened by our baby at six-forty-five. I dressed and went downstairs. The Ruppert man and the blue man weren't in sight, but our party was otherwise intact. The tobacco man was still asleep on the sofa; his hat had fallen off, or someone had taken it off. The Schaefer man had two pots of coffee percolating on the kitchen stove, and Gloria was cooking oatmeal. A moment later, the Ruppert man came in from outside; he had been shovelling snow off my footpath. The blue man never did turn up again; he had presumably walked to Ossining. I went out to the Post Road. No cars were moving, but a pedestrian said that he thought it was passable as far as Ossining. I reported this intelligence to our truck drivers, and they called their dispatchers and passed the word along, as if transmitting a front-line message to headquarters. My wife said that we were practically out of food. I made an announcement to this effect, whereupon the truckmen went outside and, with what looked like almost no effort, dug out my driveway. Then they piled into my car and we drove, quite easily, to Ossining, where we picked up a batch of supplies. On the way back, we slithered around a stalled Ruppert truck with a driver sitting in it. My Ruppert man requested me to stop, got out, chatted briefly with the other driver, and then asked me if it would be all right if the fellow came along with us. Ruppert No. 1 explained that Ruppert No. 2 was supposed to be following him into New York and that it wouldn't look good if No. 2 got in ahead of him. When we reached home, I found that my wife had collected two more truck drivers, sporting the colors of the A. & P., who had spent the night on the road, in their cab. One of them was eating breakfast, and the other soon joined him. He had been upstairs taking a shower, and was wearing my gray flannel pants.

We had lunch at eleven-thirty, and then sat around listening to weather reports on the radio until two o'clock, when the road magically opened up. My wife and I went out to the highway with our guests and waved goodbye to them as they drove off. They all promised to stop in and say hello when they next came by.

By now, everything is almost back to normal at Scarborough. The Post Road has been cleared, and traffic is moving along it at a brisk rate. One odd thing that both my wife and I have noticed, however, is that after dark the trucks don't seem to roar by as fast as they used to; our furniture hasn't trembled since the night of the storm. I'd like to tell my grandfather about this, but I can't get him out of his damned old snowdrift.

January 17, 1948

Preview

We were lolling in a sidewalk café the other afternoon when Leonard Lyons came by. "What's new?" we asked, whipping out notebook and pencil, and Mr. Lyons obligingly provided us with a minor saga that we pass along as a glimpse of what, in the dawning age on television, may soon be the experience of all parents. Mr. Lyons bought a television set four years ago (an R.C.A. model, which still works), and about that time the third of his four sons was born. This boy, Jeffrey, is, as far as his father knows, or we know, a truly exceptional child—one who has never known life without television, and who is now becoming old enough for the effects of its singular influence to be ascertainable. If Dr. Gesell will pull up a chair, we will proceed.

Up to a few weeks ago, Jeffrey had never seen any baseball games other than major-league ones, of which he had watched dozens on television. At this point, his father took him to Central Park, where his two older brothers, aged ten and eight, play ball regularly. Lyons *père* set about what he imagined would be the difficult and laborious task of initiating Jeffrey into the great American game. He started off by handing the boy a small bat. Jeffrey accepted it, looked around, spotted a flat stone about a foot square, walked over to it, tapped the bat against it three or four times, assumed a stance—legs apart, body almost erect, elbows out from the body, and bat held high—and told his father to smoke one in. Lyons blinked and lobbed a gentle pitch toward Jeffrey. Swinging with a beautiful follow-through, he slapped the ball (a lightweight, lively one, for this primary lesson) out a hundred feet, clear to the edge of the playground. An adult onlooker who had taken this in rushed over and said excitedly, "I'll be darned if he doesn't swing exactly like Joe DiMaggio." Lyons observed DiMaggio closely on television the next day, and *he* was darned if Jeffrey didn't swing exactly like Joe DiMaggio, accurately duplicating the master's every motion. He slides like DiMaggio, too. When DiMaggio gets up after sliding, he habitually brushes off his trousers just above the knees, whether there's any dirt there or not. It's a kind of reflex gesture. Jeffrey does the same thing every time. His father, who, of course, gets around, mentioned this coincidence to DiMaggio one night, and Jeffrey's prototype said he didn't understand what Lyons meant. The columnist brushed himself off, by way of demonstration. "By God, I guess I *do* do that," said DiMaggio. "I never thought about it before."

Somebody gave the Lyonses a conductor's baton, and it was passed along to Jeffrey while the radio was emitting some classical music, to see what he'd do with it. What he did with it was lead the orchestra. Not only did he wave his arms convincingly but he contorted his features into fierce and angry grimaces. His parents were puzzled until they remembered that he had seen Toscanini make his television début a month or so earlier. Jeffrey often watches dramatic programs—most of them old Wild West movies. A while ago, he wandered into his mother's bedroom as she was lying on the floor doing calisthenics. "Who shot you, Mummy?" he asked matter-of-factly. He plays cops-and-robbers a good deal more realistically than boys raised merely on the radio; he knows, for instance, how to frisk a man for a concealed firearm by patting his armpits and hips. He has seen three prizefights on television—the first Graziano-Zale affair and both Louis-Walcott bouts. In the course of these, all the participants except Walcott got knocked down at least once each. Accordingly, whenever Jeffrey plays at boxing, he crumples to the floor, in an altogether professional manner. He takes television so much for granted that on a number of occasions, while visiting the homes of friends or relatives, he has looked around their living rooms and asked, "Where's the television set?"

We are sorry to say that Jeffrey's batting form has deteriorated since his first time up. Association with amateurs, including his older brothers, who started to play baseball before television came into the household, has corrupted him. "He's beginning to play baseball like a kid," his father told us.

September 4, 1948

The Frontal Attack

Gunnar Myrdal, the Swedish sociologist whose "An American Dilemma," a study of the status of the Negro in the United States, is generally regarded as the most authoritative work in its field, writes in it that "Negroes and whites in America deal with each other through the medium of plenipotentiaries." Among the members of both these racial groups who give any thought to such matters, it is usually conceded that the ranking Negro diplomat is Walter Francis White, a dapper, pink-cheeked, and polished man of fifty-five who is so non-Negroid in appearance and on such good terms with high-level statesmen that anyone meeting him for the first time at a Washington cocktail party could easily take him for some thoroughly Anglo-Saxon ambassador. White, whose only formal title is that of Secretary of the National Association for the Advancement of Colored People, is, according to an anthropologist who once peered at the roots of his family tree, five-thirty-seconds Negro. He has fair skin, delicate features, and light-blue eyes. His hair and his mustache are now graying, but they used to be blond. The fact that he is physically indistinguishable from any run-of-the-mill, socially acceptable paleface is a constant annoyance to those of his fellow-citizens who like to think that they can, to put it in their own way, "spot a nigger any time, anywhere." White has never been spotted as a Negro by a stranger. Many years ago, he and two white lawyers called on the late Clarence Darrow to ask him to serve as counsel in a case in which the N.A.A.C.P. was interested. Darrow had not met any of the delegation before, but he had been told in advance that it would include a Negro. During their conversation, one of the attorneys, the swarthiest of the trio, made a remark about discrimination against colored people. "I understand the troubles of your race," said Darrow sympathetically. The man replied that he did not happen to be colored. "I mean *your* race," said Darrow to the other lawyer, a medium brunette. He, too, corrected Darrow. "But they told me one of you was a Negro," said Darrow, thoroughly confused, "and, surely"—here he turned to White—"it can't be *you*."

Today many people, especially Negroes, are familiar with White's looks, and it is scarcely possible for him to go anywhere by rail, for instance, without being respectfully greeted by the majority of the redcaps, Pullman porters, and dining-car waiters he encounters en route. A white passenger on a Chesapeake & Ohio train, several weeks ago, noticing the reverent treatment accorded White in the diner, called the steward over and asked if he had guessed rightly that the gentleman getting all the service was Robert R. Young. Colored people who are not familiar with White's appearance are no more intuitive than white people when it comes to identifying him as a Negro. Some years ago, while he was in Chicago investigating a race riot for his Association, another Negro, rioting at full steam and determined to shoot the first white man he saw, caught sight of White, took aim, and fired. He missed. As a rule, White is shot at only by white men. Last winter, while he was motoring from Tuskegee, Alabama, to Atlanta, Georgia, where he was born and raised, he was somewhat inhospitably welcomed back to his old home state when a couple of white men, who may or may not have known that he was to be expected along that road at that time, fired shots in the general direction of his car shortly after it crossed the Alabama-Georgia line. White did not report the incident since, as he pointed out afterward, the fellows could conceivably have been hunters who had spotted some more conventional game just as his car passed by. He has great respect for the Constitutional rights of individuals, and he would not, on the basis of such flimsy circumstantial evidence as he had on that occasion, press charges even against a white man, for he firmly believes that whites, in Georgia or any other state, are entitled to exactly the same justice as everybody else.

Every year, a substantial number of Negroes with little or none of the pigmentation characteristic of their race quietly take leave of colored society and move over into white society, where, "passing" for white, they are apt to find living conditions more agreeable. White could have passed long ago if he had wanted to, but he resolved, many years before achieving the eminence that his position as head of the N.A.A.C.P. has won him, that he didn't want to. Last year, in an article in the *Saturday Review of Literature* entitled "Why I Remain a Negro," he discussed the "enigma of a black man occupying a white body" and referred to himself as "the presentation in fact of a theory to which millions give lip service, never really believing it so— that all men are brothers under the skin." "I am not white," he wrote. "There is nothing within my mind and heart which tempts me to think I am." Some Negroes are nevertheless tempted to think he is. Shortly after the article appeared, George Schuyler, a dark-skinned, sharp-tongued writer for the Pittsburgh *Courier*, a Negro weekly, composed a rejoinder in which, playing down White's mind and heart and concentrating on his skin, he called attention to a magazine piece by "a well-known Caucasian" and said that since "our white friend" considered himself a Negro because of a smattering of Negro blood and that since he, Schuyler, had a trace of Caucasian blood, he thought he'd write a little essay on "Why I Remain a White Man." Most Negroes, however, look upon White as a bona-fide member of their race, and to many of them he is the nearest thing to a national leader they have had since Booker T. Washington died, in 1915. A prominent colored minister once acclaimed White as the modern counterpart of Moses. The testimonial was perhaps a trifle overenthusiastic, since White is hardly a universally recognized spokesman for a unified people. More than half a million Negroes—something over five per cent of all colored citizens eighteen or older—belong to his Association. By pressure-group standards, this constitutes a large body, and it is so much the biggest of its kind that White now and then is carried away by the size of his constituency and gives the impression that everything he says or does is the expressed wish of all fourteen million Negro Americans, including babes in arms. Sometimes he absent-mindedly extends his realm to take in all non-Negroes, too. A visitor to his office sat by not long ago while White received a phone call. "That man has just written a book," White remarked when he had hung up, "and he wants to see me about getting it into every American home."

In his negotiations with white Americans on behalf of colored Americans, White is a good deal less polite and restrained than are the ambassadors of most have-not nations in their dealings with the haves. When Congress was mulling over the problem of segregation in the armed forces last winter, White—who is spiritedly opposed to segregation, discrimination, and every other manifestation of Jim Crowism—sent a senator he knew a telegram blandly suggesting that the legislator and some of his colleagues put on blackface and uniforms for six weeks if they really wanted to find out how Negroes were treated in the armed forces. Not all Negroes are fond of White, but nearly all of them admire his penchant for taking resolute action of that nature in connection with their civil liberties; a dissident minority sometimes grumble that he has made a successful career out of exploiting their misfortunes. Subscribers to this viewpoint enjoy reminding one another of a probably apocryphal comic strip reputed to have been published in a Negro paper. It showed a black man saying to White, "I've finally found a solution to the race problem," and White replying, "Don't tell anybody." It is more usual, however, for White to appear in the colored press described by some glowing phrase like "the great gladiator for human rights." As a gladiator, White is voluble, aggressive, and effective. A year ago, he attended a meeting of a committee of sponsors of the Freedom Train. They had received a message from the mayor of a Southern city that their travelling exhibit of historic documents was scheduled to visit; the mayor had proposed that whites and Negroes in his bailiwick examine the display at different hours, so as not to upset a long-standing local tradition of strict segregation of the races. White sat back unassumingly until it appeared to him that the committee might approve the mayor's recommendation. Then he leaped to his feet and, quoting extensively from the itinerant documents themselves, urged that the mayor be advised that he would have to choose between segregation and the Freedom Train. The committee approved *his* recommendation. "When human rights are involved," a friend of White's who was present said afterward, "Walter is never at a loss for a word. Or even several paragraphs," he added reflectively.

White has been on the staff of the Association for thirty years, and in that period has travelled at least a million miles and made close to five thousand speeches, arguing against segregation and discrimination nearly every step and sentence of the way. He does not think that there is much likelihood of their being abolished in the near future by the governing bodies of all the forty-eight states, and his chief hope has long been pinned on the federal government. Accordingly, he has made many trips from his home base, in New York, to Washington, where he has uttered many words, most of them in favor of such still unenacted legislation as anti-lynching, anti-poll-tax, and fair-employment-practices bills. He is the author of four books and dozens of magazine articles on race problems, and he writes two weekly newspaper columns—one for the Chicago *Defender*, a Negro journal with a circulation of two hundred thousand, in which he explains to Negroes what the white world is up to, and the other for eight white newspapers, among them the Sunday *Herald Tribune*, with a total circulation of nearly three and a half million, in which he explains to white people what the Negro world is up to. This is the only column of general commentary by a Negro that has ever been syndicated in the white press. In both columns, White frequently makes it clear that although the lot of the Negro in this country may be continually improving, it isn't improving fast enough for him. This impatience keeps him from making the kinds of compromises that most ambassadors regard as part of the diplomatic game. In 1942, when the War Department announced that it planned to set up a training school for Negro pilots at Tuskegee Institute—a proposal that was applauded by many Negroes and was ultimately put into effect—White vociferously opposed the idea, arguing that the Air Forces already had plenty of schools and that it would be perfectly practicable to train whites and Negroes together. The graduates of the Tuskegee training school, among them a nephew of White's who was killed in action, compiled a creditable war record, but White, though proud of their accomplishments, never weakened in his conviction that endorsing a segregated institution of any kind, in any circumstances, would be inconsistent with his principles and thus intolerable. Although the N.A.A.C.P. has some white members in the South, including an all-white chapter at the University of Texas, its secretary's firmness about such matters has not endeared him or his organization to most white Southerners, or even to many white Southerners usually regarded as liberal. The attitude of the latter faction is that the Negro can best be helped by gradual reforms and that White is an all-or-nothing man who is doing his cause more harm than good. White's proponents reply that progress, gradual or otherwise, is rarely achieved unless its advocates demand more than they can possibly hope to get at the moment. "The Negro would never be even where he is today," one colored leader said recently, "if Walter hadn't always been in there fighting, and, what's more, always waging the frontal attack."

White often carries the assault into what he regards as enemy territory, and his arrival in Southern cities is likely to bring about some hard feelings. Several years ago, he accepted a speaking engagement in Dallas. He flew in and, on landing at the airport, found two delegations awaiting him, one of white men and one of colored. The men in the colored group, all six feet tall or more, closed in and formed a protective circle around White, who is five feet seven, as soon as he stepped off his plane. The white group stood nearby and glowered at the improvised phalanx. Both groups, in separate vehicles, escorted White to the scene of his talk, a colored Young Men's Christian Association clubhouse. (He had originally been scheduled to speak at a white Young Women's Christian Association clubhouse, but at the last minute his sponsors, with a bow to Southern womanhood, had switched locales.) White was introduced by a minister, a white man, who, noticing the band of tight-lipped white men, who had followed the visitor into the hall, delivered one of the least flowery introductions in history. "To quote Voltaire," the minister began, "'I disapprove of what you say, but I will defend to the death your right to say it.'" He paused, looked around nervously, and then concluded, "I now present Mr. White."

When White went to work for the Association, in 1918, it had been in existence for nine years. It had seventy-six branches and less than ten thousand members, about three-quarters of whom were white. Its colored members were mainly preachers, doctors, and assorted intellectuals. Today, more than nine-tenths of the N.A.A.C.P.'s five hundred and eighty thousand members are colored, a good many of them middle-class and lower-class people. There are sixteen hundred branches, the biggest of them in Detroit, Chicago, St. Louis, Los Angeles, Cleveland, and other industrial centers. There are more than seven hundred branches in the South, the biggest of them in Houston, Dallas, Birmingham, and Atlanta. The national headquarters has always been in New York, and since 1945 it has occupied two and a half floors of the Wendell Willkie Memorial Building, at 20 West Fortieth Street. The national office has a paid staff of seventy-two, four of whom are white. The organization operates on an annual budget of half a million dollars, four-fifths of which is membership dues and the rest contributions. White is the chief executive officer. His two principal assistants, both colored, are Roy Wilkins, a former Kansas City journalist, who edits the Association's monthly magazine, the *Crisis*, and Thurgood Marshall, a native of Baltimore and a graduate of the Howard University Law School, who is head of the N.A.A.C.P. legal staff. In addition to its full-time personnel, the Association, like most organizations of its type, has an impressive roster of national officers. There are sixty-six of these in all, of whom twenty-five, including Mrs. Franklin D. Roosevelt, Philip Murray, Eric Johnston, and Senators Arthur Capper and Wayne Morse, are white. The president of the N.A.A.C.P. is Arthur B. Spingarn, a white lawyer who has long been active in civil-liberties circles; the chairman of the board of directors is Dr. Louis T. Wright, a Negro surgeon and the first member of his race ever admitted to membership in the American College of Surgeons. He is also White's personal physician, and he once contributed to the advancement of colored people by picking his patient up off the floor (after White had collapsed in his apartment in Harlem early one morning with a sudden attack of appendicitis), throwing him over his shoulder, and carrying him to a hospital, seven blocks away, where, as soon as the Doctor got his breath back, he operated.

Legal representatives of the N.A.A.C.P.—either attorneys on its staff or ones who have been engaged for particular actions—have argued twenty-seven cases before the United States Supreme Court since their first appearance there in 1915 and have won twenty-four of them. All of these have touched upon matters like the disfranchisement of Negroes by the white-primary system, the extraction of confessions by torture, the denial of equal educational opportunities to Negroes, the exclusion of Negroes from juries, and the applicability of state segregation laws to passengers on interstate vehicles. Attorneys for the N.A.A.C.P. figure in some three hundred law cases a year, in one court or another. The organization takes a hand in a case only if satisfied on two points: that somebody has been the victim of an injustice solely because of his race or color, and that winning the case would be apt to establish a significant legal precedent.

White is not a lawyer and has little to do with the Association's routine legal work, but whenever something special comes up—like, say, a Supreme Court decision on an N.A.A.C.P. petition—he appears in court and becomes as excited as a bowler trying to affect the course of a rolling ball with body English. The chamber in which the Supreme Court sits has a section of seats up front near the judges' bench that are traditionally set aside for lawyers who have been admitted to practice before it. White's intense concern over the Court's pronouncements sometimes drives him to sit in this area, in order to be as close as possible to the shapers of his organization's destiny. He has never been evicted from his perch, possibly because he looks not unlike a corporation lawyer and possibly because the courtroom attendants know that he is a first-name friend of at least five of the nine justices. Last spring, when the Court was considering a case brought before it by the Association, White happened to be in Washington on the day of reckoning and happened to call up one of the justices to inquire after his health. The justice asked whether he planned to be in court that morning. "Interesting decisions of far-reaching importance are being handed down these days," he added guardedly. White can take a hint, and he went right over to the Court and seated himself way up front. After he had waited restlessly for nearly two hours, while several other matters were disposed of, the Court finally got around to the Association's case. Chief Justice Vinson talked for fifteen minutes without giving any indication of which way the decision was going, and White, at best an impatient man, grew frantic with anxiety. He looked up imploringly at the other justices on the bench, and got the impression that four of them, as he caught their eyes, mercifully favored him with an encouraging smile or nod. After the Chief Justice had at last confirmed these informal signals in legal terminology and the Court had adjourned, a friend of White's who had been sitting in the official spectators' section came forward with hand outstretched, to congratulate him on the N.A.A.C.P.'s victory. "Not now!" said White sternly, and explained that exulting over a decision while still within that courtroom by so overt an act as shaking hands would be a supreme breach of decorum.

White's cozy, nutational relationship with the judicial branch of the federal government has not distracted him from a long-time interest in, and dalliance with, the executive and legislative branches. He has been dropping in at the White House every now and then since the early days of the New Deal, and a Southern newspaper once implied, inaccurately, that he habitually approached the building through a secret tunnel from the nearby Hay-Adams House, a hotel at which he sometimes puts up. One of the most fruitful visits White ever made to the White House was in September, 1946, when he shepherded a delegation of six men—three whites and three Negroes, including himself—through the front door to an audience with President Truman. A month earlier, disturbed by signs of increasing racial friction in postwar America, White had invited representatives of forty church groups, labor unions, welfare agencies, and other social-minded organizations to a conference, sponsored by the N.A.A.C.P., in New York, at which it was agreed that a small delegation should call on the President and talk the situation over with him. At the White House meeting, Mr. Truman was told that lynching, terrorism, and other less disagreeable forms of discrimination were creating an unfortunate impression in the minds of many people in other countries who looked to the United States to set an example in civilized behavior. The President replied that, much as he deplored any abuse of civil liberties, his powers to safeguard them were limited. "Mr. President," said White, "why not have a study made to see what can be done under existing laws and to recommend the passage of whatever additional legislation seems necessary to enable the federal government to take appropriate action?" Mr. Truman was delighted with the suggestion and promptly set up the Civil Rights Committee that later issued the celebrated report that has so profoundly affected his political fortunes. When the Democratic National Convention unexpectedly revised its platform to embody many of the recommendations in Mr. Truman's controversial civil-rights program, White was as pleased as is any father when a child of his makes good. He issued a statement acclaiming the action, with paternal partisanship, as "the greatest turning point for the South and for America since the Civil War."

September 4, 1948

From Part I of a two-part Profile.

Shmoos

It was probably inevitable that we should find ourself having a chat with Al Capp, the "Li'l Abner" man, about Shmoos, the versatile creatures of his invention that have been the subject of more attention than we care to think about since their unveiling in his comic strip, last August. (On the absurd assumption that we have a reader somewhere who is unfamiliar with Shmoos, we will say briefly that they are quick-breeding animals, shaped like bowling pins, that yield milk, eggs, and cheesecake; taste like chicken or steak, depending on how they're cooked; and can be used as dress goods, building materials, and only Capp knows what else.) We met Mr. Capp in the dining room of the midtown hotel where he was staying last week. He begged us not to divulge the name of the hotel and, looking distraught, told us why. "There are members of one hundred and seventy-three Shmoo Clubs disgustingly eager to ferret me out and worship me," he said with a groan. "And the Society for the Advancement of the Shmoo, some horrible organization unhappily spawned in Connecticut, wants to abuse me because it heard that I had said that I regard the Shmoo as a loathsome little beast." "Do you?" we asked. "You can't imagine the unimaginable nightmare my life has become," he said. "I go somewhere to hear some quiet music, and they spot me coming in, and even before I'm seated, the band strikes up 'The Shmoo Rumba,' or 'The Shmoo Polka,' or some equally repulsive number. A waiter scurries over, laughing so hard he can barely hold a napkin, and he says, 'What'll it be today, Mr. Capp—a Shmoofflé?' I get sick. I can't eat. I think I have an ulcer."

Mr. Capp signalled a waiter and asked for a glass of milk. "You mean a Shmoo cocktail?" said the waiter mirthfully. Capp shuddered. "The most nauseatingly, unbearably monstrous part of it is those hideous jokes," he told us. "'What's Shmoo?' 'Happy Shmoo Year.' 'Life can be so Shmootiful.' I'm beginning to realize what President Truman must feel like when they play the 'Missouri Waltz.' I go into a bookstore looking for something intelligent to read, and some idiot clerk recommends 'The Life and Times of the Shmoo.' I pick up *Time* and find Norman Bel Geddes described as 'Shmoo-shaped.' I pick up *Life* and find a full page of editorials about the Shmoo. Now some benighted radio producer is after me to go on the 'Town Meeting of the Air' and debate the effect of the Shmoo on modern capitalism with Eric Johnston, Norman Thomas, and Robert Nathan. And my mail! Simultaneously, all over the North American continent, thousands of alert, astute Americans make the astonishing discovery that certain varieties of gourds and squashes resemble Shmoos. Can they keep this to themselves? No. They all paint up their vegetables with Shmoo features and send them to me. They send me apples and potatoes and tomatoes and eggs; some of the stuff doesn't even look like Bel Geddes. When this garbage leaves California or Toronto or wherever, maybe it smells good, but by the time it reaches me—it's inexpressible. What has happened to the American people? I watch a television show. Four beautiful girls come on the screen, and I think, How nice! Then, suddenly, before my eyes some imbecile covers them from top to bottom with Shmoo costumes. All you can see of those lovely girls is their feet. I haven't the faintest idea why the American public puts up with it."

Mr. Capp's milk arrived, and while he paused to take a sip, we asked him to enumerate some of the by-products of the Shmoo that have made, or are inexorably making, their way to market. "The list is insufferably long," he said. "Why, one day, in a snarling interview, I made some offhand remark about the probability that some fool would undoubtedly be bringing out chocolate-covered Shmoos next, and within a week three thousand or so candy manufacturers were yapping around, waving contracts. In Baltimore, there's half a factory turning out Shmoo clothes. The business is run by five sharp-featured, sharp-eyed, sharp-toothed brothers. Each of these brothers has several brothers of his own, and they all follow me around everywhere, shrieking about Shmooveralls. There are Shmoo greeting cards, balloons, dolls, other toys, jai-alai paddles, belts, suspenders, handkerchiefs, all-day suckers, dairy products, fountain pens, earrings, neckties, ashtrays, plant holders, soap, curtains, and pocketbooks. If you take the Shmoos off these pocketbooks, they make fine purses." At that moment, a pert, pretty young lady came up to Capp's table. "Could I Shmoo with you for a moment, Mr. Capp?" she asked politely. Capp regarded her stonily. "I think 'Li'l Abner' is simply Shmoopendous," she went on. "You see what I mean?" Capp said to us. "This is an apparently sane, normal girl. What can I do about her? If I kicked her, it would be bad manners." "Oh, Mr. Capp," she said, giggling, "you're just *too* Shmooey!"

January 1, 1949

Out of Practice

Lady tells us that the other day, as she neared the Delman shoe store, the employees of which have been on strike for several weeks, she became aware that one of the pickets, a substantial-looking middle-aged man, was staring at her feet. When she got abreast of him, he asked politely, "4-B, Madam?" "No," she said, "4-C." "Heavens, I *am* getting rusty!" he said.

September 17, 1949

I used to rewrite a lot of anecdotes that readers sent in to *The New Yorker*, but this one was special: The lady in question was my mother.

Human Interest

With the frustrated Shirley May France back in this country, we've had a talk with Ted Worner, a voluble press agent and sometime promoter, who engineered her through what the London *Daily Express* called "the noisiest attempt on the Channel," and we herewith record what he told us, for whom it may concern:

"I produce and direct Jackie Robinson's radio show, you see, and early this summer I saw we were going to need backing for a post-season barnstorming tour. The owner of a swimming pool at Coney Island came through, and I made a mental note to do something for him. A week later, I saw in the *Mirror* that some kid in Somerset, Massachusetts, near Fall River, had announced she would like to swim the Channel, so I called her up and offered her three hundred dollars to make a swim from the Battery to Coney Island and to come out of the water, accidental-like, on the beach next to my backer's pool. She said I'd have to ask her father, who fixes oil-burners. I did, and he said 'Sure' and invited me to promote his daughter. I never had any specific deal, but I stood to be cut in on anything the kid earned if she made the Channel. He sent me a photograph of her with a caption saying she weighed a hundred and seventy-seven pounds, and I was discouraged. But I'd been thinking. I know Gertrude Ederle very well, and I had a hunch the public might be ready for another one of those things. So I started to peddle the kid's story.

"At first, nobody would touch it, practically, but I got a break on the Coney Island thing because it was a rainy Sunday and the papers needed something to run. And when Shirley turned up that day, I found she weighed only a hundred and fifty and some pounds and had a pretty face, blue eyes, blond hair, nice teeth, and dimples. So I was encouraged, and went to the Newspaper Enterprise Association syndicate to get backing for a Channel swim. Well, it happens that N.E.A. spent nearly fifty thousand dollars in 1926, Ederle's year, on another dame who was supposed to swim the Channel, but she crossed it by riding in the boat that accompanied Trudy, and the syndicate had been hoping for a successful Channel swimmer all these years, so it bought the kid's exclusive story for a thousand dollars, with another fifteen hundred to come if she made it. The syndicate manager gave us six dozen hard-boiled eggs he'd boiled himself, and said he'd send some steaks over for the kid. The eggs spoiled, but the steaks tasted fine. I had to keep my strength up, too.

"Well, before we left, I went to see my old Army sergeant, who works for United Artists, and they were about to distribute a picture called 'Black Magic,' whose producer had decided to spend three hundred thousand dollars promoting it. He made a deal to let me have a thousand pounds of frozen English money, which he couldn't use otherwise anyway, if I'd plug the picture whenever I could. Then I promoted Shirley a wardrobe from Henry Rosenfeld, the big dress manufacturer, and I went to a friend of mine at the Kingston Watch Company—a very nice watch—and he gave us five hundred dollars and promised five hundred more if the kid made it and if she wore a Kingston waterproof during her swim. When we got set to go, I somehow found myself with a party of six—Shirley, her father, her swimming coach, her high-school French teacher, a friend of her father's who was supposed to be a money man, and a reporter for the Fall River *Herald News*. We sailed on the Nieuw Amsterdam, on July 22nd. The ship had a swimming pool, but I was the only one that went in.

"In mid-ocean, I suddenly remembered we didn't have any accommodations in England, so I radioed the London office of United Artists, and when we landed I discovered they had us staying at the Grosvenor House, at eighteen pounds a night. That must have given the press the idea that we had some real money; the *Daily Mail* described the kid's father as a Texas oil burner. I held an emergency meeting of my party that first night, and the next day we got the hell out of the Grosvenor House and went to the East Cliff Hotel at Dover—a reasonable place, where all the Channel swimmers hang out. We had fifty pounds of grease with us, by the way—lanolin—and it was more than Shirley needed, so we gave some to the European swimmers who were there. We're typical Americans—you know what I mean. About this time, the press moved in on us. For the whole six weeks we were in Europe, it was interviews, pictures, interviews, pictures. They even printed a photograph of *me* in the water. Shirley herself was completely indifferent to it all—she just wanted to swim the Channel—and the press was on me, and every so often I'd have to do something to give the story a shot in the arm. I asked the U.S. Navy for a destroyer escort, for instance, which, of course, I didn't get, and I asked Princess Margaret and Ambassador Douglas's daughter Sharman to send Shirley messages. They didn't, but the Ambassador did. And then somehow the story broke that Shirley was going to swim nude. I deny having started this, of course, but I had mentioned such a possibility casually, and when a stink was raised about it, we came out fine by issuing a very indignant and righteous statement. As a matter of fact, Shirley couldn't have swum nude, because our contract with United Artists specified that she had to wear a bathing suit with 'Black Magic' on it. I'd been brooding over what other gimmicks I could use to tie in with the picture, and one day, as I was walking along the beach near Dover, I came across an old black schooner called the Nellie Bywater. Immediately, I conceived the idea of changing its name to Black Magic and using it as a press boat during the swim. It was a slow boat, but at least it was black. The captain wanted a hundred and fifty pounds for the deal, and, what with me having to pay for everybody but the Fall River reporter, I didn't have anywhere near enough cash, but I raised the dough by telling the correspondents who were going to accompany the kid across the Channel that they could ride on the boat for fifteen pounds apiece and that I would provide food, deck chairs, and gin-rummy facilities. I also pointed out to the photographers that the kid always comes up on her left side for air and that I was arranging it so that she would come up facing the Black Magic.

"Well, after checking the weather with the Air Ministry, I picked Labor Day for the swim, but then conditions changed and I had to postpone it a day. It was a terrible mess. N.E.A. alone had fifteen men at Dover, and there were so few accommodations there that the A.P. had to sleep with the

U.P. Shirley was at Wissant, France, by then, waiting to start when I gave her the signal from Dover, and late Labor Day afternoon I called a press conference and announced that she'd take off early the next morning. Then I tried to call Shirley and tell *her*. I was informed that the telephone operator at Wissant always goes home at six o'clock. Well, here the whole world knows that the kid is going to start at dawn except the kid herself. I get frantic. I contact the chief Continental operator, or somebody, and scream 'international crisis' and throw Ambassador Douglas's name around, and after a while they somehow get word to the police at Wissant to get word to Shirley.

"I got the press boat over to the French coast, and we started back across with Shirley. Well, we finally had to pull her out, and that was that. You know, it's an amazing thing. Here was one of the greatest human-interest stories of the year—of the decade, maybe—and I didn't make a cent out of it."

September 24, 1949

Department of Amplification, Correction, and Abuse (Vicarious)

NEW YORK CITY
SEPTEMBER 12, 1949

THE EDITORS, *THE NEW YORKER*

SIRS:

It is unusual, I know, to address to you a communication complaining about an article printed in another periodical, but since the article about which I feel impelled to complain appeared in *Soviet Literature*, a journal published in Moscow, and since I might never have run afoul of the Kremlin crowd if it hadn't been for your magazine, I hope that you will understand why I am writing you.

You may recall that early in the war you were kind enough to publish a series of pieces of mine—XXXIX of them, by the exotic numbering system you used to identify them—under the general heading of "The Army Life." Some XIX or XX of these were published in book form by Simon & Schuster late in 1942 with the same title. The book had a relatively small sale—undoubtedly, I told myself consolingly at the time, because its title tended to make potential customers confuse it with the "Basic Field Manual," a useful War Department primer on Army life that was then being distributed free to every selectee inducted into the rapidly expanding Army. My book, though modestly priced, at a dollar seventy-five, and containing no official information whatever, could hardly have been expected to compete with a giveaway bearing the imprimatur of the high brass.

I haven't thought much about "The Army Life" since the war, or hadn't, at least, until a few weeks ago, when a friend of mine who persistently keeps tab on the Russian press sent me a copy of *Soviet Literature*—printed, luckily for me, in English—containing a piece by R. Samarin that deals with the wartime literary accomplishments of several American writers, principal among whom were J. Hersey and B. Mauldin. My friend appended a note saying that *Soviet Literature* is "extensively circulated outside Russia as a means of propagandizing the current work of Soviet writers and also as a means of attacking foreign writers the Soviet Union doesn't like." He directed my regard to the following paragraph:

> Among the most grossly false American books dealing with soldier-ing on the eve of the war are *The Army Life* (1942), by E. J. Kahn, *See Here, Private Hargrove* (1942), by M. Hargrove. Written, no doubt, with a view to distribution in the army, these books lay special stress on American soldiers' devotion to the laws of bourgeois ideology in the U.S.A. The alleged "democracy" of the American army is illustrated with particular cynicism in Kahn's book. The lieutenant who is training the recruits explains the peculiar beauty of the army hierarchy; it starts with the sergeant giving orders to the private, then, the lieutenant to the sergeant, and so on, until it rises to Roosevelt who gives orders to Marshall, Chief of the General Staff—thus coming full circle, the lieutenant adds enthusiastically, with the soldier-citizens giving orders to the President.

I didn't quite get the connection between Samarin's second sentence and his third, but I passed that up, my attention having been diverted by a glance through the rest of his polemic. That brief look made me gratefully aware that Hargrove and I had, on the whole, got off easier than Hersey, described as an "agent of American militarism," whose "Into the Valley" is called "a striking example of a literature that aims at corrupting the minds of the American soldiers," and Mauldin, who is credited with having believed that "the only constructive element amid the ruin and chaos" of war-torn Europe was "a drunken barbarian with his helmet set at a rakish angle and an idiotic leer on his unshaven face"—a reference to Mauldin's thoroughly lovable cartoon characters Willie and Joe, whom Samarin, in an impressive display of gross falseness, refers to throughout his article as "Billy and Joe." Poor Mauldin! Samarin also says that "Mauldin's blether thus reveals as far back as 1944 the outline of that plan of American-Nazi coöperation which has now in many cases, and despite the protests of progressive circles in the U.S.A., become an established fact." (I have just looked up "blether" in the dictionary, and, by God, there is such a word. It means "blather.") As for

American war writing in general, Samarin calls it "bestial and false in substance," "amazingly inartistic," and "a blend of imperialistic propaganda with consistent hypocrisy, seasoned with mendacious ballyhoo about the notorious American democracy." You editors ought to be ashamed of yourselves for having published such blether.

But to get back to me. When I first read the Samarin piece, his paraphrase of the chain-of-command anecdote I had related sounded accurate enough, but later, when I checked it against my text (No. V in your series), I found that my account did not start, as Samarin says, with a sergeant giving orders to a private; it started with a *corporal* giving the orders, after having himself received them from a sergeant. How could Samarin, a writer admittedly concerned with excoriating falseness and presumably concerned also with the sensitive feelings of the proletariat, thus purge from the ranks a grade of soldier traditionally considered the backbone of any respectable people's army?

The most serious charge Samarin levels against Hargrove and me is that our books were written, "no doubt," for Army consumption, the implication being that we were a couple of literary prostitutes seduced·by Washington gold. As far as Hargrove, for whom I am not authorized to speak, is concerned, his book was unquestionably distributed widely within the Army. It must have been distributed there, for it was such an enormous best-seller (it outsold my book by something like a thousand to one) that there could hardly have been enough book buyers *not* in the armed forces to account for all the copies of it in circulation. It wasn't distributed *by* the Army, though, as far as I know, and I do know that Hargrove didn't write it with such distribution in mind. He and I were both privates at the same camp in North Carolina when we were composing our respective bits of mendacious ballyhoo. Hargrove wrote his, as I recall, to make money, and so did I—a sordid, bourgeois motive that has long dominated my literary life.

Toward the end of the war, I was permanently assigned to public-relations work and stopped writing the "Army Life" series, there being nothing in the life of an Army public-relations man that could conceivably interest anybody except the unhappy fellow's next of kin. The Army did permit me, however, to write a few magazine pieces, more or less in the line of duty, on military subjects. It wouldn't let me accept any money for these. Its view was that I no more deserved to be paid extra for my writing stint than a civilian gunsmith assigned to Ordnance deserved to be paid extra every time he cleared a jammed firing pin. I thought then that the Army's treatment of me was a notable example of the practical application of the old Communistic doctrine that every man should produce according to his abilities and be rewarded according to his needs. It seems to me that Samarin, instead of blethering away like an idiot, should have given the

Army and me a pat on the back for having so conscientiously followed the Party line.

FAITHFULLY YOURS,

E. J. Kahn, II

P.S. There was not a single crack against Russia in "The Army Life," I have just ascertained. Imagine trying to get a book without one in it published today!

October 15, 1949

The Gentleman From New York

As the member of the House of Representatives from the Twenty-first Congressional District of New York, Jacob Koppel Javits, an energetic, informed, and ambitious lawyer generally addressed by the people whose backs he slaps as "Jack," is the spokesman on the national scene for the slightly more than three hundred thousand inhabitants of the upper West Side of Manhattan. Javits, who was born on the lower East Side of Manhattan, has been in Congress only three years, but he has so rapidly adjusted to his environment that he can now use a phrase like "warp and woof" in ordinary parlor conversation without blinking. He is a stocky man of forty-five, five feet nine inches in height, with a gleaming bald head and gleaming white teeth. His appearance suggests an erudite version of Jack Benny, with whom, unlike some of his legislative colleagues, he has nothing occupational in common. Javits has always been an exceptionally serious-minded man, and he is a serious-minded legislator. He has a high regard for businesslike efficiency and is himself a sturdy example of it. When he first went to Congress, another legislator asked a mutual friend what kind of political machine the newcomer had behind him. "Javits doesn't need one" was the answer. "He *is* a machine." Javits has a strong social conscience, an alert and retentive mind, a fluent tongue, a courtly manner, and an air of indomitable self-assurance. He dresses expensively and carefully but without the flashiness of many politicians. During one of the two Congressional campaigns in which he has been a candidate, a co-worker suggested to him that he enhance his visual appeal to the voters by adopting some gay sartorial symbol. The friend mentioned Al Smith's brown derby and the success that *that* had enjoyed. Javits forthwith bought himself a black fedora, and scarcely took it off his head until Election Day. There is no reason to believe that it influenced a single vote.

A congressman is, of course, supposed to espouse the views of his constituents, and Javits has tried harder than many of his colleagues to ascertain what those views are. During his 1946 campaign, he established a political precedent by engaging Elmo Roper, at a cost of two thousand dollars, to sound out the residents of the district on how they felt about things, and he ordered a similar poll taken in 1948, when he successfully ran for reëlection. On both occasions, Roper's operatives collared a thousand people of voting age, presumably a cross-section of the Twenty-first, and questioned them, for Javits' edification, about such issues as housing, the cost of living, atomic energy, China, public works, labor relations, the Soviet Union, and the quality of the performance of the Congress of the United States. Javits learned, among other things, that his potential constituents were markedly pro-labor, and after being elected he dutifully voted against the Taft-Hartley Act, to the anguish of many of his Republican colleagues, who felt, as his party irregularity since then has caused them to continue to feel, that he was being grievously disloyal to their grand old cause.

Roper's 1946 survey disclosed that only 8.8 per cent of the thousand constituents could correctly name their congressman, Javits' predecessor; that 6.9 per cent *thought* they could but came up with the wrong name; and that the remaining 84.3 per cent, many of them well informed on atomic energy and China, found the question utterly beyond them. In 1948, when the same question was asked and the right answer was, of course, "Javits," 33.1 per cent gave that name, and only 5.3 per cent somebody else's. This was enormously pleasing to Javits. A few weeks ago, guided solely by a hunch, he estimated that well over half of his constituents could now, if challenged, name their representative. If that is so, he is, by big-city political standards, remarkably well known in his district. His relative renown stems partly from the diligence with which he has looked out for the interests of his flock, and partly from his having demonstrated a nice flair for getting his name publicized not only within the narrow limits of the Twenty-first District but also in the outside world, where he has had to compete for attention with the favorite sons of the four hundred and thirty-four other Congressional districts. Javits works hard to this end. He almost never makes a speech or issues a statement without embodying in it expressions of sentiment that he regards as quotable and without distributing numerous mimeographed copies thereof. When Drew Pearson, who had once described him as "an effective operator," failed to mention him in an item that Javits thought he deserved to be counted in on, Javits hastily telephoned the columnist, fearful that he had somehow unwittingly hurt his feelings and eager to make amends. Such enterprise has paid off. Javits was, for example, the only congressman to be honored by *Forbes Magazine*, a while ago, on a page headed "Thoughts on the Business of Life," in which one of Javits' thoughts (it had to do with the responsibility of the United States to the rest of the world) was quoted alongside thoughts of Abraham Lincoln, George Eliot, Irving Berlin, and an anonymous hotel proprietor in

Syracuse who had put up a sign on his premises stating that business has never invented a substitute for customer satisfaction. Many of Javits' constituents feel that, by gaining recognition of such a high type, their congressman has brought them gratifying recognition, too. "You've put Washington Heights on the map," a pastor of that neighborhood told him a few weeks ago. Javits takes a more modest view of his achievements. "I've done a lot for the district," he says, "but the district has done a lot for me, too."

When a congressman says something on the floor, it is transcribed, and, if he has asked permission to revise and extend his remarks, it is sent to him so he can make any corrections he cares to before it is inserted in the *Congressional Record*—a protective device that leads to the excision of many grammatical bobbles, and that once enabled a representative from a dairy state who had absent-mindedly spoken favorably of oleomargarine to change a highly embarrassing "for" to a rocklike "against." A congressman may alter, add, or delete as much as he chooses, and a sentence like "I feel that we will continue to press for action for the middle-income families, which was also provided for in our bill"—the words Javits used one day in commenting on another man's housing bill—may come out something the way that one did: "I feel also that we will continue to press for action on housing for the lower middle-income families, which is not contained in his bill, but which was first provided for in the bill introduced by the ten House Republicans, later joined in by similar bills introduced by twenty-two Democratic members." Congressmen become so accustomed to editing anything they put in the *Record* that, in the process of inserting an article from the *Saturday Review of Literature* last summer, Javits edited that. Despite this careful preparation, insertions in the *Record* are still occasionally liable to misinterpretation. During the last session, Javits submitted for the *Record's* Appendix, in which congressmen may insert material not spoken from the floor, an item that began with the statement "This is an invitation to members from our twenty-six most populous states to go to the theatre." Some congressmen, who knew that Javits had introduced a bill calling for the establishment of a national theatre and who had heard through the legislative grapevine that he had just been in telegraphic communication with Oscar Hammerstein II, one of the producers of "South Pacific," read on with high anticipation, only to find that Javits' encouraging preamble was followed simply by a listing of the names of more than two hundred and fifty summer theatres in twenty-six states that a theatrical acquaintance had asked him to insert as evidence of the ubiquity of the stage. Javits had sent a telegram to Hammerstein, all right, but merely to inquire into the possibility of buying a pair of tickets for a Saturday-night performance of "South Pacific."

To a representative in Congress, it seems that the members of his particular body politic are, individually and collectively, the nicest, most generous, and most deserving people in the world. He spends about half his time looking out for their special interests, and his motto with regard to them is, as a rule, "Service with a Smile." Javits has a fine set of shining white teeth, and, though by nature a rather solemn man, he is often moved to display them in fond welcome upon the approach of a constituent, much in the manner of a maître d'hôtel upon the approach of a steady and well-heeled customer. The demands on Javits' patience, endurance, and resourcefulness are, on the whole, infinitely more severe than those a headwaiter has to cope with. Javits has served three years in Congress and during that stretch has been asked by his flock to handle around ten thousand matters. Should an ex-soldier in the Twenty-first District, which takes in the upper West Side, including the entire northern tip, of Manhattan and has a population of nearly a third of a million, feel, as one did not long ago, that the Veterans Administration was unfair in its decree that he ought to be treated by psychiatric therapy rather than by psychoanalysis, Javits is the man with whom the complaint is apt to be lodged. Should a lady be of the opinion that the Bureau of Internal Revenue is demanding of her a dollar and seventeen cents more than she owes on her federal income tax, or another lady, representing an Elizabethan Reading Club, be of the opinion that the New York Public Library carries a shamefully inadequate stock of the books favored by her society, Javits is the man who is likely to hear about it and be expected to do something about it. He is a public servant of remarkable fortitude and energy, and every few waking hours he does a favor for a constituent—sometimes without knowing about it, since he has a staff of six assistants who dispose of many such problems in his influential name.

Javits is so conscientious that he makes sure his constituents are looked after even when he is thousands of miles away from them. In the summer of 1947, while in Europe on a Congressional fact-finding expedition, he had a good deal of legislative research to attend to, over a wide area, but nonetheless he took pains during a stopover in Dublin to get in touch with the American consul regarding the issuance of a visa to a cousin of one of his constituents, who was eager to migrate to the Twenty-first District, and upon finding himself in Vienna he took equal pains to expedite the admission to this country of a rabbi, then in a displaced-persons camp, whom a group of constituents wished to import to officiate at their temple. Javits scarcely ever fails to react sympathetically to a plea for help from a resident of his district. Recently, a young man in Washington Heights wrote in to say that he thought he was losing his mind, and what did his congressman propose to do about it? "I am sure you will remain sane," Javits replied, and urged the man to feel free to call on him again if he needed further advice.

Every Saturday, barring acts of God or Congress, Javits holds open court for his constituents in his law offices, at 630 Fifth Avenue, in Rockefeller Center. Congressmen are granted free office space, when it is available, in federal buildings within their districts, and many take advantage of this prerogative, but the only eligible buildings in the Twenty-first are a couple of overcrowded post offices. Javits estimates that it would cost him at least five thousand dollars a year to maintain an office in his district, and since the law office is already set up, he uses that. On a normal Saturday, he may have around twenty appointments with constituents, and, inasmuch as they often show up in delegations, may receive as many as fifty or a hundred of them. It is a fairly simple matter for any constituent, or group of constituents, to get an appointment with him; few businessmen are as readily accessible to customers as most congressmen are to voters from their districts.

One recent Saturday, the first of Javits' callers was a colored woman employed by a federal agency, who informed him that her supervisor, in making recommendations for promotions, had been discriminating against her for eight years because she was a Negro. Javits said he would have an investigation instituted at once. Then came a Puerto Rican, who hoped Javits could arrange to have a disability pension he was drawing as a result of the Second World War paid to him in a lump sum, rather than in the monthly instalments he had been getting, so that he could start a small business. Javits said that he would inquire into the possibilities but that he was doubtful. Then came a naturalized German Jew, who carried on alternately and interminably about the revivification of Nazism in Germany and a plan he had for mixing alcohol and gasoline to take the place of fuel oil. Javits listened to him for twenty minutes, and finally said, "I understand, I understand, but what do you want me to *do?*" It turned out the man didn't have anything specific in mind; he just wanted to talk to somebody. Then came two men who were planning to make a nonpartisan survey of the state of civil rights in a portion of the West Side of Manhattan and hoped Javits would be a co-chairman, along with Representative Franklin D. Roosevelt, Jr., whose district, the Twentieth, was also involved. Javits said he'd be glad to, and asked what ground they proposed to survey. From Fifty-ninth Street to 125th, they told him, and Javits, possibly having in mind the fact that the only part of his district to be covered would be a stretch from 125th down to 114th Street, urged them to extend their northern limit to 135th. "You wouldn't want to cut Manhattanville in half, would you?" he asked sternly. They agreed that that would be an ungallant thing to do, and departed. Then came a businessman, who during the Second World War had lost a consignment of brush bristles in Switzerland. He said the Swiss government had confiscated them and had paid him only a fraction of their worth. As a German refugee to this country and technically an enemy alien he had been helpless at the time, but now he was a naturalized American citizen, and would Javits please prevail upon the State Department to intercede with the Swiss, so he could be paid in full?

"I'll do what I can," Javits told him. "But you must remember that I can't force the federal government to do anything for you. I'm only a small part of the government. All I can do is use my influence."

"That would be fine," said his visitor. "And I can't begin to tell you how much I appreciate your listening to my private troubles. I'm sorry to have taken up so much of your valuable time."

"Don't be silly," said Javits. "That's a congressman's job. That's my duty."

January 21 and 28, 1950

From a two-part Profile.

Notes and Comment

In the course of considering amendments to the present displaced-persons bill, Congress has been beset by doubts as to precisely what kinds of hapless and homeless people can be fitted into the American scheme of things without dislocating the delicate balance of our way of life. While the matter was under discussion in Washington a few days ago, the government of Czechoslovakia decreed, the Associated Press says, that all palmists, fortune-tellers, and "other specialists in the occult" must suspend operations in that country at once, on the ground that they are "medieval remains of the capitalist era." Here is a group of the dispossessed to whom the United States could readily offer haven. Let them all be invited to settle in southern California, where they could be absorbed without anyone's noticing them at all.

February 4, 1950

I Was a Gum-Moll

(For several months, faithful followers of the local afternoon press have noted with amazement the rakish course in self-enlightenment being pursued by the New York *Post*, which has been taking its readers into its confidence while it has sought, with such earnestness and

113

naîveté as would make any school child quiver with envy, to learn about Sex. The *Post* has recently found out, for instance, that there are shadowy dives in Greenwich Village that cater to homosexuals, and dance halls in Times Square that attract customers whose purpose is not always simply to dance. This last discovery was made for the paper by a typically starry-eyed *Post* reporter, a young Vassar graduate who, using a false name and with her shoulders sacrificially bared, took a job as a dance-hall hostess and was evidently surprised to perceive that some of her partners had ulterior, and in a few cases downright sinister, intentions. While devoting its columns zealously, if not exclusively, to rape, promiscuity, abortion, juvenile delinquency, degeneracy of various types and degrees, and the urgent need for psychiatric treatment for just about everybody, the *Post* has not only demonstrated convincingly that modern society is shot through with sinfulness but has aroused the suspicion among some of its more impressionable readers that hardly an aspect of life exists today in which Satan does not occupy the driver's seat. The absorbing exposé that follows consists of excerpts from the diary of a young lady recently engaged in delving into still another unsavory aspect of society for the *Post*, but whose findings have not yet been revealed there, though it is probably too much to hope that they won't be.)

MONDAY—My first day on the job! The Sweet Briar Alumnae Placement Office certainly never gave me an inkling that life on the staff of a great metropolitan newspaper would be anywhere near as exciting as this. Why, the very next desk to mine belongs to none other than Hester Van Rensselaer. Imagine! Only a year and a half out of Bryn Mawr, but she knows Sin Street and Abortion Alley like a book, and has, in fact, written a book about each of them. It was she, moreover, who did that astonishing series on motor vehicles, in which, after poking around the industry under the alias of Hot-Rod Hessie, she was able to disclose that the Nash and the Kaiser have seats that can be converted into beds. Good stories just seem to fall into her lap. This morning, taking the bus to work, she saw a male passenger wink at a girl standing down the aisle from him. Hester hasn't had time yet to look into the situation any further, but she's been instructed to write up the episode, to begin publication Thursday. It's to run for seven weeks.

WEDNESDAY—I'm told that in the old days things were quite different around here. The paper used to be so cluttered up with Samuel Grafton and *that* sort that there was scarcely any room left for revelations. The present regime will have no truck with stodgy space-fillers; it believes that a newspaper should concentrate on news. I only wish I could wangle a decent news assignment. Today, for instance, when the Managing Editor got a tip that human beings bet on horse races, and sent all the other reporters out to follow it up (all but Hester, that is, who had already made a date to take the president of the bus company to her psychoanalyst's), I had to stay behind to handle the routine stuff. The result was that I got stuck with a mid-harbor collision between two silly old ships. Darn! If only I could get a break.

FRIDAY—I have an honest-to-goodness assignment, and I hope I prove worthy of it! I was summoned by the Sensation Editor this morning. He's a terribly nice man, whom the *Post* was awfully lucky to get for the job; it seems it had been a toss-up whether he would come here or stay with the Salvation Army. He told me that he wants a probe made of the chewing-gum racket and that since Hester, who was to have done it, is unavailable, I can have a shot at it. It appears, according to the best information he has, that a lot of school children are addicts. They squander their few pitiful pennies on the stuff day after day, and things have reached the stage where they can purchase it quite openly, here and there. The S.E. directed me to go to the Costume Department tomorrow for my falsies, then to Makeup, and next Monday I'll be getting under way.

MONDAY—This is it. I have a marvellous bobby-sox-and-sweater disguise to go with my role; I'm sure nobody would ever take me for a reporter. My photographer, who is to accompany me every breathtaking step of the way, and I meandered over to a nearby subway station (the first time I had been in one!), and I had barely descended to the platform when I spotted a gang of boys, some of them no older than seventeen and some as young as sixteen, who were huddled suspiciously around a queer-looking machine. My pulse quickened. I sidled up to them and asked with airy casualness if they knew how I could obtain some chewing gum. "Got a penny, Ma'am?" one of them retorted. I pulled a marked coin from my purse and handed it to him. He put it in the machine, fiddled with some kind of lever, and with a deft, experienced flourish extracted a paper-wrapped capsule, hardly more than an inch long, which he pressed furtively into my palm. I decided to get to the heart of the matter at once. "Are you boys going to a psychiatrist?" I asked bluntly. "We're going to Bushwick Avenue, lady," one of them replied. They then quickly boarded a train before I could ask any more questions. I had time to observe, though, that they were carrying textbooks. Undoubtedly truants, I thought to myself sadly.

TUESDAY—Acting on a hunch, I went to Bushwick Avenue today, and in a subway station there, to my joy, found the same kind of machine. I knew I was getting warm. I didn't catch sight of my young hooligan friends of yesterday, but I did see one boy who was openly putting a coin into one such machine, as if he didn't give a hang what anybody thought. There was a girl with him who, though she looked young enough and innocent enough to be his sister, subsequently began to shake the machine with such relish and contempt that I knew she must be his accomplice, if not something tawdrier. I drew close to them, caught the boy's eye, and asked him, cleverly using the idiom I was sure he would grasp most readily, if he knew where I could promote a stick. He pretended not to understand me, so I decided to use a term I have heard over and over in the office. "I need your help," I began. "I want to be a gum-moll." He looked at me blankly. This boy, I realized unhappily, wasn't going to be easy to crack. "Are you *his* gum-moll?" I barked suddenly at the girl with him. "No, I'm his sister," she said, and they both scampered apprehensively away. Poor, misguided youngsters—they probably mistook me for an agent of a rival gang.

WEDNESDAY—Things aren't going as well as I had hoped, so today I tried a new tack. I went to Bushwick Avenue early, leaned against an unattended machine on the station platform, and began chewing ostentatiously on the piece of gum I obtained two days ago. It had a haunting, not entirely unpleasant taste. Pretty soon, as I had anticipated, a rascally-looking youngster sauntered toward me, as if brazenly intending to use the very machine I was lounging against. "Excuse me, Miss," he said unabashedly as he drew abreast of me. Once he had made that overture, I felt sure he was my man. I remarked languidly that you certainly couldn't get much gum for a cent, could you? He hesitated, then nodded in wary agreement. I asked him ever so offhandedly if he happened to know of any place where I could procure more than a penny's worth of the stuff. "Sure, Miss," he said. Now I was getting somewhere! I asked him if he would take me there. "Are you nuts, lady?" he said. Since he had brought the subject up, I asked him outright if he had ever had a sibling complex. He ducked that one, but I did manage to elicit from him the significant admission that his mother and father didn't know what he was doing at that particular moment and, furthermore, probably didn't care. Then I returned to the main issue. "I'll give you a quarter if you'll take me to that place you mentioned," I whispered, hoping I could square it with our business office. "What the devil!" he said, horrifyingly. "Come with me." He led me out of the station, up to the ground level, and along a drab street. While we were walking, I asked him, as if just to make conversation, what gang he belonged to. "The P.A.L.," he said. I have no idea what that is, but there may be a series in it. Then he stopped at a shabby-looking store with a sign on it reading "Stationery." That was evidently a mere front, for when we went inside, I could see that there were all kinds of goods on display, and, what's more, the proprietor unblinkingly sold the lad a whole package of gum. It cost a nickel, and contained, I later ascertained, five sticks. They were called, ironically, Juicy Fruit.

THURSDAY—When I said goodbye yesterday to my companion, who swore his name was John and his nickname Johnny, he agreed to meet me again today at the "Stationery" store if I'd give him another quarter. I showed up at the appointed time, but there was no sign of him. There wasn't anybody around except a policeman, who came up and asked me who I was. When I identified myself as a reporter, he said that for a moment he had thought I was somebody else. I asked what he meant, and he said it was nothing important; they had had a routine complaint from some kid's parents about a frowzy dame who was molesting high-school students in the neighborhood, for what sordid purpose the police didn't yet know. There's further evidence for you that beneath the placid surface of our city lies a seething, ugly stratum of life of which too few citizens are aware. I hope they catch her and put her away, for her own good. I'm sorry, though, that Johnny couldn't make it. He had half promised to tell me about a perversion he referred to as "bubble gum."

April 8, 1950

The Wayward Press
The Greenwich Tea Party

Larry Adler, the harmonica player, and Paul Draper, the dancer, are friends of mine, and I have therefore been following with far more than offhand interest the way certain elements of the press have covered a libel suit they instituted over a year ago against Mrs. John T. McCullough, of Greenwich, Connecticut. Mrs. McCullough, the wife of a *Time* editor, became upset, in the fall of 1948, when she learned that Adler and Draper were to perform the following January 21st at one of three musical evenings sponsored by the Greenwich Community Concert Association, to which series she had subscribed. She returned her tickets to the Association and explained why in a number of bristling statements that were subsequently published, most of them in the Greenwich *Time*, her home-town paper. She said that Adler and Draper were "pro-Communist in sympathy" and "exponents of a line of thinking directly opposed to every democratic principle upon which our great country has been founded." She said that "these boys had interrupted one of their concerts in Birmingham, Alabama, to give a Party-line speech." (According to the Birmingham papers, Adler and Draper, after finishing an uninterrupted performance at the Municipal Auditorium, went to a hotel and, before another audience, spoke on behalf of the Presidential aspirations of Henry Wallace, whom they were ardently supporting. The Associated Press sent out an account of the evening's events that, while it said that the Birmingham Music Club was "exceedingly embarrassed" because "a couple of performers mixed politics with art," also stated clearly that they "appeared at a joint concert . . . and later addressed a

117

Wallace-for-President rally." Despite the "later," the story was given such headlines as "Political Talk at Concert Assailed" [Des Moines *Register*], "Art for Wallace's Sake" [Cincinnati *Post*], and "Mix Politics and Art" [New York *Times*]. It may be that Mrs. McCullough, like many other people, just reads the headlines.) She said, "I do not dispute their talents, but as an American I stand opposed to Communism in any form." She said, "By purchasing tickets [for the concert], we indirectly make cash contributions to Moscow." She said, "I have learned that these two men have openly supported eight or nine Communist-front organizations. I do not know that these men are Communists, but no one who encourages Communism in any form should be supported in a capitalistic town like Greenwich. Anyone interested in Communism is interested in overthrowing our government and should be treated as a traitor." The board of directors of the Community Concert Association—a body headed by the town's first selectman, the nearest thing it has to a mayor—had an interrogatory session with Adler and Draper and then announced that it was satisfied they were not interested in overthrowing the government and that the concert would go on. It did, and shortly afterward each of the two entertainers sued Mrs. McCullough for a hundred thousand dollars. Whether or not they were justified in doing so is scheduled to be formally put up to a jury in a United States District Court at Hartford the end of this month. The case has already been tried informally by a number of columnists, including Bill Cunningham, of the Boston *Herald*; Westbrook Pegler; George Sokolsky; and Igor Cassini, the sociologist who writes for the New York *Journal-American* and other Hearst papers under the name Cholly Knickerbocker. Evidently on the assumption that a United States District Court is incompetent to handle a libel suit without extensive prompting, these gentlemen have weighed the issues themselves and have unanimously found the defendant innocent and the plaintiffs guilty. It is with the press's treatment of the case—largely with these columnists' impatient and outlandish treatment—and not with the guilt or innocence of any of the parties to it, that this article is concerned.[1]

Except in the Hearst papers, the McCullough-Adler-Draper dispute has been handled in the news columns in fairly moderate and dispassionate fashion, but it has been dwelt upon with unprecedented eagerness and voluminousness by the columnists. It is not unusual for a columnist or a commentator to go all out on a theme not touched upon by his rivals, much

[1] The writer of this article, as a friend of Adlers and Drapers, has naturally been concerned with their politics, which happen to be at odds with his own. The writer has no knowledge of, or interest in, Mrs. McCullough's politics, which may or may not be at odds with his own. Adler and Draper, who, incidentally, have both said under oath that they are not and have never been members of the Communist Party, share most, if not all, of the political views of Henry Wallace. The writer's personal view is that most of Wallace's, Adler's, and Draper's political behavior has been nonsensical. The writer has a high regard for the right of an American to be as nonsensical as he damn pleases, within the framework of our existing laws. The writer is not and never has been a member of the Communist Party.

in the manner of a single puppy grappling with a single bone; in this instance, it is as if a whole team of half-starved Eskimo huskies had suddenly sniffed the same hunk of caribou. Cassini, Pegler, et al., who seem to regard Mrs. McCullough as just about the greatest female American patriot since Molly Pitcher, and Adler and Draper as just about the most knavish rogues since Benedict Arnold and Major André, have dealt severely with the plaintiffs for having the gall to sue her and, particularly, for having permitted their attorneys to invoke against her a property-attachment law that in the columnists' view is a horrid, unfair statute. The columnists have gone after the two men much as if they were high-level State Department officials. So zealously have they applied themselves to this task that they seem even to have declared a truce on the lively competition that usually prevails among their kind. Sokolsky has referred to Cassini, in a public speech, as a dear friend and to Cunningham, in print, as "that fine Boston reporter."

Cassini, who has chewed away at Adler and Draper more persistently than any of his colleagues have—since Mrs. McCullough sent back her tickets, he has devoted some or all of about fifty of his sprightly syndicated columns to the subject—said not long ago, "Next to the Alger Hiss case it will be the most important to go before an American court."[2] Whatever it will be—it could conceivably be just a libel case—his estimate of the significance of it may have been influenced by the fact that he was the first journalist to publicize Mrs. McCullough's original charges and has been a participant in the case. It was he to whom Mrs. McCullough turned for guidance in the beginning, when she decided to make things hot for Adler and Draper. He obliged by providing her with a list of Leftist organizations with which the two men had allegedly been affiliated and by putting her in touch with J. B. Matthews, a former yeoman of the House Committee on Un-American Activities, who, in turn, furnished her with some findings of the *California* Committee on Un-American Activities, of which she has made considerable use in attempting to establish that Adler and Draper are all the things she said they were. As a result of thus getting acquainted with her, Cassini was able to scoop everybody else by running an item in his column of December 19, 1948, that began, "The fashionable community of Greenwich, Conn., is afire! And it's about the burning question of Communism. One of the prominent women of the community, Mrs. John T. McCullough . . . started the spark that may turn into a general conflagration, and may have the same importance in history as the Boston Tea Party."[3] When the directors of the Greenwich concert group issued

[2] On another occasion, he held it to be equally important. In any case, he would seem to rank it a notch above the trial of the eleven leaders of the Communist Party.

[3] According to Cassini's scale of historical values, the Tea Party is thus a notch below the Hiss case.

their statement about Adler and Draper, Cassini was furious. "Why don't you engage Stalin and Molotov next for a speaking engagement?" he asked them in print. A few days later, he sounded as if he thought Stalin and Molotov had already made a persuasive appearance in Greenwich. "It is evident by the events that have taken place following Mrs. McCullough's action," he wrote, "that the rich and arty community of Greenwich has its fill of fellow-travellers.[4] Offensive as the idea might be, Mrs. McCullough has discovered them harbored in the schools, newspapers, and civic groups. But the Adler-Draper issue has forced them to identify themselves!" The next day, he ran a meek retraction; the publishers of the Greenwich *Time*, the only newspaper in that town, had noticed the offensive idea harbored in his column and had forced him to withdraw his implied identification of *them*.

In dealing with Adler and Draper, who he has suggested ought to be sent to Russia, Cassini, by trade a high-society columnist, has seemed to be anxious to reduce the whole disagreement to the level of a plebeian brawl. In January, 1949, addressing an aside to the Greenwich concert group, he said, "Gee, what do you want, a crack on the head to persuade you that they [Adler's and Draper's activities] are [subversive in character]?" In November, 1949, he reported that Mrs. McCullough's husband, on confronting one of the plaintiffs, "had to restrain himself from punching Draper on the nose." In December, Cassini lost interest in preliminary fighters and got down to the main event. "I have been told by an excellent authority," he wrote, "that Paul Draper . . . said he was the victim of a vicious plot to ruin him and that if he ever came face to face with me he would tear me apart." Then, after a long digression in which he remarked that a friend of his had once hoped to punch *Adler* in the nose, Cassini concluded, "That brings me to Draper's statement that he'd like to tear me apart. Well, I'd love to give him the chance. And he can bring Adler along, too—and I swear I won't ask Pegler for help." Some of Cassini's loyal readers evidently felt that he ought not to chance going it alone, for two and a half weeks later he wrote, "I'm absolutely overwhelmed with emotion at the hundreds of offers pouring in from fellows who want to join the big party if I ever come face to face with Paul Draper and Larry Adler." He declined the proffered aid, however. "I want all the fun for myself," he said. Three days after that, he reported that Draper was "exercising like mad every afternoon . . . as if he were in training for a big boxing match." Eleven days later, he indicated that he had changed his mind about fighting them singlehanded. He had had further offers of help, from Harry Donovan, the son of a former middleweight champion, and two members of Donovan's family—a "professor of boxing"

[4]The voting in Greenwich for President, two months earlier, had been: Dewey, 12,697; Truman, 5,485; Wallace, 248.

and a "well-known football star." "With the Donovans on my team," Cassini wrote, "Draper and Adler better beat it fast." Two weeks after that, Cassini hinted that he was not averse to letting someone else do all his fighting for him. "Ed Luckenbach, the young shipping heir, almost fractured a couple of guys who were loudly abusing your columnist for his attacks on Draper and Adler," he wrote. "When Ed asked them to step outside they shut up like clams, the yellow-livered heroes." Some admirers of the columnist tremble to think what might happen to him if he were ever to tangle with Draper, an event that seems likely only in Cassini's truculent imagination. The dancer is taller and heavier, has a longer reach, and would have an almost incalculable edge in footwork.

Cassini and his colleagues, in their analysis of the case, have made much of the Connecticut attachment law, which has been in effect since 1805 and permits a plaintiff in a damage suit to attach a defendant's property pending settlement of the case. The idea is to prevent a defendant from liquidating his assets so he can plead poverty if he loses the suit. Recourse to this law is common procedure in the state, and Adler's and Draper's original attorneys, as all the columnists have related over and over, had an attachment put on Mrs. McCullough's property—a house, a piece of land, and a two-thousand-dollar savings account she had jointly with her husband. Attachments of this sort can be reduced, or lifted, upon application to a judge, but Mrs. McCullough never took any such step. (She could also have freed her assets by getting a surety company to post a bond for her. This would have cost her a few hundred dollars a year. Surety companies usually want, in addition, collateral equal to the value of the property involved, but they have been known to waive this requirement upon presentation by the attachee of a sworn statement showing financial responsibility. The columnists have not cluttered their readers' minds with dull details of this nature.) Last February, Adler and Draper themselves finally instructed their counsel to lift the attachment, after it had been in effect for a little over a year.

Before the plaintiffs took this action, there was considerable agitation about the attachment not only in the columns but, perhaps partly as a result of them, in the Connecticut papers. An organization called the Minute Women of Connecticut sprang into being and petitioned a special session of the state's General Assembly, its lawmaking body, to repeal the ancient statute. Among the Minute Women who testified against the law before a legislative committee of the Assembly were Mrs. McCullough and Miss Vivien Kellems, an eccentric industrialist who has often been commended in Pegler's column and who has long been on the outs with the federal government, which she maintains has no right to compel her to withhold income-tax deductions from her employees' wages. Miss Kellems told the committee, according to a news story in the *Journal-American*, "Let Connecticut strike a blow for freedom and against Communism by eliminating the law."[5] Mrs. McCullough said, according to the same story, that as a result of the iniquitous law, she and her husband had "been forced to public charity." The State Bar Association issued a statement approving of the law, and the Assembly didn't take any action.

In calling her husband and herself charity cases, Mrs. McCullough must have meant that they were relying on contributions to pay her legal bills, for the attachment didn't affect Mr. McCullough's salary. By the time she testified before the legislative committee, she had received about ten thousand dollars from all over the country, thanks to an intensive fund-raising drive initiated in Cassini's column[6] and enthusiastically helped along by Pegler, Sokolsky, Cunningham, the radio commentator Fulton Lewis, Jr., and the Yale *Daily News.*

Pegler, in a series of splenetic treatises on the case, has harped on the use by "two precious strollers" of the attachment law, or, as he calls it, "a weapon for the intimidation and the suppression of opinion both oral and on paper." He has also found Adler and Draper a convenient springboard for comments on Marshall Field, Felix Frankfurter, and Eleanor Roosevelt. In his characterization of Draper he has reached splendid, if preposterous, heights rarely before attained even by him. He has labelled Draper "the pretty pirouetician who stamps a dainty foot with hand on hip," "the dainty elf who flits like a wisp," "this mincing twirp," and "a pink and mincing dancer, rather on the elfin side."[7] He has described a Draper performance as follows: "Affecting skin-tight pants, he puts his hands daintily on his hips, tosses his head, makes a saucy mouth and whirls and flounces madly," and he has referred to Draper's "dancing dainty figures and tossing his golden curls[8] with his hands on hips." All this is not only fantastic but probably irrelevant to the question of whether Mrs. McCullough libelled Adler and Draper. Pegler's resolute clinging to it may be dictated, however, by his seeming lack of precise knowledge about the alleged libel itself. Summarizing it in one column, he said, "Mrs. McCullough only remarked that she desired not to contribute money to Draper, a dainty dancer, and Adler, a mouth-organist, because reports of a Congressional committee had said they were associated with Communist fronts." And in another column he said, "Mrs. McCullough defiantly says Draper and Adler were spreading Communist propaganda throughout the United States in the guise of entertainment."

[5] Not long after making this statement, Miss Kellems struck what she would presumably consider a blow against freedom and for Communism by, as the Bridgeport *Herald* has related, invoking the attachment law herself, against her principal business competitor.

[6] Last Christmas Day, Cassini used the old device of a letter to Santa Claus purportedly composed by his young daughter. She told Santa her Daddy would be very happy if he could send a fat check to Mrs. McCullough.

[7] Adler has got off relatively easy. He is simply "the merry piper with the melodious reeds" whose performing is "dreary wheezing on the jail-organ" or "asthma with a score."

[8] Draper has straight hair, and the brutal truth is that he is getting bald.

Pegler has accorded more space to Draper than to Adler, perhaps because the columnist used to live in Ridgefield, Connecticut, where the dancer now lives. "In Connecticut there are a great many Communists and fellow-travellers filtered in from New York," Pegler has said. He has also said, mysteriously, that Ridgefield "has quietly become infested with wealthy sixth columnists." This one was too much for the Ridgefield *Press*. "We dislike mentioning the name of Westbrook Pegler in the *Press*," it said editorially of the former Ridgefield townsman, "because we have a certain pride in keeping our paper free of evil things." Swallowing its pride, the *Press* let him have it for around five hundred buzzing words, finishing up with "What a pity that his talent could not have been directed toward building a better world."

Pegler has advised those of his readers who are patriots not only to support Mrs. McCullough with funds but to "bang this pair and knock them bowlegged" any time they may appear in the patriots' vicinity. That the two men are to be regarded as personae non gratae is a point of view that has been stressed with equal fervor, if less inventiveness, by Fulton Lewis, Jr. Last fall, he devoted nearly a solid week of daily broadcasts to Adler and Draper. On November 11th, he concluded a spirited belaboring of them with "What a lot of suckers we Americans are. Why do we do it? Is this what those men whose total sacrifice we are commemorating on this Armistice Day of 1949—is this what they gave their lives for? Is this protection and treasured guarding of the principles they tried to insure for us and the rest of the world? Answer that question yourself. That's the top of the news as it looks from here." Lewis's contention that this sort of thing constitutes news was echoed ten days afterward by Sokolsky. Referring to the interest Pegler, Cassini, and he himself had shown in the matter, he said, "We went after the story—as reporters should do but too often do not do. . . . Our business is news."

Sokolsky's business includes not only the reporting of news but the making of it. In mid-December, he was the main speaker at a well-publicized rally in Greenwich attended by more than a thousand people. According to the Greenwich *Time's* account of the occasion, Sokolsky got a "thunderous accolade" after delivering an oration about the threat to the world posed by Communism, in the course of which he gave *his* interpretation of just what had been said about Adler and Draper by Mrs. McCullough, who was present and to whom he referred as "this little girl." He said, "We can be so weakened that in time of peril or in time of war, we can be destroyed because we haven't the will to survive. That is what Mrs. McCullough tried to say when she complained to the concert committee."[9]

[9] It must have been an astonishingly effective speech; the Greenwich *Time* noted that one gentleman in the audience "took the floor to announce that he felt, by not having been aroused to the menace of Communism before this, that he had violated the Boy Scout oath, which he thereupon recited almost in its entirety."

No columnist has been more generous in his praise of Mrs. McCullough, or more scathing in his rebuke of her antagonists, than Bill Cunningham, Sokolsky's fine Boston reporter, who is also a radio commentator of influence in New England. Like Pegler, he began his journalistic career as a sportswriter, and in his essays on the lawsuit he has shown himself to be a writer of the Peglerian school.[10] He has described Adler and Draper as "the precious pair," Draper as a "male coryphee" and "masculine sprite," and Draper's dancing as "terpsichorean tiddledywinks."[11] Pegler's Back Bay counterpart didn't join the fun until November, 1949, nearly a year after Cassini had started his tea party, but one week after getting into the act he wrote, "Last Sunday, after full investigation, I told the whole story in print here, for the first time." Some things he unquestionably did say for the first time. None of the other columnists had thought before to write, for instance, "We can't let this woman go down. . . . The woman's on Our Team." He was also first with a number of errors. He said, discussing the drive to collect money for the defendant, that "slowly, some practically secret support began flowing her way." There was nothing secret about it; Cassini, Pegler, and Sokolsky had been engaging in syndicated fund-raising for months. Cunningham reported, moreover, that Mrs. McCullough had read in the New York papers that in Birmingham "'entertainers' from New York had deliberately flavored their performance with left-wing propaganda, ridiculing the United States and the capitalistic system." No such story having appeared in any New York paper, Mrs. McCullough couldn't have read it in one. In February, the fine Boston reporter did a column on a statement that had been issued by the plaintiffs' second, and current, firm of attorneys about the lifting of the attachment. He misquoted the statement and then briskly lambasted Adler and Draper on the basis of his own misquotation, intimating that they were not only unchivalrous but untruthful. The plaintiffs' lawyers, referring to the inception of the lawsuit, had said that "the attachment is a legal detail about which [the plaintiffs] had no knowledge at the time." Cunningham sliced off the last three words and, having thus revised the statement to suit his convenience, said, "The reader is left to assume that since they've just learned of these things, they've hastened to make the generous corrections. Whether that's kissin' kin of sincere apology or belated and hypocritical play for public sympathy in a battle that's now knocking their ever-lovin' ears off, is left, dear reader, to your own measuring machine. I can't call anybody, or even any brother act, a pair of self-starting, stem-winding revolving liars in print without laying

[10] Like Cassini, he doesn't think too favorably of present-day Greenwich. He considers it "a community of fat-cats." Pegler has specifically identified Mrs. McCullough's husband as a non-fat-cat.
[11] He has described Adler as a "mouth-organ maestro" and Mrs. McCullough as a "courageous young woman, holding her head very beautifully."

myself open to subpoenas, writs of replevin and whatever else it is the sons of sue use, but maybe the facts can, and here are some of the latter."[12]

Each of the three principals has made a sworn oral deposition, a procedure sometimes used in the hope of shortening a trial by getting both sides to agree in advance—through examination and cross-examination—on certain points. Mrs. McCullough made her deposition first. In it she revealed that, for a prominent resident of Greenwich, her newspaper-reading habits are unorthodox. She said that she read the *Journal-American*.[13] She also testified that she had asked her husband for information about Adler and Draper. He had dutifully brought home four clippings from the *Time* morgue, which have been put into evidence as trial exhibits and consequently have not yet been returned to the *Time* morgue. One, an item from *Time*, didn't mention Adler at all and mentioned Draper only in passing. (It was about the dancer's mother, Mrs. Muriel Draper. She is not a party to the lawsuit, and Draper swore in his deposition that he does not go along with her political views, which are outspokenly radical, but Cassini, Pegler, and the rest have dragged her in at every opportunity. Thus, Sokolsky said in one of his columns, "Then Larry Adler and Paul Draper discovered that public resistance had developed to their artistic appearances. Meanwhile, Paul Draper's mother, Muriel Draper, went off to Moscow where she indicated an attitude toward the United States not usual among loyal Americans." Cunningham dished up a paragraph about her trip to Russia and appended this postscript: "It chances to be the son, not the mother, however, who's involved in this case." He did not explain why, since that chanced to be, he had bothered to bring the mother in to begin with.) *Time*, incidentally, has run only one story on the case, despite its being more or less close to home and despite Pegler's having written, provokingly, "Mr. McCullough is an editor for the Time-Life or fui piu axis, but the magazines aren't backing the McCulloughs."[14]

The second deposition proceeding was Draper's. On the eve of his hearing, a rumor went around Connecticut newspaper circles that Pegler, Sokolsky, and Lewis also planned to appear at it, reportorially. If they had appeared, it would probably have been the first time that three such Olympian newshawks had fluttered down to the same earthy roost. Only

[12]One of the latter was the first name of Adler's and Draper's chief counsel, whom Cunningham dubbed Lawrence. His name is Frederick.

[13]This is unusual in Greenwich. When the *Sun* was absorbed by the *World-Telegram*, and Sokolsky, a former bellwether of the *Sun*, went over to the *Journal*, the Greenwich *Time* hastened to buy his column, on the theory that local fans of his might otherwise no longer get to read him.

[14]James A. Linen, the publisher of *Time*, lives in Greenwich, and he backed his employee to the extent of serving as a member of the committee that sponsored the rally addressed by Sokolsky. Gene Tunney was on the committee, too, but, as far as is known, has never offered to back Cassini in a square-off with Draper.

Sokolsky turned up. He didn't stay very long, and he was the only one of the half-dozen reporters on the scene who took no notes. The absence of Pegler and Lewis was partly compensated for by the presence of the chairman of the Yale *Daily News*,[15] a journal that has been much interested in the case, even though neither Adler, Draper, nor Mrs. McCullough went to Yale. However, the plaintiffs' current attorneys, Wiggin & Dana, have long been counsel for Yale University.[16] The Yale *News* ran a two-part editorial on the case last fall. The wording of the lead sentence of the first installment must have pained the English Department; it went: "There are probably few members of Yale who have not heard at some time or another during the past months of the suit that has been brought against Mrs. Hester McCullough of Greenwich by Larry Adler and Paul Draper, harmonica player and dancer respectably." In the second installment, the *News* said, "There seems to be no question that Mrs. Hester McCullough . . . will win her case. If she does not reason is dead and the most far-reaching of all possible curbs will be put on freedom of speech and forthright and open political discussion."[17]

When Draper was making his deposition—and, a couple of months later, when Adler was making his[18]—Mrs. McCullough's attorneys called attention to the fact that both plaintiffs' names had frequently been printed in Left Wing publications, including the *Daily Worker* and the *New Masses*. A few of the items cited referred to appearances the entertainers had made, on behalf of one organization or another, that had also been written up in non-Communist publications like the New York *Times*. Adler, in the course of

[15]The only reporter who brought a date along.
[16]Not long after the case got under way, Cassini advised the plaintiffs' first chief counsel, J. Kenneth Bradley, formerly a Republican National Committeeman from Connecticut, that if he believed in his clients, he ought to resign from the Republican Party, and Sokolsky wrote, "It is said that Kenneth Bradley wants to be the Republican candidate for Governor. . . . While a lawyer may defend any client, even a murderer, a Republican politician and State leader puts himself in a dubious position when he exacts the letter of the law in making such an American woman as Hester McCullough defenseless. . . ." Bradley stepped out a few days after that. A Philadelphia *Daily News* columnist has said there was talk that Mrs. McCullough might run for Congress, and Cassini has published a letter proposing her for Secretary of State. Cassini did not comment on this suggestion one way or the other, but he has taken the view that Dean Acheson ought not to be Secretary of State.
[17]A couple of days after the editorials appeared, the *News* published a letter from two students that went:
To the Chairman of the "News":
1. Messrs. Draper and Adler are associated with subversive organizations. (Cf. Attorney General's list.)
2. The law firm of Wiggin & Dana are associated with Messrs. Draper and Adler. (Cf. Yale *Daily News*.)
3. Yale University is associated with the law firm of Wiggin & Dana. (Cf. Yale *Daily News*.)
4. The Yale *Daily News* is associated with Yale University.
Ergo, the Yale *Daily News* is associated with subversive organizations and we don't want to hear any more about it.

making his deposition, asked one of the defendant's lawyers how it was that he was so partial to the Communist press. "To find out about certain people we are limited to certain publications," the lawyer answered. This was a curious reply, inasmuch as his own client had acknowledged that she had been dependent for her initial information about her adversaries on the *Time* morgue and on a Hearst gossip columnist.[19]

Adler made his deposition in February, 1950, shortly after flying home from Europe, where he has spent most of the past year, largely because he cannot obtain many engagements in the United States.[20] Draper has stayed on this continent, but he hasn't been working much, either. His only stage appearance this year has been in Toronto, where Adler preceded him by a few weeks. If Cassini has his way, neither of them will play a return engagement there. "I have a notion that soon the names of Draper and Adler will be mud in Canada also," he wrote on Valentine's Day. "I received a call from Toronto the other day from a gentleman by the name of Forbes Ross, who is a reader of the column. He said that in Canada few people have been informed about the McCullough case, but that he had read about it and that it was high time that something similar was done about it in Canada. I gave the man my blessing. . . . I'm only sorry that my column is not syndicated in Canada, otherwise I'd give him all the moral support he needs."

Draper's only other remunerative stint this year was a six-minute appearance on a Sunday-night television program sponsored by the Lincoln-Mercury Division of the Ford Motor Company that features Ed Sullivan, who lives in Port Chester, New York, three miles from Greenwich.[21] Sullivan is, of course, a columnist of note himself, and he has long been at

---

[18] Adler wasn't present for the taking of Draper's deposition. He was in Europe and wasn't expected to be present. It was therefore perhaps misleading for the Stamford *Advocate* to say, in a subhead over a story about Draper's testimony, "ADLER FAILS TO SHOW FOR PRETRIAL QUIZZING ON CLAIM OF LIBEL."

[19] Furthermore, you don't always find out the truth about certain people in certain publications. The *Daily Worker* not long ago referred to Draper's mother as "Miss Muriel Draper." The press of the extreme Right is just as apt to be flighty in its handling of facts as that of the extreme Left. A West Coast weekly called the *Broom* ran a story about the lawsuit last December that said that because of Adler's and Draper's nasty behavior "elderly Mrs. McCullough has not been able to pay her help, her phone, her taxes, her grocery bills and is compelled to sit helpless and alone, in her big house for a whole year already." Mrs. McCullough is thirty-two—several years younger than either of the plaintiffs.

[20] On May 17, 1949, Cassini said that Adler was "playing the harmonica and probably making speeches at the Palladium in London." Adler hasn't appeared at the Palladium since before the war.

[21] The Port Chester *Guide* has itself run stories about the case, including a long one, marked "Special to Port Chester *Guide*," that, except for one paragraph, it lifted, without credit, from the *Journal-American*. In the brand-new paragraph the *Guide* noted that Mrs. McCullough has "won the powerful journalistic support of such brilliantly eminent and nationally outstanding columnists as Westbrook Pegler, George Sokolsky, and Igor Cassini . . . and Peter F. Capeci, Editor and Publisher of the Port Chester *Guide*."

odds with Pegler, in whose published opinion Sullivan is "an inveterate but incurable adolescent . . . a stagestruck paragrapher of the Broadway-underworld beat." Cunningham doesn't think much of Sullivan, either; he has called him "the dumbest looking m.c. in yellivision," which is probably fine Bostonese for "television." Draper did a couple of dances on the program. Benson Ford, the boss of Lincoln-Mercury, happened to be in the studio audience and, according to *Variety*, "joined in the vociferous applause for Draper's performance."

There was no further applause. For the next three days, the *Journal-American* carried on as if Draper had been caught practicing vivisection on Louella O. Parsons. On Monday, it ran a bright-red forty-eight-point two-line head that swept across six columns of its front page: "PAUL DRAPER IN TV SHOW DRAWS FLOOD OF PROTESTS." Accompanying it was a photograph of Mrs. McCullough with her arm in a sling—the result, according to Cassini, of "strain." "Hundreds of protests poured in on the Columbia Broadcasting System today denouncing the appearance of dancer Paul Draper, cited as a leftist and Communist sympathizer, on the Ed Sullivan 'Toast of the Town' television program last night," the story began. It went on to note that the network, the sponsor, and the advertising agency concerned with the show had all graciously ceded to Sullivan sole responsibility for Draper's appearance on it. Sullivan was quoted as saying, "I've been battling Communism vigorously right along, but it would be awful if we reached a state of mind where performers were not hired because of unsubstantiated rumors." The following day, the *Journal-American* had another big front-page, double-bank headline on the matter, this time in black: "VETS JOIN PROTEST ON DRAPER TV ACT." The veterans were identified as the New York State Commanders of the Catholic War Veterans and the Veterans of Foreign Wars, the New York State Adjutant of the American Legion, and the Queens County Commander of the Catholic War Veterans. Next day, the early editions of the *Journal-American* carried a four-column, two-line front-page headline: "FORD PROBES DRAPER APPEARANCE ON TV." Later editions had a red four-column, two-line front-page headline: SULLIVAN MAKES DRAPER APOL-OGY." Both editions mentioned further protests by veterans, most of them Catholic War Veterans from Queens. The commander of the St. Joan of Arc Post, Jackson Heights, announced that he was calling an emergency meeting of the Post that week to consider the situation, and he added, without waiting to learn the sense of the meeting, "We will be very careful in the future about watching C.B.S. shows." As for Sullivan's apology, it consisted of a statement to the press in which the most apologetic sentence went, "I am sorry if some people were offended by the appearance of a performer whose political beliefs are a matter of public controversy."

When a big metropolitan newspaper features a news story on its front page three days running, under whopping headlines, one would expect the other city papers to do something about it, too. News is supposed to be news, after all. But while the hubbub was raging on page 1 of the *Journal-American*, the news desks of the other New York papers remained aloof.[22] It was almost as if they had decided that the commotion was in large measure the *Journal-American's* invention. (It is a not uncommon journalistic trick to call up the head of an organization—a veterans' organization, say—and ask him if he has a statement to make, and then use his statement as the basis of a news story.) The *Mirror*, which is, of course, a Hearst paper, did carry a couple of small stories about the Sullivan-Draper affair, and muted mentions of it were tucked inside the *World-Telegram & Sun*, the *Post*, and the *Compass*, but the *Times* and the *Herald Tribune* didn't consider it worth an inch of type. Neither did the *News*, Sullivan's own paper. An explanation for this reticence of the *News* was offered by *Billboard*, which, after reporting that C.B.S. and Sullivan "both appeared to be somewhat queasy this week, the result of eating a large portion of stuffed crow . . . prepared Hearst-journalism style, featuring a nauseating yellow dressing," said that the *Journal-American* had been flailing about the way it had in an attempt to lure circulation away from the *World-Telegram & Sun*. *Billboard* said the *Journal-American* figured that if it could get into a tussle with the *News*, maybe people who read about the *Journal's* anti-Sullivan crusade in the *News* in the morning would buy the *Journal* in the evening to keep posted. But the *Journal's* hopes were unfulfilled, added *Billboard*, because the *News* "didn't give the *J-A* so much as a rumble." Sullivan himself has never alluded to the episode in his column and since the night of the television program has mentioned Draper's name only once, in purely routine fashion.[23]

While the *Journal-American* was putting the screws on Draper in New York, Adler was in Chicago, about to begin an engagement, at a vaudeville house, on a bill that starred Hildegarde. His presence out there did not escape Cassini's watchful eye. "Larry Adler . . . opens at the Chicago Theatre on Friday," he reported on the preceding Wednesday. "I wonder if

[22] All the columnists, naturally, remained unaloof. Cassini took Sullivan to task for his effrontery, and later wrote, after Sullivan apologized, "This should be a warning also to men like Sullivan that you can't try to shield or apologize for any of those fellows unless you want mud splashed in your own face. Sullivan, I'm sure, has learned his lesson and won't repeat the mistake." Up in Boston, Cunningham, who had seen the television show, wrote, "I felt a sense of personal shock, when the interior of my home was suddenly turned into a stage for a featured performance of this leaper to music, whose chief plea to fame so far as I'm concerned, is his legal effort to beat dead a young woman in whose sort of citizenship I believe, and whose fighting heart, I humbly, but fully, salute." Cunningham does not write as colorfully as Pegler and does not punctuate as well, either.

[23] It was the announcement of the birth of a child to Draper's wife. Cassini said, possibly in jest: "Ed Sullivan said in his column that his pals, the Paul Drapers, had named their third youngster Kate. I should have thought they would have wanted to name her Hester McCullough."

the veterans there will do the same job of protesting that they did when Paul Draper appeared in New York." The Chicago veterans evidently didn't take the hint fast enough to please Cassini, for after waiting two days he wrote, "I hope the city desk of the paper which prints my column in Chicago, the *Herald-American*, will be as alert as the *Journal's*. It was the *Journal's* front-page stories which focussed public attention on Draper's appearance on Sullivan's show. The Chicago *Herald-American* can do the same good job with Larry Adler, who's opening tonight at a Chicago theatre, as we did with Draper." The *Herald-American's* city desk, its alertness having been challenged, ran a story that same afternoon signed by Cassini himself, under the odd headline "ADLER HERE AS TIDE OF DRAPER PROTESTS RISES." The following day, the *Herald-American* served up a news story that must have restored Cassini's ebbing faith in city desks and veterans. It began, "Hundreds of Illinois war veterans filed protests today against theatrical and other entertainment bookings" of Draper and Adler. The "hundreds" seemed to consist of "more than a score" of patients at an American Legion convalescent home, and of the commander of the Department of Illinois of the Catholic War Veterans. The convalescent men issued a statement saying, in part, "We expect the Legion and other veterans' groups to act in this emergency." By that time, Hildegarde's manager, a lady, apparently felt she ought to make a statement, too, and she did: "This is an embarrassing situation."

The next day, the *Herald-American* ran a front-page story under the headline "LEGION URGES STAGE BAN ON DRAPER, ADLER." The story was less startling; it referred to the commander of the Cook County Council of the Legion, who had given out a six-paragraph statement. It concluded, "Adler should not be permitted before an American audience." Despite all this, Adler was permitted to finish his engagement without any emergencies' being declared. Nor was there any to-do back in New York when, two weeks after the Sullivan show, Station WPIX, owned by the New York *News*, televised an old motion picture, "Sidewalks of London," in which Adler had a part. Maybe the *Journal-American's* movie critic was napping. A week before *that*, and a week after the Sullivan show, Draper had appeared, without pay, on a radio program called "Rebuttal." The fact that he was going to be on it was announced to the press in advance, but the *Journal-American* didn't run a story about it, even on an inside page, and didn't call upon any veterans to protest, even Queens veterans.

A couple of weeks after the Sullivan show, Cassini himself participated in a radio program called "Something Ought to Be Done." He had a debate with Clarence Derwent, the president of Actors' Equity, on the question of whether Adler and Draper should be allowed to earn a living. Cassini must have been ill at ease in an unfamiliar medium, for after saying, "I do believe that if a man is a law-abiding citizen he has the right to perform," he also said, without demonstrating that Adler and Draper had been non-law-abiding, that he didn't think *they* should have that right. Finally, Derwent said, "Well, maybe really this discussion should have taken place after the court had decided." Said the announcer, thereby bringing the program to an end, "And perhaps that is true." And perhaps it is.

April 15, 1950

This was 1950—with McCarthyism in full flower. The Adler-Draper libel suit ended with a hung jury. The case was never retried. The performers, still unemployable, moved to Europe. Considering the temper of the times, *The New Yorker* was very brave, I thought then and still believe, to run the piece at all.

Reprise

Last September, after the return of Shirley May France to this country from her unsuccessful assault upon the English Channel, we had an enlightening audience with Ted Worner, the press agent who promoted, and suffered through, her high adventure, and last week, a few hours before her departure on the Queen Elizabeth for another shot at the Channel, we went over to his office, at 1650 Broadway, and got briefed on the current expedition, of which he is, as before, the entrepreneur and a prominent member. He received us in a room with a tank of tropical fish embedded in one wall, and we had barely brought out our pencil when he began to talk:

"Irving Straus, president of the Westchester Aquarium, White Plains, is a client of mine, and he makes these things. I had a big fish that I called Shirley May, but it ate up all the little ones, so I had to get rid of it. I handled the opening of the Westchester Aquarium, in May, and I brought Shirley around for it, naturally. Well, here we are starting our second annual tour. Shirley's seventeen now, be eighteen August 11th, and if she makes it this time, she'll still be the youngest person ever to do it. She weighs one-sixty-one and she's feeling great. I had her tonsils taken out at New York Hospital. Cost me $124.85, but it was worth it. She's a great kid, and determined. I weigh one-ninety-three, and I expect to lose twenty-five pounds before we're through, just like last year. We didn't have much backing then, but this time the Newspaper Enterprise Association syndicate is paying all expenses, including mine. The kid's done a swimming series for N.E.A.—'Improve Your Swimming with Shirley May France'—and they've got exclusive byline-story and posed-picture rights. And Mutual Broadcasting has bought the exclusive rights to the actual swim, and a stroke-by-stroke description will be given to the American people, two or three minutes on the hour, every hour she's in the water.

"I'm going mad with endorsements this year. The Brewster Hat Company is coming out with four Shirley May hats. And there are Shirley May dresses, by Citation Frocks, a very high-class firm, and Shirley May balloons, by the Barr Rubber Company, of Sandusky, Ohio, and the Kingston Watch Company has come through again with an outright payment. Shirley'll wear a Kingston underwater watch during her swim, like she did last year. It won't be the same watch; they're pretty sturdy, Kingstons, but, after all, the Channel two years in a row . . . We get a five-per-cent royalty on sales of all Shirley May merchandise. I'm taking along fifteen Kingstons to give to my influential friends in England, and seven boxes of cigars. Cigars are very scarce over there. I have mine made in Brooklyn, and they cost me twenty-five cents apiece. When I remember how I had to scrounge around for money last time!

"I've been very busy since September, with this African explorer I'm going to Africa with in January, and the Yonkers Ferry, and a flock of other clients. I had it fixed for a ferryboat to come alongside the Queen Elizabeth with a big sign on it saying 'Good luck, Shirley May France,' but then I found out the Queen sails at midnight. We're travelling cabin class— Shirley, her father, her swimming coach, and me. It's the average-American way to travel, you know. The Cunard Line called me two days ago and said, 'Mr. Worner, would you like to have the cabin-class pool filled while the Elizabeth's in port, for pictures or anything?' I said no, that wouldn't be necessary. The British are awfully excited about Channel swimming nowadays. You know how they used to be—swim the Channel, have a spot of tea, and that would be the end of it. Now the London *Daily Mail* is offering the equivalent of four thousand dollars in prizes for a race across the Channel on August 15th or the first good day thereafter. Shirley May France will *not* be in the race. If she makes it across, four thousand will be a drop in the bucket. I get ten per cent of whatever she gets.

"Shirley's been busy, too. I went up to Fall River, where she lives, for Thanksgiving and Christmas dinner. I gave her a good, warm robe for Christmas. She left school in January and appeared at a lot of Sportsmen's Shows. Milwaukee; Omaha; Denison, Texas; somewhere in Vermont—I forget where all. I would have preferred that she stay in school. The Cinderella angle, you know. I figure she'll be ready to take to the water around the middle of July. We've got eight or ten bathing suits for her to choose from, but I have a hunch she'll wear an old green cotton number that's a favorite of hers. I approached all the bathing-suit manufacturers for a deal, but none of them will come through until they see if she makes it. If she doesn't this time, I dunno. Who wants to commute to the English Channel all his life?"

June 24, 1950

132

Cellar Game

We dispatched our man Stanley to Philadelphia last week to find out what goes on when two hopeless baseball teams meet at this late stage of the season, especially when one of them is the Philadelphia Athletics, the most chronically hopeless team in modern baseball. It finished in the first division only once in the last ten years, and wound up eighth in six of them. Stanley took in an American League doubleheader, starting at six-thirty, between the Athletics, who began the evening in seventh place, thirty-five and a half games from the top, and the St. Louis Browns, thirty-six and a half games off the pace. Stanley now batting:

"Had early dinner in hotel and found Philadelphia agog over baseball, with the Phillies lording it over National League, but didn't hear Athletics mentioned. Cabdriver amazed when I asked to be driven to Shibe Park. He brooded for a while and asked, 'You got a cousin playing, or something, Mac?' Streets near park clear of traffic as I drove up, like Wall Street on Sunday. Knew game had started, but so quiet you could have heard a mitt drop. Flags hanging limply from staffs. No lines at ticket windows. Ticket man seemed surprised when I showed up, asked where I wanted to sit; said I could sit anywhere. Thought it over and decided on behind third base. Sign on wall inside said seating capacity 33,166. Attendance didn't seem to total 1,166. 'Not a bad crowd, considering,' said man three seats from me, my nearest neighbor, after I'd sat down. Said, conversationally, Athletics must be in financial straits. 'Not them,' said man knowingly. 'They own the park, and they make money when the National League plays here, and they do pretty well selling the players they develop. And the hot dogs—there's a lot of money in hot dogs.' Hot dogs actually warm, by the way. Unusual. Ushers female, and man was hawking Coca-Cola in Pepsi-Cola hat. Very unusual. Crowd quiet; could hear infielders talking to pitcher. Foul ball dropped in lower stands. Nobody sitting within fifty feet of it; could have nabbed it myself by sprinting. Atmosphere not conducive to sprinting. Athletics' catcher slow getting ball away on pick-off play. 'Saving himself for the 1960 Series,' spectator three rows behind me yelled derisively. Later same catcher called safe at first on close and questionable play. Browns didn't even bother to squawk. Browns had two outfielders playing in infield. That kind of team. Signals of Athletics' third-base coach to batter so obvious everybody knew what they meant. So did Browns, I suppose, if they bothered to look. During traditional seventh-inning stretch, mild applause for Athletics from group directly back of home-club dugout. Players' families? Nobody at all sitting behind visitors' dugout. Black cat strolling on field near Browns' bull pen got biggest hand of night. In eighth inning, Athletics' cleanup man struck out and let go of bat, and it flew past St. Louis pitcher's head. 'Our power man!' moaned man behind me. A's lost, 2–1. Old Connie Mack, now in hundred-and-seventeenth year as manager, stuck head over roof of dugout and waved at friend in stand. 'Mr. Mack's looking pretty good, considering,' said nearest neighbor.

"Rained briskly between games. Stopped just as second game supposed to start. Dodgers never have that sort of luck. Wandered around stands, thinking to sample public opinion on Athletics, but decided impractical, not enough public present to make conclusive. Did ask man at refreshment stand why he thought the people came to game. He replied, 'What else is there to do in Philadelphia?' Returned to seat. Nearest neighbor told me he hadn't missed a Shibe Park game (both leagues, mind you) in 1947 season and had seen all of the Phillies' home games and most of the Athletics' home games this season. Must have looked at him incredulously, for he said, 'Why not?' Had me there. Philadelphia player hit what would have been sure double down right-field foul line, but stopped running on way to first base to turn around and see how umpire called it. Asked nearest neighbor why he thought batter hadn't been advised by Athletics' first-base coach. 'He's probably asleep,' man behind cut in. Browns put on three-run rally. 'These A's can't win a game!' young fan about twenty feet southwest of me cried out. 'Yes, they can, boy,' said older lady with him. 'Don't be down on them, boy. Help them along a little bit.' Philadelphia player dragged himself listlessly to plate. 'Notice that spirited enthusiasm,' groaned cynic behind me. Cleanup man batted next, struck out, bat flew out of hands toward Browns' pitcher again. 'You're bound to get him the third time. Keep trying!' hooted cynic. Athletics by now five runs behind. 'Get the shovel out,' shouted cynic. 'We're heading for the cellar again.' A's lost second game, too, and landed there. Browns, by winning both ends, only thirty-five and a half games out of first. No trouble getting cab from park. 'Must have been drab and dreary in there,' said driver.

"P.S. Just looked up official attendance figure: 1,356."

September 9, 1950

Notes and Comment

The death of Bernard Shaw followed by only a few hours the announcement of the disbanding of the Society for Philosophical Inquiry, an organization founded in this country in 1884 to encourage independent thinking, and abandoned on the ground that Americans no longer care about independent thought. "I have decided that people do not want to think," the Society's secretary-treasurer wrote to its few remaining members in revealing its dissolution. He transmitted this gloomy intelligence by postcard, a medium of communication to which Shaw was partial, too. Postcards are plain, forthright, terse, and wholly without concealment, and they suited Shaw fine. The Society may have exaggerated somewhat the current national mental attitude, but independent thought certainly seems to be less general now than it was in 1884, when Shaw was a dashing and non-conformist critic of twenty-eight. He never stopped thinking independently himself, and it was universally gratifying that his great and irreverent mind didn't peter out ahead of the absurdly frail body in which it was set. It is inevitable, we suppose, that the movie people will soon give Shaw the full biographical treatment, and we hope that Hollywood, in depicting him as a crotchety, antic, and lovable old cuss, won't fail altogether to note also that he was a marvellous symbol of philosophical inquiry, who resolutely held off, as long as he was able to wave a walking stick, the dismal onrush of convention and conformity.

November 11, 1950

Notes and Comment

While Mr. Austin and Mr. Malik were debating the cease-fire proposal at Lake Success, we were being dragged through Macy's toy department by a couple of small boys who have never heard of the Yalu River and for whom there was nothing incongruous about spending that taut moment of history gravely examining a fire engine that really squirts water. The toy department was jammed, the din was frightful, and the solemn voices of despair were only remotely audible. Macy's is featuring a new kind of balloon this Christmas. You can poke it and pummel it and, presumably, kick it, and it won't break. The boys with us were were delighted with its durability. We were impressed, too, but didn't have the notion, which they had, that it is completely indestructible, or that the world is.

Peace is getting harder and harder to define. It has become clear that the Communists, for all their talk of it, think of it as something warlike, and propose to achieve it, or their interpretation of it, in a bellicose manner. The dove still figures importantly in Left Wing symbolism, but the variety in evidence is a formidable example of what breeding can do, being capable of flying, scarcely without pause, across the high mountains of Tibet, down into the valleys around Pyongyang, and all the way to Lake Success, where it bellows instead of cooing. Peace can certainly no longer be defined as the absence of war, because there is no longer any coherent definition of war. The nations that haven't exchanged a shot since V-E and V-J Days are still technically at war with each other, and the nations that are shooting at each other at the moment of this writing are still technically at non-war. Pending

135

a clarification of terminology, we shall wistfully define peace as the state of mind of a child in Macy's toy department two weeks before Christmas.

December 23, 1950

Notes and Comment

Along with other commentators, we've had occasion from time to time to remark on the oddly celestial prose style of General MacArthur. If it will cheer him any in what may otherwise be a bleak period for him, we extend our congratulations on the terse, atypical communication he sent to John Foster Dulles approving the State Department's note to Russia on Japan. According to the papers, it said, in toto, "Reply to Malik on the Japanese peace treaty question is a honey." The admirable conciseness and simplicity of this message, and its felicitous termination, should not go unacclaimed. Our compliments to General MacArthur. It is exceedingly comforting to know that despite his long absence from our midst, he retains at least one tiny fragment of our earthy native idiom.

January 13, 1951

Notes and Comment

A Congressman has introduced a bill providing for the distribution of distinctive lapel buttons to 4-Fs. We imagine he has it in mind to spare men in that class of deferment from getting their feelings hurt, or their eyes blackened, by overzealous patriots who suspect them of dodging service. We are opposed to this piece of legislation, for a number of reasons. For one, there is a general disinclination on the part of Americans, despite the example set by President Truman, to wear lapel buttons of any kind, as the rapid disappearance of the Second World War's discharge insigne has attested. Thus, if the bill became law, many 4-Fs wouldn't wear their buttons, or would neglect to switch them from suit to suit, and the result would be even more badly hurt feelings and more blackened eyes than if the subject of buttons had never come up. For another, it would be a cinch for real draft-dodgers to equip themselves with fake insignia, just as it is a cinch for real Communists to take loyalty oaths. For still another, the proposal seems to us one more symptom of the current nationwide preoccupation with oversimplified identification tags. This country has already gone far enough in the direction of allowing men to be judged by what they superficially appear to be rather than by what they actually are.

The 1-As in Korea have recently had some experience with a short-lived identification scheme worked out over there. The troops of an American infantry division were ordered by their commanding general to grow beards, his thought evidently being that, in view of the notorious smoothness of Oriental cheeks, it would simplify the problem of recognition if a line could be conspicuously drawn between hirsute ally and beardless foe. The order had been in effect only a couple of weeks when the general was replaced. His successor at once commanded all his troops to shave, presumably to the relief of those embarrassed young G.I.s whose chins were still merely flecked with down. Nobody will ever be able to figure out a surefire way of giving all law-abiding men one kind of mien and all transgressors another. Some of the nicest faces we ever saw were in a batch of rogues'-gallery photos we pored over once after a burglar had visited our home. Our burglar's portrait wasn't among them, but he was duly caught anyway, and he wasn't a bad-looking chap.

January 27, 1951

A Reporter in Korea
No One But The Glosters

It is hard to tell at this date which battles of the Korean war military historians will ultimately single out for special mention, but it is doubtful whether they can overlook a recent two-and-a-half-day engagement that, whatever name the historians may settle on for it, is known now to those who went through it as the Battle of the Imjin, and that has already been officially characterized as "epic" by the Eighth Army. The battle began, just south of Imjin River and some twenty-five miles northwest of Seoul, on the night of April 22nd, as the Chinese were launching their spring offensive all across the front, and it continued, without letup, until midafternoon of April 25th. The great majority of the United Nations troops who participated in it were British, of the 29th Brigade, but it was nonetheless a fittingly multinational affair, involving Belgians, South Koreans, and Filipinos, as well as Americans from both the continental United States and Puerto Rico. The 29th Brigade, with a total strength of sixty-six hundred and a front-line fighting strength of four thousand, suffered more than a thousand casualties during that bloody span of time. In return, it inflicted a vastly larger number of casualties on the enemy; the exact count is indefinite, inasmuch as the British decline to assume credit for killing anybody unless they have actually seen him dead. They saw a great many dead Chinese those two and a half days, being frequently in hand-to-hand contention with the enemy, and on occasion, to conserve ammunition, being under orders to hold their fire until their attackers were only fifteen yards away. Out of something like sixty thousand Chinese who assaulted the seventeen-thousand-yard sector the brigade was holding when the battle started, it is widely, if unofficially, believed that between ten and fifteen thousand were dispatched. And what is perhaps more important—since hordes of dead Chinese were almost as commonplace as hordes of live ones in Korea that particular week—is that the steadfast resistance of the British to this massive assault was very likely the most influential single factor in the dashing of the Communists' probable hope of celebrating May Day in the capital city of the Republic of Korea.

The entire 29th Brigade saw action in the Battle of the Imjin, but the worst assault fell upon one unit, the 1st Battalion of the Gloucestershire Regiment, informally called the Glosters. Of the six hundred and twenty-two Glosters who were in the most advanced of the brigade's three echelons when the fight got under way, just five officers and thirty-four other ranks were available for duty three days afterward, and they only because they had made a near-miraculous withdrawal through enemy fire so intense and enveloping that they subsequently said they felt like human targets in a shooting gallery. Their commanding officer, a tall, taciturn, pipe-smoking lieutenant colonel named J. P. Carne, who has served with the Glosters since 1925, is missing in action, as is his regimental sergeant major, E. J. Hobbs, whose association with the outfit goes back equally far. When, on the morning of the twenty-fifth, the Glosters were so hard pressed and so inextricably cut off from all other friendly troops that they could no longer function as an effective fighting force, every man was authorized to break through the encircling Chinese as best he could. The Colonel and the Sergeant Major elected to stay with the wounded, along with the Glosters' medical officer and chaplain. The handful of Glosters who did get out brought back several versions of Colonel Carne's last words to them. The one most generally accepted is that as they took leave of him, and as he stood there among the sad and suffering remnants of the organization to which practically his entire adult life had been devoted, he said, with the perfect discipline for which his soldiering countrymen have long been noted, "Any of you chaps happen to have a spare twist of tobacco?"

The 29th Brigade, which arrived in Korea early in November, is composed of a number of units with ancient traditions, among them the 1st Battalion, Royal Ulster Rifles; the 1st Battalion, Royal Northumberland Fusiliers; the 45th Field Regiment, Royal Artillery; and the 8th King's Royal Irish Hussars, this last a cavalry outfit that was formed in 1693 and took part in the Charge of the Light Brigade at Balaklava, but is now mechanized and equipped with fifty-two-ton tanks called Centurions. The

Ulster Rifles, who wear as a device the harp of Ireland and the crown of Britain, had a rough time early this January in the brigade's one other costly action in Korea; two hundred and thirty of them were killed. This loss happened to occur in the very area assigned to the 29th Brigade in mid-April, and on their return to the unhappily familiar scene the Rifles reburied some of their dead who had fallen there, and commissioned a stonemason in Seoul to cut an obelisk to mark the spot. Dedication of the monument was scheduled for April 23rd, but the ceremonies were, perforce, postponed. April 23rd is a big day for the British. Not only is it Shakespeare's birthday but it is also the day consecrated to their patron saint, Saint George. To the Northumberland Fusiliers, who trace their martial lineage back to 1674, the holiday is especially precious, for Saint George and his dragon are represented on the badge they wear on their berets. They had planned a turkey dinner for the twenty-third, and had fitted themselves out with the red and white roses (made of cloth, on this occasion) that are the traditional cap ornaments for the day. The banquet had to be cancelled, but the Fusiliers wore their roses anyway. Some of the gunners of the Royal Artillery joined the battle sporting real roses, which they had had flown in from Japan for the holiday. But they, too, were unable to pay any further tribute to Saint George. While the battle was on, they were busy firing more rounds per weapon—the average was a thousand—than had been hurled even at El Alamein, theretofore considered the biggest show ever put on by British artillerymen. The Royal Artillery motto is *"Ubique,"* and its guns in this case were twenty-five-pounders, mounted to permit a traverse of three hundred and sixty degrees; and during the Battle of the Imjin, with Chinese assaulting some of the gun emplacements from the rear, they had to be traversed full circle. The guns have a range of thirteen miles; they were fired point-blank, over open sights, at enemy riflemen fifty yards off. Toward the end of the battle, every round of twenty-five-pound ammunition in Korea had been delivered to the British gun positions, and lorries were waiting at two air-strips for a fresh supply that had been urgently ordered from Japan. But the battle was over before the ammunition ran out.

As for the Glosters, they date back to 1694 and have acquired forty-four battle honors—more than any other British regiment. The men of the 1st Battalion—the only element of the regiment in Korea—probably earned a forty-fifth at the Imjin, and they have already been awarded an American citation for their stand there. The Glosters have streamers on their regimental colors for Waterloo, Sevastopol, and Gallipoli, among other legendary arenas, and General Wolfe is said to have died in the arms of a Gloster during the Battle of Quebec. On March 21, 1801, while arrayed against the French at Alexandria, the Glosters, who then fought in geometric rows, were surrounded, and received the order "Rear rank, rightabout face and fire!" They battled back-to-back until the French were driven off, and ever since then the members of the regiment have been entitled to wear two cap badges, one in front and one in back. They are the only British troops who enjoy this privilege. The men who were to fight virtually back-to-back again, just a month after the hundred-and-fiftieth anniversary of their most cherished day, were for the most part experienced soldiers, many of them reservists, with wives and children, who were recalled to service a year ago. Their average age was over thirty. At five minutes to eight on the morning of April 25th, when, after fighting almost without food or water or sleep for nearly sixty hours, these Glosters reported to brigade headquarters that their radio was about to run out of power and that they would appreciate having some air and artillery missiles dropped thirty yards from their own position, the brigade commander, a normally unbending brigadier, had a special message relayed to them. "No one but the Glosters could have done it," it said.

During the daytime of April 22nd, there were no particular signs of trouble to come. All along the front, to be sure, the United Nations had for several days been awaiting the Chinese offensive, but no one could anticipate precisely when it would be launched, nor did the British seem more or less likely than any other troops in the line to bear the brunt of the attack. On the twenty-first, the British, who had the 1st Republic of Korea Division on their left and the American 3rd Infantry Division on their right, had sent an exploratory patrol across the Imjin. It had travelled ten thousand yards beyond the river and had encountered only a scattering of enemy troops. A British intelligence report took note of a "large undetermined number of enemy north of the river," but concluded that nothing more worrisome than strong enemy probing patrols could be expected on the twenty-third and twenty-fourth. The brigade troops in the line were getting hot meals and, assuming that they would continue to get them, had no combat rations along. That turned out to be unfortunate, for the most any one of them had to eat during the battle was one hard-boiled egg and a slice of bread. As it soon developed, not only were the Chinese ready to undertake far more than probing patrols, but the ones on the Glosters' front were an exceptionally well-outfitted bunch of Chinese. They had new uniforms, ample rations, new Russian weapons in prime condition, and new shoes. One enemy soldier who was taken prisoner even had a spare pair of new shoes, made in Shanghai, a most unusual luxury for a Chinese infantryman—or, for that matter, a British or American infantryman—in combat. But it is to be doubted whether all the soldiers facing the brigade were as sharp as their equipment. During the battle, for instance, one Gloster rifleman saw two Chinese sitting in plain view on a ridge six hundred yards distant, eating lunch. He shot one of them, and the man toppled over. The other, scarcely a foot away, didn't even glance at the victim, but placidly went on eating.

In any event, the brigade's orders from above committed it to holding its positions, no matter what opposition might be forthcoming. On the eve of the battle, a battalion of Belgians attached to the British was deployed just north of the Imjin, on the brigade's right. Behind the river were the Fusiliers. On the left were the Glosters, in an especially rugged area, four miles broad, dotted with sheer rock cliffs rising to a height of two hundred and fifty feet. The Ulster Rifles were in reserve. The weather was clear on the twenty-second, as it was to be throughout the battle, but things were so quiet during the day that only one supporting air strike was asked of the United States Air Force and Navy fliers backing up the brigade. At six o'clock in the evening, the Belgians were attacked and almost immediately cut off; four hours later, the Fusiliers were hit. A patrol from the Rifles set off to aid the Belgians but couldn't reach them, and for most of that first night the Belgians were the main objects of concern. They stayed in their ticklish situation for another twenty-four hours, in the course of which a tank column tried, and failed, to get to them; on the night of the twenty-third, they managed to slide over to the right flank and sneak out, with relatively few casualties.

Shortly after midnight of the twenty-second, when Saint George's Day was only half an hour old, Able Company of the Glosters was attacked. By four o'clock, the whole battalion was engaged, and by six the whole brigade. The enemy came in three waves. In the first rush, Able Company lost its commander and two other officers. One walkie-talkie operator, running out of ammunition, used his rifle as a club, swinging it at the Chinese as they came into his foxhole and shouting, *"Banzai,* you bastards! *Banzai!"* A few minutes later, the radioman regained his hereditary reserve and called into his transmitter, with finality, "We're overrun. We've had it. Cheerio." By midmorning, the Glosters had at least a regiment in front of them and, because the South Koreans on their left had been driven back several thousand yards, an indefinite number on the hills behind them. By midday, the Glosters hadn't been budged from the high points they had instructions to hold, but they were completely separated from the rest of the brigade, and the Chinese had penetrated so far back that the battalion's supply echelon was overrun, too, and nine of its men were taken prisoner. Quantities of the things the Glosters needed most desperately—machine guns, ammunition, and medical supplies—were packed into straw-lined bags and dropped to them by six light observation planes. A larger-scale airdrop was set up for the following morning. At dawn on the twenty-fourth, three Flying Boxcars were poised high over the Glosters' positions, waiting for the morning mist to lift so they could descend close enough to drop their

141

cargo accurately. But when the mist rose, the pilots found the Glosters, and not a few Chinese, fighting literally inside a curtain of falling shells that the brigade's gunners and mortarmen were throwing around them. The planes couldn't dip down unless the shelling was halted, and the decision was up to the Glosters. The Glosters waved the hovering Boxcars away.

There had been three air strikes on Saint George's Day. On the twenty-fourth, there were so many that at noon a young American Air Force lieutenant who was serving as liaison between the brigade and its tactical air support stopped keeping track of individual strikes, as he had been conscientiously doing up to then. Probably some fifty planes gave the brigade a hand that morning. There were plenty of targets available to them. So many Chinese had infiltrated around the Glosters' flanks, both of which were by then exposed, that one air observer spotted some seven hundred of them standing around nonchalantly in a single group, in the open. One dive-bomber seared a Chinese-held hill with napalm. The nine Glosters captured the day before were on it, along with their guards. Several of the guards caught fire, and while they were frantically trying to beat out the flames, seven of the Glosters, who had somehow contrived to avoid being more than uncomfortably warmed, ran down the hill and escaped into the lines held by the Fusiliers and the Rifles. This was a particular relief to one of them, who had spent five years in a Nazi prisoner-of-war enclosure. The Fusiliers and the Rifles were better off than the Glosters, but they were having no picnic either. There were Chinese behind them, too, and brigade headquarters organized a makeshift reinforcement party to help them out. It was composed of what little could then be mustered for the purpose: eight tanks from the Hussars, some Royal Engineers acting as infantry, a few Royal Army Service Corps lorries—which under normal circumstances wouldn't be sent too near the enemy but whose drivers in this instance volunteered to lumber along behind the tanks right to the front—and forty green replacements who had reported to the brigade that day and had been assigned to the Fusiliers. Some of them never got to report to the Fusiliers. There were so many enemy wandering around the countryside by then that the headquarters was under small-arms fire, and mortars were being lobbed out at the enemy from behind brigade headquarters—which, as a major in charge of the mortars later remarked, was a most ungentlemanly way to wage war.

The Glosters were in pretty bad shape on the morning of the twenty-fourth. The enemy had been at them all night long. Baker Company, which, like the three other rifle companies in the battalion, had a normal strength of a hundred and fifty men, was down to one officer and fifteen other ranks. It was nearly impossible to move out of a foxhole anywhere along the battalion line without drawing machine-gun fire. The Glosters nevertheless reassembled around a hill on which the battalion command post had been established. The line had shrunk from four miles to six hundred yards, but it still hadn't been breached. The Glosters begged several times that day for a helicopter to come and evacuate their more seriously wounded. The enemy, however, was so close on all sides that no helicopter could be sent out with any real hope of accomplishing this mission. That morning, Colonel Carne was asked if he thought a relief column could get through to him. He said no. (Communications with him had been spotty for some hours; artillery fire had knocked out all the telephone wires, and only two gradually fading radios linked the Glosters with the rest of the brigade.) That afternoon, in disregard of the Colonel's opinion, the first of three attempts to rescue the Glosters was made. A battalion of Filipino infantrymen and some supporting tanks got to within fifteen hundred yards of them, and then, in a defile, the lead tank was set afire, and the entire column was blocked and had to withdraw. Neither of the two subsequent relief columns—one composed of Belgian, Filipino, and Puerto Rican infantrymen and elements of the 8th Hussars, and the other of tanks and infantrymen from the American 3rd Division—got even that close. When the third try had failed, the Glosters, by that time seven miles deep in Chinese, were on their own.

Early on the morning of the twenty-fifth, the brigade was finally instructed to pull back to new defensive positions. It had held up the Chinese long enough to disrupt their timetable all across the front. Those of the Fusiliers and Rifles who could walk managed to withdraw in fairly good order. The non-walking wounded from these units were worse off. Some two hundred of them were loaded onto the backs and sides of eight Centurions, which started off toward the rear through a narrow mountain pass. They were ambushed by the Chinese. The wounded, lying exposed on the tanks, couldn't do anything about it, and the tank crews were almost as impotent. Their vehicles were so slippery with blood and so jammed with sprawled bodies that it was impossible to traverse the gun turrets. On the way out, two tank commanders were wounded. Both remained standing in their hatchways, one fainting there and reassuming command when he came to. An officer riding on the outside of one Centurion, who while aboard ship en route to Korea last fall had entertained at a troop show by putting on a fake mental-telepathy act, was startled when one of the wounded men raised his head and said, "Beg pardon, sir, but there's something I've been wanting to ask you. How'd you do that bloody trick?" The driver of another Centurion, one that had no wounded on it and was, accordingly, buttoned up tight, was surprised to hear a thumping noise overhead. Looking up through his periscope, he saw a Chinese soldier perched above him, pounding on the hatch cover in an effort to open it. Without slowing down, the driver swerved to one side, drove the tank clean through a Korean house, brushing the interloper off, and then resumed his course.

Before daylight each morning during the battle, the Chinese had been sounding the bugle calls with which they customarily herald their armed approach. Before dawn on the twenty-fifth, the three hundred or so Glosters who were still fit to fight counterattacked in just about the only manner left to them: their bugler blew a long reveille. It rang out, clear and astonishing, and it was followed by a series of other calls—short reveille, half-hour dress, quarter-hour dress, cookhouse, and, just for the hell of it, the American variation of reveille. It was an amazing concert. For the few minutes it lasted, both sides stopped firing. Then the Glosters cheered, and the fighting started up again. At five minutes past six, shortly after daybreak, the Glosters were advised by brigade headquarters that they had permission to break out. At six-twenty, the Glosters reported that they were surrounded and couldn't break out. But they still wanted air support, and they got it. By almost split-second coördination between air and artillery, a flight of dive-bombers swooped on the enemy just one and a half minutes after the artillery lifted a barrage it had been laying on. The Glosters by then were down to one small yellow air-ground recognition panel, and it was hard for the diving aircraft to know exactly where to strafe and bomb. But the Glosters threw a couple of smoke grenades out from their perimeter—thirty-five yards is a fair throw with a smoke grenade—and the planes aimed their machine guns where the grenades landed. Then bombs were dropped, at a somewhat, but not terribly much, more cirumspect distance. The Chinese were hurt, and momentarily relaxed their pressure.

Colonel Carne summoned his company commanders to a hollow near his headquarters, where fifty or sixty stretcher cases were lying on the ground. He told them that all the hope of carrying on as a unit was gone. He said he was going to stay where he was and he gave them the option of surrendering or fighting their way out in separate groups. The commanders of Able, Baker, and Charlie Companies and their remaining men headed south, toward the United Nations line. It was the commander of Dog Company, Captain Mike Harvey, a twenty-eight-year-old officer from Portsmouth, who led out the group of thirty-nine that got back. He was in charge of Dog Company only by chance; its regular commander, a major, had gone to Japan on April 22nd for a rest. When the major arrived there, he heard that the spring offensive had started and caught the first plane back to Korea. Despite several tries, he was never able to make his way far enough forward to reach his unit. Harvey, a pink-cheeked man with horn-rimmed glasses and an unkempt mustache, is a Reserve officer who was in the Hampshire Regiment during the Second World War; up to April 22nd, he had thought of himself as a Hampshire man on loan to the Gloucestershire Regiment. Now he thinks of himself, without reservation, as a Gloster. He is unusually abstemious for a soldier, forgoing both tobacco and alcohol, principally because he has been interested in judo since the age of twelve and holds one of the highest ratings in the art. After he had assembled his withdrawal party, consisting then of twelve officers and ninety-two other ranks, he let the remnants of the three other companies start off ahead. "I stood on a hill watching them to see if they were really going," he said afterward. "It was unbelievable that things had come to this pass." He decided not to go south himself but instead to try the unexpected and proceed due north for a mile, straight toward the Chinese rear, and then swing west a couple of miles, in an outflanking movement, before turning south. He warned his group that they would have to travel fast, exhausted though they were, and that there could be no stopping to aid anybody who might be wounded.

Proceeding cautiously, Harvey and his men didn't see a single Chinese for the first three miles. His scheme was working fine. Then, just as they were veering south, they ran into a few Chinese. The Glosters shot them and moved on. When only a few miles from a point where they thought friendly troops would be, they were heartened by the appearance overhead of a Mosquito plane, generally used as liaison between ground forces and fighter aircraft. The Mosquito circled above them and wagged its wings encouragingly, and they waved back. The Mosquito began to guide them homeward through the hills. Harvey was keeping his men on low ground whenever possible, knowing that the Chinese habitually congregate on ridges. Ultimately, they came into one valley, two miles long, that was almost a canyon, with precipitous walls on both sides and a floor about a quarter-mile wide. A stream flowed through it, and they waded along this for a mile or so, until it dwindled away. As they came out on dry ground, thirty or forty machine guns opened up on them, from both flanks. The Glosters made for a ditch about a foot deep and dived into it. By then, the Mosquito had radioed for fighter planes, and they had come buzzing along and were working over the slopes as energetically as they could. But the machine guns didn't let up. The Glosters crawled forward, keeping their heads below the level of the ditch, since raising them as much as an inch above it had already proved fatal to several. The ditch, like the river bed before it, was full of stones, and the soldiers' arms and legs were lacerated. One man's shoes had fallen apart in the river, but he kept going, first in his socks and then, as those disintegrated, barefoot. Every so often, the men came to a four- or five-yard stretch where the ditch petered out, and in the stumbling race for the next ditch more were hit and dropped.

Finally, rounding a bend, they saw some American tanks down the valley, just half a mile away. They crawled ahead eagerly, and got to within five hundred yards of them. The tanks opened up with machine guns and 76-mm. cannon, and the six Glosters in the lead fell. The Mosquito pilot, horrified by this case of mistaken identity—the tank men had no idea any friendly troops were still that far north—flew frantically toward the tanks, diving almost on top of them, but they kept on firing. Harvey's single file of men, on their bellies in the ditch, were receiving fire from the front and both sides, and the men at the rear of the column, most of whom had exhausted their ammunition, were being stabbed by Chinese who had rushed down the valley behind them. Harvey tied his handkerchief and scarf to a stick, put his cap on it, and waved it at the tanks. Simultaneously, the Mosquito made another pass at the tanks and dropped them a note. The tanks, suddenly aware of their error, ceased firing. The remaining Glosters reached the tanks and crouched behind them. Using them as a partial shield against the continuing enemy fire, they withdrew another five hundred yards, to the reverse slope of a small hill. There they climbed on the tanks and rode out, for three more miles under steady enemy fire. The tank men were heartsick over their mistake. One of them took off his shoes and gave them to the Gloster who'd lost his. The lieutenant in command of the tanks kept asking how many of the Glosters his people had wounded. The Glosters, not wanting to make him feel any worse, wouldn't tell him; indeed, they didn't know for sure. The lieutenant was wounded himself getting them out.

As soon as Harvey got to a telephone, he called brigade headquarters. "I thought we had better get back, in case they wanted us again," he explained later. "Then I learned that we were the only survivors and that everyone else was missing. And everyone else is still missing." A week after the battle, the Glosters he had led out invited him to stop by for a beer. He hadn't touched the stuff in over three years, but to please them he drank a glass. "It tasted pretty awful," he said. "Being a judo man, it doesn't suit me."

The 1st Battalion of the Gloucestershire Regiment began reorganizing the day after the Battle of the Imjin ended. A few days after that, the handful of men from the old battalion and the new replacements lined up in a green Korean field for a simple memorial service. Massed around a table covered with a white cloth and bearing a cross and two candles, they stood with heads bared as their new battalion chaplain walked toward them in a white robe. Captain Harvey, now the battalions's new adjutant, distributed hymnals. The Glosters sang two hymns and, snapping to attention, a stanza of "God Save the King." After a few words from the battalion's new commander, who himself had been shot in the wrist during the Battle of the Imjin, the chaplain recited the names of Colonel Carne and Sergeant Major Hobbs, as symbolic of, respectively, the officers and other ranks listed as missing. Then the chaplain told a story from Ecclesiastes about a city under siege, and how, after all hope was seemingly gone, a good and wise man had saved it. And yet, in spite of that, the chaplain said, the poor wise man was very soon forgotten. "In England, they'll remember for a little while," he went on. "The soldier does have his day. I want to remind you this afternoon that it is not enough to remember now. We've got to show what we think of their sacrifice in the way we conduct ourselves in the days ahead. We are, as it were, a link between our past and the future, and if we are to be faithful to our past, we must hand on to future generations some of the heritage of the past. Having handed it on, we will be in some measure worthy of those who died that we might live."

May 26, 1951

Notes and Comment

Waiting for some definite and reassuring word from the conference room in Kaesong has been not unlike waiting for the obstetrician to come down from the delivery room and report on a woman who has been in unusually difficult and protracted labor. All the customary sensations are present—the uncertainty, the fear, the sense of being unable to do anything to help the direct participants, and the urge to take a nip to steady the nerves. We can only hope that the ordeal in the inner sanctum will end quickly and satisfactorily, and that the offspring, however odd it may look when first exposed to view, will be healthy, will be smart as a whip, and will enjoy a long and tranquil life.

As of this writing, the delegates are still trying to decide on a formal agenda, and in this respect they are far worse off than the expectant mother, whose agenda is never in doubt. It seems to be increasingly hard for high-level conferees like those in Kaesong to agree, no matter how many carefully chosen words they exchange, on just what it is they want to talk about. The ritual of drawing up the agenda has become a barrier as hard to get past as radar, and may be remembered as one of Communism's most peculiar contributions to contemporary civilization. Up to a few years ago, as far as we can recall, there was never anything terribly complicated about agenda. It was simply something that was on hand when a meeting was called to order, like a pitcher of ice water at the chairman's elbow.

The picture of one of the assistants on the United Nations negotiating team, an Army colonel from New York, was published in the *Times* the other day, and we noticed, with a twinge of regret, that he was sporting on the lapels of his uniform the insignia of the Judge Advocate General's Department. Up to then, we'd always thought that one of the few advantages of military negotiations over civilian was the military's saucy non-dependence on lawyers. Few civilians about to engage in delicate negotiations would dream of entering upon them without an attorney hovering close by. We'd been under the naïve impression that the armed forces, however, were singularly blessed in that they could dispatch admirals and generals to a place like Kaesong unencumbered in their mission by the cautionary whispers of counsel. Well, our illusions are shattered now, and we're resigned to the inevitability that in this drama, too, the protagonists dare not be guided solely by the precepts of such as Mahan and Clausewitz but instead find themselves, like all the rest of us, abjectly dependent on that windy and ubiquitous old Blackstone.

July 28, 1951

Notes and Comment

The death, en route to Washington, of the elephant that the King of Cambodia had presented to President Truman was a source of some disappointment to us. The President is conceded by even his most eloquent detractors to be an accomplished politician, and we had been wondering what political use he might find for the great beast. In the past, chief executives in receipt of similar presents have customarily turned them over to zoos, and such would doubtless have been the ultimate disposition of Mr. Truman's elephant. But if the President had shortly taken off on one of his cross-country speaking tours, he might have found it profitable to defer getting rid of the elephant until after the journey. Think of the effect on the inhabitants of this or that whistle-stop if, as Mr. Truman appeared at dawn on the rear platform of his train, he had been accompanied by the very symbol of the opposition, kneeling submissively at his side and, on the delivery of a telling rhetorical point, trumpeting with shrill appreciation! It might have taken a pork barrel or two full of peanuts and some intensive training to insure a coöperative performance, but it would have been worth the effort.

The Republicans couldn't very well have let such an act go unchallenged, and the logical step for the G.O.P. would have been to furnish its campaign orators with donkeys. If it had, the electorate would quickly have become so confused that both parties would have had to trade in their old mascots for new ones. The inconvenience to political cartoonists notwithstanding, we'd have been all for it. Neither animal has ever struck us as suitable for high-class leadership. An elephant, for all its massive grandeur, is apt to grow panicky at the sight of a mouse—a reaction indicative of uncertainty about its own strength and of general instability, both qualities to be deplored in time of crisis. A donkey is altogether too stubborn and ornery to merit admiration in an era when open-mindedness and pliability are so sorely needed. To any party in search of a substitute animal, we suggest the

Labrador retriever—sturdy, handsome, alert, intelligent, at home on land or water, the possessor of a firm but gentle jaw, an estimable watchdog, and terribly good with children.

September 15, 1951

Hundredth Birthday

The dependable old *Times* began its second hundred years of publication on Tuesday, September 18th, and on the afternoon before, while the birthday issue was being assembled, we visited the fourteenth floor of the paper's offices at 229 West Forty-third Street to extend our congratulations to its publisher, Arthur Hays Sulzberger. He received us cordially. "I've kept my calendar clear today and tonight because I imagined people might be dropping in," he said. "I celebrated my own sixtieth birthday last Wednesday, and I had a big party on Saturday, and I've just now come from General Adler's daughter's wedding. I am weary but unbowed." Mr. Sulzberger looked in fine fettle to us, and so did his office, brightly festooned with flowers. "The big ones there are for the *Times*, from Sloan Colt," he said, "and the others are left over from my birthday." He informed us that we shouldn't expect to find much in the way of special frills, hundredth anniversary or no. "We decided not to have a big anniversary edition and hold people up for advertising," he said. "As I told my staff, our main concern is simply to make the September 18th issue a good newspaper." He handed us a galley proof of an editorial on the centennial that was to run the next morning, and we callowly asked him who had written it. "The *Times*," he replied.

Mr. Sulzberger offered to show us around the building and we eagerly accepted the invitation. As he towed us off, he passed a secretary wrestling with a bulky package. "Another congratulatory scroll from the Chinese!" she called merrily. He led us first into the nearby office of Orvil Dryfoos, his son-in-law and assistant. Dryfoos hastily snapped off a broadcast of a ball game. "Very critical game," he said defensively. "Yanks and Indians tied, one to one, going into the ninth." Mr. Sulzberger asked if he planned to be on hand at press time. "I've got to go to my brother's birthday party," Dryfoos said, "but I'll stop in afterward."

Mr. Sulzberger guided us from floor to floor. On the eleventh, he drew our attention to a Chinese scroll hanging on a wall. "It calls us 'the throat and tongue of the world,'" he said proudly. On the tenth, he introduced us to Charles Merz. "I've written another editorial on the anniversary," Merz told him. "A nice little turn-the-column piece, I think." Mr. Sulzberger, seemingly unruffled by this breach in security, said he'd look it over shortly.

As we strolled through air-conditioned corridor after air-conditioned corridor, he called our attention to the gay color schemes that prevailed. "We've tried to make the place cheerful," he said. Cheerful it looked, too; the good gray *Times* is hatched in a gaudy nest. We encountered many of the paper's thirty-five hundred home-office employees on our tour (each was to get an individual birthday cake the next day), and most of them greeted the publisher amiably, as remote acquaintances are apt to greet each other during the Christmas-holiday season. On the seventh floor, in the photoengraving department, a photoengraver shouted to the boss, "Yankees win, two to one, in the ninth!" "Good news!" cried Mr. Sulzberger heartily. We passed through an inside, windowless corridor with "Shelter" signs prominently displayed in it. "We're not figuring on any evacuation," the publisher said. "If there's a direct hit on the *Times*, we'll all go together."

Mr. Sulzberger said he had to return to his desk then—to scan Merz's editorial, we assumed—and as we accompanied him back upstairs, he remarked, "You know, I was talking to some Army officers recently, and I told them that for us every day is a D Day, and every D Day has its H Hour. Tonight, our H Hour will be at ten-forty." He left us at Dryfoos's office.

"Rizzuto squeezed the winning run home," Dryfoos whispered to us. He added that he had just been talking with Turner Catledge, the executive managing editor, and that Catledge had told him congratulations were pouring in from everywhere. "Messages from the President, the Vice-President, and the Speaker of the House all came through within a two-minute period," said Dryfoos. "Think of it!" He informed us that the daily six-o'clock news conference of representatives of the paper's various news departments—city desk, foreign desk, national news desk, sports, business, financial—was about to be held and asked if we'd like to sit in on it. When we said we would indeed, he escorted us to Catledge's office, on the third floor, just off the city room. "Big night tonight," one of a dozen editors present was saying as we arrived. "Hear about the Toledo *Blade?*" asked Catledge. "They sent in the text of a congratulatory editorial of theirs, to run as a paid ad. The suckers! We'd have run it for free." Mr. Sulzberger came in. "I just celebrated my sixtieth birthday," he said to the room at large. "Tonight at ten-forty, we'll all be a hundred. Let's make the first one of the new century just as good as we can. That's why you're here, I know, and so without further ado I'll beat it back up to my ivory tower." There was polite laughter, and everyone stood up as he departed.

Catledge, presiding in place of Edwin L. James, the managing editor, who had been ill for some weeks, got the conference under way, asking each editor, in turn, to summarize the major items he had scheduled for the next morning's paper. It quickly developed that, what with a terrific raft of testimonials of one sort or another to be fitted in, space was going to be exceedingly tight. A man from the foreign desk said that in honor of the anniversary he was blowing up the Korean war map from its customary two-column breadth to three columns. Catledge groaned. Sports announced that the Yankees had won, 2–1. "If you got any space left, the stock market went down a little today," said Finance. "If it went down, let's leave it out," retorted Catledge, kidding. "Arnold Constable's celebrating its hundred-and-twenty-sixth anniversary," said Business. "My God, they have one every year!" said Catledge. "Last year, on the one-twenty-fifth, they wanted us to take a picture." "We took one this year," said the picture editor ruefully. "Tonight, all editions five minutes early," said Catledge.

By this time, we were resolved to actually see the *Times* through its first H Hour of its second century. Shortly before ten that night, we turned up in the city room, a vast sea of desks flecked with green eyeshades, where we found Catledge pacing the aisles, and he presently took us one flight up to the composing room. There the foreman wished him a happy centennial. "It'll be a good, orderly close," he added. At ten-fifteen, Mr. Sulzberger reappeared. "Right on the nose," Catledge told him at once. "You know, I have a young grandchild trying to get born tonight," said Sulzberger. "That would be something," murmured Catledge. "And Mrs. Sulzberger's birthday is the nineteenth," the publisher added. We reflected idly that the gift wrappings must be piling up around that family like newsprint.

We all trooped down to the pressroom, in the basement. Bells were ringing, stereotype plates were clanking, pressmen were shouting. The superintendent of the room, Alfred W. Harris, greeted us warmly. "I got over a third of the first hundred here myself— thirty-nine years," he said, and mentioned that he would be sixty-three his next birthday. At ten-thirty-seven, Catledge said, "Well, we ought to be rolling now." One minute later, Press No. 14, one of ninety-five on the premises, began to roll. Harris deftly grabbed the first copy to come off it and handed it gravely to Sulzberger. "Now for another hundred years," said the publisher. Soon presses were roaring on all sides.

We walked upstairs to the mailroom and stood there a few minutes, noting that the subscription copies of Joseph Kelemen, M.D., of Antwerp, New York, and Sidney C. Fink, of Winnetka, Illinois, were tidily wrapped and ready to be mailed. We left the building and headed east. At the southwest corner of Forty-third and Broadway, a newsstand dealer was yelling, "Morning *Times!* Morning *Times!*" A lady passing by turned to her companion and said, "Tomorrow's paper is out already."

September 29, 1951

Hi!

Having been advised by several teen-agers of our acquaintance that meeting friends under the clock at the Biltmore has lately become more fashionable than at any other time since the Fitzgerald era, we went over there at cocktail time a day or two after most of the colleges and boarding schools had recessed for the holidays. We took up a position directly beneath the clock, a timepiece of modest proportions set at the top of an arch that separates the lobby from the cocktail lounge. The arch was decorated with seasonal foliage and colored lights, and flanked with massive potted poinsettias. In the jam-packed lounge, to our north, a string ensemble was valiantly playing, but we could barely hear it over a din reminiscent of the Bird House at the Bronx Zoo. The hubbub was intermittently punctuated with the staccato cry of "Hi!," which we presently judged to be the almost universal greeting of the younger generation. Buffeted by the gentle push of countless searching shoulders, we stood and watched one intoxicating reunion after another. "Hi!" said a boy, rushing toward a girl. "Hi!" said she, linking her arm happily in his, and went on, "While I've been waiting, I've seen everybody I haven't seen in years! Now we've got to meet my mother." "Here?" he asked, astonished. "Of course not. At the St. Regis," she said. "But first we've got to get my luggage." "You have a lot?" he asked. "Just my suitcase and golf clubs," she said, and they tripped off, arms entangled.

What holding of hands! What flashing of eyes! What carols of delight from those met up according to plan, and what frowns of despair on the faces of those afraid their plans had gone awry! Near us were half a dozen boys and girls temporarily unmet and anxiously scanning their wrist-watches. Nobody glanced at the ageless clock to get the time. One boy had an orange-and-black muffler draped carelessly around his neck. Princeton was in town. Another wore dirty white shoes. Harvard was in town. There was a scattering of second lieutenants and ensigns. The world situation was in town. All the girls, some in city clothes, some still in campus clothes, had marvellously fresh, scrubbed faces. They looked as if they'd just stepped off a ski slope, and maybe some of them had.

A middle-aged man with a badge on his lapel came up and stood briefly under the clock. He seemed puzzled, and finally asked a passing bellhop where the Book Paper Manufacturers were meeting. He was directed toward some more senile part of the hotel. An exceptionally tall boy strode by, his head floating half a foot above the rest of the crowd. "That's the basketball player I was telling you about," a young man at our right said to his girl. "The one that got a scholarship whose father owns a diner." "He doesn't look so hot to me," the girl said, and we admired her for saying it, since the fellow she was with couldn't have been taller than five foot three. A woman in her late twenties paused under the clock. She, too, seemed incongruous, for she had a five-year-old boy with her, wearing a coonskin cap. "We're a little late to meet Daddy," she was telling him. "Half an hour late." We wondered if she would have been as late a decade earlier. A girl who had been standing morosely at our side for twenty minutes sighted a boy she knew, but it was the wrong one. "Have you seen Bruce, Jeff?" she asked. "He was supposed to meet me under the clock. I can't imagine where in the world he is." "Probably in the Men's Bar," said Jeff, callously. "If he doesn't show up in fifteen minutes—" she began angrily, but her tone suddenly changed, and instead of the unexpressed threat came a blissful "Hi!" as Bruce scrambled toward her, panting. "I'm sorry I'm late," he said, hesitantly touching her hand. "It's perfectly all right," the girl replied, and we could tell by the look in her eyes and the grip of her fingers that it was.

December 29, 1951

In the Pink

Walter S. Mack, Jr., an energetic, unconventional businessman who was last mentioned in these pages when he was chairman of the board of the Pepsi-Cola Company and was noted not only for his use of skywriting and jingles as advertising devices but for his vast and enthusiastic consumption of his own fizzy product, is now president of Nedicks. As such, he invited us and other journalists to a nine-o'clock breakfast party the other morning at the Nedicks off the main lobby of Madison Square Garden. The occasion was the introduction of a new type of Nedicks orange drink and a new type of orange-drink dispenser. The skies above were clear, as we arrived, of all save natural and illegible clouds. The Nedicks store itself, barred to cash customers while the party was on, was decorated with flowers and balloons. An accordionist with a huge papier-mâché orange over his head was strolling about, playing "The Farmer in the Dell" interminably. Several young ladies in Nedicks uniforms—orange trimmed with green—were passing out favors. "Our new uniforms are made of nylon and will be washed every night," we were told by a lady press agent, whom we recognized as a former member of Mack's Pepsi-Cola entourage. "The girls aren't full-fledged models but from the Conover Career Girl School. We didn't want oversophisticated-looking girls."

Mack, looking sophisticated as all getout in a trim gray flannel suit with side vents, was standing behind the serving counter, a cigarette in his mouth. Its lengthening ash hovered perilously above a heap of fresh sugar doughnuts. The publicity woman introduced us to a Mr. Phillips, of Nedicks, who said the new orange drink is much more orangey in color than its forerunner. We asked if he was a Pepsi-Cola alumnus, too. "Mr. Phillips has been with Nedicks for fifteen years," the publicity woman said. "He has a clean record." Mack stepped nimbly to one side as his ash began to go, and it fell neatly to the floor.

We grabbed a vacant seat at the counter and were served some breakfast—

orange drink, scrambled eggs and sausages, and coffee. A man at our left remarked teasingly to a lady at *his* left that to him the orange drink didn't taste terribly different from the old variety. "I'm always afraid to speak freely in these places," the lady said, looking around nervously. The man, politely changing the subject, said that Mack looked to him like General MacArthur. The fearful lady kept mum. We can't be intimidated that easily; we said Mack looked to us like General Mark Clark, and always had.

Mack stepped out from behind the counter and went over to a microphone. "Orange drinks have become a fundamental part of the lives of the American people," he said, and went on to extoll the virtues of his orange drink over all others, not to mention over mere oranges. Tex and Jinx wandered in. Mack announced that he was about to unveil a new jingle, and promised cheerfully that in the months to come it would drive us all off our rockers. At his signal, a phonograph somewhere gave forth with "Keep in the pink, with Nedicks sunshine drink," to the tune of "The Farmer in the Dell." That explained that.

Afterward, Mack had his picture taken with Jinx. We dragged him away from her and asked him how much orange drink he is currently imbibing. "I drink a lot, I drink it all day long," he replied. "I drink it at home and I'm having a cooler put in at my office. At home, we keep it in pitchers. My kids drink it all day long, and the neighbors' kids come in and help themselves." We asked, gently, what about Pepsi-Cola, which we had once heard him say his kids guzzled from dawn to dusk. "There's some Pepsi around and they can get it if they want it," he said. "The orange is kept cold, though. Pepsi's a good drink. But, personally, I'm off carbonated drinks. I'm having a lot of fun."

March 1, 1952

Plenipotentiary

On the most recent anniversary of the birth of Franklin D. Roosevelt, a memorial wreath was laid at his grave, on behalf of President Truman, by William Averell Harriman. For this particular assignment, Mr. Truman could hardly have picked a more suitable envoy. Of all the Americans who have played significant parts in the administration's conduct of foreign affairs during the phrenetic era that began with the outbreak of the Second World War in Europe, Harriman—an energetic, peripatetic, aristocratic, and somewhat enigmatic man of sixty who was recently characterized by Secretary of Defense Robert A. Lovett, an old friend and business associate, as "a remarkably public-minded man, in a strange, rather demure sort of way"—is the only one who had a position of consequence at the start of the period and has had one ever since. The other familiar names—Byrnes,

Forrestal, Hopkins, Hull, Leahy, Marshall, Stettinius, Stimson, Welles, and the rest—are now missing from the picture, but Harriman, a public servant of rugged persistence, is still around. Since last November, as Director for Mutual Security, in which capacity he supervises the allocation by this country of all military, economic, and technical aid to other countries, he has been very much around. Harriman has had eight influential government jobs in the last eleven years, and in each he has been intimately concerned with foreign affairs, especially European affairs. Not only is he, by virtue of the nature and length of his service, a unique link between the Roosevelt and Truman regimes, but he is the most durable link between the United States and the rest of the Western world.

Harriman's contribution about himself to *Who's Who in America* is a terse entry that omits many of his achievements—he does not mention in it, for instance, that he is recognized throughout Sands Point, Long Island, as the world's ace croquet strategist—but he does mention that he has lately held the rank of Ambassador Extraordinary and Plenipotentiary. Right now, Harriman is not technically an ambassador of any degree, but to all practical purposes he has been functioning as a superdiplomat ever since, late in the winter of 1941, President Roosevelt sent him to run the then-infant lend-lease program. From that now seemingly remote time on—whether presiding over the American Embassy in Moscow or in London, or, while Secretary of Commerce, heading the committee that worked out detailed recommendations for the Marshall Plan, or roaming about Europe as chief overseas operative for the Economic Coöperation Administration, or acting as Truman's personal adviser on foreign affairs, or serving as chairman of the North Atlantic Treaty Organization triumvirate known as the Three Wise Men—he has been a liaison man between the executive branch of the American government and its counterparts abroad. It is he who has conferred, in times of stress, with a Mossadegh or a Tito or a MacArthur. None of his professional contemporaries can match him. To find an apt prototype, it is perhaps necessary to go all the way back to Hermes, the fleet and tireless messenger of the Olympian theonomy. Averaging five or six transatlantic crossings a year, and embarking on countless additional journeys over land and other seas, Harriman has resolutely winged his way about the earth, pausing here, there, and practically everywhere to negotiate in his country's interest with those potent mortals who nowadays control the loudest thunder and the brightest lightning.

Even among diplomats, a traditionally well-favored lot, Harriman is a notably handsome specimen—slim, six feet one, with dark hair graying at the edges, clean-cut and delicate features, and deep-set brown eyes shaded by thick, curly brows. One lady who is herself an ornament of international society has described him as America's answer to Anthony Eden. (Dean Acheson would be a contender for this accolade, the lady added, if only he travelled about more.) Aside from his looks and his means—he is currently worth around forty million dollars—Harriman has few of the conventional attributes of a diplomat. (He sometimes seems to have few of the conventional attributes of a Democrat, either.) He is indifferent about his clothes, sometimes ordering them by telephone. He is bored by purely social gatherings, and at dinner parties occasionally falls asleep in the drawing room while the evening is still young. He has a constant, nagging impulse to work, and has no use for a dinner party that doesn't advance the progress of whatever project he may be engaged in at the moment. At many dinners attended by international figures he has been clearly impatient for the ladies to leave the table so he could talk business. In Paris, a couple of years ago, he was invited to dinner by a British peer and his wife. Harriman, who had been immersed in a conference that ran late, arrived just as the other guests were sitting down at the table, and some time after his hostess had planned to have them sit down. The dessert dishes had scarcely been removed when he excused himself, explaining, quite truthfully, that he wanted to get back to work. "Look here, Averell, you can't make up for coming late by leaving early," his host grumbled. Harriman is at home in most of the capital cities of the world, but he is fluent in no foreign tongue, not even French, the language of diplomacy. "My French is excellent, except for the verbs," he once told a friend—a remark that, inasmuch as he is an uncommonly serious-minded man, comes about as close to being a joke as anything he ever says. Harriman doesn't go in much for small talk. It was typical of him that during an eighteen-month period when George Kennan was his chargé d'affaires in Moscow, the Ambassador never once referred to the coincidence that Kennan's great-uncle, and namesake, had years before written a two-volume biography of Edward Henry Harriman, his father.

A useful diplomat ought to be a competent observer and analyst. Harriman's record would seem to indicate that he has in the main been perceptive and accurate in both capacities. In November, 1941, for instance, he declared, publicly and unequivocally, "Hitler will never destroy Russia," a statement few men would have dared make at that time without swathing it in hedges. Also, of course, a diplomat should be able to get along with and not be awed or fazed by men of stature. Important people, and especially Very Important People, or V.I.P.s, are Harriman's specialty. No one alive has known better than he has all of the Big Three who led the Allies in the Second World War. Harriman was barely in his teens when he first met Roosevelt, and he saw him frequently thereafter. Harriman had deep admiration and respect for him, and Roosevelt appreciated his sympathetic and coöperative attitude—so uncharacteristic of an industrialist of prominence—toward many, if not all, of the objectives of the New Deal. Harriman was with Churchill when the Japanese attacked Pearl Harbor, and at the Kremlin when the Japanese sued for peace. In advance of

Churchill's latest visit to Washington, it was Harriman who, at President Truman's request, called on the Prime Minister three times to sound him out on the agenda; when Churchill reached Washington, he saluted Truman and shook hands with a flock of other American dignitaries, but for Harriman he had an exclusive, affectionate pat on the arm.

For a man who has spent so many historic moments in the company of historic personages, Harriman is curiously and engagingly naïve about his associations. Recently, he told an acquaintance, solemnly and a bit shyly, "In the last ten years, I guess I've seen most of the important political characters—Beneš, de Gaulle, Chiang, Adenauer, de Gasperi, and all the rest. I've seen Stalin more than any other foreigner has, you know. Some name did come up the other day—someone I'd never met. I've forgotten who it was, for the instant. Oh, yes. Nehru." Harriman's companion got the feeling that Nehru would not long elude him. Harriman cares about rare people the way a philatelist cares about rare stamps. It has been observed by one of his friends that, while unquestionably a V.I.P. himself after all these years of illustrious fraternization, he is also what might be called a philovippist, or, in the friend's arbitrary diminution, a vippist. Recalling once that he had never made the acquaintance of Hitler, Harriman sounded almost wistful, as if lamenting the absence from his collection of a forever unattainable vippic treasure. (He bagged Mussolini in 1927, while in Italy on a non-governmental business trip.) Sometimes in conversation Harriman seems listless and inattentive, giving the impression that his thoughts are far from the subject at hand. But when he talks about big shots, and his association with them, his face lights up. "A country's policies can only work out successfully if you get to the right people," he says. "If you talk to people, you get a feel of things you don't otherwise get." According to one reflective man who has worked with him for many years, Harriman is one of the few world statesmen who think not in terms of masses but of individuals. "Averell doesn't think abstractly about situations," the man said not long ago. "You talk about French labor and he sees a French worker on the streets of Paris. You talk about British rationing and he sees a London housewife queuing up at a meat shop. He isn't often terribly articulate, in a philosophical way, but you can sense from what he says that he perceives human beings behind problems. The world is a reality to him. Places like Korea and Indo-China aren't far off to him. He feels and sees them. They're part of his visual experience."

Lately, since Harriman has actively become a political candidate, a role in which others have now and then tried to cast him since as far back as 1938 (when he was embarrassed at being hailed as Presidential timber by the president of the Union Pacific Railroad at a time when Harriman was chairman of its board), he has been seen to go out of his way to clasp hands with casual acquaintances who have no other claim to fame than that of being voters. By and large, however, Harriman is not a handshaker. One associate of his, observing recently that Harriman seemed especially contented while basking in the radiance shed by big people, added, "Averell's a power snob. His attitude always is 'There's only one guy worth talking to in any situation—the top guy—and I'm the guy who talks to him.'" Harriman's admirers parry such thrusts by pointing out that in concentrating on the movers and shakers of his day he has made the most efficient use of his time, and has, besides, managed to become so inured to world leaders that he has no fear of any of them and can, accordingly, deal with them in man-to-man fashion. When, in August, 1950, soon after General MacArthur's controversial sortie to Formosa, Harriman sped from Washington to Tokyo, as Truman's emissary, to find out what was going on, he was welcomed by the General, whom he had known for many years, with a cordial "Hello, Averell." "Hello, Douglas," replied Harriman affably. MacArthur is said to have appeared rather taken aback by the bilaterality of this greeting.

It is an indication of what a relative Johnny-come-lately Harry S. Truman is to the international scene that he never met Harriman until a couple of weeks after he became President, when Harriman, at that time Ambassador to Russia, flew home from Moscow to take in the San Francisco Conference. Harriman collects conferences, too. Throughout the war years, he attended all but one of the big Allied get-togethers—the exception being the second meeting of Roosevelt and Churchill at Quebec, in September, 1944, which conflicted with some Rumanian armistice negotiations that Harriman's diplomatic responsibilities obliged him to sit in on—and so established a figure at top-level conferences was he by then that the Associated Press considered the mere fact of his absence from the meeting in Canada worth special mention.

Harriman's presence at Casablanca, Cairo, Teheran, Yalta, Potsdam, and the rest of the far-flung spots where far-reaching decisions have been thrashed out was regarded as inevitable by most of the other participants (as his presence has been since the war at London, Paris, Rome, and Lisbon), but there was a time when his status was less certain. On the eve of the Atlantic Charter meeting off Argentia, Newfoundland, which was held in August, 1941, it began to look as if Harriman, then in England, would not be invited. In a conversation with Churchill, Harriman remarked that lend-lease matters might come up for discussion, and Churchill and he agreed that in that event it might be useful if Harriman were present. Harriman thereupon cabled Harry Hopkins suggesting that Hopkins convey the Prime Minister's sentiments to the President. Hopkins did, but Harriman, who had returned to the United States in anticipation of getting the nod, heard nothing further until after the naval convoy carrying the vanguard of

Roosevelt's party steamed up Long Island Sound toward Argentia. Harriman was staying at Sands Point, in one of five houses he owns on this continent (a sixth, in Washington, which he rents, is currently his main domicile), and as he watched the ships go by, he began to suspect that he might not after all get to join the Navy and see world history made. At the last minute, though, Roosevelt authorized him to climb aboard a plane that was transporting Sumner Welles to Newfoundland. On Churchill's next two trips across the Atlantic to consult with the President, Harriman prudently travelled with the Prime Minister. From then on, he was pretty much a fixture at conferences—he even represented the United States at a couple of Churchill-Stalin affairs that Roosevelt missed—and by the time the Yalta meeting took place, it seemed only natural that the distaff representation there should consist of Sarah Churchill Oliver, Anna Roosevelt Boettiger, and Kathleen Harriman, the younger of the Ambassador's two daughters.

A few days before the San Francisco Conference, Harriman went to the White House and reported to President Truman and his principal civilian and military advisers that, on the basis of his experiences and observations in Moscow, he believed Russia's postwar attitude toward the United States was likely to be anything but comradely. Harriman had given substantially the same pessimistic appraisal, the night before, to James Forrestal, who wrote in his diary, "He said the outward thrust of Communism was not dead and that we might well have to face an ideological warfare just as vigorous and dangerous as Fascism or Nazism." No high government official was disposed to sound the alarm publicly at that time—a time when the war with Japan had yet to be concluded, the atomic bomb had not yet been exploded, and Soviet coöperation was still judged by the Joint Chiefs of Staff to be desirable—but Harriman continued to sound it privately. At San Francisco, he expressed similar strong misgivings about Russia, at an off-the-record press conference, to a dozen eminent journalists who he thought should have his views to complement their own analyses of the international situation. Two members of the group were indignant at Harriman's intemperate attitude toward the Soviet Union. To their minds, an ambassador to an allied nation had no business speaking so disrespectfully, even off the record, about the government to which he was accredited.

Not long after Harriman and Truman finally met, Harriman urged the President to feel free to call on him at any time for any chore. Truman, who has had his personnel problems, was pleased with Harriman's exceptionally accommodating attitude. When the President was confronted with Henry Wallace's dissension from State Department policy in the fall of 1946, he had no trouble persuading Harriman to take his place as Secretary of Commerce, even though Harriman had become Ambassador to the Court of St. James, only six months earlier and had barely had a chance to look up his wartime friends in London. After Harriman left the Cabinet, in the spring of 1948, to return to Europe for the E.C.A., he customarily stopped in at the White House during his periodic visits to the home office from his office in Paris. In June, 1950, ten days before the outbreak of fighting in Korea, Truman, having decided that he wanted Harriman's counsel more regularly available, made him his Special Assistant, a theretofore nonexistent post and one that has been vacant since Harriman moved on to his present job. The idea was that Harriman would wind up his E.C.A. affairs at a leisurely pace and then report for duty. At six-thirty on the morning of June 27th, a few hours after resolving to intervene in Korea, Truman got Harriman on the phone in Paris and asked him to return as quickly as possible. Harriman, a former eight-goal polo player who is used to making fast stops and starts, arrived in Washington less than thirty hours later.

Harriman's relations with Truman have become increasingly warm. It was noted by Washington people who keep track of such things that the President asked him to the Army-Navy football game in 1950. This, however, was given not a great deal of weight, since the President habitually invites nearly *everybody* to the Army-Navy game. But then came cruises aboard the Williamsburg and a bid to the opening game of the 1951 baseball season, an event considered harder to get invited to by the President than any football game. Harriman was presently admitted to membership, too, in the Key West club, although because of his high-society origins and preference for bridge, backgammon, and bezique to poker, his membership has been a limited one. On the mantel of his Washington office is a photograph taken at the President's Florida retreat in the spring of 1951. It shows Truman, Admiral Leahy, and Harriman amid a swarm of White House staff members. The picture is in color, and does full justice to the flowery shirts sported by the President and his crew. Harriman, clad in a white shirt, black sweater, and white jacket, is a conspicuously achromatic anomaly in this garish bouquet.

Much of the credit for Harriman's having become interested in government service, and having devoted himself to it, from 1940 to the present, with industry and zeal, belongs, his friends believe, to his older sister Mary, a high-minded, intellectual woman, who when a girl surprised her social set by enrolling at Barnard, where she majored in sociology, and by founding, in her débutante year, the Junior League. These were regarded at the time as very peculiar things for the daughter of E. H. Harriman to get mixed up in. One of her closest friends was Frances Perkins, with whom she worked in several consumers' movements. They lived together in Washington in the early days of the New Deal, in which both were prominent—Miss Perkins, of course, as the first woman Cabinet member, and Harriman's sister, by then the widow of Charles Cary Rumsey, a sculptor, as chairman of the

Consumers Advisory Board of the National Recovery Administration. She and her brother Averell, both Republicans up to 1928, had left that party then to vote for Al Smith, a friend of theirs. Brother and sister both voted for Franklin Roosevelt, another friend, in 1932. Harriman, at that time chairman of the Union Pacific and a partner in the private banking firm of Brown Brothers Harriman & Company, had had almost twenty years' experience in finance and industry. He had also, though on the whole more serious-minded than most rich young blades of his generation, occasionally demonstrated a knack for indulging in the frolicsome antics for which rich young blades are celebrated. Mrs. Rumsey, who had long hoped he would develop a social conscience as driving as her own, urged him to branch out into public affairs. He made a start by becoming a member of the Business Advisory Council, set up in 1933 by Secretary of Commerce Roper to act as a liaison group between his department and the business community. A year later, to his sister's delight, Harriman took a full-time job with the N.R.A., as its New York administrator. He went on to other positions in the agency, and he was working for it in Washington as its chief administrative officer for the entire country when, late in 1934, Mrs. Rumsey died after being thrown by a horse and severely injured. Some of Harriman's acquaintances think that he has worked as hard as he has for the country since then partly as a sort of memorial to his sister and her aspirations for him.

Another good friend of Mrs. Rumsey's was the late George Russell, the Irish poet known as Æ. In the twenties, she introduced him to her brother, who recalls that Russell predicted to him then that the United States would have a historic role to play, because Americans had been the first people to adopt a planetary viewpoint. "I told him at the time that we certainly didn't seem to be behaving that way," Harriman said recently. "He replied that nonetheless he could detect signs that Americans were getting ready to assume planetary responsibilities. He said, 'You have a vision about this planet that no other nation has ever had.' Russell was right. He was a philosopher who foresaw precisely the kind of role that the United States is now playing. What so few people understand is that our hundred and fifty million citizens, constituting only ten per cent of the population of the non-Soviet world, control, in terms of gross national product, half that world's economy. Therefore, what we do affects everybody. We've got to think in world terms. It's revolutionary, but we've got to do it. We've got to the point now where we must assume the same kind of responsibility in world affairs that we're accustomed to assuming in our individual affairs. If we waver, the world wavers. If we're firm, the world is firm."

After the N.R.A. was declared unconstitutional, in 1935, Harriman re-embraced private enterprise for a while. He continued, however, to serve on the Business Advisory Council, and shortly before Harry Hopkins, whom he had got to know well, became Secretary of Commerce, Harriman was elevated to the Council's chairmanship. As such, he had the difficult mission of serving as an emissary between business and government at a time when the two poles of his particular axis were about as far apart as they have ever been. He reappeared on the Washington scene in a full-time capacity in June, 1940, when Edward Stettinius asked him to head the transportation section of the National Defense Advisory Commission, from which post Harriman moved on to become chief of the Materials Branch of the Production Division of the Office of Production Management. While he was there, his stock dipped slightly among some conventional-minded Democrats when it came out, early in 1941, in a conversation between Roosevelt and Wendell Willkie shortly after the President's victory in their race, that Harriman had contributed to the campaign treasuries of both. Harriman's explanation of this action is that in Willkie's case he was contributing solely to his campaign to get nominated, since Harriman didn't want any isolationist to have a shot at the White House that year; once two internationalist nominees were selected, Harriman says, he was exclusively for Roosevelt. In any event, the President didn't seem to be offended by Harriman's bipartisan generosity, for in March, 1941, when the lend-lease program was getting under way, he sent him to London to run that end of it.

Harriman was gratified by this assignment. For one thing, it would afford him a chance to tackle a critical task at a critical time, and for another, he would be tackling it in dangerous and exciting circumstances. He had sat out the First World War in this country, operating a shipyard, though he was only twenty-five and in good health when the United States became a belligerent. In 1920, he said to a magazine interviewer, "I felt that in no other way could I contribute half as much to the urgent needs of the nation in the supreme emergency that had arisen." As Harriman grew more mature, his friends now surmise, he came to wonder if perhaps it might not have been his shipyard rather than himself that was essential to the war effort, and this may have led him to the conclusion that if another supreme emergency arose, he would not only contribute his services but expose himself to risk. He went through a good many air raids in England, and planes he was riding in were twice fired upon by anti-aircraft—in both instances, as it happened, Allied anti-aircraft guilty of a mistake in identification. "I once mentioned to Stalin that I had been shot at by the British and the Russians but never by the Germans," Harriman said not long ago. "Stalin rather liked that."

Harriman arrived in England with the broad assignment of not only administering lend-lease but, operating under the informal title of "defense expediter," doing everything else he could, short of committing the United States to outright warfare, to help the British. He was at once whisked off by Winston Churchill to spend the weekend at the Prime Minister's country place, Chequers. They had become acquainted in Italy in 1927, and in the intervening years had had a couple of reunions. Harriman spent most of his weekends at Chequers while he was in England. In "The Grand Alliance," the third of Churchill's volumes on the war, the author tells how early one Saturday morning in May, 1941, he learned of the loss of the battleship Hood, which had been engaged in a fight on the Atlantic with the Bismarck. "I went straight to Harriman's room at the end of the corridor," Churchill writes, "and, according to him, said, 'The Hood has blown up, but we have got the Bismarck for certain.'" Harriman remembers vividly that the Prime Minister, barefoot and in a nightshirt, roused him from his sleep, but he has no idea why his host cited him as the authority for his own words. As a matter of fact, Harriman, who has an excellent memory for details, says that what Churchill says he said Churchill said is not quite precise, and that his host's exact words were "The Hood is sunk. It's a hell of a battle. We've got her."

The following month, as the British situation in Africa became increasingly precarious, Harriman flew down to see what he could do about expediting logistical support there. He carried with him a letter of introduction from the Prime Minister to General Wavell, the senior commander in the Middle East, which read, in part, "Mr. Harriman enjoys my complete confidence and is in the most intimate relations with the President and with Mr. Harry Hopkins. No one can do more for you. . . . I commend Mr. Harriman to your most earnest consideration. He will report both to his own government and to me." This was an unprecedented form of credentials for an envoy who had no official diplomatic accreditation to England and whose own country wasn't officially in the war he was inspecting. Harriman flew to the Western Desert to have a look at the tactical situation there, cruised over Africa from Eritrea to the Gold Coast, and subsequently recommended to President Roosevelt that the United States establish an air-transport route across the South Atlantic to Africa and on to the Near East. This suggestion led to the chain of air-bases that were to prove extremely handy after the United States declared war.

It was Churchill's custom to make frequent morale-building trips to various parts of England, especially to localities hard hit by German bombs, and he often took Harriman with him. Churchill believed that the sight of an eminent American would help persuade his beleaguered countrymen that the United States was standing by them, and, to indicate that American concern existed on the highest level, he would introduce Harriman around as "the President's personal envoy." One time, the two of them went by train to Bristol the morning after that city had had a harrowing night raid. Everybody was immensely bucked up to see the Prime Minister. When the time came to leave, a crowd gathered on the station platform to wave goodbye to Churchill, who was seated with Harriman in their compartment. "Churchill was waving back, and suddenly he stopped," Harriman says. "Tears began streaming down his cheeks, and he picked up a newspaper, to hide his face. 'They have such confidence,' he said to me. 'It is a grave responsibility.' You can imagine how I felt. The whole Middle East was in danger, ten per cent of every convoy was being sunk, for all anybody knew there might be an invasion of England the next day, and here was this man, standing alone and resolute. You couldn't help being profoundly moved."

While based in England, Harriman made two trips to Russia. In September, 1941, Churchill and Roosevelt dispatched him to Moscow with Lord Beaverbrook, to arrange for Anglo-American lend-lease shipments to Russia. The arrangement resulted, as far as largess from the United States was concerned, in a three-and-a-half-year flow of goods worth eleven billion dollars. In August, 1942, Harriman returned to Moscow, with Churchill, to talk about opening a second front in Europe. En route, they stopped in Iran; while there, Harriman made arrangements for operation by the United States of the supply line from the Persian Gulf to the Caspian Sea, over which much of the Soviet lend-lease bounty ultimately was shipped.

In October, 1943, Harriman was appointed Ambassador to the Soviet Union, and this time he travelled to Moscow with Secretary of State Hull, who was going to attend a Big Three conference there. Harriman's wife was in poor health during much of the war, and he took along as his hostess his daughter Kathleen, now Mrs. Stanley G. Mortimer, Jr., who had been with him most of the time he was in England, too. In Moscow, they lived at Spasso House, a spacious residence that the United States acquired for its ambassadors' use when this country resumed diplomatic relations with Russia in 1933. A detachment of N.K.V.D. men lived next door, and accompanied Harriman wherever he went. This attention was accorded only to the American, British, and Japanese envoys, and was, the Russians explained, to be construed as a courtesy and an honor bestowed because they were more important than other diplomats. As a matter of fact, the secret policemen proved quite helpful to Harriman on occasion. If his car got a flat while they were tailing it, they would hop out of their own vehicle and help change wheels. One winter weekend, Harriman and his daughter were invited to visit a British diplomat at a country place he had outside Moscow, approachable only over a rough, rutty road. The Harrimans elected to travel by jeep, and considerately advised the N.K.V.D., who they knew would tag along, to do so, too. The secret police ignored this advice, and set off behind the Ambassador, lightly clad, in a heated sedan. Their car got stuck, whereupon one determined operative piled out and took off on foot after the Harriman jeep, which obligingly slowed down so he could keep up with it. Presently, fearing that his shadow would freeze to death before they reached their destination, Harriman stopped and urged him to climb aboard. The N.K.V.D. man agreed after Harriman promised he wouldn't tell anybody.

Another time, the Ambassador, whom President Roosevelt had made responsible for all American matters, both civilian and military, that came up in Moscow, and who generally worked sixteen hours a day on them, decided to take a few hours off and go skiing. The N.K.V.D. men were apprised of his intentions and equipped themselves with skis. They did not know, however, that Harriman, whose achievements in private life had included the setting up of Sun Valley, is an expert skier. The Ambassador drove to the top of Sparrow Hill, the high, steep slope at the crest of which Napoleon stood when he watched Moscow burn. Harriman bound on his skis, pushed off, and zoomed down, checking his speed with a mere two turns. The secret police gasped. Then one of them gamely hurled himself in pursuit. He landed in a heap halfway down the slope. The next time Harriman went skiing, the N.K.V.D. deputized a champion Russian skier to shadow him.

Harriman saw Stalin on an average of once a month during the two and a half years he spent in Moscow. They got along well enough, though they never became exactly intimate. Whereas Harriman has long been "Averell" to Churchill, to Stalin, whose language has no "h," he was always "Mr. Garriman." Harriman refers to his many chats with the Prime Minister as "personal talks," and to those with the Soviet Premier as "discussions." One interpreter who sat in on a good many of these discussions thinks that Stalin respected Harriman more than he usually does outlanders because Harriman never hesitated, when the situation seemed to call for it, to talk back to him. In April, 1945, Major General Patrick J. Hurley, who is regarded in many quarters as the very model of a modern major diplomat, passed through Moscow on his way to China. Harriman escorted him over to the Kremlin to see Stalin. Russia had already reneged on a number of the Yalta agreements, and Soviet-American relations had receded markedly from their high-tide point of the preceding year. Stalin and Harriman had had several sharp debates. During the Hurley audience, Stalin brusquely accused Harriman of some fancied offense against the brotherhood of man, and Harriman responded in the same forthright spirit. Stalin counterattacked, and Harriman counter-counterattacked. Hurley, observing the exchange with mounting dismay, tried to pour a time-tested brand of diplomatic oil on the troubled waters by saying something like "Come, come, gentlemen, things can't be as bad as all that." Both Stalin and Harriman paused, looked at Hurley and then at each other with a "Who-let-*him*-in?" expression, and vigorously resumed their argument. As they were leaving the Kremlin, Hurley remarked to Harriman that he had sat in on a lot of diplomatic sessions in his day but had never seen anything like that. "That was nothing compared to what usually goes on," said Harriman equably.

Shortly after V-E Day, Stalin invited Harriman to the Kremlin to look at some motion pictures of the victory parade in Moscow. Harriman, who knows horses, commented appreciatively on a spirited mount the Chief of Staff of the Soviet Army, General Alexei I. Antonov, was shown riding. A few days later, a Russian officer called at the Embassy to announce that Stalin wished to give Harriman the horse, a stallion named Fact, and to give his daughter a gelding named Boston, which, even if it had never borne so high-ranking a burden, had the distinction of having been through the siege of Stalingrad and of then having walked from Stalingrad to Budapest and from Budapest to Moscow, a distance of over twenty-five hundred miles. For several months, the Harrimans exercised the horses at the Budenny Cavalry School in Moscow, the only place the Soviet authorities would permit them to ride. In the winter of 1946, soon after Harriman moved out of the Embassy, the Soviet government had the horses loaded on a Liberty ship at Odessa and shipped, accompanied by a retinue of three Red Army veterinarians, to the United States. Harriman stabled them at his family estate at Harriman, in Orange County, New York, where they aroused much curiosity among people who had never seen a Communist horse.

It is indicative of the rapidity with which wartime camaraderie between the Soviet Union and the United States disintegrated that by October, 1946, less than a year and a half after Stalin had presented the Ambassador with the Chief of Staff's charger, Harriman was being denounced by *Pravda* as a warmonger. (Harriman, to be sure, was by then denouncing Russia in similar terms.) By 1949, Harriman was getting the full treatment; in a book published in Moscow by a pro-Communist British journalist living there, Harriman was described—and the characterization must have come as a surprise to his acquaintances in Moscow who recalled his handsome, sensitive face, with features that have been compared on this side of the Iron Curtain to those of a poet—as "a man with the face of a criminal who is paying blackmail to avoid the revelation of his crimes, cringing as if afraid of his neighbour."

On returning to the United States from Russia, Harriman briefly contemplated retiring from public service. Then John G. Winant, the Ambassador to the Court of St. James's, retired from that post, just as the Russians began to make threatening gestures toward Iran, a nation of much concern to the British. President Truman decided that Harriman, being a man who knew his way around England, Russia, and Iran, was the logical choice to fill the vacancy. Harriman didn't remain in London long, however. The tension over Iran abated, and simultaneously the tension within the President's Cabinet grew acute, when Secretaries Byrnes and Wallace had their tiff. As Secretary of Commerce, Harriman devoted the better part of the next eighteen months to domestic problems. In addition to his Cabinet duties, though, he was appointed by the President to serve as chairman of the Committee to Report on Foreign Aid to Europe, which was known for short as the Harriman Committee and which drew up the blueprint of the Marshall Plan. Paul G. Hoffman was a member of the committee. In the spring of 1948, when the President put Hoffman in charge of the E.C.A., Hoffman requested that Harriman be his chief deputy abroad, and Truman released him from the Cabinet.

Harriman established his headquarters, known formally as the Office of the Special Representative, in Paris, first in space belonging to the American Embassy, and later in the Hotel Talleyrand, on the Rue St. Florentin just off the Place de la Concorde. The building, named after its most famous tenant, is classed by the French as a *monument historique;* one may not trifle with its façade. When the Americans began to move in, with the usual clatter of steel desks and temporary partitions, the French grew apprehensive, not knowing what might happen next. To remind the new tenants that the building had venerable associations and was to be handled with care, the French government furnished Harriman's private office, and that of his chief assistant, with elegant and costly antiques. That, in turn, made Harriman apprehensive. "What will congressmen think if they visit me and see all this stuff?" he said to an aide. "Couldn't we put a little card up somewhere, the way they do in museums, telling where the furnishings came from?" The assistant said he thought the French might resent this, but he got the facts of the matter on the record with typical American ingenuity, by writing to Drew Pearson, who helpfully explained in his column how Harriman's lavish atelier had got that way.

Harriman had a lot of territory to cover as Special Representative— seventeen countries, plus Trieste and the British and American Occupation Zones of Germany. (It was at his suggestion that recommendations for the distribution of various categories of American aid among these nineteen entities were made not in Washington but by the nineteen themselves, acting through the coördinating body to which they all belonged—the Office of European Economic Coöperation.) Harriman travelled about so much and so fast that once in a while he forgot where he was. In the spring of 1949, in the course of a rapid whirl around Scandinavia, he absent-mindedly wound up a speech he was making in Norway with a stirring tribute to the wartime gallantry of Danish seamen. During his journeyings he became unusually conversant with postwar political and economic conditions all over the Continent. He was as responsible as any man for the United States' swift endorsement of the Schuman Plan when that novel idea was first proposed. The E.C.A. was supposed to busy itself exclusively with building up the economic strength of Europe, but Harriman concluded not long after he moved to Paris that Europe would shortly need some assistance in building up military strength as well, and this point of view—shared, of course, by other statesmen—ultimately resulted in the formation of the North Atlantic Treaty Organization. A foreign correspondent who has roamed about Europe for the better part of the last fifteen years said recently, "In some ways, I think Harriman is probably the best-informed man in the world right now on the over-all structure of Western civilization."

May 3, 1952

From Part I of a two-part Profile.

Employment

A couple of hours before the commencement exercises at Columbia last Thursday, we had an illuminating chat up there with an amiable, composed young man of twenty-four who was about to be awarded a Bachelor of Science degree in Engineering and then cast loose into what college graduates used to think of as a harsh, cold, unaccommodating world. Our man, to whom we shall refer discreetly, and pseudonymously, as David Murray, had already decided on his postgraduate career. On June 16th, after a week's idling, he was going to work, at a salary of three hundred and sixty-eight dollars a month, for the du Pont Company, at the big hydrogen-bomb plant in South Carolina that du Pont is building for the government. He accepted that position—and if you don't think "accepted" is the right word, just wait—on April 9th. Since then, he has been kept busy advising fifteen other importunate corporations that he is sorry but he can't see his way clear to entering their employ. The applicants he has been constrained to turn down—ten of them made him definite offers and five of them tentative offers—are Colgate-Palmolive-Peet, United States Steel, Westinghouse, the Hughes Tool Company, Otis Elevator, Chase Brass & Copper, Continental Can, Eastman Kodak, Union Carbide & Carbon, the Electro Metallurgical Company, the Brown Instrument Company, Procter & Gamble, Ford, and two divisions of General Electric.

Mr. Murray began thinking of the future last fall, at the start of the academic year. Perhaps telepathically, many of the aforementioned outfits were thinking along similar lines, and they dispatched agents to Columbia to talk to the engineers slated to come up for degrees. "This sort of thing has been going on all over the country this year, I'm told," Murray said. "The competition among these big corporations for people with technical training, like me, has been fantastic, no matter where you stand academically. Scholastically, I guess I rank just about in the middle of our group. I have a B-plus average." Life this term has been one series of interviews after another, not to mention all-expenses-paid trips, to various plants, mills, and branches, that might make even a basketball player envious. Murray spent part of his Christmas vacation at a Procter & Gamble factory in Missouri. "That's what vacations are for," he told us. "Very nice people there. They offered me three hundred and fifty a month, but there were some features I didn't care for. It was a defense-production job—the kind that might run four years, until this war thing eases up, and then I'd be stuck. Of course, they did say that in that event they'd probably find something for me elsewhere in the organization, but I don't particularly like 'probably's."

The starting salaries Mr. Murray was offered ranged from three hundred and four a month (G.E. Manufacturing Services Division) to four hundred and twenty-five (Hughes Tool Company). He was promised no cash bonuses, no automobiles, no girls, no gold-plated slide rules. The Hughes job was the only one he took the initiative in negotiating for. "I saw an ad in the *Columbia Spectator* and applied just for the heck of it," he said. "I never talked to anybody from Hughes. Their offer came by mail. In earlier correspondence, they'd asked me to answer a whole lot of questions, and I hadn't bothered with all of them, so when they came after me anyway, I got the feeling they'd have hired *any*body. Ford offered me a job at three-sixty, by telephone. U.S. Steel bid three-twenty-five about the time I gave the nod to du Pont. I was in the middle of a series of interviews with Continental Can then, too. Nice outfit, but too much travelling involved. Westinghouse wanted me to study for nine months, but, frankly, I've had enough school for a while. Otis Elevator wanted me to work in a factory upstate, in— Gee, I can't remember offhand just where. I visited the du Pont people in Washington in March. They struck me as extremely efficient—they and Procter & Gamble. Du Pont knew what they wanted, and they have an automatic review of your salary every six months. How you make out there depends on what you do, rather than luck. I'm not afraid of getting along in a giant organization. I investigated all these places pretty thoroughly before I made up my mind. First, I weeded out the undesirables, and then the just fairs. When I wrote all the others saying I couldn't come in with them, I made a point of not insulting them. You never know, after all, when you may be looking for a job. Oh, incidentally, I did visit one factory—Johnson & Johnson—where I didn't get a definite offer. They just said they'd put my name on a list. But they were only talking in terms of three hundred, so I didn't care much."

June 14, 1952

Notes and Comment

The vet says our dog's tonsils are badly inflamed, and he has instructed us to take her to the hospital, after resting her at home for ten days and dosing her with some pills, for a tonsillectomy. Coming on top of the protracted and costly interneship at our place of a team of young tree surgeons, this latest medical responsibility, which our lawyer doubts is tax-deductible, obliges us to postpone for another six months the capping of a tooth (our own) that our dentist is eager to get his hands on. It seems to us that in our childhood pets and trees didn't run up the whopping doctors' bills they do now. They were pretty much expected to look after their own health, barring some major accident like eating glass or being struck by lightning. Now they appear to be in the same frail fix we are. It's only a question of time, we suppose, before some enterprising insurance man will come up with an animal-health or tree-health policy, affording people like us, for a modest monthly premium, protection against the indispositions of dog or dogwood. In our present mood, we'd sign up in a jiffy. We only hope our trees can pass the physical.

It used to be thought that life in the country was healthier, for the non-human as well as the human, than life in the city. An urban executive we know who has a terrace outside his office was recently presented with a young willow tree by a suburban acquaintance. It was a spindly little tree, bent over at a grotesque angle, and without a trace of green on its branches. Torn from its familiar mooring in the earth and perched nineteen stories above street level in a confining wooden tub, the willow looked to be in bad, if not moribund, shape. But a couple of weeks of bracing city air have done wonders for it; its trunk is straighter, its limbs are more robust, its head is crowned with leaves.

June 21, 1952

Notes and Comment

It has been our custom to make a dispassionate, comprehensive analysis of the political situation just before Election Day each fall, as a service to those of our readers who may be confused by all they hear and read elsewhere, but in view of the current hoopla over the Presidential nominations, we have decided to jump in and do our clarifying now. To take first things first, the choice of a Republican standard-bearer may well be determined by the votes on and of the delegates from the South, a section of the country in which nobody realized, until recently, there were any Republicans. Senator Taft's boosters have complained that many of the Southern Republicans partial to Eisenhower are really Democrats who are unsportingly trying to crash the Grand Old Party. Taft himself has stated that if he is elected, he will appoint to his Cabinet two Dixiecrats, who would presumably be known as Dixiepublicans, or, for short, Dixiecups. Keep your eye on Texas.

Taft has been widely accused, by partisans of Ike, of planning to capture the nomination by means of a steam roller, a machine the Eisenhower people claim was invented by the Senator's father, during the 1912 Republican Convention, to flatten Roughriders. The Taft people accuse the Eisenhower people of having themselves used a steam roller in New Jersey. The Russians say they invented the steam roller. *Pravda* has examined the candidates of both major parties and appears to be for Justice Douglas, who does not appear to be a candidate. Justice Douglas is for justice. Paul Douglas is for the United States Marines. Henry Ford is for Eisenhower. General Motors is for Chevrolet. Red Grange is for Taft. So is Mrs. Preston Davie, who on November 2, 1936, asserted that there was only one day left to elect a Republican and save the American way of life. Syngman Rhee is for Syngman Rhee. Mississippi is the state to watch.

Eisenhower and Taft are both fond of golf, but they haven't played much lately, and certainly not in the same foursome. Julius Boros, the new Open champion, is uncommitted. The last President to play golf while holding office was Warren G. Harding, against whom the Democrats have been ardently campaigning ever since. The Republicans are campaigning against Felix Frankfurter, who put the New Deal through law school. Taft says that Eisenhower is a New Deal Republican and that he, Taft, is the No Deal candidate. Eisenhower says *he* is the No Deal candidate. Taft and Eisenhower, while seeing eye to eye on the undesirability of deals, do not agree on how much money should be appropriated to help our allies. At the moment, near as we can make out, Eisenhower believes we are spending too much and should slash the national budget by forty billion dollars; Taft thinks Eisenhower's attitude is far too tightfisted. We live in a topsy-turvy world. To bridge one major gulf between the two principal Republican camps, John Foster Dulles has been drafted to draft the foreign-policy plank of the Party's platform. Dulles is a Dewey man. Dewey is an Eisenhower man. Eisenhower is a man from Abilene. Abilene is in Kansas, the home of Alf Landon, whose campaign manager was John D.M. Hamilton, who is currently one of Taft's strategists. Pennsylvania could be the state that turns the tide. Eisenhower is not quite certain whether he is for or against federal ownership of tidelands. Tidelands are one of the things he is being educated about. He does know about the Taft-Hartley Act, and he is for that, more or less. Hartley is for Taft. Eisenhower says his brother Milton is the one in the family who has all the brains. Milton has no delegates yet, but who can tell? Keep your eye on Milton. Milton is a college president, as is Dwight, as is Harold Stassen. Who in the world is running the colleges these days? Louisiana could be decisive.

The Republicans have all the generals, or at least all the generals who seem to want to be had. Oddly, though, the Democrats have no admirals. Politically, it has been a terrible year for admirals, many of whom have been landlocked at Panmunjom. The Democrats are resolutely united against Herbert Hoover, but otherwise their convention looks to be wide open, with Nancy Kefauver, Marie Harriman, and Jane Barkley among the more serious contenders. Senator Russell is a bachelor, but he has an eighty-four-year-old mother, who cannot be discounted. Alben Barkley, with seventy-four years, is running slightly ahead of General MacArthur, who is on inactive active unassigned assignment, which the Army interprets to mean he may keep his uniform on or take it off, depending on the humidity. One Count is a dark horse. The Democrats once had a prospective candidate named Kerr, but he seems to have got mislaid somewhere. Organized labor is beating the drums for Averell Harriman, who is so wealthy he can buy drums for everybody in the house. Harriman says he is the Democrat who can surely beat Eisenhower, and he ought to know, since Eisenhower is a good friend of his. Harriman, running on a strong pro-F.E.P.C. platform, won the primary in Washington, D.C., a Southern-type community, from Senator Kefauver, a Southerner. This was regarded as quite significant, even though nobody in Washington, D.C., is allowed to vote in a national election. Kefauver has corralled the most delegates so far, a considerable achievement in view of the fact that his kids have had the mumps. Adlai Stevenson, who may or may not be a candidate, has been feeling ill, and no wonder. The Virgin Islands could swing it one way or the other.

June 28, 1952

Three Cheers For The Blue, White, And Red

Of all the Americans whose eyes grow bright and whose pulses quicken at the sight of the Stars and Stripes and the sound of "The Star-Spangled Banner," none reacts to either patriotic stimulus more briskly than a retired advertising man named Gridley Adams, a chipper, outspoken, egocentric, and contentious old gentleman who for the better part of the last thirty years has carried on an impassioned, public love affair with the flag of the United States of America. Adams, who will be eighty-five next month, has been chairman of the National Flag Code Committee since 1924, and in 1946 founded the United States Flag Foundation, of which he is director-general, as well as sole active and supporting member. Both are conspicuously one-man organizations whose present headquarters are a four-room apartment Adams and his eighty-year-old wife, whom he married in 1898, occupy in Peter Cooper Village. Adams believes firmly and unshakably that he is the best-informed person around on the correct handling of and proper attitude toward The Flag. (To his mind, these last two words should always be capitalized when they appear in sequence.) Some of the proprieties he advocates are so finical, and so remote from common usage, that in the course of proclaiming his ardor for the flag he occasionally gives the impression that he not only regards it as his truest love but also regards himself as its only true lover. Although he has found himself at frequent and disputatious odds with other flag authorities, his own appraisal of his eminence in this field has been endorsed by such sentinels of the flag as the editors of the *American Legion Magazine*, who stated in their columns ten years ago, "Gridley Adams knows more about displaying the United States Flag than any other living person." As far back as 1929, Adams was characterized by the New York *Evening Post* as the Watchdog of the Flag, and more recently he has been hailed by *Town & Village*, a community weekly put out for residents of Peter Cooper and Stuyvesant Town, as Mr. Flag.

Nearly all Americans stand up, most of them at some approximation of attention, when they are in the vicinity of a band playing "The Star-Spangled Banner." Some of them may possibly know some of the words. Adams, a slight, white-haired, white-mustached man who holds himself unusually straight even when he is at ease and who knows all the words of all the verses, draws himself rigidly upright whenever he hears the national anthem from any source, including the loudspeaker of a household radio. It is of no concern to him that the National Americanism Commission of the American Legion holds such private gestures of respect to be supererogatory. Discussing the matter with Adams one day, an acquaintance of his remarked that he would feel silly rising to his feet every time "The Star-Spangled Banner" was wafted into a room where he was sitting alone. "Imagine demonstrating your patriotism only when company is present!" snorted Adams. He advised the man to place a small flag on top of his radio, as an added inducement to exertion whenever the hallowed notes emerged. Adams is aware that his viewpoint is unconventional. "I guess I'm a crank," he said cheerfully a while ago. "I guess I'm just a crazy nut about the flag."

Many Americans believe that it doesn't much matter how casually they treat their flag, provided they don't treat it with willful disrespect. The late Colonel James A. Moss, the founder and president-general of the United States Flag Association—a now defunct organization—once stated that a sensible policy for any American was to handle the flag as he would his mother's picture. "You wouldn't leave your mother's picture on the hood or back of a car, or soil it, or put it on the floor, or leave it out all night in the rain," he said. Adams, an old-fashioned type who uses a straight razor and wears spats, is a strong believer in respectfulness (he once threatened to cane a stranger for edging a lady out of a seat on a streetcar), but when it comes to complying with the federal and state statutes that relate to the flag, he is inclined to place the letter of the law above the spirit of it. As he roams observantly about New York or pores over newspaper and magazine illustrations, he is continually saddened and enraged to find evidences of indifference to or maltreatment, witting or unwitting, of the flag. He is at once moved to write indignant and admonitory letters to the parties he considers culpable. He does not give a hoot who the parties may be. One of his biggest and most comprehensive barrages was fired in 1938. It is wrong for the flag to be allowed to touch the ground or to be used decoratively, and specifically wrong for it to be draped over a monument that is to be unveiled (although it is right for it to be draped over a casket in a military funeral). In 1938, a monument so veiled was dedicated at Gettysburg in honor of the soldiers of both the Union and the Confederate Armies. Among those who participated in the ceremonies were President Roosevelt and representatives of the American Legion, the Daughters of the American Revolution, and the Sons of the American Revolution. Adams cut out a newspaper photograph of the scene, embellished it with an acid caption of his own, had the composite photostatted, and sent copies to several hundred people on his mailing list, as an example of a real horror. "What a shame that what foreign nations have never succeeded in doing—bringing Old Glory to earth—it remained for a group of patriotic (???) Americans to accomplish!" he wrote. "Patriotism—what crimes are committed in your name!"

Adams has written a good many exhortatory tracts on Old Glory. "The Flag is not just a piece of bright material," he declared in one. "It is the Symbol of a great Nation. It deserves to be displayed correctly, reverently. . . . The National Flag represents the living country and is itself considered a living thing . . . every star a tongue, every stripe articulate." Now and then, apparently feeling that the flag and its appurtenances, however vocal, are nonetheless illiterate, Adams undertakes to serve as their amanuensis. He once wrote the owners of a Manhattan office building a letter signed "Your two naked flagstaffs." It began, "We are a couple of stouthearted staffs . . ." The signatories went on to complain that all the other staffs in their neighborhood were happily adorned with flags but that they, alas, were bare and fretful. A few days later, Adams was delighted to see that the two staffs had flags on them. "A keen eye might have detected on the faces of those spherical staffheads an expression akin to a smile," he observed in a follow-up letter of commendation, which he signed with his own name.

Adams not only has detected in flags and flagstaffs all kinds of animate traits that might elude people with less acute aural and visual faculties, but he has found that mere propinquity to a flag or a flagstaff can give the power of speech to other normally inanimate objects. Years ago, after visiting a memorial to Alexander Hamilton in Weehawken, near where Hamilton duelled with Aaron Burr, Adams disclosed in a letter to the *Hudson Dispatch*, the morning daily that serves Weehawken, that he had heard a muted voice and had seen the lips of the bust of Hamilton move. "Here at my back is a flagstaff as bare as Eve before her fall," Adams quoted the statue as saying. "Where, oh where, has vanished the spirit of patriotism that once was so manifest?" Adams offered to buy the neglected, disillusioned staff from Weehawken and give it a decent home, but his proposition was ignored. Mrs. Adams grew up in Weehawken, and Adams has closely followed that city's behavior toward the flag, and especially toward the one that flies—or, as the case may be, doesn't fly—at Hamilton's back. In 1935, a new bust of Hamilton was installed at the memorial, and Adams read in the *Dispatch* that the dedication ceremonies were to be supervised by the Molly Pitcher Chapter of the Daughters of the Revolution, with assistance from some Boy Scouts, and that a flag was to be employed as a veil. On the day of the event, Adams betook himself to the scene, uninvited but resolute. "I listened to a namesake of Hamilton's, this Hamilton Fish, give a rasp of a political speech," Adams told a friend later, "and then the flag was hoisted from its lowly and humiliating position by three Eagle Scouts, no less. After the ceremony was over, I stood up. I told those three Eagle Scouts they had violated their Scout oath by debasing the flag, and I said to those Daughters, 'Molly Pitcher would have been insulted if she could have seen you sitting here permitting the flag she loved to be desecrated. You ought to change the name of your chapter.' A policeman came up to me and said, 'Who are you?' I told him, 'I'm the chairman of the National Flag Code Committee, and I have a right to speak here,' and he walked away. Boy! Do I sometimes feel I'm too militant, but hell and damnation, when you're fighting for the flag with your voice, you've got to fight as hard as though you were fighting for it with a gun."

Adams wages the battle less often in person than through the mails. "On my desk are two inkwells," he likes to say. "One contains ink and the other vitriol." Actually, this statement is hyperbolic, since he attends to all his correspondence on a portable typewriter, using the index finger of his right hand. The impact of the letters he writes is heightened by his letterheads, which are splendid, multicolored printing jobs embellished with a picture of the flag and with many illustrious and patriotic names, a few of them slightly misspelled. Those listed on his Flag Foundation stationery include General Douglas MacArthur (Honorary Chairman); Sergeant Alvin C. York (National Chairman); James A. Farley, William Green, and Gene Tunney (among a twenty-two-man advisory committee); and the Honorable Herbert Hoover, Captain E. V. Rickenbacker, the Honorable Harold R. Medina, General Lucius D. Clay, General William J. Donovan, Governor Thomas E. Dewey, Gilbert Grosvenor, and George E. Sokolsky (among thirty-seven members-at-large). Adams got them all to serve by writing to them, but he

175

has never called a meeting of the Foundation in its six years of existence, and is unacquainted with the majority of its sponsors.

Every so often, someone who has heard of Adams consults him before embarking on an enterprise involving the flag. Several years ago, for instance, he was asked to look over and authenticate, prior to publication, a magazine article on flag etiquette written by Emily Post. Adams says he fixed up a couple of breaches of etiquette in it, but he chivalrously professes not to recall what they were. On another occasion, a playing-card manufacturer sought Adams' opinion of the design of a new deck he was planning to bring out, which had the flag on the back of the cards. Adams, knowing that the flag is not supposed to be used for commercial gain, entered the manufacturer's office with stern visage. Grabbing a sample deck, he licked his thumb and began to deal. Suddenly he paused. "How does it strike you to see me smear the flag of the United States of America with a wet thumb?" he demanded. The manufacturer, abashed, promised not to distribute any of the cards and expose the flag to further such indignity.

Usually, Adams offers his advice without being asked. He has plenty of opportunities to do so, inasmuch as few people know the rights and wrongs pertaining to the flag. For one thing, a lot of people are unaware that when the flag is hung vertically, the union, or canton (the blue part with the stars), must be at the flag's own right, or at the observer's left—in other words, that the flag must not be simply tipped over from its conventional horizontal position. According to heraldry, the flag's own right-hand, or dexter, portion is the traditional area of honor. This goes back to the days of chivalry, when a knight's sword arm was his strong and honorable one, and, by extension, the right side of anything he was concerned with was the honorable side. (There appears to have been no provision in heraldry for left-handed knights.) Simply tipping a flag over would put the union at the flag's left, or sinister, or dishonorable, side. "You'd be surprised how many supposedly patriotic citizens aren't familiar with the implications of dexter and sinister," Adams told a friend a while back. "The apathy shown the Stars and Stripes is woeful beyond measure."

Ignoramuses are also wont to torture the flag into odd shapes for what they believe to be decorative purposes. "A few years ago, the more one could tie it into rosettes and twist it and festoon it," Adams has written, "the greater was considered one's respect for it." To impress on such sinners the outrageousness of their ways, Adams once had a picture of Abraham Lincoln, for whom he has vast respect, painted on a small square of cloth. Whenever he encountered somebody who had twisted a flag in the pursuit of art, he would haul out his Lincoln portrait and twist *it* grotesquely. "That doesn't show very much respect for Lincoln, does it?" he would ask. Adams has browsed extensively in Lincolniana and has become convinced that

Raymond Massey and other contemporary declaimers of the Gettysburg Address have been reading their lines all wrong. "Lincoln didn't say, 'government *of* the people, *by* the people, and *for* the people,'" he maintains. "He said, 'government of the *people*, by the *people*, and for the *people*.' I once ran into a fellow who said he had a friend who had heard Lincoln at Gettysburg and who recollected that Lincoln did not make a prepositional speech."

Among the crimes recurrently committed in the name of patriotism are the imprinting of handkerchiefs and napkins with the flag, the use of a worn-out flag as a horse blanket or slipcover (a worn-out one should be burned, in a dignified manner), the collecting of money in the flag (it should never be used as a receptacle), the placing of the flag so that other nations' flags are to its own right or above it (they should be to its left or at a lower level), and the crossing of two American flags (which puts one of them in the inferior, sinister position). Adams got the American Red Cross to revise its 1948 fund-raising campaign poster when he discovered that the artist's sketch, showing three flags on a lamppost, had two Red Cross flags inclined toward the dexter and a United States flag toward the sinister. A few of the indignities to which the flag is subjected have become so well established by time and precedent that not even Adams has much hope of eliminating them. "Take the Masons," he said recently. "The Masons cover a table with the flag and lay a Bible on top of it. Wrong. [So is Adams. The Masons are international and don't use anybody's flag in their ritual.] Nothing may be placed on the flag. But you can't ask the Masons to change, after a hundred years, any more than you can ask the Elks to substitute something seemly for their emblem, which superimposes an elk and a clock on the United States flag. Wrong. Absolutely wrong. A distinguished Elk—he was a Past Exalted Ruler—once said to me, 'Adams, I know we're wrong, but if I tried to do anything about it, it would cause an earthquake from coast to coast. I'd be kicked in the pants if I advocated anything like that.' Boy! Boy!"

Adams spends a good deal of his time chiding individuals or groups who superimpose words or pictures on the flag or on a likeness of the flag. (For that matter, he is equally critical of the superimposition of the flag on anything else, and he registered a vigorous protest with the Columbia Broadcasting System several months ago because, in a televised broadcast of a boxing match, it had allowed the ring to be seen through the diaphanous folds of a flag. The next time he tuned in on the fights, he was gratified to note the absence of this irregularity.) He does not let personal considerations interfere with his principles. Last year, in a nationwide pro-Americanism competition, he was awarded a hundred dollars for an anti-Communist editorial he had written in 1950 for a weekly newspaper published near Mahopac, where the Adamses' only child, Mrs. J. Brooks Emory, Jr., lives with her husband, a vice-president of Young & Rubicam, and their seven-year-old son. The sponsors of the competition, a pro-American organization called the Freedoms Foundation, concurrently bestowed a non-monetary award upon the producers of a patriotic movie short. Adams admired the movie and the sentiments behind it, but because its title and various screen credits were flashed against a flag background, he felt obliged to castigate severely the judges of the competition, among whom were the heads of ten patriotic groups with whose policies and activities he is generally in enthusiastic accord. Adams has a terribly low personal opinion of General Eisenhower for a somewhat similar reason—specifically, because the General once autographed the flag. In 1944, just after the invasion of Normandy, a veteran of the First World War living in Brooklyn sent Eisenhower a flag with the sentimental request that he sign it and fly it in liberated France that Fourth of July. The flag didn't arrive in time for that, but Eisenhower did arrange for it to be flown over Cherbourg on Bastille Day. The Mayor of Cherbourg then autographed it and stamped it with his municipal seal, after which Eisenhower appended his signature and returned it to its owner, who proudly exhibited his singular trophy to the press. Adams was shocked. "It didn't matter so much about that French Mayor," he says, "because it wasn't *his* flag. But what Eisenhower did is a clear violation of the law, and you can't make up for a thing like that by apologizing that you didn't mean any harm. Oh, the alibis I've had! Oh, I've been fighting this thing to beat the band! You have to fight it! Boy! Boy!"

Adams does not confine his interest in patriotic matters to the flag. Up to a year ago, he persistently tilted at the Girl Scouts of America, whose annual custom it has long been to raise funds by selling cookies embossed with part of the great seal of the United States, which is part of their organizational insignia. Adams contended that this constituted a great affront to the great seal, and he told the Girl Scouts so several times. He told them also that it was illegal. In 1951, perhaps weary of being chivied by Adams, the Girls got a law passed by Congress permitting them to use their insignia, seal and all, on cookies and other merchandise they sell. Part of the obverse of the unexceptionable, inedible seal is the shield of the United States—it appears across the body of the eagle clutching the olive branch and arrows—and its peculiar characteristics have also provided Adams with much scope for activity. Unlike the flag, with its seven red stripes and six white ones, the shield has seven white and six red. Moreover, its upper, blue portion has no stars. Practically *everybody* goes wrong on the shield. It is particularly dismaying to Adams, who cannot abide irresponsibility in high places, that even a President's wife, Mrs. Coolidge, was thrown by it. She once embroidered a bedspread for the Lincoln Room of the White House, artfully working into her design nine shields, grouped around a great seal. All are inaccurate portrayals. Not only did she get her stripes reversed in the shields, but in depicting the eagle on the seal, she put the arrows in the dexter talon and the olive branch in the sinister talon, instead of the other way around, and she made it three arrows instead of the correct thirteen.

Whenever Adams gets to brooding about the shield, he becomes even more annoyed with manufacturers of flags and shields than with Mrs. Coolidge. A few years ago, passing the Fifth Avenue store of Annin & Co., the country's oldest firm of flagmakers, he glanced at a show window and was appalled to see a two-foot-high cloth shield that was spattered with stars and had red stripes predominating. "I stepped inside and asked a salesman what that object in the window was," Adams says. "'Don't you know the United States shield?' he asked me. 'I sure do when I see one,' I said, and I walked out." Annin & Co. know the shield, too, actually, but while they make correct shields for government use, for civilian customers they deliberately make the kind that infuriates Adams. "We like the shield that way," one Annin executive explained recently to another passerby who stopped in. "The official shield looks like a mistake. It looks like a barber pole. We make a shield that looks like the flag. If you put our shield next to the correct one, ninety-nine out of a hundred people would pick ours as the correct one. If we put white stripes on the outside, and left off the stars, people would say, 'That's a cockeyed way to make a shield.' Who are we to stop people from getting what they want?" Adams is further embittered by flag manufacturers who bedeck flags with gold fringe and tassels, even though he admits that this is not a violation of anything and that there is sound precedent for it, since in ancient times wives and other lady camp followers of soldiers in the field used to occupy idle moments by prettying up their menfolk's colors. The Annin people say they are partial to fringe and tassels because such accoutrements set off a flag as a frame sets off a painting. Adams is unaffected by this argument. "The flag needs no passementerie," he says. "Flag designers put on those gewgaws—all that fringe and those tassels—just to add ten or fifteen dollars to the price of a flag. Those manufacturers don't know about the flag. They don't give a rap about the flag. They're in business, that's all. They remind me of the tailor who persuaded a woman to buy a two-pants suit to have her husband buried in, because it was a bargain. Oh, human nature is a funny thing!"

Still another of Adams' peeves is the widespread use of the phrase "red, white, and blue," which has been solidly entrenched in the American vocabulary ever since—if not before—an English actor named Thomas à Becket gave three cheers for it in "Columbia, the Gem of the Ocean," which he composed during a visit to Philadelphia in 1843. Adams maintains that a transient alien should not have the last word on so consequential a matter, and that the lyrics are grievously in error, because the order should be "blue, white, and red." Blue, he contends, not only is assigned the position of honor on the dexter side of the flag but, in the heraldic scheme of things,

179

ranks in importance just behind gold and silver; white before red, he says, is "traditional." Heraldry is a misty and mysterious science, full of inconsistencies, and as a result the question can perhaps never be unequivocally settled. This country's most renowned flag authority, the late Admiral George Henry Preble, in his massive "Our Flag: Origin and Progress of the Flag of the United States of America," published in 1872, agrees with Adams that blue should precede red, but he also says that the sequence in America should be "blue, red, and white." However, since all heraldic scholars rate white not as a real color but as equal to silver (as yellow is to gold), and since some heraldic scholars rank metals above colors, a case could be made for saying "white, blue, and red," if anybody wanted to make such a case. For that matter, a case could be made for "red, blue, and white," since on the letterhead of the United States Flag Foundation, which is printed on white paper, the name of the organization is in blue except for the initial letters, which are red.

In any event, Adams has crusaded lustily, and with some success, for "blue, white, and red." In 1934, when airmail service was reorganized in the United States and special collection boxes were set up around the nation, they were painted with stripes of red, white, and blue, with the red uppermost. Adams protested to Postmaster General Farley, and the boxes were repainted, with blue on top and red demoted to the bottom. Adams also got the stripes changed around on the Freedom Train of a few years back, after they had been painted on in what to him was reverse order, by protesting to the president of the Pennsylvania Railroad, which had fitted out the train. A while ago, attending an outdoor patriotic rally, Adams spotted a Daughter of Something-or-Other who was wrapped in a broad tricolor sash with the red at the top. "I went up to her and I said, 'Turn that over! You ought to know that blue comes first!'" Adams says. "She was shamefaced and said, 'Oh, the wind must have blown it around.' Golly, how some people hate to be told!"

July 5, 1952

From a Profile

Cockers

Senator Nixon's reference to Checkers, his children's black-and-white cocker spaniel, may have made most of the country cocker-spaniel-conscious these past few exhilarating weeks, but it doesn't appear to have had any pronounced effect on the cocker-spaniel world. We learned this the other day—not, unfortunately, from a cocker spaniel but from perhaps the next best source, Mr. Clark C. Thompson, who is chairman of the executive committee of the American Spaniel Club and a cocker fancier from way back. "I've been to two shows since Mr. Nixon's speech," Mr. Thompson told us, "and I didn't hear a word about his dog, or, for that matter, about him. With dogs, politics is never discussed." As a consequence, Mr. Thompson went on, he was unable to say with any assurance whether the Senator could be assumed to have the cocker-spaniel vote, or the votes of cocker-spaniel owners, in his pocket. "I would hesitate to state, however," Mr. Thompson added, measuring his words carefully, "that the Senator's gesture will be wholly without influence. He'll probably get all the wavering ones."

Mr. Thompson heard the celebrated Nixon speech over the radio. "When Nixon mentioned his cocker spaniel, it made me prick up my ears," he said. "I liked his little touch when he said he was going to keep the dog, regardless. Anybody who feels that way about cocker spaniels must be a good man." A day or so later, Mr. Thompson scrutinized a photograph of Nixon's dog he saw in the papers, and concluded that Checkers is a presentable enough specimen of the breed. "Of course, the picture I saw wasn't properly posed," Mr. Thompson said, "but I would say from looking at its head that it is a good cocker. It's certainly no mutt; it looks like a purebred to me." These days, a purebred cocker-spaniel puppy, he informed us, usually sells for between thirty-five and fifty dollars. Checkers is a perfectly suitable name for a black-and-white cocker, Mr. Thompson said, but not original. There's a well-known champion, out in Toledo, called Bar-Nan Checkers.

Cocker spaniels, we learned further from Mr. Thompson, are at present the most popular breed of dog in the United States, and have been for a generation. (A magazine called *Popular Dogs* devoted most of its September issue this year to cockers, which it hailed as "the popular choice for old and young alike." The issue went to press before Mr. Nixon's speech; just one of those coincidences.) Nowadays, more than twenty-five thousand purebred cocker pups are registered annually with the American Kennel Club, and this almost certainly doesn't include the entire national litter. Even so, Mr. Thompson is of the view that the breed isn't enjoying quite the countrywide favor that it did during the golden era of cockerdom, which he told us was roughly from 1925 to 1945. Those were the days of Flush, Katharine Cornell's co-player in "The Barretts of Wimpole Street." (Cockers are great dogs for flushing game out of hiding places, and they were recruited during the Second World War to detect enemy mines.) Those were the days, too, of Ch. My Own Brucie, the winningest cocker of them all, who took best-in-show at Morris & Essex in 1939 and at Westminster in both 1940 and 1941. My Own Brucie, an all-black cocker, was the youngest offspring of Red Brucie, a renowned sire who was, in turn, the son of Ch. Robinhurst Foreglow, who belonged to Justice Townsend Scudder, who presided at the

Snyder-Gray trial. It's strange how cocker spaniels do get involved in the sweep of history.

The American Spaniel Club has around five hundred members, Mr. Thompson told us, among them owners of cockers, springers, clumbers, Sussexes, and the rest. It's one of the oldest dog clubs in the country, having been founded in 1881 and antedating the American Kennel Club itself by three years. Senator Nixon has not yet joined the Spaniel Club, but President Truman is an honorary member, as the result of someone's presenting *him* with a cocker spaniel shortly after he took office. Truman proceeded to give his cocker away, which may prove to have been a ghastly political blunder. Cockers are said by some to have come to America on the Mayflower, as befits a breed with such distinguished associations. They can also trace their heritage back to one of the early Dukes of Marlborough, who bred spaniels for hunting on his grounds, and developed the Blenheim spaniel from a cross between a cocker and a dwarf-spaniel breed. This would seem to give Senator Nixon something in common with Winston Churchill, who, moreover, has the use of an official country home called Chequers.

October 11, 1952

Are Ducks Deductible?

Most rural homeowners have some ornament on their property—an ancient tree, a climbing rose, a Dutch oven, or whatever—of which they are especially fond. What my wife and I dote upon are the wild ducks on our pond. There is nothing terribly distinctive about the pond itself, aside from the fact that its banks, once smooth and velvety, are now pitted with treacherous holes, as the result of a family of muskrats dwelling there, uninvited, during most of last winter. But the ducks, to us, are something special. Almost every day there are a few of them swimming about on the pond or, depending on the weather, sunning themselves at the water's edge, where the muskrats used to burrow. It has become a household ritual for us and our two older boys, upon arising, to rush to a window and count the ducks with which that particular dawn has blessed us. This routine has helped the boys, aged five and three and a half, with their arithmetic. They can count ducks like nobody's business. Quite some time ago, Joey, the younger of the two, while still unable to tot up all his own fingers, could count up to fourteen ducks, the maximum we have ever spotted at once.

Joey receives no formal instruction in mathematics at the nursery school he attends, but he evidently counts ducks there, too, or reports on ducks he has counted at home before breakfast. At any rate, his teacher, whom I shall call Miss Dillon, informed his mother and me not long ago that she, and her class, had heard so much about the ducks on Joey's pond that she would like to bring the whole group over someday for a spell of duck-watching. It would make an estimable field trip for the children, she said. My wife and I, agreeably flattered, said that that would be fine, and that all she had to do was let us know when; one or the other of us (I work at home a good deal) would undoubtedly be available to run over to school in the station wagon and pick up the gang. We advised Miss Dillon that if the children were real lucky, they might even get to see our dog, a Labrador retriever, plunge into the pond and swim after the ducks, as she does interminably. The ducks let her get to within about ten feet of them, and then they fly serenely to another part of the pond, a hundred feet or so away, and settle down again. The dog thereupon shifts her course and paddles vigorously toward them until, when she is once more within a few feet of them, they languidly fly to a different spot. This performance sometimes continues for half an hour, at the end of which the dog gets tired, splashes ashore, comes indoors, and goes to sleep, still pretty wet, on a chair in my study.

The other morning, while my wife was off on an errand and I was somewhat tensely preoccupied with a visitor, an agent of the Bureau of Internal Revenue who had dropped in to chat about an old income-tax return of mine that seemed to be giving him concern, Joey's teacher telephoned. She said that the class was eager to see the ducks, and would it be convenient for my wife or me to come fetch them in fifteen minutes? At that moment, the revenue agent, elbow-deep in check stubs and just beginning to recover from the shock of my having inadvertently offered him a chair that turned out to be a trifle damp, was inquiring patiently but firmly whether I had any evidence beyond my own vague recollection that would tend to prove I had ever taken a party of four business acquaintances to dinner and "Guys and Dolls." He had already asked a lot of probing questions about similar deductions I had claimed, with a persistence I could not help admiring. I never knew a man to go on so about deductibility! Anyway, grateful for Miss Dillon's interruption, I asked her to hold on a minute, and then asked the agent—I'll call him Mr. Thomas hereafter— whether he'd mind if I took an hour or so out to show our ducks to my second dependent's classmates. He replied that he and I had so much ground still to cover in the general area of deductibility, or non-deduct- ibility, that an hour or so couldn't make much difference one way or the other. My study opens onto a lawn some fifty feet from the pond, and, glancing out a window, I saw six sleek, handsome ducks cruising leisurely across its surface, while a black retriever's head moved doggedly toward them. I told Miss Dillon I'd be right over, and I invited Mr. Thomas, during my absence, to avail himself, if he cared to, of a nearby bookshelf.

It was a chilly, blustery day, and after I reached the school, it took Miss

Dillon and her assistant several minutes to get Joey and his classmates, a dozen children in all, zipped and buttoned into their snow suits. The delaying tactics of one young boy, named George, were particularly effective; he had got hold of a stick, and as the other children were being urged into their clothes, he kept whacking them about the legs with it. Ultimately, though, the whole crowd was stuffed into the station wagon and we got under way. On arriving back at my place, I began to shepherd the group across the lawn toward the pond. As we neared my study, I saw Mr. Thomas peering at us through a window, and I waved cordially to him. He evidently thought I was summoning him, for he opened an outside door, thus creating a powerful draft. Out toward the pond blew a page of my income-tax return, and out behind it charged Mr. Thomas, uttering cries of alarm. He caught up with the precious, to him, sheet of paper some ten feet short of the water, but his frantic pursuit so alarmed my six ducks that they whirled into the air and took off past a willow tree and far over a meadow.

"There go the ducks!" I shouted, hoping that a few of Joey's classmates would at least get to witness their departure. But the children appeared to be concentrating instead on Mr. Thomas and on our dog, who, her pastime thus summarily halted, was scrambling out of the pond. Tail wagging, she approached Mr. Thomas and shook herself spiritedly, sprinkling him from head to toes.

"Did anybody get to see the ducks?" I called out.

"I did," replied Mr. Thomas, dabbing at himself with a handkerchief. "Nice ducks. You feed 'em?"

"Sometimes we do," I replied. "I don't suppose I could somehow claim—"

"No," he said. "Wild ducks are non-deductible. You run a duck farm, now, that's something else."

Miss Dillon had edged alongside during this exchange, and, understandably bewildered, she said to Mr. Thomas, "Do you run a duck farm?"

"Mr. Thomas is from the Bureau of Internal Revenue," I said. "He's come to see me about one of my tax returns."

"My!" she said, and darted at me a look of such a sort as must have crossed the face of any lady who chanced to be introduced to Al Capone in his declining years.

Meanwhile, young George had picked up a branch broken off the willow tree during a recent storm, and, sensing that he was about to whack Mr. Thomas across the shins with it, I quickly sought to create a diversion. So I pointed dramatically toward one of the gaping holes at the edge of the pond. "We used to have some muskrats living here," I said loudly. "When the pond froze last winter, you could stand on the ice and watch them swimming underfoot."

George and a girl classmate stepped forth to obtain a closeup view of the muskrats' lair. "Watch out for the hole!" Miss Dillon cried, but she was too late. George had spotted it, and he pushed the girl toward it. She tripped in it, pitched forward, and landed on her face, inches from the water. As she was falling, Mr. Thomas leaped gallantly to her aid. The girl proved to be unharmed, though scuffed, but Mr. Thomas, unfortunately, misjudged his distance and went in the water up to his ankles. I felt much as if I had been a party to slapping a cop in the face with a custard pie. Rather unstrung, I expressed my regrets that he'd got his feet soaked, offered him a dry pair of socks, and remarked, nervously, that I hoped any damage he incurred to his clothing in the course of exercising his official duties would be—

"No," said Mr. Thomas curtly. "Laundry and dry cleaning, except in very special circumstances, are non-deductible."

There was a long pause. Presently, Miss Dillon asked me if I thought the ducks would return that day, and when I expressed my doubts, she said she had probably better be getting the kids back to school. I suggested to Mr. Thomas that perhaps he'd like to dry out during my absence, but he allowed that he'd rather leave immediately, and return another day, maybe, when things would be quieter. So I bade him au revoir, loaded the children and their teachers into the station wagon again, and headed for school.

"I'm sorry about the ducks," I said to Miss Dillon as we were driving along.

"Oh, don't you worry. We'll come back some other time," she said consolingly. "It wasn't your fault that that man created such a ruckus. And, no matter what, it was an interesting social experience for the children, visiting your home like this."

I'm glad it was. Next time the kids come, however, I hope I'll have a little advance notice. If I have, I aim to lock the dog in the house, fill in the muskrat holes, and, rather than trust those flighty ducks, scatter some realistic-looking decoys on the pond. I must remember to ask Mr. Thomas, if he ever shows up again, whether decoys purchased on behalf of educational institutions are deductible.

November 15, 1952

No Bullies or Toadies

Hearing of the existence of a local group called the Friends of Frank Merriwell, whose members have banded together out of nostalgic devotion to that famous apostle of Fair Play, we looked up its president, a man named Joseph M. Graham, who works for Equitable Life. The other night, Mr. Graham invited us to attend one of the Friends' monthly meetings, which are held in a private dining room of the Press Box Restaurant, on East

Forty-fifth Street, and before the proceedings got under way, he told us a bit about the outfit. It began slightly over a year ago, when he and a handful of other Merriwell addicts got to reminiscing about their boyhood idol. "It surprised us that no one had ever become a Friend of Merriwell before," Graham said. "Frank Merriwell, I mean. We hate his brother Dick. Anyway we've been an awfully informal outfit. We chugged along very quietly and nicely until someone said, 'Let's have membership cards.' So we got cards, and now we have fifty members, and I don't even know them all. I'm afraid we're going to get even more organized tonight. Somebody's bringing a lawyer."

Mr. Graham showed us a sampling of the mail the Friends had lately received—largely as a result of a mention of the organization in the *Times*, there being several *Times* men among the members. A man in Springfield, Massachusetts, expressing the hope that Burt L. Standish's Frank Merriwell books—out of print since 1934—would soon make a comeback, said, "It would be a great thing for our country. Maybe decency and honor would once again count for something in American life." A lady in Winchester, Virginia, wanted the Friends to know that she had learned to read by borrowing her brother's Frank Merriwells, and, having mastered them, had swiftly gone on to Shakespeare.

Presently, the meeting began, with fourteen Friends on hand, all of them well past boyhood. Mr. Graham, seated beside us, rapped for attention. "We meet in the name of Frank Merriwell," he intoned solemnly. "Hear! Hear!" murmured the assemblage. A waiter brought a round of drinks. We asked Mr. Graham, in a whisper, if Frank himself ever touched the stuff. "He gambled," said Graham. "His hands trembled with excitement just at the thought of poker. He *must* have drunk." The Friend on our other side, a *Times* man, confided to us that as a youth he often had lumps on his head, inflicted by his mother in an effort, obviously vain, to wean him away from Frank Merriwell. "Frank had a friend who could suspend the law of gravity," he told us gravely. Mr. Graham asked for a report from the book-finding committee, which turned out to be another *Times* man. The committee observed glumly that the Friends possessed not a single copy of a Merriwell book. (Over a hundred million copies have been published.) "Yale University is lousy with Merriwells," the committee said. "I understand somebody left Yale a set of two hundred and seventy in his will. Maybe we could get those, because I don't think Yale much likes the idea of being associated with Frank." "Snobs!" cried a voice downtable. Mr. Graham was instructed to write a polite letter of inquiry to Yale.

"Now, about the question of being properly organized," broke in a man at the end of the table, who we quickly gathered was the lawyer. "First of all, we'll need a person of permanent address to give summonses to."

"If we could get people to return to Frank Merriwell," said Graham nervously, "maybe we could lick the comic books."

"I'm a bachelor. I don't give a hoot what the kids read," said the lawyer. "Now, it will cost you sixty dollars to incorporate. Unless maybe you'd prefer something along the lines of a joint-venture setup."

"Let's have a quiz," said Graham hastily. He read off ten questions from a paper, including "As a baseball pitcher, what puzzling delivery did Frank have?" (Ans.: Double shoot), and "Who was old Joe Crowfoot?" (Ans.: Indian who reared Frank). The replies were hurled back confidently from all sides.

"I would suggest that there have to be certain provisions made whether you incorporate or not," the lawyer was saying. "You have to protect yourselves. There are a lot of ramifications."

"I sure would like to get us some turtleneck sweaters and bulldogs," said Graham.

"It would be advisable, all things considered, for the incorporation papers to be sent at the earliest possible opportunity to the Secretary of State of New York," said the lawyer. "It occurs to me that if no stock issue is involved, perhaps it could be done for forty dollars."

"I would like to have a letterhead with 'No Bullies or Toadies Allowed' on it," said Graham.

"Now, if any of you gentlemen happens to know a Supreme Court justice who is a Frank Merriwell fan . . . " said the lawyer.

"Gee, we're getting organized," said Graham. "I feel terrible."

March 21, 1953

The Tough Guy And The Soft Guy

Unlike American football, which has been blowing hot and cold about the matter in recent years, the American theatre has steadily become more and more a field of action in which the specialist defers to the triple-threat man— so much so, in fact, that nowadays the most successful stage folk are those whose multifarious talents enable them to play both offense and defense, as it were, and coach themselves, too. Howard Lindsay produces, directs, writes, and acts, and Oscar Hammerstein II can, without fumbling, shift from the position of producer to that of writer, lyricist, or music publisher. Joshua Lockwood Logan, a volcanic, flamboyant, and inventive man of forty-four who once played left tackle for Culver Military Academy and is now regarded by both Lindsay and Hammerstein, to mention just two of his admirers, as one of the theatre's most glittering ornaments, is as protean as they come. He is co-producer and co-author, as well as director and choreographer, of "South Pacific," the biggest musical hit of all time. He was co-author and director of "Mister Roberts," one of the biggest non-musical hits of all time. He is co-producer, co-author, co-choreographer, and director of "Wish You Were Here," perhaps the biggest upset in theatrical history. He is merely co-producer and director of "Picnic," the latest presentation to carry his name—or names—but then it is a much more modestly scaled show than most of the productions he has been connected with.

Whereas Lindsay has his Crouse and Hammerstein his Rodgers, Logan is a solo act. Because of his versatility, and the fact that he has been mixed up in quite a few notable Broadway enterprises—among them the original version of "On Borrowed Time," "I Married an Angel," "Knickerbocker Holiday," "Charley's Aunt," "By Jupiter," "Annie Get Your Gun," "Happy Birthday," "John Loves Mary," and "The Wisteria Trees"—it is sometimes contended in theatrical circles that if Logan does not have a partner, then there must be two Logans. Logan himself has provided considerable evidence in substantiation of this theory. He thinks nothing of putting in a full day's work and, on top of it, a full night's work, and of sustaining this vigorous pace for days on end. At times, moreover, he bears little physical resemblance to himself. To be sure, some of his outward characteristics are more or less static—his height, of six feet one inch; his graying hair, thin on top and longish in back; his small gray mustache, which he is forever fingering—but his weight is strikingly inconsistent. While two hundred pounds or slightly thereunder is par for him, he has a tendency toward fatness. Every now and then, when his loosest-fitting suits begin to feel intolerably tight, he combines massive portions of exercise with tiny ones of food, and succeeds in paring himself down by several dozen pounds at a swoop. Then he changes to a set of smaller-size suits, which he holds in readiness for such disciplined interludes. "I have a kind of passion about health," he says. "The subject of fat is almost an obsession with me. I hate it to such a degree that it affects my attitude toward the world. When I lose weight, I'm a different person."

When Logan was in his teens, he took one of Charles Atlas's mail-order courses in body-building, and he has been a fanatic about body-building ever since. A couple of years ago, in deference to the building, or maintenance, of his own body, he cut out smoking and, save for an occasional tumbler of wine, drinking. Nonetheless, his spirits are sometimes so bubbly that even without alcoholic stimulants he gives the impression of being rollickingly drunk. When a show he is concerned with is about to go into rehearsal, he usually spends a few preparatory days at Bill Brown's Health Farm, at Garrison, New York. While chinning himself there one invigorating morning in 1949, he heard that the place was up for sale and slated to be converted into a run-of-the-mill hospital. Along with other clients of the establishment, among them a couple of lawyers and a Chinese restaurateur, Logan thereupon organized a syndicate that bought Brown's and ran it for a while. Logan occasionally drags startled playwrights into Turkish baths for story conferences; during rehearsals of "South Pacific," he engaged a trainer to come to his apartment at seven every morning and lash him through a brisk agenda of calisthenics; and he is probably as acrobatic a director as the theatre can boast. He has been known to direct a scene while standing on the narrow and flimsy arms of an orchestra seat, a balancing trick few human beings can perform even when they are not going through the exertions of ordering actors around.

Logan's respect for professional muscle men was intensified in 1936, while he was on a movie assignment in Hollywood. A couple of his cronies, Henry Fonda and James Stewart, noting that he was rather bloated, persuaded him to enroll in the academy of a physical-culture man they knew. When Logan presented himself there, the trainer appraised him thoughtfully, checked his pores, and said, "Friend, in six weeks I'll have you looking like Nat Pendleton." Logan's face fell. It seemed to him that in Hollywood, of all places, he ought to be able to do better than Nat Pendleton. He backed away, murmuring excuses. "On second thought," the trainer said hastily, "I'll have you looking like Clark Gable." "I'll take the course," said Logan, who then looked, as he has continued to look, somewhat like Alfred Lunt. Recalling the episode recently, Logan said, "In about three months, I was in perfect condition. I could see my stomach muscles. That, to me, is my constant ambition. You could scarcely keep me off the beach. I wanted as many people as possible to see my stomach muscles while they were visible."

Logan's temperament has varied almost as spectacularly as, though not necessarily in direct proportion to, his displacement. In 1941, after exhibiting manic-depressive symptoms that alarmed his family and his friends, he had himself committed for three months to a mental hospital. He was cured of his psychosis, and it has not recurred, but he is still subject to unalarming spells of alternating elation and dejection. The clinical details of this travail were narrated at length, with his approval, in a *Life* article four years ago, and they are still discussed, with animation and candor, by Logan's acquaintances and by Logan himself. Logan is an anomalous character in the world of the theatre in that he usually says exactly what he thinks. One night, during a party at an apartment he occupies in River House, he got to lecturing the British playwright Emlyn Williams, a great friend of his, on how to write plays. Soon afterward, Logan turned to another group and forgot all about the conversation. Williams, however, was offended by what he took to be Logan's gratuitous, as well as blunt, advice. "Emlyn walked out of my place boiling with rage," Logan says. "He was crossing Fifty-second Street, cursing me, when a truck almost ran him down. As he told me afterward, it suddenly occurred to him, 'What would Josh have thought if that truck had hit me? He'd have thought, Emlyn Williams threw himself in front of a truck because I insulted him. Josh would have had another nervous breakdown and got another article about it in *Life*, and that's all he wants, anyway.' So Emlyn crept back to the relative safety of the party. He was damned if he was going to give me that satisfaction."

Ever since childhood, Logan has been vexed by intimations that he is a many-faceted, if not exactly a dual-natured, creature. "There's been a kind of arty thing all through my life that goes along in a parallel line with an attempt not to be arty," he is apt to say in self-analytical moments, or, "There has always been in me a fight between the tough guy and the soft guy." A Surrealist painter who did a portrait of him as a young man depicted him with his heart fully exposed, outside his chest, and with jagged rocks and fierce flames at his back. The soft guy and tough guy inside Logan are now pretty evenly matched, but when he was a child, in the Deep South, the soft guy had the tough one on the ropes most of the time; as a small boy, he was extremely fond of flowers and poetry. In his teens, at Culver, he sought to compensate for his early mushiness by acquiring a veneer of toughness that was conspicuous even in a military academy. He still admires toughness. A young actor aware of this predilection, while trying out for a role in "Picnic" when Logan was casting it last fall, remarked, in an effort to advance his candidacy, "Mr. Logan, I was once a juvenile delinquent." "Maybe so," replied Logan, "but the trouble is it doesn't show any more," and he regretfully dismissed the aspirant. Logan has remained devoted to poetry, and his memory is richly stocked with it. William Blake and Emily Dickinson are the two poets he quotes most, and he is likely to interject fragments of their works into almost any sort of conversation. He once astounded a Rotary Club luncheon audience, before which he had agreed to appear on behalf of Bill Brown's Health Farm, by interpolating a long excerpt from Miss Dickinson into a prose eulogy of pushups and volleyball. During the early stages of his breakdown, while he was under treatment by a New York psychiatrist, Logan's interest in poetry reached new heights. He found that he could memorize long stanzas practically at a glance. His reading at the time was confined almost entirely to "The Oxford Book of English Verse." One day, he composed a long poem, called "Ode to 'The Oxford Book of English Verse' During a Manic Elation," in which he diagnosed his own condition with what appeared to him to be singular wit and grace. He showed it eagerly to his doctor, who read it without cracking a smile. Logan, outraged, abandoned the man in favor of Dr. Merrill Moore, a Bostonian and a psychiatrist who is also a prolific composer of verse and is known in some lay circles as "the galloping sonneteer." Dr. Moore read Logan's lines and was moved to gratifying bursts of laughter. "This is great!" he said when he had finished. "You ought to send it to the *Atlantic Monthly*." Logan has been his faithful friend, and contented patient, from that instant on.

William Blake and Emily Dickinson, while dear and useful to Logan, are somewhat atypical of the creative people whose work he most esteems. "My gods are the big ones—Shakespeare, Milton, Goethe, Dickens, Beethoven, Rodin, and, above all, Michelangelo," he has said. "The things that are universal and timeless are what appeal to me. The problem for any creative artist is not only to reveal his own emotions, desires, hungers, passions, and fulfillments, but to bring these to others so they can participate in them. Michelangelo did it so everybody could understand it and could see it for miles. In the theatre, you've got human beings looking at human beings, the ideal situation, and you can get to the bare principles of things—to the big, cosmic truths, the truths so blinding they can't be seen, so loud they can't be heard." In emulation of Michelangelo, Logan likes to do everything, and to do everything in a big way. Other people squeeze lemon halves on oysters; Logan eats lemon halves—skin, pulp, juice, seeds, and all. "Josh is an encompasser," a distinguished playwright said recently. "He has a voracious appetite for every imaginable experience. He wants to eat a lot, talk a lot, own a lot. I remember once I was driving along a crowded side street and got stuck behind one of those big Department of Sanitation trucks with a gaping maw in back that everything gets thrown into and gobbled up by. I watched it for a minute or two and suddenly I realized that I was thinking, Gosh, it's Josh! I was ashamed of myself afterward, because I love Josh." Most of Logan's friends express their affection for him in similar terms. "You can't just like Josh," Hammerstein remarked a while ago. "You love him. I love him."

Along with being lovable, Logan is considered by the majority of his co-workers in the theatre to be notably courageous, shrewd, and exuberant, as well as one of the most talented members of their species. Richard Rodgers and Leland Hayward, who have been associated with him in many ventures—the three of them, along with Hammerstein, are the producers of "South Pacific"—are similarly inclined to liken him to a balloon, gradually becoming inflated as his interest in a project develops, then swelling beyond what would appear to be his breaking point, but somehow never exploding. "You look at him and you tell yourself, 'A guy as tireless, as passionate, as violent as this can't last,'" Rodgers says. "You're sure he'll burst. Well, I've been looking at him for a great many years." Logan does not mind being considered potentially fulminant. "Mildness is not a virtue in the theatre," he once wrote in an essay on stage directing. So far from mild is his comportment while he is nursing a show through rehearsals that his friends feel he would never stop to rest were it not for the humanitarian rules imposed and strictly enforced by Actors' Equity, an organization holding the belief that an actor's endurance is limited, even if Logan's isn't. Most actors hugely enjoy working with him; one chorus girl kicked a drama critic in the shins because she resented his having made a disparaging comment about him. "Josh has a peculiar talent for infecting a cast with his own vital enthusiasm," Hammerstein says. "You can almost see the injections going right into them. The whole damn theatre is alive and vibrating." Logan's absorption in his work is so complete that if he happens to have a cold he goes on directing a scene even at the moment of dropping nose drops into his nostrils, with his head hanging down in the aisle. He is oblivious of all distractions when he is wrapped up in his work, and his associates sometimes amuse themselves by seeing how many objects they can load into his arms without his becoming aware of it. He has been known to direct a scene while heaped with coats, umbrellas, overshoes, and random props.

Logan not only acts explosively but reacts explosively. One night while he was travelling in Spain with his wife, who is the actress Nedda Harrigan, and the Jo Mielziners, the group perched on a hillside and watched some gypsies down below dancing by the light of the moon. It was a quiet, lovely, stirring performance. Mrs. Logan and the Mielziners expressed their appreciation in suitably muted whispers; Logan expressed his in hearty, echoing roars of approbation. Some people cannot understand how a man as impulsive and excitable as Logan is can put together a show as sensitively and deftly as he can; his acquaintances believe that it is because he has two priceless assets—sure taste and a sure touch. Dr. Moore conceived an explanation of what makes Logan tick several years ago and made his patient write it over and over on a blackboard. "I have an innate sense of self-direction," this manifesto goes. "Disaster may approach, but I somehow make the right decision." Logan's innate sense of directing other people is evident offstage as well as on. While entertaining at home, he is constantly manipulating light switches to make sure his guests are properly illuminated. "Josh is a theatre person," Paul Osborn, the playwright and a close friend of his, says. "Everything he does or sees or hears or lives, he relates to the theatre. He can't walk along a street and watch a kid pick a cigarette butt up out of a gutter without wanting to grab the kid and tell him how to pick it up better."

Everything connected with "Mister Roberts" is memorable to Logan. "'Mister Roberts' has a life of its own," he says of the play. "Sometimes I feel that I didn't help do it—that it did me." Logan and Thomas Heggen had a wonderful time writing the show. They began it in the summer of 1947, at a country place the Logans then occupied at Brookfield Center, Connecticut. They dictated the play to a stenographer, working mostly at night and enjoying their labors so enormously that a few lines were irretrievably lost because, owing to the howls of laughter emanating from their authors, the stenographer couldn't catch them. As soon as a scene, or often only a fragment of one, was typed, they would rouse Mrs. Logan, regardless of the hour, and read it to her. It took them a couple of months to write the first of the play's two acts, and three weeks to finish the first of the six scenes in the second act. Mrs. Logan concluded that they'd be at it all winter, and one day in late November she took off for New York for a day's shopping and a night's uninterrupted sleep at a hotel. At four o'clock the next morning, Logan and Heggen, after a prodigious spell of productivity, finished the play. By way of celebration, they opened a bottle of Scotch and telephoned Mrs. Logan in New York to read her what they'd done. By six o'clock, they had finished the Scotch and the phone call. They were too exhilarated to sleep, so, unable to think of anything else to do at that hour, they set up a motion-picture projector and spent the morning looking at some color films Logan had shot in 1939 while exploring Patagonia.

A day or two later, Henry Fonda arrived in New York from Hollywood. He had been a friend of Logan's since the early thirties, when both were associated with the University Players, a renowned youth movement of that era. Fonda called Logan, who asked him to accompany him to a performance of "Finian's Rainbow," in which David Wayne was featured. After the show, they joined Wayne for supper, and Logan invited both actors to meet Heggen and him the following afternoon and hear their new play. They all forgathered, and Logan read "Mister Roberts" aloud. He has the reputation of being able to read a play better than most actors can act it. Before he was through, Fonda and Wayne had alternately laughed and cried so much that they were exhausted. As soon as they had pulled themselves together, they both begged to be in "Mister Roberts," and were given leading parts. Logan had more trouble filling the less important roles, but only because his standards of casting are meticulous. Over the period of a month he auditioned nearly a thousand prospective supporting shipmates. When he had at last selected the ones he wanted, he prescribed sunlamp treatments for them, so that they could resemble the crew of a cargo ship in the Pacific without using greasepaint. Logan detests makeup. He believes it destroys the illusion of realism for the audience. To provide a further realistic touch, he had his sailors wear the same dungarees throughout rehearsals that he intended them to wear during the play's run, so the dungarees would be convincingly dirty. "By the time we had our first public performance, in New Haven, the costumes were sensational," he says. "They were so grimy the men looked as though they'd been aboard ship for two years." Then, to Logan's anguish, between New Haven and Philadelphia an overzealous wardrobe mistress sent all the filthy rags he had been nurturing out to be dry-cleaned.

193

The dramatic version of "Mister Roberts" underwent quite a few revisions in the nearly five years of its presentation. Logan is fond of raw, lusty, bawdy lines and situations, and since this was a fondness Heggen enthusiastically shared, their first script brimmed with the stuff. Much of it was gradually excised over the years—so much, in fact, that Logan finally complained to a friend, "There's not a single 'God damn' left in the show any more." Some of the lines that Logan and Heggen cherished most of all were dropped; one had to do with a sailor's inquiring of an officer about the sex of a goat that wandered aboard, and another was a brief distillation of an entire chapter that Heggen, in his basic narrative, had devoted to the subject of gonorrhea. These treasured bits were retained long enough to divert friends of the authors who saw the play at the beginning of its New York run. They were also overheard by some strangers, one of whom, an affronted lady, complained to the police. After "Mister Roberts" had been running on Broadway for three years, Logan and Hayward, its producer, sent it to Boston. Anticipating further complications there, the two men paid a formal call on the mayor in advance of the opening. They promised to cut out all conceivably objectionable references to the Deity, and then, with as much dignity as they could muster under the rather peculiar circumstances, appealed to the mayor in the name of G.I. humor to let them keep three rather broad physiological references. He consented, and the show played Boston for twenty-one weeks without any fuss.

Germany was more of a headache. The Department of Defense requested permission to put on "Mister Roberts" for its occupation forces there, and Logan consented, patriotically waiving all royalties. Here at last, he thought, was an audience whose sensibilities he did not have to worry about. After one performance, the show was closed down, on orders of a four-star general whose wife had attended the première and had issued orders to *him*.

Logan's principal ambition has been to win recognition as a writer. He had written for the stage before "Mister Roberts"—he had collaborated on the book of an unsuccessful 1940 musical comedy called "Higher and Higher" and had done a great deal of anonymous rewriting—but "Mister Roberts" was his first real literary achievement. His forte, as a dramatist, is not so much conceiving crisp or tender dialogue as planning scenes that will act well; according to Hayward, he is the greatest constructionist in the history of the theatre. Logan's writing methods are unconventional. He cannot type, and he abhors pens and pencils. Shortly after completing "Mister Roberts," he became a dictaphone addict. Not only does he keep dictaphones in both his homes but for a while he had one in a station wagon, wired to the car's battery. He learned of the possibilities of this arrangement from Dr. Moore, who uses a dictaphone in his car and in the course of motoring between Boston and New York has dictated a couple of hundred letters and perhaps a dozen or two sonnets. In the summer of 1949, while Logan was writing "The Wisteria Trees," he took his station wagon, with its dictaphone, to Europe with him. When he arrived at Antibes to visit the Irwin Shaws, who had leased a château there, the new work wasn't quite finished. He wanted Shaw to read it, so he pulled up at the front door of the château, and for a couple of hours, while his host and hostess waited to welcome him, stayed in the car, dictating the end of his play. As fast as he completed a cylinder, Mrs. Logan, a typewriter on her knees and earphones clamped to her head, transcribed his dialogue. With the car stationary, the strain on its battery proved too much, a circumstance that made Logan doubly miffed when he subsequently had to revise the ending. "To think that I practically burned up a car on that lousy third act!" he groaned.

Logan has since confined his sessions with a dictaphone to interiors where light plugs are handy. He finds the machine infinitely preferable to an animate stenographer. "A dictaphone has nice passivity," he says. "You don't have to worry about the expression on its face when you try out a line." For Logan, the dictaphone really came into its own while he was working on "South Pacific." As originally planned, he was to be merely the director and a co-producer of the show; the book was to be written by Hammerstein alone. With rehearsals already scheduled, Hammerstein still hadn't come up with a script. He had got stuck, owing to his lack of familiarity with G.I. lingo. Logan, a veteran not only of Culver but of four years in the Army, knew it well. He picked up a couple of dictaphones and rushed out to Hammerstein's country place, near Doylestown, Pennsylvania. As the two men labored together, they became increasingly optimistic. "This is going to be the Goddamnedest show ever!" Logan would cry. "It's going to win the Pulitzer Prize!" They finished in a month, and by then Logan had contributed so much that Hammerstein, while not relinquishing any of his author's royalties, did grant his collaborator equal billing on the book, thus affording Logan a chance to have his name appear three times on the program, instead of just twice. It also afforded him a chance to share in the Pulitzer Prize he had accurately forecast—an honor that came to him, however, only after the Pulitzer judges, apparently not realizing that Rodgers and Hammerstein ever need any help, had first given the prize exclusively to them. On being advised of their error, the judges sent Logan a telegram of apology, and ultimately amended the Pulitzer Prize to include him, too.

The first day of rehearsals of "South Pacific" was a momentous occasion. Everybody connected with the show sensed from the start that it was going to be unique. Many of the principals had never heard Ezio Pinza sing "Some Enchanted Evening," and were eager to do so. Logan cannot abide wasting rehearsal time; he likes to begin moving his cast about as quickly as possible.

Toward the end of the afternoon, he decided to tackle "Some Enchanted Evening." He was not much concerned about how Pinza sang it; he knew Pinza could sing. He also knew that Pinza had never acted in the legitimate theatre before, and he wanted to make sure that he got the singer off on the right track. "We were all sitting there just dying to hear this guy sing the song," Hayward recalls. "So Ezio begins. He has scarcely got going when Josh starts pushing him around, turning him, shoving his arms, doing this and doing that—directing him already, for God's sake. Halfway through the number, just when Pinza is hitting a beautiful, round, sustained note, Josh suddenly stops him. 'Now, wait a minute, Ezio,' he says. 'Let's try it this way.' The rest of us could have killed him."

By the end of the second day of rehearsals, Logan had completed two-thirds of what proved to be the final staging of "South Pacific"—an almost unheard-of accomplishment even in the case of a simple play, to say nothing of an elaborate musical. The company's troubles were by no means two-thirds over, however. Pinza, for all the glory of his singing voice, was almost wholly unintelligible when reciting dialogue. Aware of this, and distressed about it, Pinza had his wife call Hayward a couple of days before the show's out-of-town début in New Haven and suggest that maybe her husband ought to drop out. Hayward was so unnerved by this prospect that he couldn't bring himself to mention the call to Rodgers and Hammerstein and Logan until three years later.

Pinza learned fast, and in New Haven he was understood well enough to be widely acclaimed. On the other hand, "I'm Gonna Wash That Man Right Outa My Hair" and "I'm in Love with a Wonderful Guy," the two biggest musical numbers assigned to Mary Martin, whom no one had had any qualms about, fizzled. Logan was stricken. He had staged them with loving care, and he concluded that if they hadn't gone over, the whole show must be a miserable flop. He staggered off to his room at the Hotel Taft and huddled there in despair. His sister, Mary Lee Leatherbee, then a researcher at *Life* and a knowing theatregoer, was the only person except his wife—who was prudently saying nothing, lest her husband grow even more perturbed—he allowed to enter the room. He told his sister that he was sure "South Pacific" was a ghastly failure, and asked if she didn't think so, too. "Well," she replied, "I did see Mike Todd walking up the aisle mumbling something and shaking his head." Two hours later, Logan received a telegram from Mike Todd. "Greatest thing I've ever seen in my life," it read. "It was a little puzzling at the time," Logan says. "I later learned that what Todd had been saying as he walked up the aisle was 'Greatest thing I've ever seen in my life.' He'd just been shaking his head the wrong way." At three o'clock in the morning, Logan could endure his solitude no longer. He telephoned Rodgers' room, and was surprised to hear unmistakable shrieks of revelry in the background. "Where've you been?" Rodgers asked.

"We're having a party to celebrate. We've got a hit." Though Rodgers and Hammerstein assured Logan that the two Mary Martin numbers could easily be fixed, he was not really himself again for three more nights. Then, lying in his hotel-room bed brooding about some way to get an additional laugh out of the scene in which Luther Billis, the enterprising Seabee chief, wears a sarong and a brassière made of two coconut husks, he hit upon an idea. "I had kept thinking, Gee, there must be something extra I could get out of those coconuts," he has since recalled. "But what? Suddenly it struck me. Cigarettes! He keeps his cigarettes in them! Intoxicated with the gag, I began to laugh. I laughed so hard the bed shook. Nedda woke up. 'What is it?' she asked. I was laughing too hard to talk. I finally calmed down long enough to tell her the gag. She said, 'Very funny,' and went back to sleep. That was my favorite moment of the whole show."

April 4, 1953

From Part I of a two-part Profile.

A Reporter at Large
The Gentle Wolfhound

In the summer of 1951, the *Nichi-nichi Shimbun*, a daily newspaper published in Osaka, Japan, a metropolis of two million people, chose an American Army sergeant with the conspicuously alien name of Hugh Francis Xavier O'Reilly as that city's "man of the year." It was an accolade theretofore conferred only on indigenous residents of Japan. Sergeant O'Reilly, himself a native of the Bronx, and, as one might suspect, a Catholic of Irish ancestry, has never attained much celebrity at home, but at least one authority on Asia has implied that his fame over there may ultimately transcend that of General MacArthur, regardless of the disparity in their rank. This was James A. Michener, who declared, in an article that appeared in *Holiday* several months ago, "Many Americans have made lasting impressions on Japan, but I think of two in particular—Lafcadio Hearn and Sergeant Hugh O'Reilly."

Sergeant O'Reilly, whom I first met when we were both in Korea a couple of years ago—he as a soldier in the 27th Infantry Regiment of the 25th Division and I as a correspondent—made a lasting impression on me, too. He is a big, sentimental, soft-voiced man, now thirty-eight years old, with coal-black hair, a neatly trimmed black mustache, and a great beak of a nose. His primary job in Korea was that of public-relations man for his regiment, an outfit nicknamed the Wolfhounds. The 27th Infantry was ably led and stoutly manned, but its prowess might have been somewhat less widely acclaimed than it proved to be had it not been for the affectionate and articulate attention Sergeant O'Reilly paid to the exploits of his fellow-Wolfhounds. The Wolfhounds were noted throughout Korea not only as a splendid fighting unit but also as the philanthropic patrons of an orphanage back in Osaka, near which the regiment had been stationed on occupation duty before it was shipped to Korea, in July, 1950. This institution, operated by the Sisters of Charity of St. Vincent de Paul and inhabited in large part by children who lost their parents in the Second World War, is called, formally, the Holy Family Home and, informally, O'Reilly's Orphanage. Sergeant O'Reilly had sold the Wolfhounds on the idea of supporting the orphanage at Christmastime of 1949; from then on, every payday, in or out of battle, he had passed the hat among them, and the Wolfhounds had filled it amply. Their donations had averaged something over three thousand dollars a month—or slightly more than a dollar every payday for every individual on the outfit's roster. I remember seeing O'Reilly a few hours after pay call at the end of April, 1951, when he was on the point of flying from Korea to Japan to deliver that month's take, a good one, to his orphans. He was an imposing sight. Every pocket of his uniform bulged with bills—American greenbacks, military scrip, Japanese yen, and Korean won. He had about five thousand dollars' worth of currency on him.

As a public-relations man, O'Reilly was primarily concerned with getting other people to write about the Wolfhounds, but he wrote a good deal about them himself, largely for *Stars & Stripes*, the one paper that soldiers in Korea get to see with any regularity. He hardly ever wrote about the regiment without mentioning the orphanage. He also wrote a good deal about the orphanage for *Stars & Stripes*, and he hardly ever wrote about the orphanage without mentioning the regiment. He loved them both, fiercely, protectively, and unabashedly. The day I saw him festooned with cash, he was heading for Japan not only to help out the orphanage but also to try to persuade the editors of *Stars & Stripes*, in Tokyo, to devote a whole page to the Wolfhounds' fiftieth anniversary, coming up in May—a page for which he stood ready to provide appropriate text and illustrations. (He got his page all right.) The 27th Infantry was organized in the Philippines during the Moro Rebellion of 1901; General Pershing was a captain in the regiment then. Its nickname derives from its having been part of an expeditionary force sent to Siberia in 1918, when the Allies were supporting the White Russians battling Red Russians there. In 1929, the regiment, then in Hawaii, got itself a real Russian wolfhound as a mascot, and named it Kolchak, in memory of Admiral Aleksandr Vasilievich Kolchak, who had commanded the White Russian forces in Siberia. The regiment didn't have a four-footed wolfhound in Korea, but if it had had, the dog would undoubtedly have been called Kolchak, just as all Yale's bulldogs are called Handsome Dan.

Sergeant O'Reilly was a stylish operator in Korea. The most comfortable transport that many lieutenants could aspire to there was the front seat, next to the driver, of a two-and-a-half-ton truck. Sergeant O'Reilly had his own jeep, and a corporal to drive it. The corporal had other duties, too—he was the regimental photographer, for one thing—but his main function seemed to be to look after O'Reilly, the way an aide looks after a general. At the command post of the 27th Infantry, there was the usual cluster of tents— one for the commanding officer and one for each of his principal staff officers. There was also a tent for O'Reilly, set up not many yards away from that of the commanding officer. The first C.O. of the Wolfhounds in Korea was Colonel John H. Michaelis, who is still perhaps the most renowned combat officer of the Korean war. In the perilous early days of that conflict, the Wolfhounds were in Eighth Army reserve. They were thrown into the line wherever the North Koreans appeared to be pushing the hardest, and in tribute to their stemming of one Communist blow after another, the late General Walton H. Walker called them the "Fire Brigade." Michaelis, as chief of this illustrious brigade, and O'Reilly, as its leading drum-beater, complemented each other beautifully, much like Jenny Lind and P. T. Barnum. Jenny Lind had a fine voice, and there was nothing Barnum could do to make it sound better, but it didn't hurt her any to have him around to remind people how good she was. Early in 1951, when Michaelis was promoted to brigadier general and assigned to a higher post, some of O'Reilly's friends feared that his own eminence in regimental circles might be imperilled. No more exclusive tent for him, they predicted. No more jeep. No more chauffeur. Their alarms were unjustified. The wife of the new regimental commander, it turned out, was living in Osaka and for some time had been in charge of collecting old clothes there for O'Reilly's Orphanage.

Many of the war correspondents in Korea spent far more time with the Wolfhounds than with any other regiment; they seemed to gravitate toward the 27th like buffs toward a civilian fire brigade. A number of them even wore the regiment's insignia, samples of which O'Reilly always considerately had on hand when, and occasionally before, a visitor expressed a hankering for some. In advance of the Wolfhounds' fiftieth anniversary, O'Reilly conceived the notion of having every gun and mortar along the regiment's sector of the front fire one round in its honor at noon on the great day—a salvo scheduled to be the most intensive launched at the enemy at any single moment of the war up to then. The idea was approved by the higher headquarters concerned, and O'Reilly happily divulged the plan to a bunch of correspondents the night before the anniversary. Early the following morning, one wire-service reporter, eager to score a beat over his rivals, filed a colorful account of this barrage, referring to it as a "deadly fanfare." His story zipped across the Pacific and was prominently displayed in quite a few American newspapers. The writer was a little miffed at O'Reilly when noon came and there was no discernible increase of sound over the modest fanfare that had prevailed all morning. He intimated that O'Reilly had sold him a bill of goods. O'Reilly hadn't; that particular feature of the birthday party had had to be cancelled at the last moment because a patrol from an adjacent regiment had inadvertently wandered out into the territory where all the testimonial shells were to have landed.

One other thing I knew about O'Reilly when I was in Korea contributed to my picture of him as a singular G.I. Most American soldiers I encountered in the Orient were anxious to return to the United States, and they did not regard such romantic attachments as they had formed overseas as permanently binding. O'Reilly said that he was deeply in love with an Osaka girl and that he was determined to return to Japan, marry her if she would have him, and settle down in her native land. In any event, he wanted to stay there and do what he could to improve Japanese-American relations. "I'm a guy with a lot of idealistic things in my head,". he told me once. Just recently, I received word that he was back in this country, stationed at West Point, holding the rank of master sergeant and assigned to the public-information office of the Military Academy. One day, I drove up there and called on him, at his quarters. I found that he was married to his Osaka girl, the former Yuko Saito, and that they were living in a comfortable five-room apartment, with their dog, a mongrel pup, part collie and part mystery, whose name, it came as no surprise to me to learn, is Kolchak.

It was good to see O'Reilly again, and to meet his wife, a pert, attractive twenty-three-year-old girl who speaks English fairly fluently and seems to have become quite Americanized. We had scarcely been introduced when she inquired whether she was right in thinking my car was a 1951 Chevrolet. She was. I asked O'Reilly if the Wolfhounds were still supporting the orphanage, and he told me that of course they were. "When I got rotated out of Korea and out of the regiment, in July, 1951," he said, "my parting words to my successor in the public-information job were 'Your first responsibility is the orphanage. Then come the Wolfhounds.' He gave the same instructions to *his* successor. You know what the turnover in an infantry regiment is like. There's probably not a single officer or man in the 27th today who was a Wolfhound three years ago, when we were in Japan. There's probably not a single active Wolfhound who has any personal reason to be concerned about any of our orphans—a hundred and seventy of them now, I was told in a recent letter. But military tradition is a peculiar thing. Down, Kolchak! The latest report I had, the total amount raised by the Wolfhounds for the orphanage was over a hundred and thirty thousand dollars."

I asked O'Reilly what it was that had frustrated his hopes of staying in Japan. "That was a funny business," he said. "You remember how I wanted to go back to Osaka, marry Yuko, and settle down? Only I guess you never knew that when I was in Korea I didn't know Yuko's name or address, and had never had a date with her. But I'll tell you about that later. Anyway, when it came time for me to be rotated, I applied for and received an eighteen-month extension—the hitch I was on would normally have been up in a month—specifically to be allowed to stay in Japan. Well, not long after I'd found Yuko and we'd got married, out comes an order that all soldiers who were on extended tours of duty and married to Japanese nationals would have to leave Japan. Something to do with security, I heard. So here we are."

The third of five children, Sergeant O'Reilly was born on August 27, 1914, in that part of New York where the Bronx approach to the Triborough Bridge is now located. His mother had come here from Ireland. His father, born in New York of Irish parents, had started out driving a horsecar and had become superintendent of transportation for the New York Railways Company, now the New York City Omnibus Corporation. O'Reilly grew up in a rowdy neighborhood, notable for the intensity of its street fights. Two-Gun Crowley was one of the participants. "Most of the kids I fooled around with became mobsters, cops, or priests, pretty much in that order, I guess," O'Reilly says. He himself never got into any serious jams, but he recalls that he was such a troublemaker as a boy that he was kicked out of six high schools in his freshman year. (Lafcadio Hearn, for whatever it may be worth, had a similarly irresponsible boyhood.) He quit school then, and switched restlessly from one job to another, never fitting in well wherever he was. At eighteen, he enlisted in the Army and was shipped to Hawaii. He spent three years there. He became a private first class, but got into a fight with a sergeant, was busted and was discharged as a private. Returning to New York, he held a succession of odd, menial jobs for nearly six years, and in the meantime attended night school and earned enough credits to obtain a high-school diploma. Then, discouraged about getting anywhere in New York, he drifted out to California. He was working as a shipfitter's apprentice in San Francisco when the Japanese attacked Pearl Harbor. A month later, he enlisted in the Marine Corps. He was afraid that if he went back into the Army he'd be assigned, because of his previous service, to train recruits. Having been at Pearl Harbor, he wanted to get into action.

O'Reilly was presently sent to New Caledonia, thence to Guadalcanal, and on to Guam. He didn't see a great deal of combat—he was with an anti-aircraft outfit most of the time—but, on Guam, he saw enough of it to develop a violent hatred of all Japanese. On Guam, too, occurred what he describes as "the first deal I ever got mixed up with helping people out." A village called Mong Mong had been pretty well levelled by bombs, and O'Reilly and some other Marines gave the villagers whatever extra rations they could scrape up. O'Reilly was the leading benefactor; the other Marines, who up to then had called him "Pop," because he was twenty-nine years old and a comparative graybeard among them, began to call him "the King of Mong Mong."

In December, 1945, after four years in the Marine Corps, O'Reilly was discharged. He came back to New York to look for a job. His father had died during the war, and, out of respect for his memory, the bus company took his son on as a driver. O'Reilly quickly became active in the affairs of the Transport Workers Union, and he was ultimately elected a member of the executive board of Local 100 of the T.W.U. For a couple of years, he helped handle union grievance cases. "I learned what makes bus drivers as nasty as they sometimes appear to be," he told me. "I remember one kid the boss was about to fire. The kid had drawn a vehicle with a bad clutch for the Eighty-sixth Street crosstown run. He had an awful trip. There were cars parked at every bus stop, and taxis kept cutting in on him, and the streets were full of Jersey drivers, and people were asking fool questions, and everybody gave him dollar bills to change, and the driver ahead was cheating—going too fast, that is, so that as a result the kid's bus was getting extra-heavy loads. And when he reached Madison Avenue, he was just about to get a break, finally, on a traffic light, when two women climbed on the steps, and one of them kept her foot on the steps so he couldn't close the door, and she said, 'Can you tell me how to get to Staten Island?' That did it. The kid spit in her face, and he used a foul word. She wrote an indignant letter to the bus company, giving the number of the bus and reporting what had happened, explicitly. Well, the boss came to me and said he'd have to fire the driver. He was a nice kid, and he hadn't ever blown up like that before, and I wanted him to have another chance, so I said to the boss, 'Nonsense, you can't fire a man on the uncorroborated evidence of a woman who is clearly not a lady.' 'What do you mean, not a lady?' the boss asked me. 'No lady would put a word like that on paper,' I told him. The kid's still driving."

The Transport Workers Union was having its political troubles then. A number of Communists were holding key positions in the organization. O'Reilly became one of the ringleaders of an anti-Communist bloc within the union. One day, while he was operating a bus along Columbus Avenue at 166th Street, a bullet shattered the glass of the driver's window and just missed him. The chief of the anti-Communist forces in the ideological battle was a union official named Pete McCaffrey. In 1948, McCaffrey was taken to a hospital, fatally afflicted with cancer. O'Reilly lost heart for union work. That August, a week before his thirty-fourth birthday, he once again enlisted in the armed forces. This time, he went back to the Army. He had had his fill of the Marine Corps. "The Marines are too conscious of being Marines," he said to me. "All this talk of theirs about being supermen is a lot of hooey. It used to gripe me. They were forever telling us what an honor it is to die for your country. What you ought to teach a soldier is that the idea is to make the enemy die for *his* country."

In June, 1949, O'Reilly was ordered to Japan. He didn't want to go there. "I thought I disliked the Japanese intensely," he told me. "I said that if they sent me over there, I'd kick little Japanese kids in the head. It was said mostly as a joke, of course, but there was an underlying feeling of real hostility." The Army was unimpressed by O'Reilly's emotions, and in July he reached Japan. He was given his choice of two regiments in the 25th Division. When he learned that one of them was the Wolfhounds, he picked it unhesitatingly. "I'd seen the Wolfhounds when I was in Hawaii," he explained to me. "They were stationed right next to my regiment, the 21st. The Wolfhounds were a real holler outfit. One night, there was a boxing match between one of them and a guy in my regiment. The decision went against the Wolfhounds. They didn't like it. Later that night, the whole damn regiment marched into our compound and continued the fight. They beat the hell out of us. They were tough babies. I always admired them."

In Japan, the 27th Infantry was stationed at Camp Sakai, about five miles from downtown Osaka. O'Reilly was assigned to Baker Company, as a platoon sergeant, and held that post for four months. Then he heard there was a vacancy at regimental headquarters, in the public-information section. He applied for the job and got it. O'Reilly still had little use for any Japanese, young or old. When he had time off, he hung around the camp for the most part; he didn't want to see any more of the Japanese than he had to. On Christmas Day, 1949, however, he was one of about a dozen soldiers who accompanied a Red Cross field representative attached to the Wolfhounds to a holiday party at the Holy Family Home. The orphanage was in sorry shape. The Japanese government helped support it, but provided only the equivalent of twenty cents a day for each child whom the government had placed there, and nothing at all for the fair number of children who had arrived not as government wards but as doorstep foundlings. And the sums the orphanage received from other sources were negligible. What was more, the sisters and the children had just been evicted from a new building, into which they had moved while it was still being put up for them; they had run out of funds, and because the contractor hadn't been paid, he wouldn't let them continue to occupy the nearly finished structure. The orphans were living in cramped, leaky, drafty huts. O'Reilly was appalled by these conditions. On returning to camp, he buttonholed a couple of corporals from Baker Company, his old outfit, and they agreed to take up a collection for the orphans there on the next payday, December 31st. From a hundred and forty-three men in Baker Company, they wheedled a hundred and forty-three dollars. The corporals and O'Reilly took it to the orphanage on New Year's morning.

By the time the following payday rolled around, at the end of January, O'Reilly had made the plight of the orphans known to every company in the regiment. Gradually, without official directives—and for a while, indeed without the regimental commander's knowledge—the Wolfhounds came to adopt the orphanage. The regimental commander first learned what was going on in the course of searching for a bulldozer of his that none of his men seemed to be able to produce. He eventually located it at the orphanage, where it was being used to clear up rubble. O'Reilly didn't have a jeep then, and because of a strict watch the military police were keeping for potential black marketeers, it was difficult for an enlisted man to take any kind of supply-laden Army vehicle out of the camp except on official business. Daily, O'Reilly would scrounge powdered milk, soap, dried eggs, cereal, chocolate, and whatever else he could get his hands on from obliging mess sergeants; then, early in the afternoon, he would borrow the Red Cross man's jeep, pile these provisions in it, and deliver them to the orphanage. For six months, he spent five hours a day there, helping the sisters get the place fixed up. He came to know the children well. They were especially fascinated by his mustache. The Japanses for "mustache" is "*hige*"; to many of the orphans he was O'Hige San. O'Reilly had plenty of coöperation. The regiment's medical officer, for instance, suddenly discovered that he had a lot of spare vitamin tablets in stock; each child got one every day. The doctor also held sick calls twice a week at the orphanage.

Very soon after the Wolfhounds began to collect funds for the Holy Family Home, the new building was completed and the orphans moved into it for good. As word of what the 27th was doing got around, other contributions dribbled in. A Hollywood actress sent five hundred dollars. Another five hundred came in from the bus drivers and mechanics of a garage at 146th Street and Lenox Avenue—the garage O'Reilly had worked out of in civilian life. The crew of a Navy transport contributed two hundred dollars, and a bank president in St. Louis twenty-five. A number of Wolfhounds, including O'Reilly, amended their National Service Life Insurance policies to name the orphanage as beneficiary. A company of Wacs stationed in Tokyo, upon hearing that the Wolfhounds had adopted the orphanage, were moved to adopt the Wolfhounds. When the 27th went to Korea, the Wacs sent the regiment a gratifying shipment of cigarette lighters and comic books.

Meanwhile, O'Reilly had met Yuko Saito, after a fashion. The daughter of a manganese-mine operator, she was working as a salesgirl at the glove counter of a store that O'Reilly wandered into during one of his rare excursions to downtown Osaka. O'Reilly, up to then a steadfast bachelor, instantly lost his anti-Japanese bias. He went back day after day. Too shy to ask Yuko her name, he simply bought gloves. He bought mountains of gloves. Yuko had never seen anybody—not even an American service man—buy so many gloves. She thought he must be keeping a terribly demanding cabaret girl. One day, while he was buying a couple of pairs, she remarked to him that she was quitting her job. O'Reilly was dismayed. He thought he would never see her again. He didn't know what to say or do. He didn't say or do anything. He lost track of her for a couple of months, and then, on his way to buy an electric fan for the orphanage kitchen one warm spring day, he spotted her walking along the street. He jumped out of the jeep he was riding in, greeted her, and asked her if she knew where he could buy a fan. She told him. He thanked her and left, without learning her name. Yuko, who by then had become curious about this strange, timid, glove-mad American, followed him to the store she had designated. She explained when she turned up that she just wanted to be sure he had found the fan department. They parted, still without introducing themselves, and a few weeks later the Korean war began.

The 27th Infantry was one of the first American regiments to be sent to Korea. When the time to move came, O'Reilly thought the orphanage was out of luck. "I didn't see how the boys could be approached for such a thing at such a time," he told me. "But a week before our first payday in Korea, men started asking me, 'Are we going to keep up with the orphanage?' So we had the collection as usual. In Japan, we'd been way under strength. We'd had only two of our three authorized battalions, and we'd averaged around fifteen hundred dollars a month. In Korea, we got our third battalion and the average shot way up. The commander of one of the third battalion's companies asked me as soon as he heard about the orphanage what the best was that any company had done up to then on any one payday. I told him nine hundred dollars. He brought me ten hundred and twenty-four dollars. That got a platoon leader in the second battalion sore. He said his platoon could lick that company any day, and it did. It brought me eleven hundred dollars. The money rolled in whether we were fighting or not. One month, I didn't get anything from Easy Company. I telephoned the lieutenant commanding it and said I hoped he had some money for me. He said he didn't, but that by the time I got from regimental headquarters to where the outfit was he'd have some. Easy was in the line. While I was driving up, the company got into a fire fight. The lieutenant and two of his non-coms crawled from hole to hole, right in the middle of it all, and when I got there,

they had eighty-four bucks for me. I wrote the incident up for *Stars &*
Stripes, but they didn't use it. They wouldn't believe me."

Just as the Wolfhounds didn't forget the orphans, the orphans didn't
forget the Wolfhounds. They sent every company in the regiment hand-
painted greeting cards at regular intervals, with the sentiments on them
translated into English by one of the sisters. O'Reilly himself got an average
of a letter a day from one orphan or another. On his thirty-sixth birthday, a
few weeks after he reached Korea, he received a Birthday Spiritual Bouquet
from the children, advising him that they had offered 574 Rosaries, 137
Paters, 68 Glorias, 18 Credos, 10,705 Ejaculations, 340 Sacrifices, and 270
Acts of Charity in his behalf. That day, also, he received fifty bilingual
letters, one containing the verse:

> O'Reilly San, O'Hige San,
> Your mustache is very funny.
> You have a gentle face,
> O'Reilly San.

O'Reilly is convinced that the regiment was abetted in battle by its
association with the orphans. "The prayers of those kids had a lot to do with
what the Wolfhounds did," he told me. "Those kids were on their knees
every night for us while we were fighting. I don't care what people say.
Prayer helps. Prayer helps. Of course, the fact that in Mike Michaelis we
had one of the most brilliant commanding officers in the Army helped, too."

O'Reilly's last payday in Korea, at the end of June, 1951, was a
memorable one. As a sort of farewell gift for him, the regiment came up
with the record-breaking sum of ten thousand four hundred dollars.
O'Reilly presently carried it back to Japan in a cheap aluminum suitcase he
had once bought on a stroll along the Ginza in Tokyo. He had a layover
between planes that night at an airbase at Ashiya and, with a couple of other
enlisted men, went to a joint on the outskirts of the field for a beer. When he
left the place, his companions didn't follow him out, as he'd expected them
to. He was carrying the suitcase, and he set it down and went back in to see
what had happened to them. "When I came outside again a minute later, it
was gone," he told me. "I was frantic. There was nobody in sight.
Something made me turn to the left. I ran three hundred yards, at top
speed, and I bumped into three airmen. I grabbed one of them by the lapels.
'Give me that suitcase, you son of a bitch!' I yelled. 'I haven't got any
suitcase,' he said. 'That suitcase contains ten thousand dollars in cash for
orphans,' I told him, shaking him. 'Why the hell didn't you say so?' he
asked. He walked over to a nearby hedge, and from behind it he pulled my
suitcase. Then the three airmen bawled me out for being so careless with so
much money. And then they emptied their pockets and gave me everything
they had on them for the orphanage."

After delivering the money—by that time ten thousand four hundred and thirty-two dollars and fifty-five cents—to the Holy Family Home, O'Reilly began to search for Yuko. He hadn't seen her in a year. He had no idea where, in a city of two million, to look for her. One day, he decided to buy a car. A priest he knew suggested an agency that sold English Fords, and O'Reilly went there. Yuko was working in the office. O'Reilly bought a Ford, and took pains to learn her name, but he still didn't have the nerve to ask her for a date. Determined not to have her change jobs again without his knowing about it, he called the Ford agency almost every day, inventing questions about his car as an excuse. Finally, he had a legitimate inquiry. His ignition system caught fire, and he phoned Yuko and asked her to send a mechanic to the spot where he had broken down. Yuko had had enough of his bashfulness. She arrived with the mechanic and invited O'Reilly home to dinner. A few weeks later, they were engaged.

The O'Reillys were married on December 7, 1951, the tenth anniversary of Pearl Harbor. Their choice of that date, as it happened, was purely coincidental; O'Reilly had obtained a furlough beginning then. But by that time he had been named Osaka's man of the year because of his interest in the orphanage, and the Japanese press made a big thing of the wedding; several of the Japanese reporters who covered the ceremony observed that the choice of that date signified that Americans no longer regarded Pearl Harbor Day as a day of infamy. O'Reilly was taken aback by this. So was Yuko, for, like most Japanese who were schoolchildren in 1941, she hadn't known that Pearl Harbor Day was December 7th. She had been taught that the Japanese had declared war several days earlier and that the American disaster at Pearl Harbor was simply the result of puny defenses. Sixty orphans from the Holy Family Home sang hymns at the wedding, and a celebrated Japanese poet (his son is now studying, under O'Reilly's sponsorship, at a Baptist university in South Carolina) wrote a poem for the Japanese papers in which he likened the marriage of Hugh and Yuko to a rainbow bridge between the West and the East.

In July, 1952, O'Reilly was informed that, because of the regulation affecting service men married to Japanese girls, he would have to return at once to the States. He was sorry. At the time, he was assigned to the public-relations office of a headquarters called the Southwestern Command, was living, with Yuko, in a comfortable country home between Osaka and Kyoto, could visit the orphanage frequently, and was quite content. Furthermore, he was apprehensive about bringing Yuko to the United States. Walking out of a hotel in Tokyo with her shortly after their marriage, he had been slapped in the face by a Japanese woman, who evidently disapproved of American soldiers' consorting with her compatriots. O'Reilly knew that this attitude wasn't typical of the way most Japanese felt, but he didn't want Yuko to be exposed to any similar insults in his country. His own family welcomed her graciously. But when, after a furlough, he was assigned to Fort Monmouth, New Jersey, he prudently went down there alone, leaving Yuko in the Bronx with his mother while he sought a place to live where his wife wouldn't be embarrassed. He found an ideal landlady at Long Branch, near the post. She was an Italian, and when he told her what his problem was, she said, "Japanese? What's the difference? Human being." That was that.

O'Reilly spent only a month at Monmouth. The Sergeant's old boss, General Michaelis, had by then become Commandant of Cadets at the Military Academy, and O'Reilly wrote him, requesting a transfer to West Point, which the General soon arranged. Yuko finds West Point a pleasant spot. General Michaelis's chauffeur has a Japanese wife, and another Japanese married to a soldier lives right next door to the O'Reillys and shares a washing machine with Yuko. The O'Reillys' apartment is furnished partly with plain, utilitarian Army furniture and partly with relatively exotic belongings they brought from the Orient—sets of lacquerware and china; a beautifully costumed, glass-encased doll, which O'Reilly was awarded by the *Nichi-nichi Shimbun* when it named him man of the year; several paintings made for him by orphans from the Holy Family Home; and a painting done by a Japanese boy who was one of a group of sixty children O'Reilly gave English lessons to in Osaka a couple of evenings a week after he returned from Korea. One of the couple's most treasured possessions, which O'Reilly keeps hidden in a closet (Yuko showed it to me while he was on the phone), is a testimonial that was waiting for him at his mother's apartment in the Bronx last summer when he got back to the United States. It was written by one of the sisters who were running the Holy Family Home when he first visited the place and signed by three other members of her order. "Welcome home, Sergeant O'Reilly," it reads. "May the love, gentleness, and care you so generously lavished on the unwanted little children of Japan return to you a thousandfold, and may your countrymen always remember the great part you and the 'Wolfhounds' played in carrying the Real Spirit of America not only to the land of cherry blossoms but into the hearts of little almond-eyed youngsters who will miss forever their beloved O'Reilly San."

May 9, 1953

Revelation

Walter S. Mack, a dapper salesman whose career we have followed with fascination through lively romances with Pepsi-Cola and Nedicks Orange Drink, invited us and a hundred or so other guests to a "Revolutionary Revelation" lunch at the Waldorf the other day. We went. After nearly two hours' worth of drink and food, none of it notably unconventional, Mr.

Mack stood up behind a table on which were arrayed various bottles and cans, and rapped for attention. Behind him was a mirror with a printed strip saying "Nothing is so powerful as an idea whose time has come" pasted on it. "I hope you all feel in a very revolutionary spirit," said Mack, a Republican whose name was once bandied about as a possible mayor of New York. After that gambit, he plunged into an earnest spiel about such revolutionary revelations of the past as jet aircraft, television, and three-dimensional films, and then drifted into a discussion of foodstuffs. Our pulse quickened. "I'm about to reveal a fundamental change in methods of operation in the soft-drink industry," he announced gravely. "This revolution had to come. Neither you nor I nor anyone else could stop it. I am about to launch a line of soft drinks in non-returnable, no-deposit, *foolproof*, *cutproof*, *drinking* TIN CANS!" He paused triumphantly. You could have heard a pile-driver drop.

A fleet of waiters scurried out of an anteroom toward the lunch tables and gave each guest two tin cans, one stamped "C. & C. Ginger Ale" and the other "C. & C. Super Coola." They had cone-shaped tops surmounted by standard bottle caps. "Let me tell you what I found when I got mixed up in the soft-drink industry," said Mr. Mack while these revelations were being passed out. He gave a brief history of the cola business. Then he explained that National Phoenix Industries, a corporation of which he is president, two years ago bought Cantrell & Cochrane, a venerable soft-drink outfit, of which he is also president (as he is of Nedicks, too). He seized a defenseless bottle of Pepsi-Cola from the display in front of him. "Look at this!" he said scornfully, and we couldn't help remembering how he used to say he loved the stuff. That was before he switched to Nedicks. And now . . . He grabbed a bottle opener and pried the cap off the Pepsi-Cola. "Look what happened!" he shouted. "A little piece of glass broke off!"

A man at our table, sipping coffee and critically examining his unopened Super Coola can, remarked, "This has a haunting resemblance to a Pepsi-Cola can Walter was promoting three or four years ago." Mack, oblivious to the clatter of cans, went on to tell a chilling story about what happened once to a child who ran full tilt into a rock while holding a bottled soft drink in his hand. Then he explained that his new tin can is capable of withstanding high carbonation pressure, thanks to a design that the Continental Can Company (of which he is not president) developed for him. "Don't ask me what's in the lining," he said. "Ask Continental Can. They won't tell you." With one hand, he next held up a box containing twenty-four cans of Super Coola, to demonstrate how light they were. Then, straining like a wrestler, he hoisted on high a case of twenty-four Pepsi bottles. At the conclusion of this feat, puffing slightly, he declared, "An old Coca-Cola executive said to me the other day, 'Walter, this tin can of yours is greater than "Ben-Hur."'" And another thing—we have wrapped up Vitamin C in these soft drinks.

Five flavors, all vitalized. That is the reason why I have the temerity to say to you, 'Here is something in the trend of modern living—this little atomic container that you have before you today.'"

We sampled the contents of our two cans, which tasted pretty much like, respectively, all other colas and ginger ales of our experience. Then we started to leave, staggering under the weight of a giant bottle opener, or Super Coola can opener, that an attendant had urged upon us. Mack was having his picture taken, holding aloft a tray jammed with Super Coola cans. "I told the boys I wouldn't run for mayor," he was saying to a man beside him. Mack caught our eye. "Goodbye!" he called merrily. "I'm having a lot of fun. It's super-ka-dooper."

May 23, 1953

Some twenty-five years later, I read somewhere that Walter Mack, by now well into his eighties, was busily promoting a new soft drink.

Flexibility

We were on the verge of acknowledging receipt of a routine business letter from Abraham H. Berwald, director of marketing for the Eagle Pencil Company, the other day when we noticed that Mr. Berwald had signed his name in pencil. Forthwith we were off for the company's offices, at Thirteenth Street and Avenue C, to make acknowledgment in person and find out, while we were at it, whether it is the policy of the outfit to transact all its written affairs in this informal, if in the circumstances quite suitable, fashion. Mr. Berwald, a courtly gentleman of seventy-one, received us in a tenth-floor office with a commanding view of lower Manhattan. Glancing about the premises, we observed, along with a flock of pencils of all sizes, a desk pen set, a typewriter, and an old hand-wound phonograph.

We came right to the second purpose of our visit, and Mr. Berwald told us that while he, in his twenty-seven years at Eagle, has stuck faithfully to pencils, as have a few other old-timers, the pups among the company's staff don't go in much for this display of loyalty. "The pencil is a fine writing instrument," Mr. Berwald said, with feeling. Back in 1877, he continued, when Eagle marketed the first indelible pencils, business houses wrote letters and checks with them, but the practice died out after a couple of years, because of the rise of the typewriter and the fountain pen. Although Eagle makes pens, too, just as Ford makes Lincolns, pencils are the first love of present-day Eagle executives. Henry Berol, a vice-president and a member of the fourth generation of the family that founded the firm in 1856 and has run it ever since, is addicted to magenta leads. He is the only man at Eagle who is allowed to use that shade, and the source of magenta memoranda is thus readily apparent to his associates. Eagle is otherwise an exceedingly tolerant organization, Mr. Berwald assured us. Some years back, it took on a chap who had just left the Adam Hat outfit, where he had got into a dreadful jam for being observed without a hat on. After switching jobs, he wouldn't put anything but an Eagle pencil between his quivering fingers until he learned, to his relief, that he could write in blood for all his new employers cared.

We thanked Mr. Berwald, acknowledged receipt of his letter, and were about to leave when he stayed us with a wave of his hand. "Do you know about the difficulties inherent in the manufacture of colored pencils?" he asked challengingly. We confessed ignorance. "Well, sir, the old-fashioned colored leads were terribly brittle," he said. "The thick ones broke right and left. The thin ones were even worse. But look at what we have now!" He seized a handful of carmine leads, unencased in protective wood, from his desk. "In bygone years, if I had dropped one of these on the floor, it would have smashed into six or seven pieces," he said. He dropped one on the floor, and it remained intact. "If I'd slammed it on the floor, it would have smashed into I don't know how many pieces," he continued. He wound up and slammed one on the floor, and *it* remained intact. Flushed with victory, he called to his secretary for a bunch of old-fashioned leads. She fetched them at once, and he began dropping and slamming them all over the room. We ducked as lead flew about us. "There!" cried Mr. Berwald. "What's happened is that we have made colored leads flexible. Why, look how far I can bend this one without break—Oops! Well, after all, there are limits."

We said we really had to be on our way. "Wait!" cried Mr. Berwald. "You've heard of our Turquoise drawing pencils, with their needle points, haven't you?" We mumbled noncommittally. "Well, we decided the other day that nobody really knows what a needle point on a pencil means. After all, you can't sew with graphite, can you?" A younger man silently entered the room. "Mr. Saulsbury, our advertising manager," said Mr. Berwald. "Are you ready?"

"Ready," said Saulsbury, and he lifted the lid of the ancient phonograph.

"Saulsbury, here, picked this machine up in a local junk shop," Mr. Berwald said.

"The record came from the five-and-ten," volunteered Saulsbury.

We noticed that a small plastic record was resting on the venerable turntable.

"Now pay attention," admonished Mr. Berwald.

Saulsbury wound up the machine and, with a flourish, inserted in the playing arm a finely sharpened Turquoise pencil point. The turntable started revolving, and the strains of "The Star-Spangled Banner" emerged, scratchy but stirring, from the sound box. Mr. Berwald rose to his feet. After the music ended, there was a brief silence.

"You're the first to witness this demonstration," Mr. Berwald told us gravely. In awe, we marched away.

June 27, 1953

A-1

Eve Ay, Miss Pa. of '53,
Became Miss A. at Atl. C.
Her ht. and wt. made little dif.
She might still be just Pa.'s Miss if
She hadn't had one asset—viz.,
The skinniest handle in the biz.

Oh, gone the day when plump white thigh
Attracted judge's roving eye.
Farewell, tape measures, scales, et al.
It's letters that count, from Me. to Cal.
That state prevails whose beauteous repr.
Can boast a name most like an abbr.

October 3, 1953

Department of Amplification

SCARBOROUGH, N.Y., JANUARY 27, 1954
The Editors, *The New Yorker*,
DEAR SIRS:

I read with sympathetic interest James A. Maxwell's recent account in your columns of the experiences of a friend of his who had been living with thirteen pedigreed Great Danes—mother and twelve young. I gather from Mr. Maxwell's chronicle of the ordeal that his friend's main difficulty was in disposing of the litter. Was *that* all?

I have been living lately with ten pedigreed Labrador retrievers—mother and nine. (There are a human mother and three human children in my household, too, but the hell with them; nobody has had time to pay any attention to them lately—or to me, either.) Labradors, to be sure, are slightly smaller than Great Danes, and nine is a smaller number than twelve, but I suspect that I can play in Maxwell's friend's league

212

nonetheless. Great Danes, I surmise, are easier to breed and raise than Labradors. At any rate, Maxwell made no mention of his friend's continually getting to work late because of the time consumed every morning in scooping soft-boiled eggs out of their shells. Two-minute eggs, the vet told me—one per puppy. Daily.

My wife and I got involved with Labradors three and a half years ago, when we acquired, as a house pet, a female puppy from a litter bred by a neighbor of ours in Westchester, who lives on Teatown Road and had named his bitch Sable of Teatown. When we got around to choosing a formal name for ours—a family council had already settled upon Cleopatra as an apt first name—we followed my friend's precedent. We live on Holbrook Road, so Cleopatra of Holbrook she became and, as such, was duly registered with the American Kennel Club. After she grew up, we were anxious to breed her, but for one reason or another circumstances never seemed propitious until late last fall. Unfortunately, we misjudged the moment of her coming in season, with the result that when she did, we had no mate lined up for her. A friend of ours came to our rescue by recommending a friend of his—a Long Island lady who breeds Labradors. I telephoned her, explained my predicament, and asked if she had a good dog standing at stud. The Long Island lady said she did indeed, but before committing herself she wanted a few facts about my bitch's background. The only facts I had then were the names of Cleopatra's parents, which had been all anybody in Westchester cared about, since Cleo is only a pet. But that wasn't enough for Long Island. No indeedy. Long Island wanted to know did my bitch have in her some of the Timbertown strain, or some of the Arden, perhaps? I said abjectly that I hadn't any idea.
"What's the name of your bitch, anyway?" asked the Long Island lady.
"Cleopatra," I said. "Cleopatra of Holbrook."
"Mmm, Holbrook, Holbrook," said Long Island. "I don't believe I'm familiar with that particular strain."
I was obliged to confess miserably that Holbrook was not a strain at all but merely the road I live on, and no great shakes of a road at that.
The Long Island lady, after a shocked pause, directed me sternly to obtain a three-generation pedigree from the Kennel Club and report back to her. I got one all right, and learned from it, to my amazement and delight, that Cleo is chock-full of acceptable strains; one of her paternal great-grandfathers turned out to be an Arden bench champion, and her maternal ancestors included a whole host of Timbertowns. Much set up, I called the Long Island lady again, to convey this heartening information, and on the receipt of it she consented to receive my bitch and my stud fee.
I drove Cleo to Long Island and deposited her in one of the fanciest dog-and-cat hospitals I have ever seen (it resembled a funeral parlor for human

beings), and there she was successfully mated. I had already learned that sixty-three days is the usual gestation period for dogs, and it was simple enough to compute when Cleo would whelp—four days after my own birthday, according to the calendar. This not only made the anticipated date of the puppies' arrival easy to keep in mind but proved a source of considerable relief to my wife, who was planning a birthday party for me and didn't want a yelping brood of puppies underfoot.

A week or so before my birthday, I took Cleo, then promisingly bulging, to our local vet, who said she was coming along fine and predicted—with what, from my amateur viewpoint, turned out to be astonishing accuracy— that she would have between eight and ten pups. He asked me if I had ever delivered a litter, and I said only of cats. (I once had eleven cats in my house, but that is quite another story, and not a very pretty one.) The vet said he thought my wife and I could manage all right, and he warned me to keep an eye on Cleo as her accouchement drew near; dogs tend to try to have their puppies out-of-doors, he said, and I should be alert for any flurry of hole-digging by Cleo. For several days, whenever I let her out, I sneaked after her. But Cleo is no fool; she would let me tiptoe behind her for a while, and then, after I had hidden behind some bush or tree, would suddenly wheel and bark at me, pretending she thought I was a trespasser. It was an embarrassing situation for both of us.

The day of my birthday, our house was a busy place. On the theory that I could persuade Cleo to have her litter indoors, I had built a large whelping box, fitted it out with blankets and pillows, and installed it in the basement. That afternoon, my wife, with the instinct females have about each other, suddenly decided that Cleo was going to have her puppies, whenever she had them, in our bedroom, so I dragged the whelping box up there. Then I showed it to Cleo, who not only seemed to approve of it but climbed right in and went to sleep. At about that time, a piano tuner turned up to loosen a couple of stuck keys, and he was still around, sprawled beneath our piano, when my wife and I went upstairs about six-thirty, to dress.

While I was shaving, my wife, who was dressing in the bedroom, called to me in an urgent voice. The first puppy had arrived. I rushed to the head of the stairs to summon the children, who were downstairs watching television. They ran up. So did our cook, who had been preparing dinner. So did the piano tuner. In about fifteen minutes, the second puppy was born. After that, my oldest child, announcing that he now understood how *that* worked, returned to the television set. He had barely got back to it when he sounded a frantic alarm. From the tone of his voice, my wife and I could tell something was seriously wrong. We scrambled downstairs to find the kitchen full of flames. The cook had left a frying pan on the range with some oil in it, and the oil had somehow blazed up and flames were licking the ceiling. By the time we had put the fire out, the third puppy had arrived and the piano tuner had fled into the night. (We haven't seen him since, and lower C is still stuck.) The first dinner guests arrived concurrently with the fourth puppy.

The remainder of that evening is a bit hazy in my memory. My wife and I somehow finished dressing, and we took turns at the whelping box. The last puppy arrived at around one o'clock in the morning, and somewhere in the interval drinks and food must have been served. I do recall very clearly, however, my anguish when one of our guests presented me with two hundred tulip bulbs as a birthday gift, accompanied by the cheerful counsel that I should get them into the ground as soon as possible, since frost was threatening. As each new puppy emerged, my wife or I ascertained its sex, and when the litter was complete, we compared notes and calculated that we had six males and three females. Cleo had them with no trouble, and they all looked healthy and handsome. That good old Holbrook strain asserting itself, I thought smugly.

Shortly thereafter, I registered the puppies with the Kennel Club (the breeder is supposed to do this, and later the owners of individual dogs register theirs separately), noting that we had six males and three females. A few days ago, my wife and I were showing the dogs to a prospective purchaser who wanted a bitch, and we undertook to extract three females from the squirming, frolicking, fascinating mass of growing dogs that have taken over our guest room. To our consternation, we each came up with two females. It seems we must have made a mistake on my birthday. I am probably in a terrible jam with the Kennel Club for filing a false affidavit with it. Our kitchen is in a terrible jam, too, preëmpted, as it has been, by huge quantities of Pablum, cod-liver oil, mineral powder, Karo syrup, milk, soft-boiled-egg shells, oatmeal, and other foodstuffs that young Labradors seem to require, including various fancy cuts of meat. (My wife bought some ground chuck steak for the puppies the other day, but our cook inadvertently fed it to the children, who thrived on it, as well they should have, considering what it cost.) Practically the only thing that puppies don't have to be given to eat, it seems to me, is tulip bulbs. I wish they were on the list. I have two hundred of them still on hand, and the ground is frozen solid.

Sincerely,
E. J. KAHN, JR.

February 6, 1954

Closings and Openings

A possibly apocryphal story in the gossipy world of bankers, brokers, and other dealers in large figures, concerns a meeting some time back of two real-estate men who themselves deal in figures that are not exactly small—William Zeckendorf and Roger Lacey Stevens. According to the story, Zeckendorf and Stevens, who between them control some three hundred million dollars' worth of property, were comparing notes one day, and in the course of their conversation Zeckendorf remarked, "You know, Roger, I believe you're the greatest operator of them all," whereupon Stevens, who habitually wears an air of diffidence, at once replied, "Oh, no, Bill, *you* are." Zeckendorf unexpectedly took him up on it, saying, "O.K., Roger, I guess you're right. But if I'm the greatest, you're the second greatest." Shortly after this conversation is supposed to have taken place, Stevens organized a syndicate that bought the Empire State Building for fifty-one and a half million dollars, the highest price ever paid for a single building in the history of the world, and it was not long after *that* that Zeckendorf's company, Webb & Knapp, Inc., bought the Chrysler Building and enough satellite buildings to bring the total price of his purchase to an even fifty-two million. Stevens has been content to let Zeckendorf have the higher price tag as long as he has the higher structure. "You can juggle figures all you like," he once said, "but there is only one Empire State Building."

Whatever their ranking, Zeckendorf and Stevens are quite a pair, and comparisons between them are made with some frequency these days. Actually, they are not at all alike. Stevens, a casually dressed, soft-spoken, fairly inarticulate man of unassuming appearance, spends at least half his time not dealing in real estate at all but putting on Broadway shows; in the past, his flair for making money on closing profitable real-estate deals has been neatly balanced by a flair for losing it on opening unprofitable shows ("Mr. Pickwick," "An Enemy of the People," and "Barefoot in Athens," among others), although this season, having been largely responsible for the production of such Broadway hits as "Tea and Sympathy" and "Sabrina Fair," he seems to have learned the trick of coming out on top whether he is closing a deal or opening a show. Zeckendorf, an impeccably tailored, stentorian, eloquent man with a flamboyant air, is his own show. His office, elegantly decorated with trick lighting fixtures and captive trees, and densely populated with suave staff assistants, looks like something out of *House & Garden*, his home looks like something out of "Kind Sir," and he shuttles between these two dazzling establishments in an elongated limousine (a Chrysler) with the legend "1-WZ" on its license plate. Stevens has a staff of only two people, who share with him a cramped and grubby cubicle in the Empire State Building that he has borrowed from a window washer; his files are kept not in custom-built cabinets, as Zeckendorf's are, but in old cardboard packing cartons strewn about the floor. Stevens does not have a car in New York (where, conceivably to Zeckendorf's chagrin, the words "Empire State" are inscribed on the license plate of everybody's car, including his own Chrysler), and his home here is an eight-room apartment, which, although he, his wife, their fifteen-year-old daughter, and a fourteen-year-old poodle have been living in it for a year now, is still only half furnished. Zeckendorf, a man who travels widely, confers with his real-estate associates by telephone every weekday, no matter what distant part of the world he may be in. Stevens also gets about, but he is inclined to neglect to let his associates know exactly where he is, with the result that he is sometimes unavailable to them for a week at a stretch, even though he may be physically no more remote than Hartford.

Zeckendorf says that the only resemblance between Stevens and himself is that they both are bald. "And at that he's thin and I'm fat," he adds. This is a relative estimate. Zeckendorf's eating habits are those of a determined gourmet, verging at times on those of a gourmand. Stevens can take fancy foods or leave them alone—when he has a play in production, and his stomach is jumpy, he has been known to subsist exclusively on dry Martinis, pea soup, and cheese—but, notwithstanding Zeckendorf's charitable appraisal of his bulk, he, too, has a tendency toward stoutness. From time to time, Stevens tries to combat this by killing his appetite with tobacco, to which he has a long-standing antipathy. When he is in a reducing mood, he smokes quantities of cigars. "I loathe the damn things," he once said while lighting up an innocuous-looking stogie. There is no one brand that he particularly detests; he will puff, and gag, on any old kind, provided it does not strike him as ineffectually bland.

Stevens and Zeckendorf run into each other every now and then. At one meeting a couple of years ago, Zeckendorf, who, at forty-eight, refers to Stevens, who is forty-three, as a "young man," suggested that they pool their formidable talents. Stevens was to take over Zeckendorf's job as president of Webb & Knapp, and Zeckendorf would become chairman of its board. Had the proposed merger gone through, it would probably have had an effect on real estate similar to the one that the creation of United States Steel had on heavy industry, but Stevens declined the offer, feeling that both he and Zeckendorf operate best in the role of lone, if far from hungry, wolves. As competitors, moreover, they have a livelier relationship than they might have as partners. Last fall, soon after Zeckendorf picked up the Chrysler Building, Stevens and some of his co-proprietors of the Empire State invited him to lunch in their building in order to congratulate him in a straightforward, if unavoidably condescending, way on owning the second-highest building in the world. They even arranged a press conference to commemorate the occasion. This was held in a room where scale models of the two buildings rested on a table behind which the guest of honor, and various of his hosts, could be photographed. With no half mile in between to soften the contrast, as there is in real life, the Chrysler Building looked pathetically puny alongside the Empire State. Zeckendorf stalked fearlessly into this enemy territory, stole the ensuing headlines by answering all the questions asked by the reporters (he later said that he had waited politely for his hosts to answer them, but that they had seemed to be struck dumb in his presence), and, when the photographers aimed their cameras, came within a hair of achieving a really remarkable triumph by deftly picking up the model of the Chrysler Building, as if to examine it, and elevating its spire above that of the model of the Empire State. "The damn-fool photographers muffed it," he lamented afterward.

Although Stevens attended the party for Zeckendorf, he rarely turns up for the receptions that are held at the Empire State Building for other distinguished visitors, like touring royalty, who come to see it and the view from it. "I try to duck that sort of thing," he explained recently. "It's too time-consuming. I haven't been on top of the tower in a year." His first ascent was made a couple of years ago, when he and some of his colleagues were being shown around shortly before they were to take over the premises. Construction on the television mast was then in progress, and the new owners were led to some scaffolding, which consisted of narrow planks of wood edged with chicken wire, and were urged to walk around the tower on it. Stevens, who suffers mildly from acrophobia, looked down, turned green, clutched a nearby metal upright, and said, "You boys walk around. I'll wait." Later, he picked out as his office a cubbyhole, no more than eight feet wide and twenty long, on the fifth floor.

Stevens, who sometimes says he was attracted to the Empire State Building solely because it seemed to be a cheap piece of real estate (it cost fifty-two million dollars when it was erected, in 1931), got wind of the fact that it might be available when he stopped in at the banking house of Hemphill, Noyes & Co. one morning in the spring of 1951 to pass the time of day with Jansen Noyes, Jr., one of the three Noyes members of the firm. "Why don't we stir something up?" Stevens asked conversationally. Noyes had just been told, in hushed, furtive tones, by a vice-president of the Charles F. Noyes Company, a real-estate brokerage firm, that the Empire State Building might be on the market, and he now relayed this news, in a whisper, to Stevens. (While Charles Noyes is not related to the Hemphill, Noyes Noyeses, they have many dealings with his company and invariably refer to him as Uncle Charlie.) Stevens said in an offhand manner that he would be interested in seeing the building's audited statement and hearing a price, but Jansen Noyes hadn't been let in on any such arcane figures. A month later, Uncle Charlie visited Hemphill, Noyes and disclosed that the prospective sellers wanted fifty million dollars, take it or leave it. Jansen Noyes asked if he could convey this information, together with a few other statistics that Uncle Charlie had guardedly passed along, to a certain individual, and when Uncle Charlie consented, he telephoned Stevens, who was then in Detroit. In a strangely unfamiliar voice, Stevens instructed Noyes to take an option on the building. Noyes expected Stevens to come directly to New York to go into details, but he had no further word from him for three weeks. Noyes later learned that at the time of his telephone call Stevens had had the mumps, and had been too embarrassed about his predicament to mention it or to show himself on Wall Street.

Stevens made a million-dollar deposit on the Empire State Building in May, 1951, and agreed to hand over the rest of the money by November 30th. In accepting the down payment, the attorneys for the estate of John J. Raskob (he had put up the building), who were superintending the other end of the deal, granted him one out: He could withdraw from the whole business if the financial situation of the country changed materially before August 31st. Like many another current purchaser of large real-estate holdings, Stevens decided to raise part of the necessary cash, and reap certain attractive tax benefits, by selling the land out from under the building and then leasing the land back. He got the Metropolitan Life Insurance Company to agree to be the other party, provided he could arrange suitable mortgage financing. By mid-August, J. P. Morgan & Co. had promised Stevens a two-and-a-half-million-dollar loan, and he had a few more million dollars half promised, but he was still far short of his objective. His attempts to obtain mortgage money had got nowhere. Stevens nevertheless announced to all concerned that in his opinion financial conditions had not changed and that he considered himself committed to go ahead. It has since been widely conceded that he was taking a monumental risk. Mortgage money in the amount he required—somewhere around twenty million dollars was the sum he had settled on as enough—was extremely tight. But Stevens, whose sensitivity to the nuances of the money market is considered acute, knew that toward autumn some of the big insurance companies are usually loaded down with incoming premium money that they haven't yet got around to investing and are in search of ways to unload it. Before tackling any such source of help, he persuaded the Raskob estate to take a five-million-dollar purchase-money second mortgage. Then, although he had been turned down twice by the Prudential Insurance Company—or, as it is usually called in financial circles, the Pru—on a twenty-million-dollar first leasehold mortgage, he approached it again, for he had reason to believe that it was eager to find outlets for uninvested funds. This time, he asked the Prudential for a fifteen-and-a-half-million-dollar first mortgage and offered to pay five per cent interest—one-half per cent more than the maximum he had previously discussed. After some deliberation, the Prudential found this proposition interesting enough to give him an oral commitment on it, but only if he would also switch to it the land-sale-and-lease-back deal he had arranged with the Metropolitan. The Metropolitan graciously consented to withdraw, and the Prudential was in, tentatively, for thirty-two and a half million—the first mortgage and an additional seventeen million dollars for the land, or just about nine million dollars an acre. Stevens was to lease this back for a hundred years, at an annual rental that was to be a million and twenty thousand dollars for the first thirty years and to decrease over the next seventy until it amounted to a mere three hundred and forty thousand.

Although the Prudential had agreed in principle to all this, it was far from ready to hand over the money. It insisted on waiting until the lease on the land had been drawn up and carefully examined. The examination, with corollary dickering, took four solid weeks of sixteen-hour-a-day sessions, during which Stevens and his colleagues, including his lawyer, Thomas A. Halleran, a member of Cravath, Swaine & Moore, fenced with a committee of insurance executives over details. As the wrangling progressed, Stevens assumed a characteristic air of lamblike naïveté. The more the Prudential's lawyers raised their voices, the softer and more trembling his voice became. He declared abjectly that while he sympathized with the Pru's position, his lawyer, Halleran, was a temperamental dragon who, if the Pru didn't yield on its demands, might very well order him to wash his hands of the deal—a course that, by this stage of the game, Stevens felt sure the Pru had no wish to have him follow. (Stevens once asked Halleran why it was that he always seemed to get himself involved in troublesome legalities in the course of closing deals. "There's always trouble when you try to substitute ingenuity for cash," the lawyer replied.) At the end of the four weeks, Stevens got his mortgage, and the rental terms he wanted, but the Prudential's lawyers, perhaps piqued at not having won any modification of the lease—an eighty-five-page printed document that Halleran had submitted for their ratification—declined to approve it until the whole thing had been reprinted, unchanged except that the margins were a quarter of an inch wider. Reflecting on those exciting days, Ben Tobin, a longtime real-estate associate of Stevens', says, "I was scared to death. It looked as if Roger couldn't get through, but he did. If he hadn't licked the Pru, we'd have been dead. The million dollars we'd have forfeited would have been bad enough, but we could probably have offset that somehow. It was the loss of face that would have been fatal."

Meanwhile, Stevens had had to raise his equity money—fourteen million dollars, including his million-dollar deposit and the loan from J. P. Morgan. He had got Charles Noyes to come in for a million four hundred thousand by dangling before him a hundred-thousand-a-year contract to manage the Empire State Building. The Alleghany Corporation, an investment company controlled by Robert R. Young, proved good for two million one hundred thousand more. Then the families of Raskob and the late Alfred E. Smith added a million fifty thousand, mostly out of sentiment. Stevens, Tobin, and still another real-estate associate, Alfred R. Glancy, Jr., had something over two million dollars more of their own to throw into the kitty. Some other friends of Stevens' furnished the relatively trifling sum of three hundred and fifty thousand. There was one more large investor whom Stevens had been counting on to provide the remaining two million eight hundred thousand, but at nearly the last minute the man decided he wasn't interested. On November 28th, forty-eight hours before his deadline, Stevens advised the Raskob-estate lawyers that he guessed he'd have to forfeit, after all. Not wanting to start negotiating all over again with a new customer, they agreed to assume this share if he would promise to try to get somebody else to take it as soon as possible. They even suggested a prospect—Colonel Henry Crown, a Chicago investor who was a director of Columbia Pictures, the Rock Island Railroad, and the Hilton Hotels. Stevens scurried right over to see Crown's New York attorney, and presently the Colonel had joined the syndicate. As a reward for his coöperativeness, he was made chairman of the board of the Empire State Building. Stevens was pleased with the way things had worked out. "By the time I was through putting the pieces together," he said later, "I had made everybody in the deal a buccaneer—each one thought he was getting the edge on everybody else." Colonel Crown must have been pleased, too, for he has since bought up the shares of a number of his associates—including most of Tobin's interest in the venture—and now owns more than half the Empire State Building, or roughly fifty-two stories.

As Stevens was assembling his pieces, Halleran was feverishly preparing for the closing, which, after being postponed once to get the margins on the lease satisfactorily adjusted, was finally scheduled to get under way at nine-thirty on the morning of December 21st in the board room of the Bankers Trust Company's main offices, at 16 Wall Street. Stevens obviously couldn't sell the land out from under the building until he owned the building, but he couldn't buy the building until he got the proceeds from the sale of the land. Halleran concluded that these two steps, as well as a hundred and two other necessary formalities, would have to be imagined as occurring simultaneously, and he persuaded four title-insurance companies to accept this premise. Then he got up a thirty-three-page memorandum of stage directions for all the people—sellers and their lawyers, buyers and their lawyers, title-insurance-company representatives and their lawyers, notary publics and their lawyers, and others and their lawyers—who had to convene to execute the transfer of the property. This was just as well, since the transfer called for the passing back and forth of six hundred documents, bearing two thousand signatures, and the payment by one party to another of checks totalling $167,222,056.13. The strain of getting set for all this was so severe that one scheduled participant collapsed from nervous exhaustion shortly before the big day. A dress rehearsal of the closing, with the whole cast present, was held on December 20th, to make sure no one would blow his lines. "This wasn't done as a theatrical gesture," Stevens has since said. "If anything had gone wrong, all hell might have broken loose. We had to be certain the next paper in the series wouldn't be blocked because of some unforeseen legal technicality. By the day of the actual closing, I was numb. I had visions of being known for the rest of my life as the man who didn't buy the Empire State Building. It all went off without a hitch, though. There must have been a hundred people in the room when we closed, and as the last signature was put on the last sheet of paper, seven and a half hours after we'd started, they all suddenly and spontaneously burst into applause. I never in my life heard anything like it except on an opening night."

February 20, 1954

From Part II of a two-part Profile.

Our Far-Flung Correspondents
Almost in a Class with the Braves

MILWAUKEE, MARCH 25

Ever since the fall of 1941, I have had a soft spot in my heart for Wisconsin. At that time, as a result of the mysterious ways of Selective Service, I found myself assigned to the 32nd Infantry Division, which was composed mainly of National Guardsmen from Wisconsin and Michigan. I have often stood on alien soil—in an Australian forest, say—and listened proudly to our division band improbably trumpeting the strains of "On, Wisconsin." I made quite a few firm Wisconsin friends, some of them from the rural areas and some from this city, which, with six hundred and fifty thousand inhabitants, shelters about a fifth of Wisconsin's population. The state has not forgotten the 32nd Division, which is currently a Guard unit manned exclusively by Wisconsinites, any more than I have. A year or so ago, one of the main highways between Chicago and Green Bay, which passes through Milwaukee, was rechristened Route 32, in the outfit's honor. The roadside markers that identify the highways are decorated with a red arrow piercing a red line—the insigne on the shoulder patch of many an old uniform lying in a trunk in many an attic like mine.

Many of the men from Wisconsin I encountered overseas were soldiers of wide renown. Just for example, I vividly recall an incident one day, several miles outside of Port Moresby, New Guinea, when my commanding general was honored by a visit from one son of Wisconsin, Douglas MacArthur, who had in tow another son—Philip La Follette, a former governor of the state who was then a major. While I eavesdropped respectfully, General MacArthur ushered Major La Follette up to my general, saying, "Phil, I want you to meet your new commander. He will lead you to your glory or your death." Several weeks later, MacArthur reclaimed La Follette and made him a censor, thus enabling him to achieve a nice balance between those gallant alternatives. Still another eminent soldier from Wisconsin is, of course, Brigadier General Ralph Zwicker, and it was not long after his recent and sudden ascent to celebrity that I found I had to spend a few days here on business, which gave me a chance to renew some old acquaintances and to become acquainted, for the first time, with the state that Senator McCarthy has made famous.

One arrives in Wisconsin these days with an inescapable awareness of its national—and, indeed, worldwide—significance. Within the past fortnight, Milwaukee has been wonderingly scrutinized by correspondents from newspapers published in England, France, and Germany—all of them drawn here by the state's formidable junior Senator. Offhand, one might think that the state's *senior* Senator, Alexander Wiley, would more properly be the primary object of attention for such far-ranging fact-finders, since he is, after all, the chairman of the Foreign Relations Committee and perhaps the most international-minded Republican senator from this section of the country since Senator Vandenberg; but in Milwaukee, and throughout the state, there is little talk of any senator but Joe, as Wiley's colleague is known hereabouts to both friend and foe. Indeed, Senator McCarthy is a topic almost as feverishly discussed as the Milwaukee Braves. This is a singular tribute to McCarthy, for not even in Brooklyn has a major-league baseball team ever aroused the devotion that has been lavished on the Braves since their franchise was transferred here from Boston a year ago. The Braves broke all National League attendance records last season, and though they won't be through with spring training for another two weeks, they have already sold far more tickets for the coming season than most clubs can hope to dispose of by the time they have played a hundred and fifty-four games. Local mothers are urged by the fashion page of the Milwaukee *Journal*, the afternoon paper, to outfit their sons in diminutive copies of the Braves' uniform, and by department stores to buy their daughters—or, conceivably, themselves—charm bracelets with "MILWKE BRAVES" spelled out in pendants. The Milwaukee *Sentinel*, the morning paper, has been carrying daily dispatches from the Braves' training camp filed by the wife of the team's star pitcher, Warren Spahn, and last week it dedicated practically an entire page to photographs of Spahn's son imitating his daddy. A *Journal* photographer recently did his best to meet this sort of competition by rushing north a group picture—which his editors steeled themselves not to publish—of three members of the Milwaukee squad; his justification for assembling those particular men was that they all had colds.

After the fashion of many legislators, Senator Wiley sends his constituents a weekly newsletter, and in it he refers frequently and affectionately to the Braves. Senator McCarthy does not get out a newsletter, perhaps because he feels that his constituents have ample opportunity to keep up with him without one, and his public utterances about the Braves, if any, haven't made much of a splash back home. This neglect of the state's most prized jewel is thought by some of his fellow-Wisconsinites to reflect his lofty appraisal of the grip he has on their esteem. "When Joe starts plugging the Braves," one leading Republican told me the other day, "it'll be a sure sign that he's finally begun to slip." In Milwaukee itself, to be sure, Senator McCarthy has never stood high enough to be able to slip very far. In 1952, the city backed General Eisenhower but defeated McCarthy by almost a hundred thousand votes. The *Journal*, which is the more prominent of the two local dailies, has been one of McCarthy's most outspoken opponents. So aggressive is the paper's attitude toward the Senator that its chief editorial writer, who prides himself on having been the first of his trade to refer to McCarthy as Jumping Joe, came to the conclusion not long ago that he would have to ration himself to two or three anti-McCarthy editorials a week. The *Sentinel* is a Hearst paper and is friendly to McCarthy. In the *Sentinel*, Joe never jumps. Last week, it referred to him with unusual formality in a front-page news story as "Sen. McCarthy (R-Wis.)."

Milwaukee is against McCarthy principally because it is a heavily industrialized city, swarming with factory workers of predominantly Democratic persuasion. It is a fairly quiet, conservative city, too, with no night life to speak of, and although it ranks thirteenth among the country's municipalities in population (Milwaukeeans are extremely conscious of their relative standing and are apprehensive about Houston, which is sneaking up on them fast), it has an old-fashioned main street, Wisconsin Avenue, along or just off which are located most of the centers of civic life. Milwaukee's most publicized product, of the hundreds that its massed industries turn out, is beer. The Pabst Theatre, at present the only legitimate playhouse in town, stands directly opposite the Blatz Hotel. Pabst, Blatz, Schlitz, and Miller High Life are the four biggest breweries, and the city abounds not only with saloons dispensing the local specialty but with advertisements extolling one or another variety of it. To an outsider here, it seems odd at first to be interminably confronted with signs declaring that this beer is Milwaukee's finest and that that one made Milwaukee famous, but the explanation is simple enough. Each of the big breweries is sincerely anxious to be able to claim honestly that it is Milwaukee's favorite, and therefore the whole bunch of them knock themselves out trying to win and hold this laurel. Milwaukee's residents have responded loyally to all the beer advertising by consuming more of the stuff per capita than the burghers of any other American city—an average of thirty-nine gallons a year. Blatz is currently leading the field in this particular race. Miller High Life, however, has achieved the coveted sponsorship of the broadcasts of the Braves' games. It is not known which beer Senator McCarthy is most partial to. One influential local Republican I had a chat with, though, intimated that the Senator, like a good many Democrats, normally has a predilection for bourbon. In discussing the recent conflict between the executive and legislative branches of the federal government, this politician said, "If I were in Ike's boots, I'd invite Joe to the White House, close the doors, knock the top off a bottle of bourbon, and settle the whole business, man to man, in five minutes." He did not seem fazed by the thought that if the President were to carry out this forthright scheme, he might seem to be recognizing only one Senator out of ninety-six as his bargaining equal. For that matter, a lot of people in Wisconsin do not concern themselves unduly with the ninety-five others.

Many Wisconsin Republicans are eager to see Senator McCarthy's differences with the administration reconciled by one means or another, if only in the interests of Party harmony, but they are skeptical about the durability of any reconciliation, since Wisconsin politicians are a notoriously individualistic lot, indifferent to conventional party labels or disciplines. For instance, it was a Wisconsin member of the House of Representatives, Alvin O'Konski, who last year tried to negotiate unilaterally with Syngman Rhee—an adventure that, while less widely heralded and less productive of results than McCarthy's lone-wolf dealings with the Greek shipowners, was a demonstration of the same unorthodox diplomacy. And though the Socialist Party in the state is no more influential than its counterpart in New York, the incumbent mayor of Milwaukee, Frank Zeidler, is a Socialist. (He cheerfully describes himself as a freak.) Zeidler is resolutely antagonistic to Senator McCarthy, but he told me the other day—and I have heard the same sentiments expressed by politicians on both sides of the thorny McCarthy fence—that he thinks Wisconsin, despite the current agitation to institute recall proceedings against the junior Senator, would probably reëlect him to office if a vote were to be taken today. (McCarthy's term has another four years to run.) The Mayor has had no personal run-ins with Senator McCarthy, who has never conducted any field inquiries in his home state and hardly ever bothers to hector anybody here. McCarthy, in fact, pays relatively little attention of any kind to Wisconsin, but he is careful to pay more than the man he defeated in the 1946 Republican primary, the late Senator Robert M. La Follette, Jr.; toward the end of his term, La Follette nettled his constituents by practically making Washington his home. McCarthy has even found time recently to introduce a bill affecting the rights of the Menominee Indians, who are among his constituents.

Like a good many other states, Wisconsin has no political uniformity. Its urban and rural components are persistently at odds with each other. The fact that McCarthy has a measure of appeal for both groups is felt to be one of his vote-getting attributes. He was born in farm country and began his pre-political career near Appleton, an upstate community where just the other day two aroused citizens were fined four hundred and eighty dollars for impulsively shooting holes in the radiator of an automobile that belonged to a fellow who they thought was an informer against game-law violators. But McCarthy is a big-city boy, too. He attended college and law school at Marquette University, a Jesuit institution on Milwaukee's main street. He was boxing coach there while a student, and some of his constituents think that this explains his habit of bobbing and weaving his head while he talks. The university's opinion of its most noted alumnus is, to put it mildly, mixed. Some members of the faculty, which is made up of both clerical and lay instructors, exclaim of him admiringly, "He's one of our boys!"—a possessive relationship that has kept many non-Marquette Wisconsinites in his camp, too. On the other hand, a dean there said to me, "For a long time, I never could understand how this man, with a good Catholic education, could do the unjust and uncharitable things he has done. I'd always assumed that he'd had three years of liberal-arts training, with some courses in religion and philosophy, like most of our pre-law students, and I'd always wondered to myself, Who in the world here could possibly have taught him ethics? And then one day I learned, to my surprise, that Joe had merely had two years of engineering and one summer session of liberal arts before going to law school. Suddenly I thought, Gee, this is wonderful! He's not really one of our boys after all!"

A lot of people here are plainly growing tired of being held responsible—as, indirectly, they are responsible—for everything their junior Senator says and does. They would rather have a less time-consuming one. "I'm fond of Joe," one Milwaukee businessman remarked to me, "but I'm beginning to think I may have to give him up." (This impulse toward renunciation was disclosed during Lent.) Another businessman, who is unshakably devoted to Joe, told me he was absolutely convinced that McCarthy is the country's only hope of avoiding conquest by the Communists. But even with McCarthy still on the firing line this man is taking no chances. He has two rifles and three thousand rounds of ammunition cached in his basement, he said, and at the first sign of trouble he proposes to pack up this arsenal and take off for a spot he has already reconnoitered in Alaska, where he expects to live off the local game and watch Russian bombers, unaware of his presence down below, streak harmlessly overhead on their way to the factories and breweries of Milwaukee.

The Republican Party was reputedly founded a hundred years ago in a schoolhouse at Ripon, Wisconsin, about sixty miles northwest of Milwaukee, and last weekend centennial ceremonies were held there. On the eve of the centennial, the Young Republican Club of Milwaukee County held a commemorative dinner here in town. (The tickets called it a "Centenial Dinner.") They started planning the affair several weeks ago, and at that time, as a polite gesture, invited all the state's leading Republicans to drop in and say a few words. Somewhat to the hosts' surprise, they learned, through a communiqué issued by Senator McCarthy in Washington, that the Senator was planning not only to come but to deliver a major address—his reply to Adlai Stevenson's speech about him. The Senator's vigorous acceptance of the invitation had the effect of causing several Republicans who might have dropped in and said a few words to remember other engagements; as it developed, he was the only person, aside from the master of ceremonies, to say any words.

I had never seen Senator McCarthy in action, except on television, so I went around to the Plankinton Hotel, where the dinner was being held, and took in the proceedings. The Senator had been ill for a couple of days, and was perhaps not in top form—at one point he gave the impression of being close to fainting—but he put on a stimulating performance. Deadly serious at one moment, he would grin broadly the next while excoriating the Democratic Party for one or another of the twenty alleged treasonable acts he charged it with. He did not mention the Braves. His audience was large, and it was enthusiastic, but not wildly so. Several people stayed in their seats when their fellow-diners gave him a standing ovation, and the loudest applause he got was in response to a reference—quite unrelated to anything that preceded or followed it—to the late Senator Taft. Senator McCarthy was scheduled, or had scheduled himself, to speak for thirty minutes. He ran twenty minutes over, and then, gracious and smiling, shook hands for another half hour or so. He was sweating hard and mopping his brow, and watching him made me thirsty, so I wandered into the hotel's bar and had a beer—I forget which brand. While I was there, I asked a waitress what she thought of Senator McCarthy. Waitresses are supposed to be good barometers of public opinion; like barbers and cabdrivers, they hear a lot of things from all sorts of people. (The only Milwaukee cabdriver I discussed McCarthy with was sore at him and sore at the Army, too. He was sore at the Senator for not keeping him out of the Army during the Korean war, and he was sore at the Army for not releasing him from service as swiftly as it had released a certain professional ballplayer—not, the cabdriver hastily added, a member of the Milwaukee club.) The waitress, after a pause to collect her thoughts, said solemnly, "If Joe's right, he's right. If he's not right, I guess we've got to make him right. I don't know, really. I'm confused. Say, what do you think of those Braves?"

April 3, 1954

I Guess I Haven't Lived Yet

I have never seen a deer cross a road at a deer crossing,
And I have never come upon a fallen rock in a fallen-rock zone.
I have never noticed any trucks entering from right,
And the school bus never stops here, at least not when I'm there.
I have never felt the need for special caution while proceeding at my own
    risk along a stretch of highway that is officially closed to traffic,
And the hills that are slippery when wet always seem to be dry as a bone
    when I crawl down them in low gear.
What a dull life!

June 5, 1954

Worner (Cont.)

Ted Worner, the usually cheerful, eternally voluble Broadway press agent whose adventures have beguiled us in the past—it was he, you will recall, who shepherded Shirley May France through both of her vigorously publicized, if unsuccessful, assaults upon the English Channel—telephoned the other day and invited us, in a troubled voice, to call on him without delay. "I am known as a man of enterprise," he started in when we had arrived at his office, "but I am afraid I have overenterprised myself, if there is such a word. What would *you* do if you were stuck with the world's largest wristwatch?"

Worner, characteristically, did not pause for an answer. "It all began last fall," he said, "when I was leafing through *Life* and saw a picture of two guys walking into an exhibition hall in Frankfurt, Germany, and slung over the shoulder of each of them is an enormous watch, the biggest wristwatch ever. I remember the time well, because it was just before I got my ulcers. 'Ted,' I said to myself, 'this is something for you.' I found out the manufacturer's name through friends I have all over, and I dispatched a cable saying I wanted to buy one of the watches. My idea was to sell it to a watch company here as a promotion stunt—Kingston excluded. Kingston is a client of mine, and Shirley and I both wore their watches in the Channel, and I play golf and gin with Sam Schecter, their president, a very nice fellow, but I figured this watch, which I am sorry but I do not feel I should disclose what I paid for it any more than the late Dr. Rosenbach would have told you what he paid for one of his rare books, was a little too expensive for Schecter's blood. Well, anyway, after several months of complicated negotiations, and reams of correspondence deep into the Black Forest, I got the watch. Here it is!"

He grappled with a large wooden case, marked "ACHTUNG! SEHR ZERBRECHLICH!," that occupied a good deal of the floor space of his modest office, and from it extracted, with clearly mixed emotions, a veritable giant of a wristwatch, its case made of brass and its strap of brown imitation leather. "Including the strap, six feet eight inches long," he intoned. "The watch itself weighs six and a half pounds and measures fourteen inches in diameter across the face. The watch strap is five and a half inches wide. Eleven fair-sized rubies are in there serving as jewels. It runs seventeen days on a single winding. Can you conceive of the Speidel Corporation being so foolish as not to buy it and manufacture the world's largest wristwatch band to go with it? The sad truth is that nobody is interested in it. Oh, the cleaning women here are. 'Hey, girls, come look at the world's largest wristwatch!' they yell to each other all night long. And the customs men at Idlewild were interested when I claimed it. They came from far and near to examine it. I planned, of course, when I sold it, to restage its entry, with a beautiful girl. But Benrus has turned it down and Gruen has turned it down and just about everybody has turned it down and here it is and here I am. I know what the hell to do with a Channel swimmer. I even know what to do with Jimmy Randolph, my kid singer, who's going to be a big star and has already been at Grossinger's thirty-three times. He began at fifty dollars a week and had to play softball, too, and now he gets two hundred and fifty and no softball. But I do not know what to do with this watch."

On the face of the watch, where the name of the manufacturer would normally be, was emblazoned in huge letters, "WORNER." "It cost me five per cent extra to have my name put on it," he told us. "I plan to have a client's name substituted if I ever manage to unload it. Oh, I've had lots of ideas. I've thought of the giant in the circus, and the arm of the Statue of Liberty. One guy wanted me to buy him a station wagon and let him drive it from town to town, so local stores could advertise 'Come to Klotz's This Week Only to See the World's Largest Wristwatch,' but I think the guy just wanted to ride around the country in a station wagon."

Worner seized the watch, hoisted it to one shoulder, and began pacing up and down his office beneath it. "Hear how quietly it runs!" he commanded. "What is the matter with everybody these days? In Hollywood, where I was for six weeks as technical adviser on 'Dangerous When Wet,' the picture that Esther Williams swims the Channel in, I had my name on a door in the Irving Thalberg Memorial Building right next to Joe Pasternak. In New York, I am frustrated by a wristwatch. If only I could tie it in with one of my clients—my kid singer, say, or the Aluminum Boat Company of America, or my three hotels, or even my Oz Greeting Card Company that I got into all the mess with on account of Margaret Truman. She bought an Oz—'You've been investigated, you're in the clear, you've made it through another year, Happy Birthday,' it says—and mailed it to her father on his seventieth birthday, and I knocked myself out sending a release about it to all the papers, and then my client wants the story killed, because the store Margaret got it at is afraid it will lose her trade and says it will deny everything, so I knock myself out persuading all my friends on all the papers to kill the story I just sent them, and then, the next day, I am in my doctor's office, checking up on my ulcers, sitting there stark naked, when I pick up a paper and turn to a gossip column and I let out a shriek and my doctor comes running over and asks what's the matter and I point to the column, where my item that I had thought I got killed is. I told my doctor the whole story, and he said, 'Ted, if that had happened to me, I'd have ulcers, too.'"

June 26, 1954

Doggy

There are approximately twenty-two million dogs in the United States at present, of which perhaps a third are purebred. (Dog people do not use the word "thoroughbred," which they regard as too horsy.) Last year, more than three hundred thousand dogs were accepted by the American Kennel Club for registration as untainted specimens of their breed. The A.K.C. never inspects the dogs it pronounces purebred. Relying on the honesty of breeders, it confines itself to authenticating the data they furnish about their dogs' ancestors. Nevertheless, it does not bestow its imprimatur haphazardly. At least one dog, the pet of a prankish owner, has made the *Social Register*; there is no evidence that any human being has yet crashed the A.K.C.'s studbook. The club has made extensive use of an admonitory message from Albert Payson Terhune, the collie laureate, who was one of its directors from 1922 to 1926: "You owe it to your dog to have it registered; to give it the hallmark which guarantees its quality." But despite this and similar injunctions, a lot of dog owners have remained indifferent to registration, much as if they were dogs. One reason may be the frightening complexity of some of the forms the A.K.C. gets up. For example, in order to register a litter from the mating of an A.K.C. registered dog and an imported dog, if the dam was sold in whelp, three persons—the owner of the sire on the date of mating, the owner of the dam on the date of the birth of the litter, and the owner of the dam at the time of mating—must fill out a three-page form containing a total of sixty-four questions. (At that, the forms outsiders are expected to fill out are less formidable than some of the A.K.C.'s interoffice forms, one of which consists of an original and twelve carbons—four of them pink, three yellow, two orange, two blue, and one white.) Nearly ten per cent of all the various forms that are filled out and sent in to the club—applications to register litters of puppies, to register individual dogs, to transfer ownership of dogs, and so forth—are rejected as improperly executed. A stirring episode in "221," a promotional movie the club produced a couple of years ago and named for its address, showed a little girl in tears after her father's attempt to register her dog had foundered because of sloppy paperwork; in other words, if parents don't want their children to cry they had better get a grip on themselves and fill those forms out right. The A.K.C. is unyielding in its insistence on accuracy; it has even gone so far as to spurn an application filed by one of its own delegates. The club turned down one woman's application because she had not signed her name in cursive writing; it was only after she abjectly confessed that the pupils at the private school she had attended were taught only to print that the club consented to register her dog. Another woman, in the course of a protracted campaign to persuade the A.K.C. to acknowledge her ownership of a dog she had bought months before, wrote the club, "I have never in my life had so much fun transferring anything! If something isn't clear this time, please write me again—such fun should not be discontinued!" Tenacity of this sort is not universal; a lot of people whose efforts to win A.K.C. approval have bogged down in technicalities have simply given up.

A battery of female clerks processes the club's correspondence, which currently runs to a weekly total of some twelve thousand items of one kind and another. The girls who type out registration papers, pedigrees, and other such precious documents are allotted a specific number of blanks at the start of a day and are held accountable for each one, much as if they were working in the United States Mint. The A.K.C. divides purebreds into six major categories—Sporting, Non-Sporting, Hound, Working, Terrier, and Toy—and some of its clerks are correspondingly classified (which leads to many an intramural joke) as Hound Girls, Working Girls, Sporting Girls, and so on. There are girls whose only job is to make sure that dogs awaiting registration have registered parents; they are known as Sire and Dam Girls. Still others, who devote themselves exclusively to the task of passing on the acceptability of dogs' names, are called Naming Girls. In the A.K.C.'s files, in contrast to dog-show catalogues, the names of dogs are of the first importance; its voluminous records are indexed by dogs, and not by their owners. Once the club has approved a dog's name, it will under no conditions permit any change in it, since a change might snarl up the orderly tracing of bloodlines.

The Naming Girls have a lot of responsibilities. For one thing, they must make certain that there are no more than twenty dogs of any one breed, dead or alive, with the same name. (As of last month, there were still nine vacancies for "Fala" among Scottish terriers, but the quota for "Checkers" among cocker spaniels had been filled.) They must be careful that all dogs' names are seemly. When a lady who shall be called Smith, the owner of a bitch named Cleopatra, proposed christening one of the animal's female puppies Cleopatra's Concubine, the A.K.C. demurred. The word "concubine," it informed the petitioner, was too—well, er, slangy. The owner begged for a dispensation. Finally, the A.K.C. relented, but only to a degree; it entered the puppy on its rolls as Smith's Concubine. The Naming Girls are also supposed to see that, in the interest of common sense, male dogs don't get female names, and vice versa. Once, the application of a man who wanted to name a rowdy male puppy Jesse James was refused with the explanation that Jesse is a girl's name.

The Naming Girls have strict rules to follow when it comes to naming dogs after celebrated persons. This is forbidden unless the person in question gives his consent or has been dead for quite a while. It is permissible today to name a dog George Washington or Abraham Lincoln but not Franklin D. Roosevelt. With thousands of names to pass on every week, the Naming Girls inevitably slip up now and then. They approved, rightly, an application to name a borzoi Dostoievsky of Fleetstone, but they inadvertently allowed a Newfoundland to be named Little Bear's James Thurber. (In an attempt to reduce the number of lapses of this sort, the club recently gave its Naming Department a copy of *Who's Who*.) Outsiders are sometimes baffled by the fine distinctions that the A.K.C. makes in the matter of names. On the ground that nicknames don't count, the club has lately let a pointer be named Prune's Own General Ike. The owner of a bull terrier was allowed to name it General MacArthur in 1944, the A.K.C.'s reasoning being that no specific General MacArthur was necessarily meant, even though the applicant proposed Admiral Halsey as an alternative name. That same year, however, another bull terrier was not granted the name General Douglas MacArthur until after its owner had provided the A.K.C. with a letter from General MacArthur himself saying it was all right with him.

There are at present about twenty-five hundred active dog judges who have been approved by the A.K.C. to officiate at shows held under its rules. Some are eligible to judge only one breed, some to judge several breeds, and fifty-seven of them to judge all breeds. A number of the all-breed judges are professionals—men and women who, though they may have other occupations, are likely to spend nearly every weekend judging dogs, and whose customary fee is a hundred dollars a day, plus expenses. In an effort to prevent judges from judging the same dogs over and over again, the A.K.C. has decreed that none of them may judge any given breed more than once a month in an area within a radius of a hundred airline miles. A judge's lot is not an easy one. He may have a hundred or more dogs to pass on in the course of a single, broiling-hot day, or a devastatingly rainy one. He may also be harassed by the people in charge of the show to speed up his judging in order to adhere to an over-tight schedule. And since the condition of a dog's teeth is a determining factor in his findings, he may get nipped.

Dog people are forever charging one another with rascally deeds and demanding that the Kennel Club step in and set things straight. Since one man's opinion of an animal's quality may differ vastly from another's, dog-show judges, whose appraisals are necessarily based in great part on their opinions, come in for an exceptional amount of abuse. They are regularly accused of all sorts of misbehavior, ranging from the solicitation of bribes to drunkenness. A typical fracas was touched off last year by an elderly judge who was rating a class of German shepherds. As one of the entries was being paraded past him by a young lady, he peered intently at its tail, which seemed to him to have undergone surgery, in violation of a rule that tails may not be doctored. The young lady, aware of his gaze, murmured something about a car; afterward, the judge said he thought she'd said the dog's tail had got caught in a car door, and *she* said she'd said the tail had been worn down by long rubbing against seat covers of a car. Neither of these misadventures would have constituted grounds for disqualification, but an illegally fixed tail would have. The judge concluded that the tail had been wrongly tampered with, but he gave the dog a prize ribbon anyway. Later, he explained, "As I could not find evidence to justify my claim and knowing my calling for the official show veterinarian would but work a hardship on the entry at future shows, I saw fit to overlook the condition." That night, still brooding over the matter, the judge looked the dog up in the show's catalogue. He discovered that the dog belonged to a woman, and, surmising that the owner was the young lady who had exhibited it, he wrote her a long letter, reproving her in kindly-old-uncle fashion for what he thought she'd said to him in the show ring. He told her that he had been an expert on German shepherds since before she was born, that he knew a doctored tail when he saw one, and that as she grew older, she would learn better than to try to tell an experienced old hand like him a story like that one about the car door. The person to whom he addressed this letter was not, however, the girl, who had been simply a handler, but a woman who had had a pretty long association with German shepherds herself. Incensed by the suggestion that the tail of any dog of hers had been monkeyed with, she forwarded the judge's letter to the A.K.C. and attached to it a sheaf of affidavits from veterinarians that the tail had never been subjected to surgery. Since no formal charges of wrongdoing had been lodged with the A.K.C. by the judge, or by anyone else, it did not feel obliged to pass on the condition of the tail. But since the judge had been remiss in awarding a prize to a dog with a tail that in his opinion had been fixed, the club suspended his judging privileges.

Then things got complicated. *Dog World*, hearing about the contretemps, invited the judge to tell his side of the story. He wrote the magazine a letter in which he admitted that he had been wrong in giving the dog a prize, in view of his suspicions about it, and he reiterated those suspicions. *Dog World* published the letter, and presently its editor received a letter from the dog's owner's lawyer, in which he interpreted a letter to his client from the A.K.C. as evidence that the club had repudiated the judge's accusation. *Dog World* placatingly ran part of this letter, including a paragraph stating that the veterinarians' affidavits had been sent to the A.K.C. Now the judge took offense. He let it be known that he felt the wording of the lawyer's reference to the club might be construed to mean that it was endorsing the lady's contentions about the tail. It seemed as though the dispute might rage forever. Just then, though, the judge's suspension was lifted and he was allowed to go back to judging, so he mercifully threw no more fuel on the fire, and it died out. Whether a dog's tail can be doctored by the seat covers of an automobile remains unresolved to this day.

August 21, 1954

From Part I of a two-part Profile.

Spectral Vision

My love dreams in colors, I've suddenly learned;
The leaves on her reveries' trees all have turned.
The shades that she dreams in are not always true—
Violets are red, roses are blue—
But in her subconscious the spectrum holds sway;
While others dream drab dreams, she dreams them gay.

Asleep, she's aswirl in the rainbow's warm hues;
If Freud she should see then, he'd be in green shoes.
She dreams of mauve love fests and peppermint tiffs,
Of pale-yellow valleys and Shocking-pink cliffs,
Of lavender trips and vermilion returnings,
And polychromatic emotional yearnings.

The peacock who dazzles his lady by day,
Parading his glitter before her dun gray—
I wonder does he, in the shadowy night,
Dream dully, like me, in demure black-and-white?

October 2, 1954

Unusual Thing

"I seem to be giving away this race horse," reproted Ted Worner by phone, and we hurried right over to his office to hear about it. Worner is the garrulous and, to us, irresistible Broadway press agent who twice tried to shepherd Shirley May France across the English Channel, and who at our last meeting, nine months ago, was in somewhat dazed command of the world's largest wristwatch. We found him looking tanned and fit. "This new client I have, Kentucky Club pipe tobacco," he began, "gave away a horse last year at Kentucky Derby time, to the person who thought up the best name for it. There were over five hundred thousand entries. It is intriguing to me that there are so many people—men, women, and children—who would want to win a race horse. The advertising agency running the contest called me in to promote it. They wanted somebody who had done unusual things. When I went up to the agency, there were two account executives and the president of Kentucky Club, all puffing away at pipes like crazy. I was dying for a cigar—I am an Admiration Mayfair cigar smoker from way back, as you know—but I thought, Worner, wait till you feel surer of yourself. I even tried a pipe. The first day, I burned a hole in my imported cashmere sweater that this friend of mine brought me from Scotland. Have a cigar.

"This horse I'm giving away"—Worner rose from his desk and patted the nose of a larger-than-life-size cardboard photograph of a horse—"cost Kentucky Club forty-five hundred dollars at the Saratoga yearling sales. She's by Rippey out of Delphi. Rippey is the son of Pompey, and the father of Delphi is Sir Gallahad III, no less. The sire of three Derby winners! The kind of bloodlines a Vanderbilt or Whitney has! You know, I've never ridden a horse in my life, and I think I'm afraid to ride one, but this little filly I wish I could give to myself. Naturally, I am ineligible. Right away, when I got this job, I arranged for a vice-president, no less, of the Tobacco Workers' International Union to pose with my filly, and I have already placed this picture in high-class publications that you don't ordinarily get into, like the *Brotherhood of Maintenance of Way Employees Journal*. But I realized I'd have to come up with something special with a touch. So I hired myself four *two*-legged fillies to tour the country and talk about my four-legged filly. To be the gift horse's mouth, so to speak. Would you like to look a gift horse's mouth in the mouth? Norma!"

A young, blond two-legged filly trotted in. "Norma Copeland, an Australian from Sydney, Australia," said Worner. "She's been my Southern representative. I told her to go see all the sportswriters, and go on radio and television, and if she couldn't get anywhere with radio or television, to go see the mayor or the governor or somebody. Norma swept through the South telling everybody everything about my filly, which I have never seen. How many hands high is this horse of ours, Norma?"

"Five?" answered Norma.

"You know what I decided about my ulcer?" Worner went on quickly. "I decided that it was an ulcer, all right, but that it was probably just from this business of mine, so the hell with it. I went to the Miami *Herald*, where I am pretty well known on account of my association with Jackie Robinson and everything, and they said, 'Ted, we're glad to see you, but we don't go for these contests, Ted.' So I sent Norma around there three days later, and she got a full column."

"The secret is to give them glamour," said Norma. "Where it's hot, why wear a lot of clothes? In Fort Worth, to which I took a taxi from Dallas, the photographers kept shooting me so long my cab fare went up to fifty dollars."

"Is there no other transportation from Dallas to Fort Worth?" Worner asked bleakly.

"*I* got a gift in Fort Worth," said Norma. "I have a sixty-fourth interest in a Texas oil well. I understand Darryl Zanuck is one of my partners."

"I had it practically all fixed for Shirley May France to earn a thousand dollars recently," Worner said suddenly. "I was going to put her in the lobby of the Mayfair, wearing an Aqua-Lung, to promote 'Underwater!' But Howard Hughes turned it down. Everybody's turning things down. I turned down a client myself last week. It was this fellow I met in Brooklyn that wanted to operate a string of salons in New York where he would reduce women through hypnosis. Bah! I wish I could leave all this and go skiing, maybe to that ravine on Mount Washington—what's its name?— Tupperman's. But I don't know how to ski, and anyway I can't afford to take the time to break a leg. If I don't get a million people to send in names for my filly, I'll have done a bum job."

"I'm sure your contest will be successful," murmured Norma loyally. "It's being conducted on such a high plane. That's what I love about it."

"I have hi-fi and I eat well and I smoke twenty-five-cent cigars, but I still have no money," said Worner.

March 25, 1955

Notes and Comment

The Hotel Edison, as a service to its patrons, has made available to them recordings of various sounds calculated to lull them to sleep—among them, falling rain and chirping crickets. Another of the noises on tap is the lowing of cattle, from which we deduce that a lot of Edison patrons don't hit the sack until after daylight; the cattle of our acquaintance are as quiet as house dicks during the hours of darkness. In any event, the hotel would seem to attract—or hope to attract—a peculiar crowd of people. Who ever heard of falling rain putting anybody to sleep? Our life has been full of rain falling at night. The sequence of events is hatefully familiar to us: the first, gentle patter as we are dozing off; the sudden, nagging doubt, while the storm mounts, as to whether we closed the study window; the awful struggle with ourself as to whether we should get up and see if we did; the spineless resolution to forget about it and go to sleep; and then the terrible wakefulness, lasting, like as not, until dawn breaks and the cattle begin to low.

The kind of noise that jogs us to sleep in hotel rooms isn't anything imported from the country, with perhaps some mechanical distortion or amplification added, but, rather, the glamorous, mysterious sounds indigenous to the setting—a midnight knock at a nearby door, an off-key snatch or two of a mellow song, the tinkling of ice in remote glasses, or someone telephoning hoarsely for room service. Puts us off in an instant and makes us sleep like a baby.

April 2, 1955

Books
Be Sure You're Right, Then Go Ahead

"'You could keep on all night,' my grandmother said, 'with what everyone told about Davy Crockett, not counting even what he told about himself.'" The insomniac lady here quoted is the grandmother of Meridel Le Sueur, author of "Chanticleer of Wilderness Road—A Story of Davy Crockett" (Knopf), and she appears to have known Crockett in her youth. "Chanticleer" is one of a score or so of Crockett books currently on sale— some of them reprints, some lately written, and all calculated to succor the hungry Crockett fan in his year of need. There are Crockett books on hand for every taste and purse, and for every age level, though most of them, naturally, are aimed at juvenile targets. One of the lot, "Davy Crockett— American Hero" (Rand McNally), by Bruce Grant, comes in two sizes: as a Rand McNally Giant, twelve and a half by nine and a quarter inches, priced at one dollar; and as a Rand McNally Elf, eight by six and a half inches, priced at twenty-five cents. Aside from dimensions and cost, the Giant and the Elf are identical, and for each the claim is made that it "is based upon Davy Crockett's own account of his exciting life."

Fiddlesticks. This Mutt and Jeff combination would have us believe, among other things, that as a child Davy ("no one ever called him anything but Davy") had a dog named Sport, and that he went bear-hunting for the first time at the age of eleven or twelve. But in what is generally agreed to be the only authentic memoir penned by David Crockett—and David Crockett is the way he signed his name, as is attested by a reproduction of his signature on the jacket of one of the books about him—the celebrated Tennessean nowhere mentions having had a dog named Sport, and never specifies when he tried to kill his first b'ar. All of Crockett's biographers have tried earnestly to compensate for his reticence about that initial bear. Walter Blair, in "Davy Crockett: Frontier Hero" (Coward-McCann), maintains that he got a bear at six, while Enid LaMonte Meadowcroft, in "The Story of Davy Crockett" (Grosset & Dunlap), insists he was still bearless at ten. Stewart H. Holbrook, in the Random House Landmark series' "Davy Crockett," goes so far as to state flatly that Davy was eight years and two months old when he shot at—but missed—his first bear. As for the first bear shot at and killed, he has General Andy Jackson ask Davy whether it's true that he bagged a bear at three, and Davy answers no—he was nigh unto ten.

How do I know all these esoterica? Because, heaven help me, I have just clawed my way through practically the entire Crockett shelf. No rational man, save perhaps David himself, would undertake so unnerving a task in the heat of this summer, and I wouldn't have undertaken it, either, if I hadn't been pushed along by my eight-year-old son, who—to borrow an endearing epithet sometimes used by both Crockett and Jackson—is a "slangwhanger" on Crockett lore.

One of the things about Crocket lore that threaten the rationality of the rational man is the vocabulary encountered. Boy, what words! Miss Le Sueur's "Chanticleer of Wilderness Road," which favors "whangslanger" over the seemingly synonymous "slangwhanger," has by all odds the most colorful collection. It dotes unrelentingly on adverbs like "obstinaciously," "scalpaciously," "terrifcasciously," "tetociously," "fistifferously," "hossiferously," and "catifferously," and on adjectives like "fericacious," "monstracious," and "scoundratios," which may be a typographical mistake for "scoundratious," whatever *that* may be. In one book or another, such phrases as "You didn't shoot any better tonight than a cross-eyed old man with the tizzick" confront the reader. "Tizzick" is Mrs. Meadowcroft's word. Constance Rourke, in her "Davy Crockett" (Harcourt, Brace), a straightforward and adulatory biography originally published in 1934 and now enjoying a spirited renaissance, elects to string along with the plain old spelling "phthisic." Crockett's own preference in this respect is unknown, and possibly immaterial, since he admitted that when it came to spelling he was no whangslanger, or slangwhanger.

Two hard-cover editions of Crockett's autobiography are now available, one published by Citadel Press and the other, illustrated by John W. Thomason, Jr., by Scribner. David Crockett's own story of Davy Crockett was written in 1834, when he was forty-eight, and it takes in the first forty years of his life. The fact that he concentrated on the first, and happiest, part of his career is a break for young readers, and his recollections of the rigors of backwoods life—of, for instance, how he once coped with the problem of carting a keg of powder across an ice-encrusted river in late December—are full of dash and verve. In the current editions, as in earlier ones, this basic text has been augmented by some probably apocryphal material concerning his subsequent adventures in politics and in Texas— annals that have been attributed, off and on, to Crockett but are generally believed to have been set down by another hand.

Even though Crockett was a formidable celebrity in his own day (in a prefatory note to his autobiography, he concedes that "my name is making a considerable deal of fuss in the world," but adds, "I can't tell why it is, nor in what it is to end"), his own book throws little light on many of the facets of his life that have enthralled latter-day admirers. Walt Disney's lyrical assertion that he was born on a mountaintop in Tennessee is as familiar to many contemporary three-year-olds as the Lord's Prayer, but Crockett cannot be held accountable for this oddly situated delivery. He says merely that when he was born, in 1786, his family lived at the edge of the Nolachucky River, in what was shortly to become the eastern part of Tennessee. He offers little evidence that he was an exceptional shot as a child, although he does admit that by eighteen he was skilled enough to win first prize—a carcass of beef, worth five dollars—in a neighborhood shooting contest. Most of his formative years, it appears from his own account, were spent hanging around a tavern his father operated on a road between Knoxville and Abbingdon. It can't have been a very thriving establishment, for when Davy was fifteen, he was obliged to spend six months working off his father's debts. For three years before that, he had been travelling through Virginia and Maryland; he didn't like his father and was scared to go home. One result of his nomadic and impecunious adolescence was that he got no schooling at all until he was sixteen, and only a taste of it then. By eighteen, he was married and heading West. In 1813, he volunteered for the Army, and he devotes much space in his autobiography to his skirmishing— under General Andrew Jackson—against the Creek Indians, for whom he bore an understandable resentment, since the tribe had killed two of his grandparents and kidnapped an uncle. He considered himself a superior Indian fighter, but when not shooting at animals or men, he was no great shakes. After a disastrous attempt to make some money by taking two boatloads of barrel staves down the Mississippi to New Orleans—both ships sank, in part because Crockett had hired a worthless pilot—he was quickly persuaded to avoid any further commercial foolishness and take the easier course of running for Congress. He was elected three times and defeated twice, but a lot of the books about him hardly mention his defeats.

David, as distinct from Davy, Crockett emerges from his own story as a barely literate backwoodsman with a parochial view of the world, an engaging, if somewhat windy, storyteller, a legislator who was far more politician than statesman, and a man of scant humility. (He announced that he was perfectly willing to be President, if anybody wanted him.) Davy, as distinct from David, Crockett was, however, something else again—greatest hunter of his era, animal-tamer extraordinary, national folk hero, inspiration for a mythology that has outdazzled Bulfinch. This was as true in the early eighteen-hundreds as it is today. In "An Account of Colonel Crockett's Tour to the North and Down East," an apparently spurious work attributed to him in 1834, he is quoted as saying, on the occasion of attending a theatre in Boston, "I was very genteel and quiet, and so I suppose I disappointed some of them, who expected to see a half-horse, half-alligator sort of fellow." Just as David Crockett asserted he once wrestled with a bear, and just as Davy Crockett is alleged to have wrestled with a bolt of lightning, so have all the authors of all the current Crockett books wrestled with a dilemma—how to reconcile faithful biography with anecdotal myth. "The Life of Davy Crockett" (Signet Books), a paper-back reprint of an 1889 work containing the autobiography and also some of the apocrypha, claims on its cover to be "the only genuine authorized version of Crockett's own story." But after enveloping themselves in the mantle of historical accuracy, the editors backtrack rapidly. By the end of the book, they are confessing their doubts about the genuineness of a great deal of what they have resurrected. Dazedly, they sum up: "Davy Crockett was America's first Superman." One of the busiest of the Crockett chroniclers, Irwin Shapiro, who is twice represented in my Crockett library, starts off his "Walt Disney's Davy Crockett, King of the Wild Frontier" (a Little Golden Book) with the forthright warning to his readers that it is "a fanciful re-telling of the Davy Crockett legend." It is Shapiro's not unreasonable view, as expressed in his more substantial volume, "Yankee Thunder" (Messner), that Davy Crockett is, compared to David Crockett, "obviously the [more] credible, authentic, significant, and true." On this premise, he presents a cyclone-taming, amphibious Crockett, who swings a panther by the tail to make it cheer for Andy Jackson. Possibly because of its larksome approach to its protagonist, "Yankee Thunder" ends up by being the most entertaining of all the Crockett offerings. One scene is laid in the White House, where Crockett, on his way to Peak o' Day, in Tennessee, to thaw out the sun and save the world from freezing, stops off to ask Andy Jackson for the loan of a pair of ice skates. "Must be some around here somewheres," mutters the President. He excuses himself, runs up to the attic, and returns triumphant. "Found an old pair that belonged to Tom Jefferson," he announces.

Crockett had a motto—"Be sure you're right, then go ahead." His contemporary biographers are far from unanimous about the origin of this sterling moral precept. One thinks that Crockett borrowed it, when a mature man, from Andrew Jackson. Another thinks that it was an abbreviated version of a boyhood shooting rule Crockett prudently observed: "Be sure you're right, and then go ahead and pull the trigger." (David himself provides no clue.) Aileen W. Parks, in "Davy Crockett, Young Rifleman" (Bobbs-Merrill), says that he inherited the phrase from his uncle Joe Hawkins, a trigger-happy fellow who had once shot a man named Dick Kendall, mistaking him for a deer. The incident is mentioned in Crockett's autobiography, all right, but Kendall wasn't in it. He was in another incident, and he wasn't shot at all. In any event the Crockett writers seem not to have been terribly impressed by their subject's praiseworthy motto. They just go merrily ahead, apparently without a pause to be sure of anything. Take, for instance, the matter of Davy's pets. His favorite bear dog, in the opinion of nearly all but Elf and Giant, was a hound called Whirlwind—or Old Whirlwind, as we are told in "Old Whirlwind; a Story of Davy Crockett" (Macmillan), by Elizabeth Coatsworth. But did Whirlwind die when Davy was fourteen, as "Davy Crockett, Young Rifleman" asserts, or did he live on, as "Chanticleer" declares, until 1835, when Crockett was retired by his constituents from Congress at the age of forty-nine and Whirlwind, or—and, in this case, more properly—Old Whirlwind, would have been something over forty? Or take Crockett's first wife. David nowhere mentions her name in the autobiography, but she is thought to have been born Polly Finley, except by Marion Michael Null, author of a Crockett biography arrestingly entitled "The Forgotten Pioneer" (Vantage), who favors "Finlay." (Mr. Null is said to indulge in the raising of sequoia trees from seeds as a hobby. Walt Disney may latch onto *him* someday.) The roguish Shapiro, to be sure, calls her Sally Ann Thunder Ann Whirlwind, but it is doubtless just his joke, which is made more ambitious if we accept the word of "Davy Crockett, Young Rifleman" that the young man had a rifle called Sally Ann. But what are we to make of Miss Le Sueur's approach to this point? At the very start of "Chanticleer," she tells us that the lady's name was Polly Ann Whirlwind Crockett. Hardly have we got this compromise between fact and fancy securely fixed when the author herself begins to waver; before thirty-two pages have gone by, she has referred to Mrs. Crockett as, successively, Sally Ann, Polly Ann, Polly, Sally, and Sally Ann Whirlwind Polly Crockett. And what did this elusively named pioneer woman look like? Crockett himself said she was "very pretty" and "sweeter than sugar," but his biographers are not the sort to be satisfied with such vagueness. After what has apparently been extremely independent research, Holbrook has concluded she was fair-haired, Blair that she had glossy black hair, and Felix Sutton, in "The Picture Story of Davy Crockett" (Wonder Books), that she was a little old redhead.

In most of the Crockett books, Davy dies, gallantly, at the Alamo. (He was almost fifty at the time, but you'd never guess it from any of the illustrations.) In some, though, he survives the slaughter there, and is basely executed by the Mexicans who captured the fort. In still others—the fanciful ones—he escapes this fate, too, and enjoys long years of breathtaking, demigodlike adventure. As the redoubtable Mr. Shapiro concludes, "Now, some folks say Davy Crockett was killed at the Alamo, fighting for Texas. Well, what some folks don't know would fill a book." From all the evidence, we can expect it to appear shortly.

September 3, 1955

Notes and Comment

The match industry has a sort of beauty contest of its own now. Inspired by Oscars, Tonys, Emmys, Edgars, and the other Christian-name awards of our time, the industry is offering Joshuas and Henrys to outstanding match-book manufacturers and match-book collectors, respectively. (Joshua Pusey, it seems, invented the things, and Henry Rathkamp was an early collector of them.) We wince at the prospect of all the honors yet to be announced, let alone conferred: the annual Johnny, for the person who buys the most Philip Morrises; the Morris, in turn, for the fellow who borrows the most (in a single fiscal year) under the Morris Plan; the Philip, for whoever succeeds in marrying Princess Margaret; and so on, until the last name is exhausted and the last mantel topples under the weight of the trophies. It's getting so these days you can't tell an award from a hurricane.

September 24, 1955

Notes and Comment

New York is a tough city to characterize. One of the latest attempts was made by George Preston Marshall, who is the owner of the Washington Redskins, a professional football team, and is sore at New York, possibly because he believes that old tale about our having stolen it from the redskins. "New York is nothing but a collection of theatres, stores, and offices," he said. Now, hold on, George Preston Marshall. How would you like it if we were to assert that Washington is nothing but a batch of phony Greek temples surrounded by barely navigable traffic circles, with a big white house plunked down somewhere in the middle of it all? If we were to say anything of the sort, we'd probably get investigated, and we'd deserve to, for nothing merits more careful scrutiny these days than shortsightedness.

Perturbed by Mr. Marshall's diagnosis, we've reëxamined New York this week. Looks as fine as ever, we're relieved to say. Theatres, stores, and offices on every side, to be sure, and what a splendid array they are—with all the lovely ladies in their just-out-of-storage furs prancing in and out of them! The handsome trees at the Lever House offices have turned, the Tiffany store has held the first sale in its history (a muted, unheralded one), and all the girls on all the stages of all the twinkling theatres have never looked sprightlier.

We seem to have just about everything here, Marshall, that anybody with his eyes open could ask for. We've got people basking in the unaccustomed sunlight on Third Avenue, now that the "L" is all but gone; we've got our own municipal list of the ten most-wanted criminals, just like the F.B.I.'s; and, thanks to the farsighted tolerance of Robert R. Young and Patrick B. McGinnis, we've got a big Oldsmobile rotating on a turntable right in the middle of the main concourse of our main railroad depot. Last week, we even had a movie crew shooting in front of the Federal Courthouse downtown. A friend of ours who was on jury duty there says he thinks he may have got into a sequence with Judy Holliday and Paul Douglas. How about that, Marshall?

New York is a town of beguiling contrasts, George. Our civic leaders have been complaining for months that traffic here is practically paralyzed, but what do you suppose we've just acquired? A brand-new fleet of police cars with the mission of tracking down speeders, that's what. We need more cops, however. To qualify, you have to be at least five feet seven and a half. Send us your football team, Mr. Marshall; we can use them. And it appears that they won't have to go on television, no matter what the Mayor says, unless the Commissioner consents. You'd better check that point with Dr. Gulick first, though.

New York is a wide-awake, get-up-and-go town. If a Colombian diplomat wants to fly from Washington to Bogotá, the quickest way is via New York. Stick that in your hat, Marshall. But New York, praise be, is a poky town, too. As we write this, daylight-saving time is almost a week past, and the clock on the Paramount Building (theatre, stores, offices, all in one handy package) still hasn't been adjusted. In Washington, we understand, daylight saving ended this year in September, which means that its residents didn't get a chance to enjoy as many delightful fall evenings as New York's residents did. Very shortsighted on someone's part. We *have* residents, incidentally, Mr. Marshall. Eight million of them.

November 12, 1955

A Man Who

Early in the preëlection period—looking back, it is hard to believe that the late nineteen-sixties are still so fresh in our memories—the bosses of the All-

American Party assembled, as usual, to pick their standard-bearer for November. Though statesmen from widely scattered regions of the continent were present, not to mention the powerful Senatorial bloc from Hawaii and the other islands, the first session evoked gratifying unanimity on one crucial point. To a man, those in attendance were agreed that the public had wearied of the type of leader it had lived with so long, or at any rate the type that impressionable journalists had for so many unvarying years, in so many conventional biographical treatises, been solemnly portraying. The nominating committee decided, accordingly, to select someone as unlike the standard conception of a very important public figure as it could find, and in no time at all a name emerged from the roster under consideration by a subcommitee on qualifications that seemed, in its bearer's deviation from the popular norm, almost heaven-sent.

John Forbush was the man. To begin with, Forbush had been an admiral; no admiral had been tapped for political eminence since Dewey, and he hadn't got very far. Forbush was not a terribly renowned admiral. If the public had ever been served up many stories about him, these would inevitably have related that Old Blunt Mouth, as he was known in the Navy—not, of course, to his face, although he was supposed to love the nickname, as indicative of affection nicely blended with respect—had an exterior tough as granite, but that beneath this frosty façade there beat a heart uniquely soft. His deep but rarely demonstrated sentimentality toward all the sailors under his command would have been mentioned next. There would have followed a specific anecdote illustrating this estimable trait—perhaps a paragraph narrating how when some yeoman inadvertently made dates for the same night with two girls in one liberty port, the crusty Admiral had charitably rescued him from his dilemma by ordering an entire task force diverted to another port, a thousand miles away, where the yeoman's affairs were less promiscuously entangled. "I was young myself once," the old man would have been reported as confiding to his exec, while permitting a sly wink to flit across his grave countenance.

Admiral Forbush was, of course, not at all like that. There was no question about his having a granitic exterior; the engaging thing about him was that his interior was, if anything, even flintier. (When one of his own public-relations officers was discovered about to give out a story puffily attesting to the Admiral's alleged superhumanitarianism, Forbush had promptly had the fellow transferred to the Canal Zone, even though his wife was expecting.) On the high seas, in actuality, he *had* been known as Old Blunt Mouth, but he deplored the appellation, less because he doubted its accuracy than because he thought it impertinent toward the high position he held, and he was always on the alert to apprehend and suitably admonish anybody employing the tiresome phrase. Admiral Forbush's attitude toward enlisted men was unbendingly autocratic, though fair. One time, his exec, thinking he had caught his superior in a relatively pliable mood, had ventured to apprise him of an embarrassing situation faced by a romantic yeoman under his sway. The Admiral had responded characteristically by saying that he had more important things than that on his mind, and that as far as he was concerned, the fellow could damn well solve his own personal problems.

"We were all young ourselves once, sir," the exec had murmured tentatively.

"Well, we're not any longer," the Admiral had snapped, without altering his facial expression one whit, and that was the end of that anecdote.

To the subcommittee on qualifications, the Admiral's service record thus looked promising indeed. Further investigation elucidated other biographical details that really made the subcommitteemen's eyes bug. Like most other flag officers, Forbush had attended his share of postwar banquets. It developed that he had never archly complained in private about the food served to him in public. Not a jot of evidence could be found of his having told a single living soul that he just pretended to eat banquet food to be polite, or that he was glad he had an iron stomach, considering. The truth was that at banquets he generally ate everything placed in front of him, with gusto. His only obtainable comment in this respect had been made to a chap seated next to him on one splendid dais, who, seeking to draw him out in reg'lar-feller conversation, had whispered conspiratorially that he sure had to hand it to the Admiral for appearing to tackle banquet fare with so much relish. "Rubbish!" Forbush had replied, and for an instant his companion had been misled by this offhand choice of exclamations into deducing that Forbush was outwardly indistinguishable from everyone else at the head table. But the Admiral's amplifying remarks dispelled this false assumption. "I don't mind this food at all," he went on. "Most hotel chefs cook a good deal better than my wife does. They ought to; that's what they're paid for."

The more the subcommittee looked into Forbush's eating and drinking proclivities, the more excited it got. He spouted no nonsense, they quickly ascertained, about sipping an Old-Fashioned—just one, mind you—before dinner. To anyone who asked, he would answer forthrightly that he preferred several Martinis before dinner, and, when it came to that, before lunch, too. They relaxed him and sharpened his appetite and, at least in his own, possibly biassed, estimation, made him wittier. As a corporation executive, following his retirement from active duty, he had been as busy as any other man of his station ("My job isn't awfully interesting," he said, "but it pays well"), yet he had never asserted that he was so pressed for time he just lunched austerely at his desk off an egg-salad sandwich and a glass of milk. He didn't especially care for milk, and as for egg-salad sandwiches— "That's for Boy Scout picnics," he would say, "if you're unlucky enough to get roped into one." So he habitually went to a restaurant for lunch and lingered contentedly over his meal for a couple of hours. Moreover, he was suspicious of all his contemporaries who claimed to be chained to their desks at the noon hour by heavy responsibilities. It had been his experience that between twelve-thirty and two it was extremely hard to rouse anyone to do any business with, let alone anyone's secretary.

Forbush's own secretary, the subcommittee was delighted to note, was not an indispensable, devoted, self-sacrificing, middle-aged woman who had been with him practically forever, who knew and good-naturedly tolerated all his little idiosyncrasies, who was the only person extant able to decipher his handwriting, and without whom he would have felt lost. She was, on the contrary, a twenty-two-year-old Bryn Mawr graduate who, like her predecessor, had worked for him only six months. He invariably hired attractive young secretaries, and they invariably left him, less than a year later, to get married, with his blessing. He hated to be dependent on a secretary. As for his handwriting, it constituted no shining example of disciplined penmanship, but it was perfectly legible. Anybody who could read could make it out.

The discreet inquiries made about Forbush's home life, while productive of no startling intelligence, were on the whole encouraging. It seemed that he found it rather boring to sit around night after night in the bosom—the Admiral had winced when an interrogator hit this word—of his family. He admitted to a genuine fondness for going out. Puttering around the kitchen stove was, from his viewpoint, absolute anathema. He didn't think he cooked even as well as his wife did. He had a suitable quota of children and grandchildren, and he got along fine with the lot of them, but the grandchildren sometimes grated on his nerves, and he made no bones about saying so.

It was the Admiral's wife who happened to disclose, matter-of-factly, that her husband never brought work home in the evening. On being confronted with this eccentricity, he freely acknowledged it, while two subcommittee-men looked at each other and grinned broadly. He said it was his hunch that most men who lugged home heavy briefcases bulging with thick reports never gave them a glance. Anyway, he added, he wouldn't have much time for homework, because he needed and enjoyed a decent night's sleep. He knew as well as any American (How could an observant citizen help knowing it?) that it was the tradition for preoccupied men of distinction to make do with a frugal four or five hours' sleep at night, and to augment this scanty ration with daytime cat naps. Forbush, though, had never liked sleeping at odd moments. He preferred eight hours' sleep in the dark, and even after that much slumber would sometimes awake not refreshed at all. He never rose before seven-thirty, unless his grandchildren were visiting him, and not one of his underlings had ever had cause to complain that his boss had the crotchety habit of badgering him at dawn.

The Admiral had never taken the position that he would not ask any man to do anything he would not do himself. He believed that he lived in an age of specialization, and that when a specialist was called on to do a job, he should go ahead and do it, period. Forbush frequently had to make speeches, for example, and almost always he declared himself perfectly satisfied with the remarks prepared for him by a competent ghostwriter whom he kept standing by for just such occasions. Forbush hardly ever changed his speech-writer's words or scribbled his own ideas on margins. In this connection, the subcommittee was reassured to discover that he was no more eloquent when speaking informally to a small group than when delivering a set address at a large function. Indeed in a small group he was often utterly at a loss for words, especially when he felt tired.

Forbush's reading habits also came under careful scrutiny, naturally. When the subcommittee, tackling first things first, bluntly raised the critical issue, it got a swift and blunt response: Forbush could take detective stories or leave them alone. It was not altogether satisfactory to find that he had no passionate convictions about them, so one zealous interviewer asked, "Don't you find them helpful for relaxing?" Admiral Forbush was not to be outmancuvered. "I told you before I don't have any trouble relaxing," he said brusquely. It came out, furthermore, that he was not a particularly fast reader. A painstaking search unearthed nothing to indicate that he had ever been known to glance at a complex document and then, hours or days later, astound his associates by quoting it practically verbatim, as if he had a photographic memory. His memory was no better than average, and he forgot a good deal of what he heard or read.

The clincher was the subcommittee's discovery that John Forbush, influential man though he was, busy man though he was, never let his wife buy his clothes for him. "What the hell," the Admiral said. "I only buy a suit or two a year, and I'm the one who has to wear them. She's got her hands full with her own wardrobe, and anyhow she can never remember my size." On the dramatic revelation by the chairman of the subcommittee of this beguiling heterodoxy, Forbush was nominated by acclamation.

Election Day came not long after a protracted, nationwide drought, which was terminated by a hard and steady rain that began falling one morning when the Admiral had a tennis date. One of the reporters covering his campaign headquarters had already typed up his account of the candidate's reaction to the long-awaited downpour. "We sure can use it," he had Forbush saying. When, instead, the Admiral, who had already opened a new can of tennis balls, looked out the window and said "Damn!," the reporter was furious. Aggrieved at having to rewrite his copy, he avenged himself by quoting exactly what Forbush had said. The revised version made front pages everywhere, including Goa, and won its author a Pulitzer Prize, for never before in the annals of the Republic had a man who seriously aspired to the nation's highest office uttered a swearword—at least not in print. That one wayward monosyllable, it turned out, cost Forbush the farm belt, in addition, it goes without saying, to the Bible belt. He was defeated, ultimately, by a landslide. Asked to say a few words after his manager conceded, Admiral Forbush paused and composed his thoughts, following which—once again setting a national precedent—he spoke them aloud. "On the record," he said, "my opponent is an idiot, but then a lot of the people who voted for him are idiots, too, so I guess they got what they deserve."

December 17, 1955

Notes and Comment

As Christmas draws near, there seems to be less peace on the earth of the Holy Land than practically anywhere else, and we therefore wish an extra portion of good will to all who live beneath the Star of Bethlehem. We wish a surcease of rancor to the angry, a sackful of restraint to the hotheaded, and to everybody a moratorium on political debts. Our merriest Christmas wishes go to those whose lives have been harried by holiday preliminaries: to the novice skaters at Rockefeller Center, forced to take their lessons before so unusually many challenging eyes; to Salvation Army tuba players on Fifth Avenue, manfully making their music despite the double jeopardy of cold lip and jostled elbow; to a temporary saleswoman we saw at Saks with tears in her eyes and the book "Creatures of Circumstance" tucked under her arm; to a bulky, mink-clad lady we bumped into on Madison Avenue, who (a prep-school mother?) was trying to look as if she habitually walked around carrying a brace of hockey sticks; to the girl in the Barton's candy ad, nibbling self-consciously on a chocolate Christmas card; and to a young man we watched directing pedestrian traffic in front of the Lord & Taylor show windows (he was wearing a crash helmet, and we hope he survived). Our especially sympathetic regards go to those anonymous bulwarks of industry, the people who clean up offices after office parties. May they all find a bottle of Christmas cheer cached behind a filing cabinet!

We wish a Merry Christmas to the man in the moon, and also to an enterprising Long Island man who has been selling earth dwellers lots on the moon. (A Happy Light-Year to his customers.) Merry Christmas and congratulations to the ninety-two-year-old doctor to whom the Army—

which now has forty-one generals of a rank equal to or higher than the loftiest attained by George Washington—has just given a reserve promotion from captain to major. Merry Christmas to Captain Eddie Rickenbacker, who has turned sixty-five, and may he, too, make the grade ere long. Merry Christmas, when it comes to that, to the Army, which has indulgently permitted a pfc. in Korea to retain ownership of some land he impulsively bought there, for the establishment of an orphanage.

Merry Christmas to all orphans and strays everywhere, including our dog, who vanished last week. May somebody throw her a bone. Merry Christmas to all the defenders of lost and little causes, among them an animal-loving outfit beguilingly called Defenders of Furbearers. (Merry Christmas to furriers, too.) Merry Christmas to all the institutions endowed by the Ford Foundation, and a particularly rollicking Noël to one beneficiary—the hard-pressed hospital that reluctantly closed its doors on December 1st, never dreaming that succor was imminent. (What delightful evidence that Santa comes only when your eyes are shut!) Merry Christmas to the Foundation's controversial offspring, the Fund for the Republic, which is under considerable political attack at the moment and has just diplomatically added two offspring of literary men to a panel of judges for a TV-program contest it is sponsoring—Robert A. Taft, Jr., whose father wrote "A Foreign Policy for Americans," and Philip Willkie, whose father wrote "One World." Merry Christmas to one world, including all Germanys, all Koreas, all Vietnams, all Chinas, and both Inner and Outer Mongolia.

December 24, 1955

Notes and Comment

Our eight-year-old son had his first taste of hospital life over Washington's Birthday, and also his first taste of notoriety, being cited by a New England daily as one of "four who took advantage of Saturday's snowfall to break a leg skiing." While this was an accurate account of his misadventure, the paper got both his name and his address wrong. But how could one complain about the faulty reporting of a small-staffed rural paper when on the very next day the heavily manned *Times* ran a dispatch from the village of Buckland Brewer, England, also about legs, that said, in its entirety, "A competition to find the best pair of male legs in this Devonshire village was won by a retired rear admiral"? What rear admiral, for goodness' sake? And what were the terms of the competition? We think the *Times* might have queried its Buckland Brewer correspondent for a few more details.

We once broke a leg skiing ourself, when our son was an infant, and we were astonished at how similar accidents of this sort are: the awkward, flailing fall; the downed skier not arising; the victim's attempts to shrug off the injury ("I think I must have cut myself," the boy told us, sweating in the cold snow); the call for a toboggan, and the strangers who magically appear with one; the hasty, amateur diagnosis in the ski hut (people who hang around ski huts know about bones); the search for a doctor (a girl we'd never seen before flagged down one who was driving by); the long ride to the hospital, invariably in the next county; and the ceremonial cutting off of the ski pants. New England doctors hate to destroy clothing. The one who operated on our son's trousers began delicately snipping up the seams, explaining that he had high hopes the pants could recover. The child's mother, impatient and prodigal, grabbed the surgical shears herself and, with hurtless, expeditious, maternal, loving strokes, shredded the pants into irreparable tatters. Mothers know some things that doctors don't—that a boy of eight grows fast, for instance, and the pants would have been too small next year anyway.

A children's ward is a sobering place, for a child as well as his elders. Until our son was trundled in, he had never thought much more about polio than that it is a scourge that can usually be exorcised by Salk-vaccine injections. He's had two. Then he got acquainted with a polio patient in the bed alongside his, who had just had an operation on one leg. The other was withered. "I got surgery scheduled three times more before summer," the post-op lad told our son calmly. "But I know they won't work. The good leg'll go, too, sooner or later, same as the other." This philosopher was eleven years old.

A friend asked us to take our boy a holiday medallion—Washington's head sculptured in maple sugar—which prompted a three-year-old in the ward (burn case) to ask whether, if there was going to be a birthday party, he was well enough to go. We'd delivered the gift before we realized it was contraband. A nurse's aide called our attention to a sign that said, "Please do not bring fruit, candy, or food for children." We were tempted to recommend a rephrasing of this imprecise injunction, but we held our tongue, for in a hospital the dietitian properly outranks the English purist, just as the immobilized child outranks the ambulatory adult.

March 3, 1956

The Wayward Press
Cute and Not so Cute

On April 11th of this leap year, two bemused young Japanese sweethearts leaped into the crater of a volcano near Tokyo. Presently they climbed out, battered and burned but still miraculously alive—a striking testimonial to the indestructibility of love. The news of the survival of their romance against such formidable odds was flashed around the world by Reuters, but it got very little play here the next day, doubtless because the local papers were too busy preparing for their all-out pursuit of the happiness of a far more renowned couple.

On April 12th, the "Inside Fashion" column of the *Herald Tribune* ranged somewhat outside its prescribed titular limits to run an item that read, "Positively the last cute story about Grace Kelly: Her nickname for her fiancé is Ra (pronounced Rah)." The reporters already in, or en route to, Monaco were, of course, in no way affected by this pledge from a stay-at-home. In the fortnight that followed, they wrote many cute stories about Miss Kelly, and, possibly to show their impartiality, many not so cute. One, by Dorothy Kilgallen, in the *Journal-American*—a dispatch that I assayed as halfway between cute and non-cute—dealt in part with the pronunciation of Prince Rainier's nickname. Miss Kilgallen said it's "Ray." But then she led me and "Inside Fashion" into a quagmire of perplexity by adding, "The Prince loathes being called 'Ray' almost as much as he hates being called 'Shorty.'" Does he loathe "Ray" because he prefers "Rah"? And who calls him "Shorty"?

The *Herald Tribune* has been cutting down so drastically on its foreign staff in the last couple of years that it now has not a single correspondent permanently stationed in the entire sixteen and a half million square miles of Asia. Nevertheless, by April 16th it had four byliners filing copy from the three hundred and seventy-five acres of Monaco—Frank Kelley, Art Buchwald, Joe Hyams, and Clementine Paddleford. (That same day, the *Times*, which has the world's largest corps of foreign correspondents, to say nothing of a lot more news columns than the *Tribune*, published not a word of Monégasque intelligence.) "From outward appearances," Kelley was predicting even before the prospective bride and her entourage steamed into Monaco harbor on the Constitution, "the wedding will bear comparison with the 1953 Coronation of Queen Elizabeth II." As far as I know (it would be presumptuous for anyone to claim that he has read every last word about Miss Kelly's ascension to serenity), the actress' namesake was, with a solitary exception, the only American reporter who hit upon that particular analogy. The exception, oddly, was E. Clifton Daniel, Jr., of the *Times*. During a press conference that preceded his marriage to Margaret Truman, he was asked if he had ever been assigned to a story similar to his own wedding. After saying he hadn't, he sort of contradicted himself—forgivable for anyone off duty, and especially for a bridegroom—by adding, "But I covered the Coronation of the Queen of England, and it's much the same type of thing." Syllogistically, this would seem to make the Monaco and Missouri weddings more or less related, via the Coronation—which is as good a reason as any to beware of syllogisms. The brides' fathers, being hardheaded men and wary of syllogisms, avoided them. John B. Kelly was quoted as saying, "It was a grand production. I felt I was in Hollywood watching them shoot a Cecil B. deMille film." Harry S. Truman was quoted as saying, "Marriage is the most sacred of contracts. It should be solemnized with dignity and reverence."

Technically, Miss Paddleford, the *Tribune's* food columnist, seems to have been filing not from but about Monaco. She apparently sneaked over there ahead of the rest of the mob and got out, with copious notes, just before the Donnybrook started. Her April 12th story, at any rate, carried no dateline and began, "I have been visiting that pinpoint municipality, Monaco. . . ." Cf. "this postage stamp realm" (Cynthia Lowry, *Post*); "this stamp-sized principality" (Anonymous, *Post*); "this pre-shrunk principality" (Inez Robb, *World-Telegram & Sun*); "this happy confectionery principality" (Bob Considine, *Journal-American*); "this rococo little country" (Kilgallen, *Journal-American*); "this financially juicy little plum of a principality" (*Idem, ibid.*). Wherever Miss Paddleford may have been, she was serving up some juicy little plums herself. She had had to sit eight hours, she disclosed, awaiting an audience in Monaco with the palace chef. (Nonetheless, her feet hurt.) She had bought two bunches of Monégasque primroses, which cost only a quarter and lasted a week. (When the other correspondents set about compiling their expense accounts, I don't imagine they thanked Miss Paddleford for that.) Gripped by the romantic fervor that was then overcoming so many of her colleagues, she said of the proprietor of one restaurant whose cuisine she sampled, "If you are interested, Oscar will compose a song just for you, but watch out for that wet kiss he demands in payment." As if to reassure the Princess-to-be, Miss Paddleford hastily explained that this moist establishment is not a haunt of titled folk. "Only to certain restaurants goes the Prince; there, too, the Princess," she wrote, in her highly personal style. Miss Paddleford may have returned to the States early because of plain exhaustion. Attempting to describe one of the meals she had enjoyed in Monaco, she bogged down pitiably with "Salad? I can't remember."

The *Post*, as no loyal reader could have doubted, sent over Earl Wilson. ("I feel only a sense of pathos," Max Lerner, the paper's expert on compassion, brooded at home.) Wilson cabled back one day that he was giving the bride a picture frame as a wedding present; on another day that he had inspected, and found wanting, the living quarters of a Monégasque chauffeur; and on still another that he was having trouble rounding up a proper outfit for the church wedding.

Possibly because both Rainier-Kelly weddings were scheduled at around five in the morning, New York time, the local afternoon papers got a break on spot news. Deprived of revelations about the sub-par housing of Monégasque chauffeurs, the morning papers, aside from the *Tribune*, seemed discouraged in their coverage. To be sure, the *News*, by some heroic parlay of communications facilities, managed to publish a picture of the civil ceremony an hour and thirty-nine minutes after the shutter snapped, and after the church ceremony, the next day, triumphantly announced that it had broken its own record by accomplishing the same feat in an hour and *nineteen* minutes. Since, however, there appeared to be more photographers biting policemen and forming human roadblocks than taking pictures, the end scarcely seemed to justify the means. All things considered, the Monte Carlo story was a hands-down victory for the afternoon papers, and particularly for the Hearst papers, as represented by Miss Kilgallen and Mr. Considine. This was logical enough, for it was to the Hearst syndicate that Miss Kelly's mother, a couple of months earlier, had sold her reminiscent series called "My Daughter Grace." Indeed, it could be argued that the Rainier-Kelly wedding coverage didn't really get rolling until April 13th, when Miss Kilgallen arrived, bearing with her, as she had already confided to her readers, an evening gown and a brown broadtail jacket, with a golden mink collar, that some couturière friends of hers had asked her to deliver to the bride. Thus laden, she reached the main arena on the day that Frank Kelley informed his *Tribune* audience that the bride's father had patted one of her dogs; the day that Considine, already on the spot, advised the *Journal-American* of the number of hairdressers attending the bride (two); and the day that Earl Wilson said the Prince was furious because several reporters were plotting to smuggle their way into the church wedding by passing themselves off as priests, in rented clericals. (Much as I sympathized with the Prince's reaction to this contemplated sacrilege, I couldn't help smiling when Jane Cianferra, one of the two *Times* correspondents who finally turned up, revealed that Rainier's ancestors had taken over Monaco in the first place by a not dissimilar deception; they had infiltrated its fortress walls by disguising themselves as Franciscan friars.) Alas, Miss Kilgallen threw no light on what disposition she made of her cargo. She was, however, able to save the *Journal-American* considerable embarrassment by reporting, within forty-eight hours of her arrival, that she had witnessed Rainier and Miss Kelly dancing. "DOROTHY SEES THEM FONDLY CHEEK-TO-CHEEK," a headline crowed. This was a lucky break for her paper, because there had been grave doubts as to whether the engaged couple would dance in public at all, and the Hearst syndicate had already contracted for the exclusive rights to publish a new song, called "The Prince and the Princess Waltz," with lyrics that go, "Like the Prince and the Princess, let's dance through life." On that same memorable day, by the way, American politics figured mightily in the dispatches: Conrad Hilton, the hotel man, arrived from New York, representing President Eisenhower; Mrs. Matthew H. McCloskey, wife of the treasurer of the Democratic National Committee, was robbed of her jewels; and Father Tucker, the Prince's personal chaplain, reflecting on the low ebb to which his patron's relations with the press had sunk by then, suggested to Bob Considine that maybe Jim Hagerty ought to be summoned posthaste to smooth things over. Mr. Hilton had had an eventful trip, it seemed, having inadvertently departed without his passport. According to an A.P. dispatch from Paris, he had left it "at a hotel." What a blow to Hilton! It would have been no less cruel to identify McCloskey simply as treasurer of "the national committee of a political party."

By April 16th, Miss Kilgallen was beginning to pout. "I fear Grace is slipping away from us," she said. I had thought all along that the whole point of everybody's being over there was to acknowledge descriptively that Grace *was* slipping away from us, into a new environment. The same day, Earl Wilson, alluding to the succession of robberies that had plagued what Considine called the "light-fingered fairyland" (there were some twelve hundred reporters around, but none of them ever definitely established whether the total number of thefts was four, five, or six), wrote, "All wits worked overtime on the robber's theme. Journalist Art Buchwald claimed all jewel thieves would be barred by Rainier from the wedding—but that only one would be let in to represent all the jewel thieves, as is done with photographers." I wondered why, with copy so hard to come by, Buchwald should have blithely bestowed his *mot* upon a rival. It turned out that he evidently hadn't intended to at all. Thirty-six hours after Wilson quoted him, Buchwald came limping along in the *Tribune* with the copyrighted jest: "A second-story man said, 'I know we all can't get into the wedding, but since the Prince is allowing the photographers to pool their work, all we ask is that one pool jewel thief be allowed into the ceremony and steal for all of us.'" That ought to teach Buchwald to guard his gems carefully until he's ready to display them.

Some of the correspondents, unable or unwilling to borrow their stuff from a colleague, began writing complaints about one another. Mr. Considine said that a French photographer had stood outside Prince Rainier's window loudly singing smutty songs, in the hope of making the Prince angry enough to come to the window and thus put himself within camera range. Inez Robb grumbled that the worldly Father Tucker was competing unfairly with the full-time press by sending dispatches to a Boston paper. She didn't seem to mind that he was also accredited to the London *Sketch*, which, according to Miss Kilgallen, was printing wholly mythical quotations, such as one, from the Prince to his fiancée, that ran, "Courage, my darling. This is what you must face if you are to be a Princess." Miss Kilgallen, her pout deepening to irascibility, also took a few whacks at Lady Norah Docker, another brevetted British correspondent, whom she characterized as "a noisy type who gets herself barred from the Casino at regular intervals for causing scenes." (The fact that the *Journal-American* ran this slur was an inspiring demonstration of its devotion to the cause of a free press, for just a few days earlier it had been printing Lady Docker's own comments on the wedding preliminaries.) Considine, meanwhile, was disposing of the male members of the British press, of whom he wrote, "Each appears to believe he is the bridegroom." Amid all the confusion, it was understandable that still another bellwether of the Hearst stable, George Sokolsky, who stayed home, was moved to remark, "I cannot quite figure out whether Grimaldi is being married to Grace Kelly or to the female correspondents."

No reporters in Monaco worked harder than Miss Kilgallen and Mr. Considine, each of whom filed two stories daily. I therefore felt a stir of sympathy for them when, on April 17th, the *Journal* carried an interview with John B. Kelly, the bride's father, that the paper had obtained from New York, by telephone. Mr. Kelly didn't have much to say, aside from "It's a real little fairyland"—which was hardly more than an echo of what Considine had already said—but I wouldn't have blamed the Hearst pair for being miffed at this interference from the home office. They may have been further put out when Olga Curtis, who also wears the Hearst colors, transmitted to the *Mirror* another interview with Father Tucker. This time, he was saying that in six years Prince Rainier had never once waved to his subjects until Miss Kelly joined him in his fairyland. This seemed to me one of the most extraordinary statements that any correspondent had extracted from anybody over there, but Miss Curtis flubbed it; she used it down toward the end of her story, well after the rather pedestrian observation that it takes Grace Kelly an hour and a half to dress. In any event, Miss Kilgallen was spurred, or spurred herself, into spirited action. She promptly filed a dispatch that directly contradicted Miss Curtis; this said that the Prince was a far more practiced giver of royal salutes than his bride.

While the Hearst writers were gainsaying one another, the *Post* and the *World-Telegram*, following more orthodox journalistic procedure, were engaged in a disagreement as to what the bride's mother, who was not quoted much, had actually said on one of the occasions when her words did fall on reportorial ears. According to the *Post*, Mrs. Kelly had said, "The events of the last three months have been much of a surprise in our lives;" according to the *World-Telegram*, "The events of the last three months are scarcely believable." This would indicate that the average reporter can accurately take down only the first seven words of a statement and must then rely on his memory. The conflict might well be made the basis of a sales-promotion campaign for some live-wire shorthand school.

In the *News*, on April 19th, Eleanor Packard casually mentioned that Miss Kelly's honeymoon wardrobe would include a broadtail jacket with a milk collar. Kilgallen had made it! But for some unfathomable reason, she herself never once referred to her triumph, even though her dispatches sometimes ran to several thousand words, a good many of them autobiographical.

Perhaps it was modesty that made her reticent, perhaps censorship. Or maybe, by that stage of the game, she was simply too piqued to concentrate. Whatever it was, she grew increasingly acid, likening Prince Rainier's expression during his civil wedding to that of a guilty man being questioned by police, upbraiding him sternly for not looking at his bride during their church wedding, denouncing the royal linen closet for serving paper napkins at the wedding reception, and winding up with "Prince Rainier does not immediately strike the average viewer as ideal husband material . . . Grace has tackled a whopper." Miss Kilgallen did relent long enough to admit that the church ceremony was "a wedding beyond the fondest daydreams of all women who dream of weddings," but before that story left her typewriter, she had stiffened again and said, "It was somehow symbolic of our times, when in the highest and the lowest, and the most important and the most sacred moments of our lives, we are becoming actors for the entertainment of millions of people we will never know."

Conrad Hilton, on the other hand, holding no grudge against the Associated Press for its remissness about identifying hotels, told an A.P. man after the civil ceremony, "I call it well done, and I'm mighty proud to have watched it." To the *Tribune*, the President's representative confided, "The most impressive thing was the way Grace just said that 'Oui.'" It perhaps ought to be pointed out, in this connection, that Inez Robb was the victim of the whole episode's most unfortunate typographical error. "Mr. Portanier [the judge who officiated] turned to him," Miss Robb's story went, "and asked, 'May I, very respectfully, ask Your Serene Highness if he agrees to take as his wife and legitimate spouse Mlle. Grace Patricia Kelly, here present.'

"'Qui,' said Prince Rainier."

May 5, 1956

Notes and Comment

We hope Sir Winston Churchill, impeccable, old-school grammarian that he is, hasn't chanced to hear American radio or television commercials recently. It would pain him dreadfully, we're sure, to listen to the obnoxious and ubiquitous couplet "Winston tastes good, like a cigarette should." That pesky "like" is a problem for us Americans to solve, we guess, and anyway Sir Winston has his own problems. The latest is that, notwithstanding all the trouble he's gone to to avoid a dukedom, he suddenly seems to have acquired a realm of his own, a hand-me-down from the first Duke of Marlborough. Sir Winston has been revealed as the Prince of Mindelheim, Mindelheim being a principality in Bavaria that is smaller than Monaco. The incumbent Prince's subjects have never laid eyes on him, and they would naturally like him to stop by soon and accept their fealty, or whatever it is a prince of Mindelheim rates. If he does, they'll doubtless decide, unless they've been educated by the voice of commercial America, that Winston looks good, as a Mindelheimer should.

Last week, the stockholders of Twentieth Century-Fox were informed at their annual meeting that while the company hasn't been doing particularly well lately (earnings per share for first quarter of 1956 down from 1955), it has struck oil on several of its studio lots in Los Angeles. There's a movie in this if ever there was in anything, and the principal characters are obvious: impoverished extra (from Oklahoma), who loves the studio boss' daughter; daughter, who owns a portable drilling rig; studio boss, fretting over his balance sheet, who craftily gives the young couple a dowry consisting merely of company-stock options (he thinks they're worthless, but the hero knows better, having sniffed a telltale scent under the floor of the executives' dining room) and is staggered when liquid gold spouts up through the dumbwaiter. It's a picture that would make a handsome profit and cheer up those stockholders.

The Department of Commerce has made public a list of seven hundred previously *verboten* items that American exporters may now ship to the Soviet bloc of nations without a special license. Mallets, pencil plugs, and coin-operated machines have been granted security clearance, and so have all Easter-egg dyes save those with a vegetable base. (We personally deplore the shipment toward any child on earth of any Easter-egg dye that is not fully digestible.) While we are sure the Commerce Department had valid reasons for its decisions, we can't help wondering what lies behind its decree that masks and false faces are now sanctioned for unlicensed export but that "novelty false faces" are to remain proscribed. For heaven's sake, what kind of non-novelty false face would any American conceivably have occasion to export to Russia? What *is* a non-novelty false face, anyway? A disguise for a spy? We trust that Commerce won't find itself in a jam with the Central Intelligence Agency.

We went out to Westchester for the weekend, and as our host, wearing paint-spattered blue jeans trimmed with fresh-turned soil, was ferrying us from the railroad depot to his ranch, he brought his car to a jouncing halt. "My God, look at that!" he yelled, pointing to a house just off the road. We looked, but noticed nothing untoward, and asked if we'd perhaps missed some rare bird. "Rare indeed, in these parts!" he cried. "There! On the terrace!"" Then we caught on. Sprawled comfortably in a deck chair was a nattily dressed man (madras sports coat, linen trousers) with a glass in one hand, a book on his chest, and a portable radio at his fingertips. "I never realized anything like that existed outside of *House & Garden*," muttered our host shakily as he drove on.

May 5, 1956

Powder Your Face With Sunshine

Among the many reasons his detractors scoff at Guy Lombardo is that he resolutely refuses to allow his band to indulge in any of the improvisation that is the heart of true jazz. They also ridicule his rhythm section, which, they say, is muted almost to the point of being inaudible. According to an apocryphal but not irrelevant story, Lombardo once led his band through a half-hour radio broadcast without realizing that his drummer, who had been caught in a traffic jam, was not present. Lombardo does not bridle at this bit of fiction. "We've never been able to see much music in a drum," he says complacently. George Gowans, his drummer, is a sedate, professorial-looking man of fifty-one, who exasperates television directors by an apparently constitutional inability to flail his arms around and make frenzied faces. "George would be useless in an ordinary band," Lombardo says. "He can't make a racket."

Lombardo is not critical of bands that make a racket. He believes, though, that many of them have a tendency to go overboard for passing fads. "I don't play for acrobats," he says. "I never switch to a fad. There's been bop and swing, and there was a time when everybody was on a Latin-American kick, and now there's rock-and-roll. They come and they go, like waves, and we ride them out. The trouble with a fad is that if a band takes it up wholeheartedly, when the fad dies out—as it's bound to, sooner or later—the band dies with it. A lot of band leaders are deluded by listening to the disc jockeys' opinions of what's great. Why, if you tune in on a disc jockey nowadays, you begin to wonder what American music is coming to. Some of these disc jockeys don't know that there are still people around who love beautiful music."

Lombardo's own music is as consistent and as meticulously prepared as a perfect soufflé. He has three rigorous criteria for testing every one of his numbers before he serves it up: it must be easy to dance to, its melody must be easy to spot, and, above all, it must bear the unmistakable mark of the Royal Canadians. Lombardo's style is so readily recognizable that even people who are only moderately well acquainted with the individual characteristics of today's dance bands can confidently identify it after listening to no more than half a dozen bars, whatever the tune. One reason is his persistence in using a tuba instead of a bass viol, and another is the way his tuba is played. Back in the twenties, the oompah-oompah of a tuba was a routine part of the rhythm section of practically every dance band, but the instrument was gradually discarded in favor of the bass viol—by everybody except Lombardo. His tuba, however, is not of the conventional, frog-croaking variety; instead, it slurs from note to note, providing an obbligato to the slurring saxophones for which his band is equally noted, and, with them, creating an effect that one music critic has described as "a rather teary *vox-humana* tremble." Although Lombardo would not be likely to phrase it that way, he would agree with the general idea, for he firmly believes that musical instruments should come as close as possible to simulating the human voice. It may be significant that when the Mills Brothers, operating in reverse, imitate musical instruments with their voices, they sound not unlike the Royal Canadians.

The air of seeming detachment with which the oldest Lombardo conducts the band is more than offset by the ardor of brother Carmen, who acts as the energetic pace-setter for the instrumentalists. A strong disciple of the *vox-humana* theory, he does his best to duplicate the human singing voice—or, at any rate, his own singing voice, a singularly aspenlike one—and the result is his familiar quaking saxophone tones. Brother Lebert's special province is the brass section. His trumpet style has been much influenced by Carmen's vibrato technique on the saxophone. Like all the Lombardos, Lebert is essentially self-taught, but once, in a conscious attempt to improve his playing, he took a few lessons with a professional teacher, who ordered him to cut out that infernal vibrato. "For a few days, Leb obeyed his teacher," Guy says. "And he sounded as though he was playing through a gas pipe. So I told him to stop taking lessons. Music teachers don't know the first thing about vibrato. Ninety per cent of them say that you mustn't have vibrato in reeds or brass, but that you mustn't play a violin or cello or flute without it. What kind of nonsense is that—having an orchestra half with vibrato and half without? We believe you've got to have feeling in music, and feeling comes easiest with vibrato. This is a big issue with us, and we'll argue with the whole world on it—not that we have to, because we've proved our point."

Infuriated by such self-assurance, many authorities on the subject insist on prolonging the argument. One critic, writing in the magazine *Orchestra World*, described the Royal Canadians' saxophone style as "a wailing anticipation done in the throat," and objected to its "milky" quality and "the unsteadiness and noodling of its character." Other analysts have been even more cruel, calling the band's saxophones chronically sharp, or, to put it bluntly, off key. The Lombardos are not fazed by this allegation. Their leader once answered it by saying that most people sing off key, and Carmen has declared, "Our sound is down-to-earth sound of a sort the layman understands." Through the years, many people have found it hard to believe that the sounds produced by Carmen and his fellow-saxophonists can be made—as, in fact, they are made—with conventional musical instruments, undoctored in any way. From time to time, there have been rumors that the Lombardo saxophonists use trick mouthpieces or—from people susceptible to press agentry or sophomoric fantasy—that they fill the bells of their instruments with corn whiskey, warm milk, or molasses. Twenty years ago, when there were at least a dozen professional bands and nobody knows how many semi-professional ones aping the Lombardo style, youthful would-be imitators occasionally sneaked up onto the bandstand while the Royal Canadians were taking a breather, and stole a mouthpiece, or tipped a saxophone upside down to see if there was anything in it.

Professional musicians, of course, were above such gauche antics, but they had their own methods of attempting to acquire some of the Lombardo cachet. The most renowned of Lombardo's imitators was Jan Garber, whom a cartoonist once pictured as rehearsing his band by sitting in front of a radio loudspeaker, pencil and paper in hand, and taking notes on a Lombardo broadcast, thus increasing his supply of what *Down Beat* has called "the Lombardo stocks that made him a fortune." *Orchestra World* on one occasion snippily reviewed a Garber record in these words, "Jan Garber gives us a Garber-par (or Lombardo-par?) recording in 'Dear Diary' and 'Serenade in the Night.'" An eclectic leader, Garber has had bands of various types during his long career, but it is generally agreed that he achieved his greatest success when he was most nearly in the Lombardo groove. Lombardo now says that he and his former rival are the best of friends, but for a while Garber really nettled him, because he got so much closer than most band leaders to copying the Lombardo style. Lombardo never took the rest of the imitators too seriously, because of the general ineptness of their imitations, but at one point he acknowledged their competition to the extent of considering the idea of licensing bands in various parts of the country to use his carefully guarded arrangements. The popularity of most popular music is notably ephemeral, and almost every dance band's music library is subject to a rapid turnover. The shelves of Lombardo's library are widely conceded to house the industry's largest and hoariest collection of scores. As a rule, he keeps around five hundred arrangements within easy reach in a file room of the Roosevelt, and about a hundred and fifty on the bandstand itself. When he was starting out in Ontario, he and his handful of colleagues usually just improvised an arrangement until they had arrived at a pattern of sound that pleased them. Thirty years ago, in Cleveland, the band played its first formal arrangement—a treatment by the pianist Fred Kreitzer of Vincent Youmans' "Wildflower." Shortly afterward, a saxophone player named Larry Owen joined the crew, and in 1927 he became its principal arranger— a role he has filled, except for a few years' absence, ever since. Owen no longer plays in the band; he now devotes his time exclusively to figuring out ways of fitting all kinds of odd-shaped tunes into the firm Lombardo mold.

In 1940, after a quarter of a century of singing in public, Carmen

Lombardo unaccountably developed mike fright, but until that time he was the band's chief vocalist. He was one of the first crooners, reciting lyrics in an uncompromising nasal style that John Hammond has called "so awful its badness is magnificent." Carmen is the author, or co-author, of some two hundred and fifty songs—among them "Boo Hoo," "Powder Your Face with Sunshine," and "Coquette" (which a music columnist, after hearing him sing it, suggested might well be retitled "Croquette")—and when the band is playing one of these, he does not let his fear of the microphone deter him from singing it, but otherwise he pretty much sticks to the saxophone or flute. When Carmen stepped down as a soloist, Kenny Gardner was hired as his replacement. Gardner was a perfect selection, not only because he fitted snugly into the family by marrying the bosses' sister but because his singing is marked by the indomitable cheerfulness that has always been a basic characteristic of the orchestra. Guy Lombardo has said that he hasn't much use for torch songs unless their lyrics contain some promise—implicit or, better, explicit—that everything is going to turn out all right in the end. Larry Owen claims he can't make an arrangement on a rainy day. The whole band, in fact, is infected with a powder-your-face-with-sunshine spirit, and Gardner enters into this spirit with zest; he even sings "I'll Never Smile Again" with a glassy grin.

A booking agent once suggested to Lombardo that maybe he was putting in more time at the Roosevelt Grill than a band leader ought to devote to any one spot. "Look, I'm a dance band," Lombardo told him. "Dance bands have to have homes, so people will know where to find them when they want to dance. The Roosevelt is my home, and as far as I'm concerned, I can't be there too long." The Roosevelt has been home to the Royal Canadians far longer than it has to many of the individuals directly associated with its operation; Lombardo has stayed on in the Grill through the reign of seven general managers, which may be why the waiters there now call him Boss. The Roosevelt has named a suite in his honor, which is usually reserved by honeymooners; Guy, Carmen, and Lebert all maintain anonymous accommodations in the hotel, for nights when they don't feel like making the trip back to Long Island after office hours. The brothers know their way around the establishment as well as if they owned it, which some of their fans probably think they do by now. Quite a few of the people who frequent the Grill started going there in the days of prohibition, and it is not uncommon to find three generations of a family represented at one table. Lombardo has an atrocious memory (after thirty years of happy marriage, he still sometimes misspells his wife's first name, which is Lilliebell), and he can only manfully pretend that he recognizes the many dancers who stop by his bandstand to say hello and ask him to play the same number—"I'm Tickled Pink with a Blue-Eyed Baby," "I Miss a Little Miss

Who Misses Me in Sunny Tennessee," or whatever—that he played for them in the remote past. As the evening wears on, and sentimentality settles over his swaying worshippers in an ever-thickening cloud, he eliminates this difficulty by means of a dimmer on his bandstand, lowering the light in the room to a point where it is all but impossible to recognize *anybody*. One evening, after Lombardo had plied his dimmer even more drastically than usual, Howard Dietz and Arthur Schwartz, who happened to be present, were inspired to compose "Dancing in the Dark."

"Eighteen years in the orchestra business! I feel like an old man!" Lombardo said in 1932, when he was thirty. That, naturally, was hyperbole. Today, almost a quarter of a century later, the Lombardo band is still a remarkably youthful-looking institution. Obviously, it cannot go on forever, although so far there has been no perceptible slackening of its venerable pace. Lombardo thinks he may ultimately turn the organization over to Victor. Not long ago, a song publisher, after speculating at some length on where the Royal Canadians will end up, concluded that it didn't really matter. "If that band ever calls it a day, another's going to come along that sounds exactly like it," he said. "There are always going to be a lot of people who want to hear the kind of music Lombardo plays."

January 5, 1957

From Part I of a two-part Profile.

A Reporter at Home
A Bear at Large

In my part of Westchester—in the unincorporated sub-village of Scarborough, in the incorporated village of Briarcliff Manor, in the township of Ossining, twenty-eight miles from New York City—we rarely have occasion to think of ourselves as living in the forest primeval. On a clear day, you can see the Empire State Building, and on any old day you can see Sing Sing. Nonetheless, we have a gratifying, if not particularly unusual, abundance of wildlife. Squirrels, rabbits, raccoons, woodchucks, skunks, and possums roam in uninhibited freedom across our fields, and the meadow grass shelters handsome, sleek pheasants. The pond outside my window has two mallards frisking on it; for a week, it has also been the temporary home of six plump Canadian geese, who march up onto the lawn and sun themselves between dips, until Barge, my friendly Labrador retriever, runs over in the hope of getting better acquainted with them.

The sight of anywhere from one to half a dozen deer wandering about my property is common; not five minutes ago, four of the lovely, white-flagged animals walked gracefully across the lawn outside my window. (Last fall, a big buck sauntered right into my driveway one afternoon, and might have nuzzled the front door open if Barge hadn't chased him away.) We've had red foxes around, too, and the banks of the ponds, alas, have been ravaged by a resident colony of muskrats; but until just recently we've had to concede that when it comes to fauna the folks over in Connecticut, who were hosts to a stray moose several months ago, had the edge on us. Lately, however, a rather extraordinary series of events has occurred hereabouts, and I think I can best relate them, in more or less orderly sequence, by presenting some excerpts from an informal diary I keep:

FEBRUARY 2ND—Cold today. This evening's Ossining *Citizen Register* reports no groundhog shadow-casting, owing to snowfall. On arising from an afternoon nap, learned from our maid, Sarah, that two men in hunting clothes had come to the kitchen door asking leave to set traps for muskrats. Sarah, wonderful maid that she is, told them I was busy working and suggested they return tomorrow.

FEBRUARY 3RD—Trappers back. I asked them if traps could hurt dogs, cats, children, or other wildlife. They assured me there was no danger of that, so I granted them permission to go ahead. Feel sorry about harassing the muskrats, but damn near broke my neck in January stumbling in a hole they'd dug. It's a case of my neck against theirs. As the trappers were departing, one of them mentioned casually that they might catch mink in the traps, too, Mink!

FEBRUARY 5TH—*Citizen Register* says Briarcliff cops are searching for a 150-lb. black bear seen last week on Sleepy Hollow Country Club grounds. Hmm. Probably just a big dog. I remember how as a kid I was once chased across a golf course by an English sheep dog that I would have sworn at the time was a dragon. Strange, though, that just last August, Carroll Colby, the *Cit. Reg.* Adventure Editor, wrote in his column that it would not be utterly fantastic for a bear to turn up in Westchester. Out of curiosity, I checked to see what Ernest Thompson Seton had to say in his classic "Lives of Game Animals," and found that he estimated there were a few hundred black bears left in the Adirondacks—thirty years ago, that is. Come to think of it, Bear Mountain, across the Hudson and twenty miles north of here, must have got its name from bears. Seton says that the black bear (*Ursus americanus*) is elusive, speedy, a good swimmer, a loner, a nomad, and harmless. Glad to hear the last, just in case.

FEBRUARY 6TH—Paper reports bear tracks in the Sparta section of Ossining, near the river, a couple of miles from my house. Adds that Colby, who is a special game protector for the State Conservation Department—

and a many-faceted man, being, in addition to game protector and Adventure Editor, a Briarcliff village trustee, the fire commissioner, and an author and illustrator of juvenile books—had photographed the tracks and said they looked to him like those of a year-old black bear. Seems incredible.

FEBRUARY 7TH—Went to New York to straighten out a mess in the bank and heard much bear talk on the commuters' train. Awful jokes. A Merrill Lynch partner was hailed raffishly as an expert on bear habits. Ribald speculation that the bear was simply an excessively hairy neighbor taking a constitutional in the buff. Etc., etc. Became the victim of innuendoes myself as friends pointed out that bears are related to raccoons, that coons raid garbage cans, that my Barge is black and big (85 lbs.) and raids garbage cans. Ridiculous! Anyone can tell a bear from a dog. *Cit. Reg.* published one of Colby's photos of the Sparta animal tracks, showing them to be bigger than a child's hand. Tracks look peculiar.

(This is a P.S. written March 6th: Learned today the photo was printed upside down.)

FEBRUARY 9TH—The trappers inspected their traps. No muskrats. No mink. Sarah brought me the *Cit. Reg.* and pointed—with relief, I sensed—to an item from Irvington, ten miles to the south. A game warden there pooh-poohs our bear, saying that several dogs in his area were killed by an animal that he suspects is a rambunctious bull mastiff. In other words, our beast is probably canine, not ursine. Spoilsport.

FEBRUARY 11TH—The killer dog, a giant bull-mastiff bitch, was shot in some Irvington woods yesterday. Trouble there apparently is over. Hope so, because the dog show is on at the Garden, and killer dogs are terrible publicity. Funny thing—a Briarcliff resident with a bear background insists he heard a bear galumphing in his yard last night, *after* the Irvington slayer was slain. Went to monthly fire-company meeting, and heard more bear talk. Someone asked Chief Bowers when he was going to catch the bear. Big joke. In oblique reply, he informed us that the hook and ladder was dispatched this afternoon to break up a fight between a dog and a raccoon in a culvert. The firemen smoked the dog out, then put a 2½-inch line in to flush the coon out, but the coon just straddled the hose. The chief said that many side bets were made on who would prevail—coon or firemen. Coon money won when the firemen left, with their prey still in the culvert. This is getting to be a very animal-conscious neighborhood. Read the *Cit. Reg.* on getting home, and found the Hunting & Fishing Editor in a debunking mood. "Yarns of Westchester bears have a point in common with the Loch Ness monster," he wrote. "No one has managed yet to come up with a corpus delicti." Erudite but morbid. H. & F. Editor added that it seemed odd to him that no hunters had seen the bear—if there is a bear—during the hunting season, but omitted the pertinent fact that the hunting season ended December 15th, long before the bear was spotted. If there is a bear.

FEBRUARY 16TH—A clipping of one *Cit. Reg.* bear story has been pinned to the post-office bulletin board, alongside the circulars describing wanted criminals. Seems uncharitable toward what E. T. Seton called one of the friendliest animals anywhere—"timid, shy, and inoffensive." Murray Goodwin, whose house is less than a quarter mile from ours, told me at the post office that he had seen some outsize tracks in his rock garden yesterday. I said maybe my dog had made them. "Not Barge," he told me. "I know *his* tracks. They've been around our garbage cans for years." Bade him a curt good day.

FEBRUARY 19TH—The paper reports that the organist at All Saints', directly across the road from the Goodwins', saw a bear through the church window a few days ago. For goodness' sake! The bear, or whatever it was, skedaddled into the woods. Can't remember where Barge was when the bear was seen at All Saints'. The children, home from school, announced a sudden revival of local interest in Davy Crockett. No shooting is allowed here, of course, even in the hunting season. Bows and arrows only.

FEBRUARY 21ST—The bear story is getting around. The *Westchester News*, a White Plains weekly, says a bear has been pawing garbage cans all the way from Ossining to Tarrytown. Seton wrote that bears are omnivorous—that they "prefer all things eatable at all times." Just like Labrador retrievers.

FEBRUARY 24TH—Great to-do this afternoon on River Road, a mile and a half southwest of here. Jane Homes' maid was walking a baby carriage, accompanied by a pack of dogs, when, she claims, she saw a young black bear in the woods at the edge of the road, not fifteen feet from her. The dogs lit out after the bear, and the bear vanished. The police were summoned, but found nothing. Jane says she asked maid, "Have you ever seen a bear before?," and maid answered "Yes." What is one to think?

MARCH 1ST—Fresh snow last night. Out after breakfast with Barge, I found the ground already covered with animal tracks, much larger than Barge's and quite unlike them. Suspect imagination is getting the better of me. Today's Colby column in the *Cit. Reg.* is devoted to bears. Says he has had several letters about them. "And I am glad, for they are fascinating creatures, even if we seldom have a chance to see them outside of zoos." Colby also discusses tracks. The dog is a digitigrade, he explains, meaning it walks on its toes; the bear is a plantigrade, meaning it walks on the soles of its feet. I learn something every day.

MARCH 4TH—Bear! On going down to breakfast, I found Sarah in a swivet. Said she was awakened at 4:30 A.M. by sounds of something heavy nudging the garbage cans right outside her bedroom window. She thought at first it was a prowler, but then she became convinced it was an animal. She was too scared, understandably, to lift her head from the pillow. I knew it couldn't have been Barge, because he was snoring at my bedside then. Rushed outside and saw fresh tracks—big as my hand—in the snow near the garbage area. Plantigrade. Tried to call Colby, but he was out of town. Damn! Our breadman spread the word, and pretty soon some neighbors came over to gawk at the tracks. One was Robie Bucci, who brought along a Boy Scout handbook. The tracks resembled the bear-print pictures in it. Sarah was not cheered by the thought that a wild bear was only three feet or so from her pillow, even though separated by a wall.

MARCH 5TH—The trappers came by to check their traps. No muskrats, no mink, no moose, no nothing. Who cares? I drove over to Briarcliff Police Department and dropped in on Chief Johnson. He's been here, man and boy, most of his life, serving on the force for thirty-one years and as chief for twenty. Rock of probity. He told me there were several reports of the bear that hadn't reached the general public. For instance, it was thought to have been seen at Briarcliff College, but at the request of the college authorities, who were evidently reluctant to alarm the students' families unnecessarily, the story was hushed up. A snow-removal crew had also claimed to have seen the bear, at 4 A.M. on March 1st, a mere hundred yards from my driveway. That was the morning of the fresh snow—the morning I was puzzled by the tracks. The chief and I were soon deep in bear gab. He is sure the bear is a bear. Thinks maybe it wandered south out of the Catskills and crossed the Hudson while the river was frozen, but he admits that's just a guess. No matter; he is convinced that wherever the bear came from, it's here. I asked what the procedure would be if the police came face to face with the bear, and he said the only thing they could do—unless the bear acted ornery—would be to rope it; a 50-foot lasso is standard equipment in all police cars. The local cops did shoot a man once, back in the prohibition era, when a bootlegger acted ornery and pulled a gun on them. Self-defense. Same rule for bears. Johnson recalled that he and his fellow-cops used to rope a couple of runaway horses a week—twenty or thirty years ago, before the territory got built up and grew tame. He's proud of the way the local citizenry has behaved with a bear in its midst. No panic. Said I ought to talk to Colby, the ranking bear authority of the village.

MARCH 6TH—Colby back. Got him on the phone before breakfast. Told me he was just leaving to investigate two bear visits reported last night. Evidence of a real bear is piling higher almost daily—circumstantial, certainly, but then there's nothing shameful about circumstantial evidence. Ask any lawyer. Finally got to see Colby in person at his home. A real outdoor type, he has a den full of hunting licenses, woodsy relics, rifles, shotguns, bows and arrows. Has known bears since boyhood. Books he's written include "Who Went There?," a juvenile about animal tracks. "There seem to be two classes of people in Briarcliff right now," he told me. "Those who are dying to see the bear and those who don't want any part of it." He paused, presumably waiting for me to classify myself. I remained coolly noncommittal. Then he told me that he had sent some of his bear-track photos to the Museum of Natural History for possible authentication, but that the pictures were too fuzzy for positive identification. He showed me a letter from a mammalogist at the museum saying, "It would not surprise us to get reports on bear in this locality." Scientific open-mindedness. Colby said that when he first scrutinized the Sparta tracks, he was tempted to pass off the whole affair by announcing that they were probably those of a big dog—a St. Bernard, say, or a Lab, or a Newfie. But then his conscience nagged him, and made him confess the animal might be a bear. Told me that bears are not true hibernators, being often up and about during the winter, especially after a lean fall. He was not surprised that the bear was still at large. "A bear can outrun a dog, outrun a horse, outrun a deer, and beat a chipmunk up a tree." he said. "The way I feel about our bear is that so many mature, responsible people here have reported seeing it that the story must be true." I admitted sharing his slant. Sarah's hearing is both mature and responsible. Colby said that when he got the first bear report he called a game farm north of Pawling, where there are seven bear cubs in captivity. Thought maybe one had escaped. The owner said hold on, and went out and counted. Seven. Colby now thinks maybe our bear floated down the Hudson from the Adirondacks on an ice cake. Just a theory. "This is the most interesting thing that's happened in Briarcliff since I became a special protector," he told me. "I only wish I could find a perfectly beautiful paw print." I invited him down to have a gander at mine, and he accepted with alacrity. Declined a drink when we got to the house—sober, mature, responsible citizen. Guided him to an unmelted patch of snow outside Sarah's window. The ground was horribly trampled by now—dogs, cats, squirrels, skunks, deer, Boy Scouts, trappers, breadman, milkman, garbage men, Sarah, me. But two distinct, unmangled prints were still visible. Not perfect, not beautiful, but they looked persuasive to Colby. He was unwilling to make an unequivocal pronouncement on the basis of such skimpy evidence, but conceded that they were very possibly the footprints of *Ursus americanus* and, if so, the tracks of the closest wild bear there has ever been to New York City since it stopped being a village. Imagine! The most adventurous bear of them all, right in my own back yard!

Over a week has passed since that last hysterical entry, and the bear has been spotted twice more in Briarcliff, but he has done no damage to anyone, and no one, I am becoming increasingly delighted to note, has yet done any damage to him. These last few days, I have talked to a few big-city sophisticates who, like the warden in Irvington, refuse to take our bear seriously. Mainly to fortify myself with arguments against such skeptics, I telephoned Dr. W. J. Hamilton, Jr., Professor of Zoology at Cornell and the state's most eminent mammalogist. Dr. Hamilton had never previously heard of a wild bear nearer to New York City than the Catskills, but he said it seemed quite likely to him that our bear was the real thing, and, in terms of proximity to Times Square, it was therefore certainly a record-breaker. "Bears are wide-ranging creatures, and where they're concerned, nothing is impossible," he told me. "Heavens, there've been copperheads in Bronxville, so why not a bear in Briarcliff?" Why not?

March 23, 1957

Brainstorm

Herewith the latest thrilling installment of the adventures of Ted Worner, the unflagging Broadway press agent we bump into every now and then:

"I'm a clean-living fellow, as you know. I don't drink. I only smoke cigars. I go to Florida. I go to California. I have this twenty-three-foot cabin cruiser that sleeps four, with sixty horsepower, a mahogany interior, and a very beautiful anchorage off Rye. I've felt close to the water ever since I was a child, in Yonkers. Anyway, you know about these national weeks and months—Better Breakfast Month, Can Opener Week, whatever? Well, I have this client, Woolite, that I've had for two years. Woolite was conceived when my good friend Harvey Hewitt, its president, heard his wife complain that her forty-dollar cashmere sweater had shrank. Shrunk. You know what causes shrinkage? Hot water. Harvey hired a plant in California, behind a pizza emporium, and began to mix a cold-water soap. The fumes disgusted the pizza patrons, but he came up with Woolite. The thing caught on like woolfire, I mean wildfire. And we now have twenty-eight competitors. I've been promoting it until recently by sending a live sheep around the country, with a very beautiful actress attached to it by a leash. But when you have a product like a soap, you have to keep coming up with a new angle.

"Early last summer—oh, you got to plan ahead in this business!—I had a brainstorm. Why not a big spring promotion, lasting maybe a week or so, to get everyone to wash their wool garments in Woolite before mothproofing and summer storage? So I rushed my assistant to Washington to see the Chamber of Commerce of the United States, no less, and in July we got the word. We were in! The Chamber of Commerce's catalogue of special days, weeks, and months for 1957 lists us right next to Mother's Day. 'Mothproofing Month, National,' it says. 'May 1-31. Sponsor: Woolite Co., care of Ted Worner and Associates. Purpose: To acquaint the public with the most practical and effective method of preventing damage to clothing.' A whole month! And mothers only get a day!

"Well, you can understand how elated I felt. I called the Woolite brass on the Coast to break the news, and to my surprise they reacted with something less than wild enthusiasm, and said I'd hear from them. Then I got a letter from Harvey Hewitt. Listen to this: 'Regarding National

Mothproofing Month, the consensus of opinion out here is that it is quite a good idea but, unfortunately, not for us. While it is true that we sell Woolite as the perfect pre-mothproofing cleanser, we feel that such an ambitious undertaking should be confined to the mothproofing industry. We therefore would not be interested in promoting it as such.' You know what he wants me to promote for them instead? A new girdle wash!

"Well, what do I do now? The logical thing would be to try to make a tie-in with a mothproofing outfit. I understand there's one big company that makes the largest part of the mothproofing products on the market, but they do their own promotion. Still, I can't back out. National Mothproofing Month is registered in Washington in my name, and I have to save face. I got to have it properly celebrated by *somebody*. Already the requests are beginning to come in for material—from the Bureau of Advertising of the American Newspaper Publishers Association, from the National Research Bureau, from the Golden Empire Broadcasting Company, from a free-lance writer in Falls City, Nebraska. I can't let them down. I'll have to study up on my mothology, Woolite or no Woolite. I'll dig in and turn out a lot of public-service material—at my own expense, if necessary. It'll probably cost me three or four thousand dollars, which would have been enough, with my old boat, to get a very beautiful twenty-nine-foot cruiser that sleeps six I've been looking at—double-planked, with twin engines—but I feel it's my duty now to disseminate mothproofing information, and, by God, I'll do it! I'm going to get Woolite in there despite themselves, what's more! I'll prove to Harvey Hewitt he should have got behind this!"

March 30, 1957

The Wayward Press
Small Change

In 1950, when the price of a cup of coffee went up hereabouts from a nickel to a dime, the local newspapers—especially the evening ones, which tend to stress feature stories—made quite a fuss about the inflationary trend. And rightly so, for the nickel cup of coffee had been an institution, much as the nickel glass of beer and the nickel subway ride were in their day—and much as the nickel daily newspaper has been in its relatively brief day. Back in the last century, of course, most daily papers cost only a penny or two, and not long ago I read the bitter reminiscent lament of a convicted confidence man implying that he might have gone straight if, as a newsboy, he had not been disillusioned by Diamond Jim Brady, who used to give him a nickel for a two-cent daily and demand his three cents change.

As of last week, we have all become, willy-nilly, what Diamond Jim was too tightfisted to be, and there remains not a single paper in town that offers a newsboy a chance to acquire an extra couple of coppers from some expansive customer. The first inkling of a new order of journalistic things came on March 18th, when the *World-Telegram & Sun* announced that its news-stand price would jump from five to ten cents the next day. In a front-page statement, the paper cited "the steady increases in labor costs and the price of newsprint" as the reasons for taking "a step necessary to keep the *World-Telegram & Sun* at its best and to provide for its continued improvement in quality and service." The apologia also noted that this was the first increase in price for the paper since 1944, which may have puzzled some of the older readers, since in 1944 it would have cost a dime to buy both the *World-Telegram* and the *Sun*. Anyway, the band wagon was rolling. By the next morning, the *Times*, in its conscientious role of civic historian, had checked with the other papers, and it duly reported—on, of all places, its obituary page—that the *Journal-American* was going from a nickel to a dime, too; that the *Post* alone of the evening papers had no definite plans; that the *News* and the *Mirror*, at that moment in the four-cent bracket, contemplated no immediate changes; and that the *Herald Tribune* and the *Times* itself, at a nickel, were also standing pat.

The *Times* read its own mind correctly, and the *Herald Tribune* did indeed stand pat, but in other areas of the *Times'* survey there was evidence of legpulling. Only five days later, the *News* and the *Mirror*, in a touching show of camaraderie, announced concurrently that they would each cost a nickel the following day, and the day after that the *Post* followed the *World-Telegram* and the *Journal-American* into the ten-cent fold. None of the three evening papers has yet said why it didn't switch from a nickel to, say, seven or eight cents. Except in the case of their Saturday editions, for which they have charged a dime for some time, they have jacked up their price by a hundred per cent, while the *News* and the *Mirror* have gone up only twenty-five per cent. The *World-Telegram* and the *Journal-American*, in leading the way, both pledged their readers would get a good deal more for their dimes than they'd been getting for their nickels. The readers did, too. The first ten-cent *World-Telegram* weighed an ounce and a half more than the last five-cent one, and the *Journal-American* came across with the same fat dividend. In general, the *Telegram* seemed to be the more defensive of the pair. A week after it revamped its price, it observed in a news story that according to the American Newspaper Publishers Association there are now fifty-two dailies in this country that charge a dime—among them the Henryetta, Oklahoma, *Free Lance;* the San Luis Obispo, California, *Telegram-Tribune;* and the McMinnville, Oregon, *News-Register.* The proprietors of these comparatively modest journals may have been surprised to find themselves cast as bellwethers for a bunch of big-city boys. Of the Publishers Association's fifty-two ten-cent papers, incidentally, forty-five are in the Far

West, and thirty-four of these are in California. No wonder the *Journal-American's* Louis Sobol, who was in Hollywood when the change went into effect, was able to report that "the upping of N.Y. p.m. newspapers to a 10 cents tariff attracted only passing notice." They probably took it in stride in McMinnville, too.

Of late, most of the New York papers, possibly hoping to distract people from television, have been running puzzle contests, with prizes pegged at meaningful sums like sixteen, thirty-two, and sixty-four thousand dollars. (Ordinarily, I am fond of puzzles, but I find these largely unfathomable. They are disingenuously tricky, and the hardest part of all is deciphering the rules of the game.) I cannot remember any time in this high-spending era, however, when the local papers have been so preoccupied with *small* sums of money as they have been this last fortnight. The writer of a letter to the *News* may have sparked the whole business with a terse communication that the paper published on March 18th. "Can any reader tell me the value of an 1860 dime?" he asked. "At least 10 cents," the *News* coyly replied.

Only a few hours after the *News* had had its laugh about dimes, the *World-Telegram* hit the streets with its ten-cent manifesto. The lead-off dime *Telegram*, though heavier, was not notably dissimilar to its cheaper predecessor, aside from the circumstance that it carried an eye-catching advertisement of the Institute of Life Insurance. "Today's Biggest Bargain—For Just a Nickel!" the ad was headed, and the text urged each and every one of us to help check inflation by saving a nickel out of every dollar we have. Alas, the Institute could hardly have guessed that we would already have spent our extra nickel just to be exposed to its prudent counsel.

The next day, though—the first day of spring—the new *Telegram* began to kick up its heels. On its first page was a whole column of revelations about how the paper was being improved. "Packed solid with vital and entertaining reading," the column crowed. There was no doubt that the first page was packed solid, for the promotional column was occupying an eighth of the space that in bygone days had been devoted to conventional editorial matter. Crammed in tight among vital and entertaining reading inside the paper was a story to the effect that wooden nickels would be legal tender in Wichita County, Texas, during a jubilee there in May. This was an Associated Press dispatch, over whose facts the editors of the paper had little control, and I was on the whole more entertained by a eulogy to spring that a staff writer had composed, since it furnished evidence of a marked shift in editorial viewpoint. The author, John Ferris, who is apparently a confirmed city dweller, described the start of spring as "a day for the commuter, loosed from his suburban trap, to gulp the tonic city air." How callous toward their forebears these ten-cent papers are! Only two days before, the old, five-cent *World-Telegram* had soberly reported that automobile exhaust fumes give mice skin cancer. (Newspapers often behave peculiarly at the onset of spring. The *Times*, on March 21st, ran an article by James Reston, its Washington correspondent, in which he summarized the views of its Washington columnist, Arthur Krock, on the question of Presidential disability. The same day, the *Times* also ran a column by Krock summarizing Reston's views on the subject.)

Only a step behind the *World-Telegram*, the *Journal-American* swung into line, on March 19th, with a front-page announcement from its publisher, Seymour Berkson, explaining that costs had gone up and promising that "beginning tomorrow, you will find the news and feature content, of our newspaper substantially increased." Among the innovations unveiled on the twentieth was a biography of George Metesky, the Mad Bomber, who has been practically a member of the paper's family since he washed his hands of Consolidated Edison. (On March 22nd, the *Journal-American* achieved a real triumph of editorial juxtaposition by dividing one of its pages fifty-fifty between an installment of the Metesky saga and an advertisement that said, "You'll be better off with Con Edison.") The *Journal* ran the A.P.'s wooden-nickel dispatch, too, but put it on page 1. In fact, it had *two* five-cent stories on that ten-cent façade. The other concerned some boys suspected of robbing pinball machines, and was headed "BOYS IN PICKLE OVER NICKELS." Moreover, it was clear that the headline writer was determined to give the *Journal's* readers double their money's worth, for another story, on page 26, about an overweight pickle truck, bore the echoing headline "IN A PICKLE OVER PICKLES."

Other ten-cent innovations in the *Journal* were a question-and-answer health column by Dr. Joseph G. Molner and a fashion column by Constance Woodworth. Dr. Molner quickly showed his new readers that he is no chap to fool around with. The answer to the very first question asked him led off with a snarling "Write to what's-her-name, not to me, about mother-in-law troubles." I had no idea whether he meant Louella O. Parsons, Dorothy Kilgallen, or somebody else. Miss Woodworth tried to stimulate her new readers by passing along an unusual tidbit: mink-lined trench coats are coming into vogue. Unfortunately, her editors took the edge off her ten-cent revelation by printing, on a subsequent page, a nickel-type story about the current availability of mink-trimmed sofas.

On March 22nd, the *Journal* presented an exclusive and bloodcurdling account of conditions at the Municipal Lodging House, just off the Bowery. One of its reporters had spent a couple of days there, and revealed that, among other unsavory goings on, a man on crutches had been pushed down a flight of twelve steps simply because he didn't have a dime on him. Dimes! Dimes! Dimes! There seemed to be no getting away from small change. Another feature of this issue was a story about Elsa Maxwell, reprinted from *All Florida Magazine*. Why a paper that can have recourse to the vast, nationwide facilities of the Hearst press should feel compelled to borrow from an outside source for a piece on anyone as accessible as Miss Maxwell baffled me, but I concluded that the high costs of publication these days were forcing the editors to save every nickel, or dime, they could. In any event, Florida was handsomely rewarded for the loan; in an adjoining column, a somewhat subdued Dr. Molner was advising an interrogator that there is no evidence that citrus fruits cause kidney or gall stones.

Meanwhile, things were humming over at the *Telegram.* "PRICES HIT ALL-TIME HIGH," cried a headline that was splashed across six columns of page 1 on March 22nd. The story was merely a routine monthly report on the cost of living in New York, but the *Telegram* seemed delighted to have a chance to play it up just then. The cost of reading-and-recreation in the city, according to the story, had gone up two-tenths of one per cent in February; it will be interesting to see how this figure is affected in March and April by the hundred-per-cent boost in the cost of reading evening newspapers. The *Telegram* also carried a warning about inflation from Herbert Hoover, in Miami Beach, as well as an interview with Ivy Baker Priest, the Treasurer of the United States, whose signature appears on all paper money being printed today. Mrs. Priest, it appeared, has been doing her personal bit to curb inflation by autographing—or, rather, *re*-autographing—one-dollar bills for her friends and thus, as she sees it, removing this money from circulation. Incidentally, Mrs. Priest was described as being as "crisp and attractive as a new $100 bill," which seems an astonishing simile for a newspaper reporter to use, even after a jump in the cost of reading-and-recreation.

On March 24th, an otherwise quiet Sunday, the *News* and the *Mirror* announced bigger—or, at any rate, more expensive—things to come the following day. Both papers had last raised their prices in 1952, it was announced—on the front page of the *Mirror* and in the lead editorial of the *News.* "Sorry, but that's the way the ball bounces," said the *News* chattily. "We are sure you will agree with us that the *Mirror* is still a fabulous bargain at a nickel," said the *Mirror.* "We intend to keep the *News,* as always, the best newspaper buy in New York or anywhere else," countered the *News.* I could hardly wait for Monday. The *News* launched a big biographical series on Howard Hughes but, to offset that glaringly big-money item, also reported that in Livingston, New Jersey, the police have recently been putting dimes in public telephone booths for use by any dimeless citizens who have to make emergency calls. The *News* also carried an advertisement for the *Journal-American,* extolling Dr. Molner and Miss Woodworth, among others, and especially touting a new series, to start that very day, called "Help Your Husband Stay Alive!" by Hannah Lees. (I turned the *Journal,* when it came in, over to my wife; she told me later that Miss Lees had said there are a hundred ways for a wife to keep her husband breathing but that in her first teasing installment she hadn't specified a single one.)

The *Mirror* broke out with a rash of new features—as many as anyone could want for an extra penny. There was a new comic strip, "The Jackson Twins;" a new horoscope feature, "Astrology and You;" and a new television column (on the back page, where it is difficult to believe that the sports editors will countenance its tenancy once the baseball season starts), which promised "up-to-the-minute reviews of the programs you watched before you went to bed." Maybe the idea was that you would have seen them if you hadn't gone to sleep.

Like the *News*, the first five-cent *Mirror* carried an ad for the ten-cent *Journal-American*. The same day, the *Mirror* ran an ad about its new getup in the *World-Telegram*, which in its news columns was quoting Dorothy Schiff, the publisher of the *Post*, to the effect that her paper was going up to a dime because of the "sinister spiral of wage and price increases." Mrs. Schiff is the only local publisher who has detected anything sinister about it all. (The *Daily Worker*, which ordinarily might have seen sinister spirals on every side, refrained from comment; up to March 18th, the *Worker* and the *Wall Street Journal* were the only local dailies that charged a dime.) The *Post* that day ran an ad for the *Post* in the *Post*. It also ran a long statement by Mrs. Schiff, who apologized for not having been represented in the previous day's paper by a weekend column she writes. "No, I have not been vacationing in Florida," she said. (Who was this a slap at, I wondered. President Eisenhower? Herbert Hoover? William Randolph Hearst, Jr.?) "I have been grappling with one of the most serious problems we have ever faced at the New York *Post*." I knew that the problem must have been serious indeed, for the *Post* has never grappled with *any* lightweight problems.

By March 26th, a wild spate of intramural advertising was under way. The *News* had a promotional ad in the *World-Telegram*, and the *Post* had one in the *Times*. The day after that, the *News* advertised in the *Journal-American*, and the *Journal* in both the *Times* and the *Tribune*. The *Post* ad in the *Times* heralded the advent of a "daily magazine," and, as a come-on, printed the lead sentences of some of that very day's efforts by members of its enormous stable of special contributors. Mrs. Roosevelt said there was snow in Gander. Jimmy Cannon (in Florida, but not vacationing) started off, "I wouldn't spend a dime on a telephone call to prevent the fight racket from being classified as a felony under criminal law." (He probably wasn't aware that he could have made the call free from Livingston, New Jersey.) Earl Wilson was represented by a bewildering segment of his prose:

> "The only thing Hollywoodish about me," said Kathryn Grayson, tilting her turned-up nose to the world, "is that I'm still friendly with my two ex-husbands."

"Yes!" agreed a friend. "You were out with Johnny the other night."

It took all the self-control I had to wait till noon, when I learned from the *Post* itself that Mr. Wilson's column continued with the punch line:

"WHICH Johnny?" laughed Kathryn, whose first was Johnny Shelton, actor, and whose second was Johnny Johnston, crooner.

The *Post's* "daily magazine" turned out to be nothing much more than a realignment of the paper's forces. Many of its familiar standard-bearers had been plucked from their old spots and re-grouped in a central eight-page section. What had been worrying me most about the revamped *Post* was that it might change its unique headline-writing style, so that I would no longer be accosted each evening by such typical concoctions as "'I KEEP DREAMING THEY'RE CHASING ME . . .'" or "'I FEEL SO MUCH BETTER TODAY . . .'" Thank goodness, there is nothing to worry about. The March 27th *Post* headlined a Georgia-lynch-mob story with "'I DON'T KNOW WHAT HAPPENED . . .'" and a man-telling-his-wife-he-was-going-to-kill-himself story with "'I DON'T BELIEVE YOU. . . .'"

By March 27th, Hannah Lees, in the *Journal*, had leaked out two of her hundred ways to keep a husband alive: give him oodles of love, and never think that money means everything. That same day, the *Journal* printed a letter from a businessman in Connecticut, who began by saying, "I wondered what the extra five cents would give me as a reader of your newspaper." He had been given plenty, he was now ready to attest; in fact, he thought the *Journal* was a better buy at a dime than it had been at a nickel. That vote of confidence must have made Hannah Lees, Constance Woodworth, and Dr. Molner feel mighty good, though how such old-timers as Louis Sobol, Louella Parsons, and Westbrook Pegler may have taken it is something else again. Well, they can always console themselves with the reflection that while a nickel is only a nickel, a good cigar still costs more than a New York daily.

April 6, 1957

The Easygoing Method

In the opinion of many of his friends, Abe Burrows, a large, loud, and literate man of forty-six, is one of the funniest extemporaneous wits of our time. Groucho Marx, Fred Allen, George S. Kaufman, and Robert Benchley, who are, or were, among those friends, have all attested to his explosive volatility, and it is likely that the thousands of people who have seen him on television—in its early days, he used to appear, Faye Emerson-fashion, on some program or other almost every night—would go along with the general idea. On the other hand, that undoubted minority of people who know Burrows only from what they read about him in the papers might be inclined to a less ecstatic appraisal. Many of his sallies, when transmuted into the cold lead of type and divorced from his presence, his almost miraculous sense of timing, and the effervescent atmosphere that constantly surrounds him, are likely to seem fairly pallid—a fate that he shares with many of the most celebrated wags of history. Thus, when Burrows, seeing some guests to the elevator in his apartment house, told the operator, "Take these people wherever they want to go," the line may not have seemed outstandingly funny when it was quoted and requoted afterward, yet Burrows had made it sound so funny that everybody in the elevator was still laughing at it on the sidewalk. But whatever view one takes of Burrows' talents as a wit, there can be no doubt that in the seven years since he got his start on Broadway by working on the book for "Guys and Dolls," he has entertained far more people as a gifted librettist and director of musical comedies ("Silk Stockings," "Can-Can," and "Happy Hunting" also figure prominently in his dossier) than he ever has with his extemporaneous banter.

Among off-the-cuff wits and successful musical-comedy experts, Burrows is an uncommonly cerebral man. He makes a point of being exceedingly well informed. "You can't satirize the balcony scene in 'Romeo and Juliet' unless you've read Shakespeare," he says. "I'm an eclectic type of guy, and I read everything. I read at astonishing speed. I can read a couple of paragraphs at a grab. I read all the newspapers, all the magazines, all the best-sellers, and all the paperbacks. I am always dipping into Proust or Tolstoy, and I guess I've read the 'Anatomy of Melancholy' three or four times in the past fifteen years. As a kid, if I had nothing else to read, I would read the directions on a can of Bon Ami. And I basically have a memory that I can rely on the way Don Budge relies on his backhand. I have this ragbag sort of a head. I somehow seem to know a little something about everything."

Burrows, who was once a tutor of Latin, is a rapt devotee of etymology. He is, in fact, one of the few etymologists around who are likely to point out that "calibre" stems from the Latin *"qua libra"* and, in the next breath, to contend that a parapet is a pet parrot. He is obsessed with words. While "Happy Hunting" was in Boston prior to its New York opening last December, he was dictating a letter to a friend, and had just got past "The show is going great guns here," when he suddenly flagged himself down. "'Great guns,' 'great guns,'" he reflected aloud. "I'll bet that ain't derived from 'guns.' Maybe it's from 'gunwales,' or 'gunsils.' G-u-n-s-i-l—although it's got other spellings. You know what a gunsil is?" His secretary gave him a blank look. "Well, it's not a nice word to try to explain to you," Burrows went on. "At least, not according to Mencken. Where were we? Oh, yes. Change that to 'The show is going magnificently here.'"

One of Burrows' most engaging characteristics is his gruff, froggy voice, especially when he exaggerates it to utter grammatical absurdities in Brooklynese. Well realizing that all humor is based in large measure on surprise, he has polished to a high gloss the knack of expressing a philosopher's thoughts in truck drivers' jargon, but he can also speak perfectly good English. When he is in his truck-driver mood, he gives no indication of being aware that most reference books consider "isn't" preferable to "ain't." Sinclair Lewis characterized him as a bum who went to college. Burrows, who went to college (C.C.N.Y. and N.Y.U.) but never graduated, has described himself as a sea-water fish, and his outward appearance is indeed one that might endear him to an ocean-going ichthyologist. He has small feet, and a large, bald head, which he usually carries thrown back; with eyes blinking behind jutting spectacles and his mouth agape, he looks not unlike a fish—specifically, a huge, gaffed, gasping fish. Once described by *Variety* as "a hefty pixie," he weighs a hundred and ninety pounds and stands six feet one. Many people think Burrows also looks like an aging fish, but they are people whose only sight of him was in the infancy of television. Perhaps the cameras of that early time over-emphasized his baldness; in any event, his former television fans now and then express surprise on learning that he is still comfortably under fifty. "You look so much younger alive than on TV," a lady told him for the first time face to face. "You got an old set," Burrows replied affably.

A great believer in psychoanalysis, Burrows frequently lapses into introspective soliloquies on the subject of humor. "My own approach to it is a kind of disarming attack," he told a dinner guest the other evening. "It probably goes back to the Freudian business about humor being basically an adjustment to hostility. One guy will find an outlet for his hostility by punching you on the jaw, another by making a joke. For instance, I was tossing out an idea at a story conference once and asked if anybody liked it. 'Yes,' said one guy, 'because it has validity.' 'Well, a thing can have validity and still be good,' I told him. That was my way of saying that 'validity' is a pretty asinine word. Humorists, I suspect, don't want to be known as aggressive, and they make jokes because they're concerned about what people think of them. When a critic attacks a playwright with a joke, instead of letting him have it straight, it's because, deep down inside, the critic doesn't want the author to be angry with him. I once got to talking with a psychologist about the nature of humor, and after I had finished telling him all the things that I think make people laugh, he asked, 'Why don't they cry?' It was a tough question to answer. Maybe the answer has something to do with the fact that everything is physical. I'm not ruling out psychology, but psychology is just a form of anatomy. Having a thought involves nerve processes, like closing your fist. When you tell somebody a joke and come to the punch line, if it's any good it produces a nervous shock—a laugh-inducing shock. Why it's not a tear-inducing shock I don't know. I have a hunch it has to do with what's in your audience's mind. In the old days, comedians got their audiences into the right frame of mind by giving them signals. The original idea behind the red noses and funny shoes that comics still use was to signal audiences that whatever was said by a guy wearing them was supposed to be laughed at. If you don't prepare people in some way or other, it can be awful. One of our greatest playwrights, who generally writes heavy stuff, once wrote a scene he thought was hilarious. He gave it to his wife to read, and she thought it was sad and moving and burst into tears."

After a pause to let the picture of the artistic and domestic debacle crystallize, Burrows continued, "Why do people cry when a wounded cowboy slips off his horse in one movie, and laugh when a guy in another movie slips on a banana peel? Both experiences can be awfully painful. A matter of preparation. In each movie, the audience knows what to expect. I remember when my son was three years old. He brought me my shoe trees one day, and I said, 'You know where shoes come from, Jimmy? They grow on shoe trees.' He gave me a funny look. I thought he was going to cry. 'Don't do that!' he said. It wasn't a very good joke, but that wasn't the point. He just didn't like my throwing a curve at him when he wasn't ready. I got to thinking about it afterward and decided maybe he hadn't enough experience to take a joke—not prepared, you see."

Burrows' idea of a pleasant evening is to sit around trading bits of improvised humor with a group of his peers—Groucho Marx, George Jessel, George Burns, Milton Berle, Phil Silvers, and the like. "It's a gentle form of jousting, with its own rules," he says. "One is that nobody is expected to laugh. When someone pulls a good joke, all he can hope for is a grave nod of approval—a sort of 'well-played-old-man' type of thing. Another is that you don't interrupt a guy until he leaves an opening. Then you get in fast." In contrast to a Jessel or a Burns, however, Burrows doesn't go in much for the kind of joke that needs a lengthy story by way of a buildup. "I prefer the shorter ones," he says. "Like where one guy asks 'Does coffee keep you awake?' and the other guy answers 'No, but it helps.'"

An extraordinarily versatile man, Burrows has been profitably employed at one time or another not only in the theatre and in television but as a composer, a scenario writer, a nightclub entertainer, and a radio writer and performer. He is currently a member of six trade organizations—the American Federation of Television and Radio Artists, the Dramatists'

Guild, the Writers Guild of America, the American Federation of Musicians, the American Guild of Variety Artists, and the American Society of Composers, Authors, and Publishers—and he enjoys having attained this varied status as a professional. "I detest amateurs," he says. In 1954, while directing the play "Reclining Figure," which had to do with a forged Renoir, he decided to take up painting as a hobby. Many men, on being seized by such an urge, buy some artists' materials and strike out experimentally on their own, or, at most, attend a few art classes. Both these approaches struck Burrows as intolerably tyronic, so he engaged a private art teacher named Tully Filmus—a professional painter whose works included the fake Renoir used in the play. While Burrows has not yet had a one-man show, or even applied for membership in Artists Equity, he has reached the point of being able to forge a passable Filmus.

Burrows is well qualified to express strong views on amateurism. A decade ago, he was the most glittering unpaid parlor entertainer of the era. Harry Kurnitz, the author of "Reclining Figure" and a humorist of distinction himself, once said, "Hearing Abe do his own material for the first time is one of the funniest experiences a human being can have." Burrows' "material"—most of it composed, ad lib, in the early nineteen-forties—consists of some eighty musical monologues, in which he accompanies himself on the piano. The majority of them are satires on popular songs, including a home-town-type song, "Brooklyn, U.S.A." ("Oh, take me back to Brooklyn, where things was always good; that's where I always should of stood"); a memory type song, "Memory Lane" ("I am strolling down memory lane, without a goddam thing on my mind"); a French-type song, "Ron, Ron, Ron" ("Sur le pont d'Avignon, je ne sais pas, je ne sais; quelque chose, quelque chose, je vous aime"); and an A-type song, "A," which goes, in its lilting entirety, "A moon is shining. A star is gleaming. A banjo is starting to strum. A park bench is waiting. A soft breeze is blowing. A cop is chasing a bum. A tree is rustling. A nightingale's singing. A bobwhite is starting to bob. Ev'rything in the world is doing something, so why can't you find a job?" Since the impact of the Burrows monologues diminishes perceptibly when he is not performing them himself, their appeal has proved to be somewhat limited; a while back, when he was asked what his A.S.C.A.P. rating was, he replied, "It's 'Just Barely.'" Even so, there are many starry-eyed Burrows enthusiasts who can quote the lyrics of "A" as readily as disciples of Irving Berlin can quote the lyrics of "Always." Burrows fans turn up in odd quarters. A few years ago, the English drama critic Kenneth Tynan, ridiculing Christopher Fry's quaint literary style, wrote that one of the playwright's serious lines—"He took me by the scruff of my heart"—reminded him of nothing so much as Burrows' parody of the sophisticated-type love song; "You put a piece of carbon paper under your heart and gave me just a copy of your love."

Nearer home, Burrows' fans have hailed him as a man so uncommonly gifted that on one occasion he succeeded in satirizing a conventional song before it was even written. This display of prescient skill occurred during a party at Leonard Lyons' apartment in 1950. (Another time, Lyons told Burrows that a son of his wanted to go to Columbia but that he wasn't sure it was a good idea for the boy to attend a college so close to home. "Why don't you move to Boston?" Burrows suggested.) It was a typical Lyons gathering, held for the purpose of introducing Perle Mesta to Ethel Merman, who had been signed to play the part of the lady diplomat in "Call Me Madam," and among the other guests was Irving Berlin, who was writing the score for the show. Presently, Burrows was urged to do a turn—something that has never required much urging—and one of his numbers was a homespun ditty entitled "My Brain," a takeoff on many lyricists' penchant for ascribing symptoms normally associated with illness to romance. The song starts off routinely enough ("My brain is whirling, my head is spinning, I can't sleep a wink at night . . .") but ends up "I talked to the doctor, now I'm worried no longer, 'cause he said it ain't love, I'm just sick." A few months later, when "Call Me Madam" opened, one of Berlin's most sparkling contributions to the show turned out to be an aches-and-pains ballad that wound up with the line "You're not sick, you're just in love."

Burrows gets on remarkably well with his fellow-members of A.S.C.A.P., considering that no one has ever mimicked their output more flagrantly. "It used to puzzle me that all those songwriters would drape themselves over the piano when I was playing and knock themselves out laughing," he says. "After a while I realized each of them thought I was kidding some other songwriter's work. Of course, they may also have sensed that in an odd way I was paying them a compliment, because, after all, you can't put across a parody unless whatever it is you're parodying is already popular. The imitation depends for its effect on the strength of the original. Back in vaudeville, if you wanted to get a big hand, you did an impersonation of Jolson. It was Jolson's strength that got you your applause. As Max Beerbohm once said, 'Satire is based on qualified love.' Hatred never leads to good satire. That's why nobody ever really succeeded in ribbing Hitler." Burrows loves all kinds of music unreservedly if it is written and played well, and in a qualified way if it suffers from weaknesses in composition or performance—and there are enough of these flaws in every branch of the art to enable him to rib it all, from bop to opera. He once sat down at a piano and, with Marc Connelly joining him in some raffish duets, improvised an hour-long, non-stop burlesque of a Shubert operetta. When it comes to parodies of popular songs, some of his jabs have never got beyond the title stage—for example, "I Drew a Foul Ball in the Pennant Race of Love"—but that is probably enough. Another unfinished work, to be called "Oh, How We Danced on the Night We Were Wed; I Needed a Wife Like a Hole in the Head," has brought Burrows far more distinction than its faintly depressing first line warrants, for in the biographical notes appearing in the "Happy Hunting" program he is credited with having completed the composition, or, rather, *two* compositions—one entitled "Oh, How We Danced on the Night We Were Wed" and the other "I Needed a Girl Like a Hole in the Head." The editors of *Who's Who in America* have also come a cropper in trying to catalogue Burrows' peculiar titles. Among his accomplishments is an album of recordings that he modestly called "Abe Burrows Sings?" but the *Who's Who* editors—confident of their ability to spot an obvious typographical error—list it without the question mark.

A musical comedy is a mélange of all the arts and crafts of theatre, and the man in charge is in the rough spot of having to blend them—or, rather, their often fiercely individualistic exponents—into a harmonious whole. Burrows is looked upon as peculiarly fitted for such a task by virtue of his broad background of writing, composing, and performing. Russel Crouse, co-author of "Happy Hunting" and of several musicals before it, thinks Burrows is the best-equipped musical-comedy director he has ever worked with.

As a director, Burrows has come a long way in a short time. At the start, when he was working on "Two on the Aisle," he was so green that he telephoned Kaufman and said, "I thought it might be nice to have a treadmill. You've used treadmills. You think a treadmill is good?" "Depends what you have them say on it, Abe," Kaufman replied sagely. During the six years since then, Burrows has acquired a thorough familiarity with the innumerable minutiae of backstage operations—the sort of familiarity that enabled him, for example, while "Happy Hunting" was in rehearsal, to issue firm and confident instructions to the stage manager on the subject of two sound-effect recordings that he felt he might need for a brief dockside scene—one of harbor noises with sea gulls and the other of harbor noises without sea gulls. Burrows works hard at directing, but he refuses to take as solemn a view of the job as some of his colleagues do. "There've been a lot of weighty books written about things like how vital it is which side of the stage your exits are made from," he said the other day. "But as often as not your exits will eventually turn out to be dictated by the location of your star's dressing room in New York. People are always talking about the amount of preparation a director has to do. In a musical, most of the time, the director just ad-libs while trying somehow to make everything fit together. The all-important element is speed. I'll overlook a lot of things just to get a show on its feet fast."

This approach has not won Burrows universal approval. There are people who feel, to cite a current instance, that some of the crowd scenes in "Happy Hunting" are notable only for their congestion. Burrows, in rebuttal, takes the position that the purpose of this show is simply to star Ethel Merman, and that therefore the action of the rest of the cast must be subordinate to hers; indeed, he believes that in any musical the members of the chorus should never be allowed to distract attention from the principals. In 1952, while he was staging the musical "Three Wishes for Jamie," a chorus girl who had previously worked under directors eager to achieve realism at all times, even in the rear ranks, came up to him and asked, "What do I do during the big love duet?" Burrows replied, "Honey, if they're looking at you then, we're in trouble."

Despite an occasional blow of this kind to their pride, most actors, whether principals or lesser lights, enjoy working in a show Burrows is directing, because he approaches his task with an exuberance that tends to infect the whole enterprise. Moreover, he never permits himself a tantrum. "I don't believe in being tough," he says. "The schoolmaster's approach is not for me. I have a hunch that the reason so many so-called authoritarian directors act authoritarian is that they're basically uncertain of themselves. I'm easygoing, but I'm certain, which, in a sense, means I'm *not* easygoing. But that doesn't show. If you holler at an actor, he suspects right away that you're not sure of yourself. I work on the principle that a director shouldn't be the boss but a helper. It wouldn't surprise me if the first director in history was just one of the cast—back in ancient Greece, probably—and one of the other actors said to him, 'Hey, Joe, or Jove, or whatever your name is, go out front and tell us what it looks like.'"

Burrows' outwardly carefree attitude toward directing gives his rehearsals a quality of their own. His appearance is far from frightening, and at times it is almost lackadaisical. During a "Happy Hunting" rehearsal, someone sent out for coffee, and presently a delivery boy arrived with a trayful of cardboard containers. Burrows, at the moment, was supervising an intricate dance number involving thirty or forty weary but hard-driving members of the cast, while various of his minions darted here and there on weighty missions. After surveying the agitated scene, the boy selected Burrows as the person least preoccupied with the proceedings, grabbed him by the arm, and demanded that he pay for the coffee, thus bringing the rehearsal to a jarring halt. Burrows cheerfully fished in his pocket for some money, and then, as the boy retreated up the aisle, remarked to the cast, "See? There's nothing like running things with an iron hand." A couple of weeks later, while the show was in Philadelphia, Burrows gave further evidence of his airy approach to Stanislavski's art when Miss Merman, about to walk up a stage-set gangplank with a bulging jewel case in her hand, stopped and complained mildly to Burrows that the case got in her way. "I shall now make an artistic decision," Burrows gravely announced. "Merm, leave off the jewel case." After a pause, he added, "In the movies, for a decision like this a director wins an Oscar."

"A musical comedy isn't written; it's fixed" is a stock saying among show people, and Burrows is considered one of the theatre's most adept fixers, or, in the professional idiom, play doctors. A show's need for the kind of medication that only a play doctor can furnish is often not only dire but extremely urgent, and because Burrows' memory is so sharp that after seeing a new play just once he can remember every situation and bit of business in it, his services are often looked upon as essential. He established himself as a practitioner in 1951, when the musical "Make a Wish" was filling a pre-Broadway engagement in Philadelphia. "They were in such bad shape they were handing out passes to soldiers and sailors," he recalls. "The author had given up and left town. My agent looked at the show with me and thought it was ghastly, but there was something about the situation that challenged me. I didn't make it great, or even good, but at least I fixed it up so that it ran a hundred performances in New York and nobody got arrested."

Burrows has been paid as much as a thousand dollars merely to go to Philadelphia and sit through a show, without making any prior commitment to tinker with it, but even when he has to pay his own expenses he frequently cannot resist inspecting other people's productions before they reach New York. A few years ago, he found himself with nothing special to do on the evening "Paint Your Wagon" opened for a New Haven tryout, so he wandered up there to have a look. An actress in the cast, spotting him in the lobby before the curtain went up, cried out in anguish, "We haven't even opened, and he's already here to fix it!" Word rapidly went around that the show must be in a jam, because Burrows was out front, and within minutes Cheryl Crawford, the producer, made her way up to Burrows and asked frostily, "Haven't you anything better to do tonight?"

Burrows was sympathetic. "I wasn't going to touch her show, and I didn't, but her irritation was justified," he said not long ago. "She knew that usually I can't see anything without wanting to step in and try to fix it. Something happens to me when a show's in trouble. It takes on a personality for me—it comes alive. I watch it, and it becomes terribly important—as if a human being were sick, or dying. I begin to feel very much like a real doctor. I see this pathetic show groaning and squirming, and I think, Maybe I can help—maybe I can make it breathe. And, like as not, I can. I'm good in adversity. Sometimes I think I welcome it. There are certain kinds of guys who thrive on it—who aren't happy unless things aren't going well. And I'm one of them. While I was struggling with a musical of my own out of town once, I skipped a matinee and sneaked down the street to another musical that was trying out. I immediately saw what was wrong. Clear as hell. I began to wrestle with myself. First, I thought, It's a rival show—let them figure it out for themselves. Second, I thought, If I tell them, they'll be sore at me for sticking my nose in. Third, I thought, The guys involved in this are friends of mine, and in good conscience I can't *not* tell them. During the intermission, while I was still debating with myself about should I or shouldn't I, I bumped into the director and author of this poor, feverish show, and the next thing I knew I heard a voice saying didactically, 'Do this, do that, cut this, change that,' and the voice sounded frighteningly familiar, and all of a sudden I realized, Oh, my God, it's me!"

May 11, 1957

From Part I of a two-part Profile.

My Life as an Importer

It is not often that one gets a chance to experience at first hand the inner workings of an arcane business, which is what the import-export trade has always—until recently—been to me. My opportunity arose unexpectedly the other morning when I fished a letter from the Bureau of Customs, down at Bowling Green, out of my suburban post-office box. The letter was headed "ORIGINAL—Notification to Consignee (Addressee) of Mail Importation to Make Formal Entry (In Lieu of Bill of Lading)." It informed me that a shipment comprising one package of woollen wearing apparel with a declared value of over two hundred and fifty dollars had been sent to me by Davies & Son, London, W.1. I knew what the shipment was. Now and then, I have had a suit made by that firm, and when its representative was over here last winter, I went on a wild sartorial fling and ordered two suits at once. From the valuation put on my consignment, I concluded that both suits had been dispatched in a single box. What puzzled me was that on previous occasions I had been able to claim my clothes simply by paying my own postmaster the duty—usually around thirty-five dollars a suit. I had no idea what had happened this time, but I was anxious to get at, and into, my new apparel, and, being on my way to the city, I decided that when I got there I would go straight down to Bowling Green and find out.

Once I had reached town, it occurred to me that customs might be less agreeable than my local postmaster about accepting personal checks, so I went first of all to my bank, and fortified myself with seventy-five dollars in cash. I was about to board a subway for Bowling Green when I took another look at my letter. "To meet customs requirements," it said, "this notice (in lieu of bill of lading) together with invoice and other related papers, should be presented at Entry Division, Custom House, Bowling Green, New York City (after arrival of the shipment) by the addressee (consignee) or his duly authorized agent or transferee. If you are not familiar with customs requirements, write or telephone the customs officer of the address indicated before proceeding to the customhouse. This may save time and expense on your part."

Eager to save both, I went into a phone booth, called the Custom House, and was connected with—I suppose—a customs officer, to whom I explained my situation. "You got your invoice?" he asked, and I said that, not yet having been billed by my tailor, I had no papers at all beyond my "Notification to Consignee (Addressee)." He sighed, not unsympathetically, and asked if my notice had "Morgan Annex" stamped on it. It had. "Then you got to go there," he said. "Ninth Avenue and Thirtieth Street." By this time, it was ten o'clock. I had a lunch date on the East Side at twelve-thirty. I set out hurriedly for the Morgan Annex.

At the Annex, which turned out to be an adjunct of the main post office, I was sent to Room 503, where a clerk at a desk turned me over to another man, who led me into an enormous, fenced-in storage area piled high with crates and packages. "Wait there," my escort said, pointing toward a stand-up desk with a ball of twine on top of it. I complied, the man went away, and in a jiffy he returned and handed me my parcel from London. He also handed me a wicked-looking knife. "Open the package and see if you can find an invoice," he commanded. I slashed the wrapping paper loose, reached under the box lid, and quickly found an invoice nestling on a sheet of tissue paper that covered my suits. I was about to pull one of the suits out and look at it when the man said, "O.K., tie her up again."

I tied her up, but in rather slipshod fashion. The man expressed dismay at my slovenliness, but I assured him it didn't matter; I'd be carrying the suits to my office in a cab, I explained, and the box would hold together. "You're not carrying them anywhere yet," he said. "I'll retie it myself. Go on back to the desk clerk."

I conveyed my invoice to the clerk and took out my wallet. He asked what I was doing that for, and I said I wanted to pay the duty and get my suits. "Oh, you have to get an entry permit first," he said. "Go to Room 118 at Bowling Green." And as I backed off, he called cheerfully, "Better post bond while you're there. It'll save you time."

I left the Morgan Annex, hailed a cab, and accepted the driver's suggestion that we take the West Side Highway to save time. (I had already abandoned all hope of saving expense.) At Room 118, on the main floor of the massive Custom House, I presented my letter and invoice to a clerk. "You make entry over there," he said, pointing toward a desk where an official was seated, talking to a couple of men. I went there. As nearly as I could figure out, the official was telling the men that however tolerant the United States Customs might be of human frailty, it did not yet stand ready to go along with listing a boatload of umbrellas as chinaware.

Presently, his auditors slunk away, abashed, and he turned to me. "Sit down," he said. "You got a couple of hours of paperwork ahead of you." I asked how it could possibly take that long to redeem two suits. "Brother, it isn't a question of two suits any more," he said. "You might just as well have ordered a ton of jute. You get anything in one lot that's worth over two hundred and fifty dollars, you're in the import business. You're going to have four places to go upstairs after you finish here. Of course, if you don't want to bother, you can always engage a customs broker."

I sat down. I have enough brokers already—insurance, investment, real-estate, theatre-ticket, whatnot—and I decided that if I was going to have to be in the import business, I might as well learn it from the ground floor up.

For half an hour, while I waited, the man methodically filled out forms on my behalf, the principal ones being an "Entry Record Receipt Missing Documents" and a "Consumption Entry." I looked at my watch, and saw that it was nearly noon. He asked me if I was hungry, and I said I had a lunch date and perhaps had better postpone importing my suits. "Oh, don't do that," he said amiably. "You can fill out the rest of these forms yourself and bring them back this afternoon. Don't get here after four." My lunch appointment was with a man who insisted on telling me, in detail, how he and some neighbors had formed a small combine to import their own French wines, and thus avoid the retailers' markup. He said that the ringleader of this vinous mob had told him there was really nothing to it. As soon as I could, I wished him Godspeed, excused myself, and repaired to my office, where I spent the next hour filling out forms, such as a declaration of consignee, or agent, for merchandise obtained in pursuance of a purchase or agreement to purchase. In the course of all this, I found myself airily referring to myself—following the example of my man in Room 118—as an Importer of Record, Commercial, who had a Single Entry consisting of eight pounds, net quantity, of Schedule A Units, under Paragraph 1115 (a). Commodity Number 3640.100.

At three o'clock, I was back in Room 118, Custom House, where my friend greeted me warmly and nodded approvingly as he read through my sheaf of papers and rubber-stamped each of them three or four times. "You should have bought only one suit," he said pleasantly. We both laughed, he somewhat less shrilly than I, and then, on the blank side of a square of scratch paper that had been cut from some mimeographed sheet, he scribbled a list of instructions for me:

(1) Mr. Brady or Mr. Sheridan for Bond in corridor outside Room 248, opposite Window 1.

(2) Bond Desk, Window 7, 8, or 9. Room 248.
(3) Window 1, Room 248. Wait for Papers.
(4) Cashier's Office, Room 217.
(5) Return to Room 118.

Clutching, among my other documents, a new form, "Immediate Delivery and Consumption Entry Bond (Single Entry)," I headed upstairs. In a crowded corridor, near a sign that said "Lodging Consumption and Warehouse Entries," I found both Mr. Brady *and* Mr. Sheridan, who, as representatives of the Seaboard Surety Company, issued me a four-hundred-dollar bond—conceivably the smallest sum they traffic in—on payment of a dollar and a half. (Certainly that sum was too puny for them, because they could not change a five-dollar bill. I got change by momentarily arresting the headlong flight of one of several dozen men, possibly customs brokers, who were running up and down the corridor in a kind of bureaucratic relay race, passing documents back and forth like batons.) Leaving Mr. Brady and Mr. Sheridan, I went on to Window 7, where a clerk took away all my papers and gave me a slip with a six-digit number written on it (I have since forgotten what it was), which he said would identify *my* number. I asked him what my number was, and he pointed pityingly to "927686," which I then perceived, for the first time, had been profusely stamped on all my papers. I vowed never to forget it, and moved—or, rather, was shoved—out of line. Everybody seemed to be in a terrible hurry.

Window 1 reminded me of my post office back home—a tiny, grilled aperture surrounded by individual, locked boxes. As I approached it, men were rushing up, unlocking their boxes, scooping out papers, and dashing away—all timesavers, all, I surmised, customs brokers. I've never seen such an agitated bunch. Feeling like a summer tenant who has to ask for his mail at the window because he doesn't have a box of his own, I stepped up and gave my identifying number.

A few minutes later, a voice behind the window cried out "E.J.!" and—pleased at this informal, if not downright intimate, touch—I grabbed the papers that the owner of the voice was thrusting at me through the bars, and strode briskly away toward the cashier's office. But I strode right back after a teller there had glanced at my papers and said scornfully, "You only have a permit. You haven't made entry." I got back to Window 1 in time to hear a voice calling out, "Six—eight—six!" This turned out to be another local nickname for me, and presently I got some more papers, signifying that I had now somehow made entry.

From there on, it was a relative cinch. Oh, I was held up for a while at the cashier's office because I didn't have in exact change the seventy-two dollars and thirty-three cents I owed in duty, but eventually (after filling out a depositor's ticket) I got it, and persuaded a teller to accept my money. Then

I returned to Room 118, where I dropped all the papers I had on my mentor's desk. "Hey, you got *two* receipts for duty!" he said admiringly. "You're very lucky. Now you can go back to the Morgan Annex."

At the familiar old Annex, I turned in one of my receipts and asked if I could now have my suits. "No," said the man on duty. "They haven't been inspected by customs yet. Call us in two or three days."

Five days later, I got the suits. The box they were in had been stoutly trussed with copper wire, and I had to pay fifteen cents in postage due for "customs clearance and delivery." I could see that it was just as well I had finally managed to make entry; if I hadn't, there is no telling what might have happened. On the parcel were two printed labels, evidently the handiwork of British customs, one label saying that the merchandise therein should be returned to the sender if undeliverable, the other saying that once the merchandise had been mailed, it *"may in no circumstances be returned to the sender."* (Italics theirs, or at any rate not mine.)

There you have it, and if anybody has a couple of carloads of dutiable merchandise en route and wants to dispense with the services of a broker, I know the importing routine. I think it only fair to point out, though, that I have no intention of getting mixed up in the export business as well. As I was leaving Room 118 at Bowling Green, my buddy there suggested jovially that I stop in someday and let him see how one of the suits looked on me. When I replied politely that I might, if I didn't have to return them to England for alterations, his mood sobered. "You better not have to," he said, "because if you do, it'll have to be done through here." Who cares if the shoulders ride high?

June 29, 1957

Notes and Comment

As almost invariably happens after a big storm, the papers have been full of editorials bemoaning the apparent inability of our weather predictors to furnish us with precise forecasts. We don't bemoan it at all. One of the nicest things about weather is its unexpectedness. When bad weather arrives unpredicted, it is apt to create emergencies, and emergencies bring out some of the best qualities in people—resourcefulness, neighborliness, and fortitude, for instance—which as a rule these days have precious little chance to manifest themselves. Good weather—unheralded good weather, that is— makes everybody smile, and a pleasant sight that can be on Fifth Avenue on a sunny morning following a sullen eve. We think that weather should always come as a surprise. How charmless it would be if the onset of spring (not the first day of spring but the first springlike day) could be dependably foretold on an insurance agent's calendar!

The State Department has announced that henceforth passport pictures may be in color, a decision based on the theory that travellers will feel more cheerful if they can, to use the Department's phrase, put their best face forward. Presumably, Mr. Dulles and his associates hope this will lead, in turn, to friendlier relations between gadabout Americans and the natives. Aside from the question of whether most people actually do look happier in color than in black and white (we know one poor woman whom Kodacolor somehow always turns into a carrot), the only flaw in this plan would seem to be the fact that a passport, however handsomely illustrated, is a document one finds it hard to associate with cheerfulness. The people to whom passports must be presented—immigration and customs officials, to say nothing of concierges and the police—are so closely linked in the average tourist's mind with trouble, confusion, suspicion, and delay that it is nearly impossible for anyone to look his best while having his passport inspected. You take a cross, tired, trembling, pale, and perspiring tourist and stand him up alongside a passport picture of himself glowing with health and contentment, and the chances are that some sharp-eyed border guard will insist the photograph can't conceivably be his own.

March 1, 1958

Recollections of an Intourist Tourist

While it is true that one's first exposure to a Leningrad restaurant would quickly dispel any illusion of being in Paris, the food we had there, and in the other cities, was not bad at all. For the most part, we took our meals in the dining rooms of our Intourist hotels—large, chandeliered chambers served by dinner-jacketed staffs and equipped with bandstands that, come evening, were occupied by hard-working dance orchestras. The music was predominantly American, but every so often a band would assert its independence of the West by emitting a jazzed-up version of "The Song of the Volga Boatmen." The bands played imitatively, and a bit raggedly. It was as if the instrumentalists had got hep to American music by attending movies in which the sound and action were imperfectly synchronized.

A tourist in Russia is supposed to pay for his meals with coupons that Intourist doles out. Though each has a stipulated value in rubles, the sum does not appear on the ticket itself. My wife and I were travelling first class, and our coupons, we learned in due course, entitled us to fourteen rubles' worth of sustenance apiece at breakfast, twenty-four at dinner, four at tea, and sixteen at supper. (The official exchange rate for the ruble is four to a dollar, but tourists enjoy a rate of ten to one.) We never had tea, but it didn't matter, for the coupons could be used at any meal. You could buy drinks with them, too, if you had any to spare, but you needed a lot of spares. One evening, in a Continental mood, I asked a waiter to bring us a bottle of dry red wine. What we got was sickeningly sweet, and we couldn't down much of it. When our bill came, we found that the bottle had set us back seventy rubles and twenty kopecks, or seven dollars and two cents. The twenty kopecks really hurt.

Given enough time—two hours, say—a Soviet waiter can, and probably will, deliver a satisfying meal, though the chances are he'll bring the entire order, from caviar through ice cream, in one trayload. This may save trips to the kitchen, but it crowds the table. Occasionally, though, the service we got was so indifferent that we darkly suspected our waiters of ideological discrimination. In Leningrad, for instance, two dozen North Koreans trooped into the hotel dining room after four of us had been seated. We hadn't yet been able to place our order when they trooped out again, licking their lips and rubbing their stomachs. Another time, the prep-schoolers in our group got so famished while waiting for their lunch that after a stranger at the next table—he had the air of a Bulgarian—had finished his meal and departed, they lunged for a few pieces of black bread and globules of caviar he had left behind. In their frenzy, one of them smashed a glass. When the teacher in charge of them went to the lobby a few minutes later to complain that his wards were on the edge of starvation, an Intourist woman cut short his lament to say sternly, "Don't tell me about *your* troubles. I hear one of them broke a glass."

The best food we had in the Soviet Union was chicken à la Kiev, in Kiev—breast of chicken rolled in bread crumbs and deep-fried. As a rule, we did not tip our waiters; since they did not normally give us any change after accepting our coupons, they probably pocketed the difference between what these were worth and the cost of our food. In Kiev, I would gladly have tipped the waitress who served us that chicken, but when I handed her a couple of coupons, she did some rapid calculating and, reaching into the pocket of her uniform, pressed six rubles on me. I had never been tipped by a waitress before, and it was an exhilarating sensation.

The best ballet and theatrical companies of the U.S.S.R. were on vacation, or at the Brussels Fair, during our visit, but my wife and I did squeeze in an opera, a ballet, an operetta, a straight play, a circus, and a puppet show—a far more strenuous postprandial program than we would tackle at home, or in most places we would contemplate visiting regularly. The puppet show, at the State Central Puppet Theatre, in Moscow, was the most engaging of the lot. The performance, entitled "An Unusual Concert," was a spoof of conventional concert-hall virtuosos. It was staged by Sergei

Obraztsov, who was described in the program—a Russian-and-English one—as a "People's Artist of the U.S.S.R." His artistry was flawless, and funny. In Russian theatres, the electricians are customarily stationed, along with their batteries of lights, in upper boxes; the minuscule stage on which Obraztsov's puppets cavorted had its own adjoining boxes, and in one of them perched a puppet electrician, busily working tiny spotlights. The ballet and the opera were both put on, in Leningrad, by a visiting company from Lithuania. The opera was called "Vaiva," and before we went to hear it, we asked an Intourist woman to synopsize the action for us. "It's a fairy tale," she replied. "I'm not sure of the plot, but I think it has something to do with good and evil forces, and a magic belt. 'Vaiva' means 'belt' in Lithuanian, you know. The good forces win. It's their belt." Thus briefed, we carefully scrutinized each new waistline that came onstage, but it did us no good; practically every character was besashed.

Later that night, I picked up a copy of *Soviet Literature*, one of the English-language propaganda journals on sale at the hotel newsstand. A printed supplement that had been tucked inside fell out, and proved to be the text of a decision taken by the Central Committee of the Communist Party of the Soviet Union in regard to "the Correction of Mistakes in Appraisal of the Operas 'The Great Friendship,' 'Bogdan Khmelnitsky,' and 'With All My Heart.'" It had been determined on February 10, 1948, I read, that the libretto of "Bogdan Khmelnitsky," to cite just one of the trio, was guilty of major ideological defects. On May 28, 1958, though, the C.C. of the C.P.S.U. had decreed that this ten-year-old denunciation was unjustified, being "a reflection of the subjective approach to certain works of art on the part of J.V. Stalin," who, I learned as I read on, "was in large measure influenced, negatively, by Molotov, Malenkov, and Beria." I was sorry, in a way, that "Vaiva" had escaped reappraisal; I might have learned what it was all about.

The circus we saw was—in delightful contrast to so many greatest shows on earth—a one-ring affair. What is more, it took place not in an arena that could be converted overnight into a hockey rink or a revival-meeting hall but in a cozy, circular, low-roofed building, in Kiev, that had apparently been designed with circus-going children in mind. The house was packed with kids, who loved every minute of it. So did we. There were some amazingly limber acrobats; a juggler who kep three flaming torches in play while atop a galloping white horse; some clowns who rose to extravagant heights of buffoonery (one of them had a donkey whose rear end had been costumed in imitation of a man feigning to be the rear end of a donkey); and a suave, tailcoated magician, who, among other feats, turned a lady into a lion. We were a mite taken aback not to find any trained bears among the acts, but in compensation there were some trained white doves and a pack of exceptionally well-tutored dogs.

There were more dogs in that one circus act than we saw anywhere else in the Soviet Union. In Leningrad, a city of three million people, we met up with just one dog, and it may have been a tourist itself, for it was a French poodle leashed to a French-looking woman. On the streets of Moscow, we saw no dogs at all (maybe all the dogs in town had been requisitioned for space travel), and on the streets of Kiev we saw just one—a small white animal, which my wife guessed was part of the circus act, out for an airing. It therefore came as a surprise to us to find the last page of one issue of the Moscow *News* devoted to stories about dogs, complete with pictures. There was even an All-Union Dog Show in the offing, we read. Many breeds were to be represented, including some that I could tell from both pictures and text were strikingly different from the breeds recognized in the United States. There would be four kinds of Eskimos, for example, and five kinds of borzois, and one entirely new Soviet breed, the Estonian hound. It is only a question of time, I suppose, before doggy delegations from North Korea, Bulgaria, and maybe even the United States will be making trips to Russia themselves. Not that this is likely to produce any relaxation of international tensions. To judge by the pictures in the Moscow *News*, Khrushchev and Eisenhower may find it easier, in the long run, to reconcile their different standards than the All-Union Dog crowd and the American Kennel Club.

It would be fairly safe, I think, to say that all English-speaking Russians are eager to chat with all English-speaking visitors. As one member of our group, an art teacher named Margie, put it one day, "You know, one of the best parts of being here is being a novelty. When you go to other countries, they've all *seen* Americans. Here, you're *something*." Many Soviet citizens—especially the younger ones—gravitate toward the hotels where they know foreigners stay, and buttonhole them on the street outside. For that matter, Russians will accost a foreigner on any street. Recognition requires no particular deductive skill; with our Western clothes, our cameras, and our gaping mouths, we can be detected half a block away. In Kiev one night, a Russian man who picked several of us up insisted that we accompany him to a building where, he told us, we would find some real Americana. What he wanted to show us, it developed, was a poster heralding, in Russian, a forthcoming exhibit of the works of "РОКУЕЛЛА КЕНТА, США," which, after squinting a moment, we were able to decipher as "Rockwell Kent, USA." The Russian asked if we knew Kent, and when we all confessed we had never met him, demanded, "But is he not your leading people's artist?" We decided not to confuse the fellow by suggesting that to most of our people the hegemonic artist was probably Norman Rockwell.

Museums are a favorite hangout of Russians who want to practice their English. At the Russian Museum, in Leningrad, a young engineer latched eagerly on to my wife. Dismayed to learn that she was married, he latched dispiritedly, but volubly, on to me. Like many other Russians we encountered, he was exceedingly self-centered. He told me he was both a pilot and a research scientist, and had had something to do with one of the sputniks. "You know sputnik?" he asked. I said I knew. He went on to say that he played football, basketball, volleyball, and the piano, and was a prizefighter of no mean prowess. Then he switched to literature. He was familiar, he said, with Mark Twain, Theodore Dreiser, Walt Whitman, and three other writers, whom I was perplexed to hear identified—until I recalled that the Russians have no letter "h" and generally use "g" instead—as Victor Gugo, Goward Fast, and O. Genry. A moment later, he left abruptly. I thought at first that I had offended him because he had had to admit, in answer to my questioning, that he had never heard of Nathaniel Gawthorne, Sherlock Golmes, or G. Allen Smith, and I was relieved when I saw him swoop upon a seventeen-year-old girl in our party who had no rings on her fingers.

Most of the Russians we chatted with were extremely cordial, but every now and then we ran into one whose cup of grievance against the United States was so full that it spilled over onto individual Americans. At the Leningrad airport the evening we were to board a plane for Kiev, I fell into conversation with a Soviet Air Force colonel. We went through the usual ritual of such meetings—the tentative smile, the handshake, the exchange of cigarettes, the display of children's photographs, the establishment of origins. (He was from Minsk.) Presently, we got onto the subject of foreign relations, and his affability vanished as he rebuked me severely for my country's policies. "Russian people don't want war," he said.

"American people don't want war, either," I countered. With a snarl of disbelief, he turned on his heel and stalked into the waiting room.

I followed him in. Most of the other members of our tour group were standing around a piano, singing American songs. (There's no telling where one will run into a piano in Russia.) Several dozen Russians were listening. All of them seemed to be enjoying the recital, except one mother, whose baby had been roused by the din and was bawling, and the colonel, who stood by stony-faced. When our chorus soared—not too tactfully, perhaps—into the Wild Blue Yonder with the chantey that ends "Nothing can stop the Army Air Corps!" the colonel glowered. Then someone in the audience cried out, "Paul Robeson!" There were no Negroes among us, so it was clear this was not a case of mistaken identity, but the shout was taken up by other Russians until we Americans felt obliged to make some appropriate acknowledgment. Most of the males among us, I imagine, had tackled "Ol' Man River" in the privacy of the morning shower, but the lounge of the Leningrad airport at midnight, with immense portraits of Lenin, Stalin, and Mao on the walls, was something else again. Nevertheless, for the sake of international amity, we proceeded to render the song as best we could, and the reaction—surely a tribute more to Robeson's popularity than to our performance—was stupefying. The cheers drowned out the infant's howls, and even the colonel permitted himself a fleeting smile.

Our most comradely experience, all things considered, was an impromptu alliance we formed one noon with the Red Army. This took place at Petrodvorets, a lovely, glittering, fountain-bedecked palace outside Leningrad. It was demolished by the Nazis, and the Communists are now restoring it. While we were looking around, two workmen engaged in sprucing up some of the dozens of statues that decorate the grounds furtively approached a young American writer named Herbert and gave him a couple of postcard-size photographs—closeups of the bosoms of sculptured nudes. The men also gave him their names and addresses, and hinted that they'd like him to send them some reciprocal tokens of Western culture. He was slated to go from the U.S.S.R. to Paris, and figured he would have no trouble finding something suitable there. It was soon after Herbert amassed his rakish souvenirs that, at a gaudy set of fountains, we came upon some Soviet soldiers—half a dozen of them, armed with cameras. We took their picture. They took our picture. Several members of our tour posed in cozy embrace with the military. Cigarettes were swapped. One soldier had a guitar, and he was easily induced to play it. Another, whose insignia indicated that he was an officer, went into a deep-knee bend and did the *Kazachka*. A dozen or so Russian passersby stopped to watch. A boy and a girl in our group gave a demonstration of rock 'n' roll, to the guitarist's inept, but vigorous, accompaniment. Then, to exactly the same music, six of the tourists did a Virginia reel. A drunken Russian civilian vaulted into the clear space encircled by the spectators—some fifty of them by now—and danced a solo. The officer took a jew's-harp out of his pocket and joined in with the guitarist. Two members of our group did the fox trot, and two others, one of them a boy from Stockholm, the Swedish polka. (His partner, I was astonished to perceive, was my wife, a girl from East Rindge, New Hampshire.) A hundred spectators applauded. An accordion player materialized. One of the Russian soldiers did a high-stepping dance with the tipsy civilian. The officer danced with one of the American girls. Soon a dozen couples of mixed nationality were gaily skipping about. All at once, a stocky, leather-faced old woman in a quilted jacket, with a red armband girding one sleeve, pushed through the mob, which must have numbered close to two hundred. At a single, sharp command from her, the musicians stopped playing. The Russians, soldiers and civilians alike, drifted meekly away. There wasn't a murmur of protest. It was as sudden, and obliterating, as a summer thunderstorm.

December 20 and 27, 1958

From both parts of a two-part Reporter at Large piece.

The Universal Drink

No more fervent tributes have ever been paid to Coca-Cola than those that came from Allied service men who either got the opportunity to drink it or missed it unbearably during the Second World War. Take what General Carlos Romulo said in his memoirs, "I Saw the Fall of the Philippines." Describing the events of April 4, 1942, four days before he escaped from Bataan on the last plane out, he wrote:

> This day that was to mark the turning point in the Battle of the Philippines began for me with an incident that seemed of the greatest importance. In fact, so vital did it seem at the time that that night, upon my return to the tunnel on Corregidor after one of the most terrible days a man could ever experience, I wrote a detailed account of that day on my typewriter with a ribbon that could hardly make itself legible, and with trembling hands I added the important notation: "I had a Coca-Cola."

The Coke he had was one of eleven salt-incrusted bottles that some American soldiers had salvaged from a sunken supply ship. In "Winged Victory," Moss Hart had a gang of fliers about to take off for combat toast each other in Coca-Cola. One of them said, "Listen, brother, where *we're* all going we'll look back on a Coke as something out of Heaven." The Coca-Cola Company's vaults in Atlanta bulge with letters from service men attesting to the accuracy of this prediction. A young lady who lived in the Bronx passed along an excerpt from a love letter that her one and only, an Army corporal, had written in Europe: "Well, I guess you want to know now what it is I want so much, outside of you. Well, darling, it is a bottle of Coca-Cola." A private first class in Burma wrote his aunt, "To my mind, I am in this damn mess as much to help keep the custom of drinking Cokes as I am to help preserve the million other benefits our country blesses its citizens with. . . . May we all toast victory soon with a Coke—if flavored with a little rum, I am sure no one will object." The Japanese radio tortured our Marines in the Southwest Pacific by dwelling interminably on the forsaken pleasure of drinking a Coke. ("Can't you just hear the ice tinkling in the glasses?") It was fiendish.

The Coca-Cola Company itself boasted in wartime advertisements that "next to wives, sweethearts, and letters from home, among the things our fighting men overseas mention most [in their letters] is Coca-Cola." The fact that the company seemed eager to have wives and sweethearts furnish it with fighting men's letters mentioning the drink may have made a few of the citations it received something less than spontaneous, but there can be little doubt that the bulk of them were heartfelt. Without prodding, a naval lieutenant in the Pacific called Coca-Cola "nectar of the Gods." A soldier in Egypt rated it better than nectar, and an airman in the Solomons, whose vocabulary was large but imprecise, likened it to ambrosia. An Australian soldier thought it ripping. A sailor in the Mediterranean asked his sweetheart to scent her next letter with a drop of Coke and, after she had complied, wrote that it smelled to him "like heady wine, more powerful than Chanel No. 5, more tempting than the odor from a thousand roses."

Even today, Coca-Cola receives an occasional missive about its role in the war. A recent one included an account of an air crash that the writer had witnessed in the South Pacific. The only identifiable objects found in the wreckage, he wrote, in graphic detail, were the pilot's left hand and liver, and two blood-spattered but unbroken bottles of Coke. "Please write and tell me what you think of my story," he concluded. The Coca-Cola Company answers all its mail conscientiously, but in this instance it evaded a direct response, saying only, "We can readily see how this experience has made an indelible impression upon your mind." Another former G.I., who had been a German prisoner for more than a year, reported to the company a decade later that the mere image of Coke had given him the will to live. Half starved while on a six-week forced march, he'd been about to throw in his chips. Then, as he staggered through a German town, a peeling advertising poster caught his eye. "I looked at the sign a couple of minutes as we passed by, and memories started coming back to me, of home, of the drugstore where my girl friend (later my wife) and I used to sit and plan our lives together," he wrote. "Well, sir, I kept thinking of that Coke sign and what it stood for, of home, of the darling wife and child that were waiting for me, of all the good times and wonderful things that were ahead of me, if only I could get out of this mess alive. Right then and there I said to myself 'I will get out alive!' and a new feeling of hope and strength seemed to come over me. As I sit here with my darling wife and child, I often think back to that little Coke sign in Germany and say thanks, thanks a lot for helping to get me home." The Coca-Cola Company, touched, sent him a leather billfold.

When the Japanese attacked Pearl Harbor, they shot up four Coca-Cola coolers at Hickam Field. Coca-Cola quickly struck back. The company was run then, as it is now—although he is officially retired—by Robert Winship Woodruff, an urbane, astute, enormously wealthy Georgian, who had resolved as early as the nineteen-twenties that there was no place on earth too remote, geographically or culturally, to enjoy the benefits of Coca-Cola. Scarcely had the United States declared war when Woodruff announced his determination to make Coke available, at a nickel a drink, to every member of our armed forces, no matter where he might be. Woodruff's gesture was not only patriotic but practical. The Coca-Cola Company is the largest single user of pure granulated sugar on earth, and when sugar rationing went into effect, the company got nowhere near the amount it wanted for the ordinary production of syrup. (It tried hard, though. Early in 1942, it issued a propagandistic booklet, "Importance of the Rest-Pause in Maximum War Effort," which reproduced a batch of letters from civilian war workers hinting that they could hardly survive without Coke.) Even under rationing, however, the company was able to acquire virtually unlimited supplies of sugar for Coke for the armed forces.

The armed forces, for their part, were quick to enlist under the banner of Coca-Cola. Theatre commanders were authorized to order bottling plants, much as they ordered ammunition. The upshot of this agreeable collaboration—agreeable to everybody except the company's anguished competitors—was that ninety-five per cent of the soft drinks dispensed through overseas post exchanges during the war were drinks of Coca-Cola. ("What do they think this war is—the cause that refreshes?" grumbled a testy columnist in *PM*, a paper that subsequently folded.) Between Pearl Harbor and V-J Day, G.I.s gulped ten billion drinks of Coca-Cola, three billion of them bottled overseas, in five plants already established and fifty-nine additional plants that the company had resourcefully assembled. General Eisenhower, whose affection for Coca-Cola matches that of any alien head of state, had barely landed in North Africa when he requested eight plants. A plant needed in China was dismantled in India, flown piece by piece across the Himalayas, and put together again. When the Australian government, which had a less feverish view of the importance of Coke-drinking. told a bottler out there that he couldn't have all the cork he wanted for lining bottle caps, he notified the American Army tersely, "No cork, no Coke." He got his cork. At war's end, six dismantled bottling plants were bobbing gently off the coast of Japan, waiting to follow our troops ashore.

To supervise this mass migration of nectar, a hundred and sixty-three Coca-Cola men donned uniforms and shuttled back and forth across the world as technical observers—or, as they were more commonly known to the service men they ministered to, Coca-Cola colonels. (One enisled technical observer risked getting busted to Coca-Cola corporal by writing, in a communiqué to the home office, "Boy, what I wouldn't give for a good drink of Stateside Scotch!") Technical observers attached to General MacArthur's staff rigged up a portable Coke dispenser for use in jungle areas, and observers attached to the Navy devised a slender vending machine that could be lowered through the hatches of submarines. (It was perfected too late to be installed before hostilities ceased, but it is now standard equipment.) Coca-Cola resembled certain other forms of material in that some theatres of operations got more of it than others, and got it more quickly. For instance, the reputation of the Society Islands as a paradise was splendidly maintained; after the war native divers at Borabora recovered thirty thousand empty Coke bottles that had been tossed into a single placid lagoon there. In less serene regions, the scarcity of Coca-Cola was sometimes so acute that upon receiving a trickling shipment a military unit would have the chaplain dole it out, in the hope of avoiding mayhem. Individuals in arid areas who were lucky enough to latch on to a bottle—occasionally one would be shipped from home in a cotton-wrapped gift package—guarded it ferociously. A Navy lieutenant off Sicily opened his ship's safe, and, with pistol drawn, permitted an ensign to touch a bottle of Coke that nestled inside. Then the lieutenant locked the safe again. A soldier in Holland drank half a bottle his wife sent him and let a dozen of his buddies shoot craps for the other half. The first bottle to reach the Anzio beachhead was shared by nineteen admirably disciplined G.I.s.

In the Solomons, a single bottle of Coca-Cola was sold for five dollars; in Casablanca, for ten; in an Alaskan outpost, for forty. A field-artillery sergeant in Italy who got two bottles in 1944 drank one and raffled off the other among the men in his battalion, the proceeds going to swell a fund for children of members of the unit who died in action. Four thousand dollars was collected from soldiers vying for the bottle, and the man who won it was too overcome with emotion to drink it. Ernie Pyle, writing of this unusual fund-raising drive, said that the participants in the raffle hoped that the Coca-Cola Company would also contribute to the kitty. "I have no doubt they will," Pyle added. The company immediately sent two thousand dollars to the artillerymen, but in so discreet and roundabout a fashion—out of a natural desire not to be deluged with similar appeals from every battalion under arms—that many of its top officials do not know of the generous gesture to this day.

Soon after the war ended, the American Legion polled five thousand veterans on their preferences in the matter of soft drinks, and found that nearly two-thirds of them favored Coca-Cola. A complementary survey made by the Coca-Cola Company revealed that among veterans with overseas service the percentage was even higher. "What we did during the war cost us a lot of dough," one company vice-president has since said, "but it sure made these guys love us." And when the fighting stopped, not only did Coca-Cola have millions of young Americans much in its debt but it also had the sixty-four overseas bottling plants—fifty-nine of them ferried abroad, as the company's competitors have ruefully pointed out, at government expense—ready to be converted to production for civilians.

February 14, 1959

From Part I of a four-part Profile.

Notes and Comment

Now that Los Angeles has had, and won, its first World Series, the city, we gather from one of our correspondents, has achieved new and blissful stature. To some Angelenos, our man reports, New York has become simply a place where Carl Furillo and Duke Snider once had a tryout. Walter O'Malley, who is also feeling his oats these days, announced shortly after the Series moved to Los Angeles from Chicago that he had received ten thousand congratulatory telegrams, and added pointedly that neither the Mayor of New York nor the Borough President of Brooklyn had been heard from. During Los Angeles' finest hour, we learn, its citizens could not contain their pride and glee. There was, to be sure, some evidence of normality; for instance, Louella Parsons announced that Eva Gabor had "added to the excitement of the World Series yesterday by getting married." Mickey Cohen, meanwhile, added to the excitement of romance by disclosing his betrothal to a local stripteaser named Beverly Hills. But for the most part baseball clearly superseded romance and everything else. One night, the nervous author of a show that was trying out in Los Angeles was standing in the lobby during the second-act intermission, and he whispered to a companion, "Sidle up close to that couple over there and find out what they're talking about." "Gil Hodges," the friend reported. And every day, from one o'clock in the afternoon on, it was difficult to persuade Angelenos to answer the phone, and what work was done was half done. The star of a Western serial that was being filmed at a local studio for future exhibition on television acted out one stormy sequence while wearing an earphone attached to a transistor radio. He kept that side of his head away from the camera, and his viewers may conclude that he had a stiff neck. A deliveryman whose callous boss insisted that he take a glass shower door to a home where it was to be installed carried out his orders, but upon arrival, finding the lady of the house looking at the Series on television, he stood in her parlor with the door balanced on his head and refused to proceed farther. Fearing that if a Dodger hit a home run her room might be carpeted with shards of glass, the housewife coaxed him into completing his job by putting a portable television set in the bathroom. She was unhappy about the whole affair, because the distraction made her miss a double play.

To a New Yorker, observes our man—a Manhattanite of long standing—the warmth of the embrace with which Los Angeles has hugged the Dodgers to its bosom is impressive, for while Brooklyn used to hold the Dodgers in affection, Los Angeles seems to hold them almost in awe. It would be hard to imagine any Angeleno, these giddy days, referring to the team as bums. And the city's respectful adoration does not stem merely from the circumstance that a World Series has finally been staged in this palmy setting. Rather, it appears that the Dodgers have given the land of make-believe something real to cling to. "It's not our feelings about baseball that have us all stirred up," one reasonably old-time settler said the other day. "It's that this cockeyed, sprawling place has finally had a chance to become a unified city. It's the first time Los Angeles ever had a chance to become *anything*."

October 17, 1959

The Ethnocentrics

Pleased though they may be with their fellow-citizens and their physical surroundings, Alaskans reveal mixed feelings when asked about their state's future role in the Union. "A fair half of us are living in the past, and the other half are living in the future," one oldtimer remarked to me, "so the present doesn't worry us a bit." The cheery theme of a teachers' conference in Fairbanks last spring was "Tomorrow Is Here!," but one of the principal speakers was a Juneau economist named George W. Rogers, who had written shortly before, "Alaska is not something that is or has been; it is a promising potential of something that can be." Many Alaskans, optimistic about the destiny of their much-loved land, are furious at the sour-mouthed busybodies who have proposed that, since most states have abbreviations, a logical one for Alaska would be Alas. But there is so little unanimity among Alaskans that even the state's taxi-drivers neglect their traditional pose of omniscience and freely admit to uncertainty. One of them told me, "Sometimes I fear we'll end up a disgrace to the nation, and then I stop and look around and say to myself, 'Oh, what a marvellous, glorious state this can be!'"

Most Alaskans, while they await transfusions of capital from Wall Street, Tokyo, or Hong Kong, and the development of a new benevolence among the entrepreneurs and shippers of Seattle, seem to be reasonably content with what they now have. What they now have, mainly, is animals and scenery, which afford them ample recreation and solace, and will, they hope, do the same for future swarms of tourists. Game is so abundant in Alaska that some guides, on taking hunters into the bush, inquire in advance, as though they were shoe salesmen, just what size their customers want. The bush pilots who fly sportsmen in for the kill make a handsome living; one of them has bought a new airplane annually for the last seven years. When it's springtime in Kotzebue, on the Arctic Ocean, there may be as many as thirty small planes parked on the ice at a time. A leather-faced Texas farmer travelled to Kotzebue last spring, and the first day he was there he flew out over the ice and, with his first shot after the plane had landed, brought down the first polar bear he'd ever seen outside of a zoo. After the ice begins to break up, some hunters track polar bear by boat, cruising up alongside their prey and shooting without getting their feet wet. The airplane polar-bear hunters, who at least dismount, have nothing but contempt for these deck-chair sportsmen—a scorn that is perhaps exceeded only by the derision heaped on *them* by Alaskans who believe that the one sporting way to bag a polar bear is to go after it, Eskimo-fashion, with dog-sled and spear.

Nowadays, fewer and fewer Eskimos go after anything Eskimo-fashion. Recently, a man from Anchorage who made a jaunt to Kotzebue was disgusted at having an Eskimo boy try to cadge a dime off him. Many Eskimos have become ardent motion-picture fans, with a special addiction to Westerns. Kotzebue has a population of only twelve hundred, nine-tenths of it native, but it has two movie theatres. Not very long ago, one of them stationed guards at its exits when a particularly ancient picture was showing, so that its audience wouldn't be able to escape and patronize the rival theatre. There is no television in Kotzebue (as there is in Fairbanks, Anchorage, and Juneau), and Radio Moscow, which has lately been sending out programs in Eskimo, comes through better than most American stations. The only year-round hotel in town occupies the second story of a general store that, presumably because a local market exists for the stuff, stocks Rudolph the Red-Nosed Reindeer Toilet Water. There are just two other places in Kotzebue that sell merchandise of any kind. (One of them flaunts the slogan "Remember—Before You Buy—Try Us.") Up to four years ago, the only electricity in Kotzebue was that furnished by privately owned generators. Now the federal government has installed a power plant, and the local citizenry has had quite a time buying strings of blinking Christmas-tree lights, although there is not a tree of any species within a hundred miles of the place. To the dismay of those Alaskans who hate to see the encroaching refinements of civilization, Kotzebue recently built an up-to-date jail. "We're very proud of our jail," a Kotzebue civic booster told me. "The day it opened, our Mothers' Club held open house there and served coffee and doughnuts."

Not long after I had made a visit to Kotzebue, I met a lawyer in Fairbanks who was the only Alaskan I have ever heard admit that he didn't care for big-game hunting. "Some of my friends consider me a real nut because I don't hunt and I don't fish and I don't fly a plane," he said. "Personally, I think it's my own business whether I shoot a polar bear or not. When you stop to think about it, a polar-bear rug can be very impractical. First you have to have a large enough room, which can be expensive up here, and then you have to be careful whenever you walk through your own house that you don't trip over the damn thing's head."

I heard no such heretical views about Alaskan scenery. While taking their routine rides through the skies, Alaskans of many years' residence hop from one side of a plane to the other, pressing their noses against the windows in order not to miss any new views of the magnificent terrain that they so contentedly call their own. Alaskan geography can make even doctors, whose prose is ordinarily on the stuffy side, become rhapsodic; one of them wrote some months ago, "We are given the opportunity now to insure that no longer need the unrecorded medical voice be sent plaintively wailing across the waters of the Inland Passage to quiver in the Susitna Flats, or be sent rumbling toward the peaks of Mount McKinley only to wither and be dissipated in the Wilderness." What he meant was simply that a new Alaskan medical journal was coming out. (It has since recorded, among other unusual clinical experiences, a physician's vain struggle to save the lives of some Eskimos who had contracted botulism from eating beluga-whale flippers that had been preserved in seal oil.) Allusions to Mount McKinley, such as the doctor's, are not lightly made in Alaska. The mountain is the state's No. 1 symbol, even though, wearing a year-round crown of snow and ice, it contributes little to Alaskan efforts to convince tourists of the mildness of local weather. The motto of the University of Alaska is *Ad Summum*," and the undergraduate yearbook is called *Denali*, an Indian word meaning "Great One," and a common pet name for Mount McKinley. Alaska's favorite painter, the late Sydney Laurence, specialized in portraits of the Great One. A Brooklyn man, he came to Alaska in 1904, with Paris and the Boer War behind him, and before his death, in 1940, he is believed to have painted the mountain some ten thousand times. Alaskans, who bought most of the paintings, never tire of Mount McKinley, or of mountains in general.

"You remember that old child's game king-of-the-mountain?" a Fairbanks man asked me. "Well, here in Alaska we're all equal—not in the sense of having the same material possessions, but in the sense of feeling that when it comes to the land we live in, we're all sitting on top of the heap. Land fascinates me. There are parts of this country that I guess some people might call bleak, but I call them pretty. I like to divide my time between prospecting and hunting for mountain sheep, and I sometimes catch myself wondering why. You can't make any money prospecting nowadays, and it's certainly not that I like killing animals, especially sheep. Sheep-hunting is the hardest damn work in the world. Still, it gets you up high. The best thing, I guess, is that though I'm prospecting part of the time and hunting sheep part of the time, I'm looking at scenery all of the time. When you get on top of one of these mountains on a clear day and look out for miles and miles, and there's nothing, absolutely nothing, that's taller than you are, it's the most beautiful experience a man can have."

April 2, 1960

From a Reporter at Large piece.

Children's Friend

The face of Theodor Seuss Geisel—an arresting one, with soft eyes and a long, beaky nose—is not nearly as familiar as that of Santa Claus, yet its owner is an equally formidable contender for the adulation of many children. Santa Claus brings them presents. Geisel makes them laugh, and, what is more, he's real. Since 1936, under the alias of Dr. Seuss, Geisel, a plain and gentle man who is now fifty-six, has written and illustrated nineteen humorous books for children, all but three in galloping verse. Being shy, tense, and serious-minded, he tries to avoid the popping eyes and clutching hands of his disciples, but on the rare occasions when he is harried into making a personal appearance at an autographing bee, he attracts crowds that would cause a Western television hero to sway in the saddle with envy. There have been many attempts, some of them jocular, to define the age groups for which the Dr. Seuss books have the greatest appeal. Random House, which has published practically all of Geisel's books, conservatively catalogues his works in the five-to-nine-year-old bracket. A Bowling Green, Kentucky, reviewer, however, once estimated the age of the audience for "How the Grinch Stole Christmas," a Geisel variation on the theme of Scrooge, to range from two to ninety-two; a Houston, Texas, critic put it at three to ninety-three. And in *Junior Reviewers*, a seven-year-old junior reviewer wrote of "Scrambled Eggs Super!," a Geisel variation on the theme of scrambled eggs, "All ages would like it from 6 to 44—that's how old my mother is."

There has been a great deal thought, said, and written about the quality of contemporary children's books, much of it in high-flown psychological and sociological jargon. Geisel's own approach to the topic is down-to-earth. "If a book pleases me, it has a chance of pleasing children," he says. Many of the elders whom he also pleases are faithful to him because they feel that they can read, and reread, and re-reread a Dr. Seuss book to a child without imperilling their own mental balance or—by skipping paragraphs or whole pages—impairing their integrity. This is not to say that Geisel has no detractors. There are those who think his pictures and words are plain silly—a few of the leaders of this faction would just as soon seek to divert their children with the exterior of a cereal box—but most guardians of the young mind, it would appear, are willing to go along with the *Bulletin* of the Parents League of New York, which has enthusiastically endorsed Geisel's books. The League classifies them as "read-alouds." He himself fancies the description "logical insanity." The reading aloud of logical insanity, appropriately illustrated by its creator, has always been fun, but between Edward Lear's day and Dr. Seuss's the pickings, few people would deny, have been slim.

Geisel and his wife, who under her maiden name of Helen Palmer is herself the author of several successful but more or less conventional children's books—to name a few, "Tommy's Wonderful Rides," "Johnny's Machines," "Bobby and His Airplane," and "Donald Duck Sees South America"—are childless. Some of their friends consider it a shame that a man who is so beloved by so many children has none of his own. Geisel does not agree. "You have 'em, I'll amuse 'em," he has said on more than one occasion, and he has also said, "You can't write books for children if too many of them are looking over your shoulder." With no children at all looking over his shoulder, Geisel painstakingly turns out books that, in the opinion of Rudolf Flesch, the "Why Johnny Can't Read" man, will be read a hundred years hence, when, also in Flesch's opinion, Hemingway, Faulkner, Marquand, and other current favorites may be gathering dust. Flesch rates Geisel "a genius pure and simple." Bennett Cerf, the president of Random House, has stated that Geisel is the only genius on his list, though Cerf would probably not have put it so baldly had Faulkner, whom he also publishes, been in his office at the time. For the last few years, Geisel has been the best-selling author on the Random House list, and possibly on any list anywhere. Once or twice a year, the *Times* puts out a Sunday children's-book supplement and includes a roster of best-sellers; in last month's ratings three of the top four sellers were by Dr. Seuss. When Nevil Shute died, last January, his obituary in the *Times* proclaimed him the best-selling novelist of his day, adding that his yearly royalties amounted to a hundred and seventy-five thousand dollars in 1959. To date, nearly three million copies of Dr. Seuss's books have been sold, and Random House now orders a first printing of a hundred thousand copies of any book that he writes. Even this figure proved inadequate for "Happy Birthday to You!," which was issued in October, 1959; within a few weeks, stocks of the book were exhausted, and fifty thousand additional copies were run off. Geisel is staggered and a bit frightened by his opulence, for he has never learned to come to grips with money. Not quite trusting money, he hardly ever carries any, and he frequently grabs for restaurant checks only to discover that he can't pay them. He gave up trying to cope with checkbooks some thirty years ago, and turned them over to his wife. "I wish people would stop talking to me about money," he says. "All I want to do is to write books, and everybody's forever nagging at me to *keep* them."

Geisel's tastes are simple. "Ted has no extravagances," his wife says. "I can't think of anything he likes except cigarettes and rocks." His cigarette outlay runs comparatively high. A chain smoker, he now and then breaks off for a while and sucks on an unlighted corncob pipe filled with radish seeds. Whenever a compulsion to smoke sweeps over him—which is every few minutes—he waters his seeds with an eye-dropper. Once a crop of radish greens has sprouted from his pipe bowl—which he says takes about three days in a hospitable environment—he goes back to cigarettes. Rocks are his outdoor hubby. At his home, astride a hilltop in La Jolla, California, he is an earnest rock gardener, and *Publishers' Weekly* is apt to be crowded off his parlor table by some lithic journal like *Guide for Beginning Fossil Hunters*. One of his most treasured possessions is a heavy stone slab with a dinosaur's footprint in it, reputed to be something over a hundred and fifty million years old. Geisel himself is reputed to be something of a prankster, and, to his indignation, quite a few of his acquaintances refuse to believe that his hoary fossil is not homemade.

La Jolla is an upper-bracket community, and the relative austerity of the Geisels' way of life confounds their neighbors. Geisel and his wife have only one car, only one maid—part-time, at that—and only one swimming pool. After thirty-three years of married life, they are an uncommonly devoted couple, and they see no reason to have a second car, since they are rarely apart. Mrs. Geisel stopped writing books of her own fifteen years ago, so she could concentrate on helping her husband with his. This she does in part by keeping a vigilant critical eye on his output, in part by giving him the reassurance and praise for which he, like many another writer, has an insatiable need, and in part by shielding him from distractions. Along with his finances, she handles his correspondence. Geisel's—or, rather, Dr. Seuss's—mail is imposing. At the end of 1957, Random House announced that in the previous twelve months he had received nine thousand two hundred and sixty-seven pounds of it. No up-to-date statistics have been released, but whatever the avoirdupois of Geisel's current mail, it amounts to thousands of letters a week. Geisel's policy is to have his wife answer letters from teachers, librarians, sick or crippled children, and entire school classes. (Mrs. Geisel signs some of the replies "Mrs. Dr. Seuss.") The rest of his fan mail hardly ever gets to La Jolla. It is mercifully intercepted and screened by Random House, which sends the bulk of his correspondents a printed form letter that he has written and illustrated. The form letter in use until just recently explained that Dr. Seuss's mail service was unreliable, because he lived on a steep and inaccessible precipice and because his correspondence had to travel by Budget, an ungainly Seuss beast, driven by Nudget, a Seuss Budget-driver. Most children were satisfied with this reply, but now and then a persistent correspondent would grumble. "Did you get a letter from a girl named Olive or a boy named Bud?" an Oregon schoolchild wrote Dr. Seuss a year or so ago. "They are both in my classroom. Did you get their letter? I don't think you did the way your roads are but they will write to you again and then are you going to write to them again about the Budget and the Nudget? I want a letter from you again but not about the Budget and Nudget again." Geisel sought to curtail laments of this sort by fashioning a new illustrated form letter, which thanks the correspondent on behalf of Dr. Seuss himself and a friend—the Three-Muffed Apfel Moose.

It is only within the last couple of years that Geisel's fan mail and sales figures have soared into the literary stratosphere. As recently as 1954, he asked his agent, Phyllis Jackson, of the Music Corporation of America, whether she thought he could count on five thousand dollars annually from book royalties in the foreseeable future. She said he could, and now he knows he can. Not only does he write a new book or two every year but the sales of each book on his back list grow larger every year. All his old books are current best-sellers. An early one, "The King's Stilts," which was published in 1939, sold 4,648 copies the first year. By 1941, its annual sales were down to 394. In 1958, the last year for which figures are obtainable, they were up to 11,037. "The King's Stilts" has been a more sluggish mover than any other Dr. Seuss book; its cumulative sales have climbed nearly to the 75,000 mark. Another early Dr. Seuss, "Horton Hatches the Egg," which has had total sales of more than 200,000 and is still briskly hatching profits, sold 5,801 copies in 1940, the year it came out. It, too, fell off—to 1,645 the following year. In 1958, it sold 27,463 copies. What appears to have given all the Dr. Seuss books their recent boost was the publication, in 1957, of "The Cat in the Hat," which seems likely to achieve a total sale of a million copies by the end of this year. Since the book is priced at a dollar ninety-five, this would bring its retail gross to nearly two million dollars—equivalent to the gross on six million copies of a thirty-five-cent paper-back. Only two works of fiction, "God's Little Acre" and "Peyton Place," have sold as well as that in paperback form. And "The Cat in the Hat" is aseptic.

"The Cat in the Hat" evolved from a 1954 article in *Life* by John Hersey, who complained of the sorry state of children's primers and suggested that someone like Dr. Seuss ought to give the kids a break by providing them with sprightlier fare. Among those who urged Geisel to accept this challenge was William Spaulding, then the textbook editor and now the president of Houghton Mifflin. Having long felt that the "See the red ball? The ball is red" school of literature left a good deal to be desired, Geisel did not need much prodding. He was somewhat taken aback to learn that a primer was supposed to have a severely limited vocabulary—a particularly inhibiting restriction for a writer whose métier is verse—but after a long struggle he came up with a book that had a plot, had humor, rhymed, and did it all on a vocabulary of only two hundred-odd words. Houghton Mifflin issued "The Cat in the Hat" as a textbook, and Random House as a trade book. Hersey called it a "gift to the art of reading" and a "harum-scarum masterpiece." Curiously, the Random House edition, sold through bookstores, has far outdistanced the Houghton Mifflin one, sold through school channels; the explanation may be that some oldline educators have tended to be suspicious of a primer produced by a man who signs himself "Dr." but has never written a doctoral dissertation, and that others have felt the teaching process is a solemn business, not to be interrupted by avoidable laughter.

Geisel, being fond of both cats and children, was glad that he had been able to use the one species to edify the other. In real life he sometimes finds the relationship between animals and human beings cruelly bewildering—not long ago he rescued a mouse that was floundering in his pool, only to see it scamper straight into a mousetrap he had set in his garage—but in his books he manages to reconcile his innate kindheartedness with some of the nasty practices implicit in the survival of the fittest. When a situation in "McElligot's Pool," for instance, seemed to call for a picture of a worm on a hook, Geisel made it graphically clear that his worm was not skewered on his barb but instead had curled itself up there cozily. At the moment, the Geisels, who once kept twenty-five or thirty cats, have only one pet—an aging, wheezy Irish setter. Their home, though, is filled with Dr. Seuss animals—painted, carved into chair backs and chests of drawers, or sculptured by him out of any old objects that have come to hand, like shaving brushes—as well as with store-bought toy animals collected by his wife. As a wedding-anniversary present one year, she gave her husband a delicate life-size model of a cockroach. Geisel was touched, but professionally he shuns any animal that looks normal.

The animals that Geisel confects are anatomically absurd, as flexible and floppy-looking as rag dolls—or, indeed, as many children wish real pets were. "My animals look the way they do because I've never learned to draw," he explains. He does, in fact, draw very much like an untutored child; first he makes an outline of the creature he has in mind, and then he fills in the enclosed area with solid colors. In 1954, he appeared on a children's television program called "Excursion," in the course of which he attempted to demonstrate how different the same animal could look to different artists by having six young abstract painters render their impressions of a horse. Geisel did not enter this sweepstakes himself, but he commented sympathetically on the utterly dissimilar, and universally unnaturalistic, results. In private, Geisel is less indulgent toward much contemporary art. To spoof a friend who had pretensions as a collector, he once told him at length about a nonexistent abstract painter called Escorobus. "I have some of his finest works at home," Geisel said, "and he's given me permission to act as his agent in selling them." Then he went home and dashed off a wallful of Escorobuses. The friend came around to see them, and was reaching for his checkbook when Geisel owned up to the hoax. "That experience made me suspect that a lot of modern art is malarkey," Geisel says. "If I can do it myself, it can't be any good."

Over the years, many companies have besought Geisel to let them manufacture Dr. Seuss products of one kind or another. He has permitted R.C.A. Victor to record some of his books, but in the main he has steered clear of by-products that he cannot personally create. Two years ago, though, he was persuaded by Revell, Inc., a toy company in Venice,

California, to authorize, and help design, a series of Dr. Seuss toys and games. It has proved to be a challenging collaboration. Revell, which is run by Mr. and Mrs. Lew Glaser, a resourceful and articulate young couple, was geared to turning out small-scale models of ships, planes, and cars. To translate Dr. Seuss's animals into three dimensions was a different matter entirely. "None of my animals have joints and none of them balance," Geisel explained to the Glasers. "And when it comes to that, none of them are animals. They're all people, sort of." Whatever they were, not even he could clearly visualize them with flesh on their bones. Revell sent two sculptors to La Jolla, and for months, with Geisel working alongside them, they modelled Dr. Seuss creatures, shaping and reshaping hundreds of jointless legs and unbalanced heads before he was satisfied. By then, the Glasers had learned enough of Geisel's meticulous ways and second thoughts to stipulate that he give his assent in writing to each successive step of production as soon as agreement was reached on it. Mrs. Glaser, who calls herself Revell's Vice-President in Charge of Geisel, keeps a notebook containing reminders like "Test shots of eye decorations to T.G. for approval." The first Dr. Seuss toys went on the market in September, 1959, and before the year was out they had achieved retail sales of a million and a half dollars.

During the past year, two Dr. Seuss Beginner Books have come out—"One Fish, Two Fish, Red Fish, Blue Fish" and "Green Eggs and Ham." "One Fish" is actually a *pre*-beginner book, or, as the educators say, a reading-readiness book. "It's a book based on an educational theory I have, but one I unfortunately can't define," Geisel says. In essence, it is an attempt to initiate very young children into the mysteries of reading by seeing to it that almost every word in the text is neatly juxtaposed with an illustration of the object it describes. Children's memories being the marvellous things they are, a child who has once had the book read to him can go back to it and pick out the familiar words for himself, guided by the pictures. Not all educators are persuaded that this is necessarily a good idea. "One Fish" elicited from a Columbia professor the opinion that a bright four-year-old could learn from the book to read in a week—a conclusion that somewhat disturbed the professor, since many of his colleagues believe that four is a trifle young for a child to get mixed up in the reading business. Geisel's answer to such alarmists is that he may someday facilitate prenatal reading, by inventing a two-hundred-and-fifty word pill that expectant mothers can swallow.

Geisel has produced only one book—"The Seven Lady Godivas"—that was aimed at an unequivocally grownup audience. It was an unequivocal flop. An enhancement of the old legend, it dealt with seven Lady Godivas, all sisters, and seven brothers named Peeping (one, of course, was Tom), who courted them. It was published by Random House in 1939, and Geisel clearly had some misgivings about it beforehand; nailed to the Godiva family tree, which he drew for the end papers, was a small bucket of sap labelled "Bennett Cerf." One trouble was that all the Godivas were shown in the nude, a situation with which Geisel feels he did not cope adequately. "I tried to draw the sexiest-looking women I could," he explains, "and they came out just ridiculous." Although a review in the *Dartmouth Alumni Magazine* called the book "a particularly triumphant job," only twenty-five hundred copies of a first printing of ten thousand were sold. "I think maybe it all went to prove that I don't know anything about adults," Geisel says.

December 17, 1960

From a Profile.

Spring in Korea

The only authorized direct communication that there has been in recent years between North and South Korea, or is likely to be for some time, regardless of who controls the destinies of the Republic, takes place forty miles north of Seoul over two telephone wires, each a hundred and fifty yards long, that link the desks of two duty officers in a circular space, eight hundred metres (or about half a mile) in diameter, straddling the dividing line between the countries. This is the Joint Security Area of the Demilitarized Zone, and since July, 1953, it has been the scene of the wrangling meetings of the commission that was set up at the time of the cease-fire to supervise the terms of the armistice agreement. This spot—generally called Panmunjom, though the village of that name is actually a few hundred yards off, in North Korea—has become a tourist center, with busloads of people from both north and south arriving regularly to take in the sights and listen to the Communist and non-Communist members of the commission exchange invective, which is conveniently picked up by microphone and broadcast in the Joint Security Area over a public-address system. As for the Demilitarized Zone, it runs across the breadth of the peninsula for a hundred and fifty miles and is four thousand metres (about two and a half miles) wide—two thousand metres on either side of the Military Demarcation Line, which was the front line at cease-fire time. No firing is permitted in the Zone now, and as a result this buffer area teems with game. The Joint Security Area, a hilly enclave covered with scrub pine, lies spang in the center of the Zone, and the Communists and the representatives of the United Nations Command share free access to it. From it one can look out over a stretch of North Korea, which is physically indistinguishable from South Korea except that on some of its hills big

309

boulders have been painted with admonitions like "Peace Through Unification," "Yankee Go Home," and, inexplicably, "Keep Your Body Clean."

Within the Joint Security Area, each side is permitted a maximum guard detail of five officers and thirty enlisted men, none of whom may be armed with anything other than a pistol or rifle. Twice this spring, guards of the rival sides have tangled in fisticuffs. This no man's, or every man's, land is occupied by nine buildings—five put up by the Communists, four by us. Ours are huts of green-painted corrugated iron; theirs, slightly more permanent-looking, are of stucco trimmed with peeling red paint. The windows of their buildings have white curtains, which are drawn whenever somebody from the south approaches. Two of the buildings are the headquarters of the duty officers from the two sides, and it is these that are linked by the two telephones. Twin hookups are needed because, while each side will accept calls that come in over the other's wire, it will only place calls on its own wire. Near the hut of the duty officer of the Korean People's Army—as the North Koreans describe their side—is a dovecote. When the pigeons in it are let out for exercise, they settle only on the roofs of the K.P.A. buildings. Our people at Panmunjom think the reason is chemical rather than psychological; the roofs of our buildings are painted and those of our adversaries' buildings are not. When representatives of the two sides come face to face, it is in an American-built one-room shelter, sixty feet long and twenty wide, bisected by an eighteen-foot-long table, at which the principals sit. Behind them, filling either end of the building, are tables and chairs for interpreters, stenographers, aides, observers, and other attendant functionaries. The main table, astride the Military Demarcation Line, is itself divided lengthwise by the wires that connect the microphones—one for each side—to loudspeakers outside, which were originally set up so that reporters could follow the truce negotiations. (One day some weeks ago, a North Korean newspaperman covering a session asked a South Korean what time it was. The South Korean told him, and couldn't resist adding, "I don't suppose you fellows up there can afford watches." At the next meeting, the entire Communist press corps turned up sporting new wristwatches.)

The Panmunjom meetings, which can be called at the request of either side, are held on five different levels: the Military Armistice Commission, the Secretaries of the M.A.C., Joint Observer Teams, Duty Officers, and Security Officers. There are five senior, or top-level, members on each side. Our principal representative has been either a major general or a rear admiral; theirs, until a few weeks ago, was a North Korean propaganda minister wearing a major general's uniform. (Now it is a similarly costumed man who, for all anybody knows, may be merely a major general.) There is always a South Korean general officer on our team, but he has never said anything; strong and silent were the words for senior R.O.K. Army officers—until the other day. Whichever side has called a meeting speaks first. (Several weeks ago, we walked out on the Communists when they tried to get in the first word at a meeting we'd convened; the two factions later argued for hours over whether or not this abortive meeting had in fact *been* a meeting.) By now, it is fairly easy for either side to anticipate—from news reports or other intelligence about alleged violations of the armistice—what the other side's gambit is going to be, and to have a rebuttal prepared in advance. The Communists, who call the majority of the meetings, often say that we have no right ever to call one, since they never violate the armistice. Once, in the dim past, they admitted a couple of minor irregularities, but now they deny ever having done so. At one of the almost daily low-level sessions between the duty officers, our man seized the opportunity to twit his North Korean counterpart for forgetting to follow the rule that he had to wear a yellow armband while in the Joint Security Area. Hastily pulling an armband out of his pocket, the Communist called the American a liar. See, he cried as he pushed the band up over his elbow, he did, too, have it on! No minutes are ever kept of any meeting (though both sides keep transcripts), since it would presumably be impossible ever to get any minutes adopted by both sides. The two sides rarely see eye to eye on anything. In June of 1958, though, they did agree that at lower-level meetings there was no longer any need to have the proceedings translated into Chinese, inasmuch as it had been several years since the Chinese—who do sit in on every third or fourth meeting of the M.A.C.—had attended one.

All meetings are conducted with chilly formality. There are no salutes, no handshakes, no nods, no smiles. There is no sharing of matches, or even of ashtrays. Mostly, there are long-winded Communist propaganda speeches having nothing much to do with the armistice and bristling with denunciations of the United States. Several months ago, some unladylike South Korean girls who had persisted in sneaking into an American Army compound below the Demilitarized Zone were forcibly ejected, before which, to discourage them from returning, the resident soldiers shaved their heads. This raw treatment did not sit well with many South Koreans, and the North Koreans used it as a pretext for accusing Americans of killing Korean women, tearing their livers out, boiling the livers, and eating them. Eating human liver is a legendary Korean cure for leprosy, so the Communists may have been calling us leprous. They have called us practically every other uncomplimentary adjective in the book; after several months at Panmunjom, one of our officers sent home for a copy of Roget's Thesaurus, just to try to keep pace. At one of the armistice-commission meetings, we turned over to the K.P.A. two North Korean fishermen who had been captured by the South Koreans. They had been given clean clothing while in our custody. As soon as the fishermen were on the Communist side of the conference table, they were ordered by the North Korean officers to strip to their shorts, and their clothing was shoved back into our territory. At the next meeting, the shorts were returned.

Periodically, there are meetings of the security officers of each side to investigate and discuss incidents that occur in the meeting area itself. These sessions usually end in further misunderstandings, or in calls for more meetings. Early in April, the North Koreans strung a wire across a road used by our supply trucks in the Joint Security Area. The wire was too low for the trucks to get under, and twice we asked the Communists to raise it a bit. They ignored our requests. Then a soldier riding in one of our trucks got out and held the wire up so that the vehicle could pass beneath it. As soon as he touched the wire, nine Communist guards sprang out of hiding and surrounded him, glaring and muttering over his manhandling of their equipment. The security officers met about that the following day.

The Joint Observer Teams, for their frustrated part, have never yet submitted a joint report on their observations of incidents within the Demilitarized Zone, which was what they were set up to do. Each side's observers submit their own reports, and these are usually contradictory in every detail. This past winter, a North Korean carrying a machine gun wandered into the Zone and opened fire on a legitimate American outpost. Our soldiers shot him dead, whereupon a Joint Observer Team hustled to the scene. While the machine gunner's body and his weapon lay before them, the observers argued about what had happened. The North Koreans denied that the victim was one of their men; they said we had stolen one of their machine guns, forged a pocketful of identification papers, murdered a South Korean, dressed him in a stolen North Korean uniform, and planted him there, just to make trouble. The debate went on inconclusively for five long, cold hours, but in a sense this proved to be one of the most fruitful meetings of its kind ever held, exceeding the expectations of all concerned, because at the end of it the two sides had for once agreed on a single, simple fact: that the man on the ground was dead.

August 27, 1961

From a Far-flung Correspondents piece.

Notes and Comment

From the obituary columns of the *Times* we often learn about individuals we wish we'd known while they were alive. Some weeks ago, for instance, we read a skimpy item about a remarkable old lady who had died in Sarasota, Florida. She was Mrs. Madeline Zacchini, aged ninety-one. It was her husband, Ildebrando Zacchini, who perfected the circus act of shooting human beings out of cannons. The Zacchinis had sixteen children, all projectiles. (Mr. Zacchini died in Tampa in 1948, at seventy-nine, and the parents' grave marker, fittingly, is a cannon.) How amused Mrs. Zacchini must have been, in her last years, by all the fuss and clatter attendant on the takeoffs and landings of cosmonauts and astronauts, some of them shot from her own home state! *Her* daredevil offspring, she may well have reflected—those sixteen pioneer conquerors of what was once known as space—weren't tested by psychologists or centrifuges to determine their suitability for their unique calling; she simply bore and raised them. It would have been nice if she could have paid a congratulatory call on the astronauts' womenfolk over at Cape Canaveral. What a gabfest they all could have had! For surely the pleasure and pride and relief that Mrs. Zacchini felt when her children, after their explosive launching from a cannon's mouth, landed in their net would have been especially understandable to the mothers and wives of Gordon Cooper and the others. "You remember when those young sailors all clapped their hands after Major Cooper made it safely to the aircraft carrier?" we like to think that Mrs. Zacchini might have said. "I've heard that applause myself a thousand times, from kids at the circus. Big top or flattop, it's all pretty much the same thing. Just a question of figuring out the trajectory, getting your people up, and convincing them you know what you're talking about when you say everything's going to work out fine."

August 17, 1963

Notes and Comment

A banner headline in the *World-Telegram* early last week said, "THE OLD SOLDIER IS HOME." Old soldiers, of course, often have no conventional homes. General MacArthur was born in Arkansas of a Massachusetts father and a Virginia mother, and he resided, in our kaleidoscopic recollection of him, just as much in Manila or in Tokyo as here in New York. (His legal residence, we were surprised to learn after his death, was Stamford, Connecticut, formerly the headquarters of Remington Rand, of which he was chairman of the board.) Even though he was physically in our city for most of his last thirteen years, we never really thought of him as a New Yorker. After a ticker-tape parade in his honor in 1951, he holed up in the Waldorf Towers, and he just stayed there, a permanent transient who, though he was one of the authentic heroes present in this adulatory town, rarely seemed to take part in its affairs. We always had the impression that the only functions he attended were those held in his hotel—those he could get to without going out-of-doors and sniffing the winds that blow the city this way and that. But it was the Old Soldier's own wish that he come here to lie in state, and New York seemed pleased.

The Seventh Regiment Armory, at Park Avenue and Sixty-sixth Street, was the ideal setting for MacArthur's last local appearance. The place opened in 1880, the year of his birth, and the regimental rooms through which the hushed visitors filed were of heroic proportions and were furnished with old-fashioned elegance. The chamber that the General lay in had a lofty ceiling, polished-oak panelling, and a massive fireplace, which was all but obscured, on Tuesday, by wreaths. The air was richly scented with flowers. The First Army was in command. By First Army decree, all the servicemen who took half-hour turns in the honor guard were between five feet ten and a half and six feet tall, weighed between a hundred fifty and a hundred eighty, and had waistlines of no more than thirty-five inches. The dignitaries bade the General goodbye first, and one of the very first of them was Jim Farley, without whom no important New York funeral would be complete. After him came the other names and faces one associates with New York funerals—David Sarnoff, Lucius Clay, Lowell Thomas, Governor Rockefeller, Governor Dewey, Senator Javits, Cardinal Spellman, Ambassador Stevenson, John McCloy, William Zeckendorf, and a scattering of United Nations diplomats and consuls—and then a leathery-faced sergeant, who wrote in a red-leather guest book, "WWII Photographer to the General." When the sergeant got abreast of MacArthur's catafalque, the cameramen in the room were ready for him, and eagerly photographed the photographer rendering a final salute.

Tuesday afternoon, leaving the Armory, we walked up Park Avenue in the rain toward the rear of the waiting line. The queue stretched north to Seventy-second Street. School was out by then, and children carrying books were skylarking up and down the unbarricaded portion of the sidewalk. We got in line—people three abreast—five and a half blocks from the Armory, and headed back. It took about ten minutes to cover a block. At Seventieth Street, one of those street orators whom New York indulges approached at a trot, haranguing us loudly. All we could catch as he rushed past, with Demosthenean fury, was " . . . fluoridation! Think it over!" We have no idea whether he was pro or con fluoridation. At one side of us marched a Puerto Rican in his fifties, who had served under MacArthur in Korea, and at the other an Australian woman, age indeterminate, who remembered when the General had his headquarters in Brisbane. At Sixty-ninth Street, the Puerto Rican asked a policeman how many people had visited the General up to then. "We got other things to do besides count the people," the cop said. The rain came down harder.

Wednesday wasn't a nice day, either—at least not at seven-forty-five in the morning, when, in another downpour, we encamped gratefully beneath an apartment-house marquee across the avenue from the Armory. The cops around were wearing raincoats, but the servicemen stationed along both sides of the avenue had no outer garments, and were drenched. The air was still. The flag at half-mast at the summit of the Armory clung limply to its pole. The massed colors out front, where the black horses and the caisson were waiting, were motionless. Traffic had been halted not only on the avenue but on the side streets leading to it. The traffic lights blinked red and green, unneeded and unheeded. At seven-fifty-five, a siren wailed in the distance, but save for that and the rain drumming on the marquee there wasn't a sound. In that oasis of damp pageantry, the whole city seemed to be silent. At eight on the dot, a blaring bugle startled us and everyone around us. With ruffles and flourishes, the casket, now closed and flag-draped, was borne out to the caisson. Five minutes later, the parade to Pennsylvania Station began, and at the very instant that a West Point cadet, his sleeves streaked with chevrons of authority, cried out a confident and carrying "Forward *harch!*" a breeze came up and all the lethargic flags were stirred into a fluttering farewell.

Not long after that, the city went back about its business, and before the morning that had begun so mutedly was over, the presses of the *Journal-American* and the *World-Telegram* were noisily churning out the strange confidences that the General had supposedly entrusted to a couple of reporters ten years earlier.

April 18, 1964

Thank You, Madam President

Dancing is in big at the White House, and among President Johnson's partners have been quite a few women reporters—a normally hardboiled lot whose accounts of cutting a White House rug have been so gushy one can scarcely tell anymore whether one is reading United Press International or listening to the post-prom chatter at a schoolgirls' pajama party. Senator Margaret Chase Smith may not make the Presidency this election, but just as Mr. Johnson has established the dancing precedent, so has she established the running precedent. The possibility of a woman President someday is not to be dismissed lightly, and inasmuch as many more men than women write about the Washington scene, we had better start bracing ourselves right now for some such spate of prose as this:

BY WALTER LIPPMANN

Dancing last night with the President, who took notice, flatteringly, of my new cummerbund, I could not help reflecting on the sharp but not universally understood contrast between today's basic power structure and that of some years back. I was beginning to flesh the bones of my thoughts when the President interrupted, with a charming giggle. "Oh, Walter, you old *sober*sides," she said. "I declare, you're forever *comparing* things. Quick, dance me over toward the band. I think Arthur Krock wants to cut in." It is

315

her gift, I think, for the swift but graceful move, for the unhesitating decision and the nimble execution, that has placed her so securely in the forefront of those statesmen on whom, in the last analysis, the preservation of our national self-interest will surely stand or, in the lamentable event of being suddenly pushed off balance, fall.

BY ARTHUR KROCK

The patent unconstitutionality of the Twenty-sixth Amendment, so vigorously argued in Justice Mesta's eloquent dissent *(vide supra)*, was naturally much on this correspondent's mind last night when he barely succeeded in rescuing the President from a stumbling sycophant with two left feet. This department, which was wearing a midnight-blue jacket with grosgrain lapels and rolled cuffs, has often expressed its concern at the apparent fiscal irresponsibility of the administration, but never before during a cha-cha-cha. It is only meet and proper to concede, now that the ball is over, that this department has felt obliged to reappraise its appraisal *(ipso facto)* in the light of the hitherto little-known sage advice of Alexander Hamilton, who once said, as the President so vivaciously whispered into this ear on the dance floor last night, "A national debt, if it is not excessive, will be to us a national blessing." Whether or not the Court will sustain this view is, of course, problematical.

BY JAMES RESTON

It has been much too long since the White House boasted an out-and-out fan of the Washington Senators. The prospect seems brighter this morning, for, after dancing with the wire-service men last night, surely the President will regard our beloved but leaden-legged American League standard-bearers as paragons of competence. Through Hanson Baldwin, I had arranged for the Marine Corps band, when my turn came to trip the fantastic, to strike up "Take Me Out to the Ball Game." The President, who is quick to notice details (it may not be amiss to report that she was admiringly aware of the ruffled dress shirt I had our Paris bureau ship over from A. Sulka), asked me what the name of the song was, and when I told her, she said impulsively, "Would you take me out someday, Scotty?" The President's ability thus to cope with any situation is something the delegates to the forthcoming Tierra del Fuego conference are going to have to reckon with, for our Chief of State gives every evidence of that sure-footedness and sure-handedness lacking which no one ever yet made the double play around the Horn.

By Max Lerner

I was telling the President last night, while she good-naturedly put up with the polka I have not essayed in more years than I care to admit, about Schlampfheiter's meaningful but in some respects misleading three-volume work "Sex and Space," which I read in a cab on my way to the White House. I myself think Schlampfheiter attaches perhaps too much importance to the contemplated dispatch of an all-female crew of astronauts to Mars and an all-male crew to Venus. While it is obvious that the sexual connotations of the ravishment of the planets cannot and should not be underestimated, it seems to me, as I told the President bluntly, that the sickness inherent in our society can best be treated, Schlampfheiter notwithstanding, by a straightforward, healthy acceptance of who we are and what we are. The President did not break in except to compliment me, somewhat embarrassingly, on my tailcoat, which was rented. She is a remarkably intelligent woman.

By Drew Pearson

Discount all those stories about the President's going to a private dance at Joseph Alsop's. I had it on the very highest authority at the White House ball last night that, to avoid any charges of favoritism, she has decided to accept no invitations whatever to dances given by individual journalists. The President's appearance at the residence of the press attaché of the Chinese Embassy Tuesday, while in seeming conflict with this policy, actually came about because the society editor of the *People's Daily* was already en route from Peking to dance with her, and the State Department begged her not to risk precipitating an incident by standing him up. I will report next week on the President's appearance at my own forthcoming dance, which, of course, has nothing to do with official policy, because we are old, old friends and I can tango.

By May Craig

Another in this social season's series of receptions was held at the White House last night.

Among the President's guests were the Justices of the Supreme Court, the diplomatic corps, the Cabinet, the Congress, and the governors of the states, territories, and moons. The President looked tired.

May 2, 1964

Kvass vs. Coke

Not long after the Russians announced that they had a notion to put a drink called *kvass* on the world market, to compete with Coke, we had a chat with J. Paul Austin, the president of the Coca-Cola Company, who commutes between New York and Atlanta, his headquarters, where he directs operations in this country and a hundred and twenty-seven foreign lands. Mr. Austin once declared that the way to get ahead in the soft-drink business is always to run scared, but on this occasion he was relaxed and self-confident. "There's no evidence yet that the Russians have actually done anything with *kvass*," he told us. "Have a Coke." We did, and he did, and he confessed that he himself might, inadvertently, have launched the Russians on their soft-drink tangent, if it is a tangent. "I spent fifteen minutes in Moscow last December with Khrushchev and Mikoyan," he said. "Just the three of us, and an interpreter. I was travelling with a group of business-men. We were all purely tourists, and we paid our own way, but Khrushchev couldn't believe we weren't a trade mission. He had just concluded his wheat deal with Canada, and his mind was on breadbaskets rather than soft drinks, and what he cared about most was whether any of us could supply him with mineral fertilizers or, better still, mineral-fertilizer plants. When it became clear to him I was useless in that respect, he brought up Coca-Cola. At that, Mikoyan broke in. 'I want to ask you a question,' he said to me. 'I was in Havana during the missile crisis, and why did you ever let Castro take over your bottling plants?' I suspected some kind of joke was coming, but I played along, and replied, 'Why, Mr. Deputy Prime Minister, we didn't have anything to say about it.' 'Well, I'm sorry it happened,' Mikoyan said, 'because Castro turns out a *horrible* Coke.' He and Khrushchev both laughed. Of course, Castro wasn't turning out Coke at all, because we weren't shipping him anything he could have made it from. I don't know what kind of colored water he was putting in Coke bottles. Anyway, when this *kvass* business cropped up a few months later, I couldn't help suspecting that that conversation might have started the Soviet government thinking about introducing its drink into the Western world."

Mr. Austin, a tall man of forty-nine with russet hair and a ruddy complexion, is a Georgian by birth, like most Coke commissars. He is also the first president of the Coca-Cola Company to have gone to Harvard. The solidity and security of both institutions is reflected in his calm attitude toward *kvass*. He has never sampled the beverage, which has a slight alcoholic content and tastes, the knowledgeable say, like a blend of cider, wine, and soda pop. "I wouldn't know how to go about getting hold of some *kvass* if I wanted to taste it," Mr. Austin said. "I suppose I could ask the American Embassy in Moscow to send me some, but I'm not all that curious. If the Russians really want to come into our market, let them, provided they'll reciprocate by allowing us to go into theirs and by respecting our trademark. Essentially, this business of ours is very simple. All we have to do is to sell seventy-five million drinks of Coke a day. But we also have to sell seventy-five million tomorrow and seventy-five million the day after tomorrow, and then it becomes complicated. There's nothing easier than launching a new consumer product in a free-enterprise economy. The tough part is getting and keeping a share of the market, and the Russians may not be altogether aware of what they're up against. You may say, in sum, that we have heard nothing about *kvass* that impels us to change any of our projections, short-term or long-term. Whatever happens, we feel that we understand our market and can take care of ourselves in it and perhaps do a little bit better than the next fellow. That's all I know, except that I was talking to Soviet Ambassador Dobrynin in Washington the other day, and when I said, 'I understand you're now a competitor of mine,' he reacted in true ambassadorial fashion by saying something noncommittal about *kvass's* being better suited to European tastes than to American tastes."

We felt much relieved.

June 6, 1964

Unapathetic Book

The process of writing and publishing a book is normally so elephantine that we can't help being impressed by what may be a record-breaker in the field—"Thirty-eight Witnesses," a slim but stiff-spined forthcoming volume by A. M. Rosenthal, the metropolitan editor of the *Times*. He set out to write it on May 5th, and the first copies came back from the printer, ready for distribution, on June 4th. The book is based on that memorable, disturbing *Times* story—initiated by Rosenthal and written by Martin Gansberg—about the murder of Catherine Genovese, the young woman who was savagely killed in Queens while more than three dozen onlookers or listeners did nothing about it, not even call the police.

The story ran on March 27th, and was widely reprinted. Quite apart from his professional concern with the incident, Mr. Rosenthal felt a growing uneasiness about it; he couldn't get it and its implications out of his mind, and he made it the basis of a reflective article, "Study of the Sickness Called Apathy." Before this was published, John Stewart, of the paper's book-development department, saw it and suggested that Rosenthal amplify his study into a book, and McGraw-Hill expressed interest in the idea. The *Times* ran the article in its Sunday magazine for May 3rd. Two days later, Rosenthal closeted himself in a *Times* office far from his own and, between 10 A.M. and 5 P.M., wrote the book. Some of the text he culled from what the *Times* had already run, but he also churned out nearly ten thousand fresh words during that fecund stretch. That was a Tuesday. On Wednesday, Rosenthal resumed his regular editorial chores—he presides over what other papers call the city room—and that night he polished his manuscript. The book was set up in type about ten days after it was conceived. Its official publication date is July 8th, but on June 8th Robert Gutwillig, Rosenthal's editor at McGraw-Hill, distributed five hundred copies of it at the American Booksellers Association Convention in Washington.

We sought out Mr. Rosenthal, a chubby, soft-spoken man, and he presented us with a copy of the book. It is dedicated, with the words *"Bahut bahut mahabat se,"* to his wife, Ann Marie. "That's Hindi for 'With a great deal of love,'" explained the author, who for ten years was a *Times* correspondent in India and other foreign countries. "I don't know any Hindi, and neither does my wife. I got the phrase from Sunil K. Roy, the Indian Consul-General here, with whom I became friendly when we were both in Poland. The book is only eighty-seven pages long, but the way I look at it, if it has a hard cover and a Library of Congress card number, it's a book. I'm not so sure my assistant metropolitan editor, Arthur Gelb, would agree. He and his wife, Barbara, spent something over four years on a nine-hundred-page biography of Eugene O'Neill."

Mr. Rosenthal told us that since the appearance of the first *Times* report of the murder in Queens, the paper has been flooded with tips on what the city staff have come to call apathy stories. "It's as if everybody in New York were watching to see how apathetic everybody else was," he said. "Maybe 'apathy' isn't the right word after all. Maybe it should be 'callousness' or 'dissociation.' Whatever it is, there seem to be an awful lot of people who have been turning away from this or that. People don't seem to be connected to other people any more. I keep thinking about something that happened one day in New Delhi, years ago. I was walking along with another American, and a scabrous beggar grabbed my arm. I pulled away, but my companion reached into his pocket and gave the beggar a sour ball. I asked my friend why he'd done that. 'I haven't any money to give him, but I didn't want to give him nothing,' he said. 'I didn't want to break the connection.' You know, it's a strange thing. I always thought that if I wrote a book, it would be about India or Poland or Africa or Japan or some other faraway place I've spent some time in, but here I end up writing one about Austin Street, in Queens, which I've never been to at all."

June 20, 1964

Good Manners and Common Sense

At six o'clock in the morning of a raw winter day last January, a Coast Guard cutter left the Battery to go out and meet the S.S. *United States*, which had Queen Frederika of Greece and her daughter, Princess Irene, on board. On the cutter were the usual health, immigration, and customs men, some reporters and photographers, and a party of official greeters. The temperature was icy, a thirty-mile wind was blowing, the harbor waters were choppy, and most of the small boat's passengers, shivering on the open deck and enviously sniffing the aroma of coffee that wafted up from the cutter's snug but overcrowded cabin, looked glum. None of them had better reason to feel sorry for himself than the head of the welcoming delegation, Ambassador Angier Biddle Duke, the urbane, indefatigable Chief of Protocol of the United States, who had had only three hours' sleep the night before—having attended a memorial concert for his late friend Jacques Fray, the pianist and radio commentator—and had missed breakfast. But Duke, a forty-eight-year-old grandfather who keeps in shape by furiously pedalling on an Exercycle, appeared fit and fresh in his well-tailored topcoat and ambassadorial homburg, and looked as cheerful as a Chief of Protocol is always, in public, supposed to look. He was accompanied by two members of his Office of Protocol staff and by his wife, Robin, an equally tireless and glowingly attractive woman who, having once been chief of international public relations for the Pepsi-Cola Company, is never overawed by foreign dignitaries. When the small boat reached the large one, Duke hopped aboard and bade Her Majesty a gracious welcome to America. He helped her get ready for a press conference. He saw to all the arrangements for her debarkation and for the handling of her luggage. He smiled at her toy poodle. Later, after the liner was berthed, he and his wife escorted the royal ladies off the pier and, in one of the Carey limousines that our government hires on such occasions, to the Waldorf-Astoria, where he made sure that everything was to the Queen's taste. All went smoothly, and Her Majesty thanked him warmly for his attentiveness. It was accordingly with wry amusement that Duke read the opening sentence of the *Times*' account of the royal arrival the following morning. It said, "Queen Frederika of Greece shunned protocol yesterday with ease and dignity."

Duke has been Chief of Protocol since the start of the Kennedy administration, and he has functioned as both impresario and performer in a hundred and twenty-six official visits to this country. He is the by now familiar fellow with the aquiline, aristocratic nose and the thinning hair who appears in newspaper photographs presenting an arriving potentate to our President, standing slightly behind and to one side of the eminent principals in ceremonial formations, or striding a rank or two to the rear in state processions, his hands clasped solemnly behind him in an American variation of what protocol buffs have come to call the Prince Philip walk. Though technically attached to the Department of State, Duke spends so much time at the White House that Elizabeth Carpenter, Mrs. Lyndon Johnson's press secretary, has called it "Angie's second home." It is the responsibility of the Office of Protocol to greet a high-placed visitor; to cosset him and soothe him and indulge his every whim; to convince him that Americans believe him to be not only every bit as important as, in his own nation, he has understandably come to think he is but every bit as important as the head of any other outlying sovereign state, regardless of size or influence; and, at his leave-taking, to make sure that he carries off pleasant memories and hasn't lost any of his baggage. Duke is often the first consequential representative of our government that a foreign chieftain sees when he reaches the United States, the last one he sees when he departs, and the one he sees most of in between. The impression the visitor forms of this country is very likely to be conditioned by his impression of Angier Biddle Duke.

"Protocol" stems from the Greek "prōtokollon," which was a sheet of paper glued to the front of a notarial document, giving the document its authenticity. Stanley Woodward, President Truman's Chief of Protocol, defined the word in its modern connotation as "the science and art of handling people, usually official people or people in official life." Truman himself once wrote to the Foreign Service officer and author Charles W. Thayer, "Protocol and striped pants give me a pain in the neck." The word "protocol" pains Duke, too. Many people, he is achingly aware, consider him a governmental Emily Post; actually, in the more than three years he has spent in Washington he has worn striped pants only twice—at President Kennedy's inauguration and at his funeral. Duke is a stylish dresser, though. He is one of those slim, straight men who, like Prince Philip and like Duke's favorite uncle, the late Ambassador Anthony J. Drexel Biddle, Jr., looks good in a double-breasted suit. Striped pants aside, Duke's job does require him to dress up a good deal. White-tie affairs are less frequent in Washington now than they used to be, so he can get by with a single tailcoat, but to take in all the evening functions that a conscientious Chief of Protocol must attend he has to keep four dinner jackets in circulation.

In one costume or another, Duke covers a lot of social territory. Today, a hundred and fourteen political entities have permanent diplomatic missions in Washington. There has never before been such a concentration of ambassadors, ministers, and chargés d'affaires in a single national capital. The dean of the Washington diplomatic corps, Dr. Guillermo Sevilla-Sacasa, the Ambassador from Nicaragua, said not long ago, "A whole new day starts for me after six. I never feel or look tired after six, because I am circulating, and when I am circulating I am happily working." Duke circulates, too. When in Washington, he averages a dozen cocktail parties— or receptions, as they are called—a week, and also fits in half a dozen dinners and two or three luncheons. He is so often out on the town that he sometimes has to forgo sleep in order to get in his daily workout on his Exercycle. On such occasions, he is apt to become despondent about his job. "I'm lost," he said in a recent moment of despair. "Everybody thinks I'm dealing only with the externals of life. I'm lost and of no importance." Then he brightened. "But there are compensations," he went on. "It's satisfying to be as close as I've been to the sources of world power."

For the sources of power that preside over most of the non-Communist parts of the world, and over a few Communist ones, a trip to Washington is usually a pleasant and instructive experience, and often—in an era of foreign-aid appropriations—a rewarding one. During the Eisenhower years, an average of eight chiefs of state visited this country annually. Since 1961, the average has nearly tripled, as the number of independent nations has steadily mounted. The ceremonial aspects of Duke's life involve different kinds of visits. There are all-stops-out state visits, with round upon round of formal dinners and receptions and pilgrimages to the Lincoln Memorial and the Tomb of the Unknown Soldier and President Kennedy's grave at Arlington National Cemetery (where Duke's office keeps a green plastic wreath, in case a pilgrim forgets to bring his own). The high points of any state visit, of course, are the visitor's meetings with our President. These sessions—some business, some social—used to run on for three days, but President Kennedy, worried about his stamina and that of his visitors, too, mercifully imposed a two-day limit. President Johnson has retained it. Then, there are official working visits (slightly shorter in duration and conducted with less fanfare than state visits, but hardly austere even so), unofficial visits (the Queen of Greece's January trip), and private visits (the admission to a Boston hospital of King Saud of Saudi Arabia for an eye operation). Every kind of visit presents problems to Protocol, and a state visit, being the fanciest, presents the most. The United States prefers that the official members of a touring party number no more than ten (and it is only for official members that our government pays the bill), but the unofficial membership is unlimited; when the King of Morocco was here last year, he had an entourage of fifty-seven. Some rulers arrive, moreover, with a flock of journalists in tow, and they need looking after, too; when João Goulart was President of Brazil, he set the record in that category, with ninety-three. Our government suggests a maximum of ten days for a visit (the two days in Washington and eight elsewhere), and Duke is forever urging the ambassadors he treats with to expose their chiefs to a variety of American experiences. Would the honored visitor care to see a steel mill, or have a conference with the Secretary of Agriculture? Would he care to take

323

in a paratroop demonstration at Fort Bragg, like the President of Pakistan, or look over nuclear submarines at Norfolk, like the President of Italy, or visit Niagara Falls, like the President of Togoland, or visit a Lockheed plant in California, like the Shah of Iran, who pilots his own jets? It can be a arranged.

Two years ago, trying to be helpful, Duke drew up and had widely circulated what he called "A Diplomat's Tour" of the United States—an annotated list of ten places that he thought were first-rate when it came to giving visitors to this country "a new look at its traditions and a clearer insight into the minds and hearts of its people." The select ten were Williamsburg (" . . . reflects the greatest tradition of the United States: political liberty"), Los Angeles and its environs ("Disneyland . . . represents the American people's ebullience and sense of fun [and] also demonstrates that our enormous energy and imagination are not only applied to military and industrial works but to projects that add to the joy of the world"), Colorado Springs (" . . . you get a feeling for the infinite variety of the U.S."), Charleston (" . . . this country's past gives us a deep understanding and sympathy for any nation's desire for internal peace and unity of purpose"), the Tennessee River Valley (" . . . especially fascinating to Socialist-oriented diplomats"), Boston (" . . . closely identified with our rise from colonial status"), Seattle (" . . . almost every family has a boat"), Detroit ("American cars made on assembly lines are symbolic of this country's industrial genius"), West Point (" . . . visitors here are reminded of America's revolutionary past"), and Washington (the Lincoln Memorial "has the most marvellous effect on all visitors, American or foreign, especially those from the new nations of Africa"). Duke was not trying to say that these were the *only* ten places worth going to—indeed, he omitted New York City, which practically every foreigner makes a port of call—but he hadn't reckoned with the reaction of some of the communities he left out. Several congressmen and state governors told the White House that they considered Duke's diplomatic tour a most undiplomatically restrictive itinerary, and Duke had to spend a couple of days reassuring spokesmen for one peeved area of another.

A chief of state or prime minister coming here as a guest can have considerable to say about how and where he would like to meet his host. It is customary in Saudi Arabia, for instance, for a state guest to receive his host before he visits his host. Accordingly, when King Saud was here on a non-private visit, President Kennedy made the first move, dropping in at a Palm Beach house the King was occupying. Prime Minister Lester Pearson of Canada likes informal conferences; to accommodate *him*, Kennedy skipped Washington entirely and had a clubby tête-à-tête at Hyannis Port, with a minimum of fuss and only a half-dozen aides in each man's retinue. It is more difficult to handle state visitors outside of Washington than in it. Institutionally, the White House is wherever the President is, but the permanent White House building is a sturdier showcase than any temporary one, and the guardians of the principals—the Secret Service for our President and, for his guest, the State Department's security force, usually augmented by the guest's own bodyguards—always breathe easier when the big men are sequestered there. (During each visit, the State Department security people, to facilitate quick identification of safe persons, issues distinctive lapel insignia to the participants. These buttons or pins usually sport the colors of the visitor's national flag. As a gift for Duke, his wife has had a lot of them mounted and framed. At first glance, they resemble a collection of decorations for heroism in action, which in a sense they are.)

One of Duke's most self-satisfying innovations, achieved in an area where change is resisted, has been to arrange for incoming visitors to be conveyed directly to the White House lawn by helicopter. It has always been the custom for the President to personally greet his peers from abroad when they reach the capital, and Presidents had been doing so for years at Union Station, if the visitors came by train, or at one of the airports outside Washington, if they came by plane. It took a lot of time, and it was a headache for the Secret Service, the District of Columbia police, and others involved in security. Duke persuaded President Kennedy that an arrival at the White House by helicopter—either from a Washington airport or from a nearby city like Philadelphia or Williamsburg—would save time and could be staged with suitable pomp and dignity. Persuading the diplomatic corps was another matter. When Duke broached the idea to several ambassadors who had chiefs of state coming over, they all said that it sounded dandy but let somebody else try it first; they didn't want their chiefs treated differently from any previous visitors. Duke's chance came in September, 1962, when President Ben Bella of Algeria visited the United States. He had been in office so briefly that he didn't have an accredited ambassador. Duke was able to negotiate directly with Algiers, and his novel scheme was approved there. Once Ben Bella had arrived by helicopter and set a precedent, other chiefs of state fell amiably into line; they could do so without blazing trails or losing face. There were holdouts, inevitably. Emperor Haile Selassie is very conscious of his prerogatives. It is an Ethiopian tradition, moreover, that the farther a host travels to receive a guest, the greater homage he pays him. Duke heard through the diplomatic grapevine that some of the senior advisors of the Lion of Judah thought that for a President merely to take a few steps from his front door to his lawn was unacceptably effortless. President Eisenhower had once gone to Union Station for the Emperor, and President Kennedy was expected to do no less. Duke sent a Protocol man to Addis Ababa to show Haile Selassie some movies of Ben Bella's arrival, in all its ceremonial glory. The Emperor admired the pictures but stuck to the train. President Kennedy met it.

Occasionally, it is expedient to hold a state visit outside the capital. When

President López-Mateos of Mexico was invited to confer with President Johnson last February, the White House thought that Palm Springs, California, would make a pleasant setting. The weather was sure to be better out there than in Washington; in an election year, a President always finds it helpful to pay his respects to a state with a big electoral vote; and Palm Springs is only a short helicopter ride from Los Angeles, which has a larger Mexican population than any settlement except Mexico City. Along with Secret Service men, communications experts, White House social secretaries, and other advance planners, Duke was in Palm Springs long before the two Presidents arrived (he inspected and approved the private house that the Secret Service and the White House social staff had selected for Mr. Johnson to occupy), and he was on hand throughout the visit. He is a perfectionist, and although most people thought the meeting went off quite nicely, he composed a critical memorandum about it as soon as he returned to Washington. At one point, he had observed disapprovingly, the Governor of California had had to carry his own suitcase; at another, Mrs. Johnson's brother, who was on the scene, had had to walk a few blocks when there should have been a place for him in a car; and, worst of all, there had almost been a grievous lapse in coördinating the initial arrivals of the two Presidents at the Los Angeles airport. The timetable Protocol had devised called for Johnson to step out of his airplane fifteen minutes before López-Mateos stepped out of his. But something had gone wrong, and someone opened the door of the Mexican plane seven minutes too soon. As a result, López-Mateos had come dangerously close to setting foot on American soil before Johnson could be disentangled from a welcoming party and rushed across the runway to give his guest a proper greeting. It is with such procedural niceties that a Chief of Protocol must be unremittingly concerned.

All in all, though, the visit of López-Mateos was a success. At least, nobody made an attempt on his life—the ultimate disaster for Protocol. When Marshal Tito was here in October, 1963, two unfriendly Yugoslavs sneaked up a back stairway to his floor in the Waldorf-Astoria and almost got to his door before they were intercepted. On hearing of this near miss, Tito angrily threatened to cancel the rest of his stay. A Protocol man on duty at the Waldorf called Washington, where Duke, in the expectation that everything would be tranquil in New York, had gone to attend a concert given in Constitution Hall to commemorate United Nations Day. Summoned outside the auditorium, Duke was joined by General Chester V. Clifton, Jr., the White House military aide. At first, Duke was all for grabbing a plane to New York, but it would have been several hours at best before he could reach the Waldorf. Instead, the two men retired to the basement, where there was a pay telephone. From that command post, they tried to decide what to do to mollify the nation's outraged guest. By trial and error, they traced Adlai Stevenson, in New York, to a dinner party he was attending. Hearing the bad news, Stevenson said he'd go right over to the hotel and try to calm Tito down. By this time, the concert was over, the audience had left, Mrs. Duke and Mrs. Clifton were sitting on the basement stairs and yawning, maintenance men were wondering whether they were ever going to be able to shut up the hall and go home, and Duke and General Clifton had run through all their small change and all the change in their wives' purses. "You learn something from every crisis," the General said afterward. "What we learned from that one was that you need lots of nickels and dimes."

Protocol is in many ways simply a fusion of good manners and common sense. It stands to reason that the better informed a host is about his guest, the more successfully he can entertain him. Thus, as soon as a foreigner has agreed to come here the Protocol people begin compiling a dossier on his liked and dislikes, hobbies and habits, crotchets and idiosyncrasies. Information is procured, indeed, about every known member of an approaching party, so that the Americans who will mingle with them can know that this one speaks fluent French, that that one is a left-handed tennis player, and so on. A few weeks before the northward trek of one Latin-American President, the United States ambassador to his capital, in response to an inquiry from Protocol, sent word that, among other things, the President could not abide having his food seasoned, was leery of drafts, liked his bedroom warmed to an uncommonly high temperature, doted on classical ballet, and not only didn't smoke but in his own bailiwick wouldn't tolerate smoking in his presence. "He does drink champagne and Scotch," the ambassador added, "but does not like to be forced into drinking." A long, detailed set of dietary instructions was appended, and the ambassador, in a final caveat, warned Protocol not to mistranslate the Presidents's favorite breadstuff, known as *galletas de agua*, as "soda crackers" or "water biscuits." There had been confusion on this score before, and to clarify the point the ambassador went on to describe the baked goods. "These are actually big, round, moderately thick things with bubbles in them—something like ship biscuit," he said. Thoroughly briefed, Protocol laid in a copious supply of authentic *galletas de agua*, closed windows tightly, turned up thermostats, hid ashtrays, bought a bunch of ballet tickets, and ran a successful visit. The most assiduously gathered intelligence, though, is apt to have flaws or omissions. It was not until after Duke had solicitously tried to shield the King of Afghanistan with an umbrella during a shower that he learned that it is considered lèse-majesté in Kabul to interpose anything between the heavens and the royal head. And it was not until President Antonio Segni of Italy had got a good part of the way through his Washington stay last January that Duke learned that he does not like to be known as "His Excellency." Protocol had never before had a President who didn't. Duke's

327

office managed to edit the honorific out of most of its own written references to the visitor, but the discovery came too late for the White House to follow suit.

President Segni was the first important visitor to be given a reception at the White House after Lyndon Johnson took up residence there. Chancellor Erhard of West Germany had been over earlier, but he had gone to the President's home in Texas. To give state visitors a chance to catch their breath before plunging into the stiff schedule of activities laid out for them, Duke urges them to spend one day of comparative rest before the President officially welcomes them. Most visitors gratefully comply. Marshal Tito elected to spend a quiet preliminary day at Williamsburg. The Italian President, like several other chiefs of state, chose Philadelphia, where he could, in Duke's words, "compose himself with a sense of America's past." Philadelphia seemed a logical stop-off for President Segni, because he was going to arrive in Washington by train. This represented a compromise. When Duke was laying plans for President Segni's arrival with Sergio Fenoaltea, the Italian Ambassador in Washington, Fenoaltea at first proposed that President Johnson meet Signor Segni at an airport. Duke said that would be out of the question—American Presidents never meet people at airports anymore—and brought up the subject of helicopters. He was reminded politely that President Kennedy had gone to Union Station for Ethiopia; surely President Johnson would do no less for Italy? Duke didn't want to stir up anything new between *those* two nations and yielded. With that out of the way, Duke and Fenoaltea began mapping out the details of Segni's visit. The Italian wondered whether Signor Segni couldn't have a relatively intimate session with the President at the LBJ Ranch, like Chancellor Erhard. Duke explained that it had been logical for Erhard to go to Texas, because Mr. Johnson had happened to be going there (and because there happened to be a lot of Germans in Texas), but that the President had no such plans for the time of the Segni trip. (There are practically no Italians in Texas.) Fenoaltea, zealous on behalf of his president's prestige, took a new tack. He wondered if it would not be possible for Signor Segni to address a joint session of Congress. Duke said he would see what he could do. He knew that Mike Mansfield, the Senate Majority Leader, was trying to keep joint sessions to a minimum; they take up legislative time, and they are customarily attended by a lot of people—the diplomatic corps, the Cabinet, the Joint Chiefs of Staff, and others—who would just as soon not have to leave their offices to go over to the Capitol and listen to a speech in a language most of them can't understand. The Chief of Protocol wanted to please the Italians, though, if he possibly could. So Duke went to see Senator Mansfield and John McCormack, Speaker of the House. He was aware, he told them, of Congress's attitude toward joint sessions, and he thoroughly sympathized with that position. But he also felt constrained to point out that anything Congress could do at that moment to solidify relations with a member of NATO would be most helpful. (He didn't have to point out to two such astute politicians that 1964 was a Presidential election year and that there were large Italian-American voting blocs in key cities of key states.) Congress capitulated, and the Italian government was overjoyed; West Germany had had the ranch, but Italy had got the legislature.

When chiefs of state fly over here, our government sometimes sends a plane for them, but only if their country doesn't have a transoceanic airline of its own. Because Jordan Airways, for instance, does not operate beyond the Middle East, Duke and his wife flew to Amman in April to pick up King Hussein. President Segni, on the other hand, came over on an Alitalia plane. He was supposed to fly non-stop from Rome to Philadelphia and land there early in the afternoon. Duke had planned to fly up from Washington that morning to meet him, but it was snowing, so he took a train. Segni's wife was accompanying her husband, and there were several other ladies in the Italian party, so Duke took his wife along, too. When the Dukes reached Philadelphia, around noon, it was snowing hard. They went to the Bellevue-Stratford Hotel, where Segni was supposed to spend that first composed night, and found the lobby swarming with Italians also up from Washington, including Ambassador Fenoaltea and *his* wife. Duke phoned the airport and learned, not to his surprise, that Segni's plane couldn't land anywhere in the northeastern United States and was being diverted to Montreal. Segni's appointment to meet President Johnson at Union Station in Washington was at exactly noon the next day, and Duke began pondering how to get him there on time. Ambassador Fenoaltea thought that hitching a special car onto a Montreal-Washington train might be the answer, but it turned out that the earliest possible arrival time by rail was 1:20 P.M., which not only would throw the Union Station arrangements out of whack but would ruin a lunch that Dean Rusk was giving for President Segni at the State Department. There was talk of having the visiting party hole up in Montreal overnight and fly down in the morning, but Duke had his doubts about that. "I'm not sure the Italians want to throw themselves on the hospitality of the Canadian government without an invitation," he said. But in the end he had little choice, and it was decided that Segni would stay in Montreal overnight and fly to Friendship Airport, outside Baltimore, in the morning, arriving there at ten. This would enable him to board the same southbound Pennsylvania Railroad train that he would have taken from Philadelphia under the original plan.

Duke hates to waste time. It was now 2:50 P.M., and he wanted to get to Baltimore and start making arrangements there as quickly as possible. He learned that there was a three-thirty-five train from Philadelphia to Baltimore, and passed the word to head for it to all hands—Ambassador Fenoaltea, other Italian officials, other Protocol men, American and Italian journalists, State Department security men, interpreters, and the assorted fringe people who can be found in any such congregation. In Baltimore, the Dukes established themselves in a suite at the Sheraton-Belvedere and ordered drinks for everyone around, from the Italian Ambassador down to an R.C.A. technician who was tagging along to help correspondents file dispatches about Segni, assuming they ever met up with him. The Dukes felt so good about the way things were shaping up that they decided to give a dinner for the Fenoalteas and a few others in their caravan, but the party failed of total success because Mrs. Duke ordered two local specialties— fresh oysters and devilled crabs—not knowing that Mrs. Fenoaltea can't stand shellfish. During the evening, Duke learned over the phone that the ranking State Department official in Montreal, the United States consul-general, had the situation there well under control. Mrs. Duke, who was born in Baltimore, took over the phone and tracked down the Mayor of Baltimore, Theodore Roosevelt McKeldin. She told him how delighted she, as a native of the city, was to be back home, and how delighted she knew he would be to hear that one of Europe's most distinguished figures was about to honor Baltimore with his presence. Wouldn't the Mayor like to be at the airport at ten in the morning? The Mayor said he would, and was sure that he could find a key to the city lying around somewhere before then.

At seven-thirty the next morning, while having breakfast, Duke learned that the Segni plane was ahead of schedule and would touch down at nine-thirty. The night before, Duke had arranged for a military bus to take most of his group to the airport, but he didn't want to be held up by stragglers, so while he was spreading the latest word from lobby to coffee shop and up and down relevant corridors, his wife went out to hail a cab. It is one of her specialties. She has been know to hurl herself in front of taxis when her husband is desperate for transportation. This morning, with the streets still clogged with snow, there wasn't a cab in sight. She flagged down a private car and told its startled woman driver that she simply had to get to the airport to meet the Mayor of Baltimore, who was going to meet the President of Italy. The woman thought she was daft and said, with asperity, "I bet you don't even know who the Mayor of Baltimore is."

"I do, too," said Mrs. Duke. "It's Theodore Roosevelt McKeldin."

"Well, I have to get to work," said the woman, moving off down the street.

Mrs. Duke shrugged, saw a taxi drop off a passenger down the block, ran and flung herself upon it, and was soon comfortably settled inside it with her husband.

Friendship Airport is almost as close to Washington as it is to Baltimore, so it would have been logistically simpler for President Segni to be driven straight to the capital. But it would have been ceremonially unthinkable. By train he was supposed to arrive, and by train he would arrive. Duke was

330

taken aback when he stepped into an airport phone booth and found out that the Philadelphia-to-Washington train he was supposed to make connections with was running an hour and a half late, but a second call brought reassuring news: the Pennsylvania Railroad, anticipating some such eventuality, had deadheaded a three-car special from Philadelphia to Baltimore, and that train was ready for boarding. Mayor McKeldin arrived with a key to the city, a red carpet was laid out on a snow-cleared stretch of runway, the Italian plane landed, Duke greeted Segni with aplomb, the party drove behind a police escort back into Baltimore and climbed on the special train, the train pulled out, and it arrived alongside a red-carpeted platform in Washington on the dot of noon. It had all worked out, and Duke had the air of a man who had fulfilled his mission as he stepped nimbly off the train, homburg in hand, and said, in the respectful tones the occasion demanded, "Mr. President, the President of Italy."

In the hectic aftermath of President Kennedy's assassination, a lot of things had to be done, and they had to be done correctly, and it was up to the Office of Protocol to see that they were. As a diplomat in Washington put it, after the first shock waves had passed, "Protocol was the one thing that somehow made everybody live again." Duke had spent most of the morning of Friday, November 22nd, mulling over a state visit by Chancellor Erhard, which was to start the following Monday. He took a breather to have lunch at one of his favorite Washington retreats, the National Capital Democratic Club, in the Sheraton-Carlton Hotel, with his brother. A waiter told them the President had been shot, and Duke went straight to the White House, a couple of blocks away.

The office of Ralph Dungan, one of Kennedy's administrative assistants, became the focal point for the men working on funeral arrangements—Sargent Shriver, General Clifton, Duke, and a host of others who drifted numbly in and out. As the plane carrying President Kennedy's body, President Johnson, and Mrs. Kennedy approached Andrews Air Force Base, Duke drove out there with Arthur Schlesinger, Jr. One of Johnson's first executive acts had been to send word from the plane to Acting Secretary of State George Ball—Dean Rusk was on a plane himself, west of Hawaii—that he wanted no one to meet him at Andrews. Ball and the White House staff had decided that Johnson's order, issued under stress, did not have to be obeyed. The crowd that gathered at the airfield included quite a few White House people, senators and congressmen, Cabinet members, and members of the diplomatic corps; understandably, they all wanted to convey their personal regrets to Mrs. Kennedy. Reaching the scene, Duke reflected a moment and then issued an order of his own: No one—absolutely no one at all—was to speak to Mrs. Kennedy when she arrived. The order was obeyed.

Duke went back to the White House, and soon word came to him from Mrs. Kennedy that she wanted as much information as he could assemble that night on state funerals. His office had a file on President Roosevelt's death, but that was all. Duke appealed to the Library of Congress, and seven researchers went to work there studying accounts of the funerals of Presidents Washington, Lincoln, Grant, Theodore Roosevelt, and Harding, and of King Edward VII. By four-thirty in the morning, when Mrs. Kennedy returned to the White House with her husband's casket, Duke had a report waiting for her. (Not long after that, the Office of Protocol, the Department of Defense, and other agencies that play a part in state funerals began formulating plans for the burials of all living Americans entitled to these rites—the President, the ex-Presidents, and five-star generals and admirals. When General MacArthur died, every detail of his funeral had already been arranged.) Duke hardly got to his own office over the weekend. William Tonesk, his deputy chief, took charge there. The Protocol staff numbers only thirty-six, and as they reported in, one by one, it was obvious that they were too few for the job. Other State Department employees volunteered their help. One young woman did secretarial work nearly non-stop for forty-eight hours. When she was so tired that she couldn't type anymore, she was persuaded to leave; in all the confusion, nobody ever learned who she was.

On Friday evening, while Secretary Rusk's plane was heading home, Ball and Duke decided that in order to make the funeral as manageable as possible they would recommend to all nations that they be represented at it by their ambassadors already in Washington. The two men so informed Rusk when they met the Secretary at Andrews at two o'clock Saturday morning and rode back to the State Department with him. But it was too much to hope that the leaders of the world would go along with that suggestion. The President of the Philippines sent word that he would attend the funeral in person. Chancellor Erhard said that he would be there, too. As the hours ticked by, the list grew longer. It was evident that the Office of Protocol couldn't conceivably cope with all the eminent personages who were coming and who, in ordinary circumstances, would each merit special ceremonial handling. Duke had a solution. He tapped for protocolary help the Assistant Secretaries of State for the five regions of the globe, many of their deputy assistant secretaries, and most of the scores of desk officers beneath them who deal with individual countries; while Rusk and Ball would undertake to greet all incoming chiefs of state and heads of government, their subordinates would wait upon other guests from their own areas. The Washington embassies would furnish their own transportation and arrange for the lodging of their own emissaries. A Protocol officer, Thane Kuhlman, was dispatched to Dulles International Airport, where most of the guests would be landing, to regulate traffic. (Meanwhile, Tonesk was informing immigration and public-health authorities at scattered ports of entry that foreigners might be coming through who had taken off in such a hurry that they had no passports or vaccination certificates.) At one point, Kuhlman learned that a plane was on its way to Dulles from Idlewild carrying the Foreign Ministers of Algeria, Iran, Morocco, Tunisia, and Turkey. There had never been such a confluence of equal-ranking dignitaries at one swoop before, and the question was: In what order of precedence should Secretary Rusk escort them off the aircraft? Rusk didn't know, and Ball didn't know, and Kuhlman didn't know. The plane landed, and the passengers waited aboard it while Kuhlman phoned Tonesk for instructions. The deputy chief advocated that the men at the airport follow the old protocol custom of arranging individuals of identical importance in alphabetical order.

Duke was at the White House, juggling telephones. The British Ambassador wanted to know what Prince Philip should wear to the funeral. The Kennedy family had prescribed morning dress for civilians, and the Protocol office had at once arranged for a Washington clothing shop to stay open all weekend for the benefit of people who didn't have the correct dress. Duke said that morning dress would be all right for Prince Philip, but he turned up in an admiral's uniform—an appropriate gesture, Duke thought, from one naval officer to another. Somebody called to find out who would be responsible for the two ex-Presidents of the United States who were going to attend. Duke asked Averell Harriman to look out for Harry Truman and assigned a former deputy chief of Protocol, Clement Conger, to Dwight Eisenhower. The seating arrangements at St. Matthew's Cathedral were thrust upon Duke. He inspected the church Saturday and calculated that by putting folding chairs in the aisles he could squeeze in just about everybody who was coming. (He had television sets installed in the cathedral for the benefit of those mourners who had to be placed behind pillars.) Inevitably, there were slipups. The most important foreigners were supposed to sit in forward pews, five abreast. But when Haile Selassie and General de Gaulle took their places, far up front, they put their military hats (and the Emperor's sword) alongside them, with the result that there was room for only two others in their pew; the dignitaries who filed in behind them assumed that four to a pew was the idea, and Duke's plan was wrecked. Afterward, Crown Princess Beatrix of the Netherlands told him that, in the confusion, she had ended up wedged between First Deputy Premier Mikoyan of the Soviet Union and Mikoyan's bodyguard. "All I could say to Her Highness was 'I'm so glad you got a seat,'" Duke said later.

Everyone has his own especially poignant memories of that weekend. Duke has two that stand out. The Office of Protocol set up both receptions that followed the funeral—Mrs. Kennedy's at the White House and President Johnson's at the State Department. At the White House, Duke saw Mrs. Kennedy curtsy to Prince Philip, and he recalled that two years earlier, when he had been flying to London with the President and his wife, there had been a discussion about punctilio at Buckingham Palace—specifically about whether Mrs. Kennedy should curtsy to royalty—and Duke had told her, "My dear, chiefs of state do not curtsy to each other." Now, in Washington, as Mrs. Kennedy noticed Duke watching her curtsy to Philip, her mind flashed back, too. "She said, 'Angie, I'm no longer the wife of a chief of state,'" Duke says, "and my eyes filled with tears." At Mrs. Kennedy's reception, Duke presented each guest to the widow. The ex-President of Colombia, Alberto Lleras Camargo, was back toward the end of the line, and as he paused to chat with Mrs. Kennedy, Duke once again lost his composure. "They got to reminiscing about President Kennedy's state visit to Bogotá a couple of years before," Duke says, "and then he began to cry and she began to cry, and then I began to cry, and it seemed that the best thing to do was just to push him on down the line."

August 15, 1964

From a Profile.

The All-Around Orbiter

A Project Gemini astronaut may become early next year the first human to be exposed to the hazards of outer space with no protection except his space suit. . . . Air Force Capt. James A. McDivitt, named to be the spacecraft commander, said the experiment will be one of the highlights of the four-day mission. His copilot, Air Force Capt. Edward H. White 2nd, agreed. "This means the start of extra-vehicular activities," White said.— *A.P. dispatch.*

> Beyond passing courses in college or school,
> It's wise to have outside proclivities.
> For advancement's based not just on grades, as a rule,
> But on extra-curricular activities.
>
> In capsules, as classrooms, the rule holds perforce:
> The stars won't be reached by passivities.
> What no longer counts is mere progress on course;
> It's the extra-vehicular activities.

August 29, 1964

Our Far-Flung Correspondents
The Super-Express of Dreams

KYOTO, Japan

It is rare these days for a full-fledged airline to be glum about the speed of a railroad train, but that has been the situation lately in Japan. Since October 1st, when the Japanese National Railways started regular service between the nation's two largest cities, Tokyo and Osaka, with what the J.N.R. formally calls the Bullet Train and newspapers here have informally called the Super-Express of Dreams, the airlines operating on the same run have cancelled several flights and, instead of increasing their fares, as they had planned to, have been muttering about decreasing them. As the Bullet Train flies, Tokyo and Osaka are three hundred and twenty miles apart. Counting driving time between downtown areas and airports, travel by air between the two metropolises takes, in the best of circumstances, two and a half hours. The Bullet Train, even with stops at Kyoto and Nagoya, covers the distance in four. That's just for now, though. The train has a potential top speed of a hundred and fifty-nine miles per hour, but until the roadbed over which it zooms has settled, it is being held down to a maximum of a hundred and thirty-one. There hasn't been much attention paid to the Super-Express of Dreams, even in Japan. The start of scheduled service occurred only nine days before the start of the Olympics, from which it was hard to divert local attention, but most Japanese are by now proudly aware that, come next year, this latest product of their ingenuity is slated to cover the run in a flat three hours, at an average pace, the two stops notwithstanding, of a hundred and seven miles an hour. Some Japanese who were disappointed at their country's not having won any gold medals for speed in the Games are now cheerfully reflecting that, in the year of the XVIII Olympiad, at least they have shown their heels to the rest of the world when it comes to rail transit.

An English-language magazine in Tokyo noted the other day, "The progress of railway in Japan is most amazingly rapidity." Japan didn't have any trains at all until 1872. Today, it has many, and they tend to be extremely crowded. Forty percent of the country's population and seventy per cent of its industry are in the area served by the Tokyo-Osaka line, but until last month the only railroad connecting the two cities was a narrow-gauge double-track line. The old trains were rapid enough by Western standards—they rattled along, and still rattle along, at speeds as high as eighty miles per hour—but the need for a new, faster through route had been foreseen for a good while. In 1959, the National Railways began construction of a standard-gauge double-track line, with very gentle curves to accommodate really swift trains. The engineers used rail that was welded into five-thousand-foot sections and attached by means of metal mountings, called chairs, to ties of pre-stressed concrete. To hug these rails suitably, new electric trains with a very low center of gravity and a special pneumatic suspension system were built, and painted in dashing horizontal bands of blue and white. Each of the thirty Bullet Trains consists of twelve cars—two buffet, two first-class, and eight second-class, with an engineer's cab in the car at either end. Each train is an extra-fare proposition, and all seats are reserved—a comparatively startling idea in Japan, where standees sometimes fight for enough shoe space. Each train runs on a split-second schedule—its speed being subject to automatic control from signals along the line. An emergency stop can gum things up wildly. A couple of weeks ago, a Super-Express halted unexpectedly at a station along its route to let off a child suffering from what a doctor aboard had diagnosed as a ruptured appendix, and this humanitarian pause so upset the train's schedule that it was delayed for an hour and a half. (At last report, however, the sick child was doing nicely.)

After the Olympics ended, I decided to leave the furor of Tokyo for the relative tranquillity of Kyoto, and I booked a seat on a 10 A.M. southbound train on the new line. There are twenty-eight Bullet Train runs a day in each direction, departing on the hour and on the half hour between 6 A.M. and 8 P.M. The fastest trains are those that leave on the hour, making only the stops at Nagoya and Kyoto, and that are classified as Hikari, which means "Light." (At home, I most frequently ride on commuter trains, which can ordinarily be classified as murky and disagreeable at best.) The trains that leave on the half hour are called Kodama, or "Echo," and take an extra hour for the trip, but since they make eight additional stops, they can hardly be accused of pokiness.

My seat was in a first-class car, which was tastefully decorated in the new line's dominant blue and white. There were wide double-pane windows, trimmed with light-blue glass curtains and draperies of a slightly darker blue, both of them elegantly veined with gold. A strip of rich blue carpeting ran down the middle of the car under overhead fluorescent lights, which were flanked by gleaming apparatus for heating and air-conditioning. The seats, which could be tilted back and swivelled, were upholstered in gold, with crisp white antimacassars, and equipped with adjustable footrests and with little tables that popped out of the arms. I had an aisle seat. The seat next to mine was occupied by a Japanese who had placed a pint bottle of whiskey and a glass jigger on the window sill. The sill, I calculated, was slightly less than four inches wide. While we were waiting to get under way, my seatmate uncapped the bottle, threw away the cap, filled the jigger, and set bottle and jigger back on the sill. The only suit I had with me was the one I was wearing, and I began wondering what might happen to it after we hit a hundred miles an hour and the bottle and the jigger began to jiggle. I also began wondering how sedate old Kyoto might react to an American in a whiskey-soaked suit.

We set forth at precisely ten o'clock. A few minutes later, as we cruised at a calm enough clip through the outskirts of Tokyo, there was a musical flourish over a public-address system. Then a pleasant feminine voice came on to tell us, first in Japanese and afterward in English, that we would reach Nagoya at twelve-twenty-nine, Kyoto at thirteen-thirty-six, and Osaka at fourteen hundred. Her voice brimmed with confidence; there were no qualifications or doubts, explicit or implicit, in her prophecy. My seatmate gulped down the contents of his jigger, refilled it, and put it back on the narrow sill. I just gulped. A conductor and his assistant, both clad in trim blue-gray uniforms and immaculate white gloves, came into the car to check our tickets. First they favored us with smart salutes—an occurrence that would no doubt jolt a New York Central or New Haven commuter into dropping his whiskey glass.

After handing over my ticket and being rewarded with grateful smiles, I pulled from my pocket a strip map that the railroad distributes to patrons. It was entitled "Train Window Panorama," and, fully extended, it was five feet long. In pictures and text, it described points of interest along our route. Like all tourists here, I was most interested in Mount Fuji, which a thick cloud cover had blotted out when I flew into Tokyo a month earlier. It was cloudy this morning, too, but the clouds were scattered and drifting. At ten-fifty-nine—we hadn't seemed to be going especially fast out of Tokyo and through Yokohama, but even so we'd racked up over eighty miles that first hour—the mesmeric tip of that legendary mountain became momentarily visible to our west, above the clouds. I grabbed my camera and clicked away. An Englishwoman across the aisle remarked sourly that the best view of Fuji is from *its* west. (There is a spoilsport in every crowd.) Two minutes later, the public-address girl said that we would shortly be revving up to a hundred and ninety kilometres—about a hundred and eighteen miles—per hour, and that if we gazed to the west at that instant we would obtain our best view of Fuji. The Englishwoman grabbed her camera, but the mountain, I was gratified to notice, had ducked behind another cloud. Soon afterward, I tried to get a picture of some of the shrubbery in the district of Shizuoka, which my "Train Window Panorama" advised me was Japan's principal producer of green tea, but we were now moving faster than my

337

shutter seemed likely to. The window sill, however, was as steady as a teetotaller's hand.

By eleven-thirty, my companion, his bottle half empty, had tilted his chair back, removed his shoes, and stretched out to use his footrest. I was beginning to feel thirsty myself, so I walked into the next car, which housed one of the buffets. Along one side ran a sitdown counter for eating, and along the other ran a standup counter for cooking and serving and eating and drinking. Above the door at the far end was a roster of the principal cities on our route; a thermometerlike red line—for all I know, electronically controlled—moved slowly from one to the next to indicate where we were at any given moment. (We were now approaching Hamamatsu, whence, said the "Train Window Panorama," comes much of Japan's edible seaweed.) At the opposite end of the car was a speedometer. We were travelling at two hundred kilometres an hour—more than two miles a minute. Behind the standup counter was a refrigerator-like appliance bearing a sign reading "Do not drink water when lamp is out." Next to this warning was an unlit light bulb, so I ordered a beer from a girl behind the counter. The buffet car was prettied up with lots of fresh flowers. It was chrysanthemum time in Japan, and in Tokyo I had seen eye-popping displays of that imperial blossom at the Olympic Village, at the National Stadium, and almost everywhere else I turned, but the Bullet Train, as if to emphasize its uniqueness, had this morning gone in for carnations. The speedometer inched up to two hundred and ten kilometres per hour. There was a bit of swaying, but not much more than you get on a New York Central commuter car when it has come so close to a full stop that the passengers are already jumping off. According to a large electric clock that the Japanese had also thoughtfully provided for our enlightenment, it was now eleven-forty-six, and as the red line revealed that we were closing in on Hamamatsu the public-address girl announced, with evident relish, that when we got to that city we would overtake an ordinary express train that had left Tokyo half an hour before us. A minute or two later, we shot past it, and not long afterward there was another sound like a shot as we passed a Bullet Train going in the opposite direction. The other Bullet Train's twelve cars were fused into a single blue-and-white blur.

A Japanese standing next to me at the counter asked, in English, if I was an American, and when I said I was he wanted to know if I was an observer. I asked what he meant, and he explained that he'd read in a newspaper just that morning that the United States was thinking of going into the Bullet Train business on the run between Washington and Boston and also in the San Francisco area, and that American railroad men were supposed to be sniffing around to find out how the Japanese had turned the trick. Washington to Boston in four hours was the American dream, he told me, and he added that as far as he was concerned he hoped his nation would share its technological know-how with mine. I told him I was not really an observer and thanked him, and we exchanged bows. Then he asked me how it felt to be a marmot. I looked puzzled again. He must have taken me for a real dope, but he explained patiently that Japanese doctors use marmots to try out delicate surgical procedures on before they use them on human beings, and that we passengers were akin to marmots (if he had said guinea pigs, I'd have caught on more quickly) in that the railroad wouldn't introduce the three-hour Tokyo-to-Osaka run until it had determined experimentally how we stood up to the four-hour run. The conductor came into the buffet car and stopped beside us to ask the counter girl if there had been much breakage. No breakage at all, she told him. The conductor beamed. My companion offered him a cup of coffee, but he said he didn't drink while on duty. I asked the conductor how everything was going. In twenty-two years of working on the railroad, he said, he'd never had a better time, and the members of his crew—twenty or so all told, including the kitchen help—were also thoroughly enjoying themselves. You meet a higher class of people on the Bullet Train, he added. (This, I reflected, might have some connection with the higher class of fare.) Without even inquiring whether I was an observer, he volunteered the information that each Bullet Train has a capacity of nine hundred and eighty-seven passengers—a hundred and thirty-two in first class and eight hundred and fifty-five in second. On this run, his Hikari was eighty per cent full.

Gamagori, a summer resort noted, according to my map, for its "picturesque seascape," was coming up next, but when it came we tore through it so swiftly that its picturesqueness eluded me. The conductor said matter-of-factly that the train would probably be fuller than it was but for a good many Japanese who were reluctant to ride on it because they were not yet entirely convinced that it was safe. I blinked. He added hastily that of course it was safe. In a month's operation, there had been only one, minor misadventure: somebody had fired an air-rifle bullet at a Bullet Train and nicked a window in the last car. The marksman, I suggested, had probably aimed at the first car. Nevertheless, the conductor went on, quite a few Japanese appeared to be hanging back, waiting for some sort of all-inclusive guarantee. As far as the government and the railway administration were concerned, he said, the Bullet Trains had already been proved as safe as any trains could be.

Feeling not only secure but euphoric, I ate some fried prawns and returned to my seat to prepare to disembark, which I ultimately did on the dot of thirteen-thirty-six, as promised. By that time, my seatmate, who was evidently going on to Osaka, resembled an anesthetized marmot. His bottle was nearly empty, but his jugger, brimful, stood defiantly on the window sill. As well as I could make out, not a drop had spilled during the entire. trip.

November 21, 1964

Card Enclosed

"It is my belief [said John Cardasis, president-elect of the Florists' Telegraph Delivery Association] that we have to help members teach their customers that other occasions than funerals exist for selling flowers. For example, why shouldn't every man wire flowers to his mother celebrating his own birthday?"

—*The Herald Tribune.*

Happy birthday to me!
Happy birthday to me!
Happy birthday, dear Narcissus,
Happy birthday to me!

November 28, 1964

Resources and Responsibilities

Before David Rockefeller, who, at forty-nine, is the youngest of five well-known and well-to-do brothers, decided to go to Russia last July for a conference on Soviet-American relations, he gave the trip a good deal of thought. There is nothing unusual about an ordinary American's visiting Russia nowadays, but, as Rockefeller realizes, he is not ordinary. Not only would he arrive bearing an emphatically capitalistic surname, the mere mention of which is supposed to suffuse Russians with wrath, but there was also the matter of his being the president of the Chase Manhattan Bank, a worldwide power structure with over twelve billion dollars in assets and the kind of influence that that kind of money begets. Moreover, Rockefeller had heard hints that if he should get to the U.S.S.R. he would probably be invited to confer with Premier Khrushchev, and there was no telling how explosively the Communist leader might react to a confrontation, on his home ground, with a notorious international banker. For a while, accordingly, Rockefeller wasn't sure he should go. While assessing its pros and cons, he told one acquaintance, "I wouldn't want to do anything disadvantageous to the country or the bank. I want to make sure I do what's appropriate."

"Appropriate" is a word that Rockefeller often uses. He does not mean by it that he is loath to do anything others might disapprove of; he means that he wants to do what it is proper and useful for someone to do who is endowed with his unique combination of vast personal and business resources, and who, because of these, is saddled with no less vast responsibilities. For any Rockefeller to do anything *in*appropriate, he feels, would reflect unfavorably, if not damagingly, on the entire clan, and would also raise doubts about that particular Rockefeller's ability to carry his fair share of the family's heavy joint burden. David Rockefeller was once fittingly presented to a dinner audience as "a man for whom life is an obligation, not a joy ride." And he himself, upon being asked not long ago how he and his wife went about helping their children adjust to their uncommon heritage, said, "We've tried to teach them that they are fortunate but that along with their opportunities they'll have responsibilities. You can't expect to have the one without the other." Rockefeller has six children—two boys and four girls, the oldest twenty-three and the youngest fourteen. Some of his friends considered it a characteristically thoughtful touch on his part that, of the six, the one he elected to take to Russia with him was his second-oldest daughter, Neva, who is twenty and a junior at Radcliffe. The conference he attended was held in Leningrad, and her name, as it happens, is also that of the broad and handsome river that flows through the heart of the metropolis. Neva Rockefeller was actually named after her maternal grandmother, Neva Smith McGrath, but when Rockefeller arrived in Leningrad he could not resist letting the local citizenry leap to its own delighted, erroneous conclusion.

It was in Leningrad, on a Tuesday, that Rockefeller was told Khrushchev would like to see him the following afternoon at the Kremlin, in Moscow. Taking Neva with him, the banker went south by overnight train, and the next day participated with the Soviet leader in two and a half hours of what Rockefeller subsequently called "the most intensive conversation I've ever had with anyone." It was a far-ranging, if inconclusive, colloquy, covering, among other subjects, the capricious attitude of the Russians toward international copyright law, the failure of the Soviet Union to repay its wartime lend-lease obligations, and the possibility of increased trade between the two men's nations. Neither the Communist nor the capitalist arrived with any prepared memoranda; they talked off the cuff. (Khrushchev, who furnished an interpreter and some mineral water, acceded unhesitatingly to Rockefeller's request that Neva be permitted to take notes.) At one point, Rockefeller remarked that his mother had visited Russia in Czarist days—back in 1896, the year before she married John D. Rockefeller, Jr. She had been travelling with her father, Senator Nelson Aldrich, of Rhode Island. That got Khrushchev going on what he called the inevitable evolutionary progress of the entire world toward Communism. Waving a hand toward the scribbling Neva, the Soviet leader told her father that sooner or later people everywhere would spontaneously embrace Communism. "Someday your daughter Neva will think as I do," the Russian said amiably. Neither Neva nor her father replied.

Rockefeller's concern about going to the U.S.S.R. in the first place had been compounded by his awareness that although the Kremlin obviously knew who he was, there seemed to be some vagueness about this lower down the Party line. Two months earlier, he had had a letter from a Russian he'd met at a 1962 conference in the United States—a *Pravda* commentator who was also a deputy of the Supreme Soviet. In the course of plying Rockefeller with questions about the state of the American economy, this correspondent had inquired, "Is it true that you intend to enter politics, trying your chances in Ohio? If that is so, I wish you success." Whether the *Pravda* man had in mind Rockefeller's brother Nelson, the Governor of New York and then still a contender for the Republican Presidential nomination, or his brother Winthrop, then the Republican gubernatorial nominee in Arkansas, was uncertain, but the mere question was unsettling to David Rockefeller, who has steadfastly shied away from active participation in politics since 1948, when he was an elector for Thomas E. Dewey. Many Americans have hoped that David Rockefeller *would* try his chances in politics. He has been publicly proposed for Mayor of New York, and several highly placed Republicans have privately indicated that they would be delighted to support him if he should ever indicate an interest in the Presidency. Rockefeller is appreciative of such sentiments, but he is unswayed by them. For one thing, he is quite content with his present lot. "I can't imagine a more interesting job than mine, to tell you the honest truth," he said to a friend a few months ago. "The bank has dealings with everything. There is no field of activity it isn't involved in. It's a springboard for whatever interests one may have in any direction—a very good platform from which to participate in the economic advancement of the world."

Banking operations are so diverse that a very big bank, like the Chase, has a stake in nearly every legislative act. Nelson Rockefeller's political opponents periodically hint at dark conspiracies between the administration over which he presides and the bank over which his youngest brother presides. In 1963, for instance, when a bill to amend New York's liquor laws was under debate, one Albany legislator professed to espy chicanery in a provision of the statute that would make it easier for department stores—some of which have big accounts with the Chase—to sell whiskey. "Is this state being run by the Governor or the Chase Bank?" the lawmaker demanded rhetorically. Up to the Goldwater stampede, it used to be customary at Republican National Convention time for disgruntled G.O.P. conservatives to suggest that all Republican candidates were picked by the directors of the Chase Bank. The directors aren't quite as powerful as that, but the legend of their power has gained sufficient credence so that the most recent Republican candidate for governor of Illinois, Charles H. Percy, found it prudent to resign from the Chase board when he set out after the nomination. It is therefore hardly surprising if David Rockefeller goes out of his way to avoid partisan entanglement in his brother Nelson's legislative programs. "I've tried to be scrupulously careful not to give any substance to conflict-of-interest charges," David says. "I wouldn't want to do anything in the political field that seems inappropriate." He has been so scrupulous that not long ago one of his assistants at the bank complained, "I could get a lot more done in Albany when Averell Harriman was Governor."

The situation has its own backlash, too. In 1960, for instance, when Nelson Rockefeller tried to thwart the nomination of Richard Nixon for the Presidency, a number of Chase customers who stood firmly in Nixon's corner began grumbling that David ought to do something to curb his headstrong big brother, and there was pointed talk of switching large corporate accounts to banks whose officials' relatives did not go around rocking political boats. Even Chase stockholders are not above muttering hints that the Rockefellers are linked by bonds transcending mere fraternity. At the bank's last annual meeting, its directors submitted a proposal for a fifty-per-cent stock dividend. One shareholder complained from the floor that he'd rather have a cash dividend, whereupon an advocate of the board's plan, a man concerned about the income taxes that would be levied on a cash payment, jumped up and exclaimed, "Let's face it, ladies and gentlemen! If we vote for cash, we'll find ourselves in a position where David giveth and Nelson taketh away!"

The Rockefellers sometimes find the going prickly abroad, too. In the spring of 1963, the leftish *Ghanaian Times* got to brooding about ugly Americans, and concluded that Nelson and David Rockefeller were as ugly as they came. "Whilst the Governor of New York concentrates on changing the political climate in Washington to open up the trade in nuclear arms," a feature article in the paper said, "the president of Chase Manhattan is mostly concerned with commodities like copper and bananas." The *Ghanaian Times* credited the president of Chase Manhattan with a good many other imaginary sparetime activities as well; he was preventing the Organization of American States and the Alliance for Progress from interfering with private business interests in Latin America; he was trying to overthrow the governments of Bolivia and Peru, and to sustain the governments of Portugal and the Union of South Africa by furnishing them with arms; he was dominating the government of the United States through congressional stooges and a kept press; and, finally, he was using both the Central Intelligence Agency and the Department of State to watch over his and his bank's foreign investments. "His contempt for the liberty and happiness of other people doesn't embrace the whole of humanity," the paper added, "but only the sections falling under the scope of his bank's business, which dominates all other investors in Latin America, and is coming into South Africa, the Congo, Angola, and South-West Africa in a big way." Five years earlier, David Rockefeller had been instrumental in having one of his family's philanthropic outlets, the Rockefeller Brothers Fund, undertake a million-dollar program designed to accelerate the development of small local industries in Ghana.

The *Christian Science Monitor* once described Rockefeller as "a businessman who is listened to all over the world." His prestige is substantial, and it is still growing. These days, New York City is the hub of the globe's money markets, and Rockefeller's voice, though he never raises it, is one of the most respected in the financial community. A downtown investment banker who is himself attentively listened to wherever he goes said the other day, "I can't believe that if a poll were taken today to ascertain who the outstanding person in Wall Street and banking circles is, there would be anybody who could compete with David. He is the best product that the capitalistic system has produced." The rewards that that system has showered so richly on the Rockefellers have enabled them to employ a staff of several hundred simply to handle their own personal affairs, and in this group, as might be expected, the supremacy of the brothers is unquestioned. In the spring of 1964, for instance, David Rockefeller gave three lectures at Columbia University on "Creative Bank Management," for which he used a type of teleprompter that President Johnson is partial to. After Rockefeller had finished his first lecture, a member of the audience went backstage to congratulate him, and, seeing a Rockefeller staff man near the teleprompter, asked, "Isn't that the gadget President Johnson uses?" "No, this is the gadget David Rockefeller uses," the aide replied.

One of the points that Rockefeller stressed in his lecture series was that the world we live in is a variegated place. "Business methods that work in Terre Haute are not necessarily successful in Teheran," he said. Being a meticulous man, he rehearsed his delivery beforehand. A Chase Bank man who sat in at one practice session noticed that his boss had trouble pronouncing "Terre Haute;" it came out sounding like "Terreaute." The bank man expressed doubt that the name was pronounced that way in Indiana. "I guess I was giving it the French pronunciation," said Rockefeller, who is a passable linguist and can get along not only in French but in Spanish and German, and he added apologetically, "I'm afraid I'm not as familiar with Terre Haute as I am with Teheran."

Rockefeller is familiar with most of the principal cities of most of the countries on earth. One he visited recently was Perth, in Western Australia, from which he travelled three hundred miles inland to inspect a fifteen-thousand-acre tract of pasture land that he had recently bought, with a partner, as a personal investment; he also inspected a million-and-a-half-acre tract nearby, on which the Chase International Investment Corporation, a subsidiary of the bank, had started a sheep-and-cattle-raising venture. The corporation is also involved in hotels in Puerto Rico and Liberia, a Brazilian ready-mix-concrete plant, a Nigerian cotton-textile mill, a Venezuelan paint factory, and a Turkish steel mill. Bank presidents have to keep hopping nowadays. Last year, the Chase opened branch banks in, among other spots, Bangkok, Singapore, and Hong Kong, and Rockefeller, a conscientious executive, has put in a ceremonial appearance at each unveiling. (The Chase had pulled out of Hong Kong in 1951, because the bank's management at the time was leery of getting mixed up, however indirectly, in trade with Communist China. While Rockefeller, who is of a less cautious managerial breed, was in Hong Kong last January, he made a speech saying that the United States might appropriately start to think about engaging in limited trade with China.)

The Chase has over two hundred branch banks and representative offices around the world, and the resident officials of each one naturally want to make the most of it whenever a big frog from headquarters hops into their small outlying pond. The crowds that assemble to greet Rockefeller at airports—they include not only branch bank managers but finance ministers, American ambassadors, reporters, photographers—are sometimes large enough to make bystanders wonder what movie star is approaching. (When Rockefeller visited St. Croix, in the Virgin Islands, a few years ago, the leading hotel took a full page in the local newspaper for an ad headed "Welcome, David Rockefeller," and in the same issue he was further greeted by an editorial headed "Welcome!") His wife, Peggy, who is a woman of considerable charm and of a fairly acid wit, which nicely complements her husband's habitual blandness of manner, sometimes accompanies him on these jaunts. After one expedition to Pakistan and India, she remarked, "Wherever David goes, there always seem to be banks that want, more than anything else in the world, to feed him."

Rockefeller himself is undaunted by schedules that rarely leave him a free moment from eight in the morning until midnight. Inertia appalls him. A while ago, he was making a swing through the Middle East with Victor E. Rockhill, a Chase executive vice-president who was then the president of the Chase International Investment Corporation, and who is known around the bank as Rock. (This does not lead to nomenclatural confusion; no one there calls David Rockefeller Rocky.) Upon concluding some business they had in Beirut, the two men said goodbyes all around and went to the airport, only to learn that because of a last-minute hitch their plane would depart three hours late. Rockhill, who had been trying gamely to match Rockefeller's whirlwind pace, was overjoyed at the prospect of even that respite, but Rockefeller would have none of it. "As soon as David learned of the delay, he rang up a couple of men in Beirut he hadn't had time to talk to," Rockhill said afterward. "They were some sort of experts on Middle Eastern politics. They hustled out to the airport and huddled with him in one of those special side lounges where airports put people like David and sheiks, and he dug for information right up to takeoff time. With David, there's never a moment of nothingness."

Whether Rockefeller is travelling on business or for pleasure, his motto is *"Carpe horam."* He is so relentless an organizer that among friends who have taken trips with him he is known as "the cruise director." He wants to meet everybody and see everything, but because of his devotion to his job his reactions are likely to differ from those of run-of-the-mill sightseers. After a brief visit to Malaysia last January, he was asked for his impressions of the place, and he replied, "It is surprising that such a small country should have such fantastic foreign-exchange reserves." He has no difficulty getting together with experts on the foreign-exchange-reserves aspect of life; indeed, more often than not he is engulfed by financial men, so he goes out of his way to become acquainted with other kinds. "I find it terribly important to get overall impressions beyond those I get from businessmen," he says. In South Africa, where the businessmen are preponderantly white proponents of Apartheid, he arranged for a clandestine rendezvous with several underground black leaders. In Japan, he sought out professors and artists. Moreover, sensing that the resident American business community there had scarcely any contact with the academic community, he instantly went into action and gave a dinner for some Chase officers stationed in Tokyo and some Japanese university presidents.

Rockefeller rarely visits any country without paying at least a courtesy call—more often than not it is a business call—on its head of state. Such a gesture is expected of him, much as if he were a head of state himself. *(Pravda's* account of his seminar with Khrushchev, while it was constrained, accorded him a measure of coequality. "N.S. Khrushchev and D. Rocke- feller had a frank discussion of questions that are of mutual interest," the paper said.) The calls are often productive, sometimes for one side, sometimes for both. In Bangkok, three years ago, the King of Thailand told Rockefeller that his country could use some help in economic planning and statistical record keeping. Footing the bill out of his own pocket, Rockefeller immediately arranged to have Stacy May, an economist who at that time was working for the Rockefeller brothers, spend a few months in Thailand. A program that May drew up is currently under way. Rockefeller also visited Panama in 1961; *its* chief of state pinned a medal on him. Reasonably friendly relations existed then between Panama and the United States, and Panama had a special reason to feel friendly toward Rockefeller; under his direction, the Chase Bank had revitalized the country's cattle raising. In 1950, Panama was importing beef. The bank offered loans to cattle ranchers who would agree to substitute up-to-date, efficient methods for their traditional, casual ones. It accepted their livestock as collateral, the animals being branded with the bank's initials. The ranchers prospered, the brand became a sign of prestige, and the project succeeded so well that Panama not only increased its internal consumption of beef but found itself exporting it. The Chase now has five cattle experts assigned to its Latin-American branches.

When the chiefs of foreign countries visit the United States, they are likely to pay reciprocal calls on Rockefeller. Their schedules here are tight, as a rule, but they manage to make room for him. Sidney J. Weinberg, the senior potentate of Goldman, Sachs, said not long ago, "David's always got an Emperor or Shah or some other damn person over here, and is always giving him lunches. If I went to all the lunches he gives for people like that, I'd never get any work done." Rockefeller's facilities for entertaining are first-rate. At his family's principal estate, a thirty-five-hundred-acre enclave at Pocantico Hills, in Westchester, there is a building that John D. Rockefeller, Jr., put up for his children when they were young. It is called a playhouse, and it contains a tennis court, a swimming pool, two bowling alleys, a squash court, a billiard table, and a fully equipped gymnasium. There is enough ancillary floor space to accommodate fifty guests at a sit-down meal. The President of the Ivory Coast, Félix Houphouet-Boigny, spent a weekend at Pocantico Hills three years ago. Rockefeller served him a picnic lunch at an outdoor pool adjoining the playhouse, another feature of which is a fully equipped soda fountain, and, after hamburgers and strawberry floats, took his guest on a tour of the building. In the gym, some Rockefeller children were cavorting on a trampoline. M. Houphouet-Boigny watched them for a bit, then took his shoes off and began bouncing up and down himself. "He's an awfully nice man, and he enjoyed it very much," says Rockefeller, whose bank's international investment corporation not long afterward arranged with the Ivory Coast government to set up a company there to investigate and underwrite new small industries. (Similar companies have been established in Greece, Iran, and Nigeria.) Rockefeller's associates at the bank consider his high-level hobnobbing one of the Chase's most glittering assets. "You can learn just so much from routine economic analysis," an economic analyst at the bank said recently. "Around here, in determining what risks we can assume in various parts of the world, we often get our most useful intelligence from David's chats with important people."

David attended the Lincoln School, in New York—a day school of progressive leanings. When he was a fifth-grader, he and his brother Winthrop were privately tutored in the natural sciences one summer by a Lincoln teacher. David became enamored of beetles. His wife, whom he met a good many years later, likes to say that his addiction dates back to infancy; she paints a vivid and romantic word picture of the baby Rockefeller creeping into his Pocantico Hills mansion from the lawn, with insects, presumably including some beetles, clutched in his fists. Whenever it all began, Rockefeller gradually became one of the world's leading non-professional beetle men, with a collection that is large and resplendent. He devoted two adolescent summers in Maine to nature study (a fellow-student was Henry Ford II, whose family had a place on Mount Desert), and patiently scoured the local swamps for beetles. Two other summers found him at the Museum of Natural History's Station for the Study of Insects, at Tuxedo Park, where he abandoned beetles long enough to engage in experiments on the color perceptivity of bees. Winters generally found him hanging around the entomological section of the Museum itself.

Rockefeller finished Lincoln in the spring of 1932, and that fall he entered Harvard. As a freshman, he was granted special permission to take a graduate course in entomology, given by Professor William Martin Wheeler, an ant specialist; it was the only Harvard course he got an A in as an undergraduate. Extracurricularly, he put his expertise to humanitarian use by teaching a nature-study class at a settlement house. The summer following his sophomore year, he joined a scientific expedition that explored the bottom of the Grand Canyon, and he has subsequently furnished the wherewithal for the establishment of a research station near the top of an Arizona mountain and for an expedition to Mexico. Grateful scientists whose travels he has underwritten have named two beetles after him— *Acmæodera rockefelleri* (small, brownish, with yellow spots) and *Cicindela rockefelleri* (a species of tiger beetle). Specimens of both repose in his collections, along with some thirty thousand others. One of his best sources of new acquisitions nowadays is a retired Brazilian Air Force colonel who was longing for a jeep at the time Rockefeller made a 1962 trip to South America. Learning of this wish, Rockefeller gave him a jeep, and the officer, overwhelmed, promised to send him beetles as long as he lived. Rockefeller travels a great deal, and wherever he goes, he carries with him a few glass bottles with stoppers and a supply of cotton and formaldehyde. He has cajoled his wife and their six children into helping him hunt beetles, and the chase has been pursued *en famille* through poppy fields of Normandy and vineyards of the Bordeaux country. His eldest son, David, Jr., has been so thoroughly indoctrinated that he says he sometimes dreams of beetles. (He himself collects bottle caps.) Fond as David, Sr., is of beetles, beetles sometimes seem to be no less fond of him. A guest having cocktails on an outdoor terrace at Rockefeller's Pocantico Hills place last spring saw a small black bug settle on his host's forehead and perch there cozily. It was a beetle. After a bit, Rockefeller reached up and gently plucked it off. "Member of the Scolytidae family," he observed gravely, and then, as if waving a member of his own family off on some frolicsome flight, he released it to the breeze. Rockefeller houses his beetle collection in tiers of beechwood boxes nestled in a steel cabinet in an air-conditioned room on the basement floor of his Pocantico Hills place. His children have glued gold paper stars to the boxes that contain the more interesting specimens, among them some sacred Egyptian scarabs that Rockefeller himself brought back, dead, from an edifying safari along the Nile. By now, many of Rockefeller's acquaintances around the world have come to know about his hobby, and since he is a man who might reasonably be assumed to have everything, they give him beetles. The governor of the Central Bank of Japan sent him a glass-faced box of Japanese beetles—not our kind of Japanese beetles but *Japanese* Japanese beetles. Rockefeller isn't able to spend a great deal of time on his collection these days, and he is fortunate in having his own beetle curator—a protégé of his who enrolled in his settlement-house nature-study course, is now employed at the Chase Bank, and goes to Pocantico Hills on weekends to sort and mount beetles.

January 9 and 16, 1965

From a two-part Profile.

Harvard Yard

The prevailing mood at Harvard the day after Crimson blood was spilled was one of sadness. There was disbelief, too, but to a lesser degree. Belief has been suspended, if not shattered, on many campuses of late. Still, Harvard was, and probably is, and maybe will even continue to be, something different—the quintessential university, the very symbol of higher learning. One junior faculty member we ran into in the Yard at noon on Thursday, twenty-four hours after the students had occupied University Hall and seven hours after the police had bludgeoned them out, declared sadly, "Some of us are suffering today from the kind of hangover that comes only from over-indulgence in hubris." He went on, "It's all so irrational. It's surrealistic. A photographer who loves Harvard was roughed up first by the demonstrators and then by the cops. After that, he couldn't focus his camera, because he was crying. A dean who told me about this started crying, too. And the mere telling you about it is putting me in tears."

There were those in Cambridge who were saying, perhaps not without hindsight, that Harvard had been overdue for trouble; it had been lucky too long, it was too prominent, too inviting a target to be further spared. The Students for a Democratic Society had been muttering about occupying a Harvard building, but threat-making is the principal S.D.S. line of business, and few thought that what happened would happen. Indeed, at an evening meeting on Tuesday, April 8th, the S.D.S. had voted not to occupy. But its leaders had swiftly announced a meeting at noon the next day to reconsider, and even as that session was getting under way members of its more militant faction—including many students affiliated with the all-out-revolutionary Progressive Labor Party—were moving into University Hall. They were well prepared, with chains and padlocks and placards reading "Fight Capitalists—Running Dogs" and "Put Your Body Where Your Head Is." They had the occupants of the building hustled out within the hour. The evictions were accomplished without injury, except to pride. There was some pushing and jostling, and one frail, quiet, nonviolent assistant dean was carried out slung over a student's back, because he refused to leave under his own steam. He was James E. Thomas, an ordained minister who is also a nuclear physicist and a graduate student in philosophy, and who has long been acclaimed as one of the most liberal-minded Harvard administrators. His nickname is Jet. When a student he knew ordered Thomas out, he refused to go. "This building is occupied," he was told. "But surely it's big enough for both of us to occupy," Thomas said. "Oh, come on, Jet," said the student, and hoisted him onto his shoulders. As Thomas was being carted off, another student walked behind him, solicitously picking up the things that fell out of his pockets.

The S.D.S. had long since made known its demands, which, like many student demands these days, were proclaimed to be non-negotiable. The principal one was that Harvard abolish its Reserve Officers Training Corps. The Harvard administration had already stripped the R.O.T.C. of its academic standing and its instructors of their professorial rank; the faculty had voted by a ten-to-one ratio *not* to abolish the R.O.T.C. The S.D.S. apparently didn't really care. It was not the issue that mattered but the event. By midafternoon, the S.D.S. had the situation well in hand. Its occupation was reasonably orderly. Early on, the students voted against doing willful damage to the building, and against smoking marijuana while inside. Some filing cabinets were moved around, to serve as barricades, and the contents of a few of them were inspected. (On Friday, an underground paper sold in Harvard Square published some documents that purported to reveal an unsavory connection between the University and the C.I.A.) Finding a batch of blank identification cards for freshman proctors, a few students at once conferred proctorial status upon themselves; others, aware that Ivy League acceptances were about to be mailed to high-school seniors, whiled away the hours by typing on Harvard letterheads warm notes to young men around the country, congratulating them on their admission as freshmen next fall. Still others typed stencils, and one mimeograph machine churned forth a manifesto that concluded, "This is the first action of many to build a strong anti-imperialist movement in this country." Somebody painted an obscenity on the wall of the office of Fred L. Glimp, the Dean of the College; somebody else Scotch-Taped a note alongside it saying, "Dear Sir, We apologize for whoever did this. This vandalism was not a purpose of our protest." At one point, there were at least four hundred students in University Hall, perhaps half of them observers. One of the latter, a senior, told us afterward, "There were more beautiful girls at this Harvard function than at any other I've ever been to. One of them lent me a book to read. It was 'Cuba: Anatomy of a Revolution.' The thing that worried me most about many of the people in there was their ego-building. They seemed to spend half the day congratulating themselves on what they were doing."

From time to time during the afternoon and evening, the occupiers held a more or less formal meeting in the spacious faculty room, from which they voted to bar the faculty; they would communicate with the faculty, and with the administration, they further voted, only by public statements. Their friends outside provided them with food and with bedding. Other friends, and spectators, swarmed outside, in a blaze of television lights. One camera crew, it developed, was filming background scenes for a movie about a fictitious campus revolt. "Here we are in front of Jenkins Hall at Metropolitan University," an actor impersonating a television commentator was saying. "The atmosphere here is like a carnival."

Eventually, many of the two hundred students who remained in the building went to sleep. Quite a few of them still expected no trouble. They were wrong, of course. The administration had already decided—without consulting the faculty—to have them routed out at five in the morning. Some four hundred policemen were converging on the Yard. At four o'clock, to summon other students to the scene, fire alarms were set off—presumably by the S.D.S.—throughout the Harvard community. The students inside University Hall had been told by Franklin L. Ford, the Dean of the Faculty of Arts and Sciences, within a short time of their taking it over that if they didn't clear out in fifteen minutes they would be liable to charges of criminal trespass. Now, at 4:55 A.M., Dean Glimp warned them by bullhorn that they had exactly five minutes to get out with impunity. Apparently, nobody inside heard him. At five, the police moved in. There were two kinds—dark-blue shirts and light-blue shirts. The dark-blues were municipal police; their job was to clear students off the four flights of steps leading into University Hall. The light-blues were state police; their job was to get the students inside the building out. It is generally conceded that the dark-blues were the less disciplined and the more brutal. As they converged on the steps, clubs in hand, a few students inside the building leaped from windows and ran to freedom. Dozens of boys and girls were clubbed. One student in a wheelchair was hit. "I had to leave," a Radcliffe girl told us. "I thought it was too voyeuristic to stick around and watch students bare their skulls to nightsticks."

A hundred and ninety-six boys and girls were bundled into police vans and taken off to jail. Some forty were injured. The cops were gone by six-fifteen. The Yard was littered with trash and rutted by police vehicles. Buildings and Grounds men moved swiftly into University Hall and painted over Dean Glimp's profaned wall. All morning long, students milled about the Yard, in a daze compounded of sleeplessness and shock. "Whatever I think about seizing buildings—and I don't think much of it—I keep reminding myself that human beings perform these acts, not three guys whose initials are S., D., and S.," one of them told us. Some classes went on as scheduled. One bitterly anti-S.D.S. student reacted to the tumult by attending a course he hadn't been to in three months.

At eleven, while the students who had been arrested were being arraigned and, in most instances, released on their own recognizance, between fifteen hundred and two thousand moderate students held a meeting at the Memorial Church, in the Yard. The church had never before been so crowded; there were students perched atop the reredos. One of the undergraduate leaders invited his fellow-students to turn to and reflect on Hymn 256 in the hymnals on hand: O God of earth and altar,/ Bow down and hear our cry./ Our earthly rulers falter./ Our people drift and die." Professor Stanley H. Hoffmann, the social scientist, got up to speak on behalf of rationality. "This is the only university we've got," he said. "It could be improved. It can be improved. But it cannot be destroyed." He was loudly cheered. He advocated changes in Harvard's decision-making processes, but he warned against changing the processes so much that the will of the minority could prevail. "No university can function if the minority insists on winning all the time," he said. More cheers. The assembled students began debating what course of action they should take. They finally decided on a three-day strike, and they passed a number of resolutions—among others, condemning the administration for unnecessarily summoning the police, condemning the police for their brutality, and calling for the resignation of President Pusey if he didn't meet student demands. "This is the most impressive and most exciting thing I've seen in four years at Harvard," a Radcliffe senior said after the meeting. "It's the first time that moderates have dealt with radicals on their own terms. There's no longer a murky atmosphere here. The way the moderate students have reacted is electrifying." A resolution to condemn the S.D.S. was tabled. Nonetheless, some of the S.D.S. people who had got out of jail had hastened to the church and were already crying "Foul!" They said that the administration had purposely delayed their release so they couldn't get to the Memorial Church meeting in time to vote. The meeting broke up at two o'clock, amid ringing, responsible cries of "Clean the church! Clean the church!" Outside, a girl screamed "Bail money!" into the ears of a haggard passing dean. He winced. "Women shouldn't be allowed to talk in public," he said, not ill-naturedly. We caught sight of a student we know, a junior who hadn't missed a demonstration throughout his stay at Harvard. He looked crestfallen. "My alarm clock didn't go off," he said. "I slept through the bust. I've lost my honor."

The Yard was still full of clusters of disputants. Graduate students from the Business School and the Medical School had drifted over to see what was going on. A Divinity School student came by and asked no one in particular if it was all right for a lady organist to practice in the church, between meetings, for an imminent recital. Two S.D.S. members ripped an orange sign off a tree. "Hey, that's my sign!" yelled a student. "You wrote that?" one of the rippers asked scornfully. "Yeats did," said the sign's owner, even more scornfully. "The ceremony of innocence is drowned," the sign read. "The best lack all conviction, while the worst are full of passionate intensity." The S.D.S. men shrugged and yielded up the sign.

We had a word with an instructor in government. He had a booklet in one hand entitled "After Harvard—What?" He asked us if we were going to the faculty meeting. "What faculty meeting?" we asked. "There are meetings all over today," he said. "This one's at Sever Hall."

We headed toward Sever. On the way, we were stopped by an undergraduate with a solemn expression. "Would you like to hear the views of an ordinary, middle-of-the-road student?" he asked. We said we would. "I have always been incensed by the moral arrogance of S.D.S., but I'm afraid that this morning they scored a brilliant victory," he said. "Because of the administration's response to their totally unwarranted action, the issue, God help us, is no longer what S.D.S. did. The issue is cracked heads. It puts moderates like me in an uncomfortable position. I won't absolve S.D.S. of responsibility, and I won't support any strike, but I'll sign all the petitions in the world to disapprove of calling in the cops that way. Most of all, I am deeply concerned about the future of Harvard University."

So were the eighty faculty members who had gathered in Sever Hall. George Wald was there, and James D. Watson, and John Kenneth Galbraith, and everybody was sitting facing a blackboard on which someone had chalked "ON STRIKE." As we entered, a man we didn't recognize was saying, "For heaven's sake, let's 'reject,' or let's 'repudiate,' but, whatever we do, let's do anything but 'deplore.'" They agreed that the sense of their meeting was that they repudiated the occupation of University Hall, the eviction of the deans, the calling of the police, and the failure to inform the faculty that the police were being called. Professor Daniel Seltzer spoke up. "The primary purpose of the university is to teach," he said. "As long as one single student shows up for any of my classes, I'll teach him." Most of his colleagues nodded approvingly.

April 19, 1969

Wall Street Lunch

From time to time, we go down to the financial district to have lunch with an old friend named Douglas, an investment banker whose office is at 70

353

Pine Street. We picked him up there last Thursday, and he suggested that we go to Eberlin's, on New Street, a place he likes because it has an old-fashioned capitalistic air; that is, the waiters treat the customers any way they choose. We walked west on Pine Street. "I hope we can get there all right," he said. "I have a route I always try to walk because it takes me past the Subtreasury. I have a nostalgic feeling for the building, because it was there that George Washington took his first oath of office as President." There were a lot of policemen on Pine Street, standing next to an empty automobile, with flag decals fore and aft, parked at a hydrant a few feet from a "No Parking" sign. "You know, when I get out of the subway most mornings, it's like getting out of bed—unpleasant but mechanical," Douglas said. "This week, it's taken longer than usual to walk out of the station, and there's been this strange feeling of apprehension when you reach the street. On Tuesday, there were all those really enormous people around with little red-and-yellow buttons in the lapels—like those two guys over there. At first, I kept wondering, Who are these ill-at-ease-looking people wearing sports coats and open shirts? What are they doing here in Squaresville? I thought they must be construction workers, and I began to feel sorry that I had my attaché case in one hand, in case I might have to use my fists. But then I saw a button on a black guy, and I didn't think a black man would be a construction worker, so I figured they must be plainclothesmen. I asked one of them if he was a cop, and he said, 'I can't tell you,' so I knew he was. I wonder who picked those colors. Red and yellow."

We turned south on William Street. "I'm a nondoctrinaire liberal who supported L.B.J. on Vietnam up to the first bombing in the North, but I guess I've been kind of radicalized," Douglas said. "My God, my *firm* has been radicalized this week. We're all doing things we normally wouldn't. After the hard-hatted construction workers' first attack on the student dissenters in the financial district, a whole bunch of people in our office impulsively wrote a letter of congratulation to Walter Hickel, and our receptionist turned up wearing a 'Business Action for Peace' button. An investment-banking receptionist wearing a button! I mean, it just doesn't happen." We turned west on Wall Street, past an armored car flying two American flags from its front fenders, like the car of a diplomat on his way to present his credentials, and past helmeted mounted police and legions of police barricades, and almost as many foot patrolmen and plainclothesmen as there were pedestrians. A Western Union truck went by with "God Bless America" and "Bomb Hanoi" painted on its side. The steps of the Subtreasury Building were roped off, and three policemen had their bodies interposed between us and a bas-relief of George Washington, who was kneeling in prayer. "To have cops, in or out of uniform, polluting this scene of traditional history strikes me as desecration of a national monument," Douglas said, sotto voce. The policemen were wearing two-tone blue helmets. Nearby was a young man, conceivably a student, in a white helmet. No helmeted construction workers were visible, though obviously the district was prepared for them. A tough-looking middle-aged man asked a red-and-yellow-button-wearing operative where the Stock Exchange was. The plainclothesman pointed it out to him, and as the man started toward it the plainsclothesman casually followed him. We started south on Broad Street. On the door of the Exchange was a sign that read, "Visitors' Gallery Closed." On the east side of Broad, in front of the Morgan Guaranty Trust Building, there must have been at least a hundred police. Douglas stopped and looked around. "Most of us are staying off the streets unless we have to go to a conference," he said. "Even the pigeons are off the streets. Look at them huddled on that ledge. I don't like the feel of Broad Street today. Let's go by way of Broadway."

We doubled back to Wall Street and headed west, toward Trinity Church, which had an American flag and the flag of the Episcopal Church flying at its entrance. "I had a conference on a big real-estate deal at my office yesterday," Douglas said, "and at the end one lawyer said, 'All right, now how do I get out of here back to my office? I'm not going along Wall Street.' So four of us spent ten minutes mapping out a safe route for him." At the church, two men wearing "Silent No Longer" buttons were passing out flyers urging everyone to attend a Rally for America featuring Mario Procaccino. On the cemetery fence was a sign advertising a lecture series: "Illustrated Lecture on Jordan," "Garden Week in Virginia," "The Megalithic Art of Ireland," and "Outlook for Financial Markets." A white man stopped to look at it and was bumped into by a black man, who said "Sorry." "First heartening word I've heard all week," Douglas said. A street salesman walked by with a board like the boards one sees at football stadiums; it had American flags and flag pins and flag buttons affixed to it. "'Get your colors for the game,'" said Douglas. "But he seems to have only one side's." We walked south on Broadway to Exchange Place, and turned east. "We should be all right now," Douglas said. "Do you get the feeling that the atmosphere of this place is crackling? To me, it's like Czechoslovakia after the Russians came in."

At the restaurant, Douglas, who, in the best banking tradition, rarely has more than a Dry Sack-on-the-rocks, ordered a double Scotch, and when his food came he picked at it. Three uniformed policemen walked in, and he stiffened. "I've never seen cops in here before," he said. "But I guess they have to lunch somewhere." A friend of his stopped by the table to report that the Dow-Jones was down nine points at one o'clock but bonds were firm, and that that would undoubtedly make the Attorney General happy. Douglas shrugged, and replied, "I don't think the collapse in stocks has anything to do with John Mitchell's having been in bonds all his life. It would be attributing too much to him. Who cares about the market any longer anyway? The big question down here is: When will the *country* bottom out?"

We let Douglas try to make it back to his office on his own, and took the subway uptown, where things seemed comparatively normal for midtown Manhattan at midday in spring. There was a solitary hot-eyed man on Fifth Avenue wrapped in a sandwich board that said, "N.Y. Being Framed to Be H-Bombed. Don't Be Fooled."

May 23, 1970

The Meddlers

The approach of Amnesty International to the political prisoners of the world consists in large part of meddling. Under its aegis, concerned and reasonably literate individuals bombard governments with letters beseeching mercy or justice for a particular prisoner. This strategy is predicated on the assumption that most governments, like most people, read—or, at any rate, glance at—most of their first-class mail. Governments, also like people, do not always answer their mail, but a spate of patient, persistent, pleading letters can, in Amnesty's experience, wear down the most unflinching and granitic regime. Amnesty has learned what the players of an old children's game have known all along: Rock breaks scissors, scissors cut paper, paper covers rock. Amnesty's main sources of intelligence about prisoners are newspapers and broadcasts, letters from strangers, and the widespread members of the organization, who, though enjoined for obvious reasons from taking any direct action on behalf of their own restricted compatriots, are encouraged to let London know about them, so that somebody else can step in. Once Amnesty's headquarters is satisfied that an individual is "adoptable," a case sheet is made up for him.

Amnesty has generally had more failure than success in dealing with Communist nations, but its gadfly methods have not gone unrewarded even there. On a visit to Bucharest a couple of years ago, Sean MacBride, a former Minister for External Affairs of Ireland, who is now secretary-general of the International Commission of Jurists and also the chairman of the International Executive Committee of Amnesty, was asked by a Rumanian government official if he knew much about an organization called Amnesty International. Having no idea what might be coming next, MacBride replied merely that he had heard of it. "Well, it's very effective," the Rumanian said. He went on to tell how, back in 1962, his country had begun receiving letters from housewives all over the world petitioning for the release of this or that prisoner. The letters were at first ignored, and were in no instance answered, but they kept coming in and piling up. They amounted to such a nuisance that finally the government decided it was

356

spending too many hours over them, and set two thousand prisoners free. That, as it happened, was more prisoners than anyone at Amnesty had realized Rumania *had*.

Amnesty, whose symbol is a lighted candle surrounded by barbed wire, has only seventeen thousand members, but they cause commotions disproportionate to their strength. The organization was founded in 1961 by a London barrister, Peter Benenson, who was forced to withdraw from it in 1967, because of ill health. From the start, Benenson insisted that if Amnesty hoped to get anywhere it had to be politically dispassionate. Thus, in 1966, when it published a report critical of prison conditions in East Germany, it took pains to achieve political balance by simultaneously issuing adverse accounts of conditions in Rhodesia and Paraguay. Amnesty's reputation attests to its impartiality. It has been accused by Greece of being Communist, by the Soviet Union of being imperialist, and by Uganda of being anti-Ugandan. In East Berlin, the daily *Berliner Zeitung* thought Amnesty had done a fine job of exposing iniquity in Portugal but declared that to focus on East Germany was absurd, since there were no political prisoners in East Germany; anyone looking for violations of human rights in that part of the world should concentrate on *West* Germany. In South Africa, Amnesty has been called "an organization concerned with political interests rather than the plight of individuals."

Amnesty is international but not universal. It is divided into national units called sections, with each section supervising a varying number of "groups"—eight hundred and thirty-three of these in all—of from six to twenty persons each. It has no members in the Communist countries. A section was in the process of formation in Czechoslovakia a few years ago, but the events of 1968 stopped that. Amnesty still hopes that the split between Russia and China may help it expand. On a recent visit to East Berlin, the leader of Amnesty's West German forces urged an acquaintance to start up an Eastern section; the East Germans, he suggested, could concentrate on Russian prisoners in China. The East German merely laughed. Amnesty is active in Australia and New Zealand and, somewhat less vigorously, in Japan, India, Pakistan, Ceylon, Somalia, and Sudan. It is strongest in Europe, especially in the north. West Germany has become one of its bastions, with two hundred and seventy-nine groups—the highest number for any country. "If Amnesty had existed a generation ago, a lot of Hitler's prisoners might have been saved," one of its principals there says, perhaps a bit naïvely. There are sections in Italy and Israel, but it appears that many people who live near the Mediterranean (like many people in Latin America, where, aside from Mexico, Amnesty is almost nonexistent) are not much interested. The core of the Amnesty operation is the groups. At any given time, each group is supposed to be concentrating on three individual prisoners. In keeping with the parent organization's neutral position, one of the three is normally in a Communist country, one in a right-wing dictatorship, and one in a country somewhere between the extremes. Responsibility for the one hundred and thirty-two Jehovah's Witnesses in Spain has been divided among several countries, including Sweden, England, West Germany, Denmark, Norway, Scotland, Israel, Italy, Australia, Ireland, the United States, and the Faeroe Islands.

To underwrite the main Amnesty office in England, each of the eight hundred and thirty-three groups is supposed to send in thirty pounds a year. (Since hardly any of the American members belong to groups, the office here theoretically sends over twenty-five hundred dollars annually, but lately it has been in arrears.) All told, the London headquarters is run on a budget of less than eighty thousand dollars a year. The offices there, which occupy a ramshackle frame building a few blocks from St. Paul's, accurately reflect Amnesty's indigence. The top man in London, Martin Ennals, is the forty-three-year-old son of an undertaker in Walsall, a Midlands industrial town. He came to Amnesty two years ago after working for UNESCO and for the National Council for Civil Liberties, the British equivalent of the American Civil Liberties Union. "It's difficult to say where Amnesty is most effective, or why we're effective at all," Ennals says. "Some of it can be attributed to luck and some to good stage-managing. On the whole, though, most countries recognize us as having a role to play. Nobody will come right out and say we're splendid, but we can usually get to see the president or the prime minister. You have to talk to the top men, and talk to them as equals. You have to make them feel that they can talk to you, and respond to you, and even shout at you. If you're lucky, you may hear someday—perhaps much later—that they've listened to you and let someone go free. You may never know whether you were really responsible for it. But that doesn't matter. You don't care about being given credit for this or that amnesty. There's always another prisoner after the one you've got out."

August 22, 1970

From a Profile.

Notes and Comment

Yukio Mishima, aged forty-five, completed a four-volume fictional work called "The Sea of Fertility" this fall and then told a Tokyo reporter, "I feel I am finished now. I have done plays, long novels—everything. There is nothing left for me to do." But he decided that there was something left after all. Emulating the fate-ridden Nō drama (though he had little use for professional actors, theatricality fascinated him, and he had written several "modern" Nō plays), he saved his crucial last act for the public stage. Two weeks ago, Mishima and four young disciples, brandishing razor-sharp samurai swords, invaded the office of a lieutenant general of Japan's Self-Defense Forces and tied the general to his chair. Mishima then stepped out onto a balcony and harangued a crowd of more than a thousand Self-Defense soldiers about the military inadequacies resulting from the Japanese Constitution. Next, apparently following a well-constructed plot, Mishima walked back inside, knelt, disembowelled himself, and was beheaded by one of his companions. His last words before his hara-kiri were reported to be "I don't think they heard me very well."

Surely he was wrong. Most people who had listened to him lately, whether they agreed with him or not, heard him memorably. We had a long lunch with him this past spring, in a restaurant at the foot of Mount Fuji, that extraordinary symbol, for the Japanese, of eternal life and impetuous death. The staff of the establishment treated Mishima with a respect bordering on reverence. We write, of course, from hindsight, yet there was something in his bearing that day which we then attributed to his all-around brilliance and his Oriental playfulness but which we now feel stemmed more from his sense of elated fantasy—as if, in his wild scheme for reviving the samurai spirit in the twentieth century, he had found the hopeless mission that a Don Quixote needs in order to fulfill his destiny.

For Mishima told us that he thought of himself as a latter-day Quixote— "a minor Quixote," he said. He spoke of the windmill-tilter familiarly and affectionately, and, with equal fondness, he spoke of Spanish taste, which, being a true internationalist, he well understood, and which he shared to the point of furnishing his Tokyo home in Spanish baroque. When he talked, he put his shoulders back, thrust out his stiff, narrow chest, and swivelled the top of his body as if he were encased in a barrel. (He was a complicated man in every respect. An advocate of physical fitness, he spent five hours a week in a gym, body-building, yet on weekends he was a heavy cigarette smoker and Scotch drinker.) Beneath his close-cropped black hair, his black eyes flashed, like Picasso's. Even as he likened himself to Quixote, the analogy made him laugh—a disturbing, explosive laugh that seemed to burst out, then exhaust itself.

All his adult life, Mishima appeared to stand on the edge of catastrophe. He told us how he began to write—in 1944, when he was nineteen, attending college and also working in a Navy airplane factory. "From there, one midnight, I watched the big fire-bombing of Tokyo," he said. "The flames were so awful and beautiful it was unforgettable. I thought the world was going to end. So I pushed myself to write." The result was "The Temple of the Golden Pavilion," a novel about the burning of Japan's most cherished Buddhist temple by a mad young monk. "That end-of-the-world feeling became the basic feeling of my life," Mishima said. "That I am here at all is miraculous. I have survived too much."

Still, survive he did, prolifically turning out twenty novels, thirty-three plays, eighty short stories, and hundreds of articles, and becoming the idol of many young Japanese, who seemed to him to have been tragically leaderless since the end of the war and the diminution of the Emperor's stature. So in 1968 Mishima made himself a leader, of sorts, by starting up his famous private army, which he named the Shield Society. He designed its uniforms himself, including his own great-coat and floppy hat, adorned with antlers in the form of an ancient Korean crown—undoubtedly the most original commander-in-chief's headgear in Japan since MacArthur's. Mishima's para-military force, sometimes called "Fascist" in the Western press, had a top strength of a hundred, and was more a theatrical fantasy, conceived by a poet, than an army. A few days before we lunched with Mishima, the Minister of the same Self-Defense Forces whose premises the author stormed before dying had compared the Shield Society, at a press conference, to the dancers at the Takarazuka Theatre, which puts on all-girl revues; then, in a characteristically Japanese move, the Minister had swiftly phoned the writer to apologize for the slur. Each spring, Mishima trained sixty or so young men at a camp near Fuji. Here they ran, in the early dawn, toward the mountain, which would eventually crystallize out of the morning mist before them like the demon-god of Japanese legend. "I always make a point of running at the head of the column," Mishima told us. "I have a description of Fuji in the book I am working on. I mention how sometimes if you look at it in the summer, when its slopes are brown, and then quickly transfer your eyes to the sky, you get an after-image of the essence of Fuji—only, it is the mountain in the winter, snow-white. There is a saying about Fuji you may have heard: that if you have never climbed it, you are a fool; that if you have climbed it once, you are a wise man; and that if you have climbed it more than once, you are a fool. I am glad to be able to say that I have climbed it once." After the early-morning run, Mishima would lecture his troops on the samurai code of honor, according to which the Emperor, like the Pope, was both temporal and spiritual father. But at the end only a few Japanese seemed interested in joining Mishima's fanciful march.

At lunch, Mishima was brimming with explanations of what he was doing; he seemed to understand the source and the quality of his despair, and to recognize the strange character of his chosen way of life. "I am hungry for a role," he said. "Every writer is a cook. He needs raw food to cook with, and there is less and less of that in Japan. Everything is already cooked. Where can you find the raw anymore? In love? Cooked—already canned! In poverty? Cooked and eaten. But I, I found something truly raw in the Self-Defense Forces, and also in the Shield Society, and in the souls of the samurai. I am not like the intellectuals, always playing at revolution. There can be no revolution here in Japan. I sympathize with the student left, in its unrest, but I deplore its unwillingness to recognize the Emperor as the symbolic moral source of loyalty and culture."

To Mishima, as to the ancient Chinese and Japanese, the emperor clearly seemed more an artistic symbol than a source of power. Mystically, in history, the Emperor linked past to present, the outer universe to his terrestrial domain. Traditionally, he was necessary to the ordered running of the cosmos. "If there were no Emperor, how would we have proof of our continuity?" Mishima said to us. "Our society gets broader in space, but it ignores time. We have no bridge to relate us to the future anymore. The Emperor should be our source of glory."

Of dazzling intellectual achievements himself, Mishima had come increasingly to consider intellectuality sterile. In 1968, he saw the Nobel Prize go to his much older compatriot Yasunari Kawabata, the highly intellectual portrayer of a more old-fashioned, desiccating Japan, in which the aging of his protagonist is a symbol of the aging of society in general. "Intellectuals cannot excite," Mishima told us. "They want to instruct, but they cannot *do* anything. It seems to be in the modern Japanese tradition that writers should behave like nineteenth-century romantics. I disagree. I like men of action. Other people may be partial to writers who are neurotic and decadent, but I have been opposed to that concept for fifteen years. My ambition is to get out of such a world."

"What about politics?" we asked.

"I have never wanted to be a politician," Mishima said. "Politicians are concerned with the effect of an act, and effectiveness is not my motivation. My responsibility is to the act itself."

The ancient act of hara-kiri was originally suicide as a form of protest. Eventually, it became an act of the warrior in defeat, and, finally, an act reserved for warriors alone. No one of the merchant class, no woman, and no one of the professional classes could commit a meaningful hara-kiri within the context of Japanese culture. That right was reserved to the samurai. It is a painful death and a severe test. The subject kneels, stabs himself in the side of the abdomen, and draws the blade across his body, releasing the intestines. Standing behind the subject is a samurai with a sword, whose function is to behead the subject at the first sign of pain, or even the slightest alteration of the traditional posture. Mishima's incision was seventeen centimetres long, and represents, apparently, a degree of mastery over physical reflex, and over pain itself, unparalleled in modern records of this ritual.

Mishima kept the plans for his suicide secret, knowing that attempts would be made to stop him. But in a letter mailed to a close friend of his who lives in this country—a letter mailed on the day of his death—he says, "This is my last letter to you. You might be one who can understand my conclusion, influenced by Yomei philosophy. [This is a seventeenth-century form of Confucianism characterized by a preoccupation with the significance of intuition and action.] I have believed that knowing without acting is not sufficiently knowing, and the act itself does not require any effectiveness." Mishima's friend understands him to mean that the immediate effectiveness of the act itself is a question separate from the intrinsic power of knowledge and action synthesized. Once again, Mishima is declaring his responsibility to the act itself, rather than to its effectiveness. His letter, handwritten, is in English, which he taught himself. There are almost no mistakes, and only an occasional awkwardness. Some personal remarks to his friend are not included here. He speaks with concern about the proper publication in this country of "The Sea of Fertility," the last two volumes of which have not yet been translated. His American publisher, Knopf, was also the publisher of the Japanese writer Junichiro Tanizaki, whose works Knopf published only until Tanizaki's death. Mishima expresses the fear that it is a policy of Knopf to publish only living foreign writers, and he asks his friend to do everything possible to see to it that the last two volumes are translated and get into print. "I wrote everything in it, and I believe I expressed in it everything I felt and thought about through my life. I just finished the novel on the very day of my action in order to realize my Bunbu-Ryodo. ["*Bun*" means "culture arts," "*bu*" means warrior arts, and "*ryodo*" means "synthesis."] After thinking and thinking through four years, I came to wish to sacrifice myself for the old, beautiful tradition of Japan, which is disappearing very quickly day by day. I wish you the happiest and healthiest life."

December 12, 1970

Strictly speaking, the foregoing does not belong in this collection. All the rest of the contents of the book I wrote alone. This piece is a collaboration, but I include it because it is the only one I have ever written jointly with Eleanor Munro—my wife.

Thirty-One Flavors

While strolling on the upper East Side in recent weeks, we've had the impression that the longest lines of carefree spenders in town nowadays are not at the Off-Track Betting windows but at the counter of an ice-cream store at Madison Avenue and Eighty-fifth Street. It's one of nine hundred and twenty franchised outlets of the Baskin-Robbins chain (there are three others in Manhattan: one at Third Avenue and Seventy-seventh Street, one at Lexington and Sixty-eighth, and one at Broadway and 112th), which, among them, now annually dispense fifteen million gallons of exceptional ice cream, sherbet, and water ice; which have a repertoire of over four hundred flavors (including Licorice, Fresh Cantaloupe, and Blueberry Cheesecake); and which at any given moment have thirty-one of these on hand—one, the gimmick goes, for every day of the month. On last week's sultriest day, we stopped by the Madison Avenue store shortly before 11 A.M., its official opening hour, for a prearranged rendezvous with Irvine Robbins. It was he who started the whole booming, melting business, a quarter of a century ago in California, in partnership with the late Burton Baskin, who was his brother-in-law. Mr. Robbins, a relaxed impresario of fifty-three with longish gray sideburns, welcomed us and introduced us to the store owner, Don Burns, who at once pressed on us a heaping plastic spoonful of his wares. "Lemon Custard with Hot Fudge," Mr. Burns said. "It's simply out of this world." Both men apologized for being unable to offer us a seat. "In theory, there are a dozen chairs in each shop," Mr. Burns said, "but we had to take ours out to make room for people." Mr. Robbins was passing through New York en route from his national headquarters, in Burbank, California, to the Boston headquarters of the United Fruit Company, which bought Baskins-Robbins in 1967, lock, stock, barrel, and Almond Marzipan. He retains the better parts of two worlds: a mouth-watering capital gain and the presidency of United Fruit's Baskin-Robbins subsidiary. We asked him to account for the phenomenal success of his business.

"Well, you can't get away from the root cause that good ice cream, like motherhood, is a memorable part of the fun of youth," he said. "I must say that New York has surprised me, though. Either New Yorkers love ice cream more than most people do or they've been starved for it—for interesting ice cream, I mean. Most of the excitement we generate, I guess, comes from our flavors. That's where the action is—with novelties like Pink Bubble Gum Ice Cream, which children just can't resist the sound of. Our flavors originate in several ways. Burt Baskin, for instance, was single-handedly responsible for Pink Grapefruit Ice. Some suggestions come from our customers and some from our employees. My co-founder ran into a guy once who told him, 'Whoever thinks of all these flavors must be plumb nuts,' and Burt said, 'Congratulations! You just invented a new flavor—Plum Nuts.' I myself ran into an acquaintance who said he was crazy about our Chocolate Sherbet, but why not put orange peel in it? 'Why not?' I said. We kicked that one around in our testing labs without making much headway until I thought, Let's hypo it with orange *juice*, and the upshot was our Mandarin Chocolate Sherbet, a solid, steady seller."

The Baskin-Robbins stores get their ice cream from eight manufacturing plants around the country, and each store is required by the terms of its franchise to carry the same thirty-one flavors at the same time. There is a monthly turnover of five flavors. Vanilla, chocolate, and coffee, in their infinite variations, account for forty per cent of all sales. "All our coffee ice creams, including our Espresso, are made with fresh coffee," Mr. Robbins said.

We could not reply; Mr. Burns was at that moment teasing us with a morsel of Jamoca Almond Fudge, a patriarch of the Baskin-Robbins coffee family.

"But we like to cater to the adventurous spirit of contemporary America," Mr. Robbins went on. "Thus our Tanganilla—tangerine and vanilla, if you hadn't guessed—with its mysterious, alluring name. I myself am more partial to Burgundy Cherry, but actually I like them all. I've always liked ice cream. My father ran a dairy farm in Tacoma, Washington, and I go back to the rock-salt days." At his home, in California, Mr. Robbins told us, he has his own ice-cream bar, complete with fudge warmer, but he rarely stocks more than a half-dozen flavors simultaneously. Wherever he is, he consumes five or more scoops of ice cream daily, starting at breakfast (he is partial at that time to Chiquita Banana); a recent holiday in Morocco was almost ruined for him because of the unavailability of his personal staff of life.

When we asked him to enumerate some of the flavors of his own creation, he hesitated. "I guess I've had my finger in most of them," he finally said. "Better make that my 'influence.' Fresh Cantaloupe was mine, and Beatle Nut, and, although it pains me to mention it, Goody-Goody Gum Drop. That seemed sensational, and it looked beautiful, but the trouble was that when gum drops are frozen, because of their high sugar content they stay frozen. We had some consumer complaints."

It was getting near opening time, and people were pounding on the store's glass door. Mr. Robbins' eye was attracted by one supplicant, a tall, leggy blonde, and he leaped to sneak her in. Next, he hugged her. "My niece— Edie Baskin," he said. "The undisputed originator of Banana Daiquiri."

Miss Baskin nodded demurely and addressed herself to a two-scoop cone that Mr. Burns had deftly whipped up—Lemon Chiffon and Caramel Rocky Road. When she was able to speak, she said, "People are always asking me 'Don't you get sick of ice cream?' and I always say 'I could eat it every day of my life.'"

Her uncle beamed, and Mr. Burns seized the moment to honor us with a taste of Blueberries 'n Cream. Then he threw open his portals, and the pre-lunch upper-East Side crowd poured in. Mr. Robbins invited us to join him in a cone of 32nd Flavor, the components of which, he said solemnly, no one is at liberty to divulge. It seemed to us to have a maple-walnut base with a hint of something exotic. Curry powder? Lichees? Asparagus? We couldn't be sure. In return for a promise that we made Mr. Robbins not to attempt to analyze 32nd Flavor further, we besought him to give us a scoop for our readers—to divulge, if he saw fit, the five new flavors for August. He frowned, conferred sotto voce with Mr. Burns, and then unlocked a briefcase and informed us that the big five would be Blueberry Marshmallow, Peppermint Fudge Ribbon, Pistachio Almond, Mango Sherbet, and a brand-new invention—Currantly Delicious Sherbet.

July 10, 1971

Notes and Comment

After the United Nations voting on China last week, there was much speculation about the future of the People's Republic of China and of the Republic of China but relatively little about the future of the people of Taiwan—that is, of the twelve million native Taiwanese, who since 1949 have lived under martial law imposed and enforced by Chiang Kai-shek's two million émigrés from the mainland (and who in themselves outnumber the population of any one of the smaller nations making up two-thirds of the membership in the General Assembly). The native Taiwanese sometimes call themselves a silenced majority. Except for a couple of hundred thousand aborigines, who are presumed to be of Malay origin, the islanders' ancestors came, like Chiang and his followers, from the Chinese mainland— principally from around Amoy, on the Fukien coast—but over the years the Taiwanese have become such a distinct group that their language now differs from Mandarin Chinese as much as German differs from English. The Taiwanese have also developed certain national characteristics, including, to the despair of their few indigenous leaders, submissiveness and a tendency to think of themselves as people who are somehow destined by history to be pushed around. It is true that back in 1947, while Chiang was still on the mainland, they staged an uprising against his resident surrogates, but the revolt was quickly and harshly put down. Today, for all their numerical superiority, they occupy just thirty-two of fourteen hundred and forty-eight seats in the National Assembly, they hold few government jobs of any consequence, and they don't make much fuss about their subservient role. Between the older mainlanders and the older Taiwanese there is hardly any communication, in or out of government. Probably not one fifty-year-old mainlander in a thousand can speak a word of Taiwanese, and a Taiwanese of that age who has a second language is just as likely to speak Japanese as Mandarin Chinese. The Taiwanese under thirty, on the other hand, have been somewhat Sinofied, and most of them speak Chinese. And, to some degree, the younger mainlanders have been Taiwanized; among certain young intellectuals, indeed, the ability to speak Taiwanese has become a status symbol. There is even some intermarriage now between the groups. However, one mainlander we know of who has a Taiwanese wife doesn't understand a word of her native tongue, and has never seen any reason to try to learn it.

In Taipei, a year or so ago, we were lucky enough to have a talk with an islander active in the Taiwanese independence movement. Talking with us involved some risk on his part, for it is considered reckless there to voice any criticism of the Generalissimo, or of his son and heir apparent, Chiang Ching-kuo; when someone wants to discuss the reigning family in public, he is likely to identify the principals by sign language, using a thumb for the senior Chiang, a little finger for the junior. For a foreigner to talk to any member of the opposition can require a good deal of maneuvering—clandestine assignations, code messages, and all the rest. We met our man after receiving word that "the Scrabble game is on" and making a series of ostensibly impulsive trips from one hotel to another. And our man, who believed that he was shadowed around the clock by Chiang's security police, told us he had eluded them that day with the coöperation of a succession of taxi-drivers, who have an occupational distaste for the police. He had recently spent several years in jail on some such charge as trying to overthrow the government by having dinner with six friends who were not cousins. "There were a lot of so-called Communists locked up with me," he told us. "Some of them were fishermen whose boats the Generalissimo's patrons had intercepted, and were Communists principally in the sense that their homes were on the mainland. Others were Taiwan people who had attended a Communist meeting twenty or thirty years ago. Whoever they were, they shared with me in prison one indulgence that none of us enjoy anywhere else on this island—really free speech. We had some fine political arguments. Almost none of us had anything good to say about Red China. Most Taiwanese don't know much about it—wouldn't recognize Mao if they ran into him—but don't have any use for Communism. Oh, there were a few prisoners who said that since the Chinese here are the bad ones, the others had to be the good ones. And there were some who said that since Chiang had imprisoned them, only Mao could get them out. But I kept telling them, 'If the mainlanders here are bad, what makes you think the mainlanders over there are any different? Mainlanders are mainlanders wherever they are, and if the Communists took over here, they would probably treat us Taiwanese no better than anyone else has.' You know, some people say that, just as the Generalissimo has his illusions about retaking the mainland, so we have our illusions about independence. There is no denying that our movement does not have broad support. Taiwan has become so prosperous that our people have a sizable bourgeoisie, which would hate to endanger its lucrative medical practices and plastics factories in the pursuit of some chancy political goal. Also, our people have no leadership to speak of. But we do have a three-hundred-year-old tradition of resistance fighters—a small group of people who have opposed the Dutch, the Spanish, the Manchus, the Japanese, and whoever else has been in temporary control of our land. Perhaps we have no visible strength right now, but there is an underlying yearning for freedom, and there is nothing that Chiang can do to stamp it out, because, however much better he lives than the third of our people who are crowded into squatters' shacks, *he* is the squatter. This is our island. We'd be delighted if he would pack up and move somewhere else. The Generalissimo has the support only of his troops, his bureaucrats, and the United States. Not even all the mainlanders here like the government—they remember how corrupt it was when it actually had the mainland. The Kuomintang calls Taiwan 'Free China.' That's about as imprecise as you can get in any language. Whatever this island may be, it is neither Chinese nor free."

November 6, 1971

Letter from Munich

September 8

Into the unreal Olympic world, where inches and ounces and seconds are what traditionally matter most, the real world cruelly intruded at five o'clock three mornings ago. The first inkling most of the four thousand journalists here had of the dreadful events that should have terminated these now cheerless Olympics came just before 9 A.M. on Tuesday, at which hour we had been invited to attend a press conference with the American swimmer Mark Spitz, who, having won an unprecedented seventh gold medal the night before, had been crowned by the German press *"der König von München."* Like just about everything else around here, though, his gilt had been tarnished. He had carried a pair of brand-name athletic shoes to the presentation ceremony for the third medal, and had felt constrained— probably under pressure from the United States Olympic Committee and under at least indirect pressure from Avery Brundage, the crusty American octogenarian who is retiring this year after twenty years as president of the International Olympic Committee—to make a public apology to his teammates. On my way to the conference, I glanced at the first editions of the local morning papers. They featured a queen not just of Munich but of all West Germany—the sixteen-year-old high jumper Ulrike Meyfarth, who had never cleared six feet until the previous afternoon, when she went three and a half inches above that and won a hysterically applauded gold medal of her own. Her glory was brief, for we learned during our wait for Spitz to show up that the Olympic Village had been murderously invaded. While we were reeling from that shock, Spitz arrived and gave sober, clipped answers to a few meaningless questions. He remained seated throughout the session, and a factotum explained, "Mark Spitz does not want to come to the microphone, because of the Israeli incident." (He is Jewish, and nobody knew who, if anyone, might be the next target.) As a result, the swimmer's responses were all but inaudible to us. It didn't much matter, because most of the questions, dredged from the near-bottom of the sportswriters' cliché barrel, were absurd and obviously irrelevant. Indeed, all the things that had been on our minds for a week had suddenly ceased to seem very consequential—even the prodigies of the regal Spitz himself.

Until now, these Twentieth Olympics had had the potential of being a truly glorious show. The first week of competition had ended, and the crowds had been astronomical—over half a million spectators on Sunday, September 3rd, alone, and perhaps just as many more ticketless people strolling around the grounds and having to satisfy themselves with such offerings as the offbeat, noisy midway called the Spielstrasse (now closed), where, among other things, a Japanese sculptor at a stand entitled "Pollution Game" had decked three Olympic winners' pedestals with dummy heads, arms, and legs, and where various street-theatre groups were, often irreverently, re-creating past Olympiads, and a Berlin group was depicting the 2000 A.D. Olympics. There was no reference, though, to Hitler's 1936 Games, and, however many reincarnations the Olympics go through, this 1972 debacle, too, would be best forgotten.

September 5th was to have been a day off from track and field in any case, so the meticulous organizers could conduct a rehearsal of the closing ceremony, which was originally set for September 10th. It has now been postponed one day, since Brundage's committee declared a day of mourning, but debased even that by directing that competitions under way continue to their conclusion. After the Spitz conference, there was precious little hard news for hours. The Olympic Village was sealed off to the press—except for a few reporters who sneaked in—so I walked around it, outside the fence the Arabs had scaled. Nearby, seemingly oblivious of what one security man at a locked gate blandly called "the special situation this morning," some field-hockey players were whacking away at each other's shins in routine fashion. In the vicinity also were swarms of soldiers and policemen, with armored cars and walkie-talkies and submachine guns, all looking puzzled and helpless. Inside the athletes' compound, not two hundred yards from the hostages, a carefree game of touch football was under way. At the main entrance to the Village, where a large crowd was milling around aimlessly, I fell into conversation with a black American from California, who turned out to be the father of John Smith, the four-hundred-metre runner. The senior Smith was wondering how he could get in touch with his son, whom he hadn't had a glimpse of since arriving in Munich not long before. There was so little confirmed information available that the frustrated reporters wandering around (they are largely sportswriters, of course, not war correspondents) began interviewing and photographing each other. I, for instance, was asked by both Polish and Kenyan radio reporters what I thought of the morning's developments.

At that time, we knew of only one certain and one probable death in the Village, but that would have been enough to make touch football joyless for most people. Meanwhile, the terrorists, who in their first ultimatum had said they would shoot an Israeli hostage every two hours from noon onward unless their demands for the release of Arab prisoners in Israel were met, kept extending their deadline. While negotiations with them were proceeding, the reporters at the press center learned of the twenty-four-hour halt in normal athletic activities and learned that the next morning there would be a memorial ceremony in honor of the dead. Shortly before 5 P.M., when it was widely believed that the Palestinians might renew their violence, I went to another spot on the perimeter of the closed Village—a point some two hundred feet from 31 Connollystrasse, the Israeli team's quarters. The general public, thousands strong, was being pushed back from this area by police and soldiers, but the press was allowed free access to the outside of the Village fence. There must have been nearly five hundred cameramen on the scene, some on ladders and some in trees, still more on the rooftop of a building behind us. Among them I spotted a watchful film crew wearing the colors of Wolper Pictures Ltd. David Wolper, who had been charged with putting together the official film of the Twentieth Olympiad, had recruited a clutch of celebrated directors from all over the world to make ten-to-twelve-minute vignettes covering various aspects of the Games—Kon Ichikawa, for example, choosing the final of the men's hundred-metre dash, Mai Zetterling choosing weight lifters, Arthur Penn choosing the pole vault, and Claude Lelouch choosing the general category of "losers." Now, looking at this camera crew, I reflected that none of these gifted people could have anticipated either the more bizarre events of the past week or the crushing offscreen drama now in progress. Who would have dreamed that Ichikawa's final would be run without two Americans who failed to show up for a qualifying heat because their coach couldn't tell the time? Or that the polevaulter whom Penn concentrated on, the American Bob Seagren, would be rudely dethroned by the East German Wolfgang Nordwig, who hadn't been at all coöperative about the movie project? As for Lelouch and his losers, how could that director have foreseen the bleak truth that faces us here now? On Tuesday we all became losers.

From where I stood, outside the fence, I couldn't see the ground floor of the Israeli building, which had in recent hours been blocked from view by large blue shields—perhaps bulletproof ones. A few people were visible in the doorway of 33 Connollystrasse (the quarters of Dahomey and Zambia), on our side of the shields, among them the mayor of the Olympic Village,

369

Walter Troeger, who in that very morning's community paper had lectured his constituents—in an item written before the Arab incursion—on the impropriety of inviting unauthorized visitors into the theoretically well-secured enclave. At 4:47 P.M., thirteen minutes short of the terrorists' current time limit, ten men in variously colored sweatsuits appeared and ran around to the rear of the beleaguered Israeli building. They looked like athletes, but they were all carrying submachine guns. After a moment, two of them could be seen scrambling over the roof and the balconies of the Dahomey-Zambia building and then ducking into the rear of the crucial No. 31. It seemed reasonable to infer that if the Arabs began shooting hostages there would be quick retaliation. But nothing happened at five. I hung around the scene for a couple of hours longer, until sunset, and then, since nobody there seemed to know anything, and still nothing more had happened, I decided to return to the press center. Along the way, I saw another ten men, sweatsuited and unarmed, jogging around a practice track, while, not far beyond them, a cluster of Germans with tickets to a volleyball game in their hands were arguing with a door tender, who was trying to explain to them that the game would not be played as scheduled and that it really wasn't his fault. Back at the press center, I noticed that during the tense afternoon someone had posted a notice on a bulletin board informing me that although I had lost out on a drawing for a boxing ticket, I did have one for the basketball semifinals.

Willi Daume, the head of the German Olympic Committee, stopped by the center shortly after nine to tell us a little, but not much, about the delicate negotiations. "The Olympic movement should not surrender to terrorists," he said. He couldn't answer any questions, because he had to rush off to an emergency meeting of the International Olympic Committee. The Soviet Union issued a statement condemning acts of terrorism.

I returned to the Olympic Village vantage point a few minutes after ten, just in time to see three helicopters whirl into the black sky on their ill-fated hop to the Fürstenfeldbruck military airfield. At ten-forty-eight, back at the press center, Hans Klein, whose unenviable task it had been all along to handle the world's press, told us, ashenfaced, that there had been shooting at Fürstenfeldbruck. For the next two hours, Klein periodically reported what he knew, or thought he knew—that all the Arabs were dead; that all the hostages had escaped; and, at twelve-twenty-five, that the earlier news had been too optimistic. Then he revealed that one policeman and three terrorists were dead, one helicopter was aflame, the fate of the hostages was unknown, and—it was now twelve-fifty, and a speaker for the Bavarian State Government was on television—there were people lying beneath one helicopter or another, identity unclear. Everything unclear. I went to bed, and learned the stark news by radio at seven the next morning. Just who killed whom and why remains unclear sixty hours later, but yesterday afternoon two officials of the German government and the head of the Munich police tried to straighten things out by holding a press conference, at which they conceded that German sharpshooters at the airfield had opened fire first, on the order of the Munich police, and that the German authorities would never have considered letting the terrorists take their hostages off to an unknown destination and seemingly certain death. Whoever was at fault in the botched rescue effort, it will not help much to be able to assign the blame, if any, for the death of eleven more Jews in Germany.

With a memorial service originally planned for only one or two dead, a lot of people here believed that cancellation of the Games would be the most suitable response to the death of twelve—or, including the terrorists, seventeen—men. But one could understand, even if one did not sympathize with, the arguments to the contrary: The Olympics must not yield to fanatics; good is bigger than evil; and, on a more practical level, the West Germans had all this money invested in the Games, and all these tourists had bought tickets, and, whereas rowing and swimming and gymnastics were over, the poor archers and Greco-Roman wrestlers had not yet begun, and why discriminate against them? And then there was Mr. Brundage's holy devotion to his cause. I have no idea what the majority feeling is, but a German who had watched a man-in-the-street television-interview program yesterday told me that most of the Germans questioned thought that the Games should have been called off out of respect for the Israelis, and that most of the Americans who were questioned thought that they should go on, because otherwise all their carefully-made travel plans would have to be changed.

I arrived at the big stadium early for Wednesday's 10 A.M. memorial service, after passing en route a number of basketball players working out on a practice court. The Duke of Edinburgh had arrived early, too, I learned. About two thousand chairs had been set up in the field for athletes, though there were four times that number of athletes within walking distance of the spot. The flags, of course, were at half staff—they remained that way for a mere twenty-four hours—but the Olympic torch had not been dimmed, and the big question on many minds was: With the flame already extinguished figuratively, would Brundage and his I.O.C. douse it literally and end the competitions? The only sign of sport in the stadium was one steeplechase hurdle, at the water hazard over which the sensational Kenyan runner Kipchoge Keino had blithely glided to win a gold medal on Monday, which seemed aeons ago. The Munich Philharmonic Orchestra was on hand to open the proceedings with the Funeral March from Beethoven's "Eroica" Symphony. At nine-thirty-five, the athletes began to appear—wearing their team blazers but without flags or other national symbols—some marching in formation, some drifting in casually. Soon all the seats reserved for them were filled; what was left of the Israeli team sat up forward, directly in front of the speakers' stand. The Israelis were easy to spot, because of their white yarmulkes, but it was hard to identify many of the others. The electronic scoreboards were blank; their computers had not been programmed for this kind of happening. (So inflexible are these swift machines, we learned yesterday, that the names of the Israeli athletes who were killed will nonetheless appear on future starting lists of competitors—with "Not Present" after them. Klein's office has explained, "We ask you to accept this as a technical necessity, and not as a lack of reverence." When you can't remove dead men from a lineup, there must be something wrong with the system.) In the absence of announcements or flags, many of the athletes could not be assigned national origins, and at this moment of woe that was a tiny blessing; the competitors had fleetingly lost their territorial and ideological separateness. It became known afterward that, understandably, none of the Arab athletes were present—nor, puzzlingly, were any of the Russians. Of the nearly five hundred members of the United States team, probably no more than a quarter turned out. The banned Rhodesians were there, though, black and white together; it was their only chance to appear in uniform on the stadium turf. While I was trying to see who was who, I heard a sports columnist behind me say to a confrère, "I don't care what happens, I'm still going to be on the Monday plane. I got football next weekend."

Willi Daume made a speech, and he was followed by two Israelis, then by President Gustav Heinemann of West Germany. Finally, at eleven-eighteen, came the eulogist everyone had been waiting for: Avery Brundage—Mr. Olympics for the past two decades. Some of his remarks were curiously inappropriate. He alluded to his old enemy commercialism, which seemed all the more irrelevant considering that every ticket to these supposedly uncontaminated Games bears on its back advertising for Mercedes-Benz—the make of car, as it happens, that Brundage and his fellow-officials ride around in—and to the business of the African nations' heavy-handed anti-Rhodesian activities before the Games. "Naked political blackmail," Brundage called it, and one wondered why he had to rekindle that now cooled flame. (A few hours later, Mr. Brundage felt constrained to issue a rare apology of his own, regretting any "misinterpretations" of his remarks, but not the remarks themselves. "There was not the slightest intention of linking the Rhodesia question, which was purely a matter of sport, with an act of terrorism universally condemned," he said. Still, he had alluded to both in one sentence, so it was not surprising that some people had assumed he meant to link them.) Eventually, he got around to what everyone was waiting for, and said, to ringing applause from most of the eighty thousand people there, that the Games would continue. So

372

continue they will, but whatever medals are won from now on will, in the minds of many of us, bear—along with the names of the winners, and through no fault of theirs—an invisible defect. Anyway, the Games will conclude, we have already been informed, with a standing ovation to the indomitable president of the I.O.C., while the scoreboard flashes "Thank You, Mr. Brundage," and a band plays "For He's a Jolly Good Fellow."

The memorial ceremony ended at eleven-twenty-six, and people began to leave, to the strains of Beethoven's "Egmont" Overture. The Israeli contingent stayed put after almost all the other athletes had gone; then its members rose, turned around, and, for a moment, faced their half-staffed flag. At eleven-forty-two, they filed out of the stadium for the last time. Some of the young Israeli women were in tears, and German security men were trying to shield them from photographers. One of the thwarted cameramen called one of the Germans a Fascist. To a photographer, there is no such thing as a moment of private grief.

The Olympic Village had been re-opened to the press by now, and I headed that way. It was quiet at the main entrance; the amplified music that usually blares out had been stilled. The first athlete I recognized was John Smith, the four-hundred-metre man, and I asked him if his father had caught up with him. Not yet, he said; I assume that they got together. Yesterday, I learned, Smith pulled up lame in the four-hundred-metre event, in which he had been the favorite. This may have been just as well for him, in a way; his fellow black Americans Vince Matthews and Wayne Collett, who came in first and second, were subsequently banned from all future Olympics because of their casual behavior—which the I.O.C. called "insulting" and which consisted of their conspicuously failing to stand at attention when "The Star-Spangled Banner" was played—during the award ceremony.

I walked on to 31 Connollystrasse. There were names on the door of Room 3—Berger, Friedman, Halfin, Slavin. All dead. Room 4 had been—to no avail—the team's first-aid room. Next to Room 5 was tacked an invitation, in four languages, from the Central Council of Jews in Germany to a Rosh Hashanah ceremony at a Holiday Inn downtown. The door to Room 5 was ajar, and a man with red-rimmed eyes stood there silently handing out to passersby a roster of the Israeli team, whose members, alive and dead, would be departing for home the following day. At that moment, along Connollystrasse came Village Mayor Troeger and an Israeli man I didn't recognize. They placed two wreaths on the ground in front of the building—red gladioli and yellow chrysanthemums from West Germany, red carnations and white lilies from Israel.

By midafternoon Wednesday, the Games were in full swing again, and to such an incredible degree had outward normality been restored that a hostess at the press center was reprimanded by her superior for not wearing knee socks. Before the dreadful events of Tuesday, I had considered myself lucky to have tickets to what was considered a super-event—the super-heavy-weight finals in weightlifting, starring the three-hundred-and-thirty-six-pound Soviet giant Vasily Alexeyev, who can lift five hundred and eighteen pounds past his paunch and over his head. Four of the eleven dead Israelis had been involved in this activity, and until yesterday noon I had doubted whether I wanted to use the ticket. Now, however, curiosity got the better of me, and I watched the monstrous heavyweights waddle in to the recorded strains of the Tijuana Brass. After that strident introductory note, a German official asked us all to observe a minute's silence in tribute to the four missing Israelis. Perhaps because time is so important here, during the allotted minute an interpreter began giving us French and English translations of the official's remarks; suddenly, and mercifully, though, his voice broke. After an hour, I had had enough of the straining and grunting and grimacing, so I left before the giant Alexeyev emerged once more triumphant. But it was something of a relief to watch men threatening physical harm only to themselves.

September 16, 1972

Sunshine Boy

In Neil Simon's newest hit, "The Sunshine Boys," the leading characters, played by Sam Levene and Jack Albertson, are two old vaudevillians who are generally supposed to be patterned after Smith and Dale, the legendary ornaments of the Palace and the Orpheum circuit, whose Dr. Kronkhite act can still be quoted almost verbatim by their fans. (Smith: "Are you the doctor?" Dale: "Yes." Smith: "I'm dubious." Dale: "How are you, Mr. Dubious?" Etc., etc.) In the Simon play, the old-timers are reunited after a long estrangement and decide to retire together to the Actors' Fund Home. Well, we were flabbergasted to learn that the real Smith and Dale did end up together at the real Actors' Fund Home, a pleasant residence in Englewood with a resident cast—average age in the mid-eighties—of thirty-six. Charlie Dale lived there until shortly before his death, in November, 1971, in a nearby nursing home, at the age of ninety; his *Times* obituary was illustrated with a photograph of Joe Smith poking him in the chest, just as Sam Levene is forever prodding Jack Albertson in "The Sunshine Boys." Joe Smith, who will turn eighty-nine on February 16th, is still at the Englewood home, and we paid him a pre-birthday visit last week. His once black pencil-thin mustache is gray and thicker, but he is mellow, lucid, and marvellously recollective, and names like Cantor, Jolson, Ed Wynn, and

Fanny Brice trip intimately and affectionately off his tongue. He is also slightly stooped, and understandably so: during his encores, forty or fifty years ago, he would carry three men off the stage. "Charlie and I were pretty good acrobats, too," he told us. "I always felt sorry for people who were *only* acrobats. If they were good, they stopped the show. So they always had to go on opening or closing, with the audience coming in or going out. I gave up acrobatics quite some time ago. I'm a cardiac case now, as a matter of fact, and I've got emphysema, but, as the old gag goes, 'my neck hurts, my back hurts, my leg hurts, and as for myself I don't feel too bad.'"

Mr. Smith escorted us to his room, a cheerful chamber decorated with old stage photographs, some recent watercolors he had done, and, among other memorabilia, a whistle engraved "Help Joe Smith, who helped the White Plains Police November 14, 1924." "It was a widows-and-orphans affair," he told us. "If you put every benefit Charlie and I played end to end, it would be endless." Mr. Smith went on to say that he has never met Neil Simon but has seen "The Sunshine Boys" twice. "I liked it very much," he said. "Of course, it's a paraphrase, but it's very well done. They do an unfinished symphony in *their* doctor sketch, where the one fellow has a heart attack. 'Unfinished symphony'—that has funny possibilities. The trouble with the show is that people think I have something to do with it. I'm even getting letters asking for seats, with checks enclosed made out to the Broadhurst Theatre. Not that it's all that true to life. I never did poke Charlie hard, though I'd point my finger at him and, if necessary, give him a little jab when I said 'You're making a mountain out of a mothball'—but I never hurt him. And as for all that about my spitting in his face during the act when I pronounced my 't's—why, it was *he* who spat in *my* face. He would say, 'For *pity's* sake, you aggravate me,' and like to drown me with that 'pity.' At first I'd come back with 'Please don't speak so fluidly; when you talk, you speak April showers,' And then, of course, the business of our not getting along for years is totally fictional. We'd argue about the act every now and then, but we were about as close as two men could be—almost inseparable—and when I moved out here after my second wife died, that was it for Charlie. 'I want to be with you,' he said. At the end, I had to take care of him. But I'm very contented here. I've had boats and homes, and no regrets. We have so much to read here that a person doesn't have to be lonesome. I read a lot. When I had my heart attack, I had a heavy Balzac with me, and when a fellow-resident went berserk I figured if he came at me I'd let him have it with the Balzac. My favorite authors over the years have been Montague Glass, Ben Hecht, and Octavus Roy Cohen. Neil Simon? I don't think of him so much as an author as—How should I put it? As, I guess, an in-law. Sort of a brother-in-law."

Smith and Dale worked so long together it boggles the imagination. They made their first professional appearance in 1898, just off the Bowery, and their last, at a Lambs Gambol, in 1968. Both from the lower East Side of New York, they literally bumped into each other during the Spanish-American War. Joe, fourteen, was a shipping clerk, Charlie a sixteen-year-old printer's apprentice, and, on rented bicycles, they collided at the intersection of Delancey and Eldridge Streets. "A crowd gathered, and was disappointed when we didn't have a fight," Smith recalled. "I started to walk my damaged bike back to the rental place, and he did, too, and I said 'What are you following me for?' and he said 'I'm not following you. You're walking ahead of me.' Now, that was a funny remark. We kept exchanging cracks, and when we got to the bicycle store, still hot at it, the proprietor said we reminded him of Weber and Fields, and introduced us. 'You got something in common,' he said. 'Take a tandem for an hour and get acquainted. It's on the house.' Not long afterward, we were rehearsing in the Weber and Fields Music Hall, and one day we heard applause from the dark, out front, and it turned out to be Weber and Fields themselves. It was a very moving incident."

They were Joe Sultzer and Charlie Marks then. They got their stage names when Joe's brother picked up some dirt-cheap posters that read "Smith and Dale, Blackface Singing and Dancing Comedians;" a printer had got stuck with the posters when the men who'd ordered them changed their minds and decided to work instead as Moran and Mack, later also known as the Two Black Crows. Smith and Dale got jobs at a Childs restaurant downtown while looking for engagements, and, after playing places like the Atlantic Garden and the Palace Garden, went on tour. "Were you in San Francisco before the earthquake?" Smith asked us. "*We* were. Not long after that, we did what I suspect may have been the first commercial. I would say, 'Name two of the principal oceans,' and Charlie would say, 'Atlantic and Pacific,' and I'd say, 'No, that's a tea company.' We used that for about three years, and then one day a guy came around backstage and identified himself as an A. & P. lawyer, and we apologized and said we wouldn't do it anymore, and he said, 'No, no, don't take it out. Keep it in and we'll pay you twenty-five dollars a week.' So we got to wondering about other possibilities. We had one bit where I'd ask Charlie to make me a sentence with the word 'delight,' and he'd say, 'De wind blew in de window and blew out de light.' 'Delight,' naturally, led us to 'deliver,' and so I was going to ask him for a sentence with that in it, and he would say, 'Carter's little pills are good for de liver.' We wrote to the pill company, figuring we had another sponsor for sure, but they weren't interested."

The Dr. Kronkhite number originated more or less by chance in 1906. ("Is this the office of Dr. Kronkhite?" "No, I'm his nurse." "The doctor's sick, too?") It evolved from a night-school act and a delicatessen act ("What's ailing you?" "Every time I eat a heavy meal I don't feel so hungry after"), and it became their staple. "We had to change the title in Canada during the war, when German names were unpopular," Smith said. That's the First World War. So we used 'I. M. Ill, M.D.' People are always asking me how gags start, and it's hard to say. At about the same time, in 1914, we were in Columbus, Ohio, walking behind two colored fellows, and heard one of them say, 'If he's going to monkey with me, I'm going to rub him out.' Pretty soon, Charlie and I are sitting at a table onstage and he's saying, 'I don't care what you say about me. My wife likes me,' and I say, 'I know women who like monkeys,' and he says, 'Don't monkey with me. I'm a man of letters,' and I say, as we start to fight, 'Sit down, or I'll rub you out.' One gag leads to another, you see. One gag always leads to another. We had an act called 'Sweetheart! Darling!,' in which I was a cuckolded husband and Charlie one of my wife's lovers. At the end, I shot them both. Sophie Tucker played my wife, and at the start she'd say, 'I had a wonderful dream last night. I dreamed you bought me a beautiful mink coat,' and I'd say, 'Well, if you have the same dream tonight, wear it in good health.' Then I'd go off to the office, and our French maid would let a succession of lovers in, and when Charlie had Sophie in his arms I'd come back and catch them and shoot them both, and the maid would rush in and ask what happened, and I'd say 'I've shot them!' and she'd fall into *my* arms. 'Sweetheart!' 'Darling!' Well, one night I pulled the trigger of my cap gun and there was no noise and the maid rushed in anyway, and when she asked what happened I ad-libbed 'They died of fright.' Years later, I had to fall back on that again in the 'Vanities' when a gun wouldn't work, and Earl Carroll came up to me afterward and said, 'Joe, that's what I call quick thinking.' I said 'Yes.' Why should I tell him it happened before?"

Mr. Smith rose to stretch, and poked us gently in the chest. "The experiences Charlie and I had over the years! Way back when he turned eighty, instead of an ordinary birthday card, I wrote him a poem that began, 'You're shooting in the eighties, which nobody can deny; you'll never get below that, no matter how hard you try.' He liked it so much I've used it since then for Harry Hershfield and George Abbott and Rube Goldberg and Bugs Baer when *they* all hit eighty. You know, I dream about Charlie every night. I don't *mean* to dream about him, but there he is. In one dream, I asked him how much money he had on him, and he said six dollars, and if I were playing the numbers I'd have played six the next day. But I don't mind dreaming about him. They're all happy dreams."

February 10, 1973

Tenors

Between the acts at the Metropolitan Opera House on one of its closing nights, we bumped into Schuyler Chapin, the Met's usually unruffled acting general manager. He was looking a bit tense, like an Aqueduct type who has had a bad day and needs something big in the last race to get out alive. "You don't happen to know of any hot new tenors anywhere, do you?" Mr. Chapin asked us. We said we didn't, and he sighed. "The tenor is the rarest of beasts," he said. "I am always searching for tenors. If somebody told me there was a promising tenor working a ferryboat, I would drop everything to go hear him. When I'm not dreaming about tenors, I wake up in the middle of the night and fret about them. It's a nightmare."

We urged Mr. Chapin to unburden himself, and he led us into his office, a spacious chamber, where he normally entertains opera buffs and soothes divas. We noticed that the only tenor whose picture graced the profusely illustrated walls was the late Edward Johnson, costumed for "Pagliacci." "He's there not as a tenor but as a general manager," Mr. Chapin said. "I couldn't put up any living tenors, because if I had one I'd have to have them all. That goes for sopranos, too. I suspect that all opera managers are obsessed with tenors. Sunday is my only day off, but if I hear there's a tenor I'm not familiar with at the City Opera, I'll abandon my family and scoot over there. Suppose he turned out to be a great tenor and I had passed him by. I would even go to a night club to hear a tenor. Not that I would be able to tell much about him there. You've got to hear him on a stage in a big house. The opera world is the last bastion of the natural voice—no mikes, no amplifiers. A singer's got to get out there and *sing*. But where do you find singers? When the National Council of the Met was holding auditions, a few months back, in Chicago, Los Angeles, and Honolulu, I went out to all the finals, hoping to snare a tenor. And you know how many tenors there were among thirty finalists? Just three. We've got one of them under contract—a fine young lyric tenor, who's only about twenty-seven. A neophyte. A soprano's voice comes into full bloom much earlier, but a tenor's doesn't freeze into what it's going to be until he's close to thirty. I could probably use my new tenor right now, but I want to nurse him along and treat him very carefully, because you can't take chances with anything as rare as a tenor. Now, real deep basses are hard to find, but somehow they always seem to turn up. Tenors don't. The tenor is the soft underbelly of the opera; he's what makes or breaks a company. For three weeks last December, we had Jess Thomas, Jon Vickers, Helge Brilioth, Nicolai Gedda, Luciano Pavarotti, and Richard Tucker all performing here at once, and I felt so good I wanted to put them all in a big jewel box and stash them away. And do you know what we had then? Well, I'll tell you. Among them were three of the only four solidly arrived, dependable heldentenors on earth. Only four of them for the whole world! Where it really comes to the crunch is Wagner, and the reason the 'Ring' was scarcely done for twenty years or so was simply the lack of heldentenors. Somehow they are in extremely short supply these days. You can find non-heldentenors, who'll do an acceptable 'Meistersinger' or 'Lohengrin,' but for 'Tristan' and the 'Ring' you need real coin. Oh, how I'd love to discover a topflight Wagnerian tenor! In my daydreams, a stranger sidles up to me and says, 'You can be anything you want,' and I say, 'I want to be the world's greatest heldentenor and sing the 'Ring.''"

Mr. Chapin paused for breath and then plunged on. "I guess it goes back to when I was a kid. I was intoxicated by Melchior and Flagstad. They became identity symbols to me—especially Melchior, who simply never gave a bad performance. Sure, his acting might be a little off some night, or he might seem bored, but, oh, the sound! Melchior had had a falling-out with Rudolf Bing, as everybody knows. This past winter, not long before Melchior died, I wrote to him in California and invited him to the opening of 'Siegfried.' He couldn't make it, but he replied that mine was the first letter he'd had from anybody at the Met in twenty-two years, and he sent his regards to all hands. I read his letter at a cast party after the performance, and it was a memorable moment for me, because at the end the company broke into thunderous applause. Melchior has left some important souvenirs to the Met, among them his portrait as Tristan, and this is moving for me, because I got my love of tenors—and, indeed, of all opera—from him. Heldentenors are so scarce a commodity today that when you schedule the 'Ring' you attempt to find out what Hamburg or Vienna or San Francisco is planning to do at the same time. Because everybody needs these same tenors. You have to book them two or three years in advance. You try to get all your other singers lined up well ahead of time, too—that goes without saying—but what you latch onto most firmly are tenors. What makes it worse is that tenors are so prone to get sick—even more than sopranos, it seems to me—that you always have to have a tenor of equal stature to cover the tenor you've got billed. And you have to do a delicate balancing act, because if nobody *gets* sick the major tenor covering another major tenor has got to have a chance to sing, too. There seems to be an especially acute sensitivity in the tenor department."

We suggested that perhaps we ought to be returning to our seat, but Mr. Chapin ignored the thought. "A couple of weeks ago, Placido Domingo, one of the rare handful of first-class *Italian* tenors, was supposed to do 'Trovatore' one night, and he felt ill at three that afternoon," he said. "You know what? We turned this huge city upside down, and there wasn't a single available substitute in New York. It was too late to change shows, so it was a question of Domingo's singing or our sending the audience home. Happily, he finally decided he was well enough to go on, and he did, and he sang very nicely, but we had a terrible few hours. If it had been a soprano, it would have been a problem, but not *that* kind of problem. Some tenors feel that New York is a woman singer's town, incidentally—a shrine for sopranos—and there's a certain truth to that, but tenors are beginning to make themselves felt. They're getting to be glamour boys. Why, the

Canadian Broadcasting Corporation has begun to follow Jon Vickers about, doing a documentary on him, and they'll be doing it for a whole year. Vickers is tough to work with, but for all the right reasons. Some of the parts he has to sing are crushingly *brutal*. So I don't blame tenors for being temperamental. The only break they have going for them is that they usually win the lady. There are plenty of villainous baritone roles, but there's hardly ever a villainous tenor. This attracts the public to tenors, because the public dotes on heroes in every area—sort of the way, I guess, that I dote on tenors. Now, you be sure to let me know if you hear of one, won't you?"

We promised, and tiptoed out.

May 5, 1973

Letter From Oregon

SALEM, FEBRUARY 11

On May 31, 1973, a day on which the *Times* carried two brief inside-page stories about gasoline and oil shortages, Governor Tom McCall held a press conference at the State Capitol here in which he said, *inter alia*, "The energy crisis is real. . . . It is obvious, when viewing the national ripples from Oregon's energy perspective, that it is time for the states to join together to press for regional coöperation and a national energy policy. . . . The problems faced by Oregon are faced by all the states, and by the planet." Energy was not much of a universal concern eight months ago, and the next day the *Times* didn't even mention McCall's call to arms.

That the state of Oregon, with two million people, or roughly one per cent of the national population, should have got the jump on most of the rest of the country in perceiving an energy crisis does not especially surprise Oregonians. In the last seven years, they have become accustomed to all sorts of innovative and bizarre goings on. They have laws so progressive that, by comparison, many other states look doddering. In Oregon, to help conserve materials and also keep roadsides tidy, nonreturnable bottles and pull-tab cans are prohibited. Oregon is far ahead of the Supreme Court on abortions. The establishment of new industries is discouraged unless they agree to be clean ones. The state's three hundred and fifty-nine miles of Pacific Ocean coastline have been barred to real-estate developers; so that the citizenry can get to the beaches, access roads are being built at three-mile intervals. One per cent of all state highway funds have been set aside for bicycle paths. Contraceptives can be sold from vending machines. Candidates for public office cannot spend more than certain prescribed and puny amounts on their campaigns; in 1970 there were twelve aspirants for the governorship, and among them all, in both the primary and the general elections, they disbursed less than four hundred thousand dollars. The Oregon legislature, which unblinkingly confronts social and environmental issues from which many state (and national) legislators would recoil, has even discussed passing a bill legalizing some form of euthanasia. On January 14th, in keeping with its bellwether behavior, Oregon became the first state of the Union to adopt a program of voluntary gasoline rationing. Oregon has become so energy-conscious that I was not surprised when a state senator informed me, with the air of a man who has done his homework, that the entire state of Oregon could function for twenty-four hours on the energy required to supply the paper napkins that the McDonald's hamburger chain uses up in a single day.

Oregon's forward-looking achievements have occurred in spite of—one could perhaps also argue because of—its ingrained conservatism. It is a state with an exceptional rural bias, even though sixty-seven per cent of its people live on twelve per cent of its land—a verdant north-south corridor that brackets the Willamette River, west of the Cascade Mountains. Oregon has no big cities. Its biggest, Portland, perched where Washington and Oregon meet at the intersection of the Willamette and the larger Columbia River, has only four hundred thousand inhabitants. Oregonians, in whatever part of the state they reside, tend to be small-townish, middle-of-the-roadish, and Waspish. They are also fairly prudish about some things. "Last Tango in Paris" is not advertised in the big family newspapers, and when the society columns mention a cocktail party it is usually called a reception. But at the same time Oregonians have displayed an extraordinary capacity for tolerance. One of their most hidebound enclaves is Josephine County, where the natives still make moonshine and concoct sausages out of illegally slaughtered bears. Josephine's earthy reputation has attracted quite a few young people disenchanted with conventional places. They have brought their own shadowy habits with them, in deference to which the rock-ribbed county has now established a highly enlightened drug program.

In a state where the local equivalent of the John Birch Society not long ago came within a hair of capturing the Republican Party apparatus, it is all the more startling that most of the progress has been instigated by a governor who is a Republican. (But then Oregon has long been politically paradoxical: it was the state that gave Wayne Morse to the country and then took him away.) Until just a few months ago, Tom McCall was practically unknown outside the Pacific Northwest. Now he is being talked of as a national candidate for 1976, though he will be sixty-three by then and has recently undergone an operation for cancer. The "Today" show sends camera crews out to follow him around. An organization in Alabama that covets him as the principal speaker for a banquet has three times changed its date to accommodate his tight schedule. "Imagine that—their wanting a guy who still believes in school busing!" McCall said to me several days ago. He was then also pondering which of two other invitations he should accept—an appearance with Laurance Rockefeller at a large gathering of environmentalists in Boston or a conflicting appearance with Nelson Rockefeller at a large political gathering in Portland. He was leaning toward Nelson. The Governor is himself a politically balanced blend of Massachusetts and Oregon. He was born in Massachusetts but conceived, as he is careful to remind the home folks, in Oregon. One of his grandfathers was Samuel W. McCall, ten times a congressman and three times governor of Massachusetts. His other grandfather, Thomas W. Lawson, was an enormously wealthy businessman and a moderately muckraking writer (he once paid thirty thousand dollars to have a carnation named after him), who owned a thousand-acre estate on the South Shore of Massachusetts—a stretch of littoral that the Governor's eighty-five-year-old mother, who moved to Oregon as a twenty-two-year-old bride, considers, with West Coast vagueness, to be part of Cape Cod. Before he went into politics, McCall was a journalist and television commentator in Portland, where he called himself after both grandfathers: Lawson McCall. He ran for Congress, and lost, in 1954. He was elected Oregon's secretary of state—the second-highest-ranking job, inasmuch as the state has no lieutenant governor—in 1964. He was first elected governor in 1966, and since state law prohibits more than two consecutive terms, he is now a lame duck. On going into politics, he began calling himself Tom. Not Thomas—just plain Tom. He is notorious for both his informality and his candor. His public utterances are notably slangy; speculating not long ago on the energy situation in the Far East, he declared, "The People's Republic [of China] will slurp up all the oil in Indonesia." McCall writes most of his own stuff, but for a while, to lend him a literary hand, he had an avant-garde poet as a speechwriting assistant. The poet once inserted a generous hunk of the libretto of "Hair" into an address the Governor was giving to some thirty-third-degree Masons. "My talk was quite well received," the Governor told me. "Fortunately, the excerpt I used was one of the prettier parts of the show, and, besides, I don't believe many members of that particular audience were acquainted with the production." McCall's daily morning conferences with his staff are open to the press (which once watched him devote half an hour to wondering whether a solitary welfare recipient's telephone should be removed; the Governor solved the problem by taking up a collection in the room to pay the bill), and so, occasionally to the dismay of the other principals, are many of the meetings he has with lobbyists and importuning callers. Indeed, among the bills passed by the quixotic state legislature in 1973 was one specifying that all gatherings of state officials at which a decision could theoretically be arrived at—a cocktail party, say, or reception, with a majority of a legislative body in the room—must be open to the press. These days, when some state officials make conference calls to far-flung deputies, they invite reporters to listen in on the conversation, and for the benefit of those who can't eavesdrop they provide tapes. When, in the summer of 1973, the Governor had cancer surgery, he insisted that the newspapers be allowed to publish starkly clinical bulletins on his condition. After he recovered, he wrote a Sunday-newspaper piece entitled "My Head-On Confrontation with Cancer," illustrated with a diagram of the prostate.

It is one of McCall's homespun traits to keep telling people that while they are welcome to visit Oregon, he would just as soon they settled elsewhere. To his professed chagrin, his campaign has backfired; perhaps because of the considerable attention to Oregon that he has generated, the state's population has been increasing at a far greater clip than that of either California or Washington. He himself had no hand in distributing a batch of inhospitable "ungreeting cards," but he has acquiesced in his staff's doing so. Most of these cards stress the fact that it normally rains hard in Oregon. "Oregonians never water their lawns—they simply drain them," says one, and another says "People in Oregon don't tan in the summertime—they rust!" Still another goes "Tom Lawson McCall, Governor, on behalf of the citizens of the Great State of Oregon, cordially invites you to visit Washington or California or Idaho or Nevada or Afghanistan." All this, of course, is tongue-in-cheek, but McCall is perfectly serious about preserving Oregon's robust natural environment. He has been an environmentalist from way back. In 1937, fresh out of journalism school at the University of Oregon, he was an unpaid public-relations man for the Latah County Wildlife Association. In 1961, he produced a much acclaimed television documentary, "Pollution in Paradise," about the Willamette River, which was then dreadfully befouled for most of its three hundred miles. Today, the entire river is swimmable and is full of fish, owing, in part, to McCall's having appointed himself chairman of the State Sanitary Authority when he assumed the governorship in 1967. Toward the end of his first four-year term, two months before he stood for reëlection, the American Legion was about to descend, twenty thousand strong, on Portland for its annual national convention. From what seemed at the time to be reasonably reliable sources—among them Attorney General John Mitchell—Governor McCall heard that fifty thousand countercultural delegates were planning to attend a concurrent People's Army Jamboree in the same city. A conceivably nasty confrontation appeared imminent. To avert it, the Governor took some of the usual steps. He called out the National Guard. He had a helicopter revved up for crowd dispersal. He insisted, however, that the Guardsmen be unarmed and that the helicopter be loaded not with tear gas but— Portland being the City of Roses—with rose petals. There was no confrontation, chiefly because of another highly unorthodox step that McCall took. He announced that during the American Legion convention the state of Oregon would put on a ten-day Woodstocklike rock festival at McIver State Park, thirty miles outside of Portland. The festival was gratefully attended by some thirty-five thousand young people. It was the first public pot party any governor had given. (Since then, Oregon has decreed that the possession of marijuana is a trifling offense; anyone caught with it is liable merely to a fine, and does not get saddled with a criminal record.) "I gave the party because I wanted to save the most lives and the most property, and, in fact, the only damage of any kind was one busted four-by-six-inch windowpane at Portland State University," McCall told me. "The weather was warm, and at McIver there was a good deal of nude bathing and so forth. As a result, I figured that I'd get torn to pieces politically and would certainly lose the election. What I didn't know was that my opponent had just taken a poll and learned that people thought my Achilles' heel was indecisiveness. So when I went on radio and television, statewide, and proclaimed firmly that nobody was to be hassled in Oregon because he was young and bearded, on the one hand, or because he had fought for his country, on the other, people concluded, to my astonishment, that I could be very decisive after all, and they admired me for that—if not for my acceptance of grass-smoking and skinny-dipping—and I won."

Along with being perhaps the most open-minded of all extant governors, McCall is indisputably the tallest. He stands six feet five. In recent months, there have been numerous stories in Oregon and elsewhere about the Northwest's legendary Sasquatch, a huge, humanoid seven-or-so-foot creature akin to the Abominable Snowman of Tibet. The Sasquatch, which is presumed to dwell in Oregon's fathomless forests, is alleged to have left monstrous tracks all over the place, and therefore is sometimes also known as Bigfoot. A local joke has it that the Governor, whose shoe size is twelve, has made the prints himself, to scare off tourists. Like McCall, the Sasquatch is a larger-than-ordinary ornament of the scene which attracts more visitors than it repels. Oregon had ten and a half million tourists in 1971. In 1972, ungreeting cards notwithstanding, it had almost twelve million. "Think of it!" the Governor told me. "Twenty-four million feet pattering over our flora! Could it be that our visitors are destroying what they've come to visit? We've trimmed our budget for tourism to the bone, and we're confining our out-of-state advertising to things like the *National Geographic*, on the theory that its readers have greater respect for nature than those of the—well, those of other magazines." In January, a few days after gas rationing began in Oregon, the Governor disclosed that he was giving up his official Lincoln Continental and was switching to a compact Audi. A few weeks before, at a conference of Republican governors, he had made a speech about energy in which he said, "The people are fed up with garishness. They feel assaulted by blinking, flashing, rotating, ostentatious waste." He had also referred to large American automobiles as "Belchfire

Eights" and "Gas Glutton Supremes." Afterward, Governor William Milliken, of Michigan, told McCall how much he admired what the Oregonian had said. A reporter for a Detroit newspaper asked Milliken if he had also admired the Belchfire-Glutton characterizations. Milliken quickly remembered that he had missed that part of the speech.

McCall began to get concerned about the energy situation in 1971, soon after the start of his second term. Oregonians are conditioned to the fickleness of natural resources, since eighty-two per cent of their electric power is hydroelectric, and their economic stability—like that of neighboring Washington—is in thrall to the water level of the huge dams along the Columbia River. Surmising that some long-range planning might facilitate decisions that he and succeeding governors would have to make about state problems, McCall recruited a small task force of social scientists and immersed them in a think tank. On surfacing, they revealed themselves as convinced that a promising answer to some of the state's—and the world's— dilemmas was to be found through energetics, the system, devised by the environmental scientist Howard Odum, whereby everything on earth is measured in terms of net energy. McCall's tank thinkers (now formally recognized by the state legislature as the Office of Energy Research and Planning) were interested less in the cost of shoplifting measured in dollars, for instance, than in the cost of shoplifting measured in British thermal units—which, in the case of food pilferage alone, according to their arcane calculations, represented a hundred and eighty million B.T.U.s of food energy in Oregon every day.

It was a lucky thing for the Governor that he had his people concentrating on energy, because in the spring of 1973 they were swiftly able to furnish him with recommendations for action when Oregon found itself suddenly faced with an energy crisis. There had been little snow that winter. There was, uncharacteristically, little rain that spring. The reservoirs were at their lowest level in nineteen years. The electric-power situation looked disheartening, if not disastrous. On August 21, 1973, McCall declared a statewide energy emergency. "We've had the idea that energy in abundance would be forever at our fingertips," he said. "We've become careless. We've installed all the modern conveniences, used them without regard to energy supply, and now the piper must be paid. It takes six hundred pounds of coal to provide the energy to operate one sixty-watt bulb for a year. Turn off that bulb!" The Governor instructed all state employees to turn off those bulbs, to go without air-conditioning, and to do whatever else they could to conserve energy. He had the hot-water taps in state washrooms removed or rendered inoperative. Within a month, state agencies had cut their consumption of electricity by nearly thirty per cent, but McCall felt that the rest of his constituency wasn't following suit sufficiently, and he decided to take a drastic step. He ordered that all outdoor display lights be shut off.

"The risk of catastrophe is so great that we must make no exceptions," he said. The state legislature was then out of session, and there was some doubt whether McCall had the authority to issue such an edict, but he did it anyway, not so much for direct savings—all the outdoor lighting accounted for less than one per cent of the state's normal consumption of electricity—as for psychological purposes. "You couldn't expect anybody to snap off his lights at home if he could look out of his window and see a used-car lot so ablaze with lights you could also see it from Mars," McCall told me. There were yelps of indignation from all sides, especially in Portland, where the proprietors of blacked-out restaurants and motels could look out of *their* windows across the river to Vancouver, Washington, and see a firestorm of neon. Airline pilots reported that at night they could easily tell when they were over Oregon; it was that dark void between San Francisco and Seattle. Actually, not everybody obeyed the injunction. The Governor thereupon instructed his Public Utility Commissioner, Richard W. Sabin, to deal with noncompliance, after due warning, by ordering private utilities to shut off power to the transgressors. Sabin proceeded to draw up the only Enemies List in recent Oregon history. It has six hundred and eighty-six names on it. But, as it turned out, he never had to use it. (He has never made it public, either.) The Governor, for his part, rather hoped that someone grievously affected by the curtailment—someone, say, in the illuminated-sign business—would take him into court to test his authority. "There was one motel owner who I was sure would accommodate me," McCall told me. "But just before he went to see his lawyer he went to the hospital to see his dying mother, and she said, 'Son, obey the Governor,' and that was the end of that."

While he was at it, in August, McCall also told the drivers of state-owned vehicles not to exceed fifty-five miles an hour—most people in Oregon had practically never driven under seventy—and on November 13th he politely asked the public to follow suit in that respect. (Oregon is a well-mannered state: its highway signs don't just say "End Construction;" they say "End Construction—Thank You for Your Patience.") McCall chose fifty-five as the appropriate speed limit because he thinks fifty is too slow. "I tried it last week on a return trip from Portland," he announced in November, "and felt within myself that fifty-five was eminently more acceptable." The Governor also proposed that, to save heating fuel, all schools be closed from December 14th to January 14th, with the missed time to be made up later, when it was warmer. He was at once subjected to a barrage of protests from teachers, who didn't fancy having their work schedules altered, and from mothers, who pointed out that probably just as much electricity would be consumed by kids at home staring at television as by kids in school staring at blackboards. Moreover, the Governor was asked, where would the extra school days come from? Oregon produces vast quantities of fruits and vegetables (Salem is one of the nation's principal packing centers for beans and beets), and had McCall forgotten that Oregon school-closing dates in the spring have traditionally been geared to strawberry-picking time? McCall, who is nothing if not flexible, beat as dignified a retreat as he could, but he didn't entirely abandon his pursuit of schoolchildren. He proclaimed an Energy Crisis Week for early December, and had his Superintendent of Public Instruction get out a flock of instructional material to be used during it. By that time, it had begun to rain heavily, and the hydroelectric crisis was over. The outdoor lights went back on, and the Public Utility Commissioner locked his list of enemies, unpunished, in a file cabinet. (By mid-January, Oregon was experiencing its worst floods in a decade, and the Governor who had been preaching drought six months earlier found himself proclaiming much of the state a disaster area and riding around in a boat to inspect flood damage.) Energy Crisis Week was nonetheless diligently observed. The all-around feeling was that it would be good for young Oregonians to learn something about a problem that would probably be with them throughout their lives—to help create, as a handbook turned out by the Oregon Board of Education put it, "a generation of environment-conscious citizens." The book suggested that primary-school children be taught to spell "watt" and "volt;" that sixth graders be offered a prize (a battery-powered one, preferably) for the best energy-saving idea; that junior-high students study the construction of a nuclear electric facility; and that high-school students list the alternatives to automobile ownership. One school had a Sweater Day, another an Arctic Day, still another a Walking Wednesday. In Eugene, business-course students used non-electric typewriters. Cold lunches were served at some schools, and kids who habitually drove their own cars to school made the supreme sacrifice: they switched to bikes.

Thus, Oregonians of all ages were indoctrinated for the gasoline shortage when it hit them in December, and that was just as well, for it hit them particularly hard. Governor McCall himself got stuck in an endless line at a filling station; it seemed as though half the one million eight hundred thousand vehicles registered in his state were bumper to bumper ahead of him. No one has yet figured out precisely why gasoline was in shorter supply in Oregon than in most other states. There were rumors (a Portland institution called the Rumor Control Center was made privy to some of them) that wholesalers were punishing Oregon for having taken the lead in crying crisis. What was more likely was that Oregon's uncommonly high percentage of independent service stations had a harder time getting fuel from wholesalers than the wholesalers' own retail outlets. Moreover, the state's allocation for December, 1973, was based on its consumption during the same month one year earlier, and the previous December had been so cold that a lot of people had sensibly holed up at home. The Governor was holding emergency meetings (all open and duly reported) with gas-station proprietors and trying to decide how to cope with the unhappy gas situation when a young man named Don Jarvi, director of the state's Energy Information Center, which McCall had set up last September, had a revelation. It occurred to him while he was driving the fifty miles from Portland to Salem that the awful snarls at service stations (not to mention the hoarding these tieups had inspired) might be alleviated if a voluntary rationing program were to be adopted, with—Saturdays and Sundays excepted—cars bearing license plates ending in odd numbers being allowed to get gas on odd-numbered days, and even-numbered days being reserved for even-numbered plates. (Oregon also has some seven thousand plates with initials or words on them. Known as custom plates, or more widely, "snob plates," they cost twenty-five dollars extra, and the income they provide is used to clean up highway litter. They would arbitrarily be lumped in with the even-numbered crowd.) Reaching his office at eight-twenty the next morning, Jarvi at once passed along his idea to Robert G. Davis, the Governor's executive assistant. Davis, a distinctive politician himself, being the father of triplets, thought the scheme sounded great, and at eight-thirty he presented it to the Governor and to the rest of his staff at their regular morning meeting. They approved it. By nine-thirty, it had also been approved by a group of state legislators who have interim powers when the legislature is not sitting. Jarvi returned to Portland in the afternoon to attend a meeting with representatives of oil companies and service stations. They agreed to go along. The Governor forthwith announced the plan. On the six-thirty television news that evening, Jarvi heard that the brainstorm he'd had less than twenty-four hours earlier had become a *fait accompli*. Oregon can move fast. A fortnight later, the state of Hawaii—where, as it happened, Governor McCall had been sojourning during Energy Crisis Week—adopted the same plan but went even further and made it mandatory instead of voluntary. In Oregon, meanwhile, the long, irritating lines radiating out from service-station pumps had all but vanished.

On the fourteenth of January, the first day of voluntary rationing, I had a ten-o'clock appointment at Governor McCall's office, and by mischievous design I kept my speedometer needle at sixty all the way down from Portland, where I had spent the night. I had two reasons for defying the Governor. I wanted to be sure to get some gas in Salem (I had an even-numbered plate), and I wanted to find out how many cars would pass me. Nobody did. When I told the Governor that I had also had no trouble getting gas, he looked a mite envious; he has license plate "1" and had to wait until the next day to tank up. McCall's office is a rather small room—very small, considering his size—in a spacious building, but he has a larger chamber nearby that he can use for receiving delegations. It was only sixty-three degrees in his office—sixty-eight is the maximum temperature he permits in state buildings—and he was wearing a blue cardigan under a tweed jacket. Among the bric-a-brac with which his office was decorated were a model of the only seven-masted clipper ship ever built (the Thomas W. Lawson, constructed in Quincy, Massachusetts, in 1902 for his grandfather), a commemorative rifle (he is, after all, governor of a wilderness state), a plaque awarded him by the Associated Oregon Industries (inscribed "Tom McCall, Oregon's 'Livability' Governor, who has done more to restore, enhance, and preserve the enviable environment of Oregon than any other man"), and a photograph of himself with an eight-pound steelhead. "I netted her last July, just before my cancer operation, while I was fishing one of Zane Grey's old streams, the North Umpqua, in the south of the state," the Governor said. "It's the first steelhead I ever caught on a fly; when it comes to that, I've caught only eighteen of them by any means in fifty years. It took me almost an hour to land her, and she was so exhausted she died in my hands. I was so sorry I'd ever caught her." Conspicuous on his desk was the American Heritage Dictionary of the English Language. "I love words," the Governor said. "I got interested in them when we were kids on a ranch in eastern Oregon—there were five of us children in all—and there was only this little country school. My mother asked a teacher what she could do about educating us, and he asked her if she had any books at home, and she said yes, and he asked how many, and she said about five thousand, and he said, 'Read them all aloud.' So she did, for three hours every night. Before I was twelve, we'd been all the way through Tolstoy, Dickens, and Thackeray. I can't conjugate verbs or parse sentences, but I had the greatest education in the world. My mother had her first book published when she was eighty. She'd been working on it forty years, but she had a lot of other things to do."

I had expected to spend perhaps fifteen or twenty minutes with McCall, but he didn't seem to be in any hurry to get on about his business. Around noon, he pulled a package of saltines from a desk drawer, nibbled on one, invited me to stick around for lunch, and asked his secretary to rustle up some sandwiches. I learned later from Bob Davis that McCall starts getting hungry at eleven-thirty, because that's when he normally has lunch (in, normally, the employees' cafeteria, where he grabs the first vacant chair). The reason for the early hour is that the Governor often holds open house for visitors at twelve-thirty. A few weeks ago, a seventy-eight-year-old woman told him, as they exchanged hellos, that it was the first time in her life she had ever shaken hands with anybody interesting.

Through his sandwich, McCall went on to say that what he would like most to be remembered for was as the bearer of what he calls the Oregon message—"a story of innovation and regeneration that can actually be used anywhere," he explained, adding, "We're trying to export the hope and the formula, and my mail is full of letters urging that what we've started here be spread. We may have saved more energy per capita than any other state so far—somewhere around six per cent in electricity alone to date—but, if so, it's not because we're more capable than anybody else. It's simply that we were first. My neck is always out, because I approach everything with a sense of hope, trying to see how things can be done. I like to say that in the timeliness of an idea probably lies its greatest utility. You can spend two years studying something, but by the time you conclude that it's a good thing to do, the best time for doing it may have passed. Well, at least the whole country is now energy-conscious. It's great to have everybody else turned on, too. The President may have been too late and too mild, but, thank God, even he finally came along."

I asked the Governor what he had in mind after his term ends next January. "It will depend on my vigor, to begin with," he replied. "I'll know in several months whether the cancer will recur. If it doesn't there's been talk of my filling a Tom McCall Chair of Broadcast Journalism and Political Science at Oregon State University. That might be fun; I seem to get along well with the young. But I would hate to give up active participation in politics. *That's* been fun, too, and I've particularly enjoyed serving as unofficial pool man for the press at governors' conferences. I guess I've been unusually revealing about what goes on inside them, but I've never taken anything embarrassing out of a meeting. The first one I ever attended was a conference of Western governors, in 1967, at West Yellowstone. It was like a high-school operetta. Twelve nobodies, including me, sat around until, with a fanfare of trumpets and on a white horse, in rode Ronald Reagan. My reports on these conferences are apt to be couched in journalist's language, and my wife always has her foot ready to stamp on mine if my imagination gets too dominant. Just before another such meeting, at Jackson Hole, she got temporarily separated from me. A political reporter from San Francisco came up and said that he was desperate for a story that day, and I thought for a moment and reflected that Nixon was giving California more federal funds per capita than any other state—to keep Ron Reagan's support—so I came up with the observation that Reagan was holding Nixon hostage. Later, I had second thoughts about saying that, but by then it was already in the papers. Reagan arrived later that day, and he came walking in my direction and I said, 'Hi, Ron!' and he turned up his collar. 'God damn it all,' he finally said, 'all you had to do was call me in Sacramento to find out that what you said wasn't true,' and I said, 'But, Ron, if I'd done that there wouldn't have been any story.' Politicians never forgive you. At the time Wally Hickel was fired, I had a news conference and said, 'I think you'll find there'll be others. The President is clearing his decks before going after a second term. Even the Vice-President might be dropped, the way he's been running around the country carrying a knife under his shawl.' Well! There was a meeting of Republican governors at Sun Valley right after that, and

Agnew was coming. Privately, most of the other governors felt the same way about him that I did, but they wouldn't say so. When Ted arrived, he took me aside and said, 'Tom, I'm just mad as hell at you,' and I said, 'Why, you've got no business going around polarizing the country.' Then he made a speech, and a reporter asked me what I thought of it, and I said, 'One rotten, bigoted little speech.' The next morning, the governors had a private meeting with Agnew, and in the middle of it somebody handed him a piece of yellow teletype paper. He looked at it, and his hand began to tremble, and then he looked at me and said, 'Tom, you couldn't have said this.' I asked him what the trouble was now, and he said, 'You're quoted here as saying I gave a "rotten, bigoted little speech" last night.' I said, 'I'm not positive I used the word "little."' The terrible thing was that none of the other governors laughed. I was all set until then to be the chairman of the next Republican governors' conference, but my candidacy suddenly disappeared. I did get asked, though, to be on the Republican Governors' Campaign Committee for next fall and go around speaking for every nominee. I had to decline. As I said in my letter turning them down, I believe that issues are more significant than party labels, and—to quote myself—'I couldn't subscribe to a committee effort that, in certain instances, would turn out to be anathema to my conscience.' You can have a copy of my letter if you like."

In the office of one of McCall's assistants, I had noticed a bulging manila folder of letters to the Governor laid out where anyone who walked in could see it. The folder was labelled "Presidency." I asked McCall about his national ambitions, if any. "America is beginning to open up," he said. "We've got an inherently good system. We've just got to get the right people to make it work. If I had to run for President to sell the Oregon message—to encourage more innovative and daring actions, that is—I would do it. But that will depend on a lot of things, and in any event the message is more important than the messenger." At that point, Bob Davis stuck his head in the door and said there was a new crisis—something, I gathered, about Oregon construction men's being enraged by a new law that contained all sorts of stiff provisions protecting home buyers from unscrupulous builders. There was time for one last question, so I asked the Governor to tell me frankly whether or not he believed in the existence of the legendary Sasquatch. "I have no position on Bigfoot," McCall replied. "I guess it's about the only thing so far that I haven't taken a position on."

February 25, 1974

Booing at the Opera

Having heard that the Metropolitan Opera, of all genteel institutions, has lately been the scene of considerable booing, we went, as is our wont, straight to the top, and invited its general manager, Schuyler Chapin, to join us for lunch and discuss the grisly subject. Mr. Chapin looked fit enough on arrival, but he sat down gingerly and declined a drink. "My back's been bothering me ever since I helped put on the Bernstein 'Mass' when the Kennedy Center opened," he said. "And now my ulcer's acting up again. I'm afraid I had a fight this morning and lost my temper."

"With a singer?" we asked.

"Good Lord, no—with a trustee," he said. "One *expects* to fight with singers."

Mr. Chapin forwent some recommended scampi, ordered poached eggs, and plunged into the matter at hand. "I first became aware of the booing two years ago," he said. "It didn't worry me too much then, because it was usually aimed at conductors, who were, although perhaps I shouldn't say it, not always at their finest that season. But then, one night, after a practically flawless, absolutely gorgeous 'Otello,' out came James Levine for his bow, and he got booed, and I couldn't figure out why. Next, Jimmy McCracken appeared, and there were boos mixed in with his applause. He was furious. He was a wild man when he returned backstage, and he said, 'I don't care if they don't like it, but you simply don't boo somebody who's just sung "Otello."'"

Mr. Chapin paused for a sip of iced tea. "Last year, there was so much booing of artists that I didn't let one of them take a solo bow at all. I prefer not to mention his name, because, honestly, he hadn't been well, and he took a chance and went on anyway, and he failed. But conductors still got it, and get it, the worst. There is one booer around now who always boos James Levine. That I know. My ears tell me. It's the same sound every time. We've tried to zero in on him, with ushers moving down the aisles and across the front, but we haven't identified him yet, even though now, when Levine comes out, all our performers are searching the audience for him. He seems to have had a ripple effect. Last winter, Levine conducted our first performance of John Dexter's production of 'Les Vêpres Siciliennes.' Now, Dexter never goes to opening nights, but this time I'd persuaded him to, and to appear onstage. When he did, what a cascade of booing! At one point, part of the audience was booing and another part was trying to drown that part out with cheers, and the cheerers and booers were having at each other with no discernible reference to anybody else. The booing stopped when the artists came out, but I was thinking, Good God, what's going to happen when Levine appears? Oddly, that night he got warm applause—except for that one persistent booer. But it was different for poor Dexter. The booing was so *loud*. And to think I'd talked him into being there!

"These days, *I* get booed, too. I had to announce a cast change one night. There was no way our scheduled soprano could croak herself out of bed. I phrased it very carefully and got some applause, and thought to myself,

You're home free. Home free! I was out by a mile. 'Boo, Chapin!' 'Down with Chapin!' 'Bring back Bing!' There was so much of it when I came off that two stagehands were waiting to catch me, because they assumed I would faint. I'm even getting crank phone calls at home. One of them was long distance at four-thirty in the morning from a man who said he was in Texas. I could hear music in the background; it sounded like an opera, but I couldn't make out which one. 'The Met stinks' was one of the few things he had to say that weren't obscene. Another guy called and threatened my life. He said there was good precedent for it, because he was Al Capone's nephew and Capone had once threatened Mr. Bing, and, as a matter of fact, Bing did once have a bodyguard. I'm afraid I'm going to have to get an unlisted phone. It's a nuisance not being in the phone book, but it's a worse nuisance being awakened in the middle of the night for a private booing session.

"I've heard it argued that booing at the opera shows that the audience *cares*. I don't buy that. To me, it's a collapse of manners. Why do you boo somebody who's putting out his or her best? What does it accomplish except to insult the artist? Why not just withhold your applause? Which can be bad enough. We're not in Europe, after all. I've been asked if the booers are a claque of sorts, who are paid to boo. I don't know. But I wouldn't be surprised. I like to hope, though, that it isn't an organized thing. One has the feeling nowadays that certain people are coming to the opera almost *wishing* that a performance will flop—that she won't hit that high C or he that high D. I refer to the whole phenomenon of booing as a kind of opera gladiatorship. It's always been true that operagoers are very passionate people, but now you have to take a deep breath before confronting them. Every time I go out front, I feel as though I were in the Colosseum, facing a crowd that's looking forward to the lions' being loosed on me. It doesn't help the ulcer."

October 21, 1974

Boffos and Bustos

At two-thirty on the afternoon of December 3, 1973, Arthur Loeb Mayer, Adjunct Professor of Cinema at the University of Southern California, left the apartment his wife, Lillie, and he were occupying in Los Angeles and went to the U.S.C. campus for a haircut. Then, between four and six, he conducted a semi-weekly class called Cinema 562, the Economics of the Motion Picture Industry—at Von KleinSmid Hall. Next, disdaining a proffered ride and also disdaining a cane that Lillie, who was concerned about his health, had urged on him, he walked to the Faculty Center to treat a visiting East Coast friend to a cup of coffee. At seven, after walking back to Von KleinSmid, Mayer presided genially while a guest lecturer—his old friend Max Youngstein, who used to help run United Artists and recently engineered the success of "Billy Jack"—talked to a reconvened Cinema 562 about some of his experiences in the film industry.

Mayer, a gadabout New Yorker who at other times of the year is also Lecturer in Communication at Stanford and Visiting Professor of Drama and Lecturer in Film at Dartmouth, decided to become a full-time motion-picture pedagogue when he was seventy-seven. By then, he had achieved elder-statesman status in a relatively young industry. As a boy, he had seen some of the earliest movies made—the nickelodeon fare that was flickeringly unveiled in 1896, when he was ten. He had been engaged for some sixty-two years in the production, the distribution, the exhibition, the promotion, and, as a writer for various publications, the historicization of films. He had been one of the pioneer American importers of foreign films. He had operated his own New York theatre for many years. He and his wife had been lifelong film buffs. Indeed, Mayer had been involved in just about every aspect of movies except acting, and some of his students maintain that he has more than made up for that with his classroom performances, which a Stanford graduate has admiringly likened to Hal Holbrook's Mark Twain impersonation. The difference is that Mayer is portraying himself, with random digressions for imitations of such old occupational cronies as Samuel Goldwyn, Adolph Zukor, and assorted Warner Brothers. Once, hearing that a Dartmouth sophomore was scoring points at parties with impersonations of *him*, Mayer begged the student for a private demonstration. Assessing the takeoff, the Professor judged that there were certain marked technical deficiencies in his own elocution. So, at the age of eighty-five, he went out and took voice lessons.

Mayer, by his own rough reckoning, has seen at least twenty-six thousand pictures—an average of more than ten a week for more than half a century—although, sensibly, he hasn't sat clear through every one of them. He has never walked out on any of his all-time favorite directors: Ingmar Bergman, Jean Renoir, and Jean-Luc Godard. Max Youngstein—like Mayer, an uncommonly erudite pillar of their business—fancied himself an obsessive moviegoer until he met the Mayers, who do everything together, including suffering much of the way through deservedly unknown pictures. Youngstein, after his lecture at U.S.C., told some students, "When I first met Arthur and Lillie, thirty years or so ago, I couldn't believe it—they were seeing more movies than I was. If you mentioned some obscure little Polish documentary to them that they *hadn't* seen, they'd drop whatever they were doing and take off after it like bird dogs. But Arthur's importance in the industry doesn't derive from any statistical accomplishments—it derives from the fact that he was one of the first to make people aware that motion pictures were a truly international art and an international form of communication. He was, further, almost unique in the industry in that he was an intellectual. The great film magnates of history were intuitive men, who made decisions by gut reactions. To a business ruled by men like that, who tended to be condescending toward anybody who had had any formal education and hadn't worked—or clawed—his way up from the bottom, Arthur, who came from a fairly affluent family and had graduated from Harvard, brought something even more puzzling than these strange academic credentials: he brought a highly developed intelligence. You could have dinner with him and discuss *anything*, and that was a refreshing antidote to the stifling talk of most of the people in the business, who were so maniacally dedicated to their work, in or out of their offices, that their idea of a trenchant philosophical dialogue was one that began with 'How did you open up in Keokuk?' Arthur, unlike so many people of his age, is concerned—as he always has been—not with the past but with what is current: the new books, the new plays, the young directors and stars, and the whole social and cultural scene of which they and he are a part. He has been a kind of external human being in an ingrown business—a person who, to the astonishment of many of his peers, actually belongs to the outside world. The movie industry, accordingly, used to be almost afraid of him. They thought he was over-intellectualized. [*Variety* once called him "a very esoteric fellow."] They were scared of him the way politicians were scared of Adlai Stevenson. In a business of highly specialized small minds, he was one of the rare individuals with an overall concept of how that business affected the cultural and political aspects of our lives. He filled an essential need, for which he has never been given enough credit: he served as a bridge between the recognition of creative talent and the making of money out of it. And this is what he's been bringing to young people through his teaching—a sense of what the industry is all about. That he should have been relegated *only* to teaching is one of the saddest and dumbest things the industry has ever let happen. He should at least have been president of a big film company. But he was considered too intellectual, too witty, and people were suspicious of him. How could a man with a first-rate mind, they would wonder, be in the motion-picture business to begin with?"

The closest Mayer ever got to holding the kind of job that Youngstein has envisioned for him was serving for a couple of years—from 1950 to 1952—as executive vice-president and chief administrator of something called the Council of Motion Picture Organizations. "The industry needed, or thought it needed, an outfit that could represent all its diverse branches, and the council was forthwith set up, with great fanfare—practically everything but my footprints in cement," Mayer once explained. "I had a lavish suite of offices in the Paramount Building in New York, a galaxy of starletlike secretaries, and crackling letterheads with everybody's name on them. I went to meetings all over the country and made ringing speeches, and I even got paid reasonably well. But the council functioned as I thought it should only as long as the people in the industry believed that they had common interests—which turned out, not terribly much to my surprise, to be not terribly long."

A number of countries—Canada, Britain, France, several of the Iron Curtain nations—have for quite some time taken education in the field of motion pictures seriously. A few of them have national film schools. But until the mid-sixties—which, as it happened, was when Mayer began teaching full time—few institutions in the United States, let alone the government, considered movies a fit subject for sober study. No particular training was deemed necessary for employment in the industry; the way to get a job in it was to know somebody—or, better still, to be somebody's nephew. Now not a bad way is to know Arthur Mayer or to have been one of his prize students, but back in the 1963-64 academic year, according to Mayer, there were only a hundred and fifty-two college-level courses being offered anywhere in America in movie history, criticism, or appreciation, and nearly all these were given on just nine campuses. In the 1973-74 academic year, by contrast, six hundred and thirteen institutions of higher learning—in recognition of or resignation to the fact that to many of their students films were the most fascinating, and perhaps the most significant, of all cultural media—were known to be giving credit courses in motion pictures or television. A hundred and ninety-four of these institutions offered degrees in films (or in television), and more than twenty-two thousand students were enrolled in film-education programs. One upshot of this was that a whole textbook literature on films was springing up. Mayer is more keenly aware than most people of how recently motion pictures have acquired academic respectability. In 1968 at U.S.C., he was worried about one of his students who persistently cut classes in order to campaign for Eugene McCarthy. When Mayer asked a dean how he should handle this delinquency, the dean said to ignore it; if the lad had been skipping Latin or chemistry, that would have been a cause for grave administrative concern, but missing a course in the *movies* —why, it was probably more important for the student to indulge in outside civic activities than to preoccupy himself with anything like *that*.

No one, least of all Mayer himself, knows in advance in what direction one of his lectures may veer. Perhaps he will discourse on the encroachment of conglomerates like the Kinney Corporation on the industry ("Imagine!" he will say with a shudder. "Warner Brothers lumped in with coffins and comic books!"), or on the effect television has had on his beloved industry. "Television, you know, destroyed the automatic once- or twice-a-week moviegoing habit, which was the backbone of the industry in your parents' day, and, yes, even in my day," he said on one occasion. "And as there aren't many ordinary moviegoers left, so also there aren't many ordinary pictures. Today, they're either smash hits or total flops—in movie parlance, boffos or bustos. Alas, there's nothing in between."

December 9, 1974

From a Profile. At last report, Professor Mayer, who turned ninety in 1976, was still teaching.

Reunion

Learning that Larry Adler and Paul Draper were scheduled to appear at Carnegie Hall on June 15th, we consulted our record book and discovered that it would be thirty years since the harmonica player and the tap-dancer—bright stars of the entertainment firmament until they were eclipsed by the blacklist a generation ago—last worked together on that stage. Then we looked up Draper, Adler not yet having come over for the reunion from London, where he has been living since 1949. The dancer, the senior member by four years of the durable pair, admitted to having turned sixty-five. "I am two years younger than that in *Who's Who*," he told us. "But I decided recently to play it straight. Hell, if I'm older, I'm older." He looked as slim and fit as ever, and said that he would weigh in at a hundred and sixty—exactly what he weighed when he began dancing professionally, in 1931. "I keep in shape by teaching actively two to five hours daily," he said. "I don't sit on a stool and say 'Lift your leg.' I demonstrate. I assume Larry's in good shape, too. He's been doing a two-hour one-man show all over Europe, and to carry that off you've *got* to be in shape."

Draper, whose once reddish hair has indisputably turned gray, was wearing a blue sports shirt, sweat pants, and sneakers, and, if he'd had a whistle around his neck, could have passed anywhere for a high-school basketball coach. In reality, though, he has since the fall of 1969 been Andrew Mellon Professor of Drama at Carnegie-Mellon University, in Pittsburgh, where he now lives. "When I was younger, I often fantasized that if and when I ever stopped dancing I would retire as something like a professor of ancient history, even though my own formal higher education was confined to one year of civil engineering at Brooklyn Polytech," he said. "Now that this absurd dream has come true, I've become fascinated with academe. Whether it's because I like to teach or I love the kids I teach, I'm not sure; I guess it's both. It never occurred to me that what has happened could happen. Not a single one of my students, incidentally, has ever seen me dance commercially, though a lot of their parents have. I teach one kid whose uncle was a sax player in Henry Busse's band at the Chez Paree, where I spent almost a year and a quarter of my life."

Draper said that Adler has been teaching, too—regularly giving a summer course at an academy in Wales (Draper is currently teaching in the summer school of the University of Maryland), taking private pupils in London, and running a sort of global correspondence school for harmonica players. "People send him tapes of their performances, and Larry sends them back critiques," Draper said. "Many of these musicians are members of something called the Society for the Preservation and Advancement of the Harmonica, an organization one of whose principal objectives appears to be preserving Larry. And he's also blossomed in the last ten or twenty years into a writer: regular book reviewer for the London *Sunday Times,* contributor to *Punch* and *The Spectator*—I forget what all else." Draper added, in the reflective manner of a professor giving a survey course in ancient history, that it was back in 1933 that he and Adler met. The dancer and a singer named Alice Dawn had been engaged for the stage show at the Radio City Music Hall; Vincente Minnelli had designed a set with three doors; a third body was needed in a hurry; and the then nineteen-year-old Adler was recruited from a Gus Edwards revue. Adler and Draper not long afterward went their separate ways, on separate continents, but they crossed paths again in 1939, gave their first joint recital that year at Santa Barbara, first played Carnegie Hall in 1941, and for five years after that were one of the hottest attractions on the national concert circuit, giving sixty or seventy highly remunerative performances a year. "It was hard work but fun," Draper recalled. "Much of the time, we had as our accompanist the pianist John Colman, who was outstandingly irresponsible but a brilliant musician."

This week's reunion appearance was arranged by Frances Cole, the harpsichordist. "As soon as we were approached, I got in touch with John Colman, whom I hadn't spoken to for a while, and I asked him what shape *he* was in," Draper said. "He was as excited as we were about getting together again. I haven't seen much of Larry, either, in recent years. We worked briefly together in Europe during the early fifties, when I lived in London, but we've usually been a couple of thousand miles apart. Larry has done a number of concerts with symphony orchestras in Canada lately, playing some of the pieces that have been specially written for him, by people like Milhaud and Vaughan Williams, or the Robert Russell Bennett arrangement of 'Rhapsody in Blue' for mouth organ and orchestra. Larry will almost surely be doing some Gershwin at Carnegie—probably selections from 'Porgy and Bess'—and he's got Ellis Larkins to agree to accompany him in those numbers. My own public performing these past few years has been mostly on the university circuit, which I've loved, because some of the orchestras and bands are marvellous. These kids in college bands today do things with Schubert and Mozart that you wouldn't believe. Larry isn't due in till just before we go on, so how we're going to rehearse the numbers we'll do jointly I don't exactly know, but inasmuch as we've worked together hundreds of times and what we do is largely improvisational anyway, I suppose it won't be any real problem. I know that he can still play the harmonica better than anyone else, and that I can still dance, though my endurance, naturally, isn't what it used to be. But I can dance. You won't ask for your money back."

June 23, 1975

The Eve of Independency

In the months of 1776 before the signing of the Declaration of Independence, the British, who preferred the word "Independency," were naturally much concerned about what was taking place on the far-off scene of what they called "the civil war." They were not always fully or accurately informed. In fact, in the leading item in the January 18, 1776, issue of the *Gazetteer and New Daily Advertiser,* one of a flock of London dailies I have recently been browsing through, a letter-writer who signed himself "L" complained, "Little do the generality of the people in this country know what America is: the nature of the people, their capacity, their fortitude, their exercise in arms, their abilities, or their resources, nay, even that by descent they are Englishmen. Not much better acquainted with these affairs are the generality of the Country Gentlemen, not through want of capacity, but through a most shameful neglect of acquiring intelligence respecting so important a part of the British dominions. I condemn not all, but the generality are inexcusable."

What information there was about events across the Atlantic was likely to be three or four weeks out of date, or, depending on the vagaries of oceanic winds or sailing schedules, even older. (News from Paris usually took about a week to reach England, from Vienna about three weeks, from Madrid four, from St. Petersburg up to five, from Batavia nine months or so. And after the intelligence arrived at one British seaport or another, there was inevitably a further lag while it was carried on to the capital by stagecoach— eleven hours, as a rule, from Portsmouth, seventeen from Bristol, thirty-eight from Liverpool.) "The distance between England and America is too great to warrant the expence of sending a vessel home with every trifling piece of news," the *Morning Chronicle, and London Advertiser* reminded its readers on July 22nd, eighteen days after John Hancock had signed the Declaration of Independence. "More especially," the *Chronicle* went on, "as Intelligence of sufficient importance will naturally arise soon. Our readers therefore may comfort themselves with the hopes that when News does come, it will be worth their hearing."

London had no Sunday papers in 1776, but it did have a veritable swarm of dailies, most of them four pages long, with four columns to a page, and costing, at the start of the year, two or two and a half pence. In addition to the *Gazetteer* and the *Chronicle* there were the *Morning Post, and Daily Advertiser*, the *Daily Advertiser*, and the *Public Advertiser*. And there were papers that appeared three times a week, among them the *General Evening Post*, the *London Evening-Post*, and *Lloyd's Evening Post*. They obtained their foreign news in various ways. (The *Morning Post* speaks in 1776 of having set up a special channel for early intelligence "after considerable pains and expence," but I have not come across a revelation of what it was.) Some news reached the papers in the form of dispatches to the government from overseas administrators or military commanders; some in the form of reprints from foreign papers; some in the form of private letters that were gobbled up by the hungry British journals; and some from rumors, which were known as "hums." On July 25th, the *Morning Post* said, "There never arrives a ship from America, but, the friends of administration proclaim victory! and the partizans of faction on the other hand, as certainly sound the melancholy horn of sedition; giving doleful tidings of the miscarriage of the British forces; and all this, when not a single article of the dispatches have transpired, as a foundation for either to build an opinion on; but so general is this passion, that most ranks of people are in subjection to it, and think themselves at liberty to deceive each other in political matters, without incurring the imputation of lying."

Several weeks earlier, the *Chronicle* had introduced its followers to a coffeehouse character named Spec, whose countenance was reported to be a reliable political barometer: "When the Physiognomists observe Spec's face gloomy, black, and bloated, with evident streaks of anger and despair, they conclude that Spec has received unfavorable news from the M——y [Ministry]; or that the Americans have succeeded in some action or other; if on the contrary, Spec's face wears the appearance of cheerfulness, and his sourness of aspect seems to have had a momentary recess from his muscles and high cheek bones, then the company may depend upon it, that news is about to transpire, that the Americans are defeated, have run away from their camp, leaving their dinners *ready drest*, for the hungry regulars, &c. &c. and from this dubious oracle proceeds many of those speculative and visionary daily paragraphs, which their industrious writers so very frequent substitute for matters of fact." The *Chronicle* had another noteworthy source—an American lady in London, who in August said that she knew fighting had begun three thousand miles away; she could tell by the shooting of her corns, which she found, on the whole, more trustworthy than the stately columns of the *London Gazette*, the official publication issued twice weekly by the harried Ministry of King George III.

Thanks to the foresight of the Reverend Dr. Charles Burney, the eighteenth-century author and acquisitor, the British Library, which is tucked inside the massive British Museum, on Great Russell Street, has an estimable collection of 1776 London newspapers. These are not on microfilm. They are the venerable originals, bound in flaking leather but printed on rag paper that has splendidly withstood the ravages of time and research. They are not easy to read. There are no headlines to speak of. The type is small. Moreover, the hard news they contain is jumbled up with editorial comments, letters, jokes, publicity releases, advertisements, and obituaries. And then there are those infernal antique "s"es that look like "f"s. But it is a rare pleasure to be able to leaf through the two-hundred-year-old pages and reflect that one is receiving the same unfolding picture of events across the ocean that was viewed in 1776 by John Wesley, then seventy-three; Horace Walpole, fifty-nine; Sir Joshua Reynolds, fifty-three; Mrs. Sarah Siddons, twenty-one; William Cowper, forty-five; and, conceivably shoulder-to-shoulder, Dr. Samuel Johnson, sixty-seven, and James Boswell, thirty-six.

At the start of 1776, on the eve of Independency, the thirty-seven-year-old King, who had succeeded his grandfather on the throne sixteen years before, was understandably preoccupied with his vexatious American colonies, and as the fateful year progressed, there was hardly a Spec in his coterie who did not share his apprehensions. "A very extraordinary anxiety, about the next intelligence from the army in America, is discovered at St. James's," said the *Public Advertiser* on August 5th (a day when the news from North America was much more than a month delayed), "and though every person who approaches the King, clearly sees and foretells the total overthrow of the rebels, yet an uncommon uneasiness is very manifest in some countenances at Court."

Whatever side any Londoner might take in the approaching showdown, it was patently felt in the British capital at the onset of 1776 that this was to be a historic year. The *Gazetteer* reported on February 8th, "In a letter from General Washington, to his brother at Fredericksburg, dated Oct. 23, he mentions his hopes of returning home by the Christmas following, in peace." Five months later, the *Morning Post* conveyed the feelings of a British officer at Halifax that "there is very little doubt, as the Provincials in general are alike credulous, timid, and irresolute, but that we shall accomplish the business we are sent upon before Michaelmas day." King George and his Ministers professed to have an objective more or less similar to General Washington's, though it was peace at their price. They were working toward it by drawing up new tax schemes to defray the costs of the war, fitting out ships to transport soldiers and their provisions to America, and giving unflagging attention to the procurement of the necessary troops. His Majesty's regiments of Guards were one available source of manpower; even more promising were the German mercenaries who could be hired from the Landgrave of Hesse Cassel and other princely owners.

There was considerable criticism in the papers of the way His Majesty was conducting his affairs. Thus, a letter writer to the *Gazetteer*, using only the initials "T.H.H.," twitted the King by composing an encomium to his predecessor George II: "As to *America*, that illustrious Monarch well knew its worth and importance;—he encouraged its commerce, instead of destroying it—nursed his distant children like a kind and indulgent parent; and protected them with a powerful arm. . . . The good old King saw their noble intrepidity;—their undaunted courage—their unbounded generosity, with pleasing approbation, and a grateful heart;—*He* considered America as the brightest jewel in his crown. . . . *This* was the *King* they *loved—revered—lamented.*—Truly he was the *father of his people.*"

This is not to say that George III did not have his scribbling adherents. His poet laureate, William Whitehead, came through on June 4th, the royal birthday, with a suitable ode that went, in part:

> Can Britain fail?—The thought were vain!
> The powerful Empress of the main
> But strives to smooth th'unruly flood,
> And dreads a conquest stain'd with blood.

The Opera House was illuminated that day with His Majesty's coat of arms and with two figures representing Liberty and Plenty; and, the *Morning Post* reported, there was "plenty of strong beer distributed among the populace." But the *Chronicle* noted, soberingly, that during the King's birthday ball "a very shrill whistle was heard in the room, which very much alarmed the whole company; but though all diligent search was made, they could not discover by whom it was done." Worse yet, that paper reported, when His Majesty went to see the fifty-nine-year-old actor David Garrick, who had announced his retirement at the end of the theatrical season, in his final appearance as Richard III at the Drury Lane Theatre, "a gentleman . . . was then greatly concerned to hear so much disturbance before a certain person [the King, of course]; but upon recollection, thinks it may be service to convince him, that however the people of this country may bear injuries, when they are convinced of being imposed on, nothing can prevent their struggles for redress."

Not long before, the *Gazetteer* observed that some anonymous observer had jestingly wondered how much benefit had accrued to the nation since His Majesty donned the crown—"viz. *11 Royal children* born, *12 Growing Colonies* lost." Queen Charlotte, whose eleventh child, a girl, was born April 25, was not without a sense of humor of her own. The *Chronicle* said that she "laughed exceedingly" when Samuel Foote, appearing as Lady Pentweazle in the comedy "Taste," poked fun at the towering hairdos affected by leading offstage ladies of the day (these were sometimes called "noddle islands"), and that the coiffure of one nobelwoman at a palace ball "forced a smile from her Majesty." According to the *Chronicle's* description of this lady, "the lower part of her hair was like a man's wig; and the upper part terminated in a lofty peak, like a grenadier's cap, with a *bouquet* on the top of all." The dimensions and details of ladies' headdresses were accorded as much newspaper space as almost any other topic. The *Morning Post* suggested in February that the bearers of these vast loads would sooner or later have to change either their coiffures or their carriages, inasmuch as one lady out for a ride "was obliged to lean so forward on the opposite seat, that the people who passed by imagined she was seized with some violent disorder." In May, according to the *Chronicle*, a couple of "very large feathered and flowered heads fell foul of each other, by accident," and as a result "the wool, hair, pins, &c. got entangled to such a degree that the ladies heads had certainly been torne off, but for the kind interposition of the gallants who got on the benches, where, as good luck would have it, they could just reach high enough to set them at liberty." Mr. Garrick was not to be outdone by Mr. Foote in lampooning the fashion. In Garrick's farewell appearance as Sir John Brute in "The Provok'd Wife," according to the *General Evening Post*, he concocted a ludicrous headpiece to which "the addition of the yellow streamers to the enormous rampant plumes, had a whimsical effect, provoking the loudest bursts of laughter from every part of the house."

News of the theatre more than once overlapped the larger, offstage drama that was being enacted across the ocean. General John Burgoyne had just returned to the motherland at the start of 1776, and he shortly was revealed as the author of a play with which the harassed British officers in Boston were attempting to bolster the sagging morale of their troops. Commenting on the inspiration of Burgoyne's literary work, a farce entitled "The Blockade of Boston," the *Gazetteer* said, on March 5th, "The General, knowing human nature, thought it would be dangerous for them to continue without some other object to engage their attention, for which purpose he introduced his muse on the Boston theatre, and by that means diverted the people from disagreeable reflections, and restored the garrison to good humour." A December 1, 1775, letter from Boston in *Lloyd's* said "The reports of a Play-house here, is true; the Officers have acted several Pieces, and were in want of assistance." The London papers often ran identical items, and in this instance duplication was a blessing. Readers of *Lloyd's* who wondered what that item meant (Was there a shortage of stagehands? Had the officers botched their cues?) were enlightened by the *Chronicle*, whose version of the letter ran, "The officers have acted several Pieces, and very laudably given the receipts of the houses to the soldiers who had families, and were in want of assistance."

If things were bad in Boston, they seemed to London eyes to be not much better in Quebec, where General Guy Carleton, the governor, was heavily engaged with the pesky rebels, among them one high-ranking officer whom the British in 1776 held in especially low repute—a man who, "having in an intrigue with a certain citizen's wife, expended more than his finances would admit, was tempted to try his fortune on the highway," said the *Morning Post*, all in all the paper most sympathetic to the King's cause, and the story continued, "This step obliged him to decamp [from England], and to take up his residence among the saints . . . [who] derive their origin chiefly from pickpockets and reprieved felons. . . . Plunder being the subject of the Congress in the expedition to Canada, they chose, with great propriety, a thief and a robber for the leader." The officer thus excoriated was Benedict Arnold.

Among the eminent soldiers who were manifestly on the British side at the dawn of 1776 was Admiral Molyneux Shuldham, who had just relieved Admiral Samuel Graves as naval commander at Boston. Admirals' uniforms, according to a March 4th tailor's ad in the *Morning Post*, were fancier than generals': the former could be made for eighteen pounds eighteen shillings, the latter for ten pounds ten. (A civilian's dress suit of "ratteen, lined with rich sattin or feathered velvet, and rich gold or silver spangled buttons," was priced at a mere nine pounds.) Farther south in America, Lord Dunmore—while awaiting the arrival of Lord Cornwallis's army and Sir Peter Parker's fleet—was cruising off Virginia and North Carolina, sparring with uncoöperative towns like Norfolk and Portsmouth, and attempting to free slaves so they could fight against their former masters. "Hell itself could not have vomited any thing more black than his design of emancipating our slaves," said a letter from a Philadelphian that the *Chronicle* ran on January 20th. "The subject of their nocturnal revels, instead of musick and dancing, is now turned upon their liberty. I know not whence these troubles may lead us." An indigenous letter writer who called himself "No Yankee" commented acidly in the *Morning Post*, "As the Americans boast they are the only witnesses left on the globe for the sacred cause of liberty—ought they not to be aided by all men in the great and god-like work, it is virtuous; it is praise-worthy; and is not Lord Dunmore then doing a righteous act in emancipating their slaves, which makes up about one-third of the great numbers of people they so much boast of."

The ranking stars of the real-life show being performed on the Colonial stage were a brother act—the Howes. Richard Admiral Lord Howe was the elder, General Sir William Howe the younger. Both were designated Commissioners by His Majesty to treat with the Colonial Congress in Philadelphia and to make it realize the foolishness of its ways and capitulate before the King had to crack down hard on its constituency. The British press did not altogether share the royal view of the Howes and their mission. "An American correspondent thinks that nothing shews the want of judgment in our present Ministers more than their supposing the HOWES are particularly respected in North America," cautioned the *London Evening-Post*. "The fact is the reverse; for although the Americans raised a monument to their deceased brother, from the moment General Howe accepted of an American appointment, he was detested there as much as a friend in private life becoming an enemy, is ever more hated than a person who had always been criminal. It is true the Americans do not consider Mr. Howe in the light they did another General they once had to deal with, as a contemptible ASS, as well as a little tricking KNAVE; but they, however, hold him as a man destitute of all principle, and will no doubt hold his noble brother in the same light; and nothing seems more probable, than that both their characters will shipwreck upon the coast of North America."

There was also opposition by the indefatigable corps of writers of letters to the printer, who used pseudonyms like "Crito," "Humanitas," "Pacificus," "Candour," "Truth," and "Veritas." Some correspondents quoted other correspondents. An unnamed correspondent in Bishopsgate, for instance, was the conduit between the *Chronicle* and "A Virginian," who had written at the start of the year, "It is not surprising, considering how much is daily said and wrote about the subject, that the true origin of these troubles in America is known to so few? . . . Our leading men here were much more provident in the beginning than you in England are apt to imagine. . . . They imbibed such notions at first of the weakness and easiness of the K——, whose name of authority they affect to treat with the lowest contempt. . . . They ludicrously call his M——y Wiseacre, and it goes for a bye word among them. . . . Mr. Washington is just such another character as my Lord Essex, the Parliament's General in King Charles the First's time. . . . Hancock is one of the greatest desperadoes living.—Adams generally sleeps with the Memoirs of the Cardinal de Retz under his pillow. . . . We poor, distressed Americans make a fine joke of your pity. Do not imagine we desire peace, even upon those terms we seem to solicit it. Were you to agree to those terms, behold some new demands, without satisfaction for which we cannot think of laying down our arms."

As if the barbs and thrusts in the press were not bad enough, in both Houses of Parliament the King and his Ministers—notably Lord North, the Prime Minister, and Lord Germain, the Secretary of State for Colonies—were under constant and unremitting attack. There was Edmund Burke in Commons, for one, hammering away day after day, for all that a letter writer to the *Gazetteer* appraised him as a man whose "wit sometimes degenerates into buffoonery and ill-nature, and his oratory into bombast and mere fustian." In the House of Peers, there was the Duke of Grafton, who had been against the Tea Act of 1773, way back when, and who now, the *Chronicle* reported on March 15th, invited the King to state that if the

Colonies were prepared to petition him on their grievances he was prepared to suspend the fighting. "Were there no terms to be granted the Americans," the Duke demanded, "but at the point of the sword?" Grafton's resolution to suspend military operations was defeated, after eight hours of debate, by a vote of ninety-one to thirty-one, but even that comfortable margin of support apparently did not satisfy the King and Lord North. It was soon printed in the papers that His Majesty was going to designate a host of new peers, sympathetic to his viewpoint. This he proceeded to do, but not before the *London Evening-Post* had acerbically itemized their qualifications:

> Lord Polwarth— *Because his father's a Scotchman, a tool of the Court.*— A constant voter for all the bloody measures against America . . .
> Marq. of Carmarthen—Spoke warmly against America when in the House of Commons
> George Onslow—The slave of any Minister.

By July 6th, the *Chronicle* was saying, "There have been so many Peers in both kingdoms [England and Ireland] made within this month past, that there has been frequent mistakes made about their address at the levee [the royal reception]—several people of old families using the words, 'O Lord!' instead of 'My Lord.'"

As 1776 got under way in England, and as Dr. Johnson, or his hovering Boswell, or any curious eighteenth-century Englishman, betook himself to his favorite coffeehouse to peruse his favorite journals (Charles Lamb was too young; he had just turned one), he must have felt that in the months immediately ahead the papers would provide much that was consequential to ingest and reflect upon.

July 5, 1976

From a Reporter at Large piece.

Notes and Comment

Now and then, the troubles of our inflationary times can be reduced to comprehensible dimensions. The price of a cardboard container of coffee at the stand in the lobby of our building has gone up from a quarter to thirty cents. The reason, the man in charge explains, is that he is using a larger container. But the new container leaks, losing, we estimate, about one-sixth of its contents before they can be consumed.

August 16, 1976

The Morning After

Letter from a friend in Montreal scrawled on the back of a decathlon score sheet:

The morning after the Olympic closing ceremonies, a Russian I met here urged me to go out to the Soviet pavilion at Man and His World (née Expo 67) and bone up on the next big bash—the XXII Olympiad, Moscow, 1980. "In the USSR Sports Belong to the People," proclaimed a sign outside the building. People belong to sports there, too, I gathered from various statistics-spewing exhibits inside: there are more than fifty million persons in two hundred thousand physical-culture and sports collectives; two hundred and fifty thousand coaches have diplomas or advanced degrees, and there are twenty-three higher institutes of physical culture to educate still more; the Central Lenin Stadium, in Moscow, covers three hundred and seventy-one acres and has a hundred and forty sports facilities; etc. Indeed, Moscow alone already boasts (the word seems appropriate) seventy stadiums, a thousand three hundred gymnasium halls, twenty-six swimming pools, a hundred and ten soccer fields, etc. And a new Olympic velodrome is at present under construction. It looks as though the Russians had the 1980 situation well in hand.

Much of the pavilion's interior wall space was devoted to submissions in a competition that was held to choose the design of the official emblem for the 1980 Games. The winner, selected from twenty-six thousand entries, which were sent in by eighty-five hundred painters and designers, from places as far off as Great Britain and Mali (none, evidently, from the U.S.A.), consists of the traditional five interlocked Olympic rings surmounted by a rising tower of five parallel red lines—symbolizing racing lanes, an attendant told me—which, in turn, is surmounted by a red star. There were blown-up photographs on all sides: of the gymnast Olga Korbut ("Hair Braids That Shook the World," said a caption), of World Chess (non-Olympic sport) Champion Anatoly Karpov, of "Cuba's No. 1 Ice-Hockey Player"—Fidel himself, on a rink, holding a hockey stick. Three odd aspects to this picture: Premier Castro is all dressed up in a fancy military uniform, he doesn't have a cigar, and he forgot to put his skates on. Posted on another wall was an announcement of a photography contest now in progress, its theme being "The Way Canadians See Soviet Sport and Culture." Enormous gap between first and second prizes: first prize is a free trip to the U.S.S.R., and second prize is a one-year subscription to the magazine *Visit To The U.S.S.R.*

On a couple of tables in the pavilion were books in which visitors were invited to scribble their comments on the displays. Sampling of contents: "Fabulous exciting introduction to 1980," "I think your pavilion is quite good, but you put in too many things about the Olympics," "I like your exhibition but right now [child's handwriting] I'm very mad," "Why did you [spoil-sport's handwriting] omit the works of Solzhenitsyn in your literature?," "It is too bad that a great people never smile in their photos. Have you as a nation no humor?," and—with an arrow connecting the second of these to the first—"Why are Ukrainians winning medals for the Soviet Union?" and "Why don't you have someone monitoring this book at all times to have some of these slobs arrested?" There was also a scattering of anti-Soviet obscenities. Considering that the most used guestbook was made up of looseleaf pages, the curators of the pavilion are probably to be commended for not having removed the uncomplimentary remarks.

In a section of the building focussing on Estonia was a scale model of the 1980 yachting facilities, now under construction at Tallinn, on the Baltic coast, five hundred and sixty miles from Moscow. (The yachts in an adjacent photographic display all had red spinnakers.) An attendant informed me that these would be the most splendid yachting facilities ever conceived of or executed by man, and that I must be sure to look in on them four years hence. "Tallinn is very old city, first mentioned in documents in year 1154 A.D.," he went on. "If you are not familiar with Estonian folk dances, be assured that they are universally admired." He turned out, not surprisingly, to be an Estonian. He handed me a packet of literature extolling other widely esteemed glories of Estonia. Also the June, 1976, issue of *Soviet Union*, furnishing the intelligence that town planners throughout the U.S.S.R. are required by law to provide a stadium, a gymnasium, a swimming pool, and a shooting range for every thirty to fifty thousand persons within their jurisdiction; and, as a bonus, throwing in an ominous quote from the young Rumanian gymnast Nadia Comaneci: "I shall train even more thoroughly to see that the 1980 Games coincide with the peak of my sporting career." Also the June, 1976 issue of *Sport in the USSR*, quoting Michael Killanin, elsewhere known as Lord Killanin, on his view of the prospects for 1980: "We are bound to encounter problems, but I am quite certain that these will not be insurmountable, if faced realistically." The Estonian urged me again to plan to come over for the next Olympiad, and in the interests of international amity I did my best to oblige.

"Hope to see you in Moscow," I said.

"Don't forget Tallinn," he said.

On the way out, I learned from another sign on a wall that the motto for the 1980 Olympics will be "Sport—Ambassador of Peace." What a revolutionary idea!

August 16, 1976

Charlie's Boys

We like to keep up with other periodicals, and when we read in a recent issue of *The Gym Extra!* that "the reason Nina is not available for more classes now is that she spends every afternoon coaching a teeterboard act for Charlie from Barnum & Bailey circus," our curiosity was aroused. A few days later, we found ourself in the gymnasium of Muhammad's Mosque of Islam, on Woodycrest Avenue, a couple of blocks from Yankee Stadium, where a dozen ebullient black boys between the ages of ten and sixteen were practicing somersaults, back flips, shoulder balances, and other death-defying maneuvers, under the guidance of a woman wearing purple pants and—because she was manipulating a rope attached to a belt harness that kept some of her pupils from self-destruction as they essayed double back somersaults from one another's shoulders—heavy work gloves. That was Nina—Nina Krasavina, we learned when we introduced ourself. She, in turn, introduced us to her co-coach and husband, a compact, muscular, gold-toothed man named Gregory Fedin. "Krasavina and Fedin is our stage name," he told us. "We do a circus aerial act, all clowning. We recently finished an engagement in Montreal, with the Garden Brothers Circus. Until we left Russia, two and a half years ago, to seek freedom, we had been with the Moscow State Circus for twenty years."

We wondered if by any chance we could have caught their act in Russia, when we last attended a circus there, in 1958. "Probably not," said Mr. Fedin, after a moment's reflection. "That was very bad year for me. I crash from forty-five feet and break everything."

"Who's Charlie and where's Charlie?" we asked.

Mr. Fedin explained that Charlie was Charles King, a circus performer with a unicycle-and-basketball act, who was out of town at the moment, but who had lately been trying to help Ringling Brothers and Barnum & Bailey put together a black-acrobat number. "Nina and I have been twenty-five years in show business and we never heard of a black-acrobat act," he said. "These boys were discovered on the street by Charlie King—they call him King Charlie—and they've been studying with my wife and me for three months now. Ringling Brothers rents this hall for them. The boys come here five days a week, after school—two hours each afternoon. They have to work hard. They're going to end up with a complicated teeterboard act, and we haven't even reached the teeterboard stage yet. But in six more months they will be ready. As far as we know, the United States has no such act now. It's a pity, considering your resources, but circuses here have had to buy their teeterboard acts from places like Bulgaria, Poland, England and Germany." Mr. Fedin was not looking at us. "Don't bend your elbows!" he yelled across the gym at an errant back-somersaulter. Then he excused himself to help a boy named Kenny learn to stand on his teacher's head.

"Beautiful, Bobby! Beautiful!" cried Miss Krasavina as a fifteen-year-old boy, trussed in her safety harness, did a back somersault off an accommodating peer's shoulders. She espied another apprentice artist attempting to enter the premises unobserved. "You're twenty minutes late, Isaac!" she called out chidingly.

"I had to do something for my mother," said Isaac. "I could have got here sooner if I could have used my unicycle."

"Then use your unicycle," said Nina, with a shrug.

"We all have unicycles," a boy named Mark told us. He said he was twelve.

"You should see Mark ride," said Bobby. "He can reach down and pick a quarter off the street. And in acrobatics he does a back flip with a double full twist."

"On our unicycles, we're too much," said Mark. "Labor Day, we went to Brooklyn and joined a parade and rode our cycles in front of the band and got our pictures taken. We were supposed to be in another parade, but we ain't known where it was."

Taking a breather from some warmup handsprings, the tardy Isaac told us that most of the boys live on the same block of Jackson Avenue, in the Bronx, and that they got started when he, now sixteen, was nine, by scrounging old mattresses that people had thrown into the gutter, dragging them into an alley, and using them as tumbling mats. Eventually, Charlie King heard about them. "King Charlie—he the best friend we have," said Isaac. "Nina and Mr. Fedin, they teach us good, too. Nina won't let us practice big stuff outside of here, because it's too dangerous, but at home we can do handstands and splits and stretches and things like that."

Nina instructed Isaac to attach himself to her harness. "All right," she told him. "Double back somersault."

Two other boys, Leonardo and Leslie, hands cupped in front of them, braced themselves to catch his feet, and as Nina barked "One—two—three—*up!*" Isaac leaped toward them, and they flung him whirling into the air. He landed more or less upright.

"It worked nice, and I didn't help you," said Nina, indicating that her rope was slack.

Isaac beamed.

"When you try without rope?" asked Nina.

"Tomorrow," said Isaac.

We were sorry we couldn't be there.

November 1, 1976

Ceremony

Between the Super Bowl and the Inauguration, we managed to squeeze in attendance at another conceivably major event of the early new year: an appeal to the world, from the summit of the Acropolis in Athens, to save the Parthenon and the other shrines standing on what in Greece is often called the Holy Rock. It seems that the Parthenon, the Erechtheum, the Propylaea, and the Temple of Athena Nike, or what remains of them, are gravely threatened by a variety of forces of disintegration. Between 1913 and 1931, for instance, well-meaning but misguided caretakers embedded iron bars in some of the fragile ruins; the bars have rusted, and the oxidation has caused expansion and cracked the surrounding marble. Human feet tramping across the area—some three million pairs of them a year now—are having their own debilitating effect. But the worst damage has come from pollution. The population of Athens has gone way up—to over two and a half million at the latest count—and in the last fifteen or twenty years the sulphur-dioxide emissions from residential oil heaters, automobiles, and factory stacks have done dreadful things to the cherished twenty-four-hundred-year-old marble buildings. "It's the same disastrous effect you get from putting vinegar on chalk," we were told at the scene by Gérard Bolla, a deputy assistant director-general of UNESCO who is its man in charge of the world's cultural heritage.

This is not the first time, of course, that public concern has been expressed about the state of the Acropolis. In 1969, UNESCO urged the government of Greece to take ameliorative steps before it was too late, but that was the government of the colonels, and they were mostly interested in preserving themselves. In 1974, after their downfall, the new government named Constantine A. Trypanis its Minister of Culture and Sciences, and he at once set up the Working Group on the Preservation of the Acropolis Monuments. With its blessing, he had the three statues remaining on the west front of the Parthenon gently detached and installed in the adjacent Museum of the Acropolis. This fall, Mr. Trypanis besought UNESCO—which was already helping with the rehabilitation of such venerated sites as Carthage and Borobudur—for technical and financial assistance, and at a meeting in Nairobi in November the agency pledged all-out support. This, if everything goes according to expectations, will involve the collection and expenditure, over a five-to-ten-year period, of fifteen million dollars, much of it earmarked for detailed studies not only of the monuments themselves but of the holy bedrock on which they perch. Particularly difficult will be the precise location of the invisible reinforcing bars (gamma-ray photography will be used), their removal (a task as delicate as dentistry), and the substitution of bars made of a non-corroding alloy (titanium alloy, probably). Also, the Greek government hopes to be able to persuade those of its citizens who live near the Acropolis to heat their homes with a fuel that creates less pollution.

This month's ceremony at the Acropolis was exceedingly low-key: no bands, no flags, no costumed native dancers, not even much of a crowd. It took place on a cold, damp, gray morning. (As the Director of the Acropolis, George Dontas, had noted sadly in September at an International Symposium on the Deterioration of Building Stones, held in Athens, it is very rare nowadays to find in wintertime one of the city's legendary clear blue skies.) Mr. Trypanis presided; speaking in Greek, he said that "the buildings of the Acropolis of Athens, no matter how fully they express the spirit of the nation and of the period which created them, belong to the whole of humanity and are a symbol of the liberty of man as the peoples of the world see it today." He thereupon introduced the guest of honor and chief fund-raiser, the Director-General of UNESCO, Amadou-Mahtar M'Bow, who, being Senegalese, spoke in French. "The Acropolis is in danger," he began bluntly. Observing that "the treasures of the Acropolis testify in the highest degree to the creative genius of man," he appealed to the conscience of the world and asked for contributions to a special UNESCO fund from nations, foundations, museums, and individuals, including schoolchildren.

Both men's remarks were rendered in three languages—Greek, French, and English. During Mr. Trypanis's Greek-to-French, Professor Emily Vermeule, the eminent Harvard archeologist, squinted at the western end of the Parthenon and told us, "In this light, you can see the curvature—it's bending right up in the middle." Trying vainly to see it for ourself, we did see a single workman emerge from the Parthenon and, leaning against one of its dwarfing columns, take in the proceedings from that lofty vantage. During M. M'Bow's French-to-Greek, we bowed to three diplomats from the People's Republic of China (could they soon, we wondered, be asking UNESCO to help restore the Great Wall?), and said hello to some Australian schoolgirls, who just happened to be visiting the Acropolis that morning.

At a reception for M. M'Bow and others downtown in the Hotel Grande Bretagne—itself by now a revered antiquity of sorts—we chatted with Mr. Trypanis, who looks like an English don, and who, indeed, taught Greek literature and language for twenty-five years at Oxford, before doing a seven-year stint at the University of Chicago. "Believing in democracy, I came back to Greece only when democracy was restored," he said. "You know, one has the false feeling that classical monuments do not perish. Alas, they do. It's the sculptured parts that suffer the most dramatic damage. If you compare recent photographs of the frieze of the west front of the

Parthenon with photographs taken ten years ago, the difference is shocking—hands and arms and horses' legs just falling off or melting away." He said that the sculptures still *in situ*—the three remaining original caryatids of the Erechtheum, for instance—would be enshrined in a new museum, to be built at the base of the Acropolis as part of the current undertaking, and that the old museum would be torn down.

Was there any chance that Greece might get the Elgin Marbles back from the British Museum?

"I wish we could," Mr. Trypanis said. He went on to say that the fund-raising drive just launched had already produced a million drachmas (thirty thousand dollars) from American Express, three pounds from a Scottish schoolmaster, ten marks from a German woman tourist, and ten dollars from an American high-school class. Contributions in the United States, he added, can be made, tax-deductibly, through the International Fund for Monuments, a private organization based in New York.

We had a final few words with the Director-General of UNESCO, who, although he once taught classics and history at the University of Dakar (he was also for a while his country's Minister of Education), had never before been to Athens. M. M'Bow said he had been profoundly impressed by the Parthenon.

January 31, 1977

Oral History

When we heard not long ago that Wellington Koo, a Columbia B.A. and Ph.D. with a curriculum vitae that is probably as formidable as any extant, had contributed to his alma mater's oral-history annals several hundred hours' worth of taped reminiscences—the lengthiest recitation to date in the university's collection, or perhaps anywhere—we asked him to grant us an hour's worth of live talk. Over a cup of green tea in his Park Avenue apartment, he graciously obliged. Dr. Koo, a chipper eighty-nine-year-old, who gave up skiing in 1972 and tennis a year ago, has at one time or another been the Republic of China's Foreign Minister and Finance Minister; its ambassador to London, Paris, and Washington; its delegate to both the League of Nations and the United Nations; and, in 1926-27, its Premier and acting President. He has lived in New York since retiring, in 1967, from the International Court of Justice, in The Hague, on which august tribunal he had sat for a decade.

"My father was a mandarin, who handled all foreign loans in Shanghai in the reign of Tzu Hsi, the Empress Dowager, and also all foreign purchases by the Imperial Court," Dr. Koo told us. "The Empress Dowager was very fond of foreign things. Also, all customs revenue was remitted through

Shanghai, and he was responsible for counting it. At the time I was born, in 1888, everything was done according to five-thousand-year-old traditions, but I acquired an entirely new outlook when I was sent to a missionary school. I acquired the name Wellington there. We had a teacher, an Englishwoman, who couldn't be bothered with Chinese names—mine is Vi Kyuin—so she gave everybody an English name. Similarly, my present wife, at her missionary school in Tientsin, became Juliana, which was all right until we lived in Holland, where it embarrassed us for her to be called that. So she reverted to Yu Yün, her Chinese name. It was when I was fifteen or sixteen that I decided to go into diplomacy. I was moved to feel, because of a sign posted in a beautiful garden in the British Concession in Shanghai, that some improvement in the state of foreign relations was essential. The sign said, 'Dogs and Chinese not admitted.' It was bad enough in any event, but to put dogs ahead of Chinese was too much. When some of my school friends said they were going to college in the United States, I decided to join them, to the great sorrow of my mother. I was only seventeen, and she fell to her knees and grabbed my hand and begged me to stay in Shanghai. I majored in political science at Columbia, and I especially loved the extracurricular activities. I joined the debating team, and I heeled for the *Spectator*, the undergraduate paper, eventually becoming a news editor, and I was elected to a ten-man student board of representatives that dealt with the faculty and the administration. I observed that the big men on campus, the true heroes, were those with a varsity 'C' on their sweaters, so I went out for crew. The coach said, 'Koo, you're too small for anything but coxswain.' So I tried out for that, and after two days the coach said, 'Koo, you're through. To be a successful cox, you have to swear at your boat, and you can't swear.' My size did prove helpful, however, during the annual freshman-sophomore flag rush, when the sophomores would hang a flag on a high pole and defy the freshmen to pull it down. I was so small that two of the big guys in my class were able to throw me high enough into the air to grab the flag.

"After obtaining my undergraduate degree, in 1908, I returned to China, for an arranged marriage—both sets of parents had selected us for one another when we were eight or ten. She and I went through the ceremony, but on a strictly pro-forma basis. When I next went home, after receiving my Ph.D., in 1912, I looked up the Chinese civil code and found an article—the Chinese are remarkably advanced in many respects—permitting married couples to get divorced by mutual consent. So we did. In the spring of 1912, the provisional President of the Chinese Republic, Yüan Shih-k'ai, cabled to New York offering me a job as his English secretary. I wanted to turn him down, because my doctoral dissertation wasn't finished. My adviser, Professor John Bassett Moore, demurred. He had been Assistant Secretary of State under Presidents Cleveland and Harrison, incidentally, so my connections with American history, vicariously, go rather a long way back. I have known personally all your Secretaries of State from Elihu Root on. Anyway while I was pondering the offer of the position back home, Professor Charles A. Beard, under whom I had studied history, urged me to take it. He said I could receive my Ph.D. on the basis of what I'd already written. 'But I haven't done my index,' I said. 'My wife, Mary, will attend to that,' he said, 'and now you get yourself to the Trans-Siberian Railroad and go right back home as fast as you can.' I was surprised, on arriving in Peking, to be met at the station by the Prime Minister, T'ang Shao-yi, who had an elegant carriage with two beautiful black horses. He told Yüan Shih-k'ai, 'I'm going to keep Koo as *my* English secretary.' and the President said. 'But the reason he's here is that *I* sent for him.' Then it dawned on them that neither really had much for an English secretary to do, and it was arranged for me to work for them both. I was soon struck by the unsatisfactory way in which the Chinese conducted their relations with foreigners. Nobody had ever written down important conversations with envoys from abroad. So whenever the President received English-speaking visitors, I went home immediately afterward and wrote an account of the interview, for the record. Next, in 1914, I started a press bureau. Every night, I would have whatever German, French, English, and Japanese newspapers were available translated, and have a summary of what they contained submitted the following morning to the President. After a while, it got so that Yüan Shih-k'ai, who knew no language other than Chinese, couldn't enjoy his breakfast unless he had the summary. It was the first time in Chinese history that any such translations of the foreign press had been prepared.

"The following year, although I was very junior in rank, the President, who was dissatisfied with his minister in Washington, sent me to take his place. I happened to arrive just before Woodrow Wilson remarried. Your President had been kind enough some years earlier, when he was president of Princeton, to invite me to stay at his home, and now he wanted me to come to the ceremony. The State Department said I couldn't, because I had not yet formally presented my credentials. So Mr. Wilson invited me as a personal guest. I was amused, later, to see a film of the wedding and hear a commentator say, 'There was a Chinese in the retinue.' Wilson was a fine man—literally a gentleman and a scholar. He really *believed* in making the world safe for democracy. He wasn't appreciated by the American people. They thought that his Fourteen Points speech was too academic. I thought that that was what made it good. Politics is an interesting field, but in a way it's irrational. Politicians don't as a rule bother about rights and wrongs. Their only concern is power. I saw a good deal of President Wilson at the Peace Conference at Versailles, where I was a member of the Chinese delegation. It was a pity that his opponents kept the United States out of the League of Nations. The League was a lame horse from that moment on. I've known all your Presidents beginning with Theodore Roosevelt—although I merely sort of shook hands with Gerald Ford—and just about every head of state in my time except the Kaiser, Stalin, and Hitler. I got along splendidly with both George V and George VI. I knew both Franklin Roosevelt and Winston Churchill rather well—Roosevelt from back in the pre-First World War days when he was Assistant Secretary of the Navy. I had an appointment with Churchill one afternoon at 10 Downing Street, and he was late, and when he finally appeared, he said, 'You must excuse me, but I have to take a nap every afternoon and I can't sleep except in pajamas and it does take time, after all, to dress properly afterward.' I met Mussolini just once, when I went to Rome for the installation of Pope Pius XII, in 1939. Mussolini's son-in-law, Count Ciano, had been a popular consul general in China, so Chiang Kai-shek asked me to call on the Duce. All I can recall is that he had a great big desk, and that Ciano was very mild and cautious in his presence. You know, wherever I've been and whenever it was, I've always wanted to do the right thing for China, and I've always resented anybody who treated my country as an inferior nation and with insufficient respect. In my view, there were three countries in particular that did not behave toward China as they should have by the moral standards of international law—the Soviet Union, Japan, and Great Britain. I have had occasion from time to time to try to set them right. For instance, from the eighteen-seventies on, it was the tradition for the Inspector General of Customs in China, a man of considerable weight in the financial community there, to be an Englishman. When I was Foreign Minister, fifty years ago, I felt obliged to assert China's rights, dismissing the incumbent Inspector General for insubordination and appointing a Chinese in his place. The reaction was unbelievable. Nine ministers of the diplomatic corps called on me to complain, and in those days most Chinese officials were so afraid of the foreign diplomatic corps that they treated them like lords and masters. I was told by my visitors that what I had done would cause great disturbances in international money markets—which turned out not to be the case—but I informed the envoys that the matter was one of internal Chinese administration, and not their affair at all. They were quite taken aback.

"I haven't been on the Chinese mainland since 1946, but I have been to Taiwan twice since then—the last time in 1970. I saw a good deal of the Generalissimo then. He was born the year before me, and I met him for the first time in 1931, after the Japanese had invaded Manchuria. He asked me to come down to Nanking from Peking, where I was staying with the Young Marshal, Chang Hsueh-liang. I knew his father, the Old Marshal, too. The old Marshal—Chang Tso-lin—was illiterate, and a bandit chief, but even so he was quite a character. He knew how to deal with people. The Young Marshal's mistake was to dismiss his father's able counsellors—that led to his downfall. I got along very well with Chiang Kai-shek, though I was once informed—wrongly, as it happened—that he had put my name on a list of a half-dozen people who were to be exiled. He was a very interesting man. Recently, some newspapers on Taiwan published portions of his diaries, in some of which, I was interested to note, I was mentioned, especially in reference to my work at the Paris Peace Conference. I knew Mao Tse-tung less well. The first time I met him was in 1924, when I was Foreign Minister. He came to see me with some students, to protest against my disapproval of a pact that had been signed, without my knowledge or concurrence, between China and the Soviet Union in a fashion highly prejudicial to China. I remember Mao from then as a short, stout fellow who let the students do the talking and never said a word himself. Of course he was only a political activist, and younger than I was.

"I'm out of the mainstream of politics now, but I keep up by reading newspapers, international-law journals, and United Nations publications. And in retirement I've been able to read all the books I've always wanted to read—especially historical biographies of famous men and women. When I was in active life, I had little time to read for pleasure, and when I was at school, I was too serious. I preferred then to read about Chinese treaties and diplomatic history. Now I watch television once in a while, but not as religiously as my ten grandchildren. I think a lot about China. Eventually, I know, there will again be a united China, but how long that will take and who's going to do the unifying I can't at present foresee. But that doesn't matter: China is one of the oldest political entities on the map, and sooner or later it will be a single political entity once again."

April 18, 1977

The Two

We count on our readers to goad us into action. On receiving a letter from a subscriber that went "What ever happened to the new two-dollar bill that was introduced with so much Bicentennial hoopla last year on Thomas Jefferson's birthday? Has anybody seen one since?" we at once took the shuttle to Washington and shuttled the inquiry straight to James A. Conlon, who was then the director of the well-guarded Bureau of Engraving and Printing, which, in full view of seven hundred and fifty thousand gawking tourists a year, spews forth all the paper money—about three billion crisp greenbacks every twelve months—that any of us have, or owe. We discovered that Mr. Conlon, who retired from the Bureau this summer after more than thirty-five years (he began as an apprentice plate printer), is the father of our country's latest two-dollar bill, the first one having been introduced in 1776, and the penultimate one having been discontinued in

1966, because, except among some two-dollar bettors at New England race tracks, there was little discernible traffic in it.

"I first proposed to the Secretary of the Treasury way back in 1969 that we issue a new two," Mr. Conlon told us. "I mention this only to indicate how long we thought about the project and the degree of seriousness we attached to it. The idea arose from our continuing analyses of how and for what purposes our citizens use our currency. In our research, one thing stood out startlingly: seventy-five per cent of all cash transactions in the United States involve amounts of less than one dollar. That proved there was a high demand for low-denominational currency. Most major purchases nowadays, of course, are done by check or credit card. The Bureau used to print five-hundred, one-thousand, five-thousand, and ten-thousand-dollar notes, but we haven't turned out anything bigger than a hundred since 1946. Looking at the entire currency picture, moreover, we were impressed by the fact that Canada has been using a two-dollar bill very successfully. It would be difficult to find two peoples in the world more alike than Canadians and Americans. If the two-dollar bill worked so well there, we reasoned, it had an excellent opportunity to work here, and to diminish the tremendous volume of ones in circulation. We were then printing about one billion eight hundred million one-dollar notes a year, and we reckoned that if half of them could be supplanted by twos, we could eventually reduce the total volume of bills in circulation—at the time, there are eighty billion dollars' worth of them out—by about fifteen per cent. That would mean a saving to the government of about six million dollars a year. So, after a good deal more research, including a feasibility study at the Harvard Business School which was quite encouraging, we got the go-ahead from the two parties principally concerned—the Treasury Department and the Federal Reserve System. By April 13th of last year, we had two hundred and fifty million notes in twos in the pipeline. Our ultimate goal is to have one billion eight hundred million dollars' worth of them in circulation—at a four-hundred-million-note-a-year clip."

We said we wondered where they all were.

"We knew that the average citizen would use the two once it was introduced," Mr. Conlon went on. "The question was, how would he get it? The startling fact is that he doesn't ordinarily get his low-denomination money from a bank. He relies on retail merchants for that. Retail stores are the crux and the focal point. *They* must decide to use the two. Unfortunately, not enough of them have yet done so. Some seem to think there's no room in their cash registers. Nonsense. The same companies that make our registers make registers for Canada, and there has been no problem about finding space for twos up north. In any event, there was no way we could mandate the use of the two. It had to be voluntary. For a while, I was beginning to feel like a male Carry Nation. In New York, I stopped in at the Hilton one night for a cup of coffee and I gave the cashier a two. He accepted it, but he didn't put it in his cash register. He put it on top. I asked why. 'I give these to the manager, when I get them, and he takes them to the bank,' the cashier said. 'Why not give it to the next customer who needs change?' I asked. 'People don't like them,' he said. I said, 'How do you know? Tell you what. Next guy who comes in with a ten-dollar bill, let *me* ask him, "Would you mind if the cashier gives you a two in change?" ' He said O.K., and I did. Unhappily, the next guy was non-English-speaking."

Did Mr. Conlon happen to have a two on him?

"I had several this morning," the director said, pulling out his wallet, "but I used three of them to buy a six-dollar item. Ah, here's another!" He passed it across, saying, "When you look at this aesthetically, it's rather a nice bill, isn't it?"

Examining Gilbert Stuart's portrait of Jefferson on the face, and John Trumbull's painting of the signing of the Declaration of Independence on the back, we had to concur. It was the first of the Bicentennial twos we had laid eyes on.

"Notice that it's not brand-new," Mr. Conlon said triumphantly. "It's been used and used. People often ask, 'How long does a dollar bill last?' The poor things get folded, spindled, mutilated, snapped, crumpled, doused in beer, and stuffed among cosmetics in ladies' purses. The wonder is that they last as long as they do, which is nearly twenty months. The closest document to a dollar bill, in terms of use, is the road map, which has an endurance of a mere three hundred unfoldings and foldings. A dollar bill has a folding endurance of four thousand. That's because it's made not of paper but of seventy-five per cent cotton and twenty-five per cent linen. But to get back to the two. Right at the moment, we're kind of psyched up again about it. In mid-February, the Federal Reserve Bank out in Oregon initiated what we call the Portland Plan. It got together with some of the big retail people and talked with them, and persuaded them to give the two a shot. By the end of March, Portland had increased its use of the two by two thousand per cent. The evidence is very heavy that the two could be useful to stores everywhere—fewer bills to handle, fewer to count. We just have to continue to massage the factors that we feel can influence the use of it. If they don't have a problem with it in Canada, why should we have one? We give twos at our Credit Union in the Bureau to people who cash checks, but we need the coöperation of the retailers—and, yes, of the banks, too. The commercial banks, I'm sorry to have to say, have to date been less than enthusiastic. When people write us that they can't find a two at their bank, we suggest that they make their wishes strongly known. There is nothing more potent in this country than citizen demand. But it will take time for the two to catch on. I don't care what people say—it has maintained as positive a rate of growth in the past twelve months as any other denomination of currency. Take it from me, the two is in there plugging."

Back in New York, we went around to our branch of the Chase Manhattan, grandly wrote a check for a hundred dollars, and asked a teller for two twenties, three tens, two fives, and ten twos. "I don't have any twos," she said. Did anybody in the bank have any? She said she would check. She found one teller with one two. We went around to Gristede's to buy a can of coffee, tendered one of our twenties to the checkout woman, and asked if she had any twos. She shook her head. "I'd be glad to give you one if I had any," she said, "but I haven't seen one since coffee was three dollars, and I'm not even sure they're issued anymore."

July 18, 1977

Communists' Capitalist

In 1899, when Cyrus Eaton was sixteen and attending Amherst Academy, in Nova Scotia, he was awarded for scholastic achievement sets of the complete works of Charles Darwin and Thomas Huxley. Darwin, Huxley, and other rationalists have been his heroes ever since, and he tends to identify his own triumphs and travails with theirs. Eaton, though never ordained, was briefly, in his youth, the pastor of a Baptist church; like other lapsed preachers, he has been attracted to philosophers—Karl Marx among them—who had little use for organized religion. Along with Wall Street financiers, the popularizers of myths and superstitions have long been his foes. A contemporary whom he greatly admired was the late A. Eustace Haydon, himself a lapsed Baptist and for many years a professor of comparative religion at Chicago, whose 1941 book, "Biography of the Gods," was dedicated to Eaton. The dedicatee likes to avow his concurrence with the author's conclusion:

> More important than faith in God is devotion to the human ideals of which he has become the symbol. Too long the strong gods have been made to bear the burden. Wistfully man has watched for the day of divine action to dawn and ever healed the hurt of disappointment with more passionate faith. Hopes hung in the heavens are of no avail. What the gods have been expected to do, and have failed to do through the ages, man must find the courage and intelligence to do for himself. More needful than faith in God is faith that man can give love, justice, peace, and all his beloved moral values embodiment in human relations. Denial of this faith is the only real atheism. Without it, belief in all the

420

galaxies of gods is mere futility. With it, and the practice that flows from it, man need not mourn the passing of the gods.

In sharp contrast to many of his associates in the financial world, Eaton has habitually elected to spend his leisure time far removed from his business cronies. "On my vacations, for my companions I used to invite the presidents of universities and other scholars to visit me in Nova Scotia," he says. (He has a three-thousand-acre summer estate there, near Halifax.) "I found pleasure in talking to thinkers, for a change. I would sometimes take them on salmon-fishing expeditions, maybe half a dozen college presidents at a clip, casting in the daytime and in the evening discussing the best way of getting people interested in great books. Most of them were pretty good fishermen; it's not too strenuous a sport. Many of my industrial friends believed I was doing a wise thing in seeking to find recreation in contemplating intellectual matters. But I also encouraged reading of great books—in some instances successfully, I like to think—by people in the business world. I kept urging my friends there not to accept as the truth something that was merely popular but, rather, to question the finality and truth of all our dogmas, whether in religion or politics or economics."

In the nineteen-fifties, Eaton began to formalize his penchant by inviting—in collaboration with the Association of American Colleges—academics to a series of what were called Intellectual Life conferences, during which they would alternately play tennis or golf and explore Plato's "Crito" or "Gulliver's Travels." At the end of 1954, on the occasion of his seventy-first birthday, Eaton announced that he was turning his family's hundred-and-fifty-year-old home in Pugwash into a permanent site for meetings of thinkers. The following year, Bertrand Russell and Albert Einstein, increasingly perturbed about the proliferation of nuclear weapons, resolved to call a conference of scientists who, acting as individuals rather than representing nations or governments, could attempt to save the world from nuclear holocaust. One idea at the start was to hold a meeting at Monte Carlo, with Aristotle Onassis footing the bill. When that didn't work out, Eaton stepped in as patron and, because he sensed that the State Department was not of a mind to admit some Soviet and Chinese scholars who were on the guest list, proposed holding it on the more tolerant soil of Canada, and specifically in Pugwash.

The Pugwash conferences with which Eaton's name has been linked worldwide are the science conferences, and the first of these took place in July, 1957. Einstein was dead by then; one of his last memorable statements had been "We must never relax our efforts to arouse in the peoples of the world, and especially in their governments, an awareness of the unprecedented disaster which they are absolutely certain to bring on themselves unless there is a fundamental change in their attitudes toward one another as well as in their concept of the future. The unleashed power of the atom has changed everything except our way of thinking." Lord Russell was ailing and couldn't make the meeting, but he sent a recorded message with the British physicist C. F. Powell, one of three Nobel laureates (the others were Hideki Yukawa, of Japan, and H. J. Muller, of the United States) who did attend. In all, there were twenty-two distinguished scientists, from ten nations—among them, significantly, A. V. Topchiev, the general secretary of the Soviet Academy of Sciences, and Chou Pei-yuan, vice-rector of Peking University. Greeting his guests, Eaton declared, "A man's first moral obligation is to earn his living and his second is to be intelligent." After three days of non-income-producing but highly intellectual colloquy, interspersed with croquet and other undemanding diversions, the participants agreed, with one or two reservations, that man's misuse of nuclear energy could well result in his annihilation; furthermore, they resolved to hold more get-togethers to foster more joint thinking.

Over the ensuing years, in England and Ethiopia, in Italy and Quebec, in Sweden and Yugoslavia, there have been a couple of dozen assemblies of Pugwash scientists. In his autobiography, Lord Russell, who served for a while as chairman of the Continuing Committee of the Pugwash Movement, wrote, "Perhaps the unique characteristic of [the 1957] and subsequent Pugwash Conferences was the fact that the members consorted with each other in their spare time as well as during the scheduled meetings, and grew to know each other as human beings rather than merely as scientists of this or that potentially inimical belief or nation. This most important characteristic was in large part made possible by the astute understanding by Cyrus Eaton of the situation and what we wished to accomplish and by his tactful hospitality." Without the prior deliberations of the Pugwash scientists, the nuclear-test-ban treaty of 1963—unsatisfactory as many deemed it to be, because it permitted underground explosions to be continued—might not have come into being. The Pugwashites' lengthy palavers have also produced the phrase "hogwash from Pugwash." However history may ultimately assess these gatherings, the fact that they occurred at all was in large measure attributable—as Gerard Piel, the publisher of *Scientific American*, put it in 1972—to the circumstance that Eaton "recognized years ago that the fate and hope of mankind hangs upon the international community of science, the international community of rational human understanding." (Piel's statement was made at the kind of party that Eaton likes to give: He invited a bunch of scientists to Pugwash to watch a solar eclipse, and proclaimed the occasion a tribute to Simon Newcomb, the Nova Scotian astronomer who is the only Canadian in the Hall of Fame.) Eaton is no less fond of an encomium uttered at the 1957 conclave by Professor A. M. B. Lacassagne, of L'Institut du Radium, in Paris, who, Eaton recalls, "eloquently predicted that Pugwash, though only a village, would live in history with Austerlitz and Waterloo, two other villages that marked a drastic change in the course of human events."

Eaton has sometimes regarded himself as an ambassador between two opposing worlds—though, as Senator Barry Goldwater once gruffly noted, one manifestly without portfolio—and whenever he drops in at a foreign capital he makes a point of calling on the bona-fide American envoy and, if time permits, on the Canadian, British, French, Soviet, Vietnamese, and Chinese Ambassadors, too. One of his few frustrations is that he has never been to China; even from afar, though, he once declared that Mao Tse-tung "has been able to analyze our financial problems with deeper insight than a long line of American Secretaries of the Treasury." The breach between China and Russia has distressed Eaton. For one thing, it robbed him for a while of his customary niche in *Pravda*. "When I was in Moscow in 1965," he says, "I was told, 'If your name and picture are displayed on the front page, as in the past, it may suggest undue devotion to American capitalists, and it could be misunderstood in China. We hope that you, as an old friend, won't take it amiss if we leave you off. All the conferences that are planned for you will go on as scheduled, but nothing will be reported in the Soviet press.'"

It has been Eaton's feeling all along that effective coexistence between the Communist and capitalist worlds could be attained most easily by increasing commerce between them. The more trade, the less tension is his credo. He had been a proponent of doing business with the Russians years before many Americans would even bring themselves to contemplate that possibility, and he is fond of citing an encounter he had with President Nixon in June, 1973, in the course of a White House reception for Leonid Brezhnev. "With an arm around each of us," Eaton says, "Nixon told Mr. Brezhnev, 'For more than twenty years now, Mr. Eaton has been a leading advocate in this country of trade with yours, a belief that I have belatedly come around to myself.' Mr. Brezhnev laughed and agreed, adding that it made him extremely happy that my efforts had finally been vindicated."

October 10 and 17, 1977

From a two-part Profile.

Potatoes Redux

We had to skip our usual low-calorie cottage-cheese breakfast the other morning, because somebody had put it in the freezer, which may have been just as well, inasmuch as only a few hours later we heard cottage cheese being lambasted as roundly as though it were running for mayor. The occasion was a press conference in the Elizabethan Room of Marriott Hotels' Essex House, with portraits of Queen Elizabeth I and, logically, the Earl of Essex framing the speakers' stand. While waiting for the proceedings to get under way, we leafed through a press kit, which informed us that the creamed cottage cheese served with a typical beef-patty diet plate contains a hundred and forty calories, and that an identical-sized scoop of mashed potatoes with butter contains fewer calories (how many fewer was unspecified). The m.c. was Robert C. Greiner, Marriott's vice-president for the hotel's food and beverages, who, after confessing that he had dined on French-fried potatoes the night before, introduced Ronald N. Paul, co-founder and president of something called Technomic Consultants. Mr. Paul said that sixty per cent of all Americans are overweight and that sixty-seven per cent of all restaurant proprietors involved in a recent survey watch *their* weight. He alluded to a number of diet-conscious restaurants around the country, including one in Los Angeles, Ruffage, which boasts both a twenty-five-foot-long salad bar and a gymnasium. No wonder L.A. beat out N.Y. for the 1984 Olympics.

Mr. Greiner then took over again, and explained that the Marriott chain and the Potato Board, a Denver institution, had banded together to embark on a Slender Gourmet promotion. He forthwith introduced Robert L. Mercer, a founder and the executive vice-president of the Potato Board, and also the 1972 recipient, from the governor of Idaho, of a Certificate of Highest Merit for Distinguished Service to the Potato Industry. Mr. Mercer, modestly wearing no ribbons or medals, said, "When I talk about potatoes, I tend to speak too long." He went on, with commendable laconism, to assail the dietary pretensions of poor old cottage cheese, than which he insisted potatoes were, for would-be dieters, much better. "We say on the Potato Board, 'Potatoes are being maligned! Let's fight back!'" he said. "This is how the potato became involved with Marriott." It seems that the Board had a dietitian concoct two four-hundred-and-fifty-calorie entrées—a potato-and-fish plate called Omelette O'Brien (Irishman with a French mother, we imagine)—and that after test-marketing these with spectacular results in a few Marriott outlets it had been decided to launch them nationwide. Today, we would be sampling the omelette.

Mr. Greiner thereupon resumed, and introduced us, conceivably test-marketingwise, to a brand-new transitive verb. "Some people think we've already salad-barred the world," he said. He continued, shaking his head at the incongruousness of it all, "There are people who'll eat strawberry pie with whipped cream for dessert and still shy away from potatoes." One of the three dozen or so guests in attendance asked about the nutritional value of potato *skins*. Mr. Mercer fielded that one, stating authoritatively that while these are very rich in minerals, it is an old wives' tale to think that they are the sole repository of a potato's virtues. "The nutrition, in fact, is right under the paraderm," he said. "The skin is good, but it's not imperative that you eat it." Mr. Greiner provided a dermal footnote to that: There's a restaurant in Washington, he revealed without naming it, which sells French-fried potato skins at a dollar-fifty a portion, and has found this side dish to be a fantastic success.

During cocktails—the bartender told one inquiring woman that his Bloody Marys were three-hundred-calorie jobs—another lady told an inquiring man, sternly, "Don't you know that the white potato is an entirely different outfit? It has nothing to do with the yam or the sweet potato." At lunch, which was brightly lit, being recorded for cable television, and which was whipped up with gaudy flourishes by a four-skillet chef borrowed by the hotel for the affair, we nibbled at our weightless and not-at-all-bad omelette in the company of a young woman from *Fortune*—who brashly ate her roll (eighty-five calories)—and of Mr. Greiner himself. He wondered if the Marriott chain should convert the Elizabethan Room into a discothèque, on the order of Régine's. "Better hire Régine first," called out a food editor from below the salt. In answer to a question we posed, Mr. Greiner said that he didn't know to what kind of potatoes Marriott patrons were most partial but that *his* favorite was potato chips. "I'm a potato-chip freak," he said, "but unfortunately my wife won't buy them except when our daughters are home from college. So for nine long months every year I have to go without them—at home, that is. The only thing I love as much as I love potato chips is chocolate cake. I can pass up Cherries Jubilee, but I can smell a crummy old piece of chocolate cake a block away." His candor prompted us, for dessert, to engorge a fifty-calorie macaroon.

If we were in radio or television, we suppose we would have to offer the cottage-cheese industry equal time.

October 17, 1977

Playwright

It was in 1965 that we last had a chat with the playwright Guy Bolton, the longtime collaborator of, among other theatrical giants, Jerome Kern, George Gershwin, Cole Porter, and P. G. Wodehouse. At that time, Mr. Bolton had a new show opening on Broadway, and we were properly impressed; after all, he was over eighty. We renewed our acquaintance with him the other day, upon hearing that he had recently finished another play; we were even more impressed, inasmuch as he now counts himself to be ninety-five, is still exceedingly lively, and may be the oldest functioning dramatist of all time. (Shaw lived to be a mere ninety-four and three months.) During a tasty Irish-stew lunch at Bolton's home in Remsenburg, out on Long Island, where he and his fourth wife, the former ballet dancer Virginia de Lanty, have lived off and on since 1943, he told us that he is afraid he is slowing down: it took him three months to write his latest opus, "The Supper Party," as opposed to the maximum of six weeks which was characteristic of his more prolific years. "I have delivered the script to my agent, Audrey Wood," he said. "We don't have a producer yet, but I think it's a marketable play. Well, we'll see about that when I return from my annual trip to England."

Mr. Bolton was born in England, at Broxbourne, Herts. He started off his working life as an architect, after studying at the Beaux-Arts in Paris, and thus didn't have a play produced until 1911, when he was approaching the ripe old age of thirty. That first one was a comedy called "The Drone," which went on in New York but didn't make much of a splash. In 1914, he had his first success, a farce called "The Rule of Three," and the following year he teamed up with Kern and they brought forth "Nobody Home." It opened at the Princess Theatre, on Thirty-ninth Street east of Broadway— a slew of Bolton shows that played there became known as the "Princess plays"—and was the first of many Bolton hit musicals: "Very Good Eddie," "Sally," "Oh, Kay!," "Girl Crazy," "Anything Goes," and several dozen et ceteras. "Very Good Eddie" was the second Princess play, and it was reviewed for *Vanity Fair* by Pelham Grenville Wodehouse, Bolton's elder by a year or so. "I had never met Plummie until we bumped into each other on opening night during the interval," Bolton said. "I was a bit flustered then, because a couple alongside me had noticed during the first act that I wasn't laughing—that was because I never laugh at my own lines. 'If you don't like this show, why don't you go home?' one of them had said. Later that night, Jerry Kern took Plummie and me back to his apartment, to wait for the dailies' reviews, and the three of us decided to collaborate. After 1952, Plummie lived right up the road here in Remsenburg, and he and I used to walk our dogs together every day after lunch. We wrote together for fifty-four years, and one of our shows—'Oh, Lady! Lady!'—once played simultaneously at two theatres only a couple of hundred yards apart—the Princess and the Casino, at the corner of Thirty-ninth and Broadway. The Casino production was supposed to move straight on to Chicago as soon as we'd had a look at it, but it was such a success that it stayed where it was for several weeks before we sent it West." Bolton and Wodehouse teamed up on some twenty productions; and, with one collaborator or another, or on his own, Bolton has had a hand in so many plays and musicals that he has no idea what the total is, though it is well over a hundred.

Whether or not "The Supper Party" goes on the boards this season, its author is anticipating revivals of "Tip-Toes," a 1925 collaboration with Gershwin, and of "Anything Goes," which dates back only to 1934. "I probably won't get too personally involved," he told us, "because the one thing my doctor has said to me is 'Don't get in an argument.' I never lose my temper. I don't believe in arguing with people—except, of course, over something in connection with my work. I was living in England when Vinton Freedley persuaded Plummie and Cole and me to do 'Anything Goes,' and we all forgathered at Le Touquet. Very pleasant place to work. I thought that that was the best musical book I'd ever written. But by the time it went into rehearsal, I was in a hospital with blood poisoning, from a burst appendix, and Howard Lindsay and Russel Crouse were brought into the picture and they went off on a different tack. It had been a challenge story originally, like 'My Fair Lady' or 'Around the World in Eighty Days'—a show in which somebody decides to do something and the audience sits back and says, 'All right, let's see you do it,' but Howard and Buck took most of that out and put in a lot of comedy. No matter. Because of Cole's songs and Ethel Merman and the rest of the cast—incidentally, Ethel had made her début in 'Girl Crazy,' in 1930—it was a great success. Amateurs are still doing it all over the place. Ginnie and I practically live off it. I don't know where they find all the amateurs." The play of his that Bolton likes best, all things considered, is one he wrote alone, in 1970, about the Winston Churchills, called "A Man and His Wife." "We ran for six months in South Africa, to fantastic notices, with this marvellous Welshman, Emrys Jones, playing Churchill," Mr. Bolton said.

The first theatrical offering that Bolton recalls seeing was a production in England, when he was around ten, of "The Yeomen of the Guard." "I went to see it after my paternal grandmother, a very old lady of seventy, who was related in some way to the people who made Pears' soap, said to me, 'Guy, I hope you will never enter a theatre. It's one of the properties of the Devil.' I came to the United States for the first time just after that, and went to school for a while in New Rochelle. I am part American, actually. My great-great-grandfather had four clipper ships that took cotton from Savannah to Liverpool, and George III, in return for one peppercorn, gave him a piece of property near Brunswick, Georgia. I myself have crossed the Atlantic at least sixty-four times by ship—only six times by air. I can work wherever I am, but I don't type as much as I used to. I do most of my writing in longhand. I don't like dictaphones, though my friend Edgar Wallace used them all the time. He died broke, and Ginnie and I had to ship his body back to England, but he was a fine man. He would keep his plays running long after they should have closed, simply because he was fond of actors. So am I. We saw a good deal of Wallace in Hollywood, while I was out there writing films. I quite liked that. At the time of the Depression, I was getting a very nice salary out there—about two thousand a week. But I prefer the theatre."

Mr. Bolton told us that his favorite twentieth-century playwrights, exclusive of those he has worked with, are S. N. Behrman, Robert E. Sherwood, and George Bernard Shaw, with all of whom he was acquainted. "When I was living in London around 1927—Jerry Kern and I had our 'Blue Eyes' opening there—I borrowed a flat in the Adelphi from the playwright Totty Harwood," Bolton said. "Shaw lived next door. There was only a narrow space between his window and mine, and I could see him all the time puttering around in his woolly underwear. One day, he came to the window and said, 'Where is Totty Harwood?' 'In the United States,' I said. 'Well, who are you?' Shaw asked. 'I am a playwright,' I said. 'Well, I am, too,' he said. Then we chatted for a bit about playwrights—mostly, I'm bound to say, about him, which was fine with me."

January 30, 1978

The Sporting Scene
I Was Extremely Lucky

On January 23rd, at Pebble Beach, California, Tom Watson won the Bing Crosby National Pro-Am golf tournament and received a purse of forty-five thousand dollars. The day before that, at Boca West, Florida, Bjorn Borg had won the Pepsi Grand Slam of Tennis tournament and received a purse of a hundred and twenty-five thousand dollars. Borg's final match, against Jimmy Connors, lasted two hours and forty-five minutes; the Pepsi man who handed the victor his large check declared ringingly, on network television, "You're the highest paid hourly worker in the world." If Muhammad Ali was watching, he must have been amused. Borg did not long retain his questionable horal eminence anyway. On January 29th, at Las Vegas, Nevada, it took just a hundred and seven minutes for a man named Moshe (Chico) Felberbaum to win the final round in an international amateur backgammon championship, an event broadcast on closed-circuit television, and with it—thereby thumpingly shedding his amateur status—a first prize of a hundred and eighty thousand four hundred dollars. Chico—sportswriters use nicknames on very short acquaintance—was asked almost immediately after he reaped this monster harvest if he was disappointed at its size, and he said he wasn't. There was good reason for that odd-seeming question: as recently as nine days before the start of the competition, its promoters had been intimating—not much earlier, they had been flatly declaring—that the first prize would come to at least half a million dollars. A modest sum either way, perhaps, for a few minutes' hard work on the part of a champion heavyweight prizefighter, but boxers have to spend a good deal of time and money on training camps, and they also risk getting hurt. Physical violence is only rarely involved in topflight backgammon—though not as rarely as you might think.

Backgammon! The old dice game we used to play with our fathers when we couldn't find the Parcheesi board. Backgammon has come a long way in recent years. People who profess to know say that there are twenty million backgammon addicts—of varying ages and skills and means—in the United States today, and that in this afflicted country alone annual sales of backgammon sets rose between 1974 and 1976 from two million to five million. Backgammon professionals have a tour circuit of their own now, not unlike pro golfers and tennis players, and they migrate in flocks from Monte Carlo to Saint-Moritz and on to Nassau and Acapulco, vying for hefty gobs of prize money and gambling on the side—among themselves and with obliging pigeons—for enormous stakes. Backgammon has certain undeniable advantages over golf or tennis. For one thing, it can be played anywhere, under any weather conditions, for twenty-four hours at a stretch, and it frequently is. In the more or less friendly lunchtime backgammon games I sometimes join at the Harvard Club in New York, the basic stake is a dollar a point. Howard Reiling, who, at eighty-eight, is the club's oldest functioning backgammon player (and one of its best), can recall when the conventional stake there was a dime a point. Nowadays, when inveterate backgammon players say they are playing for a "dime" they mean ten dollars a point. The giants of the sport, however, who in New York hang around cockpits like the Mayfair and Cavendish Clubs, into which stratospheres I have never ventured, often play, I hear, for a thousand dollars a point, or even more. They also drift in and out of Las Vegas, where hundred-dollar bills are as mundane a medium of exchange as are subway tokens on the I.R.T.

It is hard to keep track of time in Vegas. There are few clocks in the big Strip hotels—the only one I noticed, at the Las Vegas Hilton, wasn't working—and there is little need for them, inasmuch as whatever goes on in that otherworldly community goes on around the clock. (What most people think of as Las Vegas isn't Las Vegas at all; the Hilton, the M-G-M Grand, Caesars Palace, and the Dunes—where I stayed, and where most of the backgammon action took place—are actually situated in a geographical entity debatably named Paradise Township.) Despite the absence of ordinary methods of telling time on what out there is called the Vegascene, the sun still rises and sets, and it is thus more or less possible, provided one occasionally glances through a window, to remember at least what day it is.

January 25th: I am on a Trans World non-stop flight, in economy class, from Kennedy to Vegas, hoping to improve my backgammon prowess by watching some experts perform. I sense that this is going to be an uncommon sort of pilgrimage when, only a minute or two after takeoff, a stewardess gives every passenger who wants one a complimentary deck of playing cards. I hope there will be a tournament for me to observe when we reach our destination. Last summer, a Phoenix, Arizona, former travel agent announced a forthcoming backgammon tournament at Vegas with nearly two million dollars' worth of prize money, but then various agencies of the law, including the Attorney General of the State of New York, began looking into how he was handling the entry fees he had collected, and the whole scheme blew up. The idea, though, was in the wind. Early in November, a second seven-digit-dollar tournament was announced, and this time its sponsors said that the entry fees—five hundred dollars per contestant, which included three nights' lodging in Nevada—would be paid directly into an escrow account at the Marine Midland Bank, in New York, and that nobody could touch a penny of them until the prizes were awarded. There was to be an unconditional limit of three thousand three hundred and twenty-eight participants. No one who had ever won as much as a thousand dollars in a single backgammon tournament, or who made his or her living primarily by playing backgammon, would be eligible. The first prize would be half a million dollars, the second prize two hundred thousand. The last thirty-two survivors would all be in the money. As a come-on, additional prizes were promised for the best showing among women and senior citizens. Concurrent with the main event, there would be exhibition matches between professionals who couldn't play in it, and between members of the New York Yankees and the Los Angeles Dodgers—a kind of reprise of last fall's World Series.

The nominal promoters—not counting the ubiquitous George Plimpton, who had been hired to lend his name to the competition as honorary chairman—were two men whose names are celebrated in gambling circles: Oswald Jacoby, the septuagenarian grand master at bridge, gin rummy, canasta, and, more recently, backgammon; and Paul Magriel, the thirty-one-year-old wunderkind known as the Human Computer, who gave up playing championship chess and teaching abstruse mathematics (he specialized in the theory of probabilities) to concentrate on backgammon. Magriel is the author of a thick, twenty-dollar tome published two years ago and entitled "Backgammon," and he writes a weekly column about the game for the *Times*. (He has long contended forthrightly that in any single game of backgammon—in contrast to a protracted match—mere luck is a fifty-five-per-cent factor. I can attest to the truth of that: not long ago, in New York, the Human Computer while blindfolded defeated Plimpton in one game and was then defeated unblindfolded in another game by a son of mine over whom I like to think I can usually prevail.) The real promoters were a small syndicate organized by Henry Wattson, a thirty-five-year-old New York-based scion of a California family in the tunnel-construction business, who is a broker in government bonds. Wattson belongs to the Mayfair Club and takes private backgammon lessons from Magriel, who has not entirely forsworn pedagogy. The young master charges five hundred dollars for five two-hour instructional sessions, and more than once after a sour lunch at the Harvard Club I have been tempted to give him a ring. If the promoters had assembled their full quota of three thousand-odd contestants, they would, after expenses, have netted a tidy three hundred thousand or thereabouts for themselves. According to the terms of their October agreement with Marine Midland, which was signed by Wattson and Magriel, if there was not a million dollars in escrow by January 5, 1978—exactly three weeks before the tournament was scheduled to get under way—the whole affair would be called off and everybody would get his money back. By Christmastime, it was clear that the total would fall far short of that cutoff number. On December 31st, a new escrow agreement was proposed by Magriel and by Henry Wattson's older brother Al, the president of the R. A. Wattson Corporation, in California. Now the size of the tournament was scaled down. There was no mention in the second agreement, as there had been in the first, of a million dollars, or of a half-million-dollar first prize. Instead, the arrangement was that of every five hundred dollars that came in, four hundred would go into a prize-money pool, and the promoters would sweeten the pool with an additional hundred thousand of their own. The ultimate winner would receive half of whatever the pool amounted to. With a thousand entries, there would be half a million dollars to spread around among the fortunate thirty-two survivors—fifty per cent of it going to the winner. Twenty-two hundred and fifty entries would re-create the million-dollar situation. With three thousand entries, the winner would receive six hundred and fifty thousand dollars, or even more than had initially been offered. However one looked at it, backgammon was beginning to make golf and tennis seem like peanuts.

On the plane, I remind myself that I have been warned by a friend of mine named George, who is going to play in the tournament but is booked on a later flight, to beware of hustlers. I am surprised that George is eligible. He once won eight thousand dollars in a smaller-scale Las Vegas tournament. George insists, splitting hairs too fine for me to see, that something like $7,000.05 of that was auction-pool money and only $999.95 was prize-pool money, so he cannot be said to be a thousand-dollar man. He has apparently persuaded the promoters of the reasonableness of his arithmetic. I often play against George, and we break even, all in all, but I have never won anything in any tournament. In terms of proficiency, I am to bigtime backgammon roughly what Gerald Ford is to golf. A stranger sitting across the aisle riffles his free deck of cards and says, alluringly, "Would you like to play a little gin rummy?" Who is hustling whom? From the look of him, I could take him for the cost of my entire trip before we cross the Mississippi. But I am feeling kindly. I tell him I do not know the game. Besides, I have spotted Paul Magriel sitting up ahead, and I want to talk to him. Magriel has such a cherubic, innocent face that if I didn't know who he was I might suggest a few hands of gin rummy myself.

I slide into a vacant seat next to Magriel, and he tells me that he has to write his column for tomorrow's *Times* before we land but that he can spare me a few minutes. He says he expects eight hundred players to materialize before the registration rolls are closed. I am startled. A release issued by his own office a fortnight ago said that "at least" two thousand players were expected, and only yesterday a woman at that office informed me that Marine Midland already had money from a thousand players in its custody. Maybe Magriel has been away from his office. In any event, he himself is emphatically ineligible to swell the total of contestants. In October, he won a million drachmas—nearly thirty thousand dollars—in Athens, in a head-to-head confrontation with the legendary Joe Dwek, the London-based scourge of European backgammon (each had the help of a consultant); and just ten days ago he picked up another twenty thousand dollars by taking the World Championship, at Paradise Island, just off Nassau. (It is further indicative of how greatly luck figures in backgammon that in the same tournament the year before Magriel lost in an early round without scoring a point, and that the fellow who skunked him was himself eliminated by a woman whom nobody on the backgammon circuit had ever heard of.) I cannot fathom why Magriel is not riding first class.

"Whatever happens at Vegas, we'll have about four times as many players as ever entered a tournament before," Magriel tells me, "and a prize-money pool ten times the size of any other." He says that arranging for the tournament has kept him so busy that he has had no time to work on any of nine additional backgammon books he is supposed to be writing—on such nuances of the pesky game as "Opening Moves," "Back Game," "Prime vs. Prime," "General Principles of Positional Play," and "The Doubling Cube." Backgammon has been in existence for four or five thousand years, but the doubling cube, which enables players alternately to double the original stake, according to their view of their prospects at any given moment (a player who refuses a proffered double thereupon loses the game in progress), dates back only to the nineteen-twenties, and it has given backgammon an entirely new and sometimes devastating dimension. (The cube goes from 1 to 2 to 4 to 8 and so on giddily up. The highest I personally have seen doubling stop at was 1,024, but that was in a mere half-dollar-a-point game, and, anyway, the chap who stood to lose the most in it wasn't risking much; he was playing aboard his private jet, and his pilots had standing orders that unless they were running out of gas they were never to land it until he was ahead.)

"Many people still think backgammon is a child's game," Magriel goes on, "but in fact there are still millions of things to be understood about it, in terms of theory, that nobody knows. Backgammon is very hard to learn. Everybody thinks it is simple, and it seems simple, and the fact that dice are involved in it tends to disguise the fact that it isn't anything of the sort. No one has yet studied the game the way chess and bridge have been studied. There are millions of situations in which nobody knows what the right move is. The trouble is that, my book and other backgammon books notwithstanding, we have too little literature. Imagine how backward we would be in chess today, or in bridge, if nobody had copied down the moves of games. In backgammon, we have no such thing yet, though I am planning to bring out, as still another book, a move-by-move analysis of my Dwek match in Athens. It lasted three days, and I barely beat him, 63–61. As backgammon stands today, in its relative infancy, the great players are great because of inbreeding. We play against one another all the time. I watch other good players and try to figure out why they make certain plays, and that improves my game. But the average player, lacking the appropriate literature, has no access to such a body of knowledge. People say that the top players in the world today have reached perfection. Well, if you were to let me lock myself up in a room for a hundred and fifty years to study the theory of backgammon and then come back and play the me of today, the future me would slaughter me."

At the Dunes, upon checking in, I find that it is nearly impossible to get to one's room without going through the casino. I am fortunate—I can ignore the silver-dollar slot machines, because I don't have any silver dollars on me. After unpacking, I make my way to a second-floor cluster of chambers where the tournament will start tomorrow. A fellow in the pressroom tells me, with a long face, that I was on one of the last planes to get out of New York on schedule. The East and the Midwest have been smitten by awful storms, and there are backgammon players wringing their idle hands from Maine to Minnesota. George Plimpton is snowed in at Flint, Michigan, and has phoned that he is going to try to get out of there by bus. Plimpton on a bus! There will be a book in that, you can bet your bottom silver dollar. In a second-floor corridor, kibitzer tickets are going on sale— ten dollars to watch any one day's play, twenty-five for the whole tournament. An outfit called Aries of Beverly Hills is providing nine hundred new boards for the contestants to play on; they retail at fifty dollars each but, when it's all over, will be available for purchase, slightly used, at thirty-five. I brief myself on some of the rules that will govern the play: the official tournament language will be English, and nobody may talk in any other; kibitzers may not open their mouths at all, nor may they use hand signals to communicate with players. I hear that Oswald Jacoby, in a last-minute effort to attract some local talent to the fray, is playing backgammon right now on television, and that the nearest set is downstairs in the casino. I rush to the scene. The TV set is alongside a poker table, and just as I arrive one of the poker players gets up and snaps it off in mid-Jacoby. "I have better things to do than watch somebody play checkers," says the poker player, returning to his childish pursuit. Back upstairs, I meet Henry Wattson, the promoter, who is a huge, bearded man. He says that he and his co-sponsors need fifteen hundred entrants to break even, but that, because of the weather and everything, he now anticipates only a thousand. He says there would have been more had not fifty people who tried to enter been disqualified. Wattson says that he himself, as a non-thousand-dollar-winner, would qualify, but that it would probably be unsuitable for him to compete. He says that there is nothing, though, to prevent him from playing *me*, sociably. He invites me to his lair. He will not play for less than a "nickel"—five dollars—a point. I shrug and accept his invitation. We play most of the night, oblivious of countrywide rain, hail, snow, sleet, and other irrelevant distractions. I graciously permit him to pay off in casino chips.

January 26th: This morning's Las Vegas *Sun*, which is devoted largely to stories about one of Howard Hughes's wills and about possible effects of radiation on eighty thousand people who were present during nuclear tests in Nevada in the nineteen-fifties, has a brief item in its sports section about our impending extravaganza which says, "At least 2,500 players are expected to compete." While I am puzzling over the source of that figure, my friend George phones from New York. He is inundated at the airport, and will arrive as soon as he dries out. After breakfast, I proceed to a salon where players who have managed to get to Vegas are converging to register. I hear German voices, and Israeli voices, and cascades of Spanish. Flights from Mexico are coming in nicely. Somebody says that if all who are expected to get here arrive, the countries represented in the starting lineup will also include Australia, Brazil, Bulgaria, Canada, Chile, England, France, and Japan. "This is bigger than the Super Bowl and the World Series combined," I hear one man say, in unaccented English. Somebody else says that the Yankees and the Dodgers will not put in an appearance after all ("Too bad," a publicity man comments. "It was to have been their last big fling before spring training"), but that Lucille Ball has duly arrived and will play. The less celebrated participants are milling around discussing crucial moments of bygone games ("And would you believe, a double-four, a thirty-five-to-one shot and the only one that could hit me") and, if they haven't previously sent their money in, trying to find somebody who can accept their entry fees. Only a banker who has been dispatched to Vegas by the Marine Midland can do that, it appears, and nobody knows where he is. Paul Magriel is literally running around looking for him. Like most other people in Vegas, Magriel is casually dressed; and—sensibly, in his circumstances—he has on track shoes. Toward noon, a young man arrives

434

who is easily identifiable as the banker: dark suit, with vest; shirt and tie; black shoes; short hair; horn-rimmed glasses; briefcase. He sets up a local branch of the Marine Midland, his back to a mountain of cardboard cartons containing glassware, in a small storage room off a bar. Oswald Jacoby also shows up, and is greeted with reverence befitting his elder-statesman stature; it is as if Bernard Baruch were visiting the White House. Jacoby is wearing bright-red pants and a Harry Trumanish sports shirt. (The word is out that Barclay Cooke, another of backgammon's doyens, is stuck in New York.) Jacoby seizes an empty chair, and a local reporter scurries over to pry a few quotable words out of him. Jacoby reflects for a bit, and then says, "I never stand when I can sit, and I never sit when I can lie down." Hyperbole, I infer, inasmuch as he stays in his chair. One prospective player waiting for an audience with Mr. Marine Midland asks a companion to guess the average age of the sixty or so bodies milling about the premises. The answer comes back with a computerlike immediacy that Magriel might admire: "Thirty-eight." I wander down to the casino in the hope of cashing in Henry Wattson's chips, which turn out to be redeemable at par for real money. At a nearby bar, I pause for some fresh grapefruit juice, which is delicious here, and which may be the reason that so many people seem to gravitate toward Las Vegas.

By mid-afternoon, tournament play is at last under way, though latecomers are still being allowed to register, and will be tomorrow, too. Concurrent action, I hear, has started up over at the Hilton. There are no favorites, odds-on or otherwise. Few people know who anybody else is, though Magriel did tell me in flight that he suspected that the eventual winner might be a bridge player of championship calibre. "I would predict that he will be somebody who excels at some other table sport," Magriel said. "He will have to have a berserk desire to win, and be used to excruciating tournament pressure." At the Dunes, the competition is taking place in a vast hall called the Crown Jewel Room, and two men, one with a cowboy twang, who are waiting for the signal for them to begin are indulging in a practice game. I watch them and am appalled. One seemingly doesn't know how a game is supposed to start, and the other doesn't know in which direction his pieces are supposed to move. Can this be a double hustle, or are they amateurs of egregious amateurishness? Later, when they get down to serious business, the cowboy throws a 5–4 but wrongly moves a 5–3, and his opponent doesn't notice the gaffe. As a kibitzer, I am forbidden to talk; I manage to suppress a gasp. I wish I were playing against both of them in the tournament.

Toward dusk, I bump into Henry Wattson, "The weather is killing us," he says. I stroll downstairs for a Perrier-and-lime, and, near the bar, espy the Marine Midland banker. "I've never seen anything like this," he says. "I had two hours' sleep last night, trying to get the accounts in order." I ask him when, if ever, he was in Vegas before. "My parents brought me here when I was fourteen," he says, "but this time I haven't even had a chance to put a penny in a slot machine." Word of inflation has evidently not yet reached his bank.

I betake myself to the Hilton, to observe an East-West exhibition match that has been scheduled there. Such bona-fide gods of the backgammon pantheon as Billy Eisenberg, Chuck Papazian, Stanley Tomchin, and Roger Low are supposed to be on view, but the only one I see—standing in a hallway—is Low, a twenty-year-old school dropout from New York whose father despaired of him until Roger began earning more money at backgammon than Low *père* ever had at anything. Low *fils* and Magriel occasionally amuse themselves on airplanes, while they are travelling to this or that tournament, by playing backgammon blindfolded. Well, not exactly blindfolded: they use an imaginary board and instead of throwing dice they throw out fingers at one another, and keep everything in their astonishing heads. Roger Low, wearing a broad sash with "Director" printed on it, says that the East-West matches aren't taking place right now but will resume tomorrow. This seems an odd thing to say, considering that, as it turns out, they haven't yet begun. Perhaps he should have stayed in school a trifle longer. He directs my voyeuristic attention to a table where two men are playing for two hundred dollars a point. I watch one of them count a wad of hundred dollar bills he is clutching in his hand. By my confirming audit, he has twenty-seven of them. His opponent, after a spell of bad dice, runs out of the hundreds *he* has been holding, reaches into a pocket, extracts a fresh supply, and plunges on. Neither says a word. Bored by their lack of carefree chatter, I return, at around midnight, to the Dunes, where I encounter Barclay Cooke, who has finally made it in from New York. "I'm supposed to be on the rules committee," Cooke tells me, "but there doesn't seem to be any ruling to do." His chance will come. I run into Henry Wattson, who suggests a return match. Poor sucker! He will never recoup his large entrepreneurial losses from me. Toward dawn, he graciously permits me to pay him off in travellers' checks, of which I heretofore thought I had brought along an adequate supply.

January 27th: At 7 A.M. Las Vegas time, when I have barely fallen asleep, I am awakened by a call from my wife. It is 10 A.M. in New York. How does she know I am here? I thought she thought I was in Tucson, Arizona, visiting a grandson. She says George told her. Blabbermouth George clearly has a lot to learn about male bonding. Now that she knows where I am, she says she is glad she caught me before I went off to work. She wonders how the weather is in Vegas and whether I have had a chance to stroll around town. I tell her, truthfully, that I haven't seen much of the weather and that I don't know which direction town is in. I decide I might as well get up. I can sleep on the plane going home. In the pressroom, I see a late issue of a Mexico City magazine, *El Mundo del Backgammon*. The headline over its lead article is *"El Millon de Dolares ¡Resucitado! ¿O Solo Una Ilusion?"* Somebody hands me a clipping from the *Armenian Post*, a New York City weekly—this tournament is getting a big play all over—which relates how Paul Magriel not long ago conducted a backgammon demonstration as a benefit for the Boston Symphony Orchestra. It is this sort of thing that backgammon players think gives us class; you never hear of poker or gin rummy players taking time off from their wretched pastimes to accomplish anything cultural like that.

Play is continuing in the Crown Jewel Room. A woman is complaining to one official that the hovering over her shoulder of two other officials cost her her first-round match, because they made her nervous. She has fingernails an inch and a half long, and I would hate to be in her vicinity when she got really agitated. The play is momentarily interrupted by a bewildering announcement over a public-address system: "People who have been forfeited have not been forfeited." Barclay Cooke is conferring solemnly with a bevy of other officials, who are all carmine sashed save him; he is wearing a bright-green sweater, and to drape a red sash over that would be, for a Racquet and Tennis Club man of his distinction, in unspeakably poor taste. Also, too Christmassy for January. One player has a bright-red fez on his head. He doesn't look Egyptian, or even Armenian; perhaps he is a Shriner. He has put a hand-lettered sign next to his board: "NO SMOKING KIBITZERS PLEASE!" That would have raised eyebrows at many another tournament on the pro circuit, because Philip Morris has been a no less dogged patron of championship backgammon—this Las Vegas tournament notably excepted—than of women's championship tennis. The fez man, staring reproachfully at an official with a cigar in his mouth, says, to no one in particular, "Other people deny it, but I am the best player in the world." A moment later, he loses his match, and resignedly walks over to one corner of the Crown Jewel Room to enroll—for an extra hundred dollars—in a Second Chance flight. It has been decreed that of the final thirty-two players, twenty-six will come from the first flight and the remaining six from Second Chance. I hear angry words, and approach a table where an early-round match is in progress. One player has risen to his feet, saying to his opponent, "When you get through smoking, I'll be back." The tobaccophile glares at him and puffs insouciantly away. An official arrives to clear the air. Nobody mentions that the official is smoking himself. "Try to be a gentleman," the official says to the nonsmoker. There is an impasse: A says he will not continue play unless B stops smoking; B says he cannot play unless he smokes. Golf was never like this. Ultimately, the official ordains a compromise: the smoker may not keep his ashtray alongside the playing surface but must put it on a chair, and he is not to exhale in a forward direction. How an official in a Philip Morris tournament might have handled this I have no idea. The smoker triumphs, which is only just, inasmuch as the abstainer cheated at one point. He threw a double 5, which required him to play four 5s, but he had only three 5s that he could move with impunity. However he handled the fourth, he would have to expose himself to a damaging hit from his opponent. So after fiddling around with his pieces for a while he played three 5s and a 6, and then quickly picked up his dice. His enemy didn't notice this skulduggery. I did, but my lips, of course, have to be sealed. I am beginning to learn a good deal about self-control.

The winner and the loser do not shake hands. Dismayed by this tawdry exhibition of human frailty, I wander down toward the casino for a Bloody Mary. At the bar, I meet a New Zealander who lives in London and has come here via Haiti to play. He was in retail shoes but is now in wholesale perfumes. While we are swapping curricula vitae, who should loom up but my friend George, who has finally escaped New York! George says that the first-round matches are tricky, because they are short—only seven points apiece—and would I mind serving as a sparring partner and playing him a few seven-pointers before he enters the lists? We work out for a while. George must have jet lag: taking his money is child's play. After he signifies, by hurling his dice past my ducking head at a wall, that he has had enough, we adjourn to the Crown Jewel Room, just in time to witness Lucille Ball coming onstage. She is surrounded by photographers, among them a camera crew from "60 Minutes," which has deemed this happening memorable enough to enshrine in the annals of network television, and whose invasions of privacy I had been carefully avoiding until I came out of my Tucson closet. There is an odd-looking little middle-aged fellow hanging lovingly on to Lucy, whom I identify for an inquisitive bystander as Mickey Rooney. Mickey Rooney double-crosses me by turning out to be Bobby Riggs. Miss Ball's playing area is soon engulfed by spectators, and, being no taller than Rooney-Riggs, I cannot see over their bent heads what is going on, so I stop to chat with one contestant, also from New York, who says he plays both at the Mayfair and at the Yale Club. I'd had no idea that Yale men play backgammon. I return to the casino for a straight vodka. The Marine Midland emissary is hunched wearily over the bar, his tie loose. He says nobody will know until tomorrow, when a banker more senior than he arrives from the East with all the escrow records, how many players there actually are in this benighted tournament. I get back to the Crown Jewel Room in time to see my friend George toss away his first-round match. Before my unbelieving eyes, he stupidly misplays a critical 2–1 roll, and then he neglects to double three times in a row when he is in so advantageous a position that his opponent, if he has any sense, would have to concede that particular game. George is of Greek extraction, and, after he rises and congratulates his deposer, a kibitzer says something to him in a foreign tongue. George nods. I ask him what the other fellow was saying, and in what language. "He said, "Θά ἔπρεπε νά διπλασιάσης,'" George says. I request a translation. "That's Greek to me, for 'You should have doubled,'" George tells me. He proceeds to enlist in the Second Chance ranks, and he invites me to play him once more. Lucille Ball is now engaged in some lively calisthenics alongside her playing table. (She eventually reaches the third round, but there falls to a woman wearing less lipstick.) It is nearly midnight, however, and "60 Minutes" has carted off its gear for the evening and so misses this exclusive footage. George and I play *à deux* for several lively hours. A costly mistake on his part.

January 28th: This morning's *Sun* has a headline reading "LV BACKGAMMON CONTEST SURROUNDED BY MYSTERY." The *Sun* is wondering, not illogically, why nobody can tell how many people are playing in it. At breakfast, I run into George Plimpton. He got here at midnight, he says— too late to play in the tournament. He looks so forlorn that I offer to play him myself. The first-prize winner, it has been announced, will receive not merely cash but also a leg on a trophy called the Plimpton Cup. George P. confesses that he has never laid eyes on it and did not foot the bill for it, so I suppose the trophy cannot be considered exactly analogous to the Davis Cup.

In the playing area, Henry Wattson is standing on a chair calling the roll of Second Chance survivors. George the Greek is not among them. His last tournament ship seems to have sunk at some hideous early-morning hour. Las Vegas is a dangerous place to visit in more ways than one—at four-thirty this morning, I saw a man being carried off to a hospital after slipping, literally, on a banana peel—but it has sturdy furniture: Wattson weighs two hundred and seventy-five pounds, and the chair does not even tremble. There are well over a hundred more or less normal-sized bodies left in contention—out of how many starters we still have not been informed. We do hear that there was almost a fistfight at the Hilton last night— something involving a person who thought he had lost a match, congratulatorily shook his adversary's hand, and was then advised by a loose-lipped kibitzer that he had misread his opponent's dice and hadn't yet lost at all. Barclay Cooke had to be summoned to the Hilton from the Dunes to render a decision, and he ruled against the premature handshaker. A formal protest has since been lodged, which I gather from reliable sources the appropriate officials will in due course see fit to ignore. Almost as soon as play resumes at our hotel, another argument erupts. A woman has played a 4–2, which she insists is what she threw; her opponent, before the woman scooped up her dice, saw it as 5–2. Henry Wattson lumbers over to adjudicate. "I believe that both of you believe you're right," he says, with consummate tact. He instructs them to roll one die each—the higher number to determine what the woman's move is to be. She rolls a 5, her opponent a 4, and she gets to play her 4–2 after all.

Oswald Jacoby is in the room, but he isn't watching anybody. With a large crowd watching him, he is taking on someone from California. "They don't play one another for more than a hundred dollars a point," Wattson tells me. "They'll gladly play other people for more. They'll play *you* for a *lot* more." I ask him, to change the subject, how many players there have been in the tournament, and he asks me to guess. My guess is eight hundred and twelve. He says I am not far off. While waiting for the ranks to be further thinned, I engage in a low-key, three-dollar-a-point contest with another Californian, a young woman who is covering the tournament for the magazine *Gammon*. (The press is here in full force—*Stern, Visual Images, Sports Illustrated*, and *Gambling Times*.) "I'm a second-year law student at Whittier," she tells me, "but since I took up backgammon, eleven months ago, I've been sitting in the back of the classroom studying Magriel's book during lectures." She has not been frittering her time away in law school; she relieves me of three dollars.

The rumor circulates that the number of contestants will finally be put at six hundred and thirty-eight. In any event, we are down to thirty-two of them, and by the end of this day—more accurately, by dawn tomorrow—all but four semifinalists will have vanished from contention. The thirty-two assured money-winners, whatever it may mean, are all male—eleven from California, four from New York, three each from Texas and Illinois, two each from Canada, England, Mexico, and New Jersey, and one each from Florida, Minnesota, and Wisconsin. The oldest is sixty-nine and the youngest twenty-one; their average age (shades of what the fellow in the registration room calculated two days ago!) is thirty-eight. Their surnames have a tangy international flavor: Aryeh, Jalil, Kaloudis, Malik, Manukian, Tcheurekdjian. I have never heard of any of them before.

At 6 P.M., paired by lot, they get under way. I ask Barclay Cooke, who, in view of the increasing seriousness of the moment, has switched to a dark suit (Magriel has stopped running, but he is still in track shoes), whether he is sorry he cannot take part in any of this. "Not at all," he says. "I'm glad to have the pressure off for a while." And indeed the pressure seems to be on: the players do not smile or chat; they take longer between moves than they did in earlier rounds; air-conditioning notwithstanding, there is sweat on more than one furrowed brow. At midnight, I take another spectator break. Henry Wattson invites me to play with him a little. I decline. I would as soon wrestle a bear. Instead, I join George Plimpton and George the Greek and a stray Pakistani in a less pressure-packed game. The man whose name adorns the Plimpton Cup does not consider himself as adept at backgammon as at football, baseball, ice hockey, and other comparatively sedentary sports; he will not play for over two dollars a point. The other George, trying to mount a comeback, insists that the rest of us play for twenty. I have never climbed that high before without oxygen. George P. quits early, an eighteen-dollar loser. He will probably retrieve the loss from a book about how we trounced him. By the time the other George gives up, he has run out of cash. I hope his checks, of which I seem to have a fistful, do not bounce.

At 6 A.M., the semifinalists are revealed; Ron Rubin, a broker and bridge champion fron New Jersey, and Simon Naim, a salesman from Chicago, in one bracket; and in the other Dennis Stone, a screenwriter from Van Nuys, California, and Chico Felberbaum, a businessman from Edmonton, Alberta. I fall asleep dreaming of their pots of gold.

January 29th: Play in the semifinals is slated to start at 9 A.M. Before then, at breakfast, I meet up with Magriel. He says groggily that the bankers have finally authorized the release of some figures: total contestants, 652; first prize, $180,400; second prize, $72,160; third prize, $18,040; fourth prize, $9,020; lowest prize, $902. "I'm a little disappointed," Magriel says. "But you have to keep everything in perspective. We did end up with the biggest tournament ever, and next year we'll do better, because we've established a certain credibility." Magriel eats cinnamon toast for breakfast.

I ask him if the competition has been more disputatious than in run-of-the-mill tournaments.

"The more you play for, the more intense the arguments get," he says. "After all, these guys are playing for nearly two hundred thousand dollars, which could radically change their lives."

The semis begin. It is touch and go at both boards. Finally, Rubin edges Naim, and Felberbaum squeaks past Stone. Rubin and Felberbaum have each had to win ten consecutive matches to get this far. The two finalists, as if at a title-prizefight weighing-in ceremony, repair together to one side of the Crown Jewel Room and, hemmed in by their seconds, confer in muted tones. Word soon spreads that they are trying—to no avail, it turns out—to agree to split their money, sixty per cent of their total take to the winner, forty per cent to the loser. (Splitting the money is not uncommon in such circumstances.) Bobby Riggs saunters by, enticingly waving a tennis racquet. Who could think of tennis, whatever odds Riggs might offer, at a time like this? Anyway, is it daylight or dark, clear or raining? I adjourn to the casino bar for a double Scotch. The younger Marine Midlander is there, besweatered and tieless; a couple more days of this and he'll look as scruffy as the rest of us.

The final is held in a smallish chamber from which most onlookers are barred, except for Barclay Cooke, the designated referee for the epic encounter, and a pit boss from the casino, whose mission is to keep a sharp eye on the dice. The rest of the cast—some four hundred strong—assemble in an adjoining room where we are to follow the tense proceedings on a large television screen, with Magriel furnishing a running commentary. This match will be a fifteen-pointer. There is a mild flap at the outset, about the direction in which the players should move their pieces. (Either way is perfectly acceptable.) "When you're playing for this amount of money, that can make a difference," Magriel explains. "Chico likes his home board to his left." Chico has his way. And then, as they swing into action, Chico wins further: in what seems no time at all, though it is really about an hour, he has attained a huge lead, of 10–1. But in backgammon there are no insurmountable hurdles. Ron comes clawing back, and at 14–4, one point from defeat, he needs a 7 to stay alive. He gets it, with a boldly thrown 6–1. That, though, is the last good breath he draws, and a few minutes later Chico Felberbaum joins Tom Watson and Bjorn Borg on the select roster of big-money champions.

Soon afterward, inevitably, the newly crowned champ holds a press conference. We learn that he is thirty-four, is from Israel, is a Sabra, is the father of two, is married to a photographer. (His wife is here with him, but she is too dazed by their good fortune to remove her camera from its case.) He migrated to Canada nine years ago, and is in "real-estate development" at Edmonton; he prefers not to divulge the name of his company, though it is his own. He has been playing backgammon for about fourteen years, on and off. More off than on: incredibly, he hadn't played seriously for six months prior to this tournament. There isn't anybody in Edmonton, he says wistfully, to play *with*.

What—*Gambling Times* and *Gambling* and *The New Yorker* are desperate to know all—brought him to Las Vegas?

"The prize."

What backgammon books has he found most helpful?

"I've never read a backgammon book."

How does he keep his game sharp, if he doesn't play much?

"I don't think it's sharp."

To what does he attribute his success?

"I was extremely lucky, and my opponent had the worst dice."

Has he ever played against any of the pros, and, now that he is one of them, will he be joining them on the circuit?

"I haven't got a chance against them. I think I played against people here who are better players than I am, which shows that backgammon is seventy-five per cent luck."

Soon we all go home. It has been a stimulating experience, everything considered, though following Tom Watson around a golf course might have been healthier. On the Vegascene, things are settling back to normal. The Dunes is preparing for the annual Hadassah dinner dance tonight, Billy

Graham is due at Caesars Palace tomorrow, and soon after that, over at the Hilton, Ali will be toying with young Spinks. My friend George gratefully accepts a ride in my cab to the airport, but he is flying to Detroit, not New York. He says he has a deal he hopes to make there with some automobile people. Earlier, he had mentioned that he owned a Rolls-Royce. A good enough deal and he will be close to even. Paul Magriel, for his part, is planning to pack up his track shoes and take off for Riyadh, where he has been summoned to give private lessons for a whole month, at what hourly rate of pay I dare not contemplate, to a brother of the King of Saudi Arabia.

March 6, 1978

Biko's Friend

"When I escaped from South Africa into Lesotho, the government there gave me a United Nations safe-passage document. It's quite a handsome document—in the place where most passports list which nations they are valid for travel in, this says simply 'the World'—and I've grown quite accustomed to it. I'm very conscious now of being a citizen of the world, and I must say I've been made very welcome these past four months in many parts of it. In my capacity as world citizen, moreover, I've discovered things I never knew before—that in Australia, for instance, the kangaroo is a real traffic hazard, and that in northern Scandinavia automobiles not infrequently collide with moose. It has been an ironic time for me. Being banned in South Africa means, among other things, that one may not legally travel, write, or make speeches. Since January, I have travelled more than eighty-five thousand miles, have written more words than I ever wrote as a journalist, and have done so much talking—a good deal of it, naturally, against apartheid—that I'm surprised this editor from Hicksville still has any voice."

These words were addressed to us the other day, in a commendably strong voice, by Donald Woods, formerly the editor of the East London, South Africa, *Daily Dispatch*. Mr. Woods, white, was in New York to mark the publication of the American edition of "Biko," his book about his friend Stephen Biko, black, now also dead.

"The contrast between my old life and my present one is fantastic," Mr. Woods went on. "Up to the time I knew Steve Biko, my circumstances were exceedingly agreeable. My wife, Wendy, and I had our fifth child six years ago, and at about that time I reached a stage of life where I was thoroughly settled into a comfortable rut, writing an anti-apartheid piece every second day or so, playing lots of golf and chess. Then, in 1973, I met and befriended Steve Biko, and my life inevitably turned inconvenient. Whenever I got a phone call that he had been arrested again, I knew I wouldn't be going to the golf club but, rather, would be dashing off somewhere to rustle up bail for him. It was a strain on my fat-cat existence. Even so, last July my brother and I went on a golfing holiday to Britain, to play St. Andrews and Carnoustie and Sunningdale and the other legendary courses; and we took in the cricket matches at Lord's; and if anybody had said to me then that I would be *living* in Britain six months afterward I'd have said he was stone crazy.

"But the night last September when I heard that Steve was dead, everything really changed. I was reminded then of what one Afrikaner politician said when his Nationalist Party took over our government, in 1948: 'Even the trees look different.' For me, the entire foundation of things had suddenly been cut away. While Steve was alive, I kept hoping that the situation in South Africa could be sorted out by logic. I never was and am not now in complete agreement with everything Steve stood for—I was nowhere near as radical as he—but he was my *friend*. In London the other day, I was addressing a meeting of the Royal Society, and someone said in the question period, 'A reader of your book finds it hard to accept that anyone could have been as good as you say Biko was.' I replied that I would have included Steve's warts if I'd known of any but that I couldn't manufacture them. Then Sir Robert Birley, the stately old ex-headmaster of Eton, hauled himself to his feet and leant on his stick and said, 'I'm happy to be able to bear out that I knew Steve Biko and that he was indeed a remarkable man. When Dennis Healey was going to South Africa as Secretary of State for Defense, I told him that it was most important that he seek out Biko, because that young man would assuredly someday be Prime Minister of South Africa.' Steve was still in his early twenties at that time; that was long before *I* met him. If the impact he had on me comes through in my book like too much of a good thing, that's because he was a rare human being.

"Well, after Steve's death I sort of hit the campaign trail, speaking out against the government. One chap listening to a talk of mine in Cape Town told me later that he'd said to his wife, 'They'll never let him get away with it.' But I didn't think the authorities would do much against a journalist. I thought they might eventually attempt to prosecute me under, say, their law about incitement to racial hostility, but I didn't think I'd ever be banned. If they got hold of me today, incidentally, they could sentence me to death under the broad terms of their Suppression of Terrorism Act, for advocating international sanctions against the government. In October, I was at the Johannesburg airport, about to board a plane for the United States, where I was supposed to take part in a conference, when three security men stopped me at passport control and said that I'd been banned and that they had orders from the Minister of Justice to escort me straight back to East London. As they were leading me away, I saw a couple of people I knew, and I wanted to run over to them and say, 'Hey, you know what's happening to me?' At the airport security office, my escorts went through my suitcase, and seemed disappointed to find nothing more than a couple of books on cricket and rugby. 'What are you looking for?' I asked. 'Firearms,' they said. I expected that they would fly me to East London—it's almost five hundred miles from Joburg—but they said no, they couldn't wait for a plane, their instructions were to get me on the road at once."

In September, Mr. Woods will be moving from London to Cambridge, Massachusetts, where Harvard has offered him a Nieman Fellowship. That should come in handy, because the Woodses managed to take only seven hundred rands—a bit over eight hundred dollars—out of South Africa. (His family had left the country before the alarm was raised.) "Not much when you have five children," the paterfamilias told us. "But, what with writing and lecturing, I hope to get by. I feel intellectually at home in the United States. I especially admire the openness of Americans. When I was in Washington, on an earlier visit, talking to your Vice-President in the White House, Mr. Mondale took me into the Oval Office to meet the President, and Mr. Carter was kind enough to urge me to feel welcome over here. My own government, I'm afraid, is particularly mad at me these days—the Afrikaans press has taken some nasty swipes, once even referring to a secretary at the *Dispatch* whom I hardly knew as 'his female friend'—but people I meet in the States or Australia, or wherever, do not generally perceive me to be a wild-eyed revolutionary. My children miss their friends in South Africa, and the sunshine, but the whole experience has been something of an adventure for them. In England, they saw snow for the first time, and they went quite bonkers throwing snowballs at one another. I miss my native land, too, but being a banned person there is no way to live. I was captain of the East London chess-club team, for instance, and when the colonel in charge of the local security-police office was explaining the do's and don'ts of banning to me—you're not permitted to talk to more than one person at a time, outside of your immediate family—and I asked him if I could play at the chess club, he said only if I didn't have any tea or coffee, because if I did and somebody else did simultaneously, that would constitute a common social purpose, which was taboo. To please my sense of humor, I did once go to my golf club—security policemen do not patrol golf courses—and walk into the bar and order a drink. There were three kinds of reaction: some members made a point of moving over and standing next to me; some shrank away; and the rest pretended that I was not there at all."

We asked Mr. Woods when he had last had any personal contact with Prime Minister Vorster.

"I went to dinner about three years ago at his official residence, Libertas, in Pretoria," Mr. Woods replied. "He was entertaining twenty-seven editors, and while we were having our pre-meal whiskeys he said to me—we spoke Afrikaans exclusively that evening—'Man, why do you go on and on and *on* day after day after *day* about apartheid?' I replied rather lamely that he should be grateful that there was some editor around who was letting him know how most blacks felt about his government. 'My God, with friends like you, who needs enemies?' he said. To make sure no editor would seem to be favored over any other, we drew lots for our places at the table, and, as luck would have it, I ended up at Mr. Vorster's right. 'Oh, my God, you're next to me!' he exclaimed—but not unhumorously. At the end of the evening, I could not help noticing that when he bade farewell to his guests, I was one of only two—the other was Piet Cillié, the doyen of the Afrikaans press—whom he addressed by their first names. I suppose you could safely say that since that evening my relationship with the Prime Minister has deteriorated."

May 29, 1978

Index

McCloskey, Mrs. Matthew H., 253
McCloy, John, 314
McCormack, John, 328
McCracken, James, 392
McCullough, Hester (Mrs. John T.), and
    Adler-Draper libel suit, 117–31
McCullough, John T., 120, 122, 125
MacDowell, Edward A., 34
McElligot's Pool (Dr. Seuss), 307
McGinnis, Patrick B., 243
McGrath, Neva Smith, 341
McGraw-Hill publishing company, 319–20
McIver State Park, Oregon, rock festival in,
    384
McKeldin, Theodore Roosevelt, 330, 331
McKelway, St. Clair, 11, 12, 15
McMinnville, Oregon, *News-Register*, 270
Mack, Connie, 134
Mack, Walter, S., 153–54
    and soft-drink packaging "revolution,"
    208–10
Macy's toy shop, 135, 136
Madison Square Garden, 153
    Thomas Mann at, 32
Magic Mountain, The (Mann), 32
Magriel, Paul (backgammon expert), at Las
    Vegas tournament, 430–31, 432–33,
    434, 435, 437, 440, 442, 443
"Make a Wish" (musical), 283
Malenkov, Georgi M., 291
Malik, Jacob, 135, 136
"Man and His Wife, A" (Bolton), 427
Mann, Thomas, 32–33
Mann, Mrs. Thomas, 32
Mannone, Wingy, 40
Mansfield, Mike, 328
Mao Tse-tung, 417, 423
Marble, Alice, 35
March of Dimes campaign, and Sinatra,
    71–72
Margaret, Princess, 104
Margery of Boston (medium), 58
Marie, Grand Duchess of Rumania, 35
Marine Midland Bank, N.Y., and Las Vegas
    backgammon tournament, 430–36
    passim, 438, 441
Marks, Charlie (Charlie Dale), *see* Smith and
    Dale
Marquand, J.P., 304
Marquette University, and Joseph
    McCarthy, 226
Marriott Hotels, *see* Essex House
Marshall, Gen. George C., 65–66, 106

Marshall, George Preston, his opinion of
    New York, 242–43
Marshall, Thurgood, 98
Marshall Plan, 155, 167
Martin, Mary, 196–97
Marx, Groucho, 275, 278
Marx, Karl, 420
Masons, 177
Massey, Raymond, 177
Matchbooks, "beauty contest" for, 242
Matthews, J.B., 119
Matthews, Vince, 373
Mauldin, Bill, 106
Maxwell, Elsa, 35, 37, 272–73
Maxwell, James A., 212–13
Mayer, Arthur Loeb (movie magnate), as
    professor of cinema, 393–97
Mayer, Lillie (Mrs. Arthur Loeb), 393, 394
Mayer, Louis B., 78
Mayfair Club (backgammon club), 429, 430,
    438
M'Bow, Amadou-Mahtar, 411–12
Meadowcraft, Enid LaMonte, 238
Medical insurance, for pets, trees, 169–70
Medina, Harold R., 175
Mediums, Dunninger crusade against, 57–60
Melchior, Lauritz, 379
Mencken, Henry L., 277
Menominee Indians, and Joseph McCarthy,
    225
Mercer, Robert L., 424–25
Merman, Ethel, 280, 282, 283, 427
Merriwell, Dick (juvenile book character),
    186
Merriwell, Frank, Friends of, 185–87
Merz, Charles, 149, 150
Mesta, Perle, 280
Metesky, George ("Mad Bomber"), 272
Metropolitan Life Insurance Co., 219, 220
Metropolitan Opera House
    booing at, 391–93
    tenors at, 377–80
M-G-M Grand (hotel), Las Vegas, 429
Miami *Herald*, 236
Miami Room (night club), 40
Michaelis, John H., 199, 206, 208
Michelangelo, 191
Michener, James A., 197
Mielziner, Jo, Mr. and Mrs., 192
Mikoyan, Anastas, 318, 333
Milhaud, Darius, 398
Miller High Life brewery, 224, 225
Mills Brothers, 259